The Evolving Use and the Changing Role of Interstate Compacts

A Practitioner's Guide

Best Regards,

Caroline N. Broun
Michael L. Buenger
Michael H. McCabe
Richard L. Masters

ABA
SECTION OF
ADMINISTRATIVE LAW
AND REGULATORY
PRACTICE

AMERICAN BAR ASSOCIATION
Defending Liberty
Pursuing Justice

Cover design by ABA Publishing

10 09 08 07 06   5 4 3 2 1

Cataloging-in-Publication data is on file with the Library of Congress

The evolving use and the changing role of interstate compacts / Buenger, Michael . L. Masters, Richard L., McCabe, Michael H. , Broun, Caroline N.

ISBN: 1-59031-643-6

Discounts are available for books ordered in bulk. Special consideration is given to state bars, CLE programs, and other bar-related organizations. Inquire at Book Publishing, ABA Publishing, American Bar Association, 321 North Clark Street, Chicago, Illinois 60610.

www.ababooks.org

SUMMARY OF CONTENTS

CONTENTS

ACKNOWLEDGMENTS

As with any work of this magnitude, many people are involved behind the scenes. Foremost are families, friends, and colleagues who have supported this effort. Without their understanding, support, and encouragement, the time and dedication needed to produce this book would not have existed. There are, however, several specific people who deserve recognition. Thanks to attorneys Jeff Litwak, William Morrow, Naomi Klaus, Liz Oppenheim, and Bruce Heppen for their review and critiquing of the book; to John Mountjoy, director of the National Center for Interstate Compacts, for his encouragement and support and for allowing us to leverage research and resources in completing this manuscript; to Kameron Murphy for his exactness in getting the almost 1,500 footnotes into proper Bluebook form; and lastly, to the American Bar Association, the Administrative Law Section and its Publications Committee, and particularly Rick Paszkiet, for their support of this project.

ABOUT THE AUTHORS

Michael L. Buenger currently serves as the state courts administrator for Missouri. He received his B.A., cum laude, from the University of Dayton in 1983 and his J.D., cum laude, from St. Louis University School of Law in 1989, where he was a White Fellow for Law and Public Policy. Mr. Buenger has also served as the state court administrator of South Dakota, as an adjunct professor of political science at the University of Dayton, an instructor for the Ohio Judicial College, a law clerk for the Court of Appeals of Ohio, and as the administrator and legal counsel for a court of appeals district in Ohio. He was a member of the teams that wrote the Interstate Compact for Adult Offender Supervision, the new Interstate Compact for Juveniles, which is currently under consideration by state legislatures; and, most recently, the proposed revised Interstate Compact for the Placement of Children. He has worked extensively with the Interstate Commission for Adult Offender Supervision, providing training and legal consulting services on variety of matters related to their compact. He has served as president of the national Conference of State Court Administrators and vice-chairperson of the Board of Directors of the National Center for State Courts. In addition, he serves on the board of advisors for the National Center for Interstate Compacts and the editorial board of the *Justice System Journal*. He also served on the American Bar Association's 2004 Commission on State Court Funding. Mr. Buenger has written and published in the areas of appellate practice and procedure, court management, the law of interstate compacts, federalism, judicial independence, and court funding.

Richard L. (Rick) Masters is general counsel to the Interstate Commission for Adult Offender Supervision, an interstate compact agency composed of all 50 states and territories, which is affiliated with the Council of State Governments (CSG) in Lexington, Kentucky. He received his B.A. degree from Asbury College in 1976 and his J.D. from the Louis D. Brandeis School of Law of the University of Louisville in 1979. He was assistant attorney general for the Commonwealth of Kentucky until 1982, after which he served as general counsel for CSG at its national office in Lexington. Mr. Masters is an adjunct professor of business regulation and commercial law at Asbury College and Northwood University and is a member of a law firm in Louisville, Kentucky. He has written and spoken extensively on the subject of interstate compacts, including the Interstate Compact for Adult Offender Supervision, for which he was the principal draftsman. He worked with CSG and the National Highway Traffic Safety Administration in the early 1980s to amend the Driver License Compact and is currently a CSG legal consultant with the United States Department of Justice/Office of Juvenile Justice and Delinquency Prevention for the purpose of amending the Interstate Compact for Juveniles. In addition, Mr. Masters continues to be involved in consultation, research, and writing concerning interstate compacts and constitutional law issues, most recently supervising the drafting of the new Interstate Compact for the Placement of Children.

Michael H. McCabe currently serves as the director of the Midwestern Office of the Council of State Governments (CSG), a national, nonpartisan association of state officials representing all three branches of state government in all 50 states and the U.S. territories. He received his bachelor's degree from Iowa State University in 1981 and his J.D. from the University of Illinois in 1984. Following a brief stint with a private law firm, Mr. McCabe joined CSG in 1985, serving first as a policy analyst and staff attorney and later as assistant director of CSG's Midwestern Office. In his current role as director, Mr. McCabe oversees the efforts of a 12-member team that provides research and staff support services to several groups of state officials, including the Midwestern Legislative Conference and the Midwestern Governors' Association. He was a charter member of the Policy Consensus Initiative Board of Directors and served as chairman of the Jane Addams Resource Corporation, a community development organization in Chicago. Over the years, Mr. McCabe has provided drafting and consulting assistance in connection with several interstate compacts, including the Interstate Agricultural Grain Marketing Compact, the Midwestern Higher Education Compact, the Interstate Insurance Receivership Compact, the Interstate Compact on Mental Health, and the Midwest Interstate Passenger Rail Compact. More recently, he participated in the development of the Interstate Compact for Adult Offender Supervision and the Interstate Compact for Juveniles.

Caroline N. Broun is an attorney licensed in California, Missouri, and Ohio. She received her B.S. with highest honors ftom the University of Illinois–Urbana and her J.D., magna cum laude, from St. Louis University School of Law. Ms. Broun was environmental inhouse counsel for an international consumer products company. She has practiced law with both large and small law firms and has clerked with the Missouri Supreme Court. She has published in the area of environmental law and wrote the *Toxic Torts Practice Guide, RCRA and Superfund: A Practice Guide* (3rd Edition) and *Superfund Law and Procedure* for West publications.

INTRODUCTION

Unlike the few other works that address interstate compacts, this work was developed with a bias toward the practitioner—not only the attorney who may face litigating matters controlled by a compact but also others who are involved in the drafting, management, and implementation of such agreements. While necessarily theoretical, it seeks also to provide practical guidance to those who find themselves dealing with matters controlled by interstate compacts and particularly the administrative agencies that may be charged with overseeing a compact.

In the United States, the creation of government structures is a dynamic process; a function largely of managing a vast array of federal and state relationships that are ever-changing. Managing these relationships is inherently complicated given the federal structure of government in which, at a theoretical and practical level, two sovereign entities cooperate, compete, complement, and at times conflict with one another in fashioning and implementing public policy. Over the years, many scholarly and practical works have been devoted to exploring the relationship between the states and federal government. Seemingly little has been dedicated to exploring the management of formal relationships between the states, a critical but largely overlooked element of federalism. The growth of federal power and the emergence of large national institutions of government in the last century have eclipsed discussions on state relations, and particularly how states manage their formal relationships over matters that are multilateral in nature. How these interstate relations are managed can have significant, long-term consequences. Take, for example, the Interstate Agreement on Detainers, the Washington Metropolitan Area Transit Regulation Compact, the Columbia River Gorge Compact, the Interstate Compact for Adult Offender Supervision, the Tahoe Regional Planning Compact, or the Interstate Compact on the Placement of Children. Each of these formal state-to-state agreements governs not only state relationships but, equally important, provides services to and/or controls the actions of individual citizens. Additionally, interstate compacts are perhaps the only exception to the largely held view that one state legislature cannot bind its successors in long-term, even irrevocable agreements pertaining to state affairs.

Throughout the history of the United States, interstate compacts have served an important—albeit largely unnoticed—role in shaping relationships between the states and, at times, between the states and the federal government. In the strictest sense, interstate compacts violate traditional notions of federalism by enabling states to create supra-state, sub-federal agreements that are as binding on the states as if the states were acting as true independent sovereigns adopting a treaty. Interstate compacts allow for ancillary and alternative governing mechanisms and create regulatory schemes that exist largely independent of individual state control and federal oversight. These mechanisms, while created by the member states, are not subject to control by any single state.

Although interstate compacts have long been used in the United States, their use as ongoing governing mechanisms has been a development of the twentieth century, evidenced by the emergence of the so-called "regulatory," "administrative" or "management" compact. Prior to the twentieth century, interstate compacts were used almost exclusively to settle boundary disputes or adjust jurisdictional lines. In more recent times, however, interstate compacts have been used not so much to resolve boundary disputes but rather to manage a wide array of multistate matters. This, in turn, has led to the creation of interstate administrative and regulatory bodies with specific subject matter control and specific management responsibility—for example, the Interstate Commission on Adult Offender Supervision, the Delaware River Port Authority, the Ohio River Valley Sanitation Commission, the Columbia River Gorge Commission, the Tahoe Regional Planning Agency, and, perhaps most notable among interstate compact agencies, the Port Authority of New York–New Jersey. Some compact-created entities such as the Washington Metropolitan Area Transit Commission and the Interstate Commission for Adult Offender Supervision are truly regulatory agencies, promulgating administrative rules and regulations and taking enforcement actions as one of their major functions. Other compact-created entities such as the Port Authority of New York–New Jersey and the Metropolitan Washington Airports Authority are more than regulatory agencies, encompassing within their sphere of authority not only regulation but, more important, the development and management of major governmental operations.

Although compacts have been used to settle land claims between the states as recently as 1999,[1] today they are more often used to deal with wide-

---

1. *See, e.g.*, Missouri-Nebraska Boundary Compact, Pub. L. No. 106-101, 113 Stat. 1333 (1999). In addition to settling the boundary between the states due to the shifting channel of the Missouri River, the compact also settles issues

ranging regional and national problems. The issues states seek to manage through compacts involve such diverse matters as water-resource management, pollution control, regional economic development, crime control, child welfare, education, emergency management, waste disposal, and so forth. Arguably, any matter between two or more states that is "supra-state, sub-federal" in nature can become the subject of an interstate compact. As Justice Felix Frankfurter once observed, "The combined legislative powers of Congress and the several States permit a wide range of permutations and combinations for governmental action. . . . Political energy has been expended on sterile controversy over supposedly exclusive alternatives instead of utilized for fashioning new instruments adapted to new situations."[2] At no time has the use of interstate compacts been employed more in fashioning "new instruments" than in the late twentieth and early twenty-first centuries. The new millennium evidences a growing interest in the use of interstate compacts to resolve serious multistate matters ranging from crime to child protection, to water management, to regional transportation and economic development matters.

Although compacts have emerged in recent years as effective and vital governing tools, the study of compacts has been limited to a relatively small group of people. Very little legal or political literature has been dedicated to the subject matter, notwithstanding the states' increasing reliance on compacts to manage many pressing national and regional issues. Additionally, with many compacts creating administrative agencies that are neither federal in nature nor state in scope, an entirely new area of administrative and regulatory law may be emerging, albeit in an ad hoc, quiet, non-systematic manner. As a result, there is a need for a reexamination of the law of interstate compacts, and particularly with regard to the development of supra-state administrative and regulatory agencies.

This book seeks to fill the existing void in this emerging area of law by addressing both the theoretical principles behind interstate compacts and the very practical implications of operating in the compact environment. It is intended to serve not only as a reference for lawyers, but also as a practical guide for legislators, drafters, compact administrators, students, and other

---

relating to criminal and civil jurisdictions between the respective state courts, competing claims of state sovereignty over disputed lands, taxes, title to land, and riparian rights. The agreement also allows for renegotiation of the boundary as the channel of the river changes.

2. Felix Frankfurter & James M. Landis, *The Compact Clause of the Constitution—A Study in Interstate Adjustments,* 34 YALE. L.J. 685, 688 (1925).

parties interested in the development of, or subject to, interstate compacts. Thus, some chapters provide a theoretical basis for compacts. Other chapters seek to provide a very practical perspective on compacts and the potential issues one may face in working with interstate compacts or litigating under such agreements. Finally, the book also seeks to provide both practitioners of the law and others with a perspective on the complexity of compacts and their interaction with other agreements, state laws, and federal laws.

Chapter 1

THE GENERAL LAW AND PRINCIPLES GOVERNING INTERSTATE COMPACTS

> No State shall, without the Consent of Congress * * * enter into
> any Agreement or Compact with another State, or with a for-
> eign Power[.][1]

1.1   THE HISTORICAL BASIS OF INTERSTATE COMPACTS

The Framers of the Constitution understood that the federal structure of
American government required formal mechanisms for managing interstate
relations, and particularly for managing the complex government, political
and economic allegiances that states might form between themselves. Consequently, the Constitution provides several mechanisms for "adjusting" interstate relations and addressing regional or national issues, many of which are
"supra-state, sub-federal" in nature.[2] Several examples of constitutional control over state action demonstrate that the Framers, though greatly state oriented, were also keenly aware of the need for some semblance of control over

---

1. U.S. CONST. art. I, § 10, cl. 3.
2. The term "supra-state, sub-federal" refers to those matters that are clearly
   beyond the realm of individual state authority but which, due to their nature, may not be within the immediate purview of the federal government or
   easily resolved through a purely federal response.

multilateral state action. Through the Full Faith and Credit Clause of the Constitution, for example, the Framers created a system by which the critical actions of one state received not only recognition but also enforcement in sister states, providing, in a sense, a national scheme of legal regulation over the actions of states.[3] Congress's extensive power over interstate commerce provides yet another mechanism for adjusting interstate relationships—often in an economic sense that nevertheless can have great social and political consequences.[4] The Supremacy Clause and federal preemption doctrine provide an additional control over state actions—individual and collective—by ensuring that federal law will trump state law in any legitimate competition between the two. The far-reaching power of the federal judiciary, and particularly the Supreme Court's original jurisdiction over state disputes, serves as another means of adjusting interstate relations by vesting ultimate authority over state disputes directly in the nation's highest court.[5]

Of all of the mechanisms available, none is more formal, more state-focused, more adaptable to collective *state* needs, and perhaps less understood than interstate compacts. Compacts are fundamentally negotiated agreements among member states that have the status of both contract and statutory law. Interstate compacts represent one of a limited number of processes provided in the Constitution for adjusting and regulating formal state relations, be they boundaries, substantive law, or even economic relationships. More important, compacts represent the only mechanism in the Constitution by which the states themselves can alter the dynamics of their

3. U.S. CONST. art. IV, § 1.
4. *See, e.g.,* Perez v. United States, 402 U.S. 146 (1971) (upholding under the Commerce Clause application of the Consumer Credit Protection Act to purely intrastate loan-sharking activities); Wickard v. Filburn, 317 U.S. 111 (1942) (upholding the application of the Agricultural Adjustment Act to the consumption of homegrown wheat by a small wheat farmer); N.L.R.B. v. Jones & Laughlin Steel Corp., 301 U.S. 1 (1937) (sustaining the validity of the National Labor Relations Act, and holding that activities having such a close and substantial relation to interstate commerce that their control is essential to protection of that commerce from burdens are subject to congressional regulation). *But see* United States v. Lopez, 514 U.S. 549 (1995) (Congress went beyond its Commerce Clause authority in adopting Gun-Free School Zones Act of 1990, as the act had nothing to do with commerce or any economic activity and, therefore, could not be sustained as a regulation of activity arising out of or connected with a commercial transaction, which, when viewed in the aggregate, substantially affected interstate commerce).
5. U.S. CONST. art. III, § 2.

relationships without running afoul of the authority of the federal government or reordering the federal structure of government. Thus, compacts are singularly important because through a compact, the states can create a state-based solution to regional or national problems and effectively retain policy control for the future. What Justice Brandeis observed in 1938 in *Hinderlider v. La Plata River & Cherry Creek Ditch Co.* is equally true today:

> It ignores the history and order of development of the two means provided by the Constitution for adjusting interstate controversies. The compact—the legislative means—adapts to our Union of sovereign States the age-old treaty-making power of independent sovereign nations. Adjustment by compact without a judicial or quasi-judicial determination of existing rights had been practiced in the Colonies, was practiced by the States before the adoption of the Constitution, and had been extensively practiced in the United States for nearly half a century before this Court first applied the judicial means in settling the boundary dispute in *Rhode Island* v. *Massachusetts.*[6]

The history of interstate compacts spans a broad range of time, extending well before the drafting of the U.S. Constitution or even the Articles of Confederation. Compacts are, therefore, the oldest mechanism available to promote formal interstate cooperation, having their roots in the American colonial era, when each colony was related directly to the King and, therefore, enjoyed a measure of independence from every other colony. There was no "federal" system of colonial government and no government with national scope and power. While the colonies were clearly "related" to one another through geography, economy, and culture, there was no recognition of formal governmental relationships existing separate and apart from their direct accountability to the Crown. For both philosophical and practical reasons, Britain could not allow the colonies to create alternative government structures separate from the Crown, and, consequently, no intracontinental government with national power and scope existed prior to the Revolution. As a result, all intercolonial disputes were submitted to the Crown for resolution because the colonies lacked the authority to independently resolve their differences or manage their intercolonial relations.

---

6. Hinderlider v. La Plata River & Cherry Creek Ditch Co., 304 U.S. 92, 104 (1938).

Well before the United States was established under the Articles of Confederation and Perpetual Union ("Articles of Confederation"), colonial authorities had experience using mechanisms and processes similar to compacts to resolve their disputes. Most intercolonial disputes generally involved boundary controversies that arose from the various royal land charters under which the colonies were founded. These charters were by definition and operation vague and expansive, applying to lands that lacked adequate surveys and for which formal possession was questionable. For example, the U.S. Supreme Court recently noted in *Virginia v. Maryland* that "Control of the [Potomac] River has been disputed for nearly 400 years. In the 17th century, both Maryland and Virginia laid claim to the River pursuant to conflicting royal charters issued by different British Monarchs."[7] Moreover, the Plymouth Charter of 1628 gave to Sir Henry Rosewell land whose true territorial definition was left open to wildly varying interpretations. That charter and subsequent amendments formed part of the basis for a land dispute that led to the Supreme Court's intervention in *Rhode Island v. Massachusetts.*[8]

Matters became more complicated with the expansion of the colonies geographically and in terms of their migrating populations. As populations moved further west, Atlantic Coast colonies made extravagant claims to portions of the interior continent based in part on their broad land charters and in part on the principle that possession was nine-tenths of the law. Consequently, boundary disputes between the colonies were inevitable and the Crown, through the Privy Council, was required to settle a number of border disputes. In 1727, for example, the Privy Council resolved a dispute between Rhode Island and Connecticut. This was followed by cases between New Hampshire and Massachusetts in 1740 and between Rhode Island and Massachusetts in 1746. The need for a method to continually address boundary disputes contributed to the evolution of the "compact" process first expressed in the Articles of Confederation and later carried forward and formalized in Article I, Section 10 of the U.S. Constitution.

Although frequently thought of in terms of allowing states to enter compacts, the Articles of Confederation and later the Constitution speak to interstate compacts in restrictive or limiting language, not authorizing their creation but restraining their creation. Beginning with the Articles of Confederation, the Founders restricted the ability of the states to join in formal, common enterprises or allegiances. Although they recognized that each state retained "its sovereignty, freedom and independence," the Articles of Confederation

---

7. Virginia v. Maryland, 540 U.S. 56, 60 (2003).
8. Rhode Island v. Massachusetts, 37 U.S. 657, 659-60 (1838).

placed limitations on multilateral state action by providing that no state could enter "any treaty, confederation or alliance whatever between them, without the consent . . . of Congress[.]"[9] This provision regarding interstate compacts was meant primarily as a preventive measure; that is, the provision's purpose was to limit the ability of the states to act collectively through compacts or other formal arrangements absent congressional consent.

The reasons behind the restrictive nature of the compact clauses contained in the Articles of Confederation and the Constitution rested in concern for what today is sometimes referred to as the "collective action" problem of federalism.[10] Collective action occurs when two or more states seek to maximize their sovereignty and political power through collective, joint or cooperative efforts at the expense of other states or regions, or even the federal government. The concern over collective action was so compelling that the drafters of the Articles provided that Congress alone was to be the "last resort on appeal in all disputes and differences . . . between two or more States concerning boundary, jurisdiction or any other cause whatever[.]"[11] Article IX of the Articles of Confederation created an elaborate procedural mechanism by which the "legislative or executive authority or lawful agent of any State in controversy with another" would petition Congress. In large part, the process conceived in the Articles of Confederation closely mirrored the process used by the Crown during the colonial era. Colonial disputes were either (1) negotiated, then submitted to the Crown for approval (a process similar to the compact method), or (2) appealed directly to the Crown through the Privy Council (a process similar to submitting state disputes directly to Congress).

Nevertheless, even the power the national government possessed under the Articles of Confederation regarding foreign relations was sometimes subject to the vagaries of the states, acting individually or collectively. Although the restrictions contained in the Articles of Confederation were meant to protect what little power the national government enjoyed from state encroachment, the restrictions did not prove effective with the passage of time. Concern over

---

9. Articles of Confederation, art. VI (U.S. 1781) ("No two or more States shall enter into any treaty, confederation or alliance whatever between them, without the consent of the United States in Congress assembled, specifying accurately the purposes for which the same is to be entered into, and how long it shall continue.").
10. *See, e.g.,* Note, *To Form a More Perfect Union?: Federalism and Informal Interstate Cooperation*, 102 Harv. L. Rev. 842, 844-47 (1989).
11. Articles of Confederation, art. IX (U.S. 1781).

collective state action continued to be a focus of the evolving government. The "consent" requirement set out in Article I, Section 10 of the Constitution was a carryover from the Articles of Confederation. It was intended to continue the principle that through its consent powers, the Congress would be a counterweight against potentially harmful collective state action that could erode the viability and sovereignty of the national government.

Comparisons have been made between Article I, Section 10, Clause 1 of the Constitution—the Treaty Clause—and Article I, Section 10, Clause 3—the Compact Clause. The Treaty Clause declares that "No State, shall enter into Any Treaty, Alliance or Confederation."[12] By contrast, the Compact Clause declares that "No State shall, without the Consent of Congress * * * enter into any Agreement or Compact with another State[.]"[13] The history of interstate agreements under the Articles of Confederation suggests a distinction between "treaties, alliances, and confederations" and "agreements and compacts." Congressional consent clearly was required before a state could enter into an arrangement with a foreign state or power, or before two or more states could enter into "treaties, alliances, or confederations."[14] Apparently, however, under the Articles of Confederation consent was not required for mere "agreements" between states. As the Supreme Court observed in *Wharton v. Wise*, "[t]he articles inhibiting any treaty, confederation, or alliance between the States without the consent of Congress . . . were not designed to prevent arrangements between adjoining States to facilitate the free intercourse of their citizens, or remove barriers to their peace and prosperity[.]"[15] Yet the records of the Constitutional Convention reveal no clues as to the contours of agreements governed by the Compact Clause. The lack of definition flowing from convention records suggests that the Framers employed the words "treaty," "compact," and "agreement" as terms of art, for which no explanation was required.[16] The Framers apparently perceived compacts and agreements as differing from treaties.

As a result, compacts between states have always been treated differently than treaties between states and foreign nations. Courts have been far more lenient to defining exceptions to the restrictions of the Compact Clause than they have been relative to defining the contours of the Treaty Clause. For example, the Virginia-Maryland Compact of 1785, which governed naviga-

---

12. U.S. Const. art. I, § 10, cl. 1.
13. U.S. Const. art. I, § 10, cl. 3.
14. Articles of Confederation, art. VI (U.S. 1781).
15. Wharton v. Wise, 153 U.S. 155, 167 (1894).
16. U.S. Steel Corp. v. Multistate Tax Comm'n, 434 U.S. 452 (1978).

tion and fishing rights in the Potomac River, the Pocomoke River, and the Chesapeake Bay, did not receive congressional consent. Yet no question of its validity under the Articles of Confederation ever arose. In referring to this 1785 compact in *Wharton v. Wise,* the Supreme Court noted:

> [L]ooking at the object evidently intended by the prohibition of the Articles of Confederation, we are clear they were not directed against agreements of the character expressed by the compact under consideration. Its execution could in no respect encroach upon or weaken the general authority of Congress under those articles. Various compacts were entered into between Pennsylvania and New Jersey and between Pennsylvania and Virginia, during the Confederation, in reference to boundaries between them, and to rights of fishery in their waters, and to titles to land in their respective States, without the consent of Congress, which indicated that such consent was not deemed essential to their validity.[17]

Whatever explicit understanding the Framers had behind the intent of Article I, Section 10 has been lost. In trying to reconcile competing provisions, Justice Story developed a theory that treaties, alliances, and confederations generally connote military and political accords forbidden to states. Compacts and agreements, by contrast, embraced "mere private rights of sovereignty, such as questions of boundary; interests in land situated in the territory of each other; and other internal regulations for the mutual comfort and convenience of States bordering on each other."[18] In the latter situations, congressional consent was required "in order to check any infringement of the rights of the national government."[19] Although for many years the Supreme Court's compact jurisprudence was at best inconclusive and at worst convoluted, the principles articulated by Justice Story have dominated. Courts faced with the task of applying the Compact Clause were reluctant to strike down emerging forms of interstate cooperation. The need to reconcile interstate cooperation with the broad restrictive language of the Constitution dictated a more discriminating jurisprudence. For example, in *Union Branch R. Co. v. East Tennessee & G.R. Co.,*[20] the Supreme Court of Georgia rejected a

---

17. Wharton v. Wise, 153 U.S. 155, 170-71 (1894).
18. 2 J. STORY, COMMENTARIES ON THE CONSTITUTION OF THE UNITED STATES § 1403, p. 264 (T. Cooley ed. 1873).
19. *Id.*
20. Union Branch R.R. Co. v. East Tenn. & G.R.R. Co., 14 Ga. 327 (Ga. 1853).

Compact Clause challenge to an agreement between Tennessee and Georgia concerning the construction of an interstate railroad, concluding that the Compact Clause restrained the power of the states only with respect to agreements "which might limit, or infringe upon a full and complete execution by the General Government, of the powers intended to be delegated by the Federal Constitution[.]"[21]

Courts, therefore, acknowledged early in the development of compact jurisprudence two important principles: (1) that the federal structure of the nation required a "state-based" approach for joint action to resolve interstate disputes; and (2) that some form of national control was necessary to maintaining the integrity of the newly established union.[22] The Compact Clause of the Constitution was and is viewed as a continued expression of the Framers' intent to maintain some semblance of national control over interstate relations, and particularly the amalgamation of political power in the states collectively or in more politically powerful states and regions. When the Framers spoke of congressional consent, it is clear that they sought to vindicate the legislative power of Congress *and* protect the power of the entire federal government.[23] James Madison in particular was concerned with the tendency of states and regions to "partition the Union into several Confederacies."[24] The Supreme Court has repeatedly observed that the purpose of the constitutional restriction is to limit agreements that are directed to the formation of *any* combinations tending to increase power in the states that encroach upon or interfere with the supremacy of the national government.[25] In *Port Authority Trans-Hudson Corp. v. Feeney,* the Supreme Court noted that "[t]he Interstate Compact Clause and the State Treaty Clause ensure that whatever sovereignty a State possesses within its own sphere of authority ends at its political border."[26] As one observer has stated, "[t]he basic purpose of the constitutional requirement of Congressional consent is to make certain that no such agreements [those affecting the balance of power in the federal struc-

21. *Id.* at 339.
22. Michael L. Buenger & Richard L. Masters, *The Interstate Compact on Adult Offender Supervision: Using Old Tools to Solve New Problems*, 9 ROGER WILLIAMS U. L. REV. 71, 81 (2003).
23. Milk Indus. Found. v. Glickman, 132 F.3d 1467 (D.C. Cir. 1998).
24. Letter from James Madison to Thomas Jefferson (Dec. 9, 1787), in 10 THE PAPERS OF JAMES MADISON 310, 312 (Robert A. Rutland et al. eds., 1977).
25. *See* U.S. Steel Corp. v. Multistate Tax Comm'n, 434 U.S. 452 (1978).
26. Port Auth. Trans-Hudson Corp. v. Feeney, 495 U.S. 299, 314-15 (1990).

ture] can stand against the will of Congress."[27] Without the restrictive nature of the Compact Clause, there would be no prohibition against the creation of state allegiances and confederacies, potentially resulting in the erosion of federal power and ultimately the deconstruction of the Union.

The restrictive language of the Compact Clause would seem to prohibit any states from entering into any agreements or compacts absent the consent of Congress. This was the general understanding of the Compact Clause throughout much of the eighteenth and nineteenth centuries. James Madison found the restriction so straightforward that he observed in *The Federalist 44* that "[the] remaining particulars of this clause fall within reasons which are either so obvious, or have been so fully developed, that they may be passed over without remark."[28] For part of the nation's history, therefore, the Compact Clause was seen as sufficiently broad and restrictive to render any interstate compacts void absent consent by Congress. The importance of the restrictive nature of the Compact Clause cannot be underestimated. The restrictiveness of the provision and the judiciary's application of that restrictiveness may be one of the reasons so few compacts were entered into for most of the nation's early history. Compacts were generally viewed by most legal scholars of the age as limited primarily to addressing state boundary disputes, as in the cases of *Rhode Island v. Massachusetts*[29] and *Virginia v. Tennessee*.[30] At least this was the practical effect, since all but one of some 36 compacts entered into before 1921 addressed state boundary disputes.

This colonial and early history is important in understanding the current dynamics associated with the compacting process. Interstate compacts are deeply rooted in the nation's history. Although the nature and subject matter of interstate compacts has most assuredly become more complex and would likely bewilder the Framers, the basic processes and principles underlying these agreements have not changed remarkably in the last 250 years.

1.2   THE NATURE OF INTERSTATE COMPACTS

1.2.1   General Considerations

Compacts hold a unique place in American law in part because of their growing reach and in part because of the status of the parties to such agree-

---

27. Frederick L. Zimmerman & Mitchell Wendell, The Law and Use of Interstate Compacts 22 (Council of State Governments 1976).
28. The Federalist No. 44 (James Madison).
29. Rhode Island v. Massachusetts, 37 U.S. 657, 729 (1838).
30. Virginia v. Tennessee, 148 U.S. 503 (1893).

ments. Within the federal system of American government, states occupy a quasi-sovereign status. The function and purposes of interstate compacts can only be understood and appreciated by accepting that states are not mere political subdivisions of the national government. Rather, they exist in a co-terminous relationship with the federal government, enjoying within the realm of their authority a level of sovereignty that is not dependent upon or a simple byproduct of the federal government's national sovereignty. As the Supreme Court noted in *Alden v. Maine*:

> The federal system established by our Constitution preserves the sovereign status of the States in two ways. First, it reserves to them a substantial portion of the Nation's primary sovereignty, together with the dignity and essential attributes inhering in that status. The states "form distinct and independent portions of the supremacy, no more subject, within their respective spheres, to the general author-ity than the general authority is subject to them, within its own sphere."
>
> Second, even as to matters within the competence of the national government, the constitutional design secures the founding generation's rejection of "the concept of a central government that would act upon the States" in favor of "a system in which the State and Federal Governments would exercise concurrent authority over the people."[31]

The status of states as possessing "primary sovereignty" impacts inter-state agreements and particularly interstate compacts. Rather than acting as mere political subdivisions or agents of the federal government, states have full authority within the realm of their responsibilities and powers to make limited, self-determinative agreements with sister states, each state acting in a "sovereign capacity." Moreover, because states possess sovereignty relative to each other, interstate problems can be resolved only through either the judi-cial process, entailing a litigation-based solution, or through a legislative process that embraces negotiation and self-determinative agreements. Absent judicial endorsement, one state cannot unilaterally impose its will on other states, for to do so would violate fundamental principles of sovereignty and independence, undermining the status of states as *equal* members in a union. However, only to the extent that multilateral agreements among states invade federal interests do the agreements become a concern for Congress acting to protect its interests. The ability to negotiate and enter interstate agreements that are binding is a far different power from that possessed by true political

---

31. Alden v. Maine, 527 U.S. 706, 714 (1999).

subdivisions of government, such as counties or municipalities, whose powers and authority are subject to expansion or contraction depending upon the will of central state authority. States can, therefore, through individual and collective action, enter into agreements with other states that control current and future state action. Here lies both the beauty and difficulty of interstate compacts.

One reason so few compacts have been entered into throughout the history of the nation may have to do with their oddity within the federal structure of American government. Arguably, interstate compacts violate the pure principles of federalism because they bring into formal contact independent government units and allow those units (the states) in some circumstances to create sub-federal, supra-state administrative agencies: a third tier of governing authority created by the collective action of the member states but not subject to the single authority of any one state. The use of interstate compacts as governing mechanisms addressing interstate matters beyond common boundary disputes is largely a development of the twentieth century, compelled by the explosion in interstate issues and the continuing development of government institutions in response to the economic, political, and social integration of the nation. Therefore, the use of interstate compacts to create ongoing administrative and regulatory agencies is a natural outgrowth of modern government and a necessity if states intend to manage their multilateral relationships short of federal preemption. For example, the creation of the Washington Metropolitan Area Transit Authority (WMATA) by an interstate compact[32] was arguably inevitable given the growing infrastructure needs of the Washington, D.C. metropolitan area. Absent federal intervention, an interstate compact between the District of Columbia, Maryland, and Virginia offered the only *fully binding* mechanism to resolve a complex multistate issue of exceeding importance to that region: the creation, integration and management of mass transit systems in an urban area spanning several independent and sovereign governmental units. Likewise, the air transportation needs of that area resulted in the adoption of an interstate compact between the District of Columbia and the Commonwealth of Virginia creating the Metropolitan Washington Airport Authority to administer Reagan National Airport and Dulles International Airport. Both of these compacts illustrate the need to take a regional approach to multistate regulation, an approach that recognizes that many affairs, and particularly those of large multistate metropolitan areas, ignore state boundaries and therefore can only be addressed on a regional basis with quasi-regional governments not directly answerable to any particular state.

---

32. Washington Metropolitan Area Transit Regulation Compact (1981).

The modern use of interstate compacts has raised new issues regarding congressional consent requirements, administration of compact affairs, and the breadth of topics subject to resolution through the compact mechanism. Compacts come in various natures, the subject matter of which is limited only by the creativity of the drafters, the readiness of state legislatures to adopt a compact, and the willingness of Congress to give its consent, if necessary. An unusual feature of an interstate compact does not make it invalid; the combined legislative powers of Congress and of the several states permit a wide range of permutations and combinations for governmental action.[33] Consequently, Congress and the states can construct alternative regional governments with particularized powers notwithstanding any specific constitutional principles authorizing such government units. The subject matter of an interstate compact is not, therefore, limited by any specific constitutional restrictions; rather, as with any "contract," the subject matter is largely left to the discretion of the parties, in this case the member states and Congress in the exercise of its consent authority, if applicable. As will be discussed in greater detail, when it approves a compact, Congress exercises the legislative power that the compact threatens to encroach upon, and declares that the compact is consistent with Congress's supreme power in that area. This is, in effect, the only restriction on either the compacting process or specific subject matter of the agreement short of finding the compact itself unconstitutional. Accordingly, just as Congress may itself enact a law that interferes with interstate commerce, for example, it may also give approval to a multi-state compact interfering with interstate commerce.[34] Compacts can, therefore, affect national interests, but generally only in those cases where Congress consents.

Because of the broad nature of the compact instrument, it is difficult to categorize neatly or with great specificity the types of compacts now in effect. Some have tried to categorize compacts along very fine lines of delineation, such as facilities (bridges and tunnels), marketing and development (promoting sale of agricultural products), or lottery (to administer interstate lotteries), to name just a few examples. In fact, some broader generalizations or characterizations can be made that essentially divide compacts into three categories. Perhaps the most familiar compacts are boundary compacts, which establish official borders between states. Examples of such compacts include the Virginia-Tennessee Boundary Agreement of 1803, the Arizona-California

---

33. Seattle Master Builders Ass'n v. Pac. N.W. Elec. Power & Conservation Planning Council, 786 F.2d 1359 (9th Cir. 1986).
34. Intake Water Co. v. Yellowstone River Compact Comm'n, 590 F. Supp. 293 (D. Mont. 1983).

Boundary Compact of 1963, the Missouri-Nebraska Boundary Compact of 1999, and the Virginia-West Virginia Boundary Compact of 1998. Such compacts are intended to resolve outstanding jurisdictional questions between the member states and provide the only means for adjusting borders given the sovereign status of states. Boundary compacts are truly "one-shot" agreements in the sense that they do not call for the creation of ongoing administrative agencies but nevertheless resolve an interstate dispute with a high degree of finality. Such compacts are, in the end, the simplest compacts to implement because of the immediate permanency of the outcome, although the negotiations to reach consensus can be quite contentious.

It is important to note that boundary compacts can have far-reaching effects. While perhaps simple in their immediate implementation, boundary compacts can implicate a wide array of matters extending to such issues as fishing rights, taxing authority, law enforcement, transportation, and the like. For example, the Coastal Zone Management Act of 1972[35] relied upon existing or amended interstate compacts and the principle of delimination to determine whether offshore resource development was "adjacent" to a state. This determination was important because under the Coastal Energy Impact Program (CEIP), federal financial assistance was available to those coastal states off whose shores resource development was being conducted on the outer continental shelf.[36] As a result, the geographical description of the areas "adjacent" to each coastal state and the use of interstate compacts or judicial determinations had a direct impact on the amount of funds a state could realize from the program. Boundary compacts are not inconsequential.

A second category of compacts is "advisory" compacts. Such compacts are more akin to administrative agreements between states, primarily because they lack formal enforcement mechanisms and are designed not to actually resolve an interstate matter, but simply to study such matters. An example of such a compact is the Delmarva Peninsula Advisory Council Compact between Delaware, Maryland, and Virginia.[37] While creating a formal interstate body, this compact limits the council to identifying the perceived regional problems; finding solutions that improve economic conditions, quality of

---

35. 16 U.S.C. § 1456a(b)(4)(B) (1976).
36. The Coastal Energy Impact Program (CEIP) was established under the Coastal Zone Management Act of 1972, Pub. L. No. 92-583, § 308, 86 Stat. 1280, as amended by Coastal Zone Management Act Amendments of 1976, Pub. L. No. 94-370, § 7, 90 Stat. 1013 (codified at 16 U.S.C. § 1451 (1979)).
37. DEL. CODE ANN. tit. 29, § 11101 (2003); VA. CODE ANN. § 2.2-5800 (2003).

life, and environmental concerns of the Delmarva Peninsula; and reporting
the findings to the states' leaders.

By their very terms, advisory compacts cede no state sovereignty nor
delegate any governing power to a compact-created agency. As such, advisory compacts generally do not require congressional consent because they
do not contribute to political combinations that would be detrimental to the
supremacy of the federal government. However, states may seek federal participation in advisory compacts out of concern that the end result of the study
may lead to agreements that impact federal interests—for example, studies
that may lead to agreements on management of navigable rivers or riparian
rights. Seeking federal participation in this context may be precautionary and
prudent; it is not, however, *legally* required or absolutely necessary if the end
result is merely advisory to the member states. Congress may even promote
such advisory compacts, as it arguably did by creating the Northern Great
Plains Regional Authority, charging that body with developing and coordinating economic development plans and making appropriate recommendations to the states and federal government.[38] However, one must distinguish
between federal participation in an advisory compact and the need to obtain
congressional consent to such compacts. While the federal government may
be a participant, it is questionable whether congressional consent, even if
granted, would have any legal impact because of the nonbinding advisory
nature of the agreement.

Finally, the broadest and largest category of interstate compact may be
called "regulatory" or "administrative" compacts. Such compacts, which are
largely a development of the twentieth century, embrace wide-ranging topics,
including regional planning and development, crime control, agriculture, flood
control, water-resource management, education, mental health, juvenile delinquency, child support, and so forth. Examples of such compacts include the
Southern Dairy Compact[39] (regulate and provide regional price support for
dairies); the Interstate Compact for Adult Offender Supervision (regulate the
movement of adult offenders across state lines); the Midwest Radioactive Waste

---

38. 7 U.S.C. § 2009bb-1 (2003).
39. The implementation of the federally funded farm bill program—the Milk
    Income Loss Contract (MILC), 7 C.F.R. § 1430.202 (2004)—by the U.S.
    Department of Agriculture on August 13, 2002, superseded state price sup-
    port and marketing legislation, including several dairy compacts. Conse-
    quently, state dairy compacts may be listed as dormant. However, this federal
    program runs through September 30, 2005, at which time state dairy com-
    pacts may be reactivated.

Disposal Compact (regulate radioactive waste disposal); the Columbia River Gorge Compact (zoning regulation, planning and development); the Interstate Mining Compact (establish a commission to promote conservation and standards for land restoration, and promote natural resource development); the Tahoe Regional Planning Compact (creates an administrative agency and regulates land use, development, and riparian rights in the Lake Tahoe Basin); and the Washington Metropolitan Area Transit Regulation Compact (regulates passenger transportation by private carrier). Perhaps the best-known and first truly "regulatory" compact is the 1921 Port Authority of New York–New Jersey Compact, which provides joint agency regulation of transportation, terminal, commerce, and trade facilities in the New York City metropolitan area. The New York–New Jersey Port Authority Compact represents the beginning of a shift in the use of compacts away from making border adjustments and toward regulating a broad class of interstate activities through the creation of suprastate, sub-federal administrative agencies.

Although boundary and advisory compacts continue to exist, and boundary compacts continue to be used on an irregular basis, it is the administrative compact that has become the subject of great interest in recent years.[40] Administrative compacts empower the member states, acting in their joint and collective capacity, to provide coordinated regulation on a broad range of activities largely without regard to state borders. Most important, many administrative compacts have given rise to independent and ongoing administrative agencies, such as the New York–New Jersey Port Authority, that occupy a unique space in the design of American government. Such commissions are neither federal in nature nor state in scope. Administrative compacts have created powerful governing commissions appropriately described as a "third tier" of government, a tier that occupies that space between the sphere of federal authority and the sphere of individual state authority.

1.2.2   Contracts Between States

In defining the nature of compacts, it is perhaps more useful to define what they are not. While enacted virtually identically by every party state's legislative body, compacts are not uniform laws or model laws as those terms are typically understood in the legal community. Uniform laws—such as the

---

40. One of the most recent boundary compacts is the Missouri-Nebraska Boundary Compact, which sought to address state-line issues as a result of changes in the channel of the Missouri River. *See* Pub. L. No. 106-101, 113 Stat. 1333 (1999). *See also* Red River Boundary Compact, Pub. L. No. 106-288, 114 Stat. 919 (2000).

Uniform Commercial Code, the Uniform Probate Code, and the Gifts to Minors Act—are enacted largely verbatim in each state. Model acts are designed to serve as guideline legislation that states can borrow from or adapt to suit their individual needs and conditions. Promulgated by the National Conference of Commissioners on Uniform State Laws, uniform acts represent the outcome of an effort to study and review the laws of the states and determine which areas should be uniform between the states. Legislatures are urged to adopt uniform acts exactly as written to promote such uniformity.

Although legislatures are urged to adopt uniform acts as written, they are not required to do so and may make changes to fit individual state needs. Uniform acts do not constitute a contract between the states, even if adopted by all states in the same form, and thus, unlike contracts, are not binding upon or enforceable *against* the states. Each state retains complete authority to unilaterally amend or change such codes to meet its unique circumstances. There is no prohibition in uniform acts limiting the ability of state legislatures to alter particular provisions as times change or to address the peculiar domestic political circumstances in a state. A state may, in the exercise of its authority over intrastate matters, amend or repeal a uniform law in total. Although there may be a common understanding among state legislatures that uniform acts require uniformity to be effective on a national basis, there is no legal consequence to a state ignoring the desire or need for such uniformity. The failure of a state to enact or maintain "uniformity" carries no legal consequence; one state cannot sue another state in the U.S. Supreme Court for damages or enforcement of a uniformity requirement. Consequently, there exist variations between states in their respective versions of the Uniform Commercial Code. It is not uncommon, therefore, to find many "uniform" laws distinctly non-uniform when compared on a state-to-state basis.

Neither are compacts administrative agreements between state agencies entered into to ease the flow of commerce, information, or the like across state lines. Such agreements, frequently created by comparable state executive agencies, usually subject to some prior legislative approval, have limited application and effect. For example, the Pennsylvania state legislature has specifically authorized the execution of administrative agreements between its state agencies and those of other states for the purpose of air pollution control. [41] A reciprocity provision of an act that empowers a secretary of state to ascertain which states grant reciprocity to other residents and to embody the findings in the official form of a "reciprocity agreement" does not rise to

41. One example of a legislatively authorized administrative agreement can be found at, 35 Pa. Cons. Stat. § 4103 (2003).

the level of a formal interstate compact such as to fall within the domain of the Compact Clause.[42] Statutes creating an executive department may also enable such departments to enter into reciprocal agreements with other states' agencies without further action by a state legislature.[43] Such agreements are subject to amendment through the administrative process and are clearly subject to unilateral change by individual member states, mainly because administrative agreements, even when authorized by a state legislature, cannot bind the hands of the legislature as to changing the substantive law at some future point.

Interstate compacts have qualities similar to both uniform laws and administrative agreements. They are clearly uniform between member states as evidenced by the enactment of virtually identical statutes by the legislatures of each member state. Likewise, many modern compacts address administrative matters and frequently create ongoing agencies. Compacts may even authorize the creation of "sub-compact" reciprocal agreements between member states.[44] However, compacts are a fundamental departure from the more common mechanisms of state-based adjustments to interstate relations or the creation of uniformity between states because they are fundamentally instruments for contractually allocating collective state governing authority. This in turn may require the member states to cede a portion of their individual sovereignty for the collective good of the member states. Therefore, compacts, when properly enacted, are fully enforceable contracts between the members in addition to possessing legal standing within each state. Unlike administrative agreements or uniform laws, interstate compacts are the sole example of the power of one state legislature to bind all future legislatures to certain principles governing the subject matter of the agreement. The Contracts Clause of the U.S. Constitution prohibits the impairment of contracts, and that prohibition extends to interstate compacts.

For example, in the case of the Interstate Compact for Adult Offender Supervision, all member states are bound in an enforceable agreement governing the controlled movement of adult offenders across state lines. Any subsequent legislative act by a member state, short of outright repeal pursuant to the terms of the compact, cannot substantively change the nature of the relationship between the member states nor the governing principles outlined in the compact. In effect, by agreeing to enter into a compact, member states

---

42. Bode v. Barrett, 106 N.E.2d 521 (Ill. 1952).
43. Roberts Tobacco Co. v. Michigan Dep't of Revenue, 34 N.W.2d 54 (Mich. 1948).
44. State v. Manning, 532 N.W.2d 244 (Minn. 1995).

contractually cede a portion of their individual jurisdiction, sovereignty, and authority over the subject matter of the compact in favor of certain governing principles that apply collectively to all member states. As observed in *Hellmuth v. WMATA*: "Upon entering into an interstate compact, a state effectively surrenders a portion of its sovereignty; the compact governs the relations of the parties with respect to the subject matter of the agreement and is superior to both prior and subsequent law. Further, when enacted, a compact constitutes not only law, but a contract which may not be amended, modified, or otherwise altered without the consent of all parties. It, therefore, appears settled that one party may not enact legislation which would impose burdens upon the compact absent the concurrence of the other signatories."[45] This ceding of sovereign authority is a vital consideration in determining whether an interstate agreement rises to the level of an enforceable interstate compact. It is a concession to all member states that an individual state cannot subsequently alter absent an outright repeal of the agreement (if permitted) or the consent of all other member states.

The contractual nature of compacts is evidenced by the principles underlying their adoption. Interstate compacts are initiated when member states adopt enabling statutes. The act of adoption of such statutes creates contractual obligations between the states. There is an offer (a proposal to enact virtually verbatim statutes by each member state), an acceptance (enactment of the statutes by the member states), and consideration (the settlement of a dispute, creation of an association, or some mechanism to address an issue of mutual interest). Many compacts also contain provisions for withdrawal or termination.[46] Compacts are most often entered by state legislatures adopting virtually identical statutes. However, compacts can also be activated by legislative acts authorizing entry into force by administrative action. For example, the Non-

---

45. Hellmuth v. Wash. Metro. Area Transit Auth., 414 F. Supp. 408, 409 (D. Md. 1976).
46. For example, Article XII, Section A of the Interstate Compact for Adult Offender Supervision ("ICAOS") provides, "Once effective, the Compact shall continue in force and remain binding upon each and every Compacting State; PROVIDED, that a Compacting State may withdraw from the Compact ("Withdrawing State") by enacting a statute specifically repealing the statute which enacted the Compact into law." The provision goes on to describe the procedure by which a state actually withdraws including notice requirements, the effective date of withdraw, and state's post-withdrawal responsibilities regarding assessments, liabilities, and obligations.

resident Violator Compact of 1977 specifically provides that the compact may be entered into force "by resolution of ratification, executed by authorized officials of the applying jurisdiction."[47] However, the language of the compact must specifically provide a mechanism for entry into force by administrative action for the compact to be valid and binding. If a state uses an administrative act without specific compact authorization, the compact may be null and void as to that state. For example, the Drivers License Compact of 1961 specifically provided that the compact "enter[s] into force and becomes effective as to any state when it has enacted the [Compact] into law."[48] The Pennsylvania Supreme Court held in *Sullivan v. Department of Transportation* that the compact was not in effect in that state because the legislature enacted a statute empowering the secretary of the department of transportation to enter into the compact rather than enact the specific language of the compact as required.[49] In reaching its conclusion, the court held that since the compact was a contract, Pennsylvania law required the court to interpret the compact within the four-corners of the instrument and nowhere in the instrument was administrative action authorized as a means of adoption.

It is important, therefore, to appreciate that compacts are more than mere intergovernmental agreements or informal administrative alliances. Although passed by state legislatures in essentially the same form, compacts are not "uniform laws" as that term is commonly understood. While uniform acts unify state laws as to those states adopting them, compacts provide the enforcement tools uniform laws lack, not only as to the populace but also as to the states themselves. Compacts are, therefore, a more powerful—albeit complex—tool for promoting *uniform state behavior* as to the subject matter of the compact. Compacts are binding legal contracts with their terms and conditions controlling—even trumping—the actions and conduct of the member states concerning the subject matter of the compact.[50] As one court has noted:

---

47. Nonresident Violator Compact, art. XII (1994).
48. Drivers License Compact, art. XII(a) (1994).
49. Sullivan v. Dep't of Transp., 708 A.2d 481 (Pa. 1998).
50. *See, e.g.*, Missouri v. Illinois, 200 U.S. 496, 519 (1906) ("The compact, by the sanction of Congress, had become a law of the Union. A state law which violated it was unconstitutional."). *See also* Nebraska v. Central Interstate Low-Level Radioactive Waste Comm'n, 207 F.3d 1021 (8th Cir. 2000) (State cannot unilaterally exercise a veto when such is not authorized by the compact.); Rhode Island v. Massachusetts, 37 U.S. 657, 725 (1838) ("By this surrender of the power, which before the adoption of the constitution was vested in every state * * * as in the plenitude of their sovereignty they might; they could settle them neither by war, or in peace, by treaty, compact or

An interstate compact functions as a contract and "takes precedence over statutory law in member states." The law of interstate compacts as interpreted by the U.S. Supreme Court is clear that interstate compacts are the highest form of state statutory law, having precedence over conflicting state statutes [.] Having entered into a contract, a participant state may not unilaterally change its terms.[51]

The fact that compacts are creations and creatures of individual state legislatures in no way alters their status as enforceable contractual obligations between member states. Many compacts constitute an unmistakable surrendering of state authority that is binding on subsequent state legislative action. Such compacts are, therefore, examples of the so-called "unmistakability doctrine" at work. The impetus for the modern unmistakability doctrine is found in Chief Justice Marshall's application of the Contract Clause to public contracts. Although the clause made it possible for state legislatures to bind their successors by entering into contracts, it soon became apparent that such contracts could become a threat to the sovereign responsibilities of state governments. Accordingly, courts became less willing to recognize contractual restraints upon legislative freedom of action, and two distinct limitations developed to protect state regulatory powers. One came to be known as the "reserved powers" doctrine, which held that certain substantive powers of sovereignty could not be contracted away. The other, which surfaced somewhat earlier, was a canon of construction disfavoring implied governmental obligations in public contracts. Under this rule, "all public grants are strictly construed."[52] Consequently, no "power of sovereignty, will be held . . . to have been surrendered, unless such surrender has been expressed in terms too plain to be mistaken."[53] Most administrative compacts constitute an unmistakable surrendering of state power.

---

agreement, without the permission of the new legislative power which the states brought into existence by their respective and several grants in conventions of the people. If Congress consented, then the states were in this respect restored to their original inherent sovereignty; such consent being the sole limitation imposed by the constitution, when given, left the states as they were before * * * whereby their compacts became of binding force, and finally settled the boundary between them; operating with the same effect as a treaty between sovereign powers.").

51. Doe v. Ward, 124 F. Supp.2d 900, 914-15 (W.D. Pa. 2000), *citing* McComb v. Wambaugh, 934 F.2d 474, 479 (3d Cir. 1991).
52. The Delaware Railroad Tax, 85 U.S. 206 (1874).
53. Jefferson Branch Bank v. Skelly, 66 U.S. 436 (1862).

As a contract, the terms and conditions of the compact define each party state's responsibility. For example, one term contained in the compact creating the Metropolitan Washington Airport Authority is a requirement that original jurisdiction over compact matters is vested in the courts of Virginia and that the courts "shall in all cases apply the law of the Commonwealth of Virginia."[54] Pursuant to the compact, the party states—in this case Virginia and the District of Columbia— have contractually agreed that Virginia law shall be controlling and that the courts of Virginia will be the choice of forum for resolving litigation matters. Moreover, even if suit is brought in federal court, the party states have agreed that the federal courts will apply Virginia law in any dispute or litigation. In approving this compact, Congress consented to these choice of law provisions as binding elements in the agreement.[55] Therefore, just as a contract between private parties can validly contain choice of law and choice of forum provisions, so too can an interstate compact.

This is not to say, however, that compacts are contracts on par with commercial agreements. Although termed a "contract" and effectuated by offer, acceptance and consideration, interstate compacts represent a political compromise between constituent elements of the Union. Such agreements are made to address interests and problems that do not coincide easily with the national boundaries or state lines—interests that may be badly served or not served at all by the ordinary channels of national or state political action. By entering into a compact, the member states contractually agree on certain principles and rules concerning the exercise of joint governing authority over the subject matter of the compact. As noted in *Hess v. Port Authority Trans-Hudson Corporation*, "[a]n interstate compact, by its very nature, shifts a part of a state's authority to another state or states, or to the agency the several states jointly create to run the compact."[56] For example, in a boundary compact, the member states agree to certain principles dividing their respective governing authority over a disputed boundary. In effect, they contracted away their respective sovereignty relative to certain parcels of land. While one might argue that the consideration for a boundary compact is the land, the actual consideration is the reallocation of governing authority between the two states by settling a dispute over a geographical boundary. Likewise, in the adoption of many administrative compacts, the member states have collectively and contractually agreed to reallocate governing authority away from individual states to a multilateral relationship

---

54. Va. Code Ann. § 5.1-173(A) (2003); D.C. Code Ann. § 9-901 *et seq.* (2003).

55. Washington-Dulles Transport. Ltd. v. Metro. Wash. Airports Auth., 263 F.3d. 371 (4th Cir. 2001).

56. Hess v. Port Auth. Trans-Hudson Corp., 513 U.S. 30, 42 (1994).

defined by commonly accepted principles. Depending on the terms of the compact, states may effectively cede a portion of their individual sovereignty over the subject of the agreement.

A perfect example of states ceding their sovereignty through an interstate compact can be found in Article XIV, Sections A and B of the Interstate Compact for Adult Offender Supervision. These two sections of the compact provide, in part, that (1) "[a]ll compacting States' laws conflicting with this Compact are superseded to the extent of the conflict;" and (2) "All lawful actions of the Interstate Commission, including all Rules and By-laws promulgated by the Interstate Commission, are binding upon the Compacting States." The compact further provides that, "All agreements between the Interstate Commission and the Compacting States are binding in accordance with their terms." The drafters of the compact did provide two escape clauses concerning the binding effect of the compact and its rules. First, to the extent that a provision of the compact exceeds the constitutional limitations imposed on the legislature of any compacting state, "the duties, powers or jurisdiction sought to be conferred by such provision upon the Interstate Commission shall be ineffective and such obligations, duties, powers or jurisdiction shall remain in the Compacting State." Second, a rule of the commission may be rejected by a majority vote of the member states' legislatures. These are, however, the only means by which a state's sovereign interests may be protected from the actions of the commission, the states having generally ceded to the commission their sovereignty over the interstate movement of adult offenders.[57]

Once entered, the terms of the compact and any rules and regulations authorized by the compact can, to the extent provided in the agreement, supersede any substantive state laws that may be in conflict, including even state constitutional provisions. Under the Compact Clause, the federal questions are the execution, validity, and meaning of federally approved state compacts. A compact controls over a state's application of its own law through the Supremacy Clause and the Contracts Clause of the Constitution. As observed in *West Virginia ex rel. Dyer v. Sims:*

> It has frequently been held that when a question is suitably raised whether the law of a State has impaired the obligation of a contract, in violation of the constitutional provision, this Court must determine for itself whether a contract exists, what are its obligations, and whether they have been impaired by the legislation of the State. While this Court always examines with appropriate respect the deci-

---

57. *See generally* Interstate Compact for Adult Offender Supervision (2002).

sions of state courts bearing upon such questions, such decisions do not detract from the responsibility of this Court in reaching its own conclusions as to the contract, its obligations and impairment, for otherwise the constitutional guaranty could not properly be enforced.[58]

The contractual nature of the agreement and its federal standing, where applicable, trumps individual state statutory schemes because, through the compact, the member states cede individual state authority in favor of a multilateral resolution to a dispute or in favor of multilateral regulation of an interstate matter. The member states cannot take unilateral steps, such as the adoption of conflicting legislation or the issuance of executive orders or court rules that violate the terms of a compact.[59] The standing of compacts, as contracts and instruments of national law applicable to the member states, generally nullifies any state action inconsistent with the terms and conditions of the agreement.

Therefore, once adopted, the only means available to change the substance of a compact (and the obligations it imposes on a member state) is through withdrawal and renegotiation of its terms, or through an amendment adopted by all member states in essentially the same form. The contractual nature of compacts controls over unilateral action by a state, including such actions as a state legislature's adoption of a contract under the compact clause, which could itself "impair the obligation of contracts." The "trumping" nature of compacts would extend not only to unilateral action by the state legislatures but also to unilateral actions by executive agencies and state courts. A state court could not unilaterally apply one state's law over another, absent a specific provision in the compact providing choice of law, because the signatories would not have consented to the broad application of a particular state's law to disputes.[60] For example, court rules that might conflict with a

---

58. West Virginia *ex rel.* Dyer v. Sims, 341 U.S. 22, 29 (1951). *See also* Kentucky v. Indiana, 281 U.S. 163 (1930); Indiana *ex rel.* Anderson v. Brand, 303 U.S. 95 (1938).

59. *See,* Northeast Bancorp v. Bd. of Governors of Fed. Reserve Sys., 472 U.S. 159 (1985) (reciprocal statutes passed by two states do not constitute a compact when states retain authority to unilaterally modify or repeal the statutes and the effect of the statutes is not conditioned upon the action of another state).

60. Hellmuth v. Wash. Metro. Area Transit Auth., 414 F. Supp. 408 (D. Md. 1976) (Maryland's public document act does not apply to WMATA as the compact did not contain a choice of law provision and the signatories did not agree to be bound by Maryland law).

provision in an interstate compact would most likely be void. Likewise, an executive order or departmental rules or policies that conflict with the terms and conditions of an interstate compact would also most likely be void.

The restrictive nature of a compact would not only extend to state actions, but would also extend to the actions of its political subdivisions. A county probation department could not act outside the parameters of the terms and rules of the Interstate Compact for Adult Offender Supervision in discharging its supervisory responsibilities over persons transferred into the state or in sending its probationers to another state. By entering into a compact, a state legislature binds "the state," including all of its governmental branches, departments, and political subdivisions.

There is, however, one exception to the general principle that, once adopted, member states cannot unilaterally impose individual state law on a compact or a compact-created commission. When a compact specifically reserves to the member states the authority to impose individual state law in an area governed by a compact, the imposition of that law is not nullified simply because the compact is an instrument of national law. Thus, as noted in *California Department of Transportation v. South Lake Tahoe* the application of state law to a bi-state entity is "precluded unless the Compact reserves * * * the right to impose such requirements."[61] The reservation of such rights in a compact can be a permissible element of the member states' agreement.

States are not, however, just parties to an ordinary, run-of-the-mill contract. The mere fact that the Supreme Court may exercise its very limited original jurisdiction in compact disputes is one indication of the importance the Framers attached to the status of states as sovereign members joined in a constituent union. This special status of states can present unique "contractual" issues, particularly with enforcing the terms of a compact. For example, in *South Dakota v. North Carolina,* the Supreme Court recognized the propriety of money judgments against states as part of an original action, but acknowledged that getting a state legislature to actually pay another state can present a unique problem.[62] However, the Supreme Court also noted in *Texas*

---

61. California Dep't of Transp. v. S. Lake Tahoe, 466 F. Supp. 527, 537 (E.D. Cal. 1978).
62. South Dakota v. North Carolina, 192 U.S. 286 (1904). *See also* Texas v. New Mexico, 482 U.S. 124, 130 (1987) ("The Court has recognized the propriety of money judgments against a State in an original action, and specifically in a case involving a compact. In proper original actions, the Eleventh Amendment is no barrier, for by its terms, it applies only to suits by citizens against a State." (citations omitted)). *See also* Maryland v. Louisiana, 451 U.S. 725 (1981). As to the limitations on actions to recover damages from states, *see*

v. New Mexico, "That there may be difficulties in enforcing judgments against States counsels caution, but does not undermine our authority to enter judgments against defendant States in cases over which the Court has undoubted jurisdiction, authority that is attested to by the fact that almost invariably the 'States against which judgments were rendered, conformably to their duty under the Constitution, voluntarily respected and gave effect to the same.'"[63] Thus, notwithstanding the special status of states and the challenges presented with enforcing compacts, compacts fundamentally constitute enforceable obligations between the states just as if the states were acting as private parties to a legal contract.

1.3   THE ADVANTAGES AND DISADVANTAGES OF INTERSTATE COMPACTS

Administrative compacts are advantageous in managing multistate issues that do not typically fall within the ambit of federal authority. American

---

Kansas v. Colorado, 533 U.S. 1, 7 (2001) ("Colorado contends, however, that the Eleventh Amendment precludes any such recovery based on losses sustained by individual water users in Kansas. It is firmly established, and undisputed in this litigation, that the text of the Eleventh Amendment would bar a direct action against Colorado by citizens of Kansas. Moreover, we have several times held that a State may not invoke our original jurisdiction when it is merely acting as an agent or trustee for one or more of its citizens."). *See also* New Hampshire v. Louisiana, 108 U.S. 76 (1883) (court will not assume jurisdiction over an action to recover payment on defaulted bonds that had been formally assigned to the state but remained beneficially owned by private individuals; Eleventh Amendment bars jurisdiction where the state is only a nominal actor in the proceeding); North Dakota v. Minnesota, 263 U.S. 365 (1923), (state could obtain an injunction against the improper operation of Minnesota's drainage ditches, but the Eleventh Amendment barred damages based on injuries to individual farmers where the damages claim was financed by contributions from the farmers and the state had committed to dividing any recovery among the farmers in proportion to the amount of their loss); Oklahoma *ex rel.* Johnson v. Cook, 304 U.S. 387 (1938) (to invoke original jurisdiction of the Supreme Court, a state must show a direct interest of its own and not merely seek recovery for the benefit of individuals who are the real parties in interest).

63. Texas v. New Mexico, 482 U.S. 124, 130-31 (1987) (by ratifying the Constitution, states gave Supreme Court complete judicial power to adjudicate disputes among them, and this power includes the capacity to provide one state a remedy for the breach of another).

federalism rests on the shared exercise of government authority by two sovereign bodies, and thus solutions to problems have generally been conceived in term of exclusive duality. Those matters of national concern, such as interstate commerce, foreign affairs, and national defense, rest within the exclusive authority of the federal government, while the states exercise a significant portion of the nation's general police power as entities whose sovereignty is coterminous with that of the federal government's. Even today some argue that the "Constitution requires a distinction between what is truly national and what is truly local."[64] However, the experience of recent years shows that complex regional or national problems show little respect for the dual lines of federalism or the geographical boundaries of individual states. This fact has encouraged the reemergence of interstate compacts not only as devices for adjusting interstate relations but also as instruments for governing large regional or national issues.

As early as 1921, the U.S. Supreme Court noted in *New York v. New Jersey*: "We cannot withhold the suggestion, inspired by the consideration of this case, that the grave problem of sewage disposal presented by the large and growing populations living on the shores of New York Bay is one more likely to be wisely solved by cooperative study and by conference and mutual concession on the part of representatives of the States so vitally interested in it than by proceedings in any court however constituted."[65] The practicalities of governing a large, multifaceted, federally designed nation frequently blurs distinctions between what is distinctly "national" in scope and what is distinctly "local" in scope. The emergence of broad public policy issues that ignore state boundaries and the principles of federalism have presented new governing challenges to both state and federal authorities. Currently, some 30 of the largest metropolitan areas in the United States extend across state lines affecting almost 25 percent of the population of the United States and creating regional concerns.

This is precisely where interstate compacts provide an effective solution that respects fundamental principles of federalism, recognizing the supremacy of the federal government regarding national issues while allowing the states to take appropriate collective action in addressing supra-state problems. Thus, compacts enable the states, in their sovereign capacities, to act jointly and collectively, generally outside the confines of the federal legislative or regula-

---

64. United States v. Morrison, 529 U.S. 598, 617-18 (2000) (holding unconstitutional the civil rights remedy of the Violence Against Women Act, 42 U.S.C. 13981).
65. New York v. New Jersey, 256 U.S. 296, 313 (1921).

tory process, while concomitantly respecting the view of Congress on the appropriateness of joint action. Because federal government agencies are generally politically removed from state interests, federal administrators tend not to emphasize regional concerns, thus portraying some insensitivity toward important state interests. The interstate compact provides states with the opportunity to offset this federal insensitivity. Equally important, compacts can effectively preempt federal interference into matters that are traditionally within the purview of the states but that have regional or national implications.

Unlike federal actions that impose unilateral, rigid mandates, administrative compacts afford states the opportunity to develop dynamic, self-regulatory systems over which the member states can maintain control through a coordinated legislative and administrative process.[66] The very nature of an interstate compact makes it an ideal tool to meet the need of cooperative state action in developing and enforcing standards upon the member states. Compacts also enable the states to develop adaptive structures that can evolve to meet new and increased challenges that naturally arise over time.[67] In short, through the compact device, states acting jointly can control not only the solution to a problem but also shape the future agenda as the problem changes. However, to achieve the ends of flexibility and responsiveness, states must adopt compacts that provide sufficient elasticity to allow adaptation to address future developments.

Given these general benefits, interstate compacts also offer very specific benefits. First, compacts can be fashioned to provide for a high level of responsiveness to local and state needs. States in a specific region or involved with a specific issue are generally more familiar with the circumstances surrounding such problems than federal officials, who are generally more geographically and politically removed. This in turn allows for more responsive regulation than perhaps the federal regulatory process affords. State officials are, therefore, more likely sensitive to the type of regulation needed to address the problem efficiently and effectively.

---

66. It is important to note that compact-created agencies are not per se exempt from federal and state law simply as a function of being a unique creature of state action. Thus, the Family and Medical Leave Act, the Fair Labor Standards Act, and other acts may apply equally to compact-created agencies as to another agency of the states or the federal government, subject of course to consideration of Eleventh Amendment immunity. *Cf.*, Lizzi v. Alexander, 255 F.3d 128 (4th Cir. 2001).

67. The Supreme Court has recognized the flexibility of compacts to meet both immediate and future concerns. *See, e.g.*, Colorado v. Kansas, 320 U.S. 383, 392 (1943).

Second, interstate compacts can be structured to respect the balance of power among federal, state, and local interests. While many administrative compacts provide power to regulate cross-border problems, they can be structured to do so in a manner that preserves national interests while retaining sensitivity to more parochial interests. To a large extent the Compact Clause requirement of congressional consent to those compacts impacting federal interests ensures that federal concerns are at the forefront of compact design and construction, while simultaneously enabling states to maintain functional and regulatory control over an issue. Approval by Congress provides states with the authority to regulate in an area that would otherwise be unavailable to them. It should be noted, however, that while compacts may be designed to address local matters, they remain agreements between sovereign states and are not subject to control by sub-state units of local government.

Third, interstate compacts can broaden parochial focus by allowing states to act collectively and jointly in addressing regional and national problems. Making decisions based solely on an individual state's boundary can be problematic because, as noted, boundaries do not necessarily reflect the natural or logical divisions often present in many supra-state problems. Absent a binding agreement, state legislatures and state regulators generally do not make decisions that are likely to restrict their own citizens' activities based on the need to protect a neighboring state's interests. Consequently, an interstate compact provides the opportunity to make decisions across state boundaries without resorting to federalization as the only means for resolving matters that have broad cross-state implications. While respecting the boundaries, interstate compacts can enlarge the member states' sphere of power.

Finally, depending on its design and construction, an interstate compact can provide member states with a predictable, stable, and enforceable mechanism for policy control and implementation. Generally the contractual nature of the agreement, particularly in the regulatory context, ensures its effectiveness and enforceability on the member states. The fact that interstate compacts cannot be unilaterally amended provides member states with a predictable and stable policy platform for resolving problems. By entering into an interstate compact, each party state acquires the legal right to require the other states to perform under the terms and conditions of the compact.

The principle disadvantage of compacts may be characterized as threefold: (1) the long negotiations and arduous course they must run before becoming effective; (2) the ceding of traditional state sovereignty to quasi-independent bodies as required by several administrative compacts and the reluctance of states to cede such authority; and (3) compliance and enforceability. Interstate compacts are entered into force when state legislatures adopt the compact in substantively the same form if not outright verbatim.

Thus, to be effective, the compact instrument cannot substantively be altered by individual state legislatures solely to meet unique state needs. The very purpose of an interstate compact, which is to provide for the collective allocation of governing authority between member states, does not allow much room for individualism. The requirement of substantive sameness prevents member states from passing dissimilar enactments notwithstanding, perhaps, pressing state differences with respect to particular matters within the compact. For example, in the context of Midwest Radioactive Waste Compact, it is impossible for a member state to adopt provisions that substantively change the allocation of governing authority between all member states. However, as anyone who has attempted to get legislation through a state legislature knows, individual state concerns and intrastate political interests cannot be underestimated as a source for derailment. It is difficult to get state legislatures to adopt compacts because of the strict requirement of substantive sameness between all member states and the tendency of parochial political interest to trump consideration for interstate cooperation.

Secondly, by their nature, most interstate compacts—even boundary compacts—require member states to cede some portion of their sovereignty, an act many state legislatures only reluctantly agree to do. Although boundary compacts can present difficult sovereignty questions, the matter of state sovereignty becomes particularly problematic when interstate compacts create ongoing administrative bodies that possess substantial governing power. Such compacts are truly a creation of the twentieth century as an out-growth of the modern administrative state. Any compact that seeks to allocate governing authority—as distinguished from a compact that merely calls for study— necessarily implicates a reallocation of sovereignty away from the traditional control of the state and to an intermediate administrative agency that is largely unregulated by individual state action or concerns. By entering into many administrative compacts, state authorities effectively cede some portion of state control over a matter that was traditionally "state" in nature, but which has become supra-state in scope. In place of individual state management, states have tilted toward the creation of supra-state administrative and management structures. This ceding of traditional state sovereignty to supra-state administrative bodies effectively means that individual states lose direct policy control over the issue that sparked interest in the compact.

Finally, although compacts are contracts between the member states, the state themselves are not ordinary parties in any sense. As sovereign entities, states enjoy a level of autonomy not available to any other government unit, save the federal government. Consequently, to a large degree, the effectiveness of a compact continues to rest upon the willingness of the member states to actually abide by the terms and conditions of the agreement notwithstanding its contractual nature. This is particularly the case with administrative compacts. These compacts frequently create ongoing administrative bodies charged with overseeing and implementing the agreement. These bodies are not, however, state bodies in the traditional sense. Neither do they possess characteristics of federal agencies. As one court has noted, even obtaining congressional consent does not transform a compact-created administrative body into a "federal" agency such that the Appointments Clause of the Constitution applies to its members.[68] As a result, the enforcement of many administrative compacts falls to hybrid governmental agencies that, although possessing significant powers, must rely on the commitment of the states to abide by their agreement. Ultimately, in the absence of goodwill compliance the enforcement of compacts falls to the judicial process, which can be exceedingly expensive and time-consuming.

Although compacts may be viewed as disadvantageous when viewed purely from an individual state's perspective, their advantages in maintaining some semblance of "state" control over issues far outweigh individual concerns. In the absence of adopting an administrative compact approach to resolving many multilateral issues, states are left with a checker-board approach to managing their relationships. This lack of coordination between the states invites federal preemption over what are traditionally state matters, encourages the application of federal regulatory schemes to such issues, or leaves critical multistate matters to the mercy of individual state regulators with the attendant confusion that results when 50 states individually attempt to regulate a multilateral concern. The latter consequence should be of particular concern. Given the large number of urban areas that now span state boundaries and the explosion of multistate regulatory issues, individual state regulation is at best haphazard. Interstate compacts, when properly drafted, can provide a uniform regulatory scheme so necessary today.

1.4   IMPACT OF COMPACTS ON PRIVATE INTERESTS

The contractual nature of interstate compacts as mechanisms for allocating state governing authority could lead some to minimize the impact of such agreements on private interests. Yet compacts can have a direct and substantial impact on private parties and private interests. For example, a boundary compact that moves an established state line not only impacts an array of state authorities, ranging from law enforcement to courts to taxing bodies, but also can affect the interests of individual citizens. Changes in boundaries can affect

---

68. Seattle Master Builders Ass'n v. Pac. N.W. Elec. Power & Conservation Planning Council, 786 F.2d 1359 (9th Cir. 1986).

land titles that stretch back years, change citizens' tax obligations by subjecting them to taxation by multiple states, change the terms and conditions of property ownership, and even result in boundaries that are inconvenient to private property by placing the boundary in the middle of building.[69] A court cannot grant to private parties title to land that is later determined by interstate compact or Supreme Court decree to be beyond the true boundaries of the state.[70] Such determinations by compact or decree affect the private property rights of the citizens of a state as well as those matters that pertain to a state's sovereignty over the land within the boundaries of the state. Title, jurisdiction, and sovereignty are dependent questions. The fixing of a boundary by interstate compact does not result in the divesting of citizens' titles to lands that were derived from grants under the state. Rather, the citizens' titles are invalid as a matter of law because of the intrinsic defect of title in the states.

The impact of interstate compacts on private interests has grown remarkably in more recent times given the increasing use of these instruments as a regulatory device. In general, the adoption of an interstate compact by a state, as well as regulatory decisions promulgated under a compact, act to bind not only the state in its official capacity but also the citizens of the state.[71] Consequently, while compacts may once have been used strictly to adjust state relationships with private instruments impacted as a byproduct such as adjustments, today many administrative compacts have direct and measurable consequences on private parties. This has particularly become the case involving those administrative compacts that affect property interests and, to a lesser extent, those compacts affecting the liberty interests of criminal offenders and juveniles. In both contexts, the courts have recognized the power of regulatory commissions to manage not only interstate relations, but also to affect the interests of private parties not as a byproduct of a compact but as a direct and purposeful consequence of the compact.[72]

---

69. New Jersey v. New York, 523 U.S. 767, 811 (1998) ("We appreciate the difficulties of a boundary line that divides not just an island but some of the buildings on it, but these drawbacks are the price of New Jersey's success in litigating under a compact whose fair construction calls for a line so definite.").
70. Rhode Island v. Massachusetts, 37 U.S. 657 (1838); Poole v. Lessee of Fleeger, 36 U.S. 185 (1837).
71. Hinderlider v. La Plata River & Cherry Creek Ditch Co., 304 U.S. 92 (1938) (states and their citizens are bound by the terms of compact). *See also* Frontier Ditch Co. v. Southeastern Colo. Water Conservancy Dist., 761 P.2d 1117 (Colo. 1998).
72. Badgley v. New York, 606 F.2d 358 (2d Cir. 1979).

There are many other examples of states employing administrative compacts, and sometimes their attendant commission or agencies, to create broad
regulatory schemes that affect a broad range of private interests. Courts have
recognized the authority of the Pacific Northwest Electric Power and Conservation Planning Council to promulgate the Northwest Conservation and
Electric Power Plan to meet the regional environmental and ecological concerns as mandated by the Bonneville Project Act.[73] Courts have recognized
the extensive authority of the Interstate Compact on the Placement of Children to control the movement and placement of children subject to a variety
of legal actions including temporary placement, adoption, and guardianships.
Compact commissions have been used to regulate milk price supports,[74] the
interstate movement of adult offenders,[75] and large metropolitan transit systems.[76] New York and New Jersey employed an interstate compact to create a
bi-state regulatory agency, the Waterfront Commission of New York Harbor,
to license and regulate certain employment activities on the New York waterfront in part to control the influence of organized crime.[77]

Because compacts can, to varying degrees, impact such a broad range of
private interests, courts have generally deferred to the authority of Congress,
agreements, and compact-created commissions in compact-based litigation. For
example, in *De Veau v. Braisted,* the Supreme Court upheld the validity of a
compact creating the New York Waterfront Commission even though laborers
affected by its regulations argued that the compact was an intrusion on federal
labor authority and had been preempted by several federal acts. As the Supreme Court noted, one of the fundamental objects of the compact was to
"keep criminals away from the waterfront" by imposing licensing and regulatory schemes on waterfront employment.[78] In upholding the validity of the
compact and the authority of the commission to regulate employment, including the effective exclusion from employment of certain felons, the Supreme

---

73. Seattle Master Builders Ass'n v. Pac. N.W. Elec. Power & Conservation
    Planning Council, 786 F.2d 1359 (9th Cir. 1986).
74. Organic Cow, LLC v. N.E. Dairy Compact Comm'n, 164 F. Supp. 2d 412
    (2001), *vacated* Organic Cow, LLC v. Ctr. for New England Dairy Compact
    Research, 335 F.3d 66 (2d Cir. 2003).
75. *See, e.g.,* Interstate Compact for Adult Offender Supervision (2002).
76. Washington Metropolitan Area Transit Regulation Compact (1981).
77. Waterfront Commission Act, 1953 N.Y. Laws 882, 883; 1953 N.J. Laws 202,
    203. The compact was approved by Congress in August 1953. *See* 67 Stat.
    541, c. 407 (1953).
78. De Veau v. Braisted, 363 U.S. 144, 149 (1960).

Court found that congressional authorization had effectively reconciled any conflict between the compact and federal labor law. The Commission was, therefore, duly empowered to regulate employment along the New York waterfront, and that included effectively excluding certain classes of individuals from employment by the application of its licensing and regulatory scheme.

Several examples illustrate the extent to which states have used interstate compacts as tools to regulate and manage private interests in an effort to manage interstate issues. One of the most pertinent is the Tahoe Regional Planning Compact. This compact, adopted by California and Nevada in 1968 and subsequently approved by Congress,[79] created the Tahoe Regional Planning Agency (TRPA) to manage water, land use, and development in the Lake Tahoe region. Regulatory decisions of the TRPA have been the source of significant litigation throughout the history of the compact, generally centering on regulatory control of development and land use. For example, in *Tahoe-Sierra Pres. Council v. Tahoe Regional Planning Agency*, the Supreme Court recognized the authority of the TRPA to regulate land use and to define the terms and conditions under which land use regulation constitutes a "taking" for purposes of the Due Process Clause.[80] The Court concluded that the mere enactment of the regulations by a compact-created agency that sought to implement moratoria on development did not constitute a per se taking of property. Rather, whether a taking occurred depended upon consideration of the landowners' investment-backed expectations, the actual impact of the regulation on the landowners, the importance of the public interest involved, and the reasons for imposing the temporary restriction. In effect, the Supreme Court upheld the authority of the TRPA to impose two moratoria, totaling 32 months, on development in the Lake Tahoe Basin while it formulated a comprehensive land-use plan for the area, and to do so without the need to compensate the private landowners and developers affected by the moratoria.

Dairy compacts have been another source of litigation over the years, given the broad regulatory authority possessed by their commissions, particularly in the context of price supports. In *Organic Cow, LLC v. Northeast Dairy Compact Commission,* a court held that the rules of construction of the Northeast Interstate Dairy Compact demonstrated that the intent of the compact was to establish a basic structure by which the Northeast Dairy Compact

---

79. CAL. GOV'T CODE ANN. §§ 66800-66801 (1977); NEV. REV. STAT. §§ 277.190-277.230 (1973). Congress approved the compact in 1969. *See* Pub. L. No. 91-148, 83 Stat. 360 (1969).

80. Tahoe-Sierra Pres. Council v. Tahoe Reg'l Planning Agency, 535 U.S. 302 (2002).

Commission may achieve those purposes through the application, adaptation, and development of the regulatory techniques historically associated with milk marketing and to afford the commission broad flexibility to devise regulatory mechanisms to achieve the purposes of this compact.[81] A "handler" within the meaning of the Northeast Dairy Interstate Compact is subject to the compact's over-order price obligation, regardless of the contract price the handler pays its producers.

The impact that interstate compacts have on private interests can also be more subtle than the overt examples of fixing dairy prices, establishing state boundaries (and the attendant consequences of such), settling land use policy, or controlling the movement of adult and juvenile offenders. The terms and conditions of a compact can indirectly establish rights and obligations, define the circumstances under which individuals can participate in compact activities, and regulate which laws apply in particular circumstances. In each of these examples it is the operational impact of compacts, in addition to their legal impact, that must be considered by the practitioner. Consequently, the rights and obligations of private citizens can be defined by administrative compacts and by the actions of compact-created regulatory bodies, actions that courts have generally recognized as a legitimate use of compact power and to which they have generally deferred.

---

81. Organic Cow, LLC. v. N.E. Dairy Compact Comm'n, 46 F. Supp. 2d 298 (D. Vt. 1999), *aff'd,* The Organic Cow, LLC v. N.E. Dairy Compact Comm'n, 164 F. Supp. 2d 412 (D. Vt. 2001), *vacated by* Organic Cow, LLC v. Ctr. for New England Dairy Compact Research, 335 F.3d 66 (2d Cir. 2003).

Chapter 2

THE FEDERAL GOVERNMENT'S ROLE IN INTERSTATE COMPACTS

The federal government's role in the interstate compact process can occur on several levels. The federal government has at times encouraged states to adopt compacts as a means of settling disputes or creating regulatory regimes to address ongoing problems, as evidenced by the federal prodding that led to the Interstate Compact on Adoption and Medical Assistance. Additionally, the federal government can be a member of an interstate compact as is the case with the Interstate Agreement on Detainers or the National Crime Prevention and Privacy Compact. Federal participation can also occur in less direct but equally important ways through the interaction of federal regulatory agencies with interstate compact agencies, and the application of federal laws to areas covered by interstate compacts. This most clearly happens in the field of environmental compacts given the great extent of overlapping jurisdiction between the states and federal government. Finally, and perhaps most importantly, the federal government has significant influence over the compact process through the exercise of congressional consent. Singularly taken, the act of consent, the denial of consent, or the modification of consent through subsequent congressional acts determines the fate of virtually any interstate compact falling within the ambit of the Compact Clause.

2.1   CONGRESSIONAL CONSENT REQUIREMENT

2.1.1   How Consent Is Given

The consent requirement of the Compact Clause must be read within the context of its restrictive nature. The requirement that states obtain Congress's consent to compacts does not place on Congress the concomitant requirement that it actually grant its consent to any compact presented for its consideration. Rather than empower, the Compact Clause restricts formal joint or collective state action and thus acts as a check against such action. Consequently, Congress is fully within its authority to withhold consent when, in its *political* judgment, such consent would lead to imprudent combinations, dangerous joint action, or intrusion on traditional federal matters. The granting of such consent is, therefore, a gratuity on the part of Congress not a right that the states possess under the Constitution.[1]

The Constitution does not establish specific procedures that states must follow in obtaining congressional consent to interstate compacts nor does it outline specific procedures that Congress must respect in granting consent. Although the Constitution is silent on the matter, tradition demonstrates that congressional consent is generally given in one of three ways. First, consent can be explicitly given upon submission of a compact by the member states for approval by Congress. Such consent is most often seen in compacts that resolve boundary disputes, but can occur in other areas. For example, in 1999 Congress gave its consent to the establishment of the boundary between South Carolina and Georgia.[2] Congress gave similar consent to a boundary compact between Missouri and Nebraska establishing the middle of the Missouri River as the border between the two states.[3] Such after-the-fact consent has an advantage over other forms of consent. By obtaining explicit consent after state legislatures have adopted a compact instrument, Congress has the opportunity to review the purpose of the instrument and the opportunity to express its agreement or disagreement in clear and unambiguous terms. Other forms of congressional consent are generally more expansive and nonspecific, which can lead to costly and complicated questions as to, for example, whether a specific compact was appropriately authorized by Congress.

---

1. College Sav. Bank v. Fla. Prepaid Postsecondary Ed. Expense Bd., 527 U.S. 666 (1999).
2. Pub. L. No. 106-90, 113 Stat. 1307 (1999).
3. Missouri-Nebraska Boundary Compact of 1999, Pub. L. No. 106-101, 113 Stat. 1333 (1999).

Second, Congress may give its consent broadly and in an advanced manner by adopting legislation that encourages states to enter into interstate compacts for a specific purpose or by granting consent in advance of the actual adoption of a compact by the states.[4] There are several examples of "advanced consent." Under the Crime Control Compact Consent Act of 1934, Congress authorized "any two or more States to enter into agreements or compacts for cooperative effort and mutual assistance in the prevention of crime and in the enforcement of their respective criminal laws and policies, and to establish such agencies, joint or otherwise, as they may deem desirable for making effective such agreements and compacts."[5] The Interstate Compact for Adult Offender Supervision adopted in 2002 relies upon this 1934 statute. Likewise, Congress gave its advanced consent to states authorizing the development of interstate pilot banking programs for the financing of highway infrastructure,[6] the development of radioactive waste disposal facilities,[7] coordination of mass metropolitan transit systems,[8] and for the construction of deep water ports.[9] Congress has sought to grant consent in other areas as well.[10] While such consent is legally effective, its broad and advanced nature can deprive Congress of the opportunity to review the specific purposes of the compact and express its explicit approval of the agreement. This lack of specificity can lead to questions regarding the need for congressional consent or the intent of Congress in encouraging the use of a compact. In granting advanced consent, however, Congress can attach conditions to mitigate the use of compacts as a means to preempt federal authority in certain areas.[11]

---

4. Petty v. Tennessee-Missouri Bridge Comm'n, 359 U.S. 275, 281-82 (1959).

5. 4 U.S.C. § 112 (2003).

6. Pub. L. No. 104-59, tit. III, § 350, 109 Stat. 618 (1996).

7. 42 U.S.C. § 2021d (2004).

8. *See, e.g.,* Transportation Equity Act for the 21st Century, Pub. L. No. 105-178 (1998).

9. 33 U.S.C. § 1508(d) (2004).

10. *See, e.g.,* State Revolving Funds for School Act, H.R. 1844, 108th Cong. (1st Sess. 2003) (two or more states may enter interstate compacts to effectuate cooperative agreement with Secretary of Education establishing multistate revolving school construction fund).

11. *See, e.g.,* Orderly and Timely Interstate Placement of Foster Children Act of 2004, H.R. 4505, § 3, 108th Cong. (2d Sess. 2004) ("States shall have in effect procedures for the orderly and timely interstate placement of children; and procedures implemented in accordance with an interstate compact approved by the Secretary[.]").

Finally, consent may be implied through congressional acquiescence to a compact. In the leading case of *Virginia v. Tennessee*,[12] the U.S. Supreme Court held:

> The approval by Congress of the compact entered into between the States upon their ratification of the action of their commissioners is fairly implied from its subsequent legislation and proceedings. The line established was treated by that body as the true boundary between the States in the assignment of territory north of it as a portion of districts set apart for judicial and revenue purposes in Virginia, and as included in territory in which federal elections were to be held, and for which appointments were to be made by federal authority in that State, and in the assignment of territory south of it as a portion of districts set apart for judicial and revenue purposes in Tennessee, and as included in territory in which federal elections were to be held, and for which federal appointments were to be made for that State. Such use of the territory on different sides of the boundary designated, in a single instance would not, perhaps, be considered as absolute proof of the assent or approval of Congress to the boundary line; but the exercise of jurisdiction by Congress over the country as a part of Tennessee on one side, and as a part of Virginia on the other, for a long succession of years, without question or dispute from any quarter, furnishes as conclusive proof of assent to it by that body as can usually be obtained from its most formal proceedings.[13]

Under the holding of *Virginia v. Tennessee*, congressional consent may be inferred when Congress engages in acts that demonstrate acquiescence to the compact. Such acts may include the adoption of subsequent legislation consistent with the terms of the compact or ratification of actions by state authorities and Congress that are harmonious with the purposes of the compact. Implied consent is most easily demonstrated in the context of border compacts as subsequent actions would clearly point to Congress's intentions vis-à-vis the compact. Courts have long held that in territorial disputes, possession and dominion are essential elements to claims between sovereigns and, as such, may be a factor in determining the existence of a compact or

---

12. Virginia v. Tennessee, 148 U.S. 503 (1893).
13. *Id.* at 522.

evaluating the conflicting boundary claims of the states.[14] Implied consent in other contexts—such as administrative compacts—may be more difficult to harmonize with competing congressional authority. Such method of consent can contribute to misunderstanding and misinterpretation of Congress's intent, or lead to an assumption of consent that does not exist. Therefore, as a general proposition, states seeking to adopt interstate compacts should not presume congressional consent but rather obtain either explicit consent or rest on some form of advanced consent.

2.1.2   The Breadth and Limits of Congressional Consent

In giving consent, Congress is not required to accept a compact as presented by the states, nor is Congress constrained in imposing limitations or conditions on the compact or its member states.[15] For example, 16 U.S.C Section 544 regarding the management of Columbia River Gorge provides that the "[m]andatory language of this Act respecting the powers and responsibilities of the Commission shall be interpreted as conditions precedent to congressional consent to the interstate compact described in section 5 of this Act."[16] The congressional consent given to the Northeast Interstate Dairy Compact was conditioned upon the Secretary of Agriculture finding a compelling interest to permit implementation of the compact, limited the price-setting authority of the Commission, and imposed an expiration date of September 30, 2001.[17] And the congressional consent to a 1935 interstate oil and gas compact between Texas, New Mexico, Kansas, Oklahoma, Illinois, and Colorado contained time limitations of which the compacting states have

14. *See, e.g.,* Georgia v. South Carolina, 497 U.S. 376 (1990); Michigan v. Wisconsin, 270 U.S. 295, 308 (1926); Vermont v. New Hampshire, 289 U.S. 593 (1933); Maryland v. West Virginia, 217 U.S. 1 (1910); Louisiana v. Mississippi, 202 U.S. 1 (1906); Virginia v. Tennessee, 148 U.S. 503 (1893); Indiana v. Kentucky, 136 U.S. 479 (1890); Rhode Island v. Massachusetts, 45 U.S. 591 (1846).
15. *See, e.g.,* S. 2518, § 1, 108th Cong. (2d Sess. 2004) (amends Omnibus Low-Level Radioactive Waste Interstate Compact Consent Act to provide that congressional consent is "granted only if the compact provides that all party states to the compact are jointly and severally liable for the cost of long-term liability incurred in connection with the radioactive release from a regional facility in a host state[.]").
16. 16 U.S.C. § 544o(d) (2004). *See also* 49 U.S.C. § 49104 (2004), concerning the numerous conditions and restrictions Congress has imposed on the Metropolitan Washington Airports Authority.
17. 7 U.S.C. § 7256 (2004).

repeatedly requested and received extensions from Congress.[18] Consequently, although the states may negotiate a compact and obtain universal assent to the instrument from state legislatures, Congress retains full authority to alter, amend, or set conditions upon the compact as part of granting its consent.[19] Other conditions that Congress can impose include the waiver of Eleventh Amendment immunity for compact commissions and agencies,[20] selection of the jurisdiction for resolving disputes,[21] and waiver of immunity from suit under the Rehabilitation Act of 1973.[22] Because of the purely gratuitous nature of consent, Congress may exact conditions that it might not otherwise extract in other contexts.[23]

States that adopt an interstate compact to which Congress has attached conditions, even after the fact, are deemed to have acceded to those conditions as a part of the compact. For example, in *Petty v. Tennessee-Missouri Bridge Commission*, the Supreme Court found that congressionally mandated provisions on the suability of the bridge commission were binding on the states because Congress was well within its authority to impose conditions as part of granting consent, and the states accepted the conditions by enacting the compact.[24] A more modern example of Congress mandating state compliance with conditions is found in the Columbia River Gorge Compact. Courts have held that the act authorizing the compact and its commission sets forth specific requirements that are conditions of Congress consenting to the compact. State land-use ordinances must be consistent with the enumerated use

---

18. Congress originally gave its consent to the compact on August 27, 1935, for a period of two years. The compact was then extended by the compacting states, with the consent of Congress, for successive periods without interruption, the latest extension being given in 1976. *See* Oil and Gas Conservation Compact, Extension and Renewal, Pub. L. No. 94-493, 90 Stat. 2365 (1976).

19. Columbia River Gorge United—Protecting People & Property v. Yeutter, 960 F.2d 110 (9th Cir. 1992); Seattle Master Builders Ass'n v. Pac. N.W. Elec. Power & Conservation Planning Council, 786 F.2d 1359, 1364 (9th Cir. 1986).

20. Petty v. Tennessee-Missouri Bridge Comm'n, 359 U.S. 275 (1959).

21. *See* 42 U.S.C. § 14616 (2003) ("The FBI or a Party State may appeal any decision of the Council to the Attorney General, and thereafter may file suit in the appropriate district court of the United States, which shall have original jurisdiction[.]").

22. Barbour v. Wash. Metro. Area Transit Auth., 374 F.3d 1161 (D.C. Cir. 2004).

23. Pennsylvania v. Union Gas Co., 491 U.S. 1, 43 (1988).

24. Petty v. Tennessee-Missouri Bridge Comm'n, 359 U.S. 275 (1959).

and development standards for land as set forth in the Gorge Act.[25] The states also must create a commission and the commission, in cooperation with the Secretary, must integrate these standards into a Scenic Area Management Plan. The Act did not require Oregon and Washington to enact the compact; the states were free to reject the conditions of the compact. Nevertheless, Oregon and Washington established a Commission and agreed to a compact that incorporated the terms of the act.

When it approves a compact, Congress arguably exercises the legislative power that the compact threatens to encroach upon and declares that the compact is consistent with Congress's power in that area. To the extent that a compact impacts interstate commerce, Congress exercises its power to regulate interstate commerce in approving the agreement. To the extent that a compact impacts extradition, Congress exercises the authority provided in Article IV, Section 1 of the Constitution to regulate interstate fugitives and absconders in approving such a compact.[26] Consequently, congressional approval of administrative compacts necessarily requires that the compact impede Congress's regulatory authority in that area; Congress, in effect, consents to the states' intruding on its traditional domain. To the extent that a compact intrudes on Congress's regulatory domain, it is free to define the breadth or limits of that intrusion by conditioning consent upon the states' accepting congressionally mandated terms. By vesting in Congress the power to grant or withhold consent, or to condition consent on the states' compliance with specified conditions, the Constitution ensures that Congress maintains ultimate supervisory power over cooperative state actions that might otherwise interfere with the full and free exercise of federal authority.

In granting consent, Congress does not pass upon a compact in the manner of a court of law deciding a question of constitutionality. The requirement that Congress must approve a compact is an act of political judgment concerning its potential impact on the balance of power between the states and federal government, or its impact on national interests. Congress may impose conditions necessary to ensure that national interests are not harmed by the compact. It is not a legal judgment as to the correctness of the form and substance of the agreement. Congressional consent presents a political question and the refusal of Congress to grant consent or to impose terms and

---

25. 16 U.S.C. § 544d(d)(1)-(9) (2004).
26. *Cf.*, California v. Super. Ct. of California, 482 U.S. 400, 407 (1987) (Extradition Act of 1793 proper exercise of Congress's powers under the Extradition Clause and Art. IV, § 1, to "prescribe the manner in which acts, records and proceedings shall be proved, and the effect thereof").

conditions on the member states is a nonjusticiable question. Consequently, as a rule, there are no limitations on Congress's substantive right to grant or withhold consent, or condition the granting of its consent, save a finding that the compact itself somehow violates the Constitution. Short of this concern, courts defer to the granting of congressional consent in a manner that may be unheard of in any other legislative context. This is due in large part because, as noted, the granting of consent is an act of political, not legal, judgment.

2.1.3   Withdrawal of Consent

Once Congress grants consent to a compact, it has been held that consent cannot be withdrawn nor additional conditions added *to the compact.* Although the matter has never been resolved by the Supreme Court, at least two lower courts have held in dicta that congressional consent, once given, is not subject to rescission or alteration, even by Congress itself. In *Tobin v. United States*, the U.S. Court of Appeals for the District of Columbia held:

> We have no way of knowing what ramifications would result from a holding that Congress has the implied constitutional power "to alter, amend or repeal" its consent to an interstate compact. Certainly, in view of the number and variety of interstate compacts in effect today, such a holding would stir up an air of uncertainty in those areas of our national life presently affected by the existence of these compacts. No doubt the suspicion of even potential impermanency would be damaging to the very concept of interstate compacts.[27]

The *Tobin* decision continues to be the approach taken by other courts confronted with the issue of withdrawal of congressional consent.[28] It should be noted, however, that notwithstanding *Tobin*, in at least one instance Congress has specifically reserved to itself the authority to withdraw consent by passing a law to that effect. Legislation granting consent to low-level radioactive waste disposal compacts specifically provides that "[e]ach compact shall provide that every 5 years after the compact has taken effect the Congress may by law withdraw its consent."[29] Because of the time-limited nature of these compacts, the specific reserve of authority, and the prior notice to the states, subsequent withdrawal of consent may be appropriate and defensible in this limited context. Moreover, a specific reservation of authority provides

---

27. Tobin v. United States, 306 F.2d 270, 273 (D.C. Cir. 1962).
28. Mineo v. Port Auth. of New York-New Jersey, 779 F.2d 939 (3d Cir. 1985).
29. 42 U.S.C. § 2021d (d) (2004).

ample notice to the member states that one condition of the compact is the reservation of Congress's authority to withdraw its consent to the agreement. Member states are not required to adopt the compact, but in doing so they accept the conditions Congress has imposed upon the states, including the potential that congressional consent may be withdrawn. Thus, the concern expressed in *Tobin*, that the withdrawal of consent could lead to unknown problems, may be obviated when the states accept a compact containing a condition that empowers Congress to withdraw consent. Whether a court would recognize withdrawal of consent, even under circumstances where Congress has specifically authorized such withdrawal in granting consent, has yet to be resolved. Withdrawal of consent can be particularly problematic when a compact involves boundary issues, notwithstanding a reservation of congressional right to do so.[30]

2.1.4   Subsequent Legislative Action by Congress

Although courts have been reluctant to recognize any implied constitutional power vested in Congress to amend, withdraw, or repeal its consent, there has been no hesitation to recognize Congress's authority to employ subsequent *legislative* action as a means of changing the landscape in which a compact operates. As the Supreme Court noted in *Merrion v. Jicarilla Apache Tribe*: "Contractual arrangements remain subject to subsequent legislation by the presiding sovereign."[31] Compacts, like other contracts, arguably remain subject to Congress's sovereign power, which "governs all contracts subject to the sovereign's jurisdiction, and will remain intact unless surrendered in unmistakable terms."[32] Unless Congress has unmistakably surrendered its legislative power in a certain area, the granting of congressional consent in no way limits Congress's right to exercise its legislative prerogatives, even to the extent that such an exercise significantly impacts or impairs the workings of an interstate compact. For example, in *Arizona v. California*, the Supreme Court held that the Congress was well within its authority to create a comprehensive scheme for managing the Colorado River, notwithstanding its consent to the Colorado River Compact.[33] The Court noted that "[t]he States, subject to subsequent

---

30. *See, e.g.,* Missouri-Nebraska Boundary Compact, art. IX (1999) ("The right to alter, amend or repeal this joint resolution [granting consent] is hereby expressly reserved.").

31. Merrion v. Jicarilla Apache Tribe, 455 U.S. 130, 148 (1982).

32. Bowen v. Pub. Agencies Opposed to Social Sec. Entrapment, 477 U.S. 41, 52 (1986).

33. Arizona v. California, 373 U.S. 546 (1963).

congressional approval, were also permitted to agree on a compact with different terms. Division of the water did not, however, depend on the States' agreeing to a compact, for Congress gave the Secretary of the Interior adequate authority to accomplish the division. Congress did this by giving the Secretary power to make contracts for the delivery of water and by providing that no person could have water without a contract."[34] While the states' adoption of a compact effectively binds all future state legislatures to the terms of the agreement, including conditions that Congress has imposed, the granting of consent does not in the same manner limit the authority of future congresses to adopt legislation in an area already regulated by a compact.

The lack of restriction on subsequent congressional action is because an interstate compact is, in the end, a state-to-state agreement. While congressional consent may transform an interstate compact into federal law, consent does not transform a compact into a binding agreement between the states and Congress. One exception to this principle may be the so-called "federal" compacts; that is, compacts to which the federal government is a full member, such as the Interstate Agreement on Detainers. While the adoption of an interstate compact by states effectively binds all future state legislatures and restricts the ability of states to act in contravention of a compact (either unilaterally or collectively), the mere granting of consent imposes no such restriction upon Congress. Congress may use its substantial legislative power— concurrent with or subsequent to granting consent—to significantly erode the purpose or regulatory authority of a compact. In general, a compact is not immune from subsequent or alternative federal legislation that may alter the landscape in which the compact operates or even render the compact a nullity in practice, if not under the law. As between Congress and the states, compacts are not afforded special deference different than that to which the states are otherwise ordinarily entitled.

While Congress retains authority to adopt legislation that subsequently affects the subject matter of an interstate compact, Congress can also use its consent powers as an avenue to change the application of federal law to the states or a compact commission. The granting of consent is a legislative action and, as Congress's legislative actions are limited by concerns for germaneness, Congress can employ the consent process to substantively alter the application of federal law. For example, in *McKenna v. Washington Metropolitan Area Transit Authority,* the U.S. Court of Appeals for the District of Columbia Circuit held that Congress's consent to Title III of the Washington Metropolitan Area Transit Regulation Compact (commonly called the Washington Metro-

---

34. *Id.* at 565.

politan Transit Authority (WMATA) Compact) effectively altered the application of the Federal Employers' Liability Act (FELA) to the WMATA and exempted it from liability under that act.[35] The court held that, even assuming that the WMATA was a railroad for purposes of FELA, the subsequent granting of consent by Congress to a compact that specifically exempted its members from "all laws, rules, regulations and orders of the signatories and of the United States otherwise applicable to such transit service and persons," acted as a limitation or denial of FELA coverage to WMATA workers, even though they may have been previously covered.[36] In effect, Congress used its consent powers to alter the application of federal law in a particular circumstance, an action that portrays the arguably unrestrictive nature of consent.

Additionally, just as Congress can use its legislative powers under Article I and the Compact Clause to alter the landscape in which a compact, a compact commission, and its member states operate, it can also use its consent power to substantively change the application of federal law to federal agencies whose activities and responsibilities are impacted by a compact. There is no bar, for example, against federal agencies following policies set by nonfederal agencies. The federal government has in fact agreed to be bound by state law in several areas[37] where there is a clear congressional mandate and specific legislation that makes the authorization of state control clear and unambiguous.[38] The expression of intent that a federal agency's conduct be governed by state law or an interstate compact can occur as part of congressional consent or in conjunction with other legislation as was the case when Congress permitted the development of the Colorado River Compact and specifically provided:

> The United States, its permittees, licensees, and contractees, and all users and appropriators of water stored, diverted, carried, and/or dis-

---

35. McKenna v. Wash. Metro. Area Transit Auth., 829 F.2d 186 (D.C. Cir. 1987).

36. *Id.* at 188-89.

37. *See* California v. United States, 438 U.S. 645 (1978) (federal reclamation projects must follow state water laws); Hancock v. Train, 426 U.S. 167 (1976) (federal government must comply with state air pollution standards). *See also* Columbia Basin Land Prot. Ass'n v. Schlesinger, 643 F.2d 585, 604-06 (9th Cir. 1981) (federal government must comply with state environmental standards); California v. EPA, 511 F.2d 963, 968-69 (9th Cir. 1975) (federal agencies must comply with state water pollution standards), *rev'd on other grounds*, 426 U.S. 200, 211-13 (1976).

38. Seattle Master Builders Ass'n v. Pac. N.W. Elec. Power & Conservation Planning Council, 786 F.2d 1359 (9th Cir. 1986).

tributed by the reservoir, canals, and other works herein, authorized shall observe and be subject to and controlled by said Colorado River compact in the construction, management, and operation of said reservoir, canals, and other works and the storage, diversion, delivery, and use of water for the generation of power, irrigation, and other purposes, anything in this subchapter to the contrary notwithstanding, and all permits, licenses, and contracts shall so provide.[39]

Likewise, Congress provided in the compact creating the Washington Metropolitan Area Transit Authority that "the applicability of the laws of the United States, and the rules, regulations, and orders promulgated thereunder, relating to or affecting transportation under the Compact . . . is suspended, except as otherwise specified in the Compact, to the extent that such laws, rules, regulations, and orders are inconsistent with or in duplication of the provisions of the Compact[.]"[40]

By contrast, states cannot create interstate governing agencies or enter into interstate governmental agreements as an avenue for avoiding federal regulation of matters that clearly rest within Congress's ambit of authority. In *Intermountain Municipal Gas Agency v. F.E.R.C.,* the court of appeals affirmed a determination by the Federal Energy Regulatory Commission (FERC) that Utah and Arizona could not by interstate agreement create a mutual governing entity to escape the regulatory authority given to the FERC by the Natural Gas Act.[41] Although Congress explicitly exempted municipalities from the coverage under the Natural Gas Act through the "Hinshaw Amendment,"[42] states could not authorize municipalities to form an interstate governing entity and then claim exemption from coverage as it seemed axiomatic that a state government can only create a governmental entity in its own state and not an interstate regulatory agency.[43] Therefore, while Congress may use its consent power to significantly change the landscape in which joint state action takes place, states may not conversely use the interstate compact or similar process as a means for avoiding or circumventing congressional authority in the absence of the explicit agreement by Congress that such action is permissible.

---

39. 43 U.S.C. § 617g(a) (2004).
40. D.C. Code Ann. § 9-1103.04 (2004).
41. Intermountain Mun. Gas Agency v. F.E.R.C., 326 F.3d 1281 (D.C. Cir. 2003).
42. 15 U.S.C. § 717 (c) (2004).
43. Intermountain Mun. Gas Agency, Questar Gas Co., 98 F.E.R.C. P61,216 (F.E.R.C. 2002).

Although Congress enjoys broad or even plenary authority over inter-state compacts, that authority is not unlimited. Most notable is the limitation that Congress may not use its constitutional power to coerce states into acting as mere agents of the federal government on matters that rightfully belong to the federal government. To allow such usurpation by Congress disrespects the status of states as sovereign partners in the federal structure. Thus, in *New York v. United States*, the Supreme Court held various aspects of the Low-Level Radioactive Waste Policy Amendments Act of 1985,[44] which authorized low-level radioactive waste disposal compacts, violated the Tenth Amendment.[45] The Supreme Court declared the Act unconstitutional holding, in part, that (1) monetary incentives constituted permissible exercises of congressional power under the Commerce, Taxing, and Spending Clauses of the Constitution, (2) access incentives represented permissible conditional exercise of Congress's commerce power, but that (3) the take title clause exceeded the Tenth Amendment because the take title incentives of the Act were not an exercise of congressional power enumerated in the Constitution.[46] Although the Court did not reach the constitutionality of the compacts authorized by Congress, it did make clear that acts of Congress must be in furtherance of the powers it possesses. Consequently, congressional power, including its consent power, is constrained by constitutional principles. Congress could not mandate that states enter into a compact on a particular matter. Congress could, however, encourage states to enter into compacts by providing constitutionally appropriate incentives and sanctions.

In summary, the consent powers of Congress are robust and broad, extending beyond the mere granting of consent to encompass substantive changes in federal and even state law. Granting consent to the member states conditioned on them taking specific actions can result in substantial changes to both state law and the compact regulatory process. Thus, for the practitioner involved in matters related to the regulatory authority of a compact, it is important to grasp the extent to which Congress, through the act of consent, has changed the legal landscape.

2.1.5   When Is Congressional Consent Required?

An unvarnished reading of the Compact Clause would lead one to conclude that *any* agreement between two or more states requires congressional consent. Under the Compact Clause, all interstate compacts and agreements

---

44. 42 U.S.C.S. § 2021b, *et seq.* (2002).
45. New York v. United States, 505 U.S. 144 (1992).
46. *Id.*

would seem to require congressional consent before taking effect, a matter that could be of significant consequence given the plenary nature of Congress's consent authority. However, compacts can generally be divided into two simple camps: those that require congressional consent because they affect federal interests and those that do not because federal interests are not affected by the terms of the compact.

The Supreme Court has long held that not all interstate agreements constitute formal compacts requiring Article I, Section 10 consent.[47] In *Virginia v. Tennessee,* the Court concluded that the Compact Clause requires congressional consent only with respect to those joint state agreements that intrude upon the power of the federal government or alter the political balance between the states and the national government.[48] The granting of consent is an act of political judgment by Congress and is intended to ensure that the political balance between the federal government and the states is maintained. To the extent that a compact does not shift the balance or intrude on federal interests, congressional consent is probably unnecessary.

As a result of this rather amorphous distinction between the conditions under which the consent requirement does or does not apply, it can be difficult to know when to seek congressional consent. Generally, the Constitution requires congressional consent only when the compact threatens to encroach upon the supremacy of the United States. But when does a compact intrude on the supremacy of the United States? Some have observed that a threat to the supremacy of the United States necessarily entails a threat to one of Congress's enumerated legislative powers since those powers are the source of supreme federal authority. Thus, as previously noted, when it approves a compact, Congress exercises the legislative power that the compact threatens to encroach upon and declares that the compact is consistent with Congress's supreme power in that area. This principle still leaves a vast opportunity for confusion as to the requirement or need for consent.

It is, perhaps, easier to think of the congressional consent requirement as applying in one of two principal circumstances. First, congressional consent

---

47. *See* U.S. Steel Corp. v. Multistate Tax Comm'n, 434 U.S. 452 (1978).
48. The Supreme Court in *Virginia v. Tennessee* not only affirmed the notion that only those compacts affecting the "political balance" of the federal system need consent, but also stated that consent can be implied after the fact. Thus, the Court concluded that Congress consented to the Virginia-Tennessee boundary compact by setting up judicial districts and taking a number of other actions acknowledging the boundary determined by the compact. *See generally* Virginia v. Tennessee, 148 U.S. 503 (1893).

is absolutely required when the substance of the compact would alter the balance of power between the states and federal government, potentially leading to impermissible state alliances that would diminish the power of the federal government or alter the balance of power among the states themselves. For example, congressional consent is required for boundary compacts because two states cannot unilaterally alter their political boundaries—and the authority each state exercises within those boundaries—without impacting federal interests, the stability of state boundaries, and the extent of state sovereignty and authority. Boundary compacts, left unregulated by Congress, could lead to impressible political allegiance between some states to the potential detriment of other states or the authority of the federal government. States could constantly renegotiate their boundaries, dissolve their boundaries in total, or create politically powerful alliances. Therefore, congressional consent is required when the states, acting collectively, take actions that they could not otherwise take and that may be detrimental to other states or the supremacy of the federal government.[49]

Second, congressional consent *may be* required when the subject matter of the interstate compact appears to intrude upon an area over which Congress has specific legislative authority. While arguably a compact intruding on Congress's authority may be deemed an intrusion on the supremacy of the United States, in actuality there are a vast array of compacts that would not contribute to impermissible political allegiance that threaten the existence of the federal government. Such compacts are generally regulatory in nature; rather than create impermissible state allegiances, these compacts may more correctly be characterized as preempting Congress's legislative authority and the federal government's regulatory power. For example, interstate dairy compacts that seek to create price supports and marketing programs for regional milk production intrude upon Congress's power to regulate interstate commerce. Likewise, the Supreme Court determined in *Cuyler v. Adams,* a seminal interstate compact case, that congressional consent to the Interstate Agreement on Detainers was warranted, noting that "[c]ongressional power to legislate in this area is derived from both the Commerce Clause and the Extradition Clause. The latter Clause, Article IV, Section 2, clause 2, has provided Congress with power to legislate in the extradition area since 1793 when it passed the first Federal Extradition Act."[50] The Interstate Compact on Adult Offender Supervision (ICAOS) requires congressional consent not so much because it changed the political balance between the states and federal

---

49. Abrams v. TransWorld Airlines, Inc., 728 F. Supp. 162 (S.D. N.Y. 1989).
50. Cuyler v. Adams, 449 U.S. 433, 442 n.10 (1981).

government but because the compact seeks to regulate an activity that could be subject to congressional regulation, such as extradition of probationers and parolees. In each of these examples, congressional consent is not required because the compact might lead to impermissible state allegiances that threaten the supremacy of the federal government, but because the subject matter of the compact intrudes on an area arguably delegated to Congress by the Constitution. In this context, Congress is not so much weighing the political relationship between the states and the federal government with respect to their sovereign authority, but the collective authority of the states to enter a compact that intrudes upon Congress's own legislative power.

The distinction between compacts that create impermissible state alliances and compacts that intrude on congressional authority is important for a singular reason: those compacts that may create impermissible alliances, such as boundary compacts, are generally not subject to alteration by subsequent congressional legislative action. For example, once Congress consents to a boundary compact, it cannot through subsequent legislation alter the landscape in which such compacts operate without the joint agreement of the states and Congress. Congress cannot, of its own accord, change state boundaries as though states were mere political subdivisions of the federal government. By contrast, those compacts that intrude on Congress's legislative authority—generally regulatory or administrative in nature—may be subject to significant alteration by subsequent congressional action. Congress can, for example, change water distribution schemes under its authority over interstate waterways notwithstanding the existence of a compact to which it has previously consented.[51]

If it is determined that a compact invades the legislative prerogatives of Congress, congressional consent should be sought. Two words of caution are needed, however. First, one should not assume that the granting of congressional consent—either explicit or implied—in the context of administrative compacts is Congress's final word on the matter. A compact does not deprive Congress of its legislative authority over matters delegated to it by the Constitution. As previously noted, through subsequent legislative action Congress can significantly alter the landscape in which compacts operate, notwithstanding consent. Second, state agreements, whether termed compacts or not, whose subject matter is appropriate for federal legislation but that do not threaten to increase the political power of the states at the expense

---

51. For an analysis of Congress's authority to regulate low-level radioactive waste through interstate compacts, *see generally* New York v. United States, 505 U.S. 144 (1992).

of the federal government, are not invalid for lack of consent. Many multilateral state issues can be the subject of federal legislation or regulation simply as a result of being larger than a single state's authority. However, these matters do not necessarily tread on the explicit authority of Congress or endanger the balance of power between the states and federal government. Nevertheless, in this latter context, consent should be sought to ensure that Congress is fully aware of the states' agreement and, therefore, at least tacitly respectful of the compact's arrangements.

By contrast, congressional consent is clearly not required, nor, if given, does it presumptively "federalize" a compact if the subject matter does not alter the political balance or invade congressional interests. In *New Hampshire v. Maine*, for example, the Supreme Court held that congressional consent was not needed to legitimize an agreement between Maine and New Hampshire that ended a dispute over a lateral maritime boundary.[52] The Court concluded that because the agreement did not affect the balance of power between the states and federal government or threaten the prerogatives of the national government, congressional consent was not required.

Likewise, the Supreme Court determined, in *U.S. Steel Corp. v. Multistate Tax Commission*, that congressional consent was not required for a compact creating an interstate commission whose purpose was to develop uniformity and compatibility of state and local tax laws.[53] The Court held that the Multistate Tax Compact did not give to the states any powers that they did not already possess individually nor did the agreement intrude upon a federal interest.[54] In addressing the appellant's complaint that the Court had never approved of a multistate compact creating a powerful commission absent congressional consent, the Court noted: "It is true that most multilateral compacts have been submitted for congressional approval. But this historical practice, which may simply reflect considerations of caution and convenience on the part of the submitting States, is not controlling[.]"[55] Consequently, states may enter agreements among themselves without the consent of Congress so

---

52. New Hampshire v. Maine, 426 U.S. 363 (1976).
53. U.S. Steel Corp. v. Multistate Tax Comm'n, 434 U.S. 452 (1978).
54. *Id.*
55. *Id.* at 472. *See also* Northeast Bancorp v. Bd. of Governors of Fed. Reserve Sys., 472 U.S. 159, 176 (1985) (even assuming certain actions or agreements concerning banking in New England were an interstate compact, agreement did not need congressional consent because it neither enhanced the power of the New England states at the expense of other states nor impacted the federal structure of the government).

long as those agreements do not infringe on federal interests or shift the balance of power within the federal structure of the government.[56] Even when states have customarily sought congressional consent for reasons of caution and convenience, the mere act of consent is not dispositive of whether it was required. A compact will not become federal law simply because Congress, in an excess of caution, enacts consent legislation.[57]

Compacts not requiring congressional consent are still enforceable agreements between the states, and disputes arising from such agreements may even be ripe for litigation under the Supreme Court's original jurisdiction. Such compacts are not, however, presumptively federal law under the law of the union doctrine and, therefore, are not subject to immediate federal court intervention nor enforceable under the Supremacy Clause. State courts are fully empowered to interpret and enforce interstate agreements, and federal courts are required to interpret the agreement as state law, not federal law. For example, the Interstate Compact on the Placement of Children is not a compact requiring congressional consent because it regulates an area typically within the purview of the states. As noted in *Malone v. Wambaugh,* "The Interstate Compact on Placement of Children has not received congressional consent. Rather than altering the balance of power between the states and the federal government, this Compact focuses wholly on adoption and foster care of children—areas of jurisdiction historically retained by the states. Congressional consent, therefore, was not necessary for the Compact's legiti-

---

56. *See* Cuyler v. Adams, 449 U.S. 433, 440 (1981), in which the Supreme Court held, "Where an agreement is not 'directed to the formulation of any combination tending to increase the political power of the States, which may encroach upon or interfere with the just supremacy of the United States,' it does not fall within the scope of the Clause and will not be invalidated for lack of congressional consent." Examples of compacts not requiring congressional consent include the Southern Regional Education Compact and the Interstate Compact on the Placement of Children. Also deemed to implicate compact concerns but not requiring congressional consent was the Master Settlement Agreement between the states and tobacco companies. *See* Star Science, Inc. v. Beales, 278 F.3d 339 (4th Cir. 2002) (agreement acted vertically between the states and did not implicate any political interests of the federal government in such a manner as to violate the Compact Clause). Likewise, a multistate gaming agreement was deemed not to require congressional consent. *See* Tichenor v. Missouri State Lottery Comm'n, 742 S.W.2d 170 (Mo. 1988).

57. Wash. Metro. Area Transit Auth. v. One Parcel of Land, 706 F.2d 1312 (Cir. 4th 1983).

macy. . . . Because congressional consent was neither given nor required, the Compact does not express federal law. Consequently, this Compact must be construed as state law."[58]

The lack of "federalization" can lead to inconsistent state court decisions that either render the goal of uniformity difficult to achieve or call into question whether an agreement even constitutes an enforceable compact among the member states. The Interstate Compact on the Placement of Children (ICPC) is one example of the problems that can arise concerning the enforceability of such state agreements. In *In re Adoption No. 10087 in Circuit Court*, the Maryland courts determined that the ICPC was not a compact but rather an interstate agreement effectuated by enactment of reciprocal statutes.[59] In this sense, it was more akin to a uniform law than an enforceable compact, notwithstanding its title and other court decisions finding the agreement constituted a compact between the states. Perhaps the greatest benefit, therefore, of congressional consent is the vesting in federal courts of the authority to interpret a compact in a uniform manner. Absent this consistency, the interpretation of compacts is left to the whim of the states, leading to the extreme case of one state declaring their agreement a compact (and therefore enforceable as a contract) and another state declaring their agreement a mere uniform law (subject to unilateral amendment and change). There is generally no question regarding the status or enforceability of interstate compacts that appropriately receive congressional consent.

2.1.6   The Effect of Congressional Consent on Court Jurisdiction

Compacts occupy a unique place within the nation's law, both as mechanisms for adjusting interstate relations and because of the effect of congressional consent on such agreements. The status of compacts has been a source of conflicting thought over the years. As early as 1852, the U.S. Supreme Court held in *Pennsylvania v. Wheeling & Belmont Bridge Company* that compacts sanctioned by Congress became the "law of the Union."[60] By contrast, in *People v. Central Railroad,* the Supreme Court suggested that interstate compacts could not be considered federal law. [61] Although *People v. Central Railroad* represents a period in American history when the "federal" status of compacts was questioned, this position has largely been rejected; it is now widely accepted that congressionally approved compacts are "federal-

---

58. Malone v. Wambaugh, 934 F.2d 474, 479 (3d Cir. 1991).
59. *In re* Adoption No. 10087 in Circuit Court, 597 A.2d 456 (Md. 1991).
60. Pennsylvania v. Wheeling & Belmont Bridge Co., 59 U.S. 421 (1856).
61. People v. Cent. R.R., 79 U.S. 455 (1872).

ized" for certain purposes, including their enforcement through the Supremacy Clause. Largely beginning with *Delaware River Commission v. Colburn,* the Supreme Court articulated the effect of congressional consent in interstate compacts holding:

> In *People v. Central Railroad,* . . . jurisdiction of this Court to review a judgment of a state court construing a compact between states was denied on the ground that the Compact was not a statute of the United States and that the construction of the Act of Congress giving consent was in no way drawn into question, nor was any right set up under it. This decision has long been doubted . . . and we now conclude that the construction of such a compact sanctioned by Congress by virtue of Article I, § 10, Clause 3 of the Constitution, involves a federal "title, right, privilege or immunity" which when "specially set up and claimed" in a state court may be reviewed here on *certiorari*[.][62]

It must be emphasized that congressional consent does not change the underlying contractual nature of a compact, a nature that is critical to understanding both jurisdiction and enforcement issues *between* the states. However, congressional consent has its own implications critical to understanding congressionally approved compacts.

The most far reaching consequence of congressional consent is its "transformational" effect on the states' agreement. Through congressional consent, where appropriate, the states' agreement is changed from solely being an agreement between the states into a law of the nation. One of the most recent and in-depth discussions on the effects of congressional consent is contained in *Cuyler v. Adams,* in which the Supreme Court recognized that congressional consent "transforms the States' agreement into federal law under the Compact Clause."[63] The Supreme Court has since qualified its consent analysis holding that it applies "where the subject matter of that agreement is an appropriate subject for congressional legislation."[64] Cases subsequent to *Cuyler,* however, suggest that the Court assigns great weight to congressional consent, perhaps more than is

---

62. Delaware River Comm'n v. Colburn, 310 U.S. 419, 439 (1940).
63. Cuyler v. Adams, 449 U.S. 433, 440 (1981). *See also* Waterfront Comm'n v. Elizabeth-Newark Shipping, 164 F.3d 177, 180 (3d Cir. 1998) ("Although the Compact is a creature of state legislatures, it is federalized by virtue of congressional approval pursuant to the Compact Clause.") *But see id.* at 450 ("In a remarkable feat of judicial alchemy, the Court today transforms a state law into federal law." (Rehnquist, J., dissenting)).
64. *Cuyler,* 449 U.S. at 440.

appropriate.[65] Therefore, the general principle is that once Congress gives consent, the compact is presumptively transformed into the law of the United States absent compelling evidence that consent was not required.[66]

The consent analysis articulated by the Supreme Court in *Cuyler* and its progeny is important in at least two ways. First, the act of congressional consent gives rise to an unusual feature of compacts vis-à-vis state participation in the creation of federal law. The act of consent effectively takes a contract between the member states, passed by state legislatures and implemented, in many contexts, by state-created administrative bodies, and makes the agreement and its rules an instrument of federal law, generally without any further subsequent action by Congress. This is the only context in which state legislative action quite literally becomes federal law, albeit for a limited purpose. Additionally, to the extent that a compact allows for amendment and change, the state legislatures themselves can control the landscape of federal law in the area of a specific compact, again generally without any further intervention of Congress. For example, by the terms of many administrative compacts state legislatures can agree to alter federal application and interpretation of such agreements as the Interstate Compact on Adult Offender Supervision, the Interstate Compact on Juveniles, and the Washington Metropolitan Area Transit Regulation Compact, the latter of which specifically provides that the agreement can be amended without any further con-

---

65. *See* Hess v. Port Auth. Trans-Hudson Corp., 513 U.S. 30, 56, 57 (1994) ("In reaching its conclusion, the Court attaches undue significance to the requirement that Congress consent to interstate compacts. Admittedly, the consent requirement performs an important function in our federal scheme. . . . But the clause neither transforms the nature of state power nor makes Congress a full-fledged participant in the underlying agreement; it requires *only* that Congress 'check any infringement of the rights of the national government'" (O'Connor, J., dissenting)). *See also Cuyler,* 449 U.S. at 451-52 ("In light of our recent decisions, however, it cannot seriously be contended that the Detainer Agreement constitutes an 'agreement or compact' as those terms have come to be understood in the Compact Clause. . . . Whether a particular state enactment is 'with' or 'under' the Compact Clause, however, depends on whether it requires the consent of Congress—the Clause speaks of nothing else. Whatever effect the Compact Clause may have on those laws it does cover, one would have thought it unnecessary to say that it can have no effect on those it *does not cover*" (Rehnquist, J., dissenting)).
66. *See* Old Town Trolley Tours of Wash. v. Wash. Metro. Area Transit Comm'n, 129 F.3d 201, 204 (D.C. Cir. 1997); Reed v. Farley, 512 U.S. 339 (1994).

sent from Congress and that such amendment can take effect, unless Congress essentially vetoes the changes, within one year.[67] Moreover, to the extent that a compact allows for its repeal, state legislatures can again significantly effect "federal" law without the intervention of Congress. Compacts, therefore, represent the only arena in which state legislative action is elevated to the height of federal law and in which subsequent state legislative action can change the landscape of federal law.

Second, by transforming an interstate compact into federal law, congressional consent gives rise to federal questions subject to federal construction and resolution. As the Supreme Court observed in *Carchman v. Nash*, "[A] congressionally sanctioned interstate compact within the Compact Clause is a federal law subject to federal construction."[68] In granting consent, Congress can effectively immunize state law from some constitutional objections by converting it into federal law.[69] When Congress so chooses, state actions that it plainly authorizes are invulnerable to constitutional attack. For example, when Congress consents to a compact that may negatively affect interstate commerce, Congress effectively insulates the compact and the actions of its regulatory commission from constitutional attack under the Commerce Clause.[70] Moreover, the granting of consent can have practical effects concerning access to federal funding opportunities for compact-created agencies.[71]

---

67. Washington Metropolitan Area Transit Regulation Compact, tit. I, art. VIII, § 1 (a) (1960) ("This Compact may be amended from time to time without the prior consent or approval of the Congress of the United States and any amendment shall be effective unless, within one year, the Congress disapproves that amendment.").

68. New York v. Hill, 528 U.S. 110 (2000); Carchman v. Nash, 473 U.S. 716, 719 (1985); Texas v. New Mexico, 462 U.S. 554, 564 (1983); West Virginia *ex rel.* Dyer v. Sims, 341 U.S. 22, 28 (1951); Pennsylvania v. Wheeling & Belmont Bridge Co., 54 U.S. 518, 566 (1852). In addition to the precedents of the Supreme Court, Congress has also provided through legislation that certain interstate compacts fall within the jurisdiction of the federal courts. *See, e.g.,* 33 U.S.C. § 466g-1(a) (2002).

69. Northeast Bancorp Inc. v. Bd. of Governors of the Fed. Reserve Sys., 472 U.S. 159 (1985).

70. Intake Water Co. v. Yellowstone River Compact Comm'n, 769 F.2d 568 (9th Cir. 1985).

71. *See, e.g.,* National Aquatic Invasive Species Act of 2003, H.R. 1080, § 1003, 108th Cong. (1st Sess. 2003) (interstate organization means entity created by interstate compact with the consent of Congress); National Clean and Safe Water Fund Act of 2003, S. 1539, 108th Cong. (2d Sess. 2004) (grants available to federal interstate water compact commission).

Jurisdiction in the federal courts may be conferred by a specific federal statute, by the particular terms and conditions of a compact, by the general effect of congressional consent, or by the mere fact that a dispute involves two or more states acting in their sovereign capacity. In the latter case, the U.S. Supreme Court may have original and exclusive jurisdiction over the controversy.[72] The "transformation" effect of congressional consent is not, however, to suggest that every dispute arising under an interstate compact must be litigated in the federal courts. State court jurisdiction is, for example, appropriate when citizens are contesting the terms or application of an interstate compact.[73] Nothing in the federal structure prohibits state courts from interpreting interstate compacts and, thus, over the years, both federal and state courts have construed the terms of interstate compacts.[74] The U.S. Supreme Court has not deprived state courts of jurisdiction to construe compacts and has implicitly recognized the powers of state courts in such controversies. On occasion, the Court has even remanded a compact-construction case to a state court for reconsideration. However, notwithstanding the recognition that state courts may entertain compact disputes, ultimately the U.S. Supreme Court retains the final word on the interpretation and application of congressionally approved compacts, even where the controversy concerns questions on which a state court has already spoken.[75] Where Congress has granted its consent, interstate compacts are subject to federal rather than state

---

72. 28 U.S.C. § 1251 (a) (2004). *See* Kansas v. Colorado, 514 U.S. 675 (1995) (invoking original jurisdiction over suit filed by one state against another relating to terms of CAI compact); Texas v. New Mexico, 462 U.S. 554 (1983); Guarini v. New York, 521 A.2d 1362 (N.J. Super. Ct. Ch. Div. 1985), *aff'd*, 521 A.2d 1294 (N.J. Super. Ct. App. 1986).

73. State *ex rel.* Tattersall v. Yelle, 329 P.2d 841 (Wash. 1958).

74. *See, e.g.*, NYSA-ILA Vacation & Holiday Fund v. Waterfront Comm'n of New York Harbor, 732 F.2d 292, 298 (2d Cir.) (congressional approval of Waterfront Commission Compact transformed it into federal law); Utah Int'l Inc. v. Intake Water Co., 484 F. Supp. 36, 42-43 (D. Mont. 1979) (rejecting argument that federal jurisdiction over CAI compact construction cases is exclusive); Eastern Paralyzed Veterans Ass'n, Inc. v. Camden, 545 A.2d 127 (N.J. 1988).

75. Petty v. Tennessee-Missouri Bridge Comm'n, 359 U.S. 275, 278-79 n.4 (1959); West Virginia *ex rel.* Dyer v. Sims, 341 U.S. 22 (1951) (West Virginia's obligation under multistate anti-pollution compact did not conflict with state constitution).

construction, and federal courts are free to fashion their own interpretation of an agreement even if that interpretation is contrary to that of a state court.[76]

The authority of the Supreme Court over compact disputes is not limited to only those compacts approved by Congress. Under both its original jurisdiction and its certiorari jurisdiction, the Supreme Court retains authority to settle disputes between the states, and this extends to compact disputes not involving direct federal questions. In *Delaware River Commission v. Colburn* and *State ex rel. Dyer v. Sims*, the Supreme Court considered the status of interstate compacts in connection with its certiorari jurisdiction. In both cases the Court addressed the question of whether a claim based on an interstate compact is cognizable under the Supreme Court's certiorari provisions as applied to reviewing the judgments of the highest state court where a title, right, privilege, or immunity is claimed under the Constitution, treaties, or statutes of the United States. In *Colburn,* the Court unequivocally answered this question affirmatively, holding that "the construction of such a [bi-state] compact sanctioned by Congress by virtue of Article I, § 10 cl. 3 of the Constitution, involves a federal 'title, right, privilege or immunity,' which when 'specially set up and claimed' in a state court may be reviewed here on *certiorari* under § 237(b) of the Judicial Code."[77] In reaching this conclusion, the Supreme Court firmly established that the construction of a compact by virtue of congressional consent presents a federal question subject to review through the appellate process.

Absent a controversy between two states or an expressed provision in a federal statute excluding concurrent jurisdiction, state courts may exercise jurisdiction over cases arising under federal law.[78] Although state courts are not deprived of jurisdiction in compact disputes as a result of congressional consent, such courts are constrained by the federal nature of the agreement. Under the Supremacy Clause, state courts must give force and effect to the provisions of a compact as instruments of federal, not state, law. While uniformity of interpretation by state courts is desired, it is a uniformity born not of comity but of the fact that state courts, in interpreting a compact, are expounding federal law.[79] State legislative history can have bearing on a court's interpretation, and should not be ignored. The history of the compact before

---

76. NYSA-ILA Vacation & Holiday Fund v. Waterfront Comm'n of New York Harbor, 732 F.2d 292 (2d Cir. 1984).

77. Delaware River Comm'n v. Colburn, 310 U.S. 419, 427 (1940).

78. Gulf Offshore Co. v. Mobil Oil Corp., 453 U.S. 473 (1981); Charles Dowd Box Co. v. Courtney, 368 U.S. 502 (1962).

79. Am. Sugar Refining Co. v. Waterfront Comm'n of New York Harbor, 55 N.Y.2d 11 (1982).

the Congress, by contrast, is an essential element of interpretation.[80] Where there is no clear interpretation of a compact by the U.S. Supreme Court, and there exists a split of authority among the courts of appeals for the various federal circuits, a state court is free to select the interpretation it considers most sound.[81]

As noted, jurisdiction in the federal courts can be conferred by the explicit terms of a compact,[82] by the receipt of congressional consent,[83] or under Article III of the Constitution vesting the Supreme Court with original jurisdiction in disputes between states.[84] It must be noted, however, that the right to sue in federal court under a compact does not arise from general contract principles or state common law, but from federal law pursuant to congressional consent. It is Congress, through its approval of a compact, that establishes a scheme to govern the mutual rights and obligations of the member states as a function of federal law.[85] As such, ultimate authority over the interpretation of a compact is vested in the federal courts either by an explicit granting of federal court jurisdiction[86] or by implication through the federalized nature of a compact.

Even in the absence of congressional consent, states may sue other states directly in the U.S. Supreme Court to enforce the provisions of a compact. Both the Constitution and federal code vest original and exclusive jurisdiction over controversies between two of more states in the U.S. Supreme Court. [87] The Supreme Court has consistently held that original jurisdiction

---

80. De Veau v. Braisted, 363 U.S. 144, 149-51 (1960).
81. Hagler v. Ford Motor Credit Co., 381 So. 2d 80, 82 (Ala. Civ. App. 1980) (where federal courts are split on an issue and the U.S. Supreme Court is silent on that issue, state courts may select the view they consider the more logical one).
82. Interstate Compact for Adult Offender Supervision, art. VIII & art. XII, § C (2002).
83. *See* U.S. Const. art. III, § 2.
84. Nebraska v. Iowa, 406 U.S. 117 (1972).
85. Entergy Ark., Inc. v. Nebraska, 358 F.3d 528 (8th Cir. 2004).
86. *See* 33 U.S.C. § 466g-1 (2002) (granting original jurisdiction to U.S. district courts, any federal and state courts, and the U.S. Supreme Court in any matter involving "the construction or application of an interstate compact which (A) in whole or in part relates to the pollution of the waters of an interstate river system or any portion thereof, and (B) expresses the consent of the States signatory to said compact to be sued in a district court").
87. *See* 28 U.S.C. § 1251 (a) (2004), which provides that the Supreme Court shall have original and exclusive jurisdiction of all controversies between two or

"extends to a suit by one State to enforce its compact with another State or to declare rights under a compact."[88] Nevertheless, the Court has held that its exercise of original jurisdiction is obligatory only in appropriate cases. In deciding whether to grant leave to file a complaint in a dispute arising under the Court's exclusive and original jurisdiction over disputes between the states, the Court examines the nature of the interest of the complaining state, focusing on the "seriousness and dignity of the claim."[89] In evaluating whether to accept jurisdiction over compact disputes, the Supreme Court also considers the availability of an alternative forum in which the issue tendered can be resolved.

Consequently, the Supreme Court generally has original jurisdiction where an interstate compact constitutes an agreement among sovereign states that creates rights and obligations enforceable against the states as constituent members of the Union.[90] However, to invoke the original jurisdiction of the Court, the compact controversy must involve the real interests of the states. The action must seek to enforce rights and obligations outlined in the agreement as a contract between the member states or as a function of federal law, if the compact was consented to by Congress. States seeking to invoke the Court's jurisdiction must be "real parties in interest" not merely nominal parties acting solely to create an avenue to forward the claims of individual citizens or other interests that would not otherwise be entitled to invoke the Court's original jurisdiction. States cannot be acting merely as surrogates for private or individual interests. To constitute a proper "controversy" that would invoke the Supreme Court's exercise of original jurisdiction:

> [I]t must appear that the complaining State has suffered a wrong through the action of the other State, furnishing ground for judicial redress, or is asserting a right against the other State which is suscep-

---

more states. Additionally, 28 U.S.C § 1251 (b) (2004) provides that the "Supreme Court shall have original but not exclusive jurisdiction of: (1) All actions or proceedings to which ambassadors, other public ministers, consuls, or vice consuls of foreign states are parties; (2) All controversies between the United States and a State; (3) All actions or proceedings by a State against the citizens of another State or against aliens."

88. Texas v. New Mexico, 462 U.S. 554, 567 (1983). *See also* New Jersey v. New York, 523 U.S. 767 (1998); Kansas v. Colorado, 514 U.S. 673 (1995); Virginia v. West Virginia, 206 U.S. 290, 317-19 (1907).
89. Mississippi v. Louisiana, 506 U.S. 73, 77 (1962).
90. Nebraska v. Iowa, 406 U.S. 117 (1972).

tible of judicial enforcement according to the accepted principles of the common law or equity systems of jurisprudence.[91]

Moreover, participation of nonstate parties is normally unnecessary by virtue of a state's role in representing the interests of its citizens. Nevertheless, the Supreme Court has, on occasion, allowed nonstate parties to participate in original actions as intervenors or amicus curiae.[92] The presence of nonstate parties accordingly does not deprive the Supreme Court of original jurisdiction. The Supreme Court may decline to exercise jurisdiction if a dispute lacks sufficient seriousness and dignity. Thus, the Supreme Court refused to exercise original jurisdiction in *California v. West Virginia* because an alleged breach of contract respecting athletic contests between two state universities lacked the sufficient "seriousness and dignity" necessary to an original action.[93] By contrast, compact disputes, particularly those involving regulation of state conduct, almost always present concerns serious enough to invoke original jurisdiction.

While the Supreme Court has original jurisdiction over suits between the states and can resolve compact disputes, the Court has limited the exercise of such jurisdiction in the compact context. First, the original jurisdiction of the Supreme Court is not an alternative to the redress of grievances that could have been sought in the normal appellate process, if the remedy had been timely sought, even when the matter involves a compact dispute.[94] Second, and most important from a compact commission perspective, the Supreme Court will generally not exercise its original jurisdiction in disputes between states and a compact-created commission. Compact-created commissions are not, in and of themselves, "states" for purposes of the Supreme Court's original jurisdiction any more than such commissions presumptively enjoy Eleventh Amendment immunity simply because they are creations of the states.[95]

---

91. Massachusetts v. Missouri, 308 U.S. 1, 15 (1939). *See also* New York v. Illinois, 274 U.S. 488, 490 (1927); Texas v. Florida, 306 U.S. 398, 405 (1939).
92. *See, e.g.,* Arizona v. California, 373 U.S. 546, 564 (1963).
93. California v. West Virginia, 454 U.S. 1027 (1981).
94. Illinois v. Michigan, 409 U.S. 36 (1972).
95. *See* Hess v. Port Auth. Trans-Hudson Corp., 513 U.S. 30 (1994) (self-sustaining compact agency not a "state" for purposes of Eleventh Amendment immunity). *But see* Lizzi v. Alexander, 255 F.3d 128 (4th Cir. 2001) (if properly conferred, compact-created agency receiving 44% of its funding from member states may be considered an entity of the "state" and thus shielded by Eleventh Amendment immunity). *See also* Delon Hampton & Assocs. v. WMATA, 943 F.2d 355, 359 (4th Cir. 1991).

This does not necessarily preclude the presence of a compact commission as an interested party to a suit between states, such as in the case of *Alabama v. North Carolina*.[96] The presence of a compact commission as an interested party is not fatal to invoking the Supreme Court's original jurisdiction so long as the suit unequivocally involves states suing states in their sovereign capacity. However, a compact commission may not invoke the Supreme Court's original jurisdiction on the theory that it can adequately represent the interests of member states and, therefore, stands in an equal position as a "state" for purposes of Article III jurisdiction.

Congressional consent also means that interstate compacts are enforceable within the terms and conditions of the agreement under the Supremacy Clause and as a federal law.[97] Through the Supremacy Clause of the Constitution, Congress may induce uniformity of regulation and eliminate barriers among states by using its legislative authority and consent to interstate compacts as preemption of state-by-state regulation. Stated more simply, congressional consent not only transforms an interstate compact into federal law for purposes of interpretation, it also transforms an interstate compact into substantive federal law for purposes of enforcement on the states. Consequently, any rights or obligations granted by a congressionally sanctioned

---

96. 540 U.S. 1014 (2003). Original jurisdiction in the contexts of compact disputes arise because of the nature of the parties, not because of a question of federal law per se. Illinois v. Milwaukee, 406 U.S. 91 (1972).

97. *See* League to Save Lake Tahoe v. Tahoe Reg'l Planning Agency, 507 F.2d 517, 521-22 (9th Cir. 1974) ("In arriving at our decision we do not overlook that the law of the Union doctrine may be said, under some circumstances, to present certain theoretical problems, *e.g.*, impermissible delegation of congressional legislative power to the states in cases where Congressional consent precedes the compact. The possibility, however, that there may be problems in potential cases does not alter our duty to follow the mandate of *Colburn*. . . . While the Court in *Colburn* felt it unnecessary to clearly articulate the basic premise of its decision, we conclude after careful investigation that the result there was based upon the implicit finding that the interstate compact involved must have been deemed to have been a 'statute of the United States' within the meaning of 28 U.S.C. § 1257(3). Neither logic nor policy justifies a different interpretation of the substantially similar language in 28 U.S.C. § 1331(a). Therefore, a case involving the construction of an interstate compact which requires a judicial determination of the nature and scope of obligations set forth therein 'arises' under the 'laws' of the United States within the meaning of § 1331(a).").

interstate compact are federal, not state, in character. For example, the Interstate Agreement on Detainers is considered a law of the United States whose violation is grounds for habeas corpus relief under 28 U.S.C. Section 2254 and enforceable upon the states through the Supremacy Clause.[98]

There is no doubt as to the propriety of jurisdiction in the federal courts in the cases involving congressionally sanctioned interstate compacts, despite the presence of legitimate and far-reaching interests of the member states.[99] In interpreting a federalized interstate compact, federal courts must address disputes just as if a court were addressing a federal statute. The first and last order of business of a court addressing an approved interstate compact "is interpreting the compact."[100] Consequently, unless the compact to which Congress has consented is somehow unconstitutional, no court may order relief inconsistent with its express terms no matter what the equities of the circumstances might otherwise demand. Absent a federal statute making state statutory or decisional law applicable, the controlling law is federal law; and, absent federal statutory guidance, the governing rule of decision would be fashioned by the federal court in the mode of the common law.[101] As the Supreme Court observed in *Arizona v. California,* "Courts have no power to substitute their own notions of an 'equitable apportionment' for the apportionment chosen by Congress."[102] Likewise in addressing a boundary dispute between Washington and Oregon, the Supreme Court noted that because Congress had established the boundary between Washington and Oregon, "the courts have no power to change the boundary thus prescribed and establish it at the middle of some other channel," even though changes in the waterway over the course of time seemed to demand altering the boundary line if only for equitable purposes.[103] The interpretation that courts give to interstate compacts effectively controls over a state's application of its own law as to the subject matter of the compact.[104]

---

98. *See* Bush v. Muncy, 659 F.2d 402, 407 (4th Cir. 1981).
99. League to Save Lake Tahoe v. Tahoe Reg'l Planning Agency, 507 F.2d 517 (1974).
100. Texas v. New Mexico, 462 U.S. 554, 567-68 (1983).
101. Oneida Indian Nation v. County of Oneida, 414 U.S. 661, 674-79 (1974).
102. Arizona v. California, 373 U.S. 546, 565-66 (1963).
103. Washington v. Oregon, 211 U.S. 127, 135 (1908).
104. *See* West Virginia *ex rel.* Dyer v. Sims, 341 U.S. 22 (1951). *See also* Alcorn v. Wolfe, 827 F. Supp. 47, 52 (D.D.C. 1993) ("Because the compact creating the MWAA was congressionally sanctioned in accordance with the Compact Clause, it is a federal law subject to federal construction, notwithstanding its genesis in the enabling acts of Virginia and the District of Columbia. . . . [T]he

2.1.7   Contractual Nature of Compacts

Although a congressionally approved compact is federalized, it remains a contract between the member states that generally must be interpreted and enforced within the four corners of the agreement. In interpreting and enforcing compacts, the courts are constrained to effectuate the terms of the compact as a binding contract so long as those terms do not conflict with constitutional principles.[105] For example, in *Texas v. New Mexico*, the Supreme Court sustained exceptions to a Special Master's recommendation to enlarge the Pecos River Compact commission's ruling that one consequence of a compact becoming "a law of the United States" is that "no court may order relief inconsistent with its express terms."[106] In the case of *Hellmuth v. Washington Metropolitan Area Transit Authority*, the court held that Maryland's freedom of information act did not apply to WMATA because the parties had

---

MWAA compact cannot be modified unilaterally by state legislation and takes precedence over conflicting state law.") *See also* McComb v. Wambaugh, 934 F.2d 474, 479 (3d Cir. 1991) ("Having entered into a contract, a participant state may not unilaterally change its terms. A Compact also takes precedence over statutory law in member states."); Wash. Metro. Area Transit Auth.

v. One Parcel of Land, 706 F.2d 1312 (4th Cir. 1983) (the WMATA's "quick take" condemnation powers under the compact are superior to the Maryland Constitution, which expressly prohibited "quick take" condemnations); Malone v. Wash. Metro. Area Transit Auth., 622 F. Supp. 1422, 1426 (E.D. Va. 1985) ("Because congressionally sanctioned interstate compacts within the meaning of Art. 1, § 10 of the Constitution are federal law, state laws inconsistent with the terms of these compacts are unenforceable as to agencies formed by these compacts."); Kansas City Area Transp. Auth. v. Missouri, 640 F.2d 173 (8th Cir. 1981) ("One party to an interstate compact may not enact legislation which would impose burdens upon the compact absent the concurrence of other signatories."). *See also* Seattle Master Builders Ass'n v. Pac. N.W. Elec. Power & Conservation Planning Council, 786 F.2d 1359 (9th Cir. 1986).

105. N.Y. State Dairy Foods v. Northeast Dairy Compact Comm'n, 26 F. Supp. 2d 249, *aff'd*, 198 F.3d 1 (1st Cir. 1999). (Once a compact between states has been approved, it is the law of the case binding on the states and its citizens. Congressional consent transforms an interstate compact into a law of the United States. Unless the compact is somehow unconstitutional, no court may order relief inconsistent with its express terms, no matter what the equities of the circumstances might otherwise invite.)
106. Texas v. New Mexico, 462 U.S. 554, 565 (1983).

not agreed to be bound by Maryland law and, therefore, no court could order relief inconsistent with or not supported by the terms of the particular agreement.[107] Congressional consent may change the venue in which compact disputes are ultimately litigated; it does not change the controlling nature of the agreement on the member states.

However, although courts have acknowledged that interstate compacts are contracts to the extent they are binding legal documents between member states that set forth certain terms and conditions, which must be construed and applied in accordance with the intent of the agreement, the courts have also recognized the unique features and functions of compacts. Though a contract, an interstate compact represents a political compromise between "constituent elements of the Union," as opposed to a commercial transaction.[108] Such an agreement is made to "address interests and problems that do not coincide nicely either with the national boundaries or with State lines—interests that may be badly served or not served at all by the ordinary channels of National or State political action."[109] Consequently, with regard to congressionally approved compacts, the right to sue for breach of the compact differs from a right created by a commercial contract; it does not arise from state common law but from federal law. While contract principles generally inform and control the interpretation of a compact and the remedies available in the event of a breach, the underlying action is not like a contract action at common law as heard in the English law courts of the late eighteenth century. Rather, it is a controversy that involves intertwining considerations of contract law and statutory interpretation.

The dual nature of a compact as both statutory law and a contract between the states has implication for their interpretation and enforcement. Unlike a typical contract dispute, courts may look to extrinsic evidence to determine the intent of the parties and to effectuate the desired results of the compact. Extrinsic evidence, such as a compact's legislative history or the negotiation history, may be examined by a court in interpreting an ambiguous provision of a compact.[110] Thus, unlike a standard contract dispute, where principles, such as the parole evidence rule, may restrict the influence of

---

107. Hellmuth v. Wash. Metro. Area Transit Auth., 414 F. Supp. 408 (D. Md. 1976).
108. Hess v. Port Auth. Trans-Hudson Corp., 513 U.S. 30, 40 (1994).
109. *Id.*
110. Arizona v. California, 292 U.S. 341, 359-60 (1934); Green v. Bock Laundry Mach. Co., 490 U.S. 504, 511 (1989); Pierce v. Underwood, 487 U.S. 552, 564-65 (1988); Blum v. Stenson, 465 U.S. 886 (1984).

outside evidence in interpreting a contract provision, resort to extrinsic evidence of the compact negotiations is entirely appropriate because of the dual nature of a compact as both a contract and statute.[111] In interpreting a compact within its statutory context, the general rules of statutory interpretation, not contract interpretation, may be controlling. This is particularly true in the context of congressionally approved compacts.

2.2   FEDERAL PARTICIPATION IN COMPACTS

Federal participation and use of interstate compacts is not confined to obtaining congressional consent. With increasing frequency in recent years, the federal government has become more than a mere conferrer of federal status through the consent requirement. It is now not unusual for the federal government to be involved directly in compact-created agencies either as an observer, through direct membership on a commission, or through a body over which the federal government exercises substantial direct control, such as the District of Columbia. Through several of these avenues, the federal government participates in or is actively affected by compacts. Examples include the Washington Metropolitan Transit Regulation Compact, the Interstate Compact on the Potomac River Basin, the Ohio River Valley Water Sanitation Compact, the Upper Colorado River Basin Compact, the Delaware River Basin Compact, and the Interstate Agreement on Detainers.

Federal participation in compacts takes several forms. Examples of full federal membership in an interstate compact include the Interstate Agreement on Detainers and the National Crime Prevention and Privacy Compact. While full federal participation is clearly the most overt example of Congress using compacts to manage collective state action and national affairs, other forms also exist. Most notably, interstate compacts have become instruments of federal control in such areas as criminal justice information sharing, water rights, energy regulations, and federal grant funding. In each of these areas, the federal government, either through overt participation or subtle involvement, has used the interstate compact instrument as a broad regulatory tool, controlling not only the states, but also federal agencies and even courts.

Several examples illustrate the extent to which federal participation in the compact process has been used to regulate state, federal, and individual conduct. One most notable example is the National Crime Prevention and Privacy Compact Act of 1998, the so-called "Triple III" compact. In enacting the compact, Congress specifically found "an interstate and Federal-State

---

111. Oklahoma v. New Mexico, 501 U.S. 221 (1991). *But see id.* at 245-46
      (Rehnquist, J., dissenting).

compact is necessary to facilitate authorized interstate criminal history record exchanges for noncriminal-justice purposes on a uniform basis[.]"[112] Under its terms, the U.S. Attorney General has authority to appoint a 15-member governing council, comprising of both state and federal officials vested with authority to promulgate rules and procedures governing the use of criminal justice information for noncriminal-justice purposes, the rules of which are "not to conflict with FBI administration of the III System for criminal justice purposes."[113] The FBI and member states agree to maintain detailed databases of criminal history records and to make those records available to the federal government and member states pursuant to the rules of the governing council, so long as those rules do not conflict with the FBI's administration of information systems.

The importance of this compact illustrates the power of compacts and their interaction at the federal level cannot be understated. The notion that the federal government is an "equal" member of a congressionally approved compact must be understood in the context of both federal-state relations on interstate matters and the practical effect of the federal government's participation in an agreement. Often federal participation is a means of encouraging or coercing states to undertake certain actions. Though not specifically stated, federal participation in a regulatory interstate compact also provides a direct measure of control over joint or collective state action, control that would otherwise be limited to the conditions Congress imposed as part of granting consent. Thus, the so-called "Triple III" not only ensures the regulation of information sharing among states, it also ensures that such regulation will not conflict with or supersede federal interests over the regulation of criminal justice information sharing. Clearly, Congress could have expressly limited the authority of the compact's commission and arguably did so by the construction of the compact. But Congress also added another measure of securing federal interests by requiring that the federal government be an active and equal member of the compact's governing commission. Once again, the lack of any restriction or direction on Congress's authority over interstate compacts means, in the main, that absent a constitutional prohibition, Congress is essentially free to use its consent powers as it sees fit, including imposing regulatory schemes on both the state and federal governments.

Even in the absence of direct participation, federal agencies can leverage compacts to supplement their regulatory powers. Projects financed through resource conservation loans and watershed loans must comply with interstate

---

112. 42 U.S.C. § 14611 (2003).
113. 42 U.S.C. § 14616 (2003).

compact provisions. For example, one federal regulation mandates that applicants not only comply with state and local water rights requirements, they must also "furnish evidence to provide reasonable assurance that its water rights will be or have been properly established, will not interfere with prior vested rights, will likely not be contested or enjoined by other water users or riparian owners, and will be within the provisions of any applicable interstate compact."[114] Federal agencies have used their regulatory authority to encourage the use of interstate compacts, such as in the case of the Interstate Compact on the Placement of Children,[115] and to recognize the unique status of agencies created by interstate compacts.[116]

2.3   EFFECT OF CONGRESSIONAL CONSENT ON COMPACT-CREATED AGENCIES

Many interstate compacts create ongoing administrative, regulatory, or management agencies. As previously noted, these agencies run the gamut in the scope of their authority and responsibility, managing everything from airport operations to water distribution to crime control. Since congressional consent, where applicable, effectively transforms an interstate compact into federal law under the law of the union doctrine, there naturally arises the question of whether agencies created under such agreements are "federal" in nature, "state" in nature, or some hybrid in between. Does the federal law control their activities, does state law control their activities, or does some hybrid notion of law control their activities?

The granting of congressional consent does not transform a compact-created agency into a federal agency. The status of a compact agency is not defined by congressional consent but rather by the terms and conditions of the compact. Thus, for example, the Metropolitan Washington Airports Authority (MWAA), an agency created pursuant to a compact actively promoted by the District of Columbia, Virginia, and Congress, is exempt from the Miller Act for purposes of contracting because the MWAA, by the terms of its compact, is a political subdivision that is independent of Virginia, the District of Columbia, and the U.S. government.[117] As such, the Miller Act, which required the contractor to provide a performance bond prior to construction or alteration, did not apply to the MWAA because the agency was not a

---

114. 7 C.F.R. § 1781.9 (i) (2004).
115. 25 C.F.R. § 20.513 (2004).
116. 23 C.F.R. § 450.306 (2004).
117. United States *ex rel.* Blumenthal-Kahn Elec. Ltd. P'ship v. Am. Home Assur. Co., 219 F. Supp. 2d 710 (E.D. Va. 2002).

federal agency.[118] Similarly, the Bi-State Development Agency of Missouri and Illinois is subject to Missouri's open meetings requirements, not the federal requirements, notwithstanding Congress's consent to the 1949 compact.[119] Likewise, a compact-created agency is not subject to the federal Administrative Procedures Act.[120] Compact-created agencies are free to construct their own mechanisms for their operations, including the process by which they will promulgate rules.[121] By contrast, Congress specifically required that the rules of the compact council authorized by the National Crime Prevention and Privacy Compact be published in the Federal Register.[122] Yet even here, the council is not considered an executive department or independent regulatory agency and is exempt from various executive orders regarding regulatory planning and review, federalism policy standards, and civil justice reform requirements.[123] Moreover, because 75 percent of the members of the council represent state and local governments, the rules prescribed by the council are not considered federal mandates for purposes of the Unfunded Mandates Reform Act of 1995. Thus, congressional consent may transform an interstate compact into federal law, but that fact does not extend federal status to the created regulatory body. Regulatory obligations imposed on federal agencies generally do not apply in the interstate compact context absent specific conditions set forth in a compact.

The most that can be said, therefore, regarding the effect of congressional consent on the status of a compact-created agency is that it has limited effect. Courts have repeatedly noted that compact agencies are not creatures

---

118. *Id.*
119. Mo. Rev. Stat. § 610.010(4)(G) (2004). The compact creating the Bi-State Development Agency also requires the states of Missouri and Illinois to "provide penalties for violations of any order, rule or regulation of the bi-state agency, and for the manner of enforcing same." Bi-State Development Agency Compact, art. V (1949).
120. *Cf.,* Old Town Trolley Tours v. Wash. Metro. Area Transit Comm'n, 129 F.3d 201, 203 (D.C. Cir. 1997). *See also* Organic Cow, LLC v. N.E. Dairy Compact Comm'n, 164 F. Supp. 2d 412 (D. Vt. 2001), *remanded by* Organic Cow v. Ctr. for New England Dairy Compact Research, 335 F.3d 66 (2d Cir., July 8, 2003).
121. *See, e.g.,* Interstate Compact for Adult Offender Supervision, art. VIII (2002) (rulemaking shall substantially conform to the federal Administrative Procedures Act and the Federal Advisory Committee Act).
122. 42 U.S.C. § 14616, arts. II(4), VI(a)(1) & VI(e) (2004); 28 C.F.R. § 902, *et seq.* (2004).
123. 67 C.F.R. § 70567-1 (2004).

of the federal government but rather creatures of the member states. As such, their standing and status within the structure of government is not defined so much by the act of Congress granting consent but rather by the terms and conditions of the compact.[124] Like property rights that are composed of various bundles, congressional consent is one of many considerations in the "bundle" of an interstate compact. Consent merely transforms the states' agreement into federal law for purposes of interpretation and enforcement. It does not per se turn a compact agency into a creature of the federal government.[125]

As previously discussed, however, Congress can, in the process of granting consent or approving federal participation in a compact, impose any number of requirements on a compact agency. For example, under Article VIII of the National Crime Prevention and Privacy Compact, the activities of the compact agency are subject to certain requirements of the Privacy Act of 1974 and the Federal Advisory Committee Act.[126] Thus, while congressional consent does not convert an interstate compact agency into a federal agency, Congress can use its consent powers to impose certain requirements on such agencies, particularly when the federal government is a full participant.

124. *Cf.,* Friends of the Columbia Gorge v. Columbia River Gorge Comm'n, 108 P.3d 134 (Wash. Ct. App. 2005) (while state court required to apply federal law in interpreting the compact, in the absence of specific procedural rules, state court applies state administrative law), *amended by* Friends of the Columbia Gorge v. Columbia River Gorge Comm'n, 2005 Wash. App. LEXIS 968 (May 5, 2005).
125. *See* Heard Communs., Inc. v. Bi-State Dev. Agency, 18 Fed. Appx. 438 (8th Cir. 2001) (congressional consent does not transform bi-state development agency into federal administrative agency).
126. National Crime Prevention and Privacy Compact, arts. IV & VIII (1998).

Chapter 3

CREATING INTERSTATE COMPACTS

The constitutional authority for interstate compacts is clear, and much of what is understood about compacts today is well established in case law. Less clear is the process by which interstate compacts are made, a process that continues to evolve, in the absence of constitutional directives, primarily through practice. This chapter presents an overview of the ways in which compacts are typically created. It chronicles the evolution of compact making from the relatively formal, directed process of old to the more varied, ad hoc process that prevails today. It also addresses some of the practical and political considerations that should be taken into account during the development, drafting, and introduction of interstate compacts.

3.1. COMPACT MAKING—THEN AND NOW

The U.S. Constitution says precious little about interstate compacts and nothing at all about how they are to be made. By imposing a congressional consent requirement on the states, the Compact Clause[1] preserved the federal legislature's role in the process of compact making, a prerogative that had previously been guaranteed under the Articles of Confederation.[2] But the role of state legislatures as the makers of interstate compacts was neither required nor obvious. Some of the compacts that predated the Constitution were submitted for ratification to the legislatures of the party states,[3] but the earlier compacts of colonial times were subject only to the approval of the Crown.

Nevertheless, the contractual nature of compacts opened the door to what quickly became commonly accepted practice, since the best way to ensure an

---

1. U.S. Const. art. I, § 10, cl. 3.
2. Articles of Confederation, art. VI (U.S. 1781). *See also* Chapter 1, § 1.1.
3. *E.g.*, Maryland-Virginia Compact of 1785.

enforceable and verifiable "meeting of the minds" between party states was, and is, to imbed the terms of any such agreement into legislation requiring mutual enactment by the parties. Less formal agreements between states have occasionally been negotiated by governors without recourse to the legislative process. But without specific legislative authorization, such agreements tend to lack the stature and enforceability of legislatively approved compacts, since governors generally "cannot enter into an interstate compact binding upon the state in the way that a president can make executive agreements with foreign nations."[4]

The legislative role in compact making may be the most visible step in the process, but just as written contracts between private parties often reveal little of the negotiations that precede them, so do completed interstate compacts tend to disguise the intricacies involved in their making. Even in colonial times, the success or failure of a compact depended as much on the underlying process as it did on the terms of the final agreement. But as compacts themselves have evolved over time, so has the process by which they are made.

3.1.1 The Traditional Approach: Negotiated Compacts

When George Washington invited a distinguished group of representatives from the newly independent states of Virginia and Maryland to meet at his Mount Vernon home in the spring of 1785, he did not anticipate that the meeting would set the stage for the constitutional convention that soon followed in Philadelphia. Nor could he have known that the interstate compact the delegates were charged with negotiating would prove to be the determining factor in a significant U.S. Supreme Court decision more than 200 years later.[5]

What was known by the participants in the Mount Vernon meeting (including such luminaries as Samuel Chase and George Mason) was that they had been commissioned by their respective state legislatures to negotiate a settlement to a long-standing dispute regarding jurisdictional rights on the Potomac River. The resulting agreement, hammered out during three days of

---

4. Frederick L. Zimmerman & Mitchell Wendell, The Law and Use of Interstate Compacts 20 (Council of State Governments 1976) (hereinafter Zimmerman & Wendell). The authors note that the "entire history of compact making indicates a general understanding that adoption of the interstate compact is achieved through the legislative process[.]"

5. Virginia v. Maryland, 540 U.S. 56 (2003).

negotiations, was later ratified by the Maryland and Virginia legislatures and became known as the Maryland-Virginia Compact of 1785.[6]

As an example of early interstate compact making, the creation of the Maryland-Virginia Compact was not unlike the process that would commonly be used following the ratification of the U.S. Constitution and for more than a century thereafter. Nor did it differ significantly from the process used to resolve intercolonial disputes for more than a century before. The center-piece of the traditional approach to compact making was a formal negotiation between delegates commissioned by their states or colonies to settle a multi-jurisdictional issue, usually a bi-state border dispute. The resulting agree-ment would then be submitted for approval, either to the Crown or, later, to the states themselves, with the consent of Congress.[7]

The strength of this approach rested in the formality of the negotiation itself, as well as in the process by which negotiators were commissioned.[8] Whether designated by governors or charged by legislative enactment, as in the case of the Mount Vernon negotiators, delegates commissioned to settle disputes were formally empowered to act for their states and, pending ratifi-cation, to bind them to the terms of their agreements. There was no question of their mandate to negotiate or of their authority to resolve issues on behalf of the states that would ultimately be parties to the compact.

As long as compacts were used primarily to resolve bi-state issues in a permanent fashion, the traditional approach to compact making worked well. Formally negotiated compacts were still the norm as late as the early twenti-eth century, and states continued to use the appointed commissioner model even as the nature of interstate compacts began to change.

An early example of a multistate compact established by traditional means was the Colorado River Compact, developed in 1922. Not unlike previous bi-state agreements resolving boundary disputes between neighbors, the Colo-rado River Compact envisioned the permanent settlement of a disputed subject, in this case, the apportionment of waters between river basin states. It was, in

---

6. Later superseded by the Potomac River Compact of 1958, Pub. L. No. 87-783, 76 Stat. 797 (1962). Congressional consent for the original compact, which predated the Constitution, was never expressly given by Congress. However, the U.S. Supreme Court later concluded that the required consent was implicitly given, albeit almost a century after the fact, when Congress ratified a compact-related arbitration award in 1878. Virginia v. Maryland, 540 U.S. 56 (2003).
7. ZIMMERMAN & WENDELL, *supra* note 4, at 16.
8. *Id.* at 16-17.

other words, a fixed-agreement compact requiring no further decision making or subsequent action by the parties once it took effect.

Where it differed from previous boundary agreements was in the seven-state scope of its anticipated membership. This complicated the negotiation process, which consumed almost a full year, but otherwise, the development of the compact followed a familiar pattern. The participating states each passed legislation authorizing their governors to appoint commissioners, and in due course, the commissioners convened for a series of formal negotiations, during which the terms of the compact were developed and reduced to writing. Once agreed to by the full commission, which in this case was chaired by a duly appointed representative of the federal government (then-Secretary of Commerce, Herbert Hoover), the new compact was circulated to the states for legislative ratification. This final step took several years to complete, but the agreement eventually became effective in 1929.

Another noteworthy compact from the same era was the New York–New Jersey Port Authority Compact of 1921. The enduring significance of this agreement was its unprecedented delegation of regulatory authority to a permanent interstate commission established by the compacting parties.[9] But in the process of its creation, this groundbreaking agreement owed more to the past than the future. As usual, the compact grew out of the deliberations of commissioners appointed by the party states and empowered to negotiate on their behalf. In this instance, however, the delegates were not expressly commissioned to negotiate a compact. Instead, they were charged more broadly with developing a comprehensive plan for the coordinated development of the harbor and port facilities serving both states. It was in the course of the ensuing discussions, beginning in 1917, that the idea of an interstate compact creating a permanent, bi-state regulatory commission first emerged.

Pursuing this route, the commissioners drafted a compact and recommended its adoption when they presented their final report to the New York and New Jersey legislatures. Both states adopted the agreement in 1921, and congressional consent soon followed. The outcome was the establishment of the first and best known of all interstate compact commissions, the Port Authority of New York and New Jersey.[10]

The Port Authority Compact demonstrated that the traditional approach to compact making could be used successfully to create a relatively complex and dynamic regulatory scheme. A formally negotiated agreement was achiev-

---

9. *See* Chapter 9.
10. Originally the "Port of New York Authority."

able, at least between a limited number of parties, even if the precise regulatory outcome was unknowable—and necessarily subject to change—at the
time the compact was enacted.

On the other hand, the Colorado River Compact demonstrated that the
traditional approach to compact making could be used successfully to create a
multistate agreement of regional scope. A formally negotiated compact was
achievable, even between multiple parties, provided that the terms of the agreement were precise and fixed. It remained to be seen, however, whether this
process would prove suitable for compacts that were both wider in scope and
more dynamic in nature than the bi-state boundary agreements of the past.

3.1.2   More Recent Practice: Compacts by Other Means

The traditional method of compact making survived the early evolution of
the compact mechanism, but as the concept continued to evolve, the process,
too, began to change. A significant advantage of the traditional model was that
the formal appointment of commissioners empowered to negotiate for their
states represented a preliminary expression of intent by the parties both to
cooperate in addressing an issue of mutual concern and, upon ratification, to
bind themselves to the terms of the resulting agreement.[11] It also made plain to
the world at large that the negotiators were legally authorized to pursue their
objective of creating a compact. As more recent practice has shown, neither of
these advantages is necessary to the successful development of an interstate
compact, but without them, the development process itself must inevitably be
defended once a compact proposal reaches the legislative arena.

Nevertheless, as the scope and complexity of interstate compacts grew,
the traditional approach to compact making began to reveal its limitations.
The joint commission model was well suited for the development of bi-state
agreements, especially when a fixed and permanent settlement of an issue
was contemplated. But the same approach could be unwieldy with respect to
compacts seeking the participation of numerous states, especially those that
addressed complex regulatory issues or that authorized ongoing administrative activities. Not surprisingly, new approaches began to emerge as the states
continued to experiment with the use of interstate compacts.

In the mid 1930s, a new interstate agreement governing the supervision
of parolees who legally move between states was developed pursuant to a
grant of congressional consent contained in the Crime Control Act of 1934.[12]
In addition to inviting participation from every state in the union, the pro-

11. Zimmerman & Wendell, *supra* note 4, at 17.
12. 4 U.S.C. § 112 (2005).

posed compact was unusual in that it was developed not by duly appointed commissioners representing the party states but by "an extra-legal organization" called the Interstate Commission on Crime.[13] The commission's members included a variety of state officials, but none had been officially empowered to negotiate a compact. Nevertheless, the compact that emerged from this informal and externally driven process eventually found a receptive audience when it was circulated for legislative approval in the states. The Interstate Compact for the Supervision of Parolees and Probationers initially took effect in 1937 and was ultimately enacted by all 50 states.[14]

In the years that followed, a number of other interstate compacts grew out of similarly informal development efforts. Many of these agreements were facilitated by existing entities, like The Council of State Governments (CSG) or the Southern Governors' Conference,[15] which provided forums for the development of cooperative interstate efforts. One such agreement was the Interstate Compact on Mental Health, which grew out of an informal conference held in New York City in April of 1955. There an ad hoc group of state officials and other interested stakeholders from four eastern states met to discuss ways in which their states might cooperate more effectively in connection with the hospitalization, treatment, and transfer between states of mentally ill patients. At a follow-up meeting later that month, an expanded group of participants adopted a resolution calling upon CSG to facilitate the efforts of a 10-state committee to draft a new compact on mental health.

CSG agreed to the request and subsequently facilitated two meetings of the group, during which several drafts of the proposed compact were developed and revised. In September 1955, the tentative agreement was approved by the full Northeast State Governments Conference on Mental Health and released for consideration by the states. Endorsements for the proposal were sought and obtained from the Western Regional Meeting of The Council of State Governments in November and from the Biennial Regional Conference of Northeastern States in December.[16] Only then did the process move into the more formal legislative arena. During a special session in late December, Connecticut became the first state to enact the proposed compact. The agree-

---

13. ZIMMERMAN & WENDELL, *supra* note 4, at 19.
14. It was later superseded by the Interstate Compact for Adult Offender Supervision, which took effect in 2002.
15. Now the Southern Governors' Association.
16. THE COUNCIL OF STATE GOVERNMENTS, SUGGESTED STATE LEGISLATION—PROGRAM FOR 1957, 26-27 (1956).

ment took effect the following year when New York and Massachusetts followed suit,[17] and it eventually attracted the participation of 45 states and the District of Columbia.

The facilitated approach to compact making gradually caught on. What it lacked in the way of official authority and formality was offset by the advantages of flexibility, speed, and relative simplicity. In theory, any group of state officials or interested stakeholders could, without securing prior authorization for its efforts, draft and propose an interstate compact. The creators of such agreements were, as a practical matter, limited only by their ability to win legislative approval for their final products. But that can be easier said than done, especially when lawmakers are presented with proposed legislation that must generally be accepted without revision, and which may have been developed entirely without legislative participation.

Not surprisingly, the more traditional approach to compact making has never been entirely supplanted by alternative means. The Delaware River Basin Compact, a five-party agreement enacted by four states and Congress,[18] was negotiated and drafted by a multistate task force (the Delaware River Basin Advisory Committee) formally charged by the region's governors with the responsibility of creating a new compact. Aided by this official sanction, the committee succeeded, upon the completion of its efforts, in accomplishing what an informal and unauthorized entity (the Interstate Commission on the Delaware River Basin) had previously been unable to do. After four years of development, the new compact was quickly ratified and then signed into law by President Kennedy and the governors of the four basin states in November 1961.

Subsequent attempts at compact making occasionally borrowed from the traditional approach while relying, in essence, on the unofficial efforts of informal entities at the outset. An illustrative example can be found in the development of the Susquehanna River Basin Compact, which had its genesis in Chicago in 1961. There, during a meeting of state legislators from across the country, Frederick Zimmerman, a former New York Assemblyman and a pioneer in the development of interstate compact usage, suggested to a Pennsylvania legislator that the time might be right to consider developing a state-federal compact for the Susquehanna River Basin similar to the Delaware

---

17. *Id.*

18. The federal government not only consented to but also joined the compact as a party, thus establishing a precedent for future state-federal compacts. The participating states were New York, New Jersey, Delaware, and Pennsylvania.

River agreement then nearing enactment.[19] Finding support for the idea, Zimmerman returned to New York, where he served as research director to the Joint Legislative Committee on Interstate Cooperation, an entity he helped to establish during his tenure in the Assembly.[20]

At Zimmerman's urging, an informal meeting of representatives from Pennsylvania, New York, and Maryland, as well as the federal government, was convened in Binghamton, New York, early the following year. Drawing from his experience in helping to create the Interstate Commission on the Delaware River Basin more than a decade earlier, Zimmerman successfully encouraged the Susquehanna group to adopt a set of organizational articles establishing an Interstate Advisory Committee on the Susquehanna River Basin.[21]

In a remarkable demonstration of bootstrapping, the three basin states were then persuaded to appoint delegates to the new committee pursuant to the organizational articles adopted by the original, unauthorized assemblage. What began, therefore, as an informal, ad hoc initiative driven by a small group of interested stakeholders had effectively metamorphosed into an approved, multistate pursuit featuring duly appointed commissioners charged with developing a new administrative compact.

Officers were elected, a development budget was approved (and eventually funded by the basin states), a staff was hired and then, more than two years after the process began, a drafting team chaired by Frederick Zimmerman was appointed to develop the anticipated compact.[22] Using the Delaware River Basin Compact as a framework for its efforts, the drafting team met numerous times in the latter half of 1964 and throughout the following year before finally completing its work in March of 1966. The new Susquehanna River Basin Compact was then approved by the full advisory committee before being formally unveiled in June. An aggressive outreach campaign to lawmakers and stakeholders throughout the basin followed, and the compact was eventually presented for legislative approval in early 1967.[23]

---

19. Interview with Richard Cairo, General Counsel for the Susquehanna River Basin Commission (Aug. 23, 2004).

20. WILLIAM VOIGT, JR., THE SUSQUEHANNA COMPACT: GUARDIAN OF THE RIVER'S FUTURE 51-87 (1972).

21. *Id.*

22. *Id.*

23. *Id.* at 91-140. New York and Maryland enacted the measure that spring. Pennsylvania did so the following year. Congressional approval was given in 1970, and the compact became effective shortly after President Nixon signed it into law at Camp David on Christmas Eve.

This "hybrid" approach to compact creation ultimately relied more heavily on the traditional model than did many of the compact efforts that followed. But the making of the Susquehanna River agreement demonstrated the value and importance of legitimizing the development process, even when it begins without official sanction. Many facilitated compact efforts that initially lack such formal authorization eventually achieve the legitimacy needed for success simply by being inclusive. Any proposal is more likely to meet with legislative approval if the compact makers can show that the development process was open, that the drafters were fair and responsive to input, and that the finished product was well received by key stakeholders.

3.1.3   Case Studies in Compact Creation

Whether negotiated by formally appointed commissioners or externally facilitated by interested stakeholders, most interstate compacts can be readily classified according to the general approach employed in their development. But over the years, there have been many paths to success. As the following examples illustrate, every compact ultimately reflects a unique set of circumstances, and the specific process of compact making, varies accordingly from one agreement to another.

3.1.3.1   The Colorado River Compact

The original impetus for the 75-year-old Colorado River Compact was a shared concern among state and federal officials over the equitable apportionment and use of Colorado River waters throughout the seven-state basin encompassing the river and its tributaries. A series of informal discussions about the future development of the basin began in 1918 and continued into 1920, at which time the participants approved a resolution urging the seven basin states (Arizona, California, Colorado, Nevada, New Mexico, Utah, and Wyoming) to formally appoint representatives charged with negotiating a fair distribution of the river waters.[24]

In 1921, all seven states passed legislation authorizing their governors to appoint commissioners for this purpose. Federal legislation followed in August of that year granting consent to the states to develop a river compact and authorizing the president to appoint a representative of the federal government to serve as chair of the Colorado River Commission, which would formulate the agreement. By the end of the year, the seven state commission-

---

24. Herbert Hoover Papers, Colorado River Commission: Scope and Content Note, *available at* http://www.ecommcode2.com/hoover/research/hooverpapers/hoover/commerce/crc6.htm.

ers had been appointed, and President Harding had named his Secretary of Commerce, Herbert Hoover, to lead the commission.[25]

The commission held its first several meetings in Washington, D.C. in January of 1922. Two months later, it reconvened in Phoenix, Arizona, for the first in a series of public hearings that eventually took commissioners to seven cities throughout the Southwest. But the challenge to devise a water apportionment formula that would satisfy all parties proved to be a formidable one. Although the commissioners originally intended to fashion a compact that would apportion river water on a state-by-state basis for the entire basin, they gradually realized that their most significant disagreements tended to divide groups of states representing the upper and lower river basins, rather than individual states in either area.[26] With agricultural, industrial, and commercial development proceeding much more rapidly in the lower basin states (especially California), the upper basin states feared that without adequate protection, their downstream counterparts would quickly preempt a disproportionate share of the river's waters under the well-established principle of prior appropriation (a fundamental tenet of water law that protects the rights of first users).[27]

Eventually, the negotiators abandoned their original goal in favor of a "two-basin strategy" that apportioned the river waters only between the upper and lower basins.[28] While sidestepping the more difficult state-by-state allocation, this approach satisfied the upstream states by protecting their collective share of the Colorado's waters against prior appropriation by the lower basin. The precise distribution between individual states was left undetermined until a subsequent compact between upstream states[29] established a state-by-state formula for the upper basin. A similar lower-basin agreement proved more elusive, and the respective rights of the downstream states were eventually determined only through protracted litigation.

---

25. *Id.*

26. Joe Gelt, *Sharing Colorado River Water: History, Public Policy and the Colorado River Compact,* 10 ARROYO (August 1997), *available at* http://ag.arizona.edu/AZWATER/arroyo/101comm.html.

27. Herbert Hoover Papers, Colorado River Commission: Scope and Content Note, *available at* http://www.ecommcode2.com/hoover/research/hooverpapers/hoover/commerce/crc6.htm.

28. The so-called "Hoover compromise" was proposed by Secretary Hoover after the commission appeared to be deadlocked.

29. Upper Colorado River Basin Compact (1949).

The final draft of the Colorado River Compact was approved and signed by the commissioners in Santa Fe, New Mexico, on November 24, 1922. It quickly won legislative approval in six of the seven basin states, but opposition in Arizona prevented the compact from taking effect until the end of the decade. The impasse was not broken until 1928, when Congress consented to an amendment stipulating that the concurrence of six states would suffice to render the agreement effective, provided that California was one of the six and that it would agree to additional limitation on the size of its allocation.[30] California agreed to the stipulations the following year, and on June 25, 1929, the nation's new president, Herbert Hoover, signed a proclamation declaring the compact he helped create seven years earlier to be effective. Arizona continued to hold out until 1944, but in the meantime, the enactment of the new agreement paved the way for the building of the Hoover Dam, which began in 1931.

3.1.3.2 The New York–New Jersey Port Authority Compact of 1921

Like the Colorado River Compact, the New York–New Jersey Port Authority Compact that preceded it was the product of a negotiation between appointed commissioners representing the party states. Unlike the Colorado River Commission, however, the entity that negotiated the Port Authority agreement was originally commissioned for a broader purpose and did not include federal participation. In part, this was because congressional consent for an interstate compact had not previously been requested or conferred, but inadvertently, perhaps, the federal government did play a role in launching the compact effort.

A series of disputes between New York and New Jersey over the development and regulation of commercial activity in and around the Port of New York came to a head in 1916 when the Interstate Commerce Commission (ICC) was called upon to resolve an issue pertaining to rail and shipping rates on either side of the Hudson River.[31] In settling the dispute, the ICC ordered the neighboring states to cooperate in administering their port facilities in the public interest. Accordingly, a temporary bi-state entity called the New York and New Jersey Port and Harbor Development Com-

---

30. By means of the Boulder Canyon Project Act, Pub. L. No. 70-642 (1928) (codified at 43 U.S.C. §§ 617, *et seq.* (2004).
31. Noble E. Whitford, History of the Barge Canal of New York State, ch. XXX (1922).

mission (consisting of three representatives appointed by each state's governor) was established in 1917.[32]

Tasked with formulating a comprehensive plan for the future development of the port and its freight handling facilities, the commission spent the next several years studying the underlying challenges and issues before submitting its *Joint Report with Comprehensive Plans and Recommendations* to the legislatures of both states. The hallmark of the commission's work was its proposal to establish a permanent interstate agency entrusted with regulatory authority over the shared port district and charged with implementing the comprehensive plan for its future development. Modeled in part after the Port of London Authority created in 1908, the proposed Port of New York Authority was to be established by means of an interstate compact between New York and New Jersey.[33]

The draft compact negotiated and recommended by the commission was quickly approved by both states in early 1921, and congressional consent for the agreement followed within months.[34] The new interstate agency it created immediately picked up where the previous bi-state commission left off, and by the end of the year, the Port of New York Authority (known today as the Port Authority of New York and New Jersey) had fulfilled its first statutory obligation by finalizing the proposed comprehensive plan for the future development of the port district. The plan was subsequently submitted to the party state legislatures in 1922 and approved, thus establishing the initial framework for the Port Authority's future pursuit of its mission.[35]

3.1.3.3   The Interstate Compact on the Placement of Children

In contrast to the formally negotiated compacts described above, the Interstate Compact on the Placement of Children is an example of a facilitated compact developed informally by interested stakeholders acting without an official charge. The need for a compact governing the interstate movement of children was first recognized in the 1950s by a group of social service administrators and legislators from several eastern states that met informally to study the problems associated with cross-border placements for

---

32. Major Elihu Church, *Development of the Port of New York*, Lecture published by the Pennsylvania Railroad, 1924.

33. PORT AUTHORITY OF NEW YORK AND NEW JERSEY, HISTORY OF THE PORT AUTHORITY, *available at* http://www.panynj.gov (2005).

34. 42 STAT. 822 (1921). President Harding signed the consent legislation into law on August 23, 1921.

35. NOBLE E. WHITFORD, HISTORY OF THE BARGE CANAL OF NEW YORK STATE, ch. XXX (1922).

adoption or foster care.[36] The group concluded that existing state and federal laws offered inadequate protection for children transferred between states and that without an interstate compact, no state could compel a sister state to provide such children with the support services they needed.[37]

In response to these concerns, the New York Joint Legislative Committee on Interstate Cooperation took the lead in proposing a compact establishing procedures for the interstate placement and protection of children. The final draft was reviewed and approved by participants in an informal 12-state conference held in January 1960 and then circulated to legislatures for their consideration.[38] Two months later, New York became the first state to enact the new agreement, but several others soon followed suit, and with no need for congressional consent, the compact took effect the same year the draft was approved by its developers.

By 1990, all 50 states, the District of Columbia, and the U.S. Virgin Islands had adopted the compact, making it one of the few truly national interstate compacts on the books. The agreement is also noteworthy for the relative speed with which it proceeded from development to enactment. As noted previously, this can be one of the advantages of the facilitated approach to compact making, provided that the process is open and responsive to the concerns of key stakeholders.

3.1.3.4 *The Emergency Management Assistance Compact*

The Emergency Management Assistance Compact (EMAC) is one of many interstate compacts to have been developed by an association of state officials, in this case, the Southern Governors' Association (SGA). The EMAC initiative was launched in 1992 after Hurricane Andrew stormed ashore and devastated much of south Florida. Frustrated by the lack of efficient means for states to assist each other in times of emergency, then-governor of Florida Lawton Chiles urged his southern counterparts to explore the creation of an interstate mutual aid agreement that would facilitate cooperative responses to disasters of all kinds.[39]

---

36. AMERICAN PUBLIC HUMAN SERVICES ASSOCIATION, GUIDE TO THE INTERSTATE COMPACT ON THE PLACEMENT OF CHILDREN 2 (2002).

---

37. OFFICE OF INSPECTOR GENERAL, U.S. DEP'T OF HEALTH AND HUMAN SERVICES, INTERSTATE COMPACT ON THE PLACEMENT OF CHILDREN: IMPLEMENTATION 1-2 (1999).

38. THE COUNCIL OF STATE GOVERNMENTS, SUGGESTED STATE LEGISLATION—PROGRAM FOR 1961, 49 (1960).

39. Richard J. Dieffenbach, *Help Is Just a State Away*, STATE GOV'T NEWS 28

The SGA responded with a resolution endorsing the idea and then established a working group to develop a compact proposal. The committee, consisting of emergency management officials, attorneys, National Guard representatives, and governors' staff members,[40] was assisted in its efforts by Virginia's Department of Emergency Services.[41] By the summer of 1993, the committee had completed its developmental work, and in mid-August, SGA members signed the proposed Southern Regional Emergency Management Assistance Compact (SREMAC) during a meeting in Tulsa, Oklahoma.

It was not long, however, before the concept behind the compact outgrew its regional origin. Even before all of the originally intended parties could enact the proposed legislation, the governors voted in 1995 to amend the agreement by opening it up to national participation. At that point, "Southern Regional" was dropped from the compact name, and EMAC was born.[42] During the months that followed, SGA began working with the National Emergency Management Association (NEMA) to facilitate a transfer of secretariat responsibilities for the new compact to an entity of national scope.

By 1996, the transition was complete, and the compact had already taken effect in several southern states. Congressional ratification followed that same year, and interest in the agreement quickly spread to other regions. Endorsements from several other regional and national associations of governors, legislators, and attorneys general fueled the effort to extend the compact's reach,[43] and by the beginning of the new century, most of the states were on board. Among the few that were not was New York, which nevertheless received EMAC assistance from many states in the immediate aftermath of the terrorist attacks on September 11, 2001. Three days later, New York enacted the compact, and by 2005, 49 states, two territories, and the District of Columbia were members.[44]

3.1.3.5 The National Crime Prevention and Privacy Compact

A more recent compact developed through nontraditional means is the National Crime Prevention and Privacy Compact (NCPPC), which took ef-

(December 1998).

---

40. Interview with Trina Sheets, Executive Director, National Emergency Management Association, Aug. 23, 2004.
41. NATIONAL EMERGENCY MANAGEMENT ASSOCIATION, EMAC GUIDEBOOK & STANDARD OPERATING PROCEDURES A-3 (2004).
42. Interview with Trina Sheets, *supra* note 40.
43. NATIONAL EMERGENCY MANAGEMENT ASSOCIATION, *supra* note 41.
44. Interview with Trina Sheets, *supra* note 40. Hawaii has yet to join the com-

fect in the spring of 1999, upon enactment by the first two of its 21 member states. The NCPPC grew out of a shared desire on the part of state and federal law enforcement officials to establish some common ground rules governing the exchange and dissemination of fingerprint-based criminal history records for certain noncriminal-justice purposes (e.g., background checks on those seeking employment requiring close contact with children or the elderly).[45]

The initial effort to address this challenge was facilitated by a national, nonprofit organization called SEARCH, The National Consortium for Justice Information and Statistics. A state-driven organization serving all 50 states, SEARCH provided a forum for state and federal officials to begin working together in the late 1970s in an attempt to develop improved information-sharing mechanisms. These informal discussions continued for more than fifteen years, during which time the notion of establishing a state-federal interstate compact took root.[46]

A draft compact was eventually developed in collaboration with the Criminal Justice Information Services (CJIS) Division of the FBI. The proposal envisioned an active role for the federal government and the establishment of a Compact Council vested with rulemaking authority to facilitate implementation of the Interstate Identification Index System, a cooperative federal-state system for the exchange of criminal history records.[47] Upon completion, the draft agreement was formally endorsed by SEARCH and by the CJIS Advisory Policy Board, as well as the National Sheriffs' Association.[48]

Armed with these endorsements, the developers of the proposal next sought congressional enactment of the compact. A bill introduced by Ohio Senator Mike DeWine was passed and signed into law by President Clinton in October 1998. State legislation followed within months, and the compact became effective after Montana and Georgia ratified the agreement in early 1999. Since then, 21 additional states have joined the compact, which is open to 50-state participation.[49]

---

pact.

45. BUREAU OF JUSTICE STATISTICS, U.S. DEP'T OF JUSTICE, NATIONAL CRIME PREVENTION AND PRIVACY COMPACT: RESOURCE MATERIALS 1, 15 (1998).
46. Interview with Wilbur Rehman, NCPPC Council Chair and Project Manager, Criminal Justice Information Services, Montana Dep't of Justice, Aug. 20, 2004.
47. National Crime Prevention and Privacy Compact, art. VI, § (1)(a) (1998).
48. BUREAU OF JUSTICE STATISTICS, *supra* note 45.

3.1.3.6 The Interstate Compact for Adult Offender Supervision

Another compact of more recent vintage, the Interstate Compact for Adult Offender Supervision differs notably from those discussed above in that it was specifically designed to replace an existing 50-state agreement, the Interstate Compact for the Supervision of Parolees and Probationers. The old compact, dating back to 1937, had provided a framework for the interstate transfer of supervision responsibilities when criminal offenders on parole or probation legally moved between states. The system worked well for more than half a century, but as the offender population grew and became more mobile, it gradually became apparent that the original agreement was no longer adequate to meet the challenges of a changing society.

By the mid-1990s, compact administrators and other practitioners in the field had begun to express a number of concerns related to the day-to-day operation of the compact. In response to these concerns, the National Institute of Corrections (NIC), a federal agency housed within the U.S. Department of Justice, Federal Bureau of Prisons, empowered an ad hoc committee to examine the underlying issues and report back to the NIC Advisory Board. A survey of practitioners and a public hearing were conducted in 1997, and based on the committee's resulting recommendations, the NIC Advisory Board decided in 1998 to pursue a revision of the existing compact.[50]

Later that year, a project advisory group, including compact administrators and other key stakeholders, was established under the auspices of the NIC to begin exploring various options. By the end of the year, the group had concluded that a comprehensive revision of the 1937 agreement was needed. At that point, the NIC entered into a cooperative agreement with The Council of State Governments (CSG), and together the two organizations facilitated the efforts of a nine-member drafting team, which again included existing compact administrators and other interested stakeholders, to develop a new compact.[51]

A final draft was completed at the end of 1999 and circulated for legislative consideration beginning in 2000. Because the transition from an existing compact to a new system threatened to complicate the transfer of offenders between states until all were subject to the same agreement, the drafters of the proposed ICAOS deliberately established a high threshold for enactment of the new compact. The legislation provided that the new agreement would not become effective until 35 states had adopted it, thus ensuring that the original

---

49. Interview with Wilbur Rehman, *supra* note 46.

50. THE COUNCIL OF STATE GOVERNMENTS, COMPACT PROJECT BACKGROUNDER AND HISTORY (2002).

51. *Id.*

compact would remain in full force and effect until a critical mass of member states agreed to support the new framework.

As a result, although eight states followed Colorado's lead in adopting the new compact in 2000 and 16 more signed in the following year, the new agreement did not become effective until the summer of 2002, when the number of participating states reached 35. Most of the remaining states soon joined as well, and by 2005, al 50 states, the District of Columbia, the U.S. Virgin Islands, and Puerto Rico were members of the ICAOS.[52]

3.2   FROM CONCEPT TO COMPACT: FIVE KEYS TO SUCCESS

Because the elements of a binding compact, like those of an ordinary contract, are few and fairly straightforward, the process of making a compact may at first glance appear deceptively simple. But as the preceding examples illustrate, there is more than one way to make an interstate compact, and the preferred path inevitably depends on the specific circumstances giving rise to a particular initiative. That is because compacts, for all their simplicity, are not ordinary contracts at all but rather creatures of an inherently political exercise. As such, they demand more from their makers during the development stage, and attention to process is essential throughout.

Whether the original impetus for a particular agreement is a potential crisis, a festering problem, a congressional directive, or simply a desired end, a successful compact process invariably begins with the recognition of a need for states to cooperate in addressing a common challenge. Where it goes from there may depend on any number of possible factors, including such variables as the level of public concern over the central issue, the urgency of finding a solution to the problem, the number and awareness of key stakeholders (both within and beyond the official government arena), and the likelihood of reaching an amicable agreement. Together, these and other factors may dictate the need for a formally negotiated compact between officially designated commissioners representing the party states, or they may suggest that an alternative approach is either necessary or preferable.

In the more likely event that a proposed compact is developed through informal channels, the specific steps in the process can vary significantly from agreement to agreement. Nevertheless, the experience of compact mak-

---

52. Massachusetts became the 50th state to adopt the compact in 2005. The U.S. territories are also eligible to participate. *See* Interstate Compact for Adult Offender Supervision, art. I (2002).

ers in recent years has shown that there are at least five keys to success in the development of any interstate compact.

3.2.1   An Inclusive Process

First, the process must be inclusive. The importance of including as many key stakeholders as possible early on in the development of an interstate compact simply cannot be overstated. Because of the contractual nature of compacts and the corresponding requirement that legislatures adopt substantially identical language when enacting them, proposed compacts may not be freely amended after introduction, as might an ordinary piece of legislation. This leaves lawmakers and other interested stakeholders who might have concerns about a proposed compact with little recourse to effect change once a proposal reaches the legislative arena. Short of introducing an amendment requiring concurrence by all party states, there is little alternative to simply opposing the agreement in its entirety if key stakeholders find fault with a proposal after its formal introduction.

For these reasons, most successful compact efforts include ample opportunity during the development stage for stakeholder input and participation. At a minimum, this means providing all interested parties with notice of the proposed initiative and a chance to present comments and suggestions at a point in the process when input can still be received and incorporated into any final proposal. This was the purpose, for example, behind the series of public hearings convened by the Colorado River Commission during the formulation of the Colorado River Compact in 1922.

But even if key stakeholders are afforded opportunities to review and comment on draft proposals, agreements developed without the direct participation of interested parties remain vulnerable to criticism, whether well founded or not, from those who are excluded from the process. This can result in additional obstacles for compact proponents when forced to defend their development strategy during the legislative consideration of a proposed compact. Regardless of the merits of their case, their chances for success may suffer if excluded opponents can attack the process, as well as the results of the initiative.

In an effort to preempt such opposition, some of the most successful compact development efforts in recent years have included multiple opportunities for stakeholder input from the very beginning. When the National Institute of Corrections, for example, decided in 1998 to pursue a revision of the Interstate Compact for the Supervision of Parolees and Probationers, its first step was to assemble a project advisory team consisting not only of existing compact administrators but also other interested stakeholders such as representatives of crime victims, state court administrators, attorneys general, and state departments of corrections. In fact, the NIC had already solicited and received broad stakeholder input even before deciding to establish this advisory group.

As development of the new Interstate Compact for Adult Offender Supervision continued during the next two years, stakeholder participation was built into every step of the process. The drafting team that drew up the proposed agreement was as representative of the varied interests at stake as was the advisory group that oversaw the effort, and before a final draft was released for legislative consideration, two other significant steps were taken. First, comments and suggestions in response to preliminary drafts were solicited and received from almost 300 individuals, agencies, and associations likely to be affected by the new compact. Then in the fall of 1999, a legislative briefing was held in Chicago in an effort to educate select lawmakers from across the country about the initiative and to solicit their guidance and input before releasing a final draft compact that no single legislature would be at liberty to amend unilaterally.

Each of these steps was carefully calculated to give the final draft proposal the best possible chance of winning legislative approval by ensuring that all stakeholders had multiple opportunities to be heard during the development process. This emphasis on inclusiveness also helped to produce genuine stakeholder "buy-in" prior to legislative consideration of the proposal, which, in turn, made it easier for the developers of the new compact to mobilize a broad-based show of support for the agreement as it moved through the nation's legislatures.

3.2.2   An Effective "Sales Pitch"

Like any other piece of legislation, a proposed interstate compact must compete with numerous other issues and initiatives for the attention of lawmakers as it wends its way through the legislative process, and even a well-conceived proposal will languish along the way if unassisted by an effective sales pitch. While the appeal for passage must always be tailored to reflect the specific proposal (as well as an understanding of the unique dynamics of each legislature), an effective pitch usually includes at least three elements and invariably begins with a compelling case on the merits.

This is the essence of the appeal for action and must, at a minimum, encompass the need to be addressed or the issues to be resolved, the key elements of the specific proposal, the thinking behind them, and the reasons why the proposed compact will likely produce the desired results. To the extent applicable, the case on the merits should also include an explanation of the consequences of inaction, especially if federal intervention or preemption of the field is a possible result. This is often a compelling argument in favor of a proposed agreement, especially with respect to regulatory issues, since interstate compacts can permit states to reap the benefits of uniform regulatory schemes without relinquishing state authority to the federal government.

The second element of an effective sales pitch is an explanation of the compact mechanism itself. Given the unique characteristics of interstate compacts with respect to other statutes and the fact that legislators only rarely deal with them in the course of their work, any appeal for the passage of a proposed compact should include enough general information about such agreements to provide lawmakers with a basic understanding of their mechanics and usage. A candid explanation of the strengths and weaknesses of the compact mechanism can go a long way toward making even wary legislators more comfortable with a statutory tool that requires them to set aside the amendatory prerogative they enjoy when considering other legislation. It can also serve as a helpful reminder that compacts are not that unusual, that virtually every state in the union has entered into numerous interstate compacts over the years, and that there are enough safeguards built into most agreements to allay any fears that lawmakers might have about sharing regulatory sovereignty with their sister states.

A third element that should be incorporated into the sales pitch is an explanation of the process by which the proposal was developed. This is especially important with respect to informally facilitated compacts developed, without official sanction, outside the legislative arena. Lawmakers are not unaccustomed to receiving draft legislative proposals from interested outsiders, but when they come with the caveat that they may not be substantially altered before passage, it becomes even more important to defend the development process. Specifically, the advocates of a proposed agreement should be prepared to demonstrate that the development effort was inclusive of key stakeholders and that it was carefully designed to anticipate and address the significant issues requiring resolution. Unanticipated substantive issues or significant opposition from excluded stakeholders could quickly stop a proposed compact in its tracks, especially if left unanswered by proponents during legislative consideration of the agreement.

3.2.3 A Broad-Based Marketing Strategy

Just as important as a compelling message is the plan for its dissemination, and not just to legislators. Since lawmakers often rely on the advice and expertise of agency officials and other interested parties in their own states when considering proposed legislation, the proponents of an interstate compact must take care to ensure that their outreach efforts reach a broad audience. Getting the word out, not only to key stakeholders but also to the public at large, can be an important part of any effort to win passage of an interstate compact.

The developers of the Susquehanna River Basin Compact, for example, devised an elaborate public relations plan that began with the production of a promotional film even before the draft compact was complete.[53] The 21-minute film was used to highlight the general need for a collaborative effort to govern the use of the river, rather than to promote a specific regulatory solution, but it set the stage for the interstate compact that followed. As the Interstate Advisory Committee on the Susquehanna River Basin put the finishing touches on the final draft in the spring of 1966, the outreach campaign intensified with a continuous flow of information to key stakeholders throughout the basin. Then, when the compact was ready to be released, the official rollout began with a set of media-oriented "announcement luncheons" held simultaneously in the three basin states that summer. These were followed by aggressive efforts to promote the compact throughout the region prior to formal legislative consideration the following year.[54]

Similarly, the developers of the Interstate Compact for Adult Offender Supervision paid careful attention to the marketing of their proposal thirty years later. The cooperative agreement between the National Institute of Corrections and The Council of State Governments, under which the draft compact was created, provided funding for the development of various educational tools, including printed materials, an informational video, and a Web site providing answers to frequently asked questions and other resources. Technical assistance in the form of consultation and legislative testimony was also provided to the states as the proposed compact made its way through the legislative process. Press releases were used to keep the media informed of the initiative's progress, and articles were placed in numerous publications, including magazines, association newsletters, and more. All of these efforts helped to generate awareness and a better understanding of the proposed compact as the process continued.

3.2.4   A Network of Champions

Given the challenge of winning support from legislators and key stakeholders in multiple states, the developers of any interstate compact must also work to build and mobilize a network of advocates on its behalf. Given also

---

53. William Voigt, Jr., The Susquehanna Compact: Guardian of the River's Future 145-46 (1972).
54. *Id.* at 146-71.

the fact that local advocates working on the inside tend to be more effective in most legislative arenas, the breadth of the network should ideally reflect the anticipated membership of the compact: the more states invited to participate, the more "champions" needed.

In addition to ensuring that key stakeholder concerns are addressed early on, an open and inclusive development process also tends to facilitate the recruitment of advocates. Once stakeholders buy into a proposed compact, and especially if they do so in any formal sense (e.g., a resolution adopted by an association), they can often be mobilized to work for its passage as well. For instance, the administrators of the Interstate Compact for the Supervision of Parolees and Probationers, both individually and through their association,[55] played a key role in winning passage of a successor agreement, the Interstate Compact for Adult Offender Supervision (ICAOS). This kind of support can provide a tremendous boon to a proposal's chances for success. But in the end, there is no substitute for allied insiders once a compact reaches the legislative arena.

In developing the proposed ICAOS, for example, the project advisory group convened by the National Institute of Corrections sought legislative guidance and input throughout the process. Developers also used a pair of informational briefings both to educate lawmakers about the concept and to help identify potential champions who might be willing to carry the proposed legislation in each state. This network of legislative advocates proved invaluable, not only in facilitating bill introductions, but also in providing reliable intelligence regarding the status of the proposal and, ultimately, in securing its passage.

3.2.5   A Proactive Transition Plan

Successful compact making also requires an effective and proactive plan for the transition period that begins when the first state passes a proposed agreement. Unlike other legislation, which is usually implemented soon after passage, an interstate compact might not take effect until years after its initial adoption, depending on the number of states required to perfect the agreement and the time it takes to secure their approval. This aspect of compact creation poses a unique set of challenges for the developers of such agreements, whose work is not truly finished until enough states have adopted a given proposal to render it effective.

The trick is to sustain the momentum generated in those states that first approve a compact while continuing to work for its passage elsewhere. This

---

55. The Parole and Probation Compact Administrators' Association (PPCAA).

can be a more or less daunting task, depending on the nature and geographic scope of the proposed agreement, but even when the anticipated parties are few in number, the lag time between initial passage and eventual implementation can make for a challenging transition if left unaddressed by compact developers.

One way to mitigate the potential impact of this problem is by making lawmakers and other stakeholders aware of it from the outset, so that all parties know what to expect. Advocates who appreciate this challenge and who represent states that are early parties to an agreement can sometimes be effectively mobilized to assist in reaching out to other eligible states. But sustaining interest in, and awareness of, a proposed compact in a state that has already adopted it can be difficult if the period between passage and implementation proves lengthy.

The key to success in this regard is a well-conceived communication plan incorporating a network of likely administrators or other key officials in those states that first adopt a proposed compact. Even before the agreement wins passage in enough states to become effective, developers who build and begin working with such a network are likely to be rewarded for their efforts with a smoother transition in the end. Such was the case when the developers of the Interstate Compact for Adult Offender Supervision passed the baton to the new interstate commission created by that agreement in 2002. The relative ease and speed of this successful transition was due in part to the facilitated efforts of an informally recruited interim planning group composed of representatives from several early parties to the agreement. By making good use of the period between the compact's initial approval in 2000 and its effective date two years later, the developers and future administrators of the proposal avoided many of the potential pitfalls of a lengthy, unplanned transition and laid a solid foundation for the compact's future success.

3.3   CONSIDERATIONS IN DRAFTING

As important and politically charged as the development process may be at the outset, in the long run, the success or failure of any interstate compact may depend as much, or more, on the care and precision that goes into its drafting. Long after the practical and political hurdles to a compact's creation have all been cleared, what remains is a statute that must be implemented, interpreted, and enforced. In this respect, at least, interstate compacts are not unlike other statutes, and their long-term viability may depend in part on the foresight exercised by drafters in determining their appropriate content and structure. At a substantive level, what goes in and what stays out of a particular agreement may depend on various factors that are specific to the issue or to the interests of key stakeholders. But once the basic components have been agreed to, it is up to the drafters to craft a compact that will stand the test of time.

3.3.1   General Considerations

As with any statute, clarity and precision of language are highly valued commodities with respect to interstate compacts, the more so because of the multistate reach and effect of the finished product. In striving for these qualities, compact drafters are well advised to bear in mind the general canons of statutory construction, but they must also anticipate and seek to prevent potential disputes arising from disparate meanings being given to common terms in the various member states. One way to do this is through the inclusion of definitions binding the members to common understandings of the most important compact terms. Such definitions should seek to harmonize the compact's provisions with the existing laws of member states whenever possible, but when deviations from the norm are necessary to achieve the compact's purposes, the definitions provided in the compact itself will, like the substantive provisions of the agreement, take precedence over any state laws with which they conflict.[56]

Another means to prevent ambiguity is the inclusion of language conveying the purpose or intent of the compact. Such language can accompany and clarify specific provisions within the agreement, or it may stand alone in the form of a preamble or a separate article.[57] Either way, statements of intent can be extremely useful to both the makers and the readers of interstate compacts, but these, too, must be carefully drafted to avoid exacerbating the very problems of interpretation they are often meant to avoid.

Attention should also be paid to the internal organization of the compact itself in order to ensure a logical and "user-friendly" flow from beginning to end. Interstate compacts can and do assume a wide variety of forms, but they typically begin with one or more preliminary provisions (e.g., statement of purpose, definitions) before proceeding directly to the essence of the agreement and the primary substantive provisions (e.g., the establishment of an interstate agency charged with specific powers and duties). Many compacts also include a number of secondary provisions designed to effectuate their

---

56. FREDERICK L. ZIMMERMAN & MITCHELL WENDELL, THE LAW AND USE OF INTERSTATE COMPACTS 27 (Council of State Governments 1976).

57. *Id.* at 28-29. The authors caution that a purpose statement in preamble form, though potentially useful, is less enforceable than comparable language set forth in the body of a compact.

primary purposes (e.g., financial provisions or procedural requirements governing an interstate agency's exercise of regulatory authority), and some include additional terms that, though not strictly necessary, are considered desirable for practical reasons (e.g., provisions recognizing the judicial enforceability of compact obligations against member states).

3.3.2   Deciding What Goes In

The precise form a compact should take depends initially on the nature of the agreement between the states. Compacts that embody fixed agreements between the parties can be relatively simple instruments, but those that establish interstate entities with ongoing responsibilities and duties typically require more elaborate statutory schemes. With respect to the latter category especially, drafters often have to make numerous judgment calls in determining what to include and what to leave out of the compact itself. Several factors may enter into this equation, but in the end, the trick is to strike an appropriate and salable balance between competing objectives. On the one hand, the compact must include enough structure and detail to ensure its smooth implementation and the successful fulfillment of its stated objectives. On the other hand, it must remain sufficiently general to accommodate changing circumstances and to preserve the operational flexibility that may be desired. Too little detail can result in important issues remaining unresolved and can open the door to future misunderstandings between the parties. Too much can invite undue scrutiny during the adoption process or needlessly tie the hands of those charged with the compact's administration following enactment.

Though there is no "right way" to structure a compact that will, in all cases, produce the desired balance between these objectives, several important factors should be considered by drafters when determining where to draw the appropriate lines. At a minimum, these include the purpose of the proposed compact, the significance of the issues to be addressed, the nature of the proposed solution, the risk of unintended consequences, and the likelihood of winning approval for whatever is finally put forward.

As a general proposition, terms that are essential to the fundamental agreement between the parties should always be included in the compact, even if they go to issues that might be considered more tactical in nature or of secondary importance in other contexts. For example, a compact that confers substantive regulatory responsibilities upon a new interstate agency arguably requires more language specifying the procedures to be employed by such an entity than does a compact that creates a purely advisory commission. But even with agreements that create new regulatory bodies, drafters should exercise careful discretion in determining the appropriate level of procedural detail to include in the compact itself. Many operational issues of a more internal nature, for example, can safely be delegated to a regulatory entity that is empowered to adopt its own bylaws. This approach offers the twin advantages of a more streamlined compact document and a greater degree of flexibility for the authorized agency, which usually retains the ability to amend its bylaws as well.

Another consideration in determining whether a compact should address a given issue is the potential need for future amendments. Because compacts are generally difficult to alter, secondary issues that are susceptible to changing circumstances are sometimes better left to the appropriate administrative authority or simply omitted altogether. Conversely, the difficulty in amending interstate compacts can be a compelling factor in favor of addressing those issues and points of agreement that the parties wish to insulate from administrative change.

With respect to administrative compacts that establish and empower new interstate agencies, drafters usually have additional options to consider in deciding what to include in the compact itself. Substantive issues that might be satisfactorily resolved through the agency's rulemaking process need not be addressed in the compact, but the drafters can, if they wish, ensure that such issues are eventually dealt with by requiring the agency to promulgate rules on specified subjects or within designated time frames.[58] The compact can also require, rather than simply authorize, the adoption of procedural bylaws governing the agency's operations.[59]

Options such as these permit compact drafters to perform a sort of strategic triage in deciding how best to address various issues. The most important elements of the agreement between the parties, including provisions that establish the necessary structure and framework for subsequent decision making, should generally be reflected in the compact itself. Secondary issues of a substantive nature, especially those that are susceptible to changing circumstances, should be left to the discretion of the new interstate agency pursuant

---

58. *See, e.g.*, Interstate Compact for Adult Offender Supervision, art. VIII (2002), which required the new compact commission to promulgate rules in 10 specified areas within 12 months following its first meeting.

59. *See, e.g.*, Midwestern Higher Education Compact, art. III (1991), which required the compact commission to adopt "suitable bylaws governing its management and operations."

to the exercise of its rulemaking authority, whether mandated or permitted. Finally, those issues of a more internal or purely operational nature can be designated for inclusion in the agency's bylaws.

Among the other factors that drafters should consider in deciding what to put into an interstate compact are the ancillary benefits that might be derived from incorporating select provisions of a more extraneous nature (e.g., purpose statements to aid in determining legislative intent or language that expressly acknowledges the special status of interstate compacts relative to other laws). Such provisions, even if legally unnecessary, can be useful for practical and political purposes, both during and following enactment.

3.3.3   Typical Provisions

The flexibility of the compact mechanism is evident not only in the wide range of subjects covered by such agreements but also in the variety of forms they take. The simplest compacts have been relatively brief, containing only a few sections and substantive terms.[60] Others have been much more elaborate, featuring numerous articles and detailed provisions.[61] The specifics can, and do, vary considerably, but most compacts include terms covering some or all of the following areas.

3.3.3.1 Purpose, Goals, Objectives

Statements of purpose outlining the need for an interstate compact and identifying the principal goals or objectives to be pursued are fairly common. As indicated previously, they are not essential to the viability of any such agreement, but they often serve one of two important functions. Initially, they can be useful tools during the effort to win passage of a proposed compact by calling attention to the underlying policy issues and presenting a case for the stated objectives. Thereafter, they can also be helpful aids to users or to courts in interpreting the intended meaning of a compact and in determining the appropriate construction to be given to any ambiguous or disputed terms.

Some compacts include preambles that articulate findings or assumptions upon which the body of the statute is based and that suggest the need for an interstate agreement in order to fulfill a specific purpose. Often, these preambles resemble legislative resolutions in that they are presented as a series of recitals followed by a simple declaration adopting the substantive

---

60. *See, e.g.*, Interstate Compact for the Supervision of Parolees and Probationers (1954), *superseded by* Interstate Compact on Adult Offender Supervision (2002).
61. *See, e.g.*, Interstate Insurance Receivership Compact (1996).

terms of the proposed compact. For example, the preamble to the New York–New Jersey Port Authority Compact reads, in part, as follows:

> Whereas, In the year 1834 the states of New York and New Jersey did enter into an agreement fixing and determining the rights and obligations of the two states in and about the waters between the two states, especially in and about the bay of New York and the Hudson River; and
>
> Whereas, The future development of such terminal, transportation and other facilities of commerce will require the expenditure of large sums of money, and the cordial cooperation of the states of New York and New Jersey in the encouragement of the investment of capital, and in the formulation and execution of the necessary physical plans; and
>
> Whereas, Such result can best be accomplished through the cooperation of the two states by and through a joint or common agency;
>
> Now, Therefore, The said states of New Jersey and New York do supplement and amend the existing agreement of 1834 in the following respects[.][62]

To ensure that statements of intent are given the same weight and effect as the substantive compact terms they accompany, drafters often incorporate purpose provisions directly into the body of the compact instead of breaking them out in preamble form. For example, the Interstate Compact on the Placement of Children includes the following provision:

> It is the purpose and policy of the party states to cooperate with each other in the interstate placement of children to the end that:
>   (a) Each child requiring placement shall receive the maximum opportunity to be placed in a suitable environment and with persons or institutions having appropriate qualifications and facilities to provide a necessary and desirable degree and type of care[.][63]

3.3.3.2 *Substantive Terms of Agreement*

Although many compacts establish mechanisms for the subsequent development of specific solutions to common problems or the ongoing exercise of interstate regulatory authority, others spell out, in fixed terms, the full

---

62. New York-New Jersey Port Authority Compact, *Preamble* (1921).
63. Interstate Compact on the Placement of Children, art. I (1960).

extent of the agreement between the parties. Bi-state boundary agreements
are typical of such compacts in that instead of establishing a means to resolve
a particular matter, they usually include substantive language that settles the
issue. For example, the Missouri-Nebraska Boundary Compact includes a
provision stating. "The permanent compromise boundary line between the
states of Missouri and Nebraska shall be fixed at the center line of the main
channel of the Missouri River as of the effective date of the compact."[64]

Similarly, the Colorado River Compact sets forth the precise terms of a
negotiated water allocation between the member states:

> There is hereby apportioned from the Colorado River system in
> perpetuity to the upper basin and to the lower basin respectively
> the exclusive beneficial consumptive use of seven million five hun-
> dred thousand (7,500,000) acre-feet of water per annum, which
> shall include all water necessary for the supply of any rights which
> may not exist.[65]

In theory, there are no limits to the potential scope or specificity of such
provisions. In practice, however, the difficulty in obtaining multistate legislative approval for a single, detailed set of substantive terms can be considerable. Drafters often conclude, as a practical matter, that "less is more" especially
when a compact establishes appropriate means for filling in the details after
enactment (e.g., through rulemaking by an authorized entity).

3.3.3.3 Compact Administration

Regardless of whether a compact embodies a fixed agreement between
the parties or establishes an ongoing interstate regulatory process, it should
include appropriate provisions to ensure the successful implementation and
administration of the statutory plan. With respect to fixed agreements, this
can be as simple as a provision specifying the appropriate oversight authorities in the party states and authorizing them to work together as necessary.
The Colorado River Compact, for example, includes the following language:

> The chief official of each signatory state charged with the adminis-
> tration of water rights, together with the director of the United States

---

64. The Missouri-Nebraska compact also includes language providing for the
    future adjustment of the prescribed boundary in the event that the course of
    the Missouri River should change. Missouri-Nebraska Compact, art. VIII
    (1999).
65. Colorado River Compact, art. III(a) (1921).

reclamation service and the director of the United States geological
survey shall cooperate, ex officio:

(i) To promote the systemic determination and coordination of the
facts as to flow, appropriation, consumption and use of water in
the Colorado River basin, and the interchange of available information in such matters[.][66]

On the other hand, compacts that delegate substantive regulatory authority
to designated representatives of the party states, or that establish new interstate
entities for similar purposes, often include more elaborate statutory schemes.
These may effectively limit broad grants of authority to the designated administrators by specifying in greater detail the respective rights and obligations of
the party states, or they may specifically define such authority by enumerating
various administrative powers and duties. In either case, the key provision is
usually an article designating or establishing the appropriate administrative
authority and describing its role in general terms. The Interstate Compact on
the Placement of Children, for instance, provides as follows:

The executive head of each jurisdiction party to this compact shall
designate an officer who shall be general coordinator of activities
under this compact in his jurisdiction and who, acting jointly with
like officers of other party jurisdictions, shall have power to promulgate rules and regulations to carry out more effectively the terms
and provisions of this compact.[67]

The remainder of this compact contains additional provisions governing
the mutual obligations of the party states but is silent concerning the manner
in which the designated administrators are to carry out their duties. By comparison, the Ohio River Valley Water Sanitation Compact includes this provision, which establishes a new interstate commission:

The signatory states hereby create the "Ohio River Valley Water Sanitation Commission," hereinafter called the Commission, which shall
be a body corporate, with the powers and duties set forth herein, and
such additional powers as may be conferred upon it by subsequent
action of the respective legislatures of the signatory states or by act
or acts of the Congress of the United States.[68]

66. *Id.*
67. Interstate Compact on the Placement of Children, art. VII (1960).
68. Ohio River Valley Water Sanitation Compact, art. III (1940).

Subsequent sections of the same compact spell out the various powers and duties referred to in this article. Such provisions are fairly common to compacts that create new interstate agencies, whether they are regulatory (as in this case) or purely advisory in nature.[69]

3.3.3.4 Agency Powers and Duties

Compacts that create new interstate agencies frequently include one or more articles specifying the agency's discretionary powers and required duties. In some cases, these are neatly divided into separate provisions, which can be helpful to compact users and interpreters alike.[70] The Great Lake Basin Compact, for example, includes a single article identifying 14 powers that may be exercised by the Great Lakes Commission.[71] Specific duties that must be performed by the commission are identified elsewhere in the agreement. Similarly, Article V of the Washington Metropolitan Area Transit Regulation Compact enumerates 13 "general powers" that may be exercised by the compact authority,[72] whereas required agency duties are specified in subsequent provisions.[73]

In other instances, agency powers and duties are intermingled and are distinguishable only by the extent to which they are cast in mandatory or permissive terms. For example, a single article within the Central Interstate Low-Level Radioactive Waste Compact includes the following language:

> *(C)* The Commission shall elect from among its membership a chairman. The Commission shall adopt and publish, in convenient form, bylaws and policies which are not inconsistent with this compact.
>
> *(D)* The Commission shall meet at least once a year and shall also meet upon the call of the chairman, by petition of a majority of the membership or upon the call of a host state member.
>
> *(F)* The Commission may establish such committees as it deems necessary for the purpose of advising the Commission on any and all matters pertaining to the management of waste.

---

69. *See, e.g.*, Midwestern Higher Education Compact, art. III (1991), which enumerates the powers and duties assigned to an advisory commission.
70. *See, e.g.*, Susquehanna River Basin Compact, art. III, §§ 3.4, 3.5 (1970), which sets forth commission powers and duties.
71. Great Lakes Basin Compact, art. VI (1968).
72. Washington Metropolitan Area Transit Authority (WMATA).
73. *See* Washington Metropolitan Area Transit Regulation Compact, tit. III, art. VI (1966), which requires the WMATA board to develop and adopt a regional mass-transit plan.

(G) The Commission may employ and compensate a staff limited only to those persons necessary to carry out its duties and functions.

(I) The Commission shall keep accurate accounts of all receipts and disbursements.[74]

Sometimes, however, commission powers and duties are almost indistinguishable at a glance, with mandatory and permissive terminology appearing in the same provision, or even the same sentence. The Tri-State Lotto Compact, for instance, includes an article entitled "Powers and Duties of the Commission," which reads, in part:

1. *Operation and administration; rules.* The commission shall have the power and it shall be its duty to operate and administer Tri-state Lotto and to promulgate rules[.]
2. *Licensed sales agents.* The commission, or its designee, shall also have the power and it shall be its duty to license sales agents to sell Tri-state Lotto tickets. . . . The commission may require a bond[.][75]

The specific powers conferred upon interstate agencies vary from agreement to agreement, but at a minimum, drafters should strive to ensure that compact entities are adequately empowered to carry out their required duties. This usually means the inclusion of provisions addressing operational and administrative matters of a relatively generic nature, as well as others that reflect the specific objectives of a particular agreement. Thus, a typical compact might confer upon a new interstate agency some or all of the following powers:

- to adopt bylaws;
- to elect officers;
- to establish committees;
- to develop budgets;
- to collect and disburse agency funds;
- to borrow resources;
- to accept donated funds and other services;
- to enter into contracts;
- to buy, sell, or lease property;

---

74. Central Interstate Low-Level Radioactive Waste Compact, art. IV (1986).
75. Tri-State Lotto Compact, art. IX, §§ 1 & 2 (1983).

- to establish offices;
- to purchase insurance and bonds;
- to hire staff;
- to adopt personnel policies;
- to sue and be sued.

Depending on both the purpose of the compact and the functions it entails, additional provisions might also be included, granting to the interstate agency the general powers:

- to collect data;
- to issue reports;
- to develop policy recommendations;
- to promulgate rules;
- to resolve disputes;
- to enforce compliance.

By way of example, Title III, Article V of the Washington Metropolitan Area Transit Regulation Compact confers many of these general powers upon the regional transit authority it creates:

In addition to the powers and duties elsewhere described in this title, and except as limited in this title, the Authority may:

(a) Sue and be sued;

(b) Adopt and use a corporate seal and alter the same at pleasure;

(c) Adopt, amend, and repeal rules and regulations respecting the exercise of the powers conferred by this title;

(d) Construct, acquire, own, operate, maintain, control, sell and convey real and personal property and any interest therein by contract, purchase, condemnation, lease, license, mortgage or otherwise but all of said property shall be located in the zone and shall be necessary or useful in rendering transit service or in activities incidental thereto;

(e) Receive and accept such payments, appropriations, grants, gifts, loans, advances and other funds, properties and services as may be transferred or made available to it by any signatory party, any political subdivision or agency thereof, by the United States or by any agency thereof, or by any other public or private corporation or individual, and enter into agreements to make reimbursement for all or any part thereof;

(f) Enter into and perform contracts leases and agreements with any person, firm or corporation or with any political subdivision or agency of any signatory party or with the federal government, or any agency thereof, including, but not limited to, contracts or agreements to furnish transit facilities and service;

(g) Create and abolish offices, employments and positions (other than those specifically provided for herein) as it deems necessary for the purposes of the Authority, and fix and provide for the qualification, appointment, removal, term, tenure, compensation, pension and retirement rights of its officers and employees without regard to the laws of any of the signatories;

(h) Establish, in its discretion, a personnel system based on merit and fitness and, subject to eligibility, participate in the pension and retirement plans of any signatory, or political subdivision or agency thereof, upon terms and conditions mutually acceptable;

(i) Contract for or employ any professional services[.][76]

The same article then goes on to grant several additional powers to the agency that reflect the unique substantive purposes of this particular compact. These include the powers to:

(j) Control and regulate the use of facilities owned or controlled by the Authority, the service to be rendered and the fares and charges to be made therefore;

(k) Hold public hearings and conduct investigations relating to any matter affecting transportation in the zone with which the Authority is concerned and, in connection therewith, subpoena witnesses, papers, records and documents; or delegate such authority to any officer. Each director may administer oaths or affirmations in any proceeding or investigation;

(l) Make or participate in studies of all phases and forms of transportation, including transportation vehicle research and devel-

---

76. Washington Metropolitan Area Transit Regulation Compact, tit. III, art. V (1966). *See also* Interstate Compact for Adult Offender Supervision, art. V (2002) (creates regulatory commission and grants general administrative powers to interstate compact agency); Midwestern Higher Education Compact, art. III (1991) (creates an advisory commission).

opment techniques and methods for determining traffic projec-
tions, demand motivations, and fiscal research and publicize and
make available the results of such studies and other information
relating to transportation[.][77]

Similar examples of substantive, compact-specific agency powers can be
found in numerous other agreements as well, including the Great Lakes Basin
Compact (which empowers the Great Lakes Commission to "consider means
of improving navigation and port facilities in the Basin"[78]); the Interstate
Mining Compact (which authorizes the Interstate Mining Commission to "study
the conservation, adaptation, improvement and restoration of land and related resources affected by mining"[79]); and the Delaware River Basin Compact (which permits the Delaware River Basin Commission to "conduct such
special ground water investigations, tests, and operations and compile such
data relating thereto as may be required"[80]).

Compacts that establish interstate regulatory bodies often include both a
general grant of rulemaking authority and additional provisions imposing
procedural requirements that must be observed by the compact agency when
promulgating rules. Sometimes, the desired procedural safeguards are simply
incorporated by reference to external standards. Article VII of the Interstate
Insurance Receivership Compact, for example, provides in part that
"rulemaking shall substantially conform to the principles of the federal Administrative Procedure Act, 5 U.S.C.S. section 551 et seq., and the Federal
Advisory Committee Act, 5 U.S.C.S. app. 2, section 1 et seq., as may be
amended." A similar reference can be found in the Interstate Compact for
Adult Offender Supervision. However, the ICAOS goes on to provide that
when promulgating a rule, the compact commission shall:

- publish the proposed Rule stating with particularity the text of
  the Rule which is proposed and the reason for the proposed Rule;
- allow persons to submit written data, facts, opinions and arguments, which information shall be publicly available;
- provide an opportunity for an informal hearing; and

77. Washington Metropolitan Area Transit Regulation Compact, tit. III, art. V
    (1966).
78. Great Lakes Basin Compact, art. VI, § 4 (1940).
79. Interstate Mining Compact, art. IV, § 2 (1970).
80. Delaware River Basin Compact, art. III, § 3.6 (e) (1961).

- promulgate a final Rule and its effective date, if appropriate, based on the rulemaking record.[81]

Such due process concerns are frequently reflected in the rulemaking provisions contained in administrative compacts. But some agreements also include terms specifying the substantive scope of an agency's rulemaking powers or preserving for the members the right to veto unwelcome rules, either unilaterally or through collective action. The New York-New Jersey Port Authority Compact of 1921, for example, conditioned the effectiveness of any rules promulgated by the Port Authority upon authorization or concurrence by the legislatures of both member states and reserved to each party the right "to provide by law for the exercise of a veto power by the governor thereof over any action of any commissioner appointed therefrom."[82]

The Interstate Insurance Receivership Compact includes a provision permitting individual member states to unilaterally reject commission-approved rules within two years of their promulgation, in which case they immediately cease to be enforceable against the rejecting state:

All Rules and amendments shall become binding as of the date specified in each Rule or amendment; PROVIDED, that if a Compacting State expressly rejects such Rule or amendment through legislative enactment as of the expiration of the second full calendar year after such Rule is promulgated, such Rule or amendment shall have no further force and effect in the rejecting Compacting State.[83]

The agreement goes on to provide that if "a majority of Compacting States reject a Rule, then such Rule shall have no further force and effect in any Compacting States."[84] Without requiring the affirmative rejection of a rule to render it invalid, the Washington Metropolitan Area Transit Regulation Compact effectively permits the same result by stipulating that commission rules remain subordinate to any existing or subsequent conflicting laws in the member states.[85]

---

81. Interstate Compact for Adult Offender Supervision, art. VIII (2002).
82. New York-New Jersey Port Authority Compact of 1921, arts. XVI & XVIII (1921).
83. Interstate Insurance Receivership Compact, art. VII, § 4 (1996).
84. *Id. See also* Interstate Compact for Adult Offender Supervision, art. VIII (2002) (provides for the invalidation of a commission rule upon legislative rejection by a majority of member states).
85. *See* Washington Metropolitan Area Transit Regulation Compact, tit. III, art. XVI (1966).

In addition to enumerating an agency's discretionary powers and required duties, either of which may be substantive or administrative in nature, some compacts include supplemental "catch all" provisions designed either to accommodate unforeseen circumstances or to ensure that the agencies they create possess sufficiently broad authority to pursue general objectives. The Tri-State Lotto Compact, for example, provides that its commission shall possess "such additional powers, incidental to the express powers granted to it by this compact, as may be necessary or proper for the effective performance of its functions."[86] Likewise, the Washington Metropolitan Area Transit Regulation Compact provides that the transit authority it establishes may exercise, "subject to the limitations and restrictions herein imposed, all powers reasonably necessary or essential to the declared objects and purposes of this title."[87] A similar provision also appears in the Great Lakes Basin Compact, but it includes an additional caveat that highlights the purely advisory nature of the Great Lakes Commission's authority by stipulating that "no action of the Commission shall have the force of law in, or be binding upon, any party state."

3.3.3.5 Finance

Another important consideration in the development and drafting of interstate compacts is the question of finance. Especially with respect to those agreements that anticipate ongoing activities or that establish new interstate agencies, provisions are essential that specify the financial obligations of the party states and the means by which compact functions are to be funded.

Depending on the nature and purpose of a given compact, the necessary financing can be obtained through a variety of mechanisms. Typical funding sources include periodic contributions from the member states themselves, proceeds and fees derived from compact-related activities, and revenues generated through borrowing. Many compacts specify multiple sources, as did the New York–New Jersey Port Authority Compact of 1921, which obligated the party states to make annual appropriations in equal amounts to support the compact commission's activities "unless and until the revenues from operations conducted by the port authority are adequate to meet all expenditures[.]"[88]

This strategy, which anticipated an eventual transition from appropriated funds to revenues derived directly from compact activity, is reflected in nu-

---

86. Tri-State Lotto Compact, art. IV(e)(6) (2005).
87. Washington Metropolitan Area Transit Regulation Compact, tit. III, art. V(m) (1966).
88. New York–New Jersey Port Authority Compact, art. XV (1921).

merous subsequent agreements as well. The Central Interstate Low-Level Radioactive Waste Compact, for instance, envisioned that initial member state contributions (capped at $25,000 per year) would eventually be replaced by revenues derived from surcharges levied upon the users of the waste disposal facilities established under the agreement:

> Funding for the Commission shall be as follows:
> (1) The Commission shall set and approve its first annual budget as soon as practicable after its initial meeting. Party states shall equally contribute to the Commission budget on an annual basis, an amount not to exceed Twenty-five Thousand Dollars ($25,000.00) until surcharges are available for that purpose.
> (2) Each state hosting a regional facility shall annually levy surcharges on all users of such facilities, based on the volume and characteristics of wastes received at such facilities, the total of which:
> a. shall be sufficient to cover the annual budget of the Commission[.][89]

By comparison, the Tri-State Lotto Compact relies solely on revenues generated from compact activity (the sale of lottery tickets) to fund its commission,[90] but the Interstate Insurance Receivership Compact envisions permanent dependence on a combination of member state contributions and commission-generated revenues:

> The Commission shall levy on and collect an annual assessment from each Compacting State and each Insurer authorized to do business in a Compacting State, and writing direct insurance, to cover the cost of the internal operations and activities of the Commission and its staff in a total amount sufficient to cover the Commission's annual budget.[91]

Some compacts, especially those that authorize significant capital projects, permit borrowing, or anticipate multiple revenue streams, contain financial provisions that are much more detailed. The Washington Metropolitan Area Transit Regulation Compact, for example, includes separate and lengthy ar-

---

89. Central Interstate Low-Level Radioactive Waste Compact, art. IV (1986).
90. Tri-State Lotto Compact, article entitled "Collection and disposition of revenue."
91. Interstate Insurance Receivership Compact, art. X, § 3 (1996).

ticles covering capital financing, operating budgets, and revenue bonds.[92] On the other hand, compacts that create purely advisory commissions often depend exclusively upon appropriations from member states and contain relatively simple financial terms. The Midwestern Higher Education Compact, for example, provides as follows:

> The monies necessary to finance the general operations of the Commission not otherwise provided for in carrying forth its duties, responsibilities and powers as stated herein shall be appropriated to the Commission by the compacting states, when authorized by the respective legislatures, by equal apportionment among the compacting states.[93]

Even those compacts that do not establish interstate entities usually contain provisions assigning financial responsibilities between the parties for any expenses growing out of compact-related transactions. The original Interstate Compact on Juveniles, for example, allocated to the affected member states the costs of transporting juveniles from one state to another based on the circumstances necessitating the transfer.[94] Similarly, the Interstate Compact on Mental Health provided that the costs of transporting patients between party states would generally be borne by the sending state.[95] A more recent agreement, the Emergency Management Assistance Compact, assigned the costs of any assistance provided under the compact to the states receiving such aid, although it also permitted two or more party states to negotiate their own cost allocations if they so choose.[96]

In addition to apportioning financial responsibilities between the parties, some compacts include additional language intended to protect the agencies and political subdivisions of the member states against unintended financial consequences. For example, the Interstate Compact on Mental Health contains the following provisions:

---

92. Washington Metropolitan Area Transit Regulation Compact, tit. III, arts. VII-IX (1966). *See also* Delaware River Basin Compact arts. XII & XIII (1961).
93. Midwestern Higher Education Compact, art. V (1991).
94. Interstate Compact on Juveniles, arts. IV (b), V (b), & VII (d) (1955).
95. Interstate Compact on Mental Health, art. VII (b) (1972). The same provision, however, permits affected states to negotiate their own cost allocations.
96. Emergency Management Assistance Compact, art. IX (1996).

(c) No provision of this compact shall be construed to alter or affect any internal relationships among the departments, agencies and officers of and in the government of a party state, or between a party state and its subdivisions, as to the payment of costs, or responsibilities therefore.

(d) Nothing in this compact shall be construed to prevent any party state or subdivision thereof from asserting any right against any person, agency or other entity in regard to costs for which such party state or subdivision thereof may be responsible pursuant to any provision of this compact.[97]

Such language reflects the fact that while interstate compacts are fundamentally contractual agreements between states, the practical impact of the administrative and financial obligations they impose on their parties sometimes comes home to roost at a much more local level or within a particular state agency. This, too, is an important factor that compact drafters must bear in mind.

3.3.3.6 *Dispute Resolution and Enforcement*

Many interstate compacts provide for the resolution of disputes between the parties or for their own enforcement against member states that fail to comply with their terms. Dispute resolution mechanisms can be especially useful as a means of avoiding expensive litigation, and, when combined with provisions for compliance assistance, they can help to ensure the success of a compact.

Compacts that establish interstate agencies frequently empower or require those entities to referee disputes between the parties. The Central Midwest Interstate Low-Level Radioactive Waste Compact is typical of such agreements in that it requires the commission it establishes to "hear, negotiate, and, as necessary, resolve by final decision disputes which may arise between the party states regarding this compact."[98] On the other hand, all that the Interstate Insurance Receivership Compact requires of its commission is an "attempt" at resolving such disputes.[99]

---

97. Interstate Compact on Mental Health, art. VII(c) (1972). Comparable language was included in the Interstate Compact on Juveniles, art. VIII (1955).
98. Central Midwest Interstate Low-Level Radioactive Waste Compact, art. III (j)(3) (1983).
99. Interstate Insurance Receivership Compact, art. VIII, § B, 1 (1996).

In similar fashion, the Interstate Compact for Adult Offender Supervision requires the commission it creates to attempt dispute resolution in some instances, but it goes a step further by also requiring the commission to enact a bylaw or promulgate a rule "providing for both mediation and binding dispute resolution for disputes among the Compacting States."[100] A much more detailed provision for the resolution of disputes by arbitration can be found in the Multistate Tax Compact, although the mechanism provided is geared more toward disputes between individual taxpayers and member state agencies than it is toward disagreements between the parties themselves.[101]

Failing the successful resolution of disputes through such alternative means, resort to litigation may be required. Noncompliance with a compact's terms can also lead to legal action initiated by one or more member states, or by a compact agency, against the defaulting party. Accordingly, many compacts include provisions specifying the rights and duties of the parties, or the agencies they create, to seek judicial enforcement when necessary.[102] For instance, the Susquehanna River Basin Compact requires its commission to:

> Investigate and determine if the requirements of the compact or the rules and regulations of the commission are complied with, and if satisfactory progress has not been made, institute an action or actions in its own name in any state or Federal court of competent jurisdiction to compel compliance with any and all of the provisions of this compact or any of the rules and regulations of the commission adopted pursuant thereto. An action shall be instituted in the name of the commission and shall be conducted by its own counsel.[103]

Some compacts also provide for intermediate steps that may be taken by the parties themselves, or by a compact commission, in an effort to compel compliance and, ultimately, to enforce the agreement. These can be as simple as the provision of remedial training and technical assistance to willing recipients.[104] Additional steps can range from the imposition of fines and other sanctions to the suspension of specified rights or even the termination of a

---

100. Interstate Compact for Adult Offender Supervision, art. IX, § B (2002).
101. Multistate Tax Compact, art. IX (1967).
102. *See* chapter 6 for a discussion of issues related to the enforcement of interstate compacts.
103. Susquehanna River Basin Compact, art. III, § 3.5, 5 (1970).
104. *See, e.g.*, Interstate Compact for Adult Offender Supervision, art. XII, § B (2002).

defaulting state's membership. The Interstate Insurance Receivership Compact, for example, provides that any party state that defaults in the performance of its obligations shall suffer the suspension of its "rights, privileges and benefits" under the compact, pending the timely cure of its default. Should the defaulting state fail to remedy the situation as required, "the Defaulting State shall be terminated from the Compact upon an affirmative vote of a majority of the Compacting States and all rights, privileges and benefits conferred by this Compact shall be terminated from the effective date of termination."[105]

Though such measures are rarely necessary in practice, a provision allowing for the termination of a defaulting party's membership was invoked against the state of Michigan in 1991, resulting in that state's controversial expulsion from the Midwest Interstate Low-Level Radioactive Waste Compact.[106] Twelve years later, the state of Nebraska was ousted from the Central Interstate Low-Level Radioactive Waste Compact pursuant to a similar provision contained in that agreement.[107] In both instances, the underlying issue leading to the default and termination was the proposed siting of a radioactive waste disposal facility in the recalcitrant state.

Compacts that allow for the involuntary termination of a defaulting party's membership sometimes permit such states to subsequently be reinstated as well. By way of example, the Western Regional Higher Education Compact provides, "Any such defaulting state may be reinstated by: (a) performing all acts and obligations upon which it has heretofore defaulted, and (b) application to and the approval by a majority vote of the commission."[108] The Interstate Compact for Adult Offender Supervision contains similar language but requires in addition that the terminated state reenact the compact before being readmitted into membership.[109]

Consideration in drafting must also be given to the potential impact of a member state's withdrawal or termination upon the rights and obligations of the other parties. To minimize the potential hardship on the remaining members, and to prevent other consequences that may be undesired, some compacts provide that a departing state's unfulfilled obligations will survive its

---

105. Interstate Insurance Receivership Compact, art. XII, § B, 1 (1996). *See also* Western Regional Higher Education Compact, art. XII (1953).
106. Midwest Interstate Low-Level Radioactive Waste Compact, art. VIII, § d (1983).
107. Central Interstate Low-Level Radioactive Waste Compact, art. VII, § e (1984).
108. Western Regional Higher Education Compact, art. XII (1953).
109. Interstate Compact for Adult Offender Supervision, art. XII, § B (2002).

separation from the compact and remain fully enforceable against that state for a specified time, or until fully satisfied. The Interstate Compact on Juveniles, for example, stipulates that the duties and obligations of a state that renounces the compact "shall continue as to [cooperatively supervised] parolees and probationers residing therein at the time of withdrawal until retaken or finally discharged."[110]

Some agreements also include language recognizing the jurisdiction and role of courts in enforcing compact provisions and the actions of interstate agencies. The Ohio River Valley Water Sanitation Compact, for instance, provides that:

> [A]ny court of general jurisdiction or any United States district court in any of the signatory states shall have the jurisdiction, by mandamus, injunction, specific performance or other form of remedy to enforce any such order [of the compact commission] against any municipality, corporation or other entity domiciled or located within such state[.][111]

By comparison, the Washington Metropolitan Area Transit Regulation Compact provides more generally that:

> The Unites States District Courts shall have original jurisdiction, concurrent with the courts of Maryland, Virginia and the District of Columbia, of all actions brought by or against the Authority and to enforce subpoenas issued under this Title. Any such action initiated in a State or District of Columbia Court shall be removable to the appropriate United States District Court[.][112]

Other agreements cover all the bases by specifying that the enforcement powers of courts encompass the duly promulgated rules and bylaws of interstate commissions, as well as the compacts under which they are established.[113]

---

110. Interstate Compact on Juveniles, art. XIV (1955). *See also* Interstate Compact on the Placement of Children, art. IX (1960).
111. Ohio River Valley Water Sanitation Compact, art. IX (1940).
112. Washington Metropolitan Area Transit Regulation Compact, tit. III, art. XVI (1966).
113. *See, e.g.*, Interstate Compact for Adult Offender Supervision, art. XII, § C (2002).

3.3.3.7 Ancillary Matters

3.3.3.7.1 Eligibility and Entry into Force

Most interstate compacts contain several additional provisions address-ing such ancillary matters as their establishment and duration, their force and effect once enacted, and their amendment by the parties. At a minimum, a compact should specify the states that are eligible to participate and the num-ber of members that are required to render the agreement effective. A typical provision to this effect was included in the Great Lakes Forest Fire Compact, which stated, "This Compact shall become effective for those States ratifying it whenever any two or more of the States of Michigan, Minnesota and Wis-consin have ratified it."[114]

It should be noted that whereas the enabling legislation adopting a com-pact in a given state usually becomes effective in that jurisdiction within the same timeframe and by the same means applicable to any other statute,[115] the compact itself does not take effect unless all other conditions precedent re-quired by its terms (e.g., the receipt of congressional consent, the passage of a specified date, the occurrence of a certain event) have been satisfied, and until it has been adopted by the required number of member states. Thus, depending on the number of parties required, a compact may be adopted but remain ineffective in a given state for a considerable period of time.

Many compacts require only two parties to become effective, even if broader participation is permitted and desired. Others specify a much higher threshold. The Interstate Compact for Adult Offender Supervision, for ex-ample, did not become effective until it was enacted in 35 states,[116] and the proposed new Interstate Compact for Juveniles requires approval by the same number.[117] Both agreements specified high adoption thresholds, because they were intended to replace existing 50-state compacts. The drafters in each instance sought to minimize the potential for confusion during the transition period from the old compact to the new by requiring a substantial commit-ment of participation before the new agreement would take effect.

Though most thresholds for effectiveness refer only to enactment by a prescribed number of states, other models are possible. The proposed Inter-state Insurance Product Regulation Compact, for example, contains an un-usual provision specifying that the compact "shall become effective and binding

---

114. Great Lakes Forest Fire Compact, art. II, § 2.1 (1952).
115. *See* chapter 3, § 3.4, *infra*.
116. Interstate Compact for Adult Offender Supervision, art. XI (2002).
117. Interstate Compact for Juveniles, art. X (Proposed Official Draft 2002).

upon legislative enactment" by just two states, but it goes on to condition the full effect of its terms by stipulating that the interstate commission it creates:

> [s]hall become effective for purposes of adopting Uniform Standards for, reviewing, and giving approval or disapproval of, Products filed with the Commission that satisfy applicable Uniform Standards only after twenty-six (26) States are Compacting States or, alternatively, . . . States representing greater than forty percent (40%) of the premium volume for life insurance, annuity, disability income and long-term care insurance products, based on records of the NAIC for the prior year[.][118]

3.3.3.7.2   *Construction and Severability*

Also typical of many compacts are provisions governing the construction and severability of their terms. The usual intent of such provisions is to ensure that a compact is construed in accordance with its stated purposes and that the remaining terms survive in full force and effect if any portion of the agreement is declared unconstitutional. For example, Article XII of the Multistate Tax Compact provides as follows:

> This compact shall be liberally construed so as to effectuate the purposes thereof. The provisions of this compact shall be severable and if any phrase, clause, sentence or provision of this compact is declared to be contrary to the constitution of any state or of the United States or the applicability thereof to any government, agency, person or circumstance is held invalid, the validity of the remainder of this compact and the applicability thereof to any government, agency, person or circumstance shall not be affected thereby. If this compact shall be held contrary to the constitution of any state participating therein, the compact shall remain in full force and effect as to the remaining party states and in full force and effect as to the state affected as to all severable matters.[119]

3.3.3.7.3   *Amendments and Supplemental Agreements*

Less common but also frequently included are provisions stipulating the means by which a compact may be amended. Strictly speaking, no such pro-

---

118. Interstate Insurance Product Regulation Compact, art. XIII, § 2 (proposed).
119. Multistate Tax Compact, art. XII (1967). Identical or substantially similar boilerplate language appears in numerous other compacts. *See, e.g.*, Southern Growth Policies Agreement, art. XIII (2005).

visions are required, since it is well understood that in the absence of such language, the parties may, subject to applicable limitations (e.g., congressional consent), alter or sever the terms of their original agreement by the same means used in its establishment (i.e., through legislative enactment by the members). Nevertheless, some compacts expressly permit or prohibit the enactment of amendments by other means or by fewer than all of the party states. The Nurse Licensure Compact, for example, expressly recognizes the ability of its members to amend its terms, but provides that no amendment "shall become effective and binding upon the party states unless and until it is enacted into the laws of all party states."[120] Similarly, the Interstate Compact for Adult Offender Supervision, which authorizes the commission it establishes to propose compact revisions, prohibits any such amendments from taking effect until adopted by all parties.

By contrast, the Gulf States Marine Fisheries Compact takes a more permissive approach by allowing for the possibility of amendments adopted by fewer than all of the member states. As provided in Article X, such amendments are binding only against those states that adopt them:

> It is agreed that any two or more states party hereto may further amend this compact by acts of their respective legislatures subject to approval of Congress as provided in article I, s. 10, of the Constitution of the United States, to designate the Gulf States Marine Fisheries Commission as a joint regulating authority for the joint regulation of specific fisheries affecting only such states as shall be compact, and at their joint expense. The representatives of such states shall constitute a separate section of the Gulf States Marine Fisheries Commission for the exercise of the additional powers so granted but the creation of such section shall not be deemed to deprive the states so compacting of any of their privileges or powers in the Gulf States Marine Fisheries Commission as constituted under the other articles of this compact.[121]

Some compacts effectively allow the substantive agreement between the parties to be altered at a later date without the necessity of a legislatively enacted amendment. The Missouri-Nebraska Boundary Compact, for example, fixes the boundary between the party states in Article II, but later, in Article VIII, allows for future adjustments of that boundary by negotiation between

---

120. Nurse Licensure Compact, art. X, § d. (2004).
121. Gulf States Marine Fisheries Compact, art. X (1949).

the parties. In this case, the inclusion of the second provision ensures that a negotiated adjustment of the boundary prescribed in the earlier article actually complies with the original compact instead of requiring its amendment.

Provisions recognizing the rights of parties to enact supplementary agreements that complement, rather than amend, the terms of a compact are also fairly common. The Gulf States Marine Fisheries Compact, for example, provides that "[n]othing in this compact shall . . . prevent the enactment of any legislation or the enforcement of any requirement by a signatory state imposing additional conditions and restrictions to conserve its fisheries."[122] In similar fashion, the Emergency Management Assistance Compact stipulates that "nothing herein contained shall preclude any state from entering into supplementary agreements with another state or affect any other agreements already in force between states."[123]

3.3.3.7.4   *Withdrawal and Termination*

Just as important as provisions governing the entry into force of a compact are those that address the withdrawal of parties and the termination of the agreement. Withdrawal terms are usually designed to require the provision of adequate notice to all members and typically contain sufficient safeguards to ensure the satisfaction of any outstanding obligations by the withdrawing party, as well as the continued operation of the compact between any remaining members. A typical provision was included in the Midwest Interstate Passenger Rail Compact, which stated, "Withdrawal from this compact shall be by enactment of a statute repealing the same and shall take effect one year after the effective date of such statute. A withdrawing state shall be liable for any obligations which it may have incurred prior to the effective date of withdrawal."[124]

A more specific notice requirement was incorporated into the withdrawal provision contained in the Driver License Compact:

> Any party state may withdraw from this compact by enacting a statute repealing the same, but no such withdrawal shall take effect until six months after the executive head of the withdrawing state has given notice of the withdrawal to the executive heads of all other party states. No withdrawal shall affect the validity or applicability

---

122. Gulf States Marine Fisheries Compact, art. IX (1949).
123. Emergency Management Assistance Compact, art. VII (1996).
124. Midwest Interstate Passenger Rail Compact, art. IX (2004).

by the licensing authorities of states remaining party to the compact of any report of conviction occurring prior to the withdrawal.[125]

Provisions governing the termination of a compact can be as simple as this one, which appeared in the Colorado River Compact, stating:

> This compact may be terminated at any time by the unanimous agreement of the signatory States. In the event of such termination all rights established under it shall continue unimpaired.[126]

However, agreements that establish interstate agencies or that permit the joint ownership or management of assets typically require more elaborate provisions with respect to termination. The Great Lakes Forest Fire Compact, for example, provides as follows:

> In the event of termination of this compact, any property acquired as the result of this compact which is held jointly by the member states shall become the property of the state where the property is located at the time of termination upon payment by that state to the other member states of the fair market value of the other member states ownership in the property. In the event the state where the property is located does not desire to acquire sole ownership of the property, the property shall be disposed of as provided by the laws of the state where the property is located and any proceeds shall be returned to the member states in proportion to their ownership in the property.[127]

3.3.3.7.5 *Relations with Nonparties*

Another concern addressed in some interstate compacts is the relationship between member states and nonparties. One approach to this issue is embodied in the Interstate Forest Fire Suppression Compact, which provides simply that agreements between party and nonparty states are not affected by the compact:

> Nothing contained in this compact shall be construed to abrogate or impair any agreement which a party state may have with a nonparty state for the confinement, rehabilitation or treatment of inmates nor

---

125. Driver License Compact, art. X (b) (1958).
126. Colorado River Compact, art. X (1921).
127. Great Lakes Forest Fire Compact, art. XII, § 12.2.

to repeal any other laws of a party state authorizing the making of cooperative institutional arrangements.[128]

But some compacts go considerably further by specifying the circumstances under which interaction between member states (or an interstate agency) and nonparties is desirable and the means by which nonparty states may participate in compact-related activities or share in compact-related benefits. For instance, the Pest Control Compact, which establishes an interstate insurance fund to be used in financing specified pest control operations, provides in part that:

> The Governing Board or Executive Committee shall authorize expenditures from the Insurance Fund to be made in a nonparty state only after determining that the conditions in such state and the value of such expenditures to the party states as a whole justify them. The Governing Board or Executive Committee may set any conditions which it deems appropriate with respect to the expenditure of moneys from the Insurance Fund in a nonparty state and may enter into such agreement or agreements with nonparty states and other jurisdictions or entities as it may deem necessary or appropriate to protect the interests of the Insurance Fund[.][129]

3.3.3.7.6   *Other Issues*

Other ancillary matters requiring more or less attention from drafters, depending on the nature and purpose of a particular interstate compact, include such issues as: liability for the actions of member state officials or interstate agency employees in connection with compact-related activities;[130] immunity from suit, defense and indemnification;[131] the exemption of compact property and activities from taxation;[132] the voting powers of member

---

128. Interstate Forest Fire Suppression Compact, art. VIII (2004). The reference to the handling of inmates is relevant to the compact's authorization of the use of criminal offenders in connection with forest fire suppression efforts.
129. Interstate Pest Control Compact, art. VIII (c) (2004).
130. *See* New England Compact on Involuntary Detention for Tuberculosis Control, art. IV (proposed) for one approach to the issue of liability.
131. *See, e.g.*, Interstate Insurance Receivership Compact, art. V, § D (1996); Interstate Compact for Adult Offender Supervision, art. VI, § D (2002).
132. *See, e.g.*, Delaware River Basin Compact, art. XIV, § 14.3 (1961); Washington Metropolitan Area Transit Regulation Compact, tit. III, art. XVI (1966).

states;[133] and any operational or administrative matters of an internal nature that are not otherwise delegated to the discretion of a compact agency or assigned to its bylaws (e.g., meeting and quorum requirements, the powers and duties of compact officers, and personnel policies for compact staff).

3.3.4   Enabling Legislation

Interstate compacts are usually enacted by member states through the adoption of enabling statutes that incorporate the full text of the proposed agreement. Unlike the compact language itself, which must be substantially identical in every participating state, enabling legislation can be customized to satisfy the procedural and technical requirements of each state's legislative process and codification system. This permits, for example, the accommodation of state-specific format, numbering, and drafting conventions, without requiring alterations to the substantive compact language itself.

More important, enabling legislation can be used to condition a state's participation in a compact,[134] or to fulfill state-specific obligations imposed upon the parties by the terms of the agreement. For example, an enabling statute might designate the appropriate state official to serve on an interstate commission established by the compact, or it might provide for the appropriation of funds to satisfy a financial participation requirement. It can also be used to assign responsibilities for the in-state administration of compact-related activities to the appropriate state agencies or to make any other elections required or permitted by the compact.

Enabling statutes also provide a potential outlet for the resolution of any compact-related concerns that might be addressed through the enactment of additional statutory language in a given state, provided that such terms are not inconsistent with and do not materially alter the compact itself.[135] Of course, the practical effect of any enabling legislation is limited to the state that adopts it, and no substantive provisions that go beyond the terms of the compact itself are binding upon the other parties to the agreement.

It should be noted that some enabling statutes merely authorize the subsequent gubernatorial execution of the compacts they embody, rather than rendering them immediately effective in accordance with their terms. This process, though used with some regularity beginning in the 1930s, has been largely abandoned, since it essentially gives the executive two passes at a

---

133. *See, e.g.*, Susquehanna River Basin Compact, art. 2, § 2.5 (1970).
134. Zimmerman & Wendell, *supra* note 4, at 20.
135. *Id.*

legislative enactment.[136] More recently, compacts have tended to be "self-executing" in that their effectiveness, in accordance with their own provisions, has depended only on the enactment of their enabling legislation.

3.3.5   Resources for Drafters

Among the resources available for reference by compact drafters are several useful tools provided by The Council of State Governments (CSG), a national, nonpartisan association of state officials with a long history in the field of interstate compacts. Over the years, CSG has facilitated the development, drafting, and implementation of numerous such agreements, and it remains an invaluable repository for compact-related information. The Council's Web site, www.csg.org, currently provides ready access to the full texts of almost 200 interstate compacts, and a more comprehensive, fully searchable database containing additional information on compacts in all 50 states and the U.S. territories was under development in the fall of 2004.

The database is part of a larger effort by CSG to establish a National Center for Interstate Compacts, which, when fully operational, will serve as an information clearinghouse and will provide training, technical assistance, legal support, and facilitation services to the developers and administrators (including state officials and interstate commissions) of interstate compacts. In the meantime, additional information about the National Center, updates on recent state and federal compact-related activities and a growing online library of interstate compact reference materials are already available on the Council's Web site.

Also available through CSG is a periodic directory of compacts entitled *Interstate Compacts & Agencies*, the most recent edition of which was published in 2003. The directory contains brief purpose statements, statutory citations, and contact information for almost 200 active compacts, as well as separate listings of compacts by state and by subject, citations to more than 60 dormant or defunct compacts, a list of more than 100 interstate compact agencies, and the full texts of several recent agreements.

---

136. *Id.* at 19-20. The authors argue that the so-called "execution method" unnecessarily gives the governor two bites at the apple, and that gubernatorial approval of an enabling statute should be sufficient to render a compact effective without requiring it to be separately executed.

Chapter 4

COURT JURISDICTION OVER INTERSTATE COMPACTS

4.1 THE JURISDICTION OF FEDERAL AND STATE COURTS IN THE ENFORCEMENT OF COMPACTS

The question of which courts, state or federal, have jurisdiction to enforce an interstate compact depends in part on whether the compact has received, or is required to receive, congressional consent. The contractual nature of compacts is such that all member states are bound to the provisions of the compact as a fully enforceable contractual agreement, with or without congressional consent. The fact that compacts are creations of individual state legislatures does not alter their status as contracts with enforceable obligations between member states. Therefore, once adopted, there are only two means available to change the substance of a compact and the obligations it imposes on member states: withdrawal and renegotiation of its terms or an amendment adopted by all member states in essentially the same form. The contractual character of the compact prevails over any unilateral action by a state, as no state is allowed to adopt any law interfering with a contractual relationship,[1] including that established under a contract adopted by a state legislature pursuant to the Compact Clause.[2]

States are not simply parties to an ordinary contract. The mere fact that the Supreme Court may exercise its very limited original jurisdiction in compact disputes is one indication of the importance the Framers attached to the status of the states as sovereign members joined in a constituent union. For example, in *South Dakota v. North Carolina*, the Supreme Court recognized the propriety of money judgments against a state as part of an original action, but acknowledged that forcing a state legislature to actually pay another state can present a unique problem.[3]

However, the Supreme Court also pointed out in *Texas v. New Mexico*: "That there may be difficulties in enforcing judgments against States counsels caution, but does not undermine our authority to enter judgments against defendant States in cases over which the Court has undoubted jurisdiction, authority that is attested to by the fact that almost invariably the States against which judgments were rendered, conformably to their duty under the Constitution, voluntarily respected and gave effect to the same."[4]

Thus, notwithstanding the special status of states and the challenges presented in enforcing compacts, compacts fundamentally constitute enforceable obligations between states just as if the states were acting as private parties to a legally binding contract.

As has been discussed, Article I, Section 10, Clause 3 of the Constitution has been interpreted by the Supreme Court to permit states to enter into enforceable agreements among and between themselves without the consent of Congress, so long as those agreements do not infringe on federal interests or shift the balance of power within the federal structure of the government.[5] The Supreme Court recognized in *Cuyler v. Adams* that congressional consent "transforms" the states' agreement into federal law under the Compact Clause.[6] Consequently, congressional consent places the interpretation and enforcement of interstate compacts squarely within the purview of the fed-

---

1. U.S. CONST. art. I, § 10, cl. 1.
2. *See* West Virginia *ex rel.* Dyer v. Sims, 341 U.S. 22, 33 (1951) (Reed, J., concurring). *See also* Hinderlider v. La Plata River & Cherry Creek Ditch Co., 70 P.2d 849 (Colo. 1937), *rev'd*, 304 U.S. 92 (1938).
3. South Dakota v. North Carolina, 192 U.S. 286, 320-21 (1904). *See also* Texas v. New Mexico, 482 U.S. 124, 130 (1987) (discussing the degree to which the Eleventh Amendment would act as a bar to such actions).
4. *Id.* at 131 (1987).
5. *See* Cuyler v. Adams, 449 U.S. 433, 440 (1981).
6. *Id.*

eral judiciary.[7] In construing a related federal question jurisdictional statute, the Ninth Circuit Court of Appeals noted:

> Neither logic nor policy justifies a different interpretation of the substantially similar language in 28 U.S.C. section 1331 (a). Therefore, a case involving construction of an interstate compact that requires a judicial determination of the nature and scope of obligations set forth therein "arises" under the "laws" of the United States within the meaning of section 28 U.S.C. section 1331(a)[8].

However, not every dispute arising under an interstate compact must be litigated in the federal courts. Under the Supremacy Clause, state courts have the same obligation to give force and effect to the provisions of a compact as do the federal courts. It is ultimately the U.S. Supreme Court that retains the final word on the interpretation and application of congressionally approved compacts given their now federalized nature.[9]

In addition to precedent of the Supreme Court, Congress has also provided that certain interstate compacts fall within the jurisdiction of the federal courts, as in the following statute, which provides in part:

> (a) The United States district courts shall have original jurisdiction (concurrent with that of the Supreme Court of the United States, and concurrent with that of any court of the United States or of any State of the United States in matters in which the Supreme Court, or any other court, has original jurisdiction) of any case or controversy–
> (1) which involves the construction or application of an interstate compact which—
>> (A) in whole or in part relates to the pollution of waters of an interstate river system or any portion thereof, and
>> (B) expresses the consent of the States signatory to said compact to be sued in a district court in any case or controversy involving the application or construction thereof.[10]

Provisions such as this are also contained in the express language of various compacts and are "choice of forum" requirements, not a mandate that

---

7. *See* League to Save Lake Tahoe v. Tahoe Reg'l Planning Agency, 507 F.2d 517 (9th Cir. 1974).
8. *Id.* at 521-22.
9. *See* West Virginia *ex rel.* Dyer v. Sims, 341 U.S. 22, 28 (1951).
10. 33 U.S.C. § 466g-1(a) (2002).

all litigation involving an interstate compact must be conducted in federal court. They act only to bind the states and any compact-created administrative body as to the forum for bringing actions regarding the enforcement and interpretation of a compact as to the member states. State courts, subject to the Supremacy Clause, would be required to defer to a compact's terms and conditions just as any federal court is required to do when confronted with compact issues. State court jurisdiction over compact disputes would presumably extend to enforcing the terms of the compact on state officials, and even declaring a state statute, rule, or constitutional provision void as conflicting with the terms of a compact to which that state is a member. A state court's jurisdiction would not, of course, extend to enforcing a compact's terms and conditions on other states, that matter resting clearly with the federal courts.

The Supreme Court has considered the status of interstate compacts in connection with its certiorari jurisdiction.[11] In these cases, the Court addressed the question of whether a claim based on an interstate compact is cognizable under the Supreme Court's certiorari provisions as applied to reviewing the judgments of the highest state court where a title, right, privilege or immunity is claimed under the Constitution, treaties, or statutes of the United States.[12] In *Colburn*, the Court unequivocally answered this question affirmatively, holding:

> [T]he construction of such a [bi-state] compact sanctioned by virtue of Article I, section 10, clause 3 of the Constitution, involves a federal "title, right, privilege or immunity," which when specially set up and claimed in state court may be reviewed here on certiorari under section 237 (b) of the Judicial Code.[13]

In reaching this interpretation of the certiorari statute, the Supreme Court in *Colburn* and its progeny has firmly established that the construction of a compact, by virtue of congressional consent, presents a federal question.

4.2   APPLICATION OF FEDERAL AND STATE LAW TO COMPACT DISPUTES

Because interstate compacts are agreements among the states, suits be-

---

11. *See* Delaware River Comm'n v. Colburn, 310 U.S. 419, 427 (1940); West
     Virginia *ex rel.* Dyer v. Sims, 341 U.S. 22, 28 (1951).
12. *Id.*
13. Delaware River Comm'n v. Colburn, 310 U.S. 419, 427 (1940).

tween the parties over their interpretation and enforcement or to vindicate rights arising under them usually have been suits in the U.S. Supreme Court. Since the federal Constitution provides original jurisdiction over suits between states, recourse has been made in that manner.[14] Additionally as has been noted, interstate compacts that have received congressional consent are transformed into federal law. Therefore, an interstate compact requiring judicial determination of the nature and scope of the obligations thereunder is subject to federal construction.[15]

Some disputes arising under an interstate compact may properly be litigated in the state courts, particularly with respect to interstate compacts for which congressional consent is neither given nor required. While compacts such as the Interstate Compact for Adult Offender Supervision and the Interstate Compact for Juveniles have choice of forum requirements, such restrictions act only to bind the states and any compact-created administrative body as to the forum for bringing actions regarding that enforcement and interpretation of the compact as to the member states. These provisions do not automatically preclude a private citizen from suing in state court, nor do they prevent state courts from enforcing the terms of a compact as a collateral matter to other litigation.[16] However, particularly where congressional consent has been given, state courts, subject to the Supremacy Clause, are required to defer to the compact's terms and conditions, just as any federal court is required to do when confronted with compact issues.

By entering into a compact, the member states contractually agree on certain principles and rules pertaining to the subject matter of the compact. Once entered, the terms of the compact, as well as any rules authorized by the compact, supersede substantive state laws that may be in conflict, including state constitutional provisions unless exempted by the compact's provisions.[17] This applies to prior state law[18] and subsequent statutes of the signatory states.[19] Moreover, states must not take unilateral actions, such as the adoption of

---

14. Frederick L. Zimmerman & Mitchell Wendell, The Law and Use of Interstate Compacts 14 (1976).
15. *See* Carchman v. Nash, 473 U.S. 716 (1985); Cuyler v. Adams, 449 U.S. 443 (1981).
16. *See* Hinderlider v. La Plata River & Cherry Creek Ditch Co., 304 U.S. 92 (1938).
17. West Virginia *ex rel.* Dyer v. Sims, 341 U.S. 22 (1951).
18. *See* Hinderlider v. La Plata River & Cherry Creek Ditch Co., 70 P.2d 849 (Colo. 1937), *rev'd*, 304 U.S. 92 (1938).
19. *See* Green v. Biddle, 21 U.S. 1, 92 (1823).

conflicting legislation or the issuance of executive orders or court rules, that violate the terms of a compact.[20] Based on this principle, a number of lower courts have also reaffirmed the principle that the provisions of a compact take precedence over statutory law in member states.[21]

4.3 APPLICATION OF CONTRACT LAW TO COMPACTS

Interstate compacts are initiated by the adoption of enabling statutes by the legislatures of the member states. As formal agreements between states, they have the characteristics of both statutory law and contractual agreements. As both statutes and contracts, the substantive law of contracts is applicable to them.[22]

4.3.1 Offer

Using the contract law analysis, the proposed compact statute adopted by the first state to enact, and which invites other states to become a party to the agreement, constitutes the *offer.* As with any other contract, the inception of a compact must be in a form of an offer to make a binding agreement. Since a compact is an instrument that is also a statute, and always has the force and effect of any other statutory law, the offer must be made in a manner that produces such law in the jurisdiction in which the offer is made. The compact provisions typically identify the jurisdictions to which the enacting jurisdiction (offeror) offers to bind itself.[23]

4.3.2 Acceptance

The *acceptance* of the offer occurs when any subsequent state legislature (offeree) enacts the compact statute in substantially identical form to that contained in the offering state's enactment. It is a fundamental requirement in the substantive law of contracts that no act constitutes an acceptance unless it is an acceptance of the offer that has been made. Consequently, the same problems raised by the variance in the terms of the offer and acceptance in

---

20. *See* N.E. Bancorp v. Bd. of Governors of Fed. Reserve Sys., 472 U.S. 159, 175 (1985).

21. *See* Wash. Metro. Area Transit Auth. v. One Parcel of Land, 706 F.2d 1312, 1319 (4th Cir. 1983); Kansas City Area Transp. Auth. v. Missouri, 640 F.2d 173, 174 (8th Cir. 1981).

22. Frederick L. Zimmerman & Mitchell Wendell, The Law and Use of Interstate Compacts 2 (1976).

23. *Id. at* 7-8.

the common law of contracts also can create similar problems in the negotiation of interstate compacts. Because compacts are statutes, it is impossible to enter into them orally or by an exchange of other communications that would otherwise lead to many of the troublesome controversies with other types of contractual agreements. However, care should be taken to enact identical texts in the statutory law of all compacting jurisdictions.

4.3.3 Mutual Consent or "Meeting of the Minds"

Where the statutory texts of a compact putatively entered into by eligible states have not been identical, the problem raised has been the customary one in contract law: Are the variations in the relevant statutory enactments sufficiently similar to permit a reasonable person to conclude that an agreement has been reached?

For example, due to its adoption of a version of an earlier draft of the compact statute that it mistakenly believed was the final draft, the State of New Hampshire's initial attempt to become a party to the Interstate Compact on Juveniles failed. Because all the other states that adopted the measure had in fact adopted the most recent version, the New Hampshire compact statute was not identical in all material respects. The errant provisions concerned the prescribed method of affecting the return of a runaway or escapee, as well as a provision that specified gubernatorial participation in the requisitioning process required for the return of such juveniles, while the versions enacted by the other states made this unnecessary and permitted a direct court-to-court approach. Subsequently, the legislature corrected this error by enacting the provisions of the Interstate Compact on Juveniles as adopted by the other states and successfully joined the compact. A different result was reached in the case of a Vermont enactment of a civil defense compact where its version of the compact statute was identical to the compact statutes adopted by the other member states in almost all respects with the exception of the immunities given to civil defense workers from another state sent to render aid. In that case it was determined by mutual agreement of Vermont and the other member states that they were contractually bound to one another to the extent of the similarity in the respective versions of the compact.[24]

Notwithstanding these concerns, the enabling legislation does not have to be uniform in each compact statute and can be utilized "to fit variations into the compactual pattern."[25] Provisions in the enabling legislation can be used to condition the impact of a compact in a state. Last-minute developments

---

24. *Id.* at 9.
25. *Id.* at 20.

that inevitably arise during the legislative process can be handled through provisions in the enabling legislation in order to avoid the need for amendment of the compact statute. The only limitation on this approach is that a state is prohibited from making reservations in the enabling legislation that "materially change" a compact in the absence of specific consent by the other member states. "There is no reason why a state cannot participate in a compact arrangement for certain of its purposes but not for others if the other member states subscribe to such limited participation. The state enabling legislation is another tool for adjustment of the compactual pattern."[26]

4.3.4   Consideration

The *consideration* for the agreement is the settlement of the dispute or creation of an association, agency, or some other mechanism to address an issue of mutual interest. While the principle of consideration has far less practical meaning than in the field of private contracts, almost invariably an interstate compact involves either the settlement of a dispute or a joint or common undertaking by the member states. In the case of the settlement of a dispute, such as a state boundary, the acceptance of the agreed solution and abandonment by each party of their inconsistent claims constitutes consideration for the compact agreement. "This situation is analogous to an agreement to submit to arbitration and to be bound by the award, or to a settlement out of court."[27] With respect to compacts that provide for a joint undertaking or reciprocal cooperation, such as the supervision of offenders on probation or parole who wish to move from one state to another, the consideration is the reciprocal obligation to perform the agreement including any financial or other contribution to the joint enterprise.[28]

4.3.5   Amendment, Termination, and Withdrawal

After a compact comes into force, it continues in accordance with its terms. Many compacts have specific provisions for termination, amendment, and withdrawal by a party state. However, where such provisions are incomplete or nonexistent, both termination and amendment may be accomplished by agreement of all member states, evidenced by the appropriate action in each such state in the same manner as the repeal or amendment of any other statute. In the event that the compact provisions are the product of adminis-

---

26. *Id.* at 21.
27. *Id.* at 9.
28. *Id.* at 10.

trative action by officials of the executive branch pursuant to statutory authority, it may be permissible for those same officials to take appropriate action to amend or terminate the agreement in the absence of a provision to the contrary.[29]

In most cases, the withdrawal of a member state or the termination of a compact will present no problems related to disposition of assets. Where the compact is primarily for the purpose of rendering services by state agencies, generally no property is involved, and withdrawal or termination only involves the discontinuation of the services. However, compacts that establish separate interstate agencies may involve the disposition of substantial property and assets. Where these consist only of office supplies and equipment, any such concerns are likely to be de minimis. On the other hand, expensive public works could be involved, and in some such compacts provisions exist for the disposition of property. Even if there are no provisions for distribution of assets in the compact text, it is probable that the applicable law in most cases would be drawn from statutes pertaining to the disposal of assets on dissolution of other public or not-for-profit enterprises generally. In compacts that establish boundary lines, the question of termination is not usually relevant. Once such boundary is established and accepted, any territory involved is incorporated into the existing states, and the compact is fully performed.[30]

4.3.6   Contract Interpretation

Like any other contract, an interstate compact must be enforced consistent with the terms and conditions of the compact. No court has authority to provide relief that is inconsistent with the compact.[31] However, in interpreting a compact, courts have latitude in attempting to discern the purposes of the agreement. In interpreting a "federalized" interstate compact, federal courts must address disputes just as if a court were addressing a federal statute. The first and last order of business of a court addressing an approved interstate compact "is interpreting the compact."[32] In the absence of a federal statute making state statutory or decisional law applicable, the controlling law is federal law; and absent federal statutory guidance, the governing rule of decision would be fashioned by the federal court in the mode of the common law.[33]

---

29. *Id.*
30. *Id.* at 11.
31. Texas v. New Mexico, 462 U.S. 554 (1983).
32. *Id.* at 567-68.
33. Oneida Indian Nation v. County of Oneida, 414 U.S. 661, 674-79 (1974).

Even though courts have acknowledged that interstate compacts are contracts to the extent they are a binding legal document among and between party states that set forth terms and conditions that must be construed and applied in accordance with the intent of the agreement, courts have also recognized the unique features and functions of compacts as compared with other sorts of contractual agreements. Though a contract, an interstate compact represents a political compromise between "constituent elements of the Union," as opposed to a commercial transaction.[34] Such an agreement is made to "address interests and problems that do not coincide nicely either with the national boundaries or with State lines—interests that may be badly served or not served at all by the ordinary channels of National or State political action."[35] Consequently, with regard to congressionally approved compacts, the right to sue for breach of the compact agreement differs from a right created by a commercial contract; it does not arise from state common law but from federal law. While contract principles may inform the interpretation of a compact and the remedies available in the event of breach, the underlying action is not like a contract action at common law as heard in the English law courts of the late eighteenth century.[36]

4.3.7 Parol Evidence

Extrinsic evidence may be considered by courts, when appropriate, to determine the intent of the parties to an interstate compact and to effectuate the desired purpose of the compact. Such evidence as the compact's legislative history or negotiation history may be examined in interpreting an ambiguous provision of a compact in the same manner as any other contract.[37] Thus, unlike in standard contract disputes, where the parol evidence rule is more restrictive of the admissibility and influence of outside evidence in contract interpretation, resort to extrinsic evidence of the compact negotiations is entirely appropriate. As the Court stated in *Oklahoma v. New Mexico*, "The use of extrinsic evidence to interpret and enforce a compact arises from the dual nature of such agreements as both statutory and contractual in nature."[38]

---

34. Hess v. Port Auth. Trans-Hudson Corp., 513 U.S. 30, 40 (1994).
35. *Id.*
36. *See* Interstate Commission for Adult Offender Supervision, *Training Outline* 11 (2004), *available at* http://www.interstatecompact.org.
37. Arizona v. California, 292 U.S. 341 (1934). *See also* Green v. Bock Laundry Mach. Co., 490 U.S. 504 (1989); Pierce v. Underwood, 487 U.S. 552 (1988); Blum v. Stenson, 465 U.S. 886 (1984).
38. Oklahoma v. New Mexico, 501 U.S. 221 (1991).

Chapter 5

STRUCTURES FOR ADMINISTERING INTERSTATE COMPACTS

One of the hallmarks of the interstate compact mechanism is its flexibility. Compacts can and do serve many purposes, and they assume a variety of forms, ranging from simple, bi-state agreements that permanently resolve discrete issues to complex, multistate regulatory schemes of a far more dynamic nature. Similarly, the means by which compacts are administered, and the frameworks they establish for their own implementation, vary widely depending on the purpose, scope, and intricacy of a particular agreement. This chapter looks at some alternative structures for the governance and administration of interstate compacts. It also highlights the strengths and weaknesses associated with each option.

5.1   ADMINISTRATION BY EXISTING STATE AGENCIES AND OFFICIALS

Self-executing compacts that permanently settle an interstate issue between the parties (e.g., bi-state boundary agreements) typically embody the full extent of the agreement between the participating members and, therefore, require little or no administrative machinery to ensure their successful implementation. In those instances, however, where compliance with the terms of such an agreement is not a simple matter to achieve or ascertain, at least some provision is usually made for the implementation and administration of the deal. One approach is to assign general oversight duties to existing agencies or officials within the member states. For example, the Colorado River

Compact, which prescribed a fixed allocation of waters between states in the upper and lower Colorado River basins, included an article assigning basic administrative and compliance responsibilities for the agreement to the appropriate officials in each party state. Specifically, Article V of the compact provided:

> The chief official of each signatory State charged with the administration of water rights, together with the Director of the United States Reclamation Service and the Director of the United States Geological Survey shall cooperate, ex officio:
>
> (a) To promote the systematic determination and coordination of the facts as to flow, appropriation, consumption, and use of water in the Colorado River Basin, and the interchange of available information in such matters.
>
> (b) To secure the ascertainment and publication of the annual flow of the Colorado River at Lee Ferry.
>
> (c) To perform such other duties as may be assigned by mutual consent of the signatories from time to time.[1]

The agreement also provided for the contingent appointment by the member states' governors of commissioners empowered to resolve any disputes that might arise among the parties related to the administration and enforcement of the compact.[2] Beyond these relatively simple terms, however, no additional administrative provisions were required by, or included in, the agreement.

A more recent example of this approach to compact administration was provided by the Interstate Corrections Compact, which permits the cooperative incarceration and rehabilitation of criminal offenders. Without establishing any new entities or requiring the designation of any particular authorities, the compact instead places the burden of its administration variously upon the "duly constituted authorities," "appropriate officials," "appropriate authorities," and "duly accredited officers" of the party states, thus giving the participating jurisdictions a great deal of flexibility to determine for themselves how best to distribute compact-related powers and duties within their own existing agencies.[3]

---

1. Colorado River Compact, art. V (1921).
2. Colorado River Compact, art. VI (1921).
3. Interstate Corrections Compact, art. IV, §§ (a), (b), & (f); art. V, § (a) (1997).

This form of compact administration works best with respect to self-executing, fixed agreements that require little or no ongoing oversight and those agreements, like the Interstate Corrections Compact, that can adequately be administered (in this case, pursuant to the terms of more detailed subsidiary agreements between the parties[4]) through existing state entities. One obvious advantage of this approach is that it is relatively inexpensive. Another is that it allows participating states to pursue cooperative goals without expanding their own bureaucracies. This can be a strong selling point for a proposed compact, especially when financial resources are in short supply. On the other hand, reliance on existing state agencies can undermine a compact's potential effectiveness if, for example, the internal distribution of administrative responsibilities within member states is not sufficiently clear, or if the specified administrative authorities are not adequately equipped with the resources they need to fulfill their compact-related duties.

5.2 "COMPACT ADMINISTRATORS"; NEW STATE ENTITIES

Many interstate compacts go at least one step beyond the simple (and often unspecified) delegation of administrative responsibilities to existing state agencies by requiring party states to affirmatively designate official compact administrators. Though the states usually retain considerable discretion with respect to such appointments, some compacts require the selection of administrators who possess certain qualifications or who represent specified agencies within their states. The Driver License Compact, for example, provides that, "The head of the licensing authority of each party state shall be administrator of this compact for his state."[5] Similarly, the proposed New England Compact on Involuntary Detention for Tuberculosis Control requires that each participating state's compact administrator "shall be the head of the state agency responsible for tuberculosis control."[6]

The powers and duties assigned by compacts to their designated administrators can vary, but most agreements that rely on this model for their administration provide generally that the authorized administrators shall be responsible for the initial implementation of the compact, for the internal enforcement of its terms, and for the oversight of any ongoing compact-related activities. Some compacts also require their administrators to serve as official liaisons on behalf of their respective states, to help ensure effective

---

4. *Id.* at art. III.
5. Driver License Compact, art. VII (a) (1958).
6. New England Compact on Involuntary Detention for Tuberculosis Control, art. VI (proposed 1997).

communication between the parties, and many specifically authorize or direct their administrators to act jointly for certain purposes, such as the promulgation of any rules that might be necessary to the fulfillment of compact objectives.

The Interstate Compact on Mental Health, for example, provides in typical fashion as follows:

> (a) Each party state shall appoint a "compact administrator" who, on behalf of his state, shall act as general coordinator of activities under the compact in his state and who shall receive copies of all reports, correspondence, and other documents relating to any patient processed under the compact by his state either in the capacity of sending or receiving state. The compact administrator or his duly designated representative shall be the official with whom other party states shall deal in any matter relating to the compact or any patient processed thereunder.
> (b) The compact administrators of the respective party states shall have power to promulgate reasonable rules and regulations to carry out more effectively the terms and provisions of this compact.[7]

A variation of this approach can be found in select recent agreements that assign internal oversight and administrative authority for compact-related matters to new in-state entities. The Interstate Compact for Adult Offender Supervision (ICAOS), for instance, not only requires the appointment of "compact administrators"[8] (as well as the establishment of an interstate regulatory commission) but also provides for the establishment within each participating jurisdiction of a new "state council" charged with various administrative duties. These include oversight, advocacy, and the "development of policy concerning operations and procedures of the compact within that state."[9]

As a practical matter, the ICAOS requirement that such state councils be established can be fulfilled either by creating a wholly new state entity or by conferring a new role, including all compact-required duties, upon an existing state agency. Either way, the result is the establishment of an internal administrative structure that exceeds in scope the simple designation of an individual compact administrator.

---

7. Interstate Compact on Mental Health, art. X (1972). *See also* Driver License Compact, art. VII (1958); Interstate Compact on Juveniles, art. XII (1955).
8. Interstate Compact for Adult Offender Supervision, art. IV (2002).
9. *Id. See also* Interstate Compact for Juveniles, art. IX (proposed 2003).

The chief benefit of these approaches to compact administration is that by going beyond sole reliance upon existing state agencies, they help to ensure that participating states pay closer attention to their own compact-related commitments and duties. Whether limited to the appointment of individual administrators or expanded to include the establishment of new in-state entities, the compact-specific nature of such administrative schemes can serve to raise the visibility of the compact itself within the member states. This, in turn, can help to bring about a greater degree of compliance with compact obligations than might otherwise be achieved in the absence of such provisions. A potential downside is the diversion of resources that might be necessary to satisfy a compact requirement that states designate specific administrators or establish new oversight authorities.

5.3   ADMINISTRATION BY ASSOCIATIONS

Associations of various kinds can, and often do, play key roles with respect to the administration of interstate compacts. This is true even though compacts rarely either expressly require or specifically authorize the participation of associations in their administration. Instead, such associations typically either grow out of various compact-required collaborations between designated administrators representing the member states, or they are recruited by compact-created entities to assist with the implementation and day-to-day administration of compact activities.

An early example of "administration by association" grew out of the Interstate Compact for the Supervision of Parolees and Probationers, enacted in 1937. That agreement expressly authorized the gubernatorial appointment in each member state of "an officer who, acting jointly with like officers of other contracting states, if and when appointed, shall promulgate such rules and regulations as may be deemed necessary to more effectively carry out the terms of this compact."[10]

Not long after the compact took effect, the administrators appointed pursuant to this provision found it desirable to form their own association, and in 1945, they established the Parole and Probation Compact Administrators' Association (PPCAA) to assist their collective rulemaking efforts and to provide a forum for the exchange of information among members.[11] For more

---

10. Interstate Compact for the Supervision of Parolees and Probationers § 5 (1946).
11. The Probation and Parole Compact Administrations Association (PPCAA) claimed legal authority for its existence under the compact provision quoted above. *See* PPCAA MANUAL, ch. 1 (August 2003). This claim is, at best,

than 50 years thereafter, the PPCAA served as the de facto administrative authority for the compact while facilitating the cooperative efforts of the duly authorized compact administrators.

Several other compacts requiring designated administrators to act jointly in pursuit of various objectives have also resulted in the establishment of associations to facilitate their collective efforts. The Association of Juvenile Compact Administrators, for example, was established shortly after the enactment of the Interstate Compact on Juveniles and continues to assist the duly authorized administrators of that agreement in their cooperative endeavors. Likewise, and for similar reasons, the administrators of the Interstate Compact on the Placement of Children formed their own association in 1974.

Some of these associations have, in turn, enlisted the assistance of other organizations to support their ongoing activities, usually by providing secretariat services to the principal association. The Association of Administrators of the Interstate Compact on the Placement of Children, for example, relies upon the American Public Human Services Association (APHSA) for secretariat services,[12] and similar assistance is provided to the Interstate Compact Coordinators for Mental Health/Mental Retardation-Developmental Disabilities (the administrators of the Interstate Compact on Mental Health) by the National Association of State Mental Health Program Directors.

In some instances, associations that currently play key roles in the administration of interstate compacts either predated or contributed to the creation of the agreements they serve. For instance, the Nurse Licensure Compact was originally developed and promoted by the National Council of State Boards of Nursing, which now assists in administering the agreement by providing secretariat services to the Nurse Licensure Compact Administrators. Another example is provided by the Emergency Management Assistance Compact (EMAC), which delegates administrative authority in each state to "the legally designated state official who is assigned responsibility for emer-

---

debatable, since the compact itself speaks only to the administrators' authority to promulgate rules. Though not prohibited, neither was the establishment of such an association expressly authorized by the compact, a fact that temporarily acquired relevance during the externally led effort to develop and implement a successor agreement, the Interstate Compact for Adult Offender Supervision. *See* discussion, Michael L. Buenger & Richard L. Masters, *The Interstate Compact on Adult Offender Supervision: Using Old Tools to Solve New Problems,* 9 ROGER WILLIAMS U. L. REV. 71, 110 n.106 (2003).

12. APSHA also provides secretariat services to the Association of Administrators of the Interstate Compact on Adoption and Medical Assistance.

gency management[.]"[13] Although an association of emergency managers already existed at the time the compact was being developed by the Southern Governors' Association (SGA), no role in the administration of the agreement was envisioned for the National Emergency Management Association (NEMA) until EMAC's original geographic scope was expanded to permit national participation. Soon thereafter, however, NEMA inherited the secretariat duties originally performed by the SGA, and it continues to play the lead role in administering EMAC today.

Even those compacts that provide for the establishment of new interstate agencies to oversee their implementation occasionally rely on assistance from outside associations. The Interstate Compact for Adult Offender Supervision, for instance, specifically empowered the commission it created to "contract for services of personnel,"[14] which it did when the commission entered into a cooperative agreement with The Council of State Governments (CSG) for interim staff support during the start-up phase of its operations. Pursuant to similar authority contained in the Midwest Interstate Passenger Rail Compact and the bylaws of the commission it creates, CSG also provides administrative support on an ongoing basis to the Midwest Interstate Passenger Rail Commission.[15]

Reliance on associations for assistance in administering interstate compacts makes the most sense in connection with those agreements that require joint action on the part of designated in-state administrators. In those instances where collective decision making is required only occasionally and where other administrative demands are relatively limited, informal associations of compact administrators may be sufficient with little or no outside support. By the same token, those agreements requiring more frequent policy decisions or the close oversight of ongoing activities may demand more from the associations employed in their administration. In addition to providing forums for meetings and deliberations between representatives of the party states, they may be called upon to meet a wide range of other needs, including public outreach, staff resources, and substantive expertise.

Associations can provide a flexible and relatively affordable alternative to the establishment of permanent administrative structures. They are particularly appealing when alternative mechanisms are not provided by compact, but assistance is required to ensure the fulfillment of stated objectives. On the other hand, for all the advantages of this approach, the procurement

---

13. Emergency Management Assistance Compact, art. II (1996).
14. Interstate Compact for Adult Offender Supervision, art. V (2002).
15. The commission is staffed by Council of State Governments' Midwestern Office.

of professional secretariat services and other association support can be more expensive than simple reliance upon existing state agencies for the administration of compacts. It can also be insufficient to meet the needs of more complex interstate agreements.

5.4   ADMINISTRATION BY INTERSTATE AGENCIES

Compacts that govern complex, high-volume transactions or that address ongoing multistate concerns requiring the development of shared regulatory solutions, often provide for the establishment of new interstate agencies to oversee their implementation and administration. Numerous compacts of recent origin have created regulatory commissions charged with developing and enforcing specific policies to solve the very problems that inspired the parties to enact compacts in the first place. In other words, instead of resolving the underlying issues up front, such compacts serve instead to establish frameworks for the subsequent development of the desired solutions.

This approach to interstate regulation goes well beyond the simple question of compact administration, since what it really entails is the establishment of new governing authorities whose members play active roles as policy makers, as well as administrators. Therefore, compacts that establish such regulatory entities often include numerous provisions defining their composition, describing their specific powers and duties and providing the means for their continuous operation.

The first compact to establish a permanent interstate agency was the New York–New Jersey Port Authority Compact of 1921, which conferred unprecedented regulatory authority upon the commission it established. Though sparse in detail compared to compacts of more recent vintage, the Port Authority agreement included provisions specifically authorizing or requiring the appointment of commissioners, the adoption of bylaws, the promulgation of rules, the acquisition and management of port facilities, the submission of annual reports to the party states, and the exercise of various other commission powers.[16] It also contained additional terms providing for the election of officers, the appointment of staff, and the appropriation of funds to support the operations of the new commission.[17] Given the size and complexity of the bureaucratic structure that eventually resulted,[18] these provisions are notable for their relative simplicity:

----

16. New York–New Jersey Port Authority Compact of 1921, arts. IV-VII & XVIII (1921).
17. *Id.* at arts. XIV-XV (1921).
18. The Port Authority of New York and New Jersey employs thousands of workers and operates on an annual budget that exceeded $4.5 billion in 2004.

- *Article XIV*. The port authority shall elect from its number a chairman, vice chairman, and may appoint such officers and employees as it may require for the performance of its duties, and shall fix and determine their qualifications and duties.
- *Article XV*. Unless and until the revenues from operations conducted by the port authority are adequate to meet all expenditures, the legislatures of the two states shall appropriate, in equal amounts, annually, for the salaries, office and other administrative expenses, such sum or sums as shall be recommended by the port authority and approved by the governors of the two states, but each state obligates itself hereunder only to the extent of one hundred thousand dollars in any one year.[19]

Another early administrative compact was the Ohio River Valley Water Sanitation Compact, which also established an interstate commission vested with rulemaking authority. In many ways, this agreement resembled the port authority compact in that the provisions governing the establishment and general operations of the Ohio River Valley Water Sanitation Commission (ORSANCO) were fairly simple.[20] However, whereas the former compact had circumscribed the broad rulemaking power of the Port Authority by reserving to the member states the right to veto the actions of their own commissioners,[21] the latter agreement included no similar checks, thus effectively giving ORSANCO wider latitude to exercise its discretionary rulemaking powers.

As the use of interstate compacts to address complex regulatory matters gradually became more common, the administrative schemes contained in such agreements also continued to evolve. Administrative compacts of more recent origin have tended to include more detailed provisions prescribing the powers and duties of the commissions they create,[22] and some have introduced new tools. The Waterfront Commission Compact, for example, was the first to empower an interstate agency to levy taxes. Specifically, the compact authorized the new commission to partially finance its own operations by collecting assessments from the employers of various waterfront workers required to be licensed under the agreement.[23]

---

19. New York–New Jersey Port Authority Compact of 1921, arts. XIV-XV (1921).
20. Ohio River Valley Water Sanitation Compact, arts. III-V (1940).
21. New York–New Jersey Port Authority Compact of 1921, art. XVI (1921).
22. *See, e.g.*, Washington Metropolitan Area Transit Regulation Compact, tit. III (1966).
23. Waterfront Commission Compact, art. XIII (1953).

Some compacts that establish interstate agencies include elaborate voting procedures or detailed provisions governing the appointment of commissioners. By way of example, one that does both is the Tahoe Regional Planning Compact, under which the states of California and Nevada established the Tahoe Regional Planning Agency. The compact requires the appointment of seven commissioners from each of the two party states, but in an effort to ensure adequate representation of both state and local interests on the governing body, it goes on to require that the 14 appointments be made by a total of 13 different authorities, including the governors of both states, county boards in four specified counties on both sides of the border, municipal authorities in two cities, legislative leaders in California, and designated executive officials in Nevada.[24]

The same compact is also noteworthy for its inclusion of language specifying three different commission voting standards, depending on the type of action being contemplated by the agency. The most important matters require affirmative votes from a majority of commissioners within each state delegation. Others require a higher number of votes, but from only one of the two state delegations, and still others may be approved by a simple majority of all commissioners without regard to state affiliation.[25]

Of course, simpler schemes can also be found, even in compacts that authorize significant regulatory activity or that permit the participation of numerous party states. The Delaware River Basin Compact, for example, delegates broad regulatory responsibility for the management and protection of water resources in the Delaware River Basin to an interstate commission comprised of just one representative from each party to the agreement[26] and requires only the vote of a simple majority of all members for the approval of any matter before the commission.[27] Similarly, the Pest Control Compact, which has been enacted in 35 states,[28] is administered by a "governing board" that includes one representative from each party state and requires the vote of a simple majority of all members for the approval of any action.[29]

Some administrative compacts contain detailed provisions governing the operations and resources of the interstate agencies they create. For instance, the

---

24. Tahoe Regional Planning Compact, art. III (a) (1981).
25. *Id.* at art. III (g).
26. The parties include the states of Delaware, New Jersey, New York, and Pennsylvania, as well as the federal government.
27. Delaware River Basin Compact, art. 2, § 2.5 (1961).
28. As of March 2004.
29. Pest Control Compact, art.IV (b) (1968).

Susquehanna River Basin Compact specifically empowers the commission it establishes to borrow money, to issue bonds, to accept grants and contributions, and to acquire property by a variety of means, including eminent domain.[30] And the Washington Metropolitan Area Transit Regulation Compact includes elaborate provisions covering such commission activities as planning, financing, and procurement. It also includes a detailed section on labor policy and even authorizes the establishment of a special police force.[31]

Other compacts are far less specific with respect to the administrative machinery that might be required by the regulatory agencies they establish. The Tri-State Lotto Compact, for example, provides simply as follows:

> *1. Commission functions.* The commission's functions shall be performed and carried out by its members and by such advisory committees or panels, or both as the commission may establish, and by such officers, independent contractors, agents, employees and consultants as may be appointed by the commission. All such officers, independent contractors, agents, consultants and employees shall hold office at the pleasure of the commission, unless the commission otherwise decides, and the commission shall prescribe the person's powers, duties and qualifications and fix their compensation and other terms of their employment.[32]

Interstate agencies can be as useful in administering purely advisory agreements as they are in implementing administrative compacts. As noted previously, some such commissions are aided in their efforts by associations that provide them with various forms of assistance ranging from occasional secretariat services to ongoing operational support.[33] Others rely on one or more of their members for administrative help. For example, the Compact Council established pursuant to the National Crime Prevention and Privacy Compact, to which the federal government is a party, receives direct staff support from the FBI. Still other such agencies go it alone and, like many of their regulatory counterparts, either provide for themselves pursuant to general grants of compact authority or are equipped with the resources they need by the compacts that authorize their establishment.

---

30. Susquehanna River Basin Compact, arts. 13 & 15 (1970).
31. Washington Metropolitan Area Transit Regulation Compact, tit. III, arts. VI, VII, IX, X, XIV & XVI (1966).
32. Tri-State Lotto Compact, art. II, § d (1983).
33. *See, e.g.,* the Midwest Interstate Passenger Rail Commission, which is supported by the Midwestern Office of The Council of State Governments.

One example is provided by the Interstate Oil and Gas Compact Commission (IOGCC). Established almost 70 years ago, pursuant to the Interstate Compact to Conserve Oil and Gas, the IOGCC was empowered to encourage the conservation of oil and gas through the prevention of waste and "to recommend the coordination of the exercise of the police powers of the several States within their several jurisdictions to promote the maximum ultimate recovery from the petroleum reserves of said States, and to recommend measures for the maximum ultimate recovery of oil and gas."[34]

The compact made no provision for the resources necessary to support the activities of the commission and expressly stipulated that its terms imposed no financial obligations upon its members.[35] Moreover, the commission's bylaws later provided that the IOGCC's expenses were to be paid "from voluntary contributions by the Member States and from other sources of revenue approved by the Commission."[36] Nevertheless, the IOGCC has, over the years, generated sufficient funding from its members and through various grants and contracts to support its activities, and it continues to serve as a forum for the exchange of information and as an advocate on behalf of the nation's oil and gas producing states.

Other nonregulatory and advisory compacts often include more specific provisions for the administrative agencies they create and typically rely heavily upon required contributions from participating states for the support of commission activities. For example, the nonregulatory New England Higher Education Compact, one of four regional agreements that authorize interstate agencies to administer various programs for the advancement of higher education,[37] requires party states to pay membership dues in support of the compact commission (the New England Board of Higher Education). It even specifies the formula to be used in determining the appropriate amounts to be paid by each state:

> Each state agrees that, when authorized by the legislature pursuant to the constitutional processes, it will from time to time make available to the board such funds as may be required for the expenses of the

---

34. Interstate Compact to Conserve Oil and Gas, art. VI (1967).
35. *Id.* at art. VII.
36. Interstate Oil and Gas Commission, Bylaws, art. VII (2004), *available at* http://www.iogcc.oklaosf.state.ok.us/ABOUTIO1.HTM#BYLAWS.
37. The other three are the Western Regional Higher Education Compact (1953), the Southern Regional Education Compact (1948), and the Midwestern Higher Education Compact (1991).

board as authorized under the terms of this compact. The contribution of each state for this purpose shall be in the proportion that its population bears to the total combined population of the states who are parties hereto as shown from time to time by the most recent official published report of the Bureau of the Census of the United States, unless the board shall adopt another basis in making its recommendation for appropriation to the compacting states.[38]

In contrast, compacts that anticipate the availability of other revenue streams often rely on those sources to fund the operations of the commissions they create. This is true even with respect to commissions that exercise only limited regulatory authority while administering activities that include more substantial operations. Thus, for instance, the Historic Chattahoochee Compact between the states of Alabama and Georgia empowered the Historic Chattahoochee Commission to accept governmental appropriations, but did not require the party states to make them. Instead, anticipating that sufficient revenues might be derived through other sources, such as "admissions, inspection fees, gifts, donations, grants, bequests [and] loans,"[39] the compact granted the commission broad authority to acquire and manage various assets and specifically empowered it to borrow funds, issue bonds, accept gifts, dispose of property, and promulgate rules governing the operation of its facilities,[40] all of which could potentially generate the revenues necessary to support the commission's administrative efforts.

Regardless of their precise form, interstate agencies can be extremely effective as tools for the implementation of interstate compacts. Whether serving as forums for the exchange of information and ideas between the parties, as advocates for the implementation of best practices and suggested solutions, as administrators of cooperative ventures and other ongoing activities, or as governing authorities with significant policy-making and regulatory powers, compact agencies are uniquely well suited to pursue shared interstate objectives. This is due in part to the special legal status of interstate compacts, relative to other state statutes, but there are other, more practical advantages as well.

If nothing else, the establishment of an interstate agency can increase the chances of a compact's success simply by ensuring that someone takes ownership for its implementation. Without an oversight entity of some kind to

---

38. New England Higher Education Compact, art. VI (1954).
39. Historic Chattahoochee Compact, art. VII (1978).
40. *Id.* at art. VIII.

coordinate the efforts of the parties, compacts that rely solely on existing state agencies or designated officials may languish through neglect or because they lack sufficient administrative machinery to effectuate their purposes. Interstate agencies, on the other hand, can help the parties to more effectively focus their efforts and marshal their resources in pursuit of compact objectives. They also provide a useful "home" for compact-related issues and can assist in raising the visibility of the underlying concerns they are meant to address.

The agency approach to compact administration is as flexible as the compact mechanism itself. This, too, is a significant advantage, since the agency model can be tailored to meet the specific needs of virtually any agreement. Compact agencies need not require the establishment of extensive bureaucratic support structures (although some do, and the cost can be high). Many that perform nonregulatory duties or that serve primarily in an advisory capacity function well with only limited staff resources and operational support.

Nevertheless, the agency model arguably best serves those compacts that address complex regulatory matters or that entail significant operations requiring continuous oversight. As multijurisdictional governing authorities often charged with significant policy-making powers, compact agencies are far better positioned than single-state agencies acting independently, or loosely organized associations of compact administrators to oversee the implementation and administration of interstate agreements.

But the very attributes that render interstate agencies so useful in the administration of compacts are also, occasionally, a source of concern among lawmakers or others who are not familiar with the compact mechanism itself or who, for various reasons, question the delegation of state authority to such entities. Some fear the loss of state sovereignty inherent in any delegation of power to an agency that the delegating state does not unilaterally control. Others question whether such delegations are even permissible on constitutional grounds, a concern that goes directly to the legal status of compact agencies.

The status question is understandable in light of the relatively unusual nature of compact entities. As joint instrumentalities of all states that participate in their creation, interstate agencies are equally responsible to each, though subject only to the collective governance of their principals in accordance with the terms of their compact charters. And like the statutes that authorize their establishment, any administrative rules duly promulgated by compact agencies enjoy a special, presumptively superior status relative to other state laws. Despite these unique characteristics, however, the status of interstate commissions as legally permissible entities is now well understood. Moreover, the U.S. Supreme Court has held that a state legislature's ability to delegate regulatory authority to an administrative agency is "one of the axioms of modern government" and that this ability extends as well to the creation of interstate commissions by compact.[41] Generally, therefore, neither the establishment of such entities nor their exercise of regulatory power is legally problematic with respect to constitutional prohibitions against the delegation of state authority.

As for concerns related to the loss of individual state sovereignty, there is no question that the parties to interstate compacts necessarily give up the right to unilaterally control the joint agencies they create. But when measured against the nature of congressional intervention and the loss of state authority that can result from federal preemption of a particular field, the legislative and regulatory control that states jointly retain under interstate compacts is usually preferred by states. Viewed through this lens, the decision to empower an interstate agency is more likely to be seen as a welcome protection of "collective state sovereignty" than it is to be resisted as an unacceptable sacrifice of individual state authority.

Of course, the parties to an interstate compact ultimately retain the ability to terminate the agreement altogether, and they can, if they so desire, build other mechanisms into the statute to limit the discretion delegated to an interstate agency or to protect the prerogatives of individual states. For example, some compacts reserve to their parties specified veto powers over the actions of the agencies they create,[42] while others include mechanisms allowing their members to jointly reject,[43] or to individually "opt out" of the enforcement of,[44] individual rules promulgated by interstate commissions. Such provisions also serve to further illustrate the wide variety of ways in which interstate agencies can be structured and empowered to ensure the successful administration of the compacts under which they are created.

---

41. West Virginia *ex rel.* Dyer v. Sims, 341 U.S. 22 (1951).
42. *See, e.g.*, New York–New Jersey Port Authority Compact of 1921, art. XVI (1921).
43. *See, e.g.*, Interstate Compact for Adult Offender Supervision, art. VIII (2002).
44. *See, e.g.*, Interstate Insurance Receivership Compact, art. VII (1996).

Chapter 6

ISSUES WITH THE ENFORCEMENT OF INTERSTATE COMPACTS

6.1   RECURRENT PROBLEMS WITH AND COMMON
OBSTACLES TO ENFORCING COMPACTS

One of the great virtues of written legal instruments, including interstate compacts, is that they tend to reduce the necessity of enforcement proceedings. The reduction of the potential for controversy over the terms of the agreement, as well as the obligations assumed under it, improves the chances of satisfactory performance by the parties to the compact. In addition, the good faith that is generally presumed among the parties to a contract also applies to the state governmental units that are members of an interstate compact, and provides some assurance that the compact obligations will be performed and discharged. While these factors have militated in favor of performance, as in all legal relationships, ignorance of compact provisions and rules, differences of opinion and practice, as well as occasional recalcitrance of the member states requires the issue of enforcement to be considered in the compact context, particularly with respect to the increasing prevalence of interstate compacts that create ongoing interstate agencies.

One of the "perennial" complaints about compact agencies is that they are "toothless," at least in practice.[1] There are a growing number of compacts that are formed for the purpose of providing both regional and national legal channels for intergovernmental action including the compacts dealing with parole and probation, juveniles, detainers, driver licensing, civil defense and disaster, placement of children, and environmental resource management. While some of these compacts establish intergovernmental agencies, as some commentators have observed, the states, in many instances, have not utilized the compact process to its full potential and are "to blame for not charging the interstate commissions with adequate regulatory and enforcement powers."[2] This deficiency has provided substantial impetus for recent revisions to the Interstate Compact for Parolees and Probationers, which has been supplanted by the Interstate Compact for Adult Offender Supervision that has now been adopted by 50 states, the District of Columbia, Puerto Rico, and the U.S. Virgin Islands. Similar efforts are actively under way with the new Interstate Compact for Juveniles, which has been adopted by 28 states and is currently under consideration by most of the remaining nonmember state legislatures, and with the Interstate Compact for the Placement of Children, which is being redrafted under the auspices of the American Public Human

---

1. *See* Jill Elaine Hasday, *Interstate Compacts in a Democratic Society: The Problem of Permanency*, 49 FLA. L. REV. 1, 22 (1997).
2. *See* JEROME C. MUYS, INTERSTATE WATER COMPACTS: THE INTERSTATE COMPACT & FEDERAL-INTERSTATE COMPACT 323 (National Water Commission Legal Study 1971).

Services Association in conjunction with the Council of State Governments. In each of these compacts, enforcement problems have been amplified by the lack of a formal governing structure. Although providing for appointment of an officer by the governor of each member state, to promulgate rules and regulations deemed necessary, none of these compacts provided any formal definition of the powers or duties of any joint body created by these three compacts.[3] There was no clearly delineated authority and thus questionable legal standing, making it practically impossible to obtain state compliance with either the provisions of the compact statutes or the rules promulgated thereunder.[4]

The comprehensive redrafts of these compacts exemplify the emerging understanding and use of the power of interstate compacts and the rise of a new and potent form of compact that creates ongoing agencies vested with substantial authority to regulate not only substantive issues, but also individual state responses to those issues. As recent experience leading to the adoption of the Interstate Compact for Adult Offenders (ICAOS) has shown, one of the critical problems to avoid is "creating compact agencies with so little authority that they are inescapably ineffectual[.]"[5] In this regard the ICAOS is one of the foremost examples of the use of the compact device to create a supra-state administrative agency to regulate an issue of regional and national concern. Beginning in 1998, under the auspices of the National Institute of Corrections and the Council of State Governments, a concerted effort was made to substantially amend and completely replace the 1937 Interstate Compact for the Supervision of Probationers and Parolees. The end result of that process was the ICAOS. The importance of it must be viewed in the context of both its policy implications and its legal standing. In light of *Cuyler v. Adams*[6] and subsequent cases, the ICAOS and the administrative rules adopted by its newly formed Interstate Commission function as "the law of the United States" applicable to the member states under both the terms of the compact and through the operation of the Supremacy Clause.[7]

---

3. *See* Michael L. Buenger & Richard Masters, *The Interstate Compact on Adult Offender Supervision: Using Old Tools to Solve New Problems,* 9 ROGER WILLIAMS U. L. REV. 71, 110 (Fall 2003).
4. *Id.* at 112.
5. Jill Elaine Hasday, *supra* note 1, at 1, 41.
6. 449 U.S. 433 (1981).
7. *See* Carchman v. Nash, 473 U.S. 716, 719 (1985) ("The agreement is a congressionally sanctioned interstate compact within the Compact Clause and thus is a federal law subject to federal constructions."). *See also* Alabama v. Bozeman, 533 U.S. 146 (2001).

Adoption of the ICAOS has "nationalized" and "federalized" the movement
of adult offenders with state convictions, while simultaneously retaining policy
direction and operational control in member states. The most significant difference between the old and the new compact, however, rests in the creation
of a formal and powerful administrative and enforcement structure that can
supersede individual state autonomy.

Other issues that have raised enforcement problems in the field of interstate compacts include financial obligations of states that are parties to compacts. In *Virginia v. West Virginia,*[8] the Supreme Court considered what has
been characterized as the most prolonged litigation directly involving obligations assumed under a compact.[9] This case arose from the unwillingness of
West Virginia to pay a portion of a debt of the Commonwealth of Virginia,
which it had assumed by means of a compact agreement as part of the final
settlement after its separation from Virginia, which occurred during the Civil
War. The importance of this decision is the unequivocal holding of the U.S.
Supreme Court that it would enforce a compact although the precise means
that it would employ are not described in the decision. Ultimately, West
Virginia performed its obligations to pay the debt it had assumed under the
terms of the compact but only after lengthy litigation. Since the obligation to
perform was a financial one, it was necessary for the legislature of West
Virginia to appropriate the required funds in order to satisfy the legal liability
resulting from the affirmation of the Supreme Court of the validity of the
compact and the obligations created by its provisions.

Similarly, in *State of West Virginia ex rel. Dyer v. Sims, State Auditor,*[10]
the auditor of West Virginia refused to release funds appropriated by the state
legislature for the purpose of satisfying its financial obligation to support the
operation of the Ohio River Valley Sanitation Commission. The commission
was established by an interstate compact to control pollution in the Ohio
River system of which West Virginia was a member along with seven other
states. The litigation was initiated in order to compel the required dues payments to be remitted to the compact commission by the auditor. The U.S.
Supreme Court held that West Virginia's enactment of the compact statute
contractually bound the state to comply with its terms, including the financial
obligations, and that it could not unilaterally change those terms or refuse to
perform its obligations without being in breach of the agreement.

---

8. 246 U.S. 565 (1918).
9. *See* Frederick L. Zimmerman & Mitchell Wendell, The Law and Use of Interstate Compacts 4 (The Council of State Governments 1976).
10. 341 U.S. 22 (1951).

The fundamental principle in this regard is not that enforcement problems will not arise, but that an interstate compact is a contractual legal instrument that can be enforced, if the need arises, more effectively than other less-formal arrangements, administrative alliances, or uniform laws as shown in the following analysis.

6.2 COMMON MISUNDERSTANDINGS ABOUT THE STATUS OF INTERSTATE COMPACTS

An understanding of compact enforcement issues requires an appreciation of the legal status of interstate compacts within the constitutional framework. Interstate compacts, particularly those receiving congressional consent, have a dual or binary nature. Compacts are state laws adopted by state legislatures that bind sister states to fully enforceable contracts. Thus, compacts are concurrently statutory (within a member state) and contractual (between member states). However, compacts are also creatures of state governments that, under particular circumstances, function as the "law of the United States," enforceable not only as contracts between member states, but also against individual member states under the Supremacy Clause of the Constitution. It is this dual or binary nature of compacts—statutory and contractual, state and federal—that gives them a unique legal standing and facilitates determination of enforcement issues.

Interstate compacts are initiated by the adoption of enabling statutes by the legislatures of the member states. It is the act of adoption of such statutes that creates contractual obligations between the states. Using the compact law analysis, the proposed compact statute adopted by the first state to enact constitutes an offer to each state to accept the offer by enactment of the compact statute in substantially identical form. The consideration for the agreement is the settlement of the dispute or creation of an association, agency, or some other mechanism to address an issue of mutual interest. "The principle of consideration while applicable to compacts has far less practical meaning than in the field of private contracts."[11]

It is equally important to note that compacts are not mere intergovernmental agreements or informal alliances and are significantly different from "uniform laws" as those terms are commonly understood. While compacts are legally enforceable contracts with terms and conditions that control—and that even trump—the actions and conduct of the member states, uniform laws are not contractual in nature.

---

11. FREDERICK L. ZIMMERMAN & MITCHELL WENDELL, *supra* note 9, at 9.

Uniform Acts are promulgated by the National Conference of Commissioners on Uniform State Laws in an effort to study and review the laws of the states to determine which areas should be uniform between the states. Legislatures are urged to adopt Uniform Acts exactly as written to promote such uniformity. Model Acts, however, are designed to serve as nothing more than guideline legislation, which states can borrow from, or adapt, to suit their individual needs and conditions. Uniform Acts do not constitute contracts between the states, even if adopted by all states in the same form, and thus, unlike contracts, are not binding upon or enforceable against the states. While uniform laws unify state law as to those states adopting them, compacts, can provide enforcement tools not only as to the populous but also as to the states themselves. Compacts are, therefore, a more powerful, albeit complex, tool for promoting uniform state behavior as to the subject matter of the compact. A state's failure to adopt a uniform law exactly as proposed has no impact on the state's relation to other similarly situated states as sovereigns within a constituent union.

6.3   MATERIAL AND NONMATERIAL DIFFERENCES IN COMPACT STATUTES

Another potential enforcement problem may arise if variations occur with respect to the text of the compact statutes enacted by and between the member states. As a contract, in order for the compact agreement to have the force of law in a jurisdiction that wishes to enter into the agreement, it must be accepted in precisely the same terms that constitute the offer—enactment of a statute entering into the compact and embodying the text, or execution of an agreement binding on the jurisdiction pursuant to specific statutory authorization. In order for the requisite "meeting of the minds" to occur with respect to the terms of the compact, no act constitutes acceptance unless it is an acceptance of the offer that has been made. Consequently, the same problems that arise by the variance in the terms of the offer and acceptance in the common law of contracts as to the existence of a binding contract also produce similar problems in the enforcement of interstate compacts. The statutory character of compacts makes it impossible to enter them orally or by simple exchange of letters, and these alternative methods of entering into contractual agreements, which give rise to most of the offer and acceptance disputes in private contractual relationships, are not available in the negotiation of an interstate compact. Thus, care should be taken to enact identical texts in the law of all compacting jurisdictions. Where the statutory texts of compacts putatively entered into by party states have not been identical, the problem raised has been the customary one in contract law: Are the variations sufficiently similar to permit a reasonable person to conclude that an agreement has been reached?

Due to its adoption of an earlier draft of the compact statute, which it mistakenly believed was the final draft, the state of New Hampshire's initial attempt to become a party to the Interstate Compact on Juveniles failed. Because all of the other states that adopted the measure had, in fact, adopted the most recent version, the putative New Hampshire compact statute was not identical in all material respects. The errant provisions concerned the prescribed method of effecting the return of a juvenile who had escaped or absconded, as well as a provision that specified gubernatorial participation in the requisitioning process required for the return of such juveniles. The versions enacted by the other states made this unnecessary and permitted a direct court-to-court approach. Subsequently, the legislature corrected this error by enacting the provisions of the Interstate Compact on Juveniles as adopted by the other states and successfully joined the compact.[12]

A different result was reached in the case of a Vermont enactment of a civil defense compact where its version of the compact statute was identical to that adopted by the other member states in almost all respects with the exception of the immunities given to civil defense workers from another state sent to render aid. In that case, it was determined by mutual agreement of Vermont and the other member states that they were contractually bound to one another to the extent of the similarity in the respective versions of the compact.[13]

Notwithstanding these concerns, the enabling legislation does not have to be uniform in each compact statute and can be utilized "to fit variations into the compactual pattern."[14] Provisions in the enabling legislation can be used to condition the impact of a compact in a state. Last-minute developments, which inevitably arise during the legislative process, can be handled through provisions in the enabling legislation in order to avoid the need to amend the compact statute. The only limitation on this approach is that a state is prohibited from making reservations in the enabling legislation that "materially change" a compact in the absence of specific consent by the other member states. "There is no reason why a state cannot participate in a compact arrangement for certain of its purposes but not for others if the other member states subscribe to such limited participation. The state enabling legislation is another tool for adjustment of the compactual pattern."[15]

---

12. *Id.*
13. *Id.*
14. *Id.* at 20.
15. *Id.* at 21.

6.4   CONFLICT WITH ESTABLISHED STATE LAWS

By entering into a compact, the member states contractually agree on certain principles and rules. Depending on the terms of the compact, a state may effectively cede a portion of its individual sovereignty over the subject of the agreement, as is the case with the Interstate Compact for Adult Offender Supervision. Once entered, the terms of the compact, as well as any rules and regulations authorized by the compact, supersede substantive state laws that may be in conflict, including state constitutional provisions, unless a specific exemption applies.[16] This applies to prior law (and subsequent statutes of the signatory states.[17] In *Dyer,* the Court also made clear that an interstate compact cannot be "given final meaning by an organ of one of the contracting states." Moreover, member states must not take unilateral actions, such as the adoption of conflicting legislation or the issuance of executive orders or court rules, that violate the terms of a compact.[18] Based on this principle, a number of lower courts have more recently declared that the provisions of a compact or its administrative rules take precedence over statutory law in member states.[19] The legal standing of compacts as contracts and instruments of national law applicable to the member states nullifies any state action in conflict with the compact's terms and conditions. Therefore, once adopted, the only means available to change the substance of a compact (and the obligations it imposes on a member state) are through withdrawal and renegotiation of its terms, or through an amendment adopted by all member states in essentially the same form. The contractual nature of the compact controls over any unilateral action by a state; no state is allowed to adopt any laws "impairing the obligation of contracts," including a contract adopted by state legislatures pursuant to the Compact Clause.[20]

---

16. *See* West Virginia *ex rel.* Dyer v. Sims, 341 U.S. 22, 29 (1951).
17. *See* Green v. Biddle, 21 U.S. 1, 92 (1823).
18. *See* N.E. Bancorp v. Bd. of Governors of Fed. Reserve Sys., 472 U.S. 159, 175 (1985).
19. *See* Wash. Metro. Area Transit Auth. v. One Parcel of Land, 706 F.2d 1312, 1319 (4th Cir. 1983); Kansas City Area Transp. Auth. v. Missouri, 640 F.2d 173, 174 (8th Cir. 1981); Doe v. Ward, 124 F. Supp. 900 (W.D. Pa. 2000).
20. *See* U.S. Const., art. I, § 10, cl.1 ("No state shall pass any bill of attainder, ex post facto law, or law impairing the obligation of contracts[.]"). *See also* West Virginia *ex rel.* Dyer v. Sims, 341 U.S. 22, 33 (1951); Hinderlider v. La Plata River & Cherry Creek Ditch Co., 304 U.S. 92 (1938).

6.5   CONFLICTS BETWEEN COMPACTS AND FEDERAL STATUTORY OR REGULATORY LAW

While every interstate compact must win the approval of the member state legislatures, as has previously been noted, only those compact agreements that "encroach upon or interfere with the just supremacy of the United States" must receive congressional consent.[21] However, Congress, unlike the states, is not bound by the compacts it approves. It can condition its consent or simply supersede its approval legislation with subsequent law.[22] The Supreme Court has also held that Congress has the right to reject compacts to which federal consent is required and to consent conditionally.[23]

6.6   COMPACT RULES THAT ARE BROADER THAN OR CONFLICT WITH THE COMPACT

In *West Virginia ex rel. Dyer v. Sims,* the Supreme Court considered, among other issues, the question of whether the state of West Virginia had authority under its Constitution to enter into a compact that delegated rulemaking authority to an interstate agency. In deciding this issue, the Court observed, "That a legislature may delegate to an administrative body the power to make rules and decide particular cases is one of the axioms of modern government."[24] Referring to the delegation of such power to an interstate agency as "a conventional grant of legislative power," and upholding the validity of the West Virginia Legislature in this regard, the Court found that "[t]he Compact involves a reasonable and carefully limited delegation of power to an interstate agency."[25]

Based upon the *Dyer* analysis, the Supreme Court clearly regards the legislative delegation of authority to an interstate compact agency as no dif-

---

21. U.S. Steel Corp. v. Multistate Tax Comm'n, 434 U.S. 452, 471 (1978), *quoting* New Hampshire v. Maine, 426 U.S. 363, 369 (1979), *quoting and affirming* Virginia v. Tennessee, 148 U.S. 503, 519 (1893).
22. *See* Louisville Bridge Co. v. United States, 242 U.S. 409, 418 (1917). *See also* Pennsylvania v. Wheeling & Belmont Bridge Co., 59 U.S. 421, 433 (1855).
23. *See* Cuyler v. Adams, 449 U.S. 433, 439-40 (1981); Petty v. Tennessee-Missouri Bridge Comm'n, 359 U.S. 275, 281-82 (1959); James v. Dravo Constructing Co., 302 U.S. 134, 148 (1937) (citing Arizona v. California, 292 U.S. 341, 345 (1934)).
24. West Virginia *ex rel.* Dyer v. Sims, 341 U.S. 22, 31 (1951).
25. *Id.*

ferent from that granted by a state legislature or, for that matter, the Congress to one of its own administrative agencies. Accordingly, such delegations of authority are subject to the limitation that the rules promulgated by the administrative agency do not exceed the scope of the statutorily delegated authority.[26] Where the rules or regulations fail to comport with this standard, they are considered ultra vires and, as such, are null and void. However, it must be emphasized that judicial review is limited, and courts usually defer to the experience and expertise of the administrative agency. Perhaps the most significant factor limiting review by the courts of action of administrative agencies generally, although undoubtedly variable in degrees appropriate to particular agencies, is the scope of the power that has been given the administrative agency by statute and the informed and expert judgment of the agency based upon its experience in the matter addressed by the statute. Courts often aver to the expertness, special competence, specialized knowledge, or experience of the administrative agency that fortifies the judgment of the agency. While due deference is generally afforded to the administrative agency, overly broad delegations of authority by the legislative body may also result in unconstitutional encroachments including violation of the constitutional doctrine of separation of powers.[27]

6.7   JUDICIAL ENFORCEMENT OF INTERSTATE COMPACTS

When considering the issue of judicial enforcement, it is useful to distinguish the two contexts in which enforcement issues may arise, the first being enforcement between the states that are parties to the agreement and the second being enforcement as it applies to compliance by third parties whether private persons or other legal entities. While compacts are ultimately enforceable in the courts as contractual obligations, as in any other legal transaction, it is desirable to minimize or avoid litigation whenever possible. One means of doing so is through explicitly providing for enforcement in the text of the interstate compact. Several compacts explicitly designate the judicial forum in which enforcement actions are to be filed both for resolution of disputes between states that are members of the compact in question and enforcement actions pertaining to third parties.[28]

---

26. *See* FTC v. Ruberoid Co., 343 U.S. 470, 487 (1952).
27. *See* INS v. Chadha, 462 U.S. 919 (1983).
28. *See* Interstate Compact for Adult Offender Supervision, Article VII (2002); Interstate Compact for Juveniles, Article XI (1955); Ohio River Valley Sanitation Compact, Art. IX (1940); Tri-State Sanitation Compact, Art. X (1935).

6.7.1   Enforcement of Compacts by Federal Courts

Under the Supremacy Clause, state courts have the same obligation to give force and effect to the provisions of a compact as do the federal courts. It is, however, ultimately the U.S. Supreme Court that retains the final word on the interpretation and application of congressionally approved compacts given their now federalized nature.[29] It is equally clear that these cases may reach the Supreme Court either on a writ of certiorari or an original action brought by a state. In either case, the power of the Court is the same. In the interpretation and enforcement of these agreements, both the federal and state courts are constrained to effectuate the terms of the compacts as binding contracts as long as those terms do not conflict with constitutional principles.[30] Although congressional consent may change the venue in which the compact disputes are ultimately litigated to federal court, it does not change the controlling nature of the agreement on the member states. Moreover, the congressional approval of a compact allows the compact provisions, which have the status of a "law of the United States," to circumscribe the scope of judicial relief available to the states that are parties to the compact. Where such forum restrictions exist, it is important to point out that they act to bind the member states and any compact-created administrative body as to the forum for bringing actions regarding the enforcement and interpretation of a compact as to the member states. These restrictions would not necessarily preclude a private citizen or entity from suing in state court, nor would they prevent state courts from enforcing the terms of a compact as a collateral matter to other litigation. However, in the absence of a specific provision in the text of the compact language, it is the Supreme Court that has original jurisdiction to adjudicate disputes involving the interpretation and enforcement of the provisions of the compact.[31]

6.7.2   Enforcement of Compacts by State Courts

Not every dispute arising under an interstate compact must be litigated in the federal courts. Compacts for which congressional consent has neither been given nor required do not express federal law and, consequently, must be construed as state law.[32] Thus, state courts are the customary forum in

---

29. *See* Delaware River Comm'n v. Colburn, 310 U.S. 419, 427 (1940).
30. N.Y. State Dairy Foods v. N.E. Dairy Compact Comm'n, 26 F. Supp. 2d 249, 260 (D. Mass. 1998), *aff'd,* 198 F.3d 1 (1st Cir. 1999).
31. *See* Texas v. New Mexico, 462 U.S. 554, 564 (1983). *See also* Rhode Island v. Massachusetts, 37 U.S. 657, 720 (1838).
32. *See* McComb v. Wambaugh, 934 F.2d 474 (3d Cir. 1991).

which such compacts are most often interpreted and enforced. Notwithstanding the exercise of its jurisdiction by a particular state, the provisions of an interstate compact for which no congressional consent is given or required are entitled to the same protections under the federal Constitution's prohibition against any law impairing the obligation of contracts. Where the states themselves dispute the nature and scope of their obligations under an interstate compact, the Supreme Court will continue to have the ultimate authority to decide the controversy. In *Dyer* the Supreme Court explained, "A State cannot be its own ultimate judge in a controversy with a sister State. To determine the nature and scope of obligations as between States, whether they arise through the legislative means of a compact or the 'federal common law' governing interstate controversies, is the function and duty of the Supreme Court of the Nation."[33] The *Dyer* Court also noted, "It has frequently been held that when a question is suitably raised whether the law of a State has impaired the obligation of a contract, in violation of the constitutional provision, this Court must determine for itself whether a contract exists, what are its obligations, and whether they have been impaired by the legislation of the State. While this Court always examines with appropriate respect the decisions of state courts bearing upon such questions, such decisions do not detract from the responsibility of this Court in reaching its own conclusions as to the contract, its obligations and impairment, for otherwise the constitutional guaranty could not properly be enforced."[34]

State courts, when enforcing an interstate compact sanctioned by congressional consent, would be required by the Supremacy Clause to defer to a compact's terms and conditions just as any federal court is required to do when confronted with compact issues. State court jurisdiction over such compact disputes would presumably extend to enforcing the terms of the compact on state officials, and even declaring a state statute, rule, or constitutional provision void as conflicting with the terms of a compact to which that state is a member. A state court's jurisdiction would not, of course, extend to enforcing a compact's terms and conditions on other states, that matter as noted herein resting clearly with the federal courts.

6.7.3   The Effect of Conflicting State Court Decisions Relative to Member States

One of the likely consequences in the administration of an interstate compact for which congressional consent is neither given nor required is the

---

33. West Virginia *ex rel.* Dyer v. Sims, 341 U.S. 22, 28 (1951).
34. *Id.* at 30.

lack of uniformity and consistency of interpretation, application, and enforcement of the compact's terms and conditions by the various state courts called upon to construe such a compact. The longer the period of existence and the more complex the provisions of a compact, the greater potential for conflicting state court decisions. One of the foremost examples of this situation has arisen with respect to the Interstate Compact for the Placement of Children. At least one federal court has held that because the ICPC has not received congressional consent, "the Compact does not express federal law." Consequently, this Compact must be construed as state law.[35] As a consequence, over the 50 years of the ICPC's existence and the thousands of adoptions and other placements of children in which it has been involved, literally hundreds of conflicting state court decisions have arisen. The situation has reached crisis proportions in which both administration and enforcement of the provisions of the ICPC have become difficult, if not impossible, giving rise to threatened congressional action and spurring a concerted effort to comprehensively amend the compact and to seek to resolve this enforcement problem by the American Public Human Services Association and the Council of State Governments.

6.8 MEDIATION AND ARBITRATION OF COMPACT DISPUTES

Arbitration and mediation provisions have become a fixture in modern business agreements in which the parties agree to employ alternative means of dispute resolution to resolve controversies ranging from employment discrimination claims to credit card disputes. Such procedures are also being employed by state agencies to resolve such divergent issues as professional licensure and disciplinary matters, occupational health and safety citations, and environmental disputes. These arrangements are also being used in interstate compacts. As with other such provisions, the purpose for the inclusion of such clauses is that which is articulated for alternative dispute mechanisms in general, namely to provide a means of adjustment of disputes arising under an interstate compact agreement without the necessity of recourse to litigation in the judicial forum.

6.9 DETERMINING PROPER JURISDICTION FOR RESOLVING COMPACT DISPUTES

The determination of proper jurisdiction for resolving compact disputes is determined in much the same way that litigants and counsel make such determinations in other contexts. A careful examination of the text of the

---

35. McComb v. Wambaugh, 934 F.2d 474 (3d Cir. 1991).

compact in question will reveal whether or not it contains an explicit provision concerning jurisdiction for purposes of disputes arising under the compact. In addition, a determination must be made whether or not the compact in question is one that has received congressional consent. In the absence of a compact provision or rule to the contrary, the compact will presumptively be subject to jurisdiction in the federal courts either based upon the precedent of the U.S. Supreme Court set forth herein or through various provisions of the U.S. Code that certain interstate compacts fall within the jurisdiction of the federal courts.[36] In the absence of such provisions, in the case of a compact for which congressional consent is provided, original jurisdiction would appear to lie in the U.S. Supreme Court.

6.10 REMEDIES IN THE ENFORCEMENT OF INTERSTATE COMPACTS

Compact provisions expressly providing sanctions that may be imposed in the event of a failure to comply with its provisions and its authorized rules are enforceable. Because congressional consent places the interpretation of an interstate compact in the federal courts, those courts also have the authority to enforce both the terms and conditions of the compact. No court can order relief inconsistent with the purpose of the compact.[37] However, where the compact does not articulate its enforceability, courts have wide latitude to fashion remedies that are consistent with the ultimate purpose of the compact. Such remedies can include both injunctive relief and monetary damages. The U.S. Supreme Court addressed this matter, observing, "That there may be difficulties in enforcing judgments against States['] counsels caution, but does not undermine our authority to enter judgments against defendant States in cases over which the Court has undoubted jurisdiction, authority that is attested to by the fact that almost invariably the 'States against which judgments were rendered, conformably to their duty under the Constitution, voluntarily respected and gave effect to the same.'"[38]

---

36. *See, e.g.*, 33 U.S.C. & 466g1(a) (2002).
37. *See* New York State Dairy Foods v. N.E. Dairy Compact Comm'n, 26 F. Supp. 2d 249, *aff'd,* 198 F.3d 1 (1st Cir. 1999) (once compact between states is approved, it is the law of the case binding on the states and its citizens, and absent constitutional defect, no court may order relief inconsistent with its express terms no matter what the equities of the circumstances might otherwise invite).
38. Texas v. New Mexico, 482 U.S. 124, 130-31 (1987). Remedies may also include the imposition of monetary penalties on the breaching state. *See also*

6.11 TEN POINTS A PRACTITIONER OR JUDGE SHOULD KNOW ABOUT ENFORCING INTERSTATE COMPACTS

Recapping the salient principles relating to enforcement of interstate compacts as discussed herein is the following list:

1. Interstate compacts are concurrently statutory (within a member state) and contractual (between member states).
2. Interstate compacts are creatures of state governments that, under particular circumstances, function as a "law of the United States" enforceable not only as contracts between member states, but also against individual member states under the Supremacy Clause of the Constitution.
3. Interstate compacts are contractual obligations, and the legal analysis interpreting the meaning and effect and enforcing the obligations under interstate compacts is generally controlled by contract law.
4. Because a compact is a contract and must be enforced within the terms and conditions of the compact, no court has authority to provide relief that is inconsistent with the compact.
5. An interstate compact takes precedence over conflicting state statutes or regulations, including the provisions of uniform laws under the Contract Clause of the Constitution and where congressional consent has been granted under the Supremacy Clause of the Constitution.
6. States may validly agree, by use of an interstate compact with other states, to create and delegate to interstate commissions or administrative agencies legislative and administrative powers and duties and may promulgate rules that have the same legal force and effect as the provisions of the interstate compact under which such rules are made.
7. Both the statutory provisions of the compact that has received congressional consent and rules that it is authorized to promulgate, become laws of the United States under the Supremacy Clause of the Constitution and trump both conflicting state statutes and regulations as well as state constitutional provisions, unless an exemption is expressly provided by the compact.

South Dakota v. North Carolina, 192 U.S. 286, 320-21 (1904); Texas v. New Mexico, 482 U.S. at 130 (court recognizes propriety of money judgments against a state in an original action involving a compact; Eleventh Amendment is no barrier, for by its terms it applies only to suits by citizens against a state); Kansas v. Colorado, 533 U.S. 1, 7 (2001).

8. Interstate compacts without congressional consent are more likely to give rise to conflicting interpretations by state courts.
9. Compacts may provide for alternative dispute resolution, including both mediation and arbitration.
10. Remedies available to courts in the enforcement of interstate compacts, even in the absence of express provisions, may include injunctive relief, damages, and monetary penalties.

Chapter 7

SPECIAL PROBLEMS

7.1 LIABILITY AND ELEVENTH AMENDMENT IMMUNITY FOR COMPACT AGENCIES

Many compacts now create ongoing administrative, regulatory, or management agencies that oversee compact operations. Examples of such agencies include the Interstate Commission for Adult Offender Supervision (regulating the movement of adult offenders across state lines); the Columbia River Gorge Commission (implementing zoning regulations, planning, and development along the Columbia River); the Washington Metropolitan Area Transit Authority (responsible for planning, developing, operating, constructing, acquiring, and improving mass transit facilities in the Washington metropolitan area); and the Ohio River Valley Sanitation Commission (regulating pollution control in the Ohio River Basin). Perhaps the best-known compact agency in the nation is the Port Authority of New York–New Jersey, which provides joint agency management over transportation, terminal, and commerce and trade facilities in the New York metropolitan area. These are but a few examples.

The creation of such agencies necessarily leads to important questions not only regarding the breadth of their authority (largely defined by the terms and conditions of the compact), but also the extent to which they are legally responsible for their actions (largely defined by case law). A significant body of case law has developed over the course of the last 50 years concerning the immunity compact agencies enjoy, and particularly whether they enjoy Eleventh Amendment immunity. Compact-created agencies are clearly not federal agencies, but neither are they de facto state agencies for purposes of Eleventh Amendment immunity.[1] They are, as the Supreme Court has observed, "diffuse; they lack the tight tie to the people of one State that an instrument of a single State has[.]"[2] Whether a compact-created agency

---

1. Although not federal agencies, at least one compact-created agency has been treated as such for purposes of determining whether it was liable for torts committed in the conduct of its operations. In *Sanders v. Washington Metropolitan Area Transit Authority*, 819 F.2d 1151 (D.C. Cir. 1987), the court applied a federal concept of "governmental function" used in Federal Tort Claims Act litigation in determining whether WMATA was liable for certain acts. The court held:

   > In granting immunity from tort actions to WMATA's "governmental" functions, the Compact seems to us to have accepted the *Dalehite* conception which we have just outlined. In construing the Federal Tort Claims Act—the federal consent-to-suit on tort claims—*Dalehite* had given the definitive understanding of those torts as to which Congress had consented (in that Act) to actions against the federal government. The "governmental function" language of the Compact's section 80 likewise concerns torts, and torts alone. The parallel is apparent, and it is especially appropriate to follow the congressional understanding, in tort cases, of "governmental function."

   Id. at 1155. Likewise, in *KiSKA Constr. Corp., U.S.A. v. Wash. Metro. Area Transit Auth.*, 321 F.3d 1151, 1159 (D.C. Cir. 2003), the court held that:

   > To determine whether an activity of the Washington Metropolitan Area Transit Authority is discretionary, and thus shielded by sovereign immunity, a court applies a two-part test culled from the Federal Tort Claims Act's "discretionary function" jurisprudence. First, a court asks whether any statute, regulation, or policy specifically prescribes a course of action for an employee to follow. If a course of action is so prescribed, sovereign immunity does not bar suits based on an employee's failure to follow the prescribed course of conduct. If the governing statutes or regulations leave room for the exercise of discretion, however, a court asks a second question: whether the exercise of discretion is grounded in social, economic, or political goals. If the exercise of discretion is so grounded, and hence susceptible to policy judgment, the activity is governmental, thus falling within the retention of sovereign immunity[.]

2. Hess v. Port Auth. Trans-Hudson Corp., 513 U.S. 30, 42 (1994).

enjoys immunity from liability as an agent of the member states is generally defined on a case-by-case basis, looking in part at the terms of the compact and in part at the extent to which the member states have a vested interest—particularly a financial interest—in the actions of the agency.

Administrative or regulatory compacts typically establish ongoing agencies. Some agencies are purely administrative or managerial and others purely regulatory in character. Most, however, have the hallmarks of being both administrative and regulatory in nature. Many compact agencies are empowered to make rules applicable to the member states and their citizens and/or to decide controversies that arise between member states. These agencies, in effect, regulate or administer multistate matters on behalf of the member states, even to the extent of regulating the states themselves. Thus, obligations imposed by a duly authorized interstate commission are enforceable on the states and its citizens to the extent provided in the compact.[3]

Because such agencies regulate on behalf of the states, one might presume that such agencies are "the state" for most purposes. Yet courts have not generally viewed compact-created agencies as true agents of the state. In *Hess v. Port Authority Trans-Hudson Corporation,* for example, the Supreme Court noted that bi-state agencies are typically the creation of three sovereigns, two states, and the federal government.[4] For purposes of Eleventh Amendment immunity, the Court noted:

> Suit in federal court is not an affront to the dignity of a Compact Clause entity, for the federal court, in relation to such an enterprise, is hardly the instrument of a distant, disconnected sovereign; rather, the federal court is ordained by one of the entity's founders. Nor is the integrity of the compacting States compromised when the Compact Clause entity is sued in federal court. As part of the federal plan prescribed by the Constitution, the States agreed to the power sharing, coordination, and unified action that typify Compact Clause creations. Again, the federal tribunal cannot be regarded as alien in this cooperative, trigovernmental arrangement.[5]

Thus, the Port Authority was too far removed from the states and did not owe its existence to "any one of the United States." It could not, therefore, be

---

3. *See* West Virginia *ex rel.* Dyer v. Sims, 341 U.S. 22, 30 (1951). *See also* Hinderliter v. La Plata River & Cherry Creek Ditch Co., 304 U.S. 92 (1938).
4. 513 U.S. 30, 40 (1994).
5. *Id.* at 41-42.

considered a "state" within the application of the Eleventh Amendment.[6] Moreover, the states may, as part of a compact, waive Eleventh Amendment immunity,[7] or such may be abrogated by Congress as part of granting consent.[8] The mere act of Congress granting consent does not confer upon a compact-created agency the status of a "state" for purposes of Eleventh Amendment immunity.[9] Where it is unclear whether the states intended to confer Eleventh Amendment immunity on a compact-created agency, the presumption will run against recognizing such immunity.[10] In the absence of a general immunity, some compacts contain provisions for qualified immunity and indemnification of compact officials.[11] Whether the creation of such provisions absolves a compact agency of any Eleventh Amendment immunity it would otherwise be entitled to enjoy is an open question.

However, to assert that all compact-created entities are left unshielded by the Eleventh Amendment oversimplifies the issue. One factor compelling the result in *Hess* was the complete financial independence of the Port Authority from the member states.[12] As the Eleventh Amendment was intended fundamentally to protect state treasuries from the federal courts,[13] there is no "state" interest at stake in a suit involving a compact agency for which the states have no direct financial responsibility. However, where considerations of state responsibility for compact-related action arise, compact-created agencies may be shielded by the Eleventh Amendment.[14] Thus, the structure of the compact itself may impart on such agencies the status of "state" for purposes of the

---

6. *Id.*
7. Petty v. Tennessee-Missouri Bridge Comm'n, 359 U.S. 275 (1959).
8. *Cf.*, Port Auth. Trans-Hudson Corp. v. Feeney, 495 U.S. 299 (1990).
9. Lake Country Estates, Inc. v. Tahoe Reg'l Planning Agency, 440 U.S. 391 (1979).
10. *Cf.*, Peters v. Delaware River Port Auth., 16 F.3d 1346 (3d Cir. 1994) (compact creating DRPA does not evidence any intent by the states to confer immunity on the authority).
11. *See* Interstate Compact for Adult Offender Supervision, art. VI, § D (2002).
12. *Id.* at 45 ("Conceived as a fiscally independent entity financed predominantly by private funds * * * the Authority generates its own revenues, and for decades has received no money from the States.").
13. Pennhurst State School & Hosp. v. Halderman, 465 U.S. 89 (1984) (Stevens, J., dissenting); *see also* Petty v. Tennessee-Missouri Bridge Comm'n, 359 U.S. 275, 276 n.1 (1959); Missouri v. Fiske, 290 U.S. 18, 27 (1933).
14. *Cf.*, Abdulwali v. Wash. Metro. Area Transit Auth., 315 F.3d 302 (D.C. Cir. 2003).

Eleventh Amendment.[15] In structuring a compact, the combined power of the states and Congress can waive immunity for some acts and retain immunity for others.[16] Even in instances where such agencies have the authority to initiate and defend litigation, this fact does not necessarily constitute a waiver of Eleventh Amendment immunity from suit against states or their political subdivisions in federal court.[17]

Thus, some agencies exercising state power have been permitted to invoke the Eleventh Amendment in order to protect *the state treasury* from liability that would have the same practical consequences as a judgment against the state itself.[18] This same principle would appear to apply to an administrative agency established by an interstate compact, so long as there exists "good reason to believe that the States structured the new agency to enable it to enjoy the special constitutional protection of the States themselves, and that Congress concurred in that purpose."[19] However, with respect to congressionally approved compacts, Congress has the authority to impose conditions that include the waiver of Eleventh Amendment immunity to compact commissions and agencies.[20] Antithetically, Congress can, through its consent power,

---

15. Morris v. Wash. Metro. Area Transit Auth., 781 F.2d 218, 219-20 (D.C. Cir. 1986) (states can confer Eleventh Amendment immunity upon instrumentalities of the state). *See also* Washington Metropolitan Area Transit Regulation Compact, tit. III, § 80 (1981) ("The Authority [WMATA] shall be liable for its contracts and for its torts and those of its Directors, officers, employees and agents committed in the conduct of any proprietary function, in accordance with the law of the applicable signatory (including rules on conflict of laws), but shall not be liable for any torts occurring in the performance of a governmental function.").

16. *See* Smith v. Wash. Metro. Area Transit Auth., 290 F.3d 201, 206 (4th Cir. 2002) (WMATA immunity waived in certain circumstances, *e.g.*, when engaged in proprietary functions or for certain torts).

17. *See* Fla. Dep't of Health & Rehab. Servs. v. Fla. Nursing Home Ass'n, 450 U.S. 150 (1981); *accord* Trotman v. Palisades Interstate Park Comm'n, 557 F.2d 35, 39-40 (2d Cir. 1977). *See also* Lizzi v. Alexander, 255 F.3d 128, 132 (4th Cir. 2001) ("sue and be sued" provision in Washington transit compact did not constitute blanket waiver of immunity; states clearly sought to confer immunity for certain action on transit authority).

18. *See* Edelman v. Jordan, 415 U.S. 651 (1974). *See also* Ford Motor Co. v. Dep't of Treasury of Ind., 323 U.S. 459 (1945).

19. *See* Lake Country Estates v. Tahoe Reg'l Planning Agency, 440 U.S. 391, 401 (1979).

20. *See* Petty v. Tennessee-Missouri Bridge Comm'n, 359 U.S. 275 (1959).

concur in the granting of Eleventh Amendment immunity to compact-created agencies.[21]

Of equal concern to compact agency officials are considerations related to other types of liability that may not be barred by the Eleventh Amendment. Whether compact officials enjoy immunity may turn on the activity that is the subject of the dispute. For example, compact officials may enjoy absolute immunity to the extent that their activities are akin to a legislative function.[22] By contrast, to the extent such actions can be classified as administrative or executive in nature, immunity may be significantly more circumscribed.[23] As a general proposition, officials do not enjoy absolute immunity from civil liability for their public acts. In recent years, the availability of the defense of sovereign immunity has been substantially reduced by state legislatures.

The extent to which an official may be liable for conduct resulting in injuries to others is generally governed by two types of classifications of public acts, discretionary acts or ministerial acts. A discretionary act is defined as a quasi-judicial act that requires the exercise of judgment in the development or implementation of public policy. A discretionary act is generally indicated by terms such as "may" or "can" or "discretion." Whether an act is discretionary depends on several factors: (1) the degree to which reason and judgment is required; (2) the nature of the official's duties; (3) the extent to which policy making is involved in the act; and (4) the likely policy consequences of withholding immunity.[24]

A ministerial act, also called an operational act, involves conduct over which a state official has no discretion. Officials have an affirmative duty to comply with instructions or legal mandates or to implement operational policy. Ministerial acts are generally indicated by terms such as "shall" or "must." A ministerial act is defined as an act "that involves obedience to instructions or laws instead of discretion, judgment, or skills."[25]

7.2   IMMUNITY WAIVER

In general, officials are not liable for injuries related to discretionary acts because the states have not waived their sovereign immunity in this regard.[26]

---

21. Abdulwali v. Wash. Metro. Area Transit Auth., 315 F.3d 302 (D.C. Cir. 2003).
22. Jacobson v. Tahoe Regional Planning Agency, 566 F.2d 1353 (9th Cir. 1977).
23. *Id.*
24. Heins Implement Co. v. Missouri Hwy. & Transp. Comm'n, 859 S.W.2d 681, 695 (Mo. banc. 1993).
25. BLACK'S LAW DICTIONARY 1011 (7th ed. 1999).
26. King v. Seattle, 525 P.2d 228 (Wash. 1974).

The public policy behind maintaining immunity is to foster the exercise of good judgment in areas that call for judgment, for example, policy development. Absent such immunity, officials may hesitate to assist the government in developing and implementing public policy. Many states have waived sovereign immunity for the failure to perform or the negligent performance of ministerial acts. Consequently, the failure to perform a ministerial act or the negligent performance of such an act can expose officials to liability if a person is injured as a result. Whether an act is discretionary or ministerial is a question of fact. The nature of the act, not the nature of the actor, is the determining consideration.[27]

Some compacts have specifically waived immunity for willful and wanton acts of their officials.[28] This mirrors the policy of most states, which generally exempt willful and wanton conduct from immunity to state liability coverage, deeming such conduct to lie outside the scope of employment.[29] Likewise, an official who violates federal law is generally stripped of official or representative character and may be personally liable for his or her conduct; a state cannot cloak such an officer in its sovereign immunity.[30]

7.3   NEGLIGENT SUPERVISION

Because several compacts involve crime control or oversee persons subject to state control, it is important for compact and state officials to be aware of issues related to negligent supervision. In determining whether a state official is liable for negligent supervision, a court may consider the following factors:

- Misconduct by a non-policy-making employee that is the result of training or supervision "so reckless or grossly negligent" that misconduct was "almost inevitable" or "substantially certain to result."[31]
- The existence of special custodial or other relationships created or assumed by the state in respect of particular persons. A "right/duty" relationship may arise with respect to persons in the state's custody or subject to its effective control and whom the state knows to be a specific risk of harm to themselves or others. Additionally, officials

---

27. Miree v. United States, 490 F. Supp. 768, 773 (1980).
28. *See, e.g.*, Interstate Compact for Adult Offender Supervision, art. VI, § D (2002).
29. *See, e.g.*, Hoffman v. Yack, 373 N.E.2d 486 (Ill. 1978).
30. *Ex parte* Young, 209 U.S. 123 (1908).
31. Vinson v. Campbell County Fiscal Court, 820 F.2d 194 (6th Cir. 1987).

may be liable to the extent that their conduct creates a danger from which they fail to adequately protect the public.[32]

- The foreseeability of wrongful actions by a private actor and the foreseeability of the harm those actions may create. Even in the absence of a special relationship with the victim, officials may be liable under the "state-created danger" theory of liability when that danger is foreseeable and direct.[33] The state-created danger exception to the general rule that the state is not required to protect the life, liberty, and property of its citizens against invasion by private actors is met if: (1) the harm ultimately caused was foreseeable and fairly direct; (2) the state actor acted in willful disregard for the safety of the plaintiff; (3) there existed some relationship between the state and the plaintiff; and (4) the state actors used their authority to create an opportunity that otherwise would not have existed for the third party's crime to occur.

- Negligent hiring and supervision in cases where the employer's direct negligence in hiring or retaining an incompetent employee who the employer knows, or by the exercise of reasonable care should have known, was incompetent or unfit, thereby creating an unreasonable risk of harm to others.[34] Liability may be found where supervisors have shown a deliberate indifference or disregard to the known failings of an employee.

- The obligation of officials to fulfill ministerial acts, which are not open to discretion. For example, an officer can be held liable for failing to execute the arrest of a probationer or parolee when there is no question that such an act should be done.[35]

---

32. *See* Withers v. Levine, 615 F.2d 158 (4th Cir. 1980) (prison inmates under known risk of harm from homosexual assaults by other inmates); Davis v. Zahradnick, 600 F.2d 458 (4th Cir. 1979) (inmate observed under attack by another inmate); Woodhous v. Virginia, 487 F.2d 889 (4th Cir. 1973). *Cf.*, Orpiano v. Johnson, 632 F.2d 1096, 1101-03 (4th Cir. 1980) (no right where no pervasive risk of harm and specific risk unknown); Hertog v. City of Seattle, 979 P.2d 400, 407 (Wash. 1998) (city probation officers have a duty to third persons, such as the rape victim, to control the conduct of probationers to protect them from reasonably foreseeable harm; whether officers violated their duty was subject to a factual dispute).
33. Green v. Philadelphia, 92 Fed. Appx. 873 (3d Cir. 2004).
34. Wise v. Complete Staffing Servs., Inc., 56 S.W.3d 900, 902 (Tex. App. 2001).
35. Taylor v. Garwood, 98 F. Supp. 2d 672, 680 (E.D. Pa. 2000).

7.4 42 U.S.C. SECTION 1983 LIABILITY

A violation of an individual's civil rights committed by a state official acting under color of state law creates a state and federal right of action for damages under 42 U.S.C. Section 1983. That statute provides:

> Every person who, under color of any statute, ordinance, regulation, custom, or usage, of any State or Territory or the District of Columbia, subjects, or causes to be subjected, any citizen of the United States or other person within the jurisdiction thereof to the deprivation of any rights, privileges, or immunities secured by the Constitution and laws, shall be liable to the party injured in an action at law, suit in equity, or other proper proceeding for redress, except that in any action brought against a judicial officer for an act or omission taken in such officer's judicial capacity, injunctive relief shall not be granted unless a declaratory decree was violated or declaratory relief was unavailable[.][36]

In general, conduct by persons acting under color of state law that is wrongful under 42 U.S.C. Section 1983 or 42 U.S.C. Section 1985(3) cannot be immunized by state law.[37] A construction of the federal statute that permitted a state immunity defense to have controlling effect would transmute a basic guarantee into an illusory promise; and the Supremacy Clause of the Constitution insures that the proper construction may be enforced.[38] The immunity claims raise questions of federal law.[39] Generally, 42 U.S.C. Section 1983 liability will not be imposed where the consequences of state action are too remote to be classified as state action. Thus, the relatives of a person murdered by a paroled offender do not have a right of action against the state because the actions of the offender are too remote, the parole board owed no greater consideration to the victim than to any other member of the public, and the offender was not acting as an agent of the state for purposes of federal civil rights liability.[40]

---

36. 42 U.S.C. § 1983 (2005).
37. *Id. See also* 42 U.S.C. § 1985 (2003).
38. *See* McLaughlin v. Tilendis, 398 F.2d 287, 290 (7th Cir. 1968).
39. Hampton v. Chicago, 484 F.2d 602, 607 (7th Cir. 1973).
40. *See* Martinez v. California, 444 U.S. 277, 284 (1980) (conduct of persons acting under color of state law, which conduct is wrongful under 42 U.S.C. § 1983, cannot be immunized by state law). *See also* Howlett v. Rose, 496 U.S. 356, 370-71 (1990) (conduct wrongful under 42 U.S.C. § 1983 cannot be immunized by state law even though the federal cause of action is being asserted in state court).

In at least one case involving an interstate compact, a court has held that the Interstate Compact on Probation and Parole (ICPP) did not create a federally enforceable right under 42 U.S.C. Section 1983 for those subject to its provisions (parolees and probationers). In *Orville Lines v. Wargo*, the court held that nothing short of a right unambiguously conferred by Congress would support a cause of action by an out-of-state parolee challenging Pennsylvania's sex offender registration requirements.[41] The court found that the ICPP manifested no intent on the part of Congress to confer a new individual right on parolees. The successor to the ICPP, the Interstate Compact for Adult Offender Supervision, likewise manifests no intent by Congress to create a new individual right for adult offenders.

7.5 CHOICE OF LAWS ISSUES

Conflict of laws problems generally are resolved with reference to the concept of domicile and vested rights. Under the Full Faith and Credit Clause of the U.S. Constitution, a number of principles have been developed for determining what state law governs in particular types of cases. For example, a state is free to apply its own scheme of worker's compensation if it has "sufficient contact" with a case to satisfy due process. Being in the place of injury has been found to be sufficient contact.[42] Issues relating to the rights of parties in a case involving a fraternal benefit society must be governed by the law of the state that chartered the society.[43] The issue of statutory assessment of shareholders in a corporation for corporate debts up to the par value of stock is governed by the law of the state of incorporation.[44] These concepts have little or no application with respect to disputes arising under an interstate compact as to the obligations of the party states. These disputes must clearly be resolved under federal law.[45]

As with other types of contracts, a choice of law provision in a compact is binding upon the parties, and one must carefully review the compact in question to make an initial determination as to such a provision. In an ordinary contract, if the forum provided is federal, the court would ordinarily be required to apply the choice of law rules of the state in which it sits to determine

41. Orville Lines v. Wargo, 271 F. Supp. 2d 649 (W.D. Pa. 2003).
42. *See* Carroll v. Lanza, 349 U.S. 408 (1955).
43. *See* Order of United Commercial Travelers v. Wolfe, 331 U.S. 586 (1947).
44. *See* Converse v. Hamilton, 224 U.S. 243 (1912).
45. *See* Carchman v. Nash, 473 U.S. 716 (1985); Cuyler v. Adams, 449 U.S. 443 (1981).

which state laws should be used to decide the dispute.[46] In construing a compact, a court may look at the law of the member states for a determination of the applicable rules of contract construction, such as those pertaining to the admissibility of extrinsic evidence to determine the intent of the parties.[47]

7.6 STANDING

It appears that standing to sue under an interstate compact is subject to the same considerations applicable to challenges of other statutes. In *Bootery Inc. v. Washington Metropolitan Area Transit Authority,* the court held, "Given the federal government's presence on the Commission and its role in the creation of the Compact, we believe that plaintiffs' standing to sue in this case is governed by the same standards as are plaintiffs who challenge action under any federal statute."[48]

Utilizing these standards, the determination of whether parties other than the party states have standing to sue under a compact will turn on the extent to which the provisions of the compact and its rules, if any, impinge directly upon the interests of other persons or entities. To establish the requisite basis for standing, the putative plaintiffs must demonstrate that they would suffer injury in fact from the action of the compact agency and that their interests are arguably within the zone of interests to be protected or regulated by the statute sued upon. "To hold that the Compact is an agreement between the political signatories imputing only to those signatories standing to challenge actions pursuant to it would be unduly narrow in view of the direct impact on plaintiffs and other taxpayers."[49]

---

46. *See* Klaxon v. Stentor Elec., 313 U.S. 487 (1941); Griffen v. McCoach, 313 U.S. 498 (1941); Erie R.R. v. Tompkins, 304 U.S. 64 (1933).

47. *See* Oklahoma v. New Mexico, 501 U.S. 221, 247 (1991) (construing the provisions of the Canadian River Compact).

48. Bootery Inc. v. Wash. Metro. Area Transit Auth., 326 F. Supp. 794, 798-99 (D. D.C. 1971). *See also* Ass'n of Data Processing Service Orgs., Inc. v. Camp, 397 U.S. 150 (1970); Barlow v. Collins, 397 U.S. 159 (1970); Scanwell Labs., Inc. v. Thomas, 424 F.2d 859 (D.C. Cir. 1970); Ballerina Pen Co. v. Kunzig, 433 F.2d 1204 (D.C. Cir. 1970).

49. Borough of Morrisville v. Delaware River Basin Comm'n, 399 F. Supp. 469, 479 n.3 (E.D. Pa. 1975).

Chapter 8

PRESENT TRENDS IN THE USE
OF INTERSTATE COMPACTS

In some respects, interstate compacts are fairly simple tools requiring only a few basic elements. Reduced to their legal essence as binding, enforceable contracts between party states, even the earliest such agreements bear a close resemblance to those of more recent origin. But over the years, the use of interstate compacts has grown and evolved in some notable ways. Though not uncommon even during the earliest days of the nation's history, compacts have been used much more frequently during the last century and especially during the last 60 years. The scope and purposes of such agreements have also changed to meet the needs of states facing increasingly broad and relatively complex policy issues. This chapter examines some of the recent trends reflected in that evolution and looks ahead at what the future might hold as well.

8.1 FREQUENCY AND STRUCTURAL TRENDS

Though the earliest interstate compacts predated the ratification of the U.S. Constitution, widespread use of the compact mechanism to address concerns of regional and even national scope is a fairly recent phenomenon. Through roughly the first 140 years of the nation's existence, fewer than 40 interstate compacts were enacted, most of which were bi-state agreements settling boundary disputes between the parties. Only in the 1920s did the frequency of compact usage begin to increase, with approximately 25 new agreements being enacted during the next 20 years.[1] But that was just a prelude to the boom that followed during the next three decades, when more than 100 new compacts were enacted.[2] Since then, the growth in numbers has slowed somewhat,[3] but today there are more than 200 interstate compacts on the books, and interest in the pursuit of new agreements remains strong.

That this is true is due largely to the flexibility of the compact mechanism, as evidenced by several structural trends that have characterized the period of compact expansion. For example, compacts have proven to be just as effective in addressing issues of broad geographic scope as they always were in resolving disputes between two neighboring states. To be sure, bi-state agreements, like the boundary compacts of old, are still being enacted today, and they continued to account for the lion's share of all interstate compacts until well into the twentieth century.[4] More recently, however, most new compacts have been designed for regional or national participation, a trend that seems likely to continue. To date, only about 10 percent of all interstate compacts count more than half of the states among their members, and only a handful of those that are open to all comers have actually attracted full 50-state participation.[5] Others have come close, however, and some are still actively recruiting new members.

Even more noteworthy is the trend toward greater reliance upon interstate agencies for the administration of compacts. Prior to the historic enactment of the New York–New Jersey Port Authority Compact of 1921, compacts were routinely administered by existing agencies and officials

---

1. Patricia S. Florestano, Interstate Compacts: The Invisible Area of Interstate Relations 23 (September 1993) (unpublished manuscript on file with the Council of State Governments), *available at* http://www.csg.org/NR/rdonlyres/eosjjs6qbc2otwxfv5gxcqkrpiaqqimpyyztfobfklggtcknrkpywabo6yavq2k3pcitqgxg5m7xuujn26zd4blohjb/Interstate+Compacts+-+The+Invisible+Area+of+Interstate+Relations+-+Florestano.pdf#search='Patricia%20S.%20Florestano'.
2. *Id.* at 11.
3. *Id.* at 12-17.
4. *See, e.g.*, the Virginia-North Carolina Interstate High-Speed Rail Compact (2004). One study concluded that by 1970, regional and national compacts combined accounted for 55 percent of all interstate compacts. Florestano, *supra* note 1, at 11.
5. Ann O'M. Bowman, *Trends and Issues in Interstate Cooperation*, THE BOOK OF THE STATES—2004, 36 (The Council of State Governments 2004).

within the party states. The Port Authority agreement was the first to estab-lish an interstate agency for this purpose, and use of the agency model quickly caught on in the decades that followed, especially as states began jointly tackling issues of greater complexity and broader geographic scope. During the 50 years that followed the establishment of the Port Authority of New York and New Jersey, the share of all compacts that established interstate agencies of some kind grew to almost half,[6] and new joint com-missions have been established by a majority of the compacts enacted since 1970. This trend, too, seems likely to continue as the states grow more accustomed to the administration of compacts by interstate agencies and more familiar with the advantages of this approach.

Though many interstate compact agencies perform important adminis-trative and oversight functions, others are purely advisory in nature, and until recent decades, only a few played significant regulatory roles. That began to change with the advent of such diverse agreements as the Delaware River Basin Compact, the Washington Metropolitan Area Transit Regulation Com-pact, the Tahoe Regional Planning Compact, and, more recently, the Inter-state Compact for Adult Offender Supervision. The rise of the interstate administrative compact commission may, in fact, be the most significant of the various structural trends evident in the recent evolution of the compact mechanism. One reason is the critical ability it gives states to reap the ben-efits of uniform regulatory systems governing far-reaching or high-volume interstate activities without sacrificing state sovereignty to the federal gov-ernment. Another is the flexibility that such commissions provide states to adjust to changing circumstances without the need to alter their fundamental agreements. Still another is the promise that this approach holds as an effec-tive means for developing new cooperative solutions to the increasingly com-plex regulatory challenges facing twenty-first-century states. For all of these reasons, the recent growth in the number of interstate compacts authorizing the establishment of interstate regulatory entities is likely a portent of things to come.

8.2   SUBSTANTIVE TRENDS

Another byproduct of the rapid growth in the number of interstate com-pacts that began about 80 years ago was a significant expansion in the breadth of substantive areas covered by such agreements. The earliest compacts dealt primarily with boundary disputes, and, to a lesser extent, with issues related to the use and management of water resources. Today, interstate compacts

---

6. Patricia S. Florestano, *supra* note 1, at 12.

govern a wide array of issue areas ranging from health, education, taxation, and transportation to corrections, child welfare, energy, and the environment, to name just a few.[7]

This expansion has been uneven over time, with some areas attracting far more attention than others at various points along the way. Compacts addressing environmental issues, for example, ballooned in number during the 1960s and 1970s, owing perhaps to a nationwide surge of environmental activism during those decades. But increasing resort during that period to the compact mechanism as a potentially useful tool in addressing such specific concerns as hazardous waste management, mining, and water quality may also have been due to a growing recognition of the success of several earlier compacts in dealing with resource protection issues of an inherently multistate nature.[8] Similarly, the growing pains and concerns associated with urban expansion and other forms of development, especially in border areas, have— beginning with the New York–New Jersey Port Authority Compact of 1921— given rise to various regional planning and development compacts, although these have sometimes come decades apart.[9]

Criminal justice, civil defense, and higher education were the subjects of notable interstate compacts enacted in the 1930s, 1940s and 1950s. By contrast, the 1970s and 1980s saw flurries of activity in areas such as transportation, river waters, and natural resource protection. Still more recently, compact initiatives have focused on issues ranging from emergency management and corrections to economic development and licensure.[10] The substantive breadth of these initiatives clearly demonstrates that the interstate compact mechanism may be readily adapted for use in almost any field. The possibilities are truly limitless, and as recent developments suggest, the range of subjects covered by such agreements is likely to continue growing in the years to come.

---

7. *See* chapter 9 for an extensive survey of the current uses of interstate compacts.
8. *See, e.g.*, the Atlantic States Marine Fisheries Compact (1942); Ohio River Valley Water Sanitation Compact (1940).
9. *See, e.g.*, Bi-State Development Agency Compact (1959); Tahoe Regional Planning Compact (1980).
10. *See, e.g.*, Emergency Management Assistance Compact (1996); Interstate Compact for Adult Offender Supervision (2002); Chickasaw Trail Economic Development Compact (1997); Interstate Compact of Participants in Horse Racing with Pari-Mutuel Wagering (2001).

8.3   RECENT DEVELOPMENTS; FUTURE COMPACT ACTIVITY

The future of compact making will undoubtedly be shaped in part by the ever-shifting policy priorities of the states and the federal government. New substantive fields will certainly be explored, and others will be expanded. But if several recent initiatives are any indication, the future may also include an occasional return to the past, as the states work to revise or replace existing agreements that no longer adequately meet contemporary challenges.

8.3.1   Amendments and Rewrites

During the last 10 years or so, the administrators of several long-standing interstate compacts and representatives of key stakeholder groups affected by them have undertaken various efforts to update and strengthen those agreements. A case in point related to the Interstate Compact for the Supervision of Parolees and Probationers, which for more than 60 years provided the framework governing the interstate transfer of supervisory authority for criminal offenders who legally move between states. Despite its unquestioned utility spanning a period of decades, the compact gradually began showing its age and eventually came under scrutiny as the mobility of the offender population began to rise and states started restructuring their parole and probation systems. An earlier effort to strengthen the compact, primarily by amending its rules, was followed in the late 1990s by a more fundamental and comprehensive effort to replace it with a wholly new agreement. That effort proved successful when the new Interstate Compact for Adult Offender Supervision (ICAOS) became effective in 2002.

Even before the new ICAOS took effect, a companion effort to replace the Interstate Compact on Juveniles (ICJ) with a new agreement modeled closely on the adult compact was launched. A key difference between the two original agreements was that unlike the old parole and probation compact, the ICJ had actually been amended prior to the rewrite attempt. However, three distinct amendments[11] had variously been adopted by several combinations of parties to the original agreement, resulting in an unworkable patchwork of provisions that were unevenly binding across the country.[12] Thus,

---

11. The amendments included additional provisions governing the return of runaways, the rendition of juveniles charged with being delinquent, and out-of-state confinement.

12. *See* Policy and Procedure Manual § 1 (Association of Juvenile Compact Administrators 2005), *available at* http://www.acja.us/manual/section1/ SignatoryMatrixRepage.pdf.

there was arguably an even greater need to replace the ICJ with a new, more uniform agreement. The proposed successor to the original compact was submitted to the states for legislative approval beginning in 2003 and is rapidly attracting new parties.

Both of these rewrite efforts were facilitated by The Council of State Governments (CSG) at the request of, and in cooperation with, key stakeholders. These included the associations of compact administrators responsible for the implementation and oversight of the original compacts.[13] Federal funding in support of the initiatives was provided by the National Institute of Corrections (NIC) and the Office of Juvenile Justice and Delinquency Prevention (OJJDP) under separate cooperative agreements with CSG.

Another 50-state compact of more recent origin is also currently undergoing a potentially extensive overhaul. Originally enacted in 1960, the Interstate Compact on the Placement of Children (ICPC) governs the movement and protection of children who are transferred between states for purposes of adoption or foster care. A network of participating state representatives, the Association of Administrators of the Interstate Compact on the Placement of Children (AAICPC), was established in 1974 and is supported in its efforts by the American Public Human Services Association (APHSA).

In its role as secretariat to the compact, APHSA responded to growing concerns about the utility and enforceability of the original agreement by establishing, in 2003, an ICPC Task Force to explore possible ways of strengthening the existing compact. By the spring of 2004, the task force had concluded that while several procedural improvements could be implemented with relative ease, the compact itself would need to be amended in order to achieve the full extent of the desired reforms.[14] APHSA subsequently endorsed the task force's proposal and committed to facilitating the efforts of an ICPC Drafting and Development Team to revise, or even rewrite, the existing compact. The team was to enlist the help of The Council of State Governments while inviting input and participation from a wide variety of key stakeholder groups. It met for the first time in July 2004, and the anticipated development work was expected to continue through the end of the year.[15]

---

13. The Parole and Probation Compact Administrators Association (PPCAA) and the Association of Juvenile Compact Administrators (AJCA), respectively.
14. Interstate Compact for the Placement of Children Task Force Report, American Public Human Services Association (March 2004), *available at* http://www.aphsa.org/Policy/Doc/ICPC%20Task%20Force%20Report.pdf.
15. Interstate Compact for the Placement of Children Rewrite Charter—Development and Drafting Team, American Public Human Services Association (June

The sense of urgency behind the ICPC rewrite initiative was heightened by the introduction during the 108th Congress of federal legislation that would effectively usurp the ICPC's governance of interstate placements.[16] Though intended to streamline the typically lengthy process, the proposed legislation would federalize certain elements of the ICPC framework by mandating that the states comply with various requirements that are inconsistent with the compact's terms. In hopes of forestalling such intervention while preserving to the states the flexibility and regulatory prerogatives they enjoy under the existing compact, APHSA and its allies have focused on the proposed rewrite of the ICPC as the best means of introducing the kinds of procedural improvements that all parties seem to agree are in the best interests of any affected children. In September 2004, CSG adopted an interim policy statement formally endorsing the collaborative effort to revise the ICPC and urging Congress both to consent to the compact and to include in any federal legislation a sunset provision that would take effect once a revised compact is enacted by the states.[17]

Two other existing compacts designed for national participation, the Driver License Compact and the Nonresident Violator Compact, are also currently under review. Eventually, they are likely to be replaced by a new agreement that will draw from both while establishing a more streamlined system for the interstate exchange of driver and conviction information. Presumably, the new compact will also include enhanced identification security requirements to protect the integrity of the driver license system. The effort is being facilitated by the American Association of Motor Vehicle Administrators (AAMVA), which provides secretariat services to the administrators of the two existing compacts. In October 2004, a preliminary draft of the proposed new Driver License Agreement (DLA) was unveiled to the administrators for review and comment. Following the incorporation of several proposed revisions, a final draft of the new agreement was scheduled to be released in January 2005.

Recent evidence suggests that efforts such as these may become more common in the years ahead as lawmakers and interested stakeholder groups work to replace obsolete compacts and to breathe new life into those agreements that

---

2004), *available at* http://www.aphsa.org/Policy/Doc/ICPC%20Rewrite %20Charter—Development%20and%20Drafting%20Team.pdf.

16. Safe and Timely Interstate Placement of Foster Children Act of 2004, H.R. 4504, 108th Cong. (2004); Orderly and Timely Interstate Placement of Foster Children Act of 2004, S.2779,108th Cong. (2004).

17. Interim Policy Resolution on the Interstate Compact on the Placement of Children (The Council of State Governments, Sept. 29, 2004).

may simply be in need of a "tune-up." According to a 2004 survey of compact administrators conducted by The Council of State Governments, more than 46 percent of respondents saw a need for their compacts to be revised.[18]

8.3.2 Expanded Participation; New Compacts

Even without taking into account any new agreements that may be on the horizon, the growing prevalence of compacts designed for regional and national participation virtually ensures that individual states will continue to consider compact-related legislation in the coming years. Numerous compacts of fairly recent origin, though already effective as between their parties, continue to invite participation from other eligible states, and agreements like the Emergency Management Assistance Compact and the National Crime Prevention and Privacy Compact are likely to continue expanding their memberships. So too, occasionally, will older agreements like the Wildlife Violator Compact and the Interstate Agreement on Qualifications of Education Personnel, both of which added new parties in 2004.[19] Various other proposals, each thus far enacted by a single state, currently remain effective only as offers awaiting acceptance by one or more additional parties before they, too, will become binding as interstate compacts.[20]

In the immediate future, however, even greater attention will likely be paid to several new or recently proposed agreements, such as the Interstate Insurance Product Regulation Compact (IIPRC). Developed under the auspices of the National Association of Insurance Commissioners (NAIC), the IIPRC seeks to modernize the existing state-based insurance regulatory system by establishing a centralized and more efficient certification process that should make it easier for insurers to introduce new products into the national marketplace.[21] The proposal grew out of a widely recognized need on the part of state regulators to streamline the existing process, but it was also motivated by the threat of additional federal intervention into a field that has traditionally been within the province of the states.

---

18. John J. Mountjoy, *National Center for Interstate Compacts: A New Initiative*, 77(4) SPECTRUM: THE JOURNAL OF STATE GOVERNMENT 9 (The Council of State Governments, Fall 2004).
19. Michigan and Hawaii, respectively.
20. Ann O'M. Bowman, *Trends and Issues in Interstate Cooperation*, THE BOOK OF THE STATES—2004, 35 (The Council of State Governments, 2004).
21. Telephone interview with Andrew Beal, General Counsel for the National Association of Insurance Commissioners (Aug. 17, 2004).

The development work began in earnest in 2002 after earlier NAIC efforts to promote greater regulatory efficiency through voluntary means proved unsuccessful. An Interstate Compact Working Group was established in March of that year, and a preliminary draft of the IIPRC was released for review and comment in December. Several minor changes were subsequently incorporated into a final proposal, which was approved by the NAIC the following summer. Endorsements for the initiative were then sought and obtained from other organizations, including the National Conference of State Legislatures and the National Conference of Insurance Legislators. Formal legislative consideration and a series of "roll-out meetings" designed to educate stakeholders about the proposed compact soon followed, and by the fall of 2004, nine states had enacted the IIPRC.[22] The new agreement will become fully effective once adopted by 26 states, or by a lesser number that collectively accounts for at least 40 percent of the premium volume for life insurance, annuity, disability income, and long-term care insurance products.[23]

Another new compact initiative was launched recently by the Council of Great Lakes Governors (CGLG), which is working to ensure the protection and conservation of water resources in the Great Lakes Basin. As part of its commitment to improve the region's water management system in accordance with principles set forth in the 1985 Great Lakes Charter and the Charter Annex of 2001 (both of which were voluntary, good-faith agreements signed by the governors and premiers of the Great Lakes states and provinces), the CGLG established a Water Management Working Group charged with developing an appropriate annex implementation strategy. Three years later, the Working Group unveiled a comprehensive proposal that called, in part, for the adoption of a new interstate compact between and among the eight Great Lakes states. The proposed Great Lakes Basin Water Resources Compact was intitially released for public comment in July 2004.[24] A revised draft was later approved by the region's governors in December 2005 and has been submitted to the states for formal adoption.

---

22. *Id.*
23. Interstate Insurance Product Regulation Compact, art. XIII (proposed), *available at* http://www.naic.org/compact/compact_draft.htm. The nine states that had adopted the compact by the fall of 2004 together accounted for just 8% of the specified premium volume. Telephone interview with Andrew Beal, General Counsel for the National Association of Insurance Commissioners (Aug. 17, 2004). By the summer of 2005, 15 states had adopted the compact.
24. Telephone interview with Peter R. Johnson, Senior Program Manager with the Council of Great Lakes Governors (Nov. 12, 2004).

A proposed Compact for Education Research and Development (CERD) is also likely to be taken up by the states in the near future. Developed only recently by the Strategic Education Research Partnership (SERP), a non-profit organization established under the auspices of the National Academies, the CERD is intended to foster improved teaching and learning in the nation's schools through a sustained program of research and development.[25] Notably, and unlike most other compacts, the CERD expressly permits an interested party to join the agreement by means of an executive order signed by the governor, provided that legislative enactment of the compact language follows within two years.[26] Through the fall of 2004, the proposal had yet to attract its first participating member, but SERP was optimistic that the four states required to render the agreement effective[27] would soon come on board.[28]

8.3.3 Continued Experimentation

As compact usage continues to evolve and new agreements are developed, states are likely to continue experimenting with new or relatively uncommon arrangements. One area that seems ripe for expansion relates to federal participation in interstate compacts. Though the first agreement permitting the federal government to participate directly as a party is now more than 40 years old (and was predated by at least one compact that provided for federal participation on an interstate commission[29]), the state-federal compact model that debuted upon enactment of the Delaware River Basin Compact has been used only sparingly. Perhaps this is because direct federal participation arguably runs counter to the notion that compacts are advantageous precisely because they allow states to avoid federal intervention. Nevertheless, the state-federal model was later replicated in such agreements as the Susquehanna River Basin Compact, the Agreement on Detainers and, more recently, the National Crime Prevention and Privacy Compact. As the national spotlight and shifting circumstances occasionally conspire to focus increased federal attention on such traditional areas of state preeminence as education and insurance, the frequency of instances in which direct federal participation in interstate compacts might be desirable (for practical and political reasons) may well increase. If so, the compact mechanism may serve as a useful tool for establishing new state-federal partnerships.

25. Compact for Education Research and Development, art. I (proposed).
26. *See id.* at art. VIII, § C.
27. *See id.* at art. VIII, § B.
28. Telephone interview with Suzanne Donovan, SERP Project Director (Nov. 16, 2004).
29. *See* Ohio River Valley Water Sanitation Compact (1940).

In any event, whether through direct participation, compelling incentives or threatened intervention, the federal government is likely to remain an influential player in the development of future compacts. Sometimes federal assistance of state-led efforts to forge new interstate agreements can be invaluable, as it was when the National Institute of Corrections provided critical funding and technical support during the development of the Interstate Compact for Adult Offender Supervision.

Another area in which interstate compacts are likely to find new uses is the international arena. Despite the obvious limitations of the mechanism with respect to cross-border enforcement, a few compacts already permit the good-faith participation of international parties, usually Canadian provinces.[30] As states increasingly find it useful to cooperate with their international neighbors in addressing issues of mutual concern, similar agreements are likely to emerge, although their precise forms may vary.

A recent example of such efforts was provided by the International Emergency Management Assistance Compact (a regional derivative of the Emergency Management Assistance Compact designed for nationwide participation in the United States).[31] The agreement grew out of a commitment made by members of the New England Governors and Eastern Canadian Premiers to cooperate in providing cross-border emergency assistance pursuant to the terms of model legislation that each jurisdiction would adopt. As between the participating states, the agreement constituted a binding interstate compact, but since the resulting contractual obligation was not subject to international enforcement, the parties employed another mechanism to cement the understanding between the states and participating provinces. The instrument they used for this purpose was an international memorandum of understanding, which the governors and premiers agreed to sign after their respective states and provinces first enacted enabling legislation containing the substantive terms of the agreement. Accordingly, the International Emergency Management Assistance Memorandum of Understanding (IEMAMOU) was duly executed by the governors and premiers of Maine, New Hampshire, Nova Scotia, and Prince Edward Island in July 2000, and by most of their regional counterparts during the two years that followed.[32]

---

30. *See, e.g.*, Northeastern Forest Fire Protection Compact (1952); Great Lakes Forest Fire Compact (1952).
31. WILLIAM K. VOIT, INTERSTATE COMPACTS AND AGENCIES—2003, 106 (The Council of State Governments 2003).
32. *Id.*

Similarly, the two-part proposal recommended recently by the Council of Great Lakes Governors for the implementation of the Great Lakes Charter Annex of 2001 calls for the adoption of a good-faith international agreement among the 10 Great Lakes states and provinces[33] as well as the enactment of a binding interstate compact between the eight Great Lakes states.[34] In this instance too, the proposed ratification of an international agreement in conjunction with the adoption of an interstate compact is both a concession to the practical limits of the compact mechanism and a reflection of the parties' desire to achieve by other means that which cannot be guaranteed by a contract enforceable only against states.

8.3.4 New Fields; Future Compacts

The expansion into new substantive fields that characterized the evolution of compact usage in the last 60 years is likely to continue well into the future. The ever-changing relationship between the states and the federal government has, in recent years, resulted in an increase of state authority in some areas, even as Congress has intervened in others. Not surprisingly, new challenges requiring more effective interstate cooperation have also emerged, some of which will inevitably be addressed through interstate compacts. Among these are several issues that have captured the limelight in the wake of recent world and national events.

For example, the post-9/11 concerns about homeland security and emergency preparedness go well beyond the sudden impetus that propelled the Emergency Management Assistance Compact to enactment in all but one of the states that had not already signed on. Left unaddressed were several related concerns, including the need for improved bioterrorism preparedness, that seem to demand the sort of mutual commitments that interstate compacts are well suited to provide.

Likewise, growing concerns in recent years about the reliability and security of the nation's electric power grid might best be addressed through interstate administrative compacts of regional or national scope. Such agreements could facilitate the cooperative siting and maintenance of transmission lines, while helping to ensure access to a reliable and uninterrupted supply of electricity.

---

33. Great Lakes Basin Sustainable Water Resources Agreement (proposed).
34. Great Lakes Basin Water Resources Compact (proposed). *See also* chapter 8, § 8.3.2.

If legislation introduced in the 108th Congress is enacted,[35] the states may soon receive express consent to begin formulating new compacts in these and other areas ranging from health care and insurance to education and transportation. The insurance field in particular is likely to see increased activity, given both the recent introduction of the Interstate Insurance Product Regulation Compact and the impact of federal incursions into regulatory territory that was long controlled almost exclusively by the states. Other areas that may be ripe for new interstate compact activities include prescription drug purchasing, election administration, utility regulation, licensure, and the taxation of interstate sales. With respect to the latter, for instance, a cooperative interstate effort to create a simplified sale and use tax system (in hopes of encouraging Congress to permit the states to collect sales taxes from out-of-state vendors) is currently being facilitated by the National Conference of State Legislatures. The centerpiece of the Streamlined Sales Tax Project is a voluntary interstate accord called the Streamlined Sales and Use Tax Agreement, which specifies uniform standards that participating states are encouraged to incorporate into their own tax codes. Although almost half of all states had, by the middle of 2004, indicated their intent to reform their tax structures in accordance with the agreement,[36] their levels of compliance with the voluntary standards varied, and it remained to be seen whether the expressed objective of the project would be achieved. In the event that more rigorous adherence to uniform interstate standards should prove necessary to protect the integrity of the state sales tax system, one or more interstate compacts may be needed to ensure the desired level of compliance.

As for the field of licensure, the potential for new compacts in this area is suggested by the recent success of at least two initiatives. The Interstate Compact on Licensure of Participants in Horse Racing with Pari-Mutuel Wagering was introduced in 2000 and quickly won passage in 10 states, including most of the major racing jurisdictions. Similarly, the Nurse Licensure Compact, which provides for the mutual interstate recognition of registered nurses, licensed practical nurses, and vocational nurses, was developed by the National Council of State Boards of Nursing (NCSBN) in 1998 and has been adopted by 20 states. On the heels of this success, the NCSBN developed in

---

35. *See, e.g.,* Regional Comprehensive Emergency Preparedness, Response, and Coordination Act of 2003, H.R. 3274, 108th Cong. (2003), and Electric Reliability Security Act of 2003, S.1754, 108th Cong. (2003).
36. National Conference of State Legislatures, Report on the Streamlined Sales Tax Implementing States and Its Conforming States Committee (2004), *available at* www.ncsl.org.

2002 a companion agreement, the Advanced Practice Registered Nurses Compact. The new agreement is open to participation by any state that has adopted the original Nurse Licensure Compact, and in the spring of 2004, Utah became its first member.[37] These efforts could easily serve as models for future licensing compacts governing the building trades, select professional fields and other regulated activities.

---

37. *See* information on the Nurse Licensure Compact, *available at* www.ncsbn.org.

Chapter 9

SURVEY OF THE CURRENT USES OF ADMINISTRATIVE COMPACTS

Beginning in the twentieth century, the states and federal government began using interstate compacts to create a wide variety of multilateral administrative schemes, controlling everything from the use of water, to interstate economic development, to harbor management, to crime control, and child welfare.[1] In many instances, the states acted on their own accord in constructing these arrangements. In more limited instances, their construction resulted after strong encouragement from Congress.[2] Today Congress is using its power to either overtly encourage states to adopt compacts, or prompt their adoption more subtly by giving advanced consent to agreements that address concerns with the security of the nation's electric grid, passenger rail service in the northeast corridor, traffic congestion, and public health.[3] The U.S. Supreme Court at times has encouraged states to use the legislatively empowered compact process to resolve differences rather than resort to the adversarial judicial process, which seemed to have a more limited opportunity for success. As the Supreme Court once noted:

> The reason for judicial caution in adjudicating the relative rights of the States in such cases is that, while we have jurisdiction of such disputes, they involve the interests of quasi-sovereigns, present complicated and delicate questions, and, due to the possibility of future change of conditions, necessitate expert administration rather than judicial imposition of a hard and fast rule. Such controversies may appropriately be composed by negotiation and agreement, pursuant to the compact clause of the federal constitution."[4]

---

1. In this publication, the term "administrative compact" is used broadly to embrace not only purely administrative agreements but also regulatory and management agreements.
2. *See, e.g.,* 42 U.S.C. § 21021 (d)(2) (2004) (encouraging low-level radioactive disposal compacts). *See also* 42 U.S.C. § 673a (2004) (encouraging Secretary of Health and Human Services to assist states in developing compacts to protect the interests of adopted children).
3. *See, e.g.,* Electric Reliability Security Act of 2003, S.1754, 108th Cong. §§ 103, 216 (1st Sess. 2003); Passenger Rail Investment Reform Act, H.R. 3211, 108th Cong. § 103 (1st Sess. 2003); Metropolitan Washington Regional Transportation Act, H.R. 2882, 108th Cong. § 5 (1st Sess. 2003); States' Right to Innovate in Health Care Act of 2003, H.R. 2979, 108th Cong. § 2004 (1st Sess. 2003).
4. Colorado v. Kansas, 320 U.S. 383, 392 (1943).

The need to resolve interstate controversies through negotiation and agreement is as real now as in years past and, if anything, is growing with the development of regionalization and economic integration in the United States.

Today most administrative compacts establish ongoing agencies vested, in some cases, with broad and expansive powers. The need for such ongoing agencies is propelled by the number and complexity of modern interstate controversies and the need to provide more dynamic frameworks adjustable to meet future changes. In short, negotiation and agreement between the states may often lead to a more effective solution than litigation precisely because it provides a more flexible solution than narrowly focused judicial resolutions. For example, in 1921 New York and New Jersey created the Port Authority to administer common harbor interests between the two states and to resolve a dispute that had long festered between the two states. The compact giving rise to the Port Authority was the first of its kind and represents the beginning of administrative compacts that create ongoing agencies. Today the Port Authority of New York–New Jersey is a semiautonomous commission that regulates transportation and economic development in a bi-state area of some 1,500 square miles with a population well in excess of 10 million people. The Port Authority's powers extend to the management of ports, bridges, tunnels, airports, surface transportation systems, and buildings. It has its own 1,300-member police force. The budget of the Port Authority in FY 2004 will exceed $4.5 billion (larger than some state budgets), and its operations extend to offices in England, Taiwan, China, Korea, and Japan. The Port Authority has construed its mandate to provide itself with significant autonomy, including determining its internal structure and independently financing its operations with bonds issues in its own name and user fees it collects on facilities under its jurisdiction.

Historically, the Port Authority compact is important for three reasons. First, today the governance structure of many administrative compacts mirror the permanent, multistate commission model developed for the Port Authority some 80 years ago. The Port Authority is the first permanent compact-created agency and the longest continuing interstate compact commission in operation. This model is now generally accepted as a necessity of the administrative compact, and it has resulted in the creation of other powerful agencies, such as the Tahoe Regional Planning Agency and the Washington Metropolitan Area Transit Authority. Second, the Port Authority Compact first demonstrated that ongoing regional issues can be effectively managed through interstate cooperation and multilateral management. Today, multilateral management by compact-created agencies occurs on a significant scale in some the nation's most densely populated regions and even on a national level. Absent creating and empowering entities such as the Port Authority, the Interstate Commission on Adult

Offender Supervision, the Columbia River Gorge Commission, the Ohio River Valley Sanitation Commission, and other like entities, states cannot retain practical and policy control over issues that supersede their individual boundaries. In place of creating such agencies, states invite and may even compel federal intervention. Finally, the Port Authority Compact was the first to use the device to manage multiple subjects. Prior to the establishment of the Port Authority, compacts were singularly focused on resolving single issues, such as boundaries, not managing ongoing regional or national problems. Following the establishment of the Port Authority, states—particularly in the 1950s and 1960s—began creating multisubject agreements to govern both regional issues and national topics. This is perhaps the most important development in the field of interstate compacts over their 200-plus year history.

With the Port Authority as the starting point for the administrative compact, states have launched into the development and use of these instruments on a broad scale. Today administrative compacts surpass in number and scope all other types of compacts. Administrative compacts address issues of economic development, waste disposal, crime, environmental control, water rationing, education, and energy development. At the same time, however, administrative compacts present unique legal and governance issues. As originally conceived, interstate compacts were used to settle interstate disputes and were, as noted, generally limited to resolving boundary and jurisdiction disputes. Early compacts, while negotiated through an interstate body, did not create ongoing administrative agencies because once the compact was adopted, the dispute was deemed resolved with no further action needed. The notion of states collectively regulating beyond their boundaries seemed contrary to notions of state sovereignty, federalism, and the national government's authority. More important, as administrative compacts have grown in number, complexity, and authority, they have confronted more traditional notions of statehood, state authority, and fundamental questions of democratic accountability. Administrative compacts may vest their ongoing administrative bodies with significant rulemaking and administrative authority that can, under some circumstances, trump individual state authority. For example, the Interstate Compact for Adult Offender Supervision declares that its rules adopted by an appointed commission are the equivalent of statutory law and, as such, are binding on the member states in their sovereign capacity. Contrary state laws adopted by an elected legislature must yield to the commission's rules unless a majority of the states' legislatures reject a particular rule.[5] It is doubtful that the Founding Fathers would have conceived of compacts being employed

---

5. Interstate Compact for Adult Offender Supervision, arts. V & VIII (2002).

with such continuing breadth or as a fundamental ingredient in governing the modern administrative state.

The pages that follow are a survey of some of the current uses of administrative compacts in several important topical areas. While not intended to be all-encompassing, inclusive, or conclusive, this survey portrays the breadth of subjects, structures, and schemes in use today. The survey also points out some of the problems that administrative compacts can face in their implementation, governance, and operation. Key to the issue is what status interstate agencies should hold in the national structure of government and what law should apply in interpreting and applying compacts. The survey is divided into key subject areas, and specific compacts are explored as an avenue for identifying the myriad of issues that can arise in the use of administrative compacts.

9.1   CRIME CONTROL AND CORRECTIONS COMPACTS

This section surveys the following topics:

- General Considerations in Crime Control Compacts
- Interstate Compact for Adult Offender Supervision
- The Interstate Agreement on Detainers
- The Interstate Juvenile Compact
- The National Crime Prevention and Privacy Compact
- The Driver License Compact
- The Nonresident Violator Compact
- Proposed Driver License Agreement

9.1.1   General Considerations

There are a number of interstate crime control and corrections compacts, most having received congressional consent through the Crime Control Consent Act of 1934.[6] This advanced consent is the basis for such compacts as the Interstate Compact for Probation and Parole (now preempted by the Interstate Compact for Adult Offender Supervision), the Interstate Juvenile Compact, and the Interstate Corrections Compact. The Interstate Agreement on Detainers, of which the federal government is also a signatory, is another example of using compacts in the crime control arena. Crime control compacts generally seek to create regulatory schemes to manage the interstate

---

6. 4 U.S.C. § 112(a) (2004).

movement of adult and juvenile offenders, or to provide cross-border coordination of crime control efforts. Several crime control compacts, such as the Interstate Compact for Adult Offender Supervision, the Interstate Agreement on Detainers, and the Interstate Corrections Compact effectively bypass traditional notions of extradition as applied to already adjudicated persons by providing a less formal, more expedient "retake and return" process.

Although there are some 18 crime control compacts in effect, not all compacts are created equal, either in scope or application. For example, the New England State Police Compact between Connecticut, Maine, Massachusetts, New Hampshire, Rhode Island, and Vermont establishes procedures for the application of mutual aid in controlling prison and other riots, as well as law enforcement emergencies generally. The compact creates the New England State Police Administrators Conference and the New England State Police Intelligence Network to assist in coordinating and administering the compact. However, this compact is limited in scope to three service areas: (1) detection and apprehension of those engaged in organized crime; (2) establishment and maintenance of a centralized intelligence bureau for the participating states; and (3) provision of mutual aid and assistance in police emergencies, as well as the authority, duty, and immunity for those engaged in such mutual aid. By contrast, the Interstate Agreement on Detainers embraces a more difficult issue and affects a much wider audience, both geographically and substantively.

Of the crime control compacts currently in effect, only one, the Interstate Compact for Adult Offender Supervision, creates a well-defined and ongoing administrative agency to manage compact affairs, the Interstate Commission for Adult Offender Supervision. In place of formal commissions, criminal control compacts have historically relied on joint action by state administrative officers to manage compact activities and, if appropriate, promulgate rules. For example, both the Interstate Compact on Probation and Parole (recently superseded by the Interstate Compact for Adult Offender Supervision), and the Interstate Juvenile Compact authorize each governor of a member state to "designate an officer who, acting jointly with other like officers of other party states, [to] promulgate rules and regulations to carry out more effectively the terms and provisions of this Compact."[7] However, neither compact formalized the membership of "like officers" or created formal rulemaking procedures. As a result, there has always been some question regarding who possesses the authority to manage the problems the compacts seek to address.

---

7. Interstate Compact for Juveniles, art. XII (1955).

The failure of many administrative compacts, particularly in the crime control arena, to formalize a management structure and procedures for adopting rules and administering affairs has led to problems. This lack of clarity has, too often, relegated management of compact affairs to professional associations such as the Association of Juvenile Compact Administrators (AJCA) or the Parole and Probation Compact Administrators Association (PPCAA), which have assumed responsibility over particular compacts on a presumptive, not assigned, basis. This has led some to question the actions of such associations, at least insofar as they seek to bind states and enforce the associations' will upon the states.[8] While it is true that these associations may have "like officers" as members, the rules promulgated by such associations have generally not been done by "like officers" nor have they been promulgated pursuant to any formal rulemaking procedures. It is arguable, therefore, whether associations such as the AJCA or the PPCAA actually have authority to promulgate administrative and regulatory rules binding on the states, notwithstanding the fact that they have done so. As compacts are solemn contracts, they must be interpreted within the confines of the agreement entered into by the states and, thus, a specific delegation of a member state's authority would seem necessary. Whether such associations constitute groups of "like officers" authorized to promulgate rules is questionable given that their memberships are not confined to the gubernatorially appointed state officials but extends to a fairly broad range of individuals.

The administrative problems long associated with interstate crime compacts is being corrected by the adoption of crime control agreements similar to the Interstate Compact for Adult Offender Supervision and the newly revised Interstate Compact on Juveniles. These agreements seek to formalize governance in an interstate commission with clearly delineated membership, clearly defined authority, and established formal rulemaking procedures. The formalization of governing authority for commissions is a critical element in establishing clear and enforceable agreements between the states in the area of crime control. Although there is no need to review every interstate crime control compact, several compacts deserve special attention.

9.1.2   Interstate Compact for Adult Offender Supervision (ICAOS)

Beginning in 1998 under the auspices of the National Institute of Corrections and the Council of State Governments, a concerted effort was made to

---

8. Michael L. Buenger & Richard L. Masters, *The Interstate Compact on Adult Offender Supervision: Using Old Tools to Solve New Problems,* 9 ROGER WILLIAMS U. L. REV. 71, 110-11 n.106 (2003).

substantially amend or completely replace the Interstate Compact on Probation and Parole (ICPP) of 1937. The end result of that process was the Interstate Compact for Adult Offender Supervision (ICAOS), which now has
replaced the ICPP throughout the United States as the principal means for
transferring supervision of nonincarcerated adult offenders across state lines.
Adoption of the ICAOS has, in a very tangible sense, "nationalized" and
"federalized" the movement of adult offenders with state convictions given
that the compact has received congressional consent pursuant to 4 U.S.C.
Section 112.

The underlying purpose of the ICAOS is defined in its preamble:

> It is the purpose of this compact and the Interstate Commission cre-
> ated hereunder, through means of joint and cooperative action among
> the compacting states: to provide the framework for the promotion
> of public safety and protect the rights of victims through the control
> and regulation of the interstate movement of offenders in the com-
> munity; to provide for the effective tracking, supervision, and reha-
> bilitation of these offenders by the sending and receiving state; and
> to equitably distribute the costs, benefits, and obligations of the com-
> pact among the compacting states.[9]

The ICAOS creates a formal and, by typical crime covered compact
standards, powerful administrative and enforcement scheme that supersedes
individual state autonomy in managing issues and resolving problems relative to the interstate movement of adult offenders.[10] Because ICAOS is a
replacement compact, several distinctions between it and the prior regulatory
scheme under the ICPP are noteworthy. Where the 1937 compact addressed
policy issues concerning the interstate movement of parolees and probationers, the ICAOS is silent as to the specifics of such policy matters. Where the
1937 compact had scant detail regarding governance and management of
compact affairs, the ICAOS is largely devoted to creating a governance structure of state councils and an interstate commission to oversee the compact.
Where the 1937 compact was a compact to regulate the movement of parolees and probationers, the ICAOS is a compact that potentially governs the
movement of all adult offenders through a system of rules applicable to party
states and their subdivisions.

---

9. Interstate Compact for Adult Offender Supervision, art. I (2002).
10. *See, e.g.,* Interstate Comm'n for Adult Offender Supervision v. Tennessee,
    No. 04-526-ICSF (E.D. Ky. June 13, 2005) (granting permanent injunction
    against Tennessee for violating the compact).

Under the ICAOS, regulation of compact operations is vested in two bodies: state councils that address intrastate affairs and an interstate commission that handles interstate affairs, administers the compact nationally, and establishes regulatory rules governing state officials in their management of adult offenders. The state councils provide compact administrators and state policy makers with a forum for addressing intrastate issues, such as ensuring adequate funding for compact operations and remedying intrastate activity that could pull the state out of compliance with the ICAOS.[11] As the movement of adult offenders embraces all three branches of state government and many community interests, the state councils provide a long-needed forum for the coordination and intrastate management of interstate adult offenders.

Notwithstanding the intrastate function of the state councils, the power of the ICAOS rests in its interstate governing structure and particularly its commission, which is comprised of one voting member from each member state and several ex officio members representing interested organizations. The interstate commission is charged with the following duties:

> (1) establish uniform procedures to manage the movement between states of the adults placed under community supervision and released to the community under the jurisdiction of courts, paroling authorities, corrections or other criminal justice agencies which will promulgate rules to achieve the purposes of this compact; (2) ensure an opportunity for input and timely notice to victims and to jurisdictions where defined offenders are authorized to travel or to relocate across state lines; (3) establish a system of uniform data collection, access to information on active cases by authorized criminal justice officials, and regular reporting of Compact activities to the heads of state councils, state executive, judicial and legislative branches and criminal justice administrators; (4) monitor compliance with rules governing the movement of offenders and initiate interventions to address and correct non-compliance; and (5) coordinate training and education regarding regulations of interstate movement of offenders for officials involved in such activity.[12]

Of its powers, perhaps none is more important than that of rulemaking. The commission is vested with broad authority to set the terms and conditions under which the supervision of adult offenders can be transferred between states, to collect and manage data, to assist in dispute resolution, and to

---

11. *Id.* at art. IV.
12. *Id.*

bring enforcement actions against a member state that violates the terms and conditions of the compact.[13] The commission thus governs the conduct of state officials in carrying out the provisions of the compact and its rules. All rules adopted by the commission must be done under procedures that substantially comply with the principles established by the Administrative Procedures Act,[14] the Federal Advisory Committee Act,[15] and the Government in the Sunshine Act.[16]

The rules adopted by the commission are more than administrative regulations. According to the terms of the ICAOS, rules adopted by the commission are on a par with state statutory law and are subject to enforcement by the courts as such. Moreover, the member states have contractually agreed that to the extent there is a conflict between state law and the rules of the commission, the rules must prevail. As a result, state legislatures have delegated a portion of their legislative authority to the commission, a delegation courts have recognized as appropriate in the limited context of interstate compacts.[17] State legislatures have retained the ability to oversee the rulemaking process, but only through the mechanism of a majority of state legislatures adopting legislation specifically rejecting a commission rule.

In addition to its rulemaking authority, the commission also possesses significant enforcement powers directed at ensure state compliance with the terms and conditions of the compact. Special note should be given to the independence of the commission in enforcing its rules and policies. The commission shall "in the reasonable exercise of its discretion" enforce the terms of the compact.[18] The compact specifically vests the commission with the power to (1) impose fines, fees and other costs in such amounts as the commission deems appropriate; (2) require remedial training for state officials charged with administering the compact; or (3) after all reasonable efforts have been taken, suspend or terminate a state's membership in the compact.[19] Of the enforcement tools available, the power to impose fines or suspend and terminate membership are the most unique. In effect, the states have agreed that an independent commission of state officials is empowered to tax a state's treasury or even terminate its membership within the compact without fur-

---

13. *See id.* at arts. IV, VIII, IX, XII.
14. 5 U.S.C. § 551, et seq. (2004).
15. 5 U.S.C. app. 2, § 1 (2004).
16. 5 U.S.C. § 552(b) (2004).
17. West Virginia *ex rel.* Dyer v. Sims, 341 U.S. 22 (1951); State *ex rel.* List v. County of Douglas, 524 P.2d 1271 (Nev. 1974).
18. Interstate Compact for Adult Offender Supervision, art. IX (E) (2002).
19. *Id.* at art. XII (B).

ther intervention by a state legislative body. The states have also agreed that to enforce its decisions the commission may institute legal action in the U.S. District Court for the District of Columbia or the federal district where the commission has its principle offices.[20] Legal action would most likely be in the form of obtaining injunctive relief to compel or prohibit a state from taking certain actions or obtaining an order to enforce a sanction issued by the commission.

Although the ICAOS has features similar to many other compacts, the unique features of the agreement pertaining to rulemaking and enforcement make it distinctive among most compacts. Oddly, the powers the commission possesses are not directed at the offender population it seeks to control but rather at the states themselves. For example, the compact does not specifically give the commission power to sanction an individual offender, nor has the commission sought to enter this arena through its broad rulemaking powers. However, the compact does specifically give the commission broad enforcement powers regarding the conduct of states and state officials. By entering the agreement, the states have ceded to an independent commission not only the authority to set the rules governing the movement of offenders, but also the conduct of states in following and enforcing those rules. This is a significant concession of power by sovereign states and may mark the beginnings of the creation of a third tier of governing authority in the United States that is truly supra-state, sub-federal in nature.

Finally, to finance the activities of the compact and its commission, the states have agreed to vest the commission with what may be characterized as taxing authority. By adopting the compact, the states have agreed to finance the activities of the commission at a rate established by the commission. The amount a state owes for commission activities is formula driven, but the formula itself is set by the commission taking into account state population and the volume of compact cases in each state. The compact specifically provides that the commission shall levy on and collect from each state an assessment that must be sufficient to cover the total operating budget of the commission.[21] Furthermore, the commission "shall promulgate a rule binding on all compacting states which governs said assessment."[22] Like any other commission rule, the rule on assessments is judicially enforceable.

---

20. *Id.* at art. XII (C). Most legal actions are commenced in the Eastern District of Kentucky because the commission's principal office is in Lexington, Ky.
21. *Id.* at art. X.
22. *Id. See also* Interstate Commission for Adult Offender Supervision Rule 2.103 (March 12, 2004).

The Interstate Compact for Adult Offender Supervision has been adopted by all 50 states, the District of Columbia, and Puerto Rico. The compact now controls the movement of offenders between the member states. The compact does not control the movement of offenders between the member states and the remaining state and any territory that has failed to adopt the compact. As to the state and those territories that are not members, the movement of offenders is governed by the 1937 Interstate Compact on Probation and Parole to the extent that state legislatures did not repeal that agreement when enacting the ICAOS. Where the Interstate Compact on Probation and Parole was repealed by enactment of the ICAOS, there is no mechanism to monitor and control the movement of adult offenders between states operating exclusively under the ICAOS and nonmember jurisdictions.

The ICAOS is a new compact, and, consequently, there is little judicial interpretation of, or guidance for, the agreement. The commission has promulgated rules that govern the procedural requirements for two classes of offenders: all felons and a limited class of misdemeanants. As to the misdemeanants, the commission has decided, at least in its formative years, to govern only those misdemeanor offenders involved in an offense in which a person has incurred direct or threatened physical or psychological harm, a subsequent offense of driving while impaired by drugs or alcohol, a sexual offense requiring registration as a sex offender, or an offense committed with a firearm.[23] All other misdemeanor offenders would not be subject to the compact and, therefore, not bound by the commission's rules. In effect, non-covered offenders are not eligible to have their parole or probation supervision transferred, but neither is their movement controlled or restricted. This fact has led to a dispute between Pennsylvania and the commission with the former suing the latter challenging the method by which the misdemeanor provisions of the rule were adopted.[24]

The ICAOS imposes on a receiving state certain substantive supervisory requirements. The first and most important of these requirements is

23. Interstate Commission for Adult Offender Supervision Rule 2.105 (a)(1)-(4) (Oct. 26, 2004).
24. Pennsylvania v. Interstate Comm'n for Adult Offender Supervision, Case No. 1:04CV00741 (D. D.C. 2004), *appeal dismissed,* Commw. Bd. of Prob. & Parole v. Interstate Comm'n for Adult Offender Supervision, 2005 U.S. App. LEXIS 3151 (D.C. Cir. 2005).

that an offender transferred under the compact is supervised in a manner to be determined by the receiving state.[25] With the exception of the duration of supervision, a sending state does not determine the manner of supervision once the offender leaves its jurisdiction.[26] However, the receiving state is required to supervise a transferred offender in the same manner as it supervises offenders sentenced by its courts. Consequently, the receiving state cannot impose extraordinary conditions on an out-of-state offender if it would not impose similar conditions on it own offender. Stated simply, a receiving state cannot discriminate. A receiving state can impose special conditions on an offender if such conditions would also be imposed on its own citizens, even if such conditions would not ordinarily be imposed in the sending state.[27]

If an offender is eligible for transfer under the compact, several procedural rules define the terms and conditions of such transfer. Moreover, transfers fall into two classes, mandatory and discretionary. Under the mandatory transfer provisions of the rule, a receiving state must accept the transfer of the offender's supervision if the offender: (1) has more than three months' remaining on a term of supervision; (2) is in substantial compliance with the terms of probation or parole; and (3) is a resident of the receiving state or (a) has resident family in the receiving state who are willing to assist in the plan of supervision, and (b) the offender can obtain meaningful employment.[28] Offenders who do not meet these criteria may still apply for and receive transfer of their supervision but solely at the discretion of the receiving state. When an offender is eligible for transfer, both the sending and receiving state must follow certain procedural requirements. First, an offender is not permitted to travel to a receiving state prior to that state's accepting the transfer of supervision.[29] There are several narrow exceptions to the principle that an offender may not travel to or relocate in a receiving state prior to acceptance by that state.[30] The sending state must submit to the receiving state certain mandatory information, and the receiving state must be given an opportunity to review the information prior to accepting supervision.[31]

---

25. Interstate Commission for Adult Offender Supervision Rule 4.101 (Nov. 4, 2003).
26. *Id.* at Rule 4.102.
27. *Id.* at Rule 4.103.
28. *Id.* at Rule 3.101.
29. *Id.* at Rule 3.303(a).
30. *Id.* at Rule 3.103(b).
31. *Id.* at Rule 3.102.

One of the purposes of the ICAOS is not only to allow for the transfer of offender supervision between states but also to allow for the easy return of offenders who violate the terms and conditions of their supervision. To this end, both in the language of the compact and the rules of the commission, the states have agreed that officers of a sending state may at all times enter into a receiving state and "retake" an offender.[32] This "retake" provision of the compact acts as a more informal procedure and substitutes for traditional extradition proceedings. Arguably, Congress has agreed to this "retake" procedure in place of extradition in its consent to the agreement, advanced though it may be. Additionally, the commission's rules require the offender to execute a waiver of extradition at the time supervision is transferred.[33] The commission's rules recognize that, with limited exception, the decision to retake an offender lies solely within the discretion of the sending state.[34] Generally, a sending state may not retake an offender who is facing criminal charges in the receiving state.[35] If a receiving state reports that a transferred offender has committed three or more significant violations of probation or parole, the sending state is required to retake and return the offender within 30 days.[36] However, consistent with the Supreme Court's decisions in *Morrissey v. Brewer*[37] and *Gagnon v. Scarpelli*,[38] the offender must be afforded a probable cause hearing consistent with due process standards before being returned to a sending state unless the offender has waived the hearing accompanied by an admission of the violations.[39] Several courts have recognized that "retaking" is different from extradition and have generally ap-

---

32. Interstate Compact for Adult Offender Supervision, art. I (2002).
33. Interstate Commission for Adult Offender Supervision Rule 3.109 (Nov. 4, 2003).
34. *Id.* at Rule 5.101(a).
35. *Id.* at Rule 5.101(b).
36. *Id.* at Rules 5.103 & 5.105.
37. Morrissey v. Brewer, 408 U.S. 471 (1972).
38. Gagnon v. Scarpelli, 411 U.S. 778 (1973).
39. Interstate Commission for Adult Offender Supervision Rule 5.108 (Nov. 4, 2003). It must be noted that the nature of the hearing to be provided to the offender is in some question, given that a retaking hearing does not constitute per se a revocation hearing. *See* INTERSTATE COMMISSION FOR ADULT OFFENDER SUPERVISION, BENCHBOOK FOR JUDGES AND COURT PERSONNEL § 4.4 (2004), *available at* http://www.interstatecompact.org/legal/benchbook.pdf.

proved of this less formal means for returning out-of-state offenders under probation or parole.[40]

One final note for practitioners: the compact specifically provides that the commission is entitled to service of process in any judicial or administrative proceeding in a compacting state that may affect the powers, responsibilities, or actions of the commission.[41] Additionally, the commission may, in the exercise of its discretion, intervene in such proceedings for all purposes and shall have standing to intervene.[42] Although this provision has not yet been interpreted by a court, it appears that the compact makes the commission an indispensable party in any proceedings that affect the commission or its actions.[43] Consequently, failure to join the commission in a proceeding to which it is entitled to service could result in dismissal of the litigation or provide hollow and not complete relief to the parties.[44] Therefore, the parties should ensure that the commission is served with pleadings in any proceedings that challenge, the actions of the commission in state court or before a state administrative body.

Because the movement of adult offenders is now controlled by the commission, state officials, offenders, and those representing offenders who are seeking to relocate to another state should become familiar with the rules. The ICAOS creates a significant regulatory regime through the use of administrative rules and various enforcement tools. Among the rules critical to understanding interstate offender transfer are those governing eligibility for transfer, the process for transfer of offenders and the process for return of violators.

9.1.3 Interstate Agreement on Detainers (IAD)[45]

The Interstate Agreement on Detainers (IAD) is an interstate compact that provides a mechanism by which state authorities and the federal government can detain individuals incarcerated in one state for return to and trial in the state lodging the detainer based on untried charges. The purpose of the agreement is to encourage the expeditious and orderly disposition of criminal

---

40. Mercer v. Sheriff, Cumberland County, 1997 U.S. App. LEXIS 28636 (1st Cir. 1997); Warner v. Parke, 1996 U.S. App. LEXIS 23239 (7th Cir. 1996).
41. Interstate Compact for Adult Offender Supervision, art. IX (A) (2002).
42. *Id.*
43. FED. R. CIV. P. 19.
44. *Cf.*, California v. Arizona, 440 U.S. 59 (1979).
45. *See* discussion, Donald M. Zupanec, Annotation, *Validity, Construction, and Application of Interstate Agreement on Detainers*, 98 A.L.R. 3d 160 (1980).

charges and the determination of the proper status of any detainers issued on untried indictments, informations, or complaints. The IAD is not only a procedural mechanism available to state and federal officials, but also a mechanism allowing incarcerated persons to demand the prompt disposition of pending charges in a state other than the state in which they are imprisoned. In this sense, the IAD is operational on two fronts. First, it provides state and federal officials with a mechanism to detain incarcerated persons. Second, and equally important, the IAD allows incarcerated persons to require the prompt disposition of cases so as to minimize any uncertainty regarding their status in states other than the state in which they are incarcerated. The IAD is designed to protect prisoners and rehabilitation programs by (1) eliminating uncertainty that pending charges may create for the prisoner by requiring prompt disposition of charges, and (2) ensuring that interruptions of a prisoner's incarceration are minimized so the prisoner's continuous presence in rehabilitative programs is guaranteed.[46] One aspect of the IAD that is unique is that the federal government is a signatory to the compact; in effect it is a full partner that is bound by the terms and conditions of the agreement just as it if were a member state. The IAD applies to transfers of sentenced prisoners for unrelated trials between two states, to transfers from the federal government to the states, and from the states to the federal government. The IAD does not apply to transfers of federal prisoners between the judicial districts of the federal courts for trial on federal charges.[47]

To accomplish the goal of prompt disposition of outstanding charges, the IAD provides rules and procedures under which a prisoner may demand the speedy disposition of charges pending against him or her in another jurisdiction, as well as procedures by which a state may obtain custody of an out-of-state prisoner for trial on pending charges. Generally, a detainer notifies custodial authorities that charges are pending elsewhere against an inmate, and requests that custodial authorities notify its sender—usually a prosecuting attorney, governor, or other law enforcement agency—before releasing the inmate. The IAD further mandates that whenever a person is imprisoned in a correctional institution of a party state or the federal government, and there is pending in any other party state any untried indictment, information, or complaint forming the basis of a detainer, the prisoner must be brought to trial within 180 after the prosecuting officer and the appropriate court have been notified in writing of the place of imprisonment and a request has been made for a final disposition. The remedy for failure to comply with the IAD may be dismissal of the underlying case.

---

46. Stewart v. Bailey, 7 F.3d 384 (4th Cir. 1993).
47. *See* United States v. Stoner, 799 F.2d 1253 (9th Cir. 1986).

The IAD is an example of an interstate compact that is simultaneously state law and federal law. Not only did Congress consent to the IAD by way of the Crime Control Consent Act of 1934, it has codified the IAD as a federal procedural mechanism for managing the flow of incarcerated people between the states and between the states and federal government.[48] The Supreme Court has upheld the validity of the IAD on the theory that the extradition clause provides one source of authority for Congress's consent to the agreement.[49] The Court has also upheld the validity of federal participation in the IAD as both a sending and receiving entity.[50] Although certain aspects of the IAD have been challenged over the years, most notably with regard to its procedural requirements, courts have consistently upheld the underlying validity of the agreement. Stated another way, while courts have been presented with many occasions to question how authorities are implementing the IAD, there is no question of its legal sufficiency as an appropriate interstate agreement for managing the movement of incarcerated individuals for trial on outstanding charges.[51]

The provisions of the Interstate Agreement on Detainers become operative only (1) when the agreement has been adopted by both the state in which a prisoner is incarcerated and the state in which charges are pending against him or her, and (2) only following the filing of a detainer based on an untried charge against a prisoner who is serving a term of imprisonment. Consequently, the Supreme Court has held that the IAD does not apply in the context of probation revocation proceedings. Although a probation violation might be based on the commission of a criminal offense, it does not result in the probationer being prosecuted or brought to trial for that offense.[52] Moreover, a writ of habeas corpus ad prosequendam issued by a federal court to state authorities directing the production of a state prisoner for trial on criminal charges is not covered by the IAD.[53] The dismissal provisions of the IAD as a remedy for violations by the states or federal government are construed narrowly within the meaning of the agreement. Violations that do not fit within the dismissal provisions will not result in a dismissal of the indictment, information, or complaint even though the violations may be substan-

---

48. 4 U.S.C. § 112(a) (2004), 18 U.S.C. app. § 2 (2004).
49. Cuyler v. Adams, 449 U.S. 433 (1981).
50. United States v. Mauro, 436 U.S. 340 (1978).
51. Reed v. Farley, 512 U.S. 339 (1994).
52. Carchman v. Nash, 473 U.S. 716 (1985).
53. United States v. Mauro, 436 U.S. 340 (1978).

tial.[54] The speedy trial requirements of the IAD do not apply to probation violations.[55]

Like most crime control compacts, the IAD as a regulatory agreement is light on administrative structure and heavy on procedural requirements. Consequently, unlike the Interstate Compact for Adult Offender Supervision, the IAD follows the traditional model of other compacts by ignoring overall governance concerns and focusing instead on specific procedural requirements for moving incarcerated persons. Like the 1937 Interstate Compact for Probation and Parole and the new ICAOS, the IAD authorizes officers "who, acting jointly with like officers of other party states, shall promulgate rules and regulations to carry out more effectively the terms and provisions of this agreement, and who shall provide, within and without the state, information necessary to the effective operation of this agreement."[56] Unlike ICAOS, the IAD does not specifically define when such officers are to meet, the subject matter of the rules, or the extent of authority granted to any body of "like officers." Notwithstanding authorization for some continuing administrative body, no such body has ever been convened, and the rulemaking authority provided in the IAD appears, in practical terms, to be more dicta than substance. The administrative workings of the IAD have fallen to each individual member and the courts, not a coordinated commission of "like officers acting jointly."

The fact that the agreement authorizes the creation of an administrative rulemaking body does not render the matter irrelevant for lack of activity. An IAD body could be convened and administrative rules promulgated. Presumably, as an interstate compact authorized by Congress, any rules adopted by an administrative body would carry considerable weight in a contest with state law. The federalized nature of the IAD would also federalize any rules that might be promulgated, particularly given that the federal government is a member of the compact. The current lack of administrative rules may be attributable, in part, to the procedural heaviness of the IAD and its very narrow subject matter. The design of the agreement and its lack of uniform rules have left much of the operational details in the hands of the courts instead of an on-going agency. This has produced a wide and confusing variance in legal interpretation and practical application of the IAD.

The IAD has been adopted by 50 states, Puerto Rico, the Virgin Islands, and the federal government. It is the only interstate agreement for the con-

---

54. United States v. Lualemaga, 280 F.3d 1260 (9th Cir. 2002).
55. United States v. Roach, 745 F.2d 1252 (9th Cir. 1984).
56. Interstate Agreement on Detainers, art. VII (1970).

trolled movement of incarcerated persons between states and the federal government for the limited purpose of resolving outstanding charges. The IAD should not be confused with the Uniform Criminal Extradition Act (UCEA). Where the former is a valid interstate compact, the latter is a uniform state law, generally binding on those states that have adopted it.[57] The IAD governs those situations involving incarcerated persons who are charged with crimes in other states. The UCEA governs those persons who have fled justice to another state. Therefore, a detainer placed on an incarcerated person does not trigger extradition concerns.[58] However, a prisoner incarcerated in a jurisdiction that has adopted the UCEA may be entitled to its procedural protections before being transferred to another jurisdiction under the IAD. This protection includes the right to a pretransfer hearing if the prisoner has not waived that right. As the Supreme Court noted in *Cuyler v. Adams* when the IAD is implicated:

> The remedial purpose of the Agreement supports an interpretation that gives prisoners the right to a judicial hearing in which they can bring a limited challenge to the receiving state's custody request. In light of the purpose of the Detainer Agreement, as reflected in the structure of the Agreement, its language, and its legislative history, we conclude as a matter of federal law that prisoners transferred pursuant to the provisions of the Agreement are not required to forfeit any pre-existing rights they may have under state or federal law to challenge their transfer to the receiving State.[59]

This ruling has no application, however, to prisoners serving federal sentences because the United States has neither adopted the Uniform Extradition Act nor enacted any other statute providing the right of hearing.[60] This demonstrates that interstate compacts, regardless of their legal status, can interplay with other state and federal statutes governing the same or similar matter.

Notwithstanding the substantive validity of the IAD, the operational validity of the agreement has been questioned on multiple occasions, particularly with regard to its failure to require that prisoners whose custody is requested by another state be informed of their right to contest the request or be afforded the right to judicial review of the request. The IAD imposes on

---

57. Michigan v. Doran, 439 U.S. 282, 289 (1978).
58. Stewart v. Bailey, 7 F.3d 384 (4th Cir. 1993).
59. Cuyler v. Adams, 449 U.S. 433, 449-50 (1981).
60. Mann v. Warden, 771 F.2d 1453 (11th Cir. 1985) (per curiam).

state and federal officials certain procedural requirements, the violation of which may result in dismissal of the case on which the detainer was issued. While the IAD is sanctioned by Congress and creates federal rights that may properly be addressed by a federal writ of habeas corpus, the issuance of a detainer is generally considered a state act based on its laws and process.[61] Consequently, a detainer is a custodial hold by the issuing state, and a prisoner challenging a confinement in federal court must generally proceed under 28 U.S.C. Section 2254, which governs writs issued "on behalf of a person in custody pursuant to the judgment of a State court."[62] Prisoners challenging detainers must first exhaust remedies available under the IAD before seeking relief in federal courts. However, the Supreme Court has authorized a separate civil rights action for damages caused by an alleged violation of the IAD.

The lack of any binding governing rules for proceeding under the IAD may be the cause for much conflicting litigation regarding its procedural implementation. Several illustrations demonstrate the lack of consistency in the application of the IAD. For example, generally, the IAD has been held not to violate the due process or equal protection rights of prisoners.[63] This position is not, however, universally held. A number of courts have taken the position that a prisoner whose custody is requested pursuant to the IAD has the right to notice and some type of due process hearing at which the detainer request can be reviewed.[64] Where prisoners were not brought to trial within 180 days of their requests for disposition of the underlying charges, the delays have been held reasonable in some cases and not reasonable in others.[65] No doubt, the lack of uniform procedural rules, the fact-sensitive nature of each case, and the subject matter of the compact contribute to confusion in implementing the IAD.

---

61. Echevarria v. Bell, 579 F.2d 1022, 1023-24 (7th Cir. 1978).
62. *See* Braden v. 30th Judicial Cir. Ct., 410 U.S. 484 (1973); United States *ex rel.* Hoover v. Franzen, 669 F.2d 433, 441-42 (7th Cir. 1982).
63. Wertheimer v. State, 201 N.W.2d 383 (Minn. 1972) (detainer acts as notice to the incarcerated person, and the right to counsel applies only when the person is in danger of a loss of liberty); State v. Thompson, 336 A.2d 11 (N.J. 1975).
64. State *ex rel.* Garner v. Gray, 201 N.W.2d 163 (Wis. 1974); People v. Koren, 449 N.E.2d 191 (Ill. App. Ct. 1983).
65. *Compare* United States v. Cephas, 937 F.2d 816 (2d Cir. 1991) *with* Hoss v. State, 292 A.2d 48 (Md. 1972).

9.1.4   Interstate Compact on Juveniles (ICJ)

The Interstate Compact on Juveniles (ICJ) was established in 1955 to assist states in managing the movement of adjudicated juvenile offenders, runaways, and the return of youths to states where they have been charged with delinquent acts. The ICJ applies not only to juvenile delinquents but also to status offenders—that is, youthful offenders whose acts would not constitute a crime if committed by an adult. One class of juvenile status offenders that the ICJ specifically seeks to regulate is runaway youths. The ICJ seeks to protect juveniles by providing for cooperative supervision of delinquent juveniles on parole or probation; the return of delinquent juveniles who have escaped or absconded from a state; the return of nondelinquent juveniles who have run away from home; and any additional measures that two or more states may desire to undertake cooperatively. The compact provides procedural means to regulate the movement of juveniles across state lines subject to the jurisdiction of a court or youth authority. The ICJ is the only law in the United States specifically directed at managing the interstate movement of juvenile offenders. The current compact applies to any juvenile who has been adjudicated delinquent and who remains subject to the jurisdiction of a court or who is under supervision by an agency or institution pursuant to court order.[66] The compact is constitutional notwithstanding its lack of full procedural protections normally afforded in other proceedings.[67]

It is generally thought that Congress consented to the ICJ through the general consent provisions of the 1934 Crime Control Consent Act discussed previously. However, the necessity of congressional consent to juvenile agreements, such as the ICJ, has been called into question in recent years.[68] As previously discussed, congressional consent is deemed necessary in two circumstances: (1) when the agreement changes the balance of power between the states and federal government; or (2) when the agreement intrudes on one of Congress's enumerated powers thereby interfering with the right of Congress to regulate a particular interstate or national matter. Courts have long recognized that juvenile delinquency and youthful offenders generally fall under the exclusive purview of the states, and thus congressional consent may not be necessary or appropriate in the context of such agreements.

---

66. Interstate Compact on Juveniles, art. III (1955).
67. *In interest of* W., 377 So. 2d 22 (Fla. 1979).
68. *See* McComb v. Wambaugh, 934 F.2d 474, 478 (3d Cir. 1991) (ICPC does not encroach on federal interests and, therefore, does not require congressional consent to be effective).

Although in recent years the federal government has taken a distinct interest in juvenile delinquency in response to increasing juvenile crime, it is questionable whether the federal government has a distinct, definable constitutional interest in managing the population served by the ICJ. The status of the ICJ relative to national interests has been a source of uncertainty. One court has noted:

> Although a juvenile petition does not technically charge a crime, the rendition procedures established by the Compact for juveniles charged with delinquency are designed to be essentially the same as those long established for the extradition of adults charged with crimes. For this reason we find the Supreme Court cases arising under the Extradition Clause persuasive authority in the context of the Juvenile Compact."[69]

However, that same court concluded that the extradition clause does not apply to juveniles, notwithstanding that the clause makes no distinction between juvenile and adult offenders.[70] The need for congressional consent has not been resolved, and there are arguments both supporting such a need and supporting the current status of the compact as state, not federal, law. Nevertheless, the absence of consent does not erode the underlying validity of the agreement as between the member states.[71] Agreements such as the ICJ remain enforceable notwithstanding the absence of congressional consent

Like many crime control compacts, the governance of the ICJ has been a matter of question and concern for years. The current compact mirrors older crime control compacts by authorizing the governor of each member state to appoint an official who, acting jointly with officers from other member states, can adopt rules to implement the goals of the agreement.[72] However, also like other crime control compacts, the ICJ utterly fails to define what constitutes such a group, the extent of their authority, or the rulemaking procedures to be employed. Thus, over the years, administration and management of the agreement has fallen to the Association of Juvenile Compact Administrators (AJCA), which has promulgated rules governing the movement of juveniles across state lines.[73] The AJCA assumed the task of writing rules even though no

69. *In re* O.M., 565 A.2d 573, 583 (D.C. 1989).
70. *Id. See also* A Juvenile, 484 N.E.2d 995 (Mass. 1985).
71. *In re* D.B., 431 A.2d 498 (Vt. 1981).
72. Interstate Compact on Juveniles, art. XII (1955).
73. For the rules governing the administration of the ICJ, *see* Association of Juvenile Compact Administrators, 2003 Rules & Regulations, at http://ajca.us/list_forms.php?formname=rr2003.

formal delegation of state authority can be found to support this role. There-fore, the rules promulgated by the AJCA have been viewed as more akin to voluntary conventions than rules binding on the states. Management of the compact is complicated by the fact that not all states have adopted amendments to the agreement addressing such considerations as runaways, rendition, and out-of-state confinement. As currently written, the ICJ contains two provisions on runaway youths, the original provision found at Article IV and the runaway amendment to the agreement. This has produced two different and arguably conflicting regulatory schemes.[74] Consequently, the uniformity of the agreement has been compromised and one could argue that there are now several ICJs in operation, not a single compact.

One final complicating factor in managing compact affairs can be found in Article X. This provision authorizes states to enter into "supplementary agreements." These agreements may address a broad range of matters including such critical issues as due process, jurisdiction, and custody. Yet these agreements do not require consent by any compact body and, therefore, are left unregulated. One may conclude, therefore, that the current ICJ has led to a patchwork of conflicting agreements, rules, and procedures that have eroded the overall goal of the compact, which is to provide for a uniform and regulated approach to managing the interstate movement of juvenile offenders.

Several aspects of the present ICJ deserve special exploration as they have contributed to significant confusion and litigation throughout the years. The lack of enforceability has no doubt been a key ingredient to the confusion as states have reached differing positions on important elements of the ICJ without the benefit of a single interpretation available to compacts that clearly fall within the scope of congressional consent and thus the federal courts. Perhaps the areas of the ICJ that have created the greatest confusion center on the rendition of juveniles, requisition, jurisdiction, and the interplay of the ICJ with the Uniform Child Custody Jurisdiction Act (UCCJA). While an entire treatise could be written on the interaction between the ICJ and several other statutes, a brief discussion of practice considerations is warranted to convey the complexity of the ICJ in action.

The handling of juveniles under the ICJ differs depending on their status as escapees or absconders,[75] or as runaways.[76] This has contributed to notice-

---

74. *Compare* Interstate Compact on Juveniles, art. IV (1955) *with* Interstate Compact on Juveniles, Runaway Amendment (1955).

75. Interstate Compact on Juveniles, art. V (1955).

76. *Id.* at art. IV.

able confusion and contradictory court decisions. The matter is made more complicated because not all member states have adopted the so-called "runaway amendment" or the "rendition amendment" to ICJ. Effectively, therefore, patchwork procedures exist that apply depending on whether both the sending and receiving states are acting under the original provisions of the ICJ, the amendments to the ICJ, or a combination thereof. Runaways under Article IV are granted a measure of procedural due process not afforded delinquents under Article V. Although the requisition for a juvenile is similar, runaways are provided the opportunity not only to contest the requisition but also to have a court in the sending state determine whether returning the juvenile is in the interests of the child. Article IV provides, in part:

> The judge of the court to which this application is made may hold a hearing thereon to determine whether for the purposes of this compact the petitioner is entitled to the legal custody of the juvenile, whether or not it appears that the juvenile has in fact run away without consent, whether or not he is an emancipated minor, and whether of not it is in the best interest of the juvenile to compel his return to the state.[77]

Although clear on its face, this provision has been the subject of conflicting court cases. Some courts have held that determinations regarding "the best interests of the juvenile" are matters to be determined by the home state, not the asylum state.[78] Other states have held that the courts in the asylum state have a paramount interest in determining the best interest of the child before granting a requisition request.[79] Even if a court determines that transfer to the requesting state is in the best interests of the juvenile, the asylum state may continue to hold the person if it has brought charges against the juvenile and those charges remain outstanding.[80]

By contrast, Article V treats juvenile delinquents differently and limits the inquiry that an asylum state can make into a requisition request. Article V provides that upon receipt of a request for return, a court or executive officer in the asylum state must issue an order directing that the juvenile be detained and taken into custody. However, prior to being returned to the home state, the juvenile must be given a hearing at which a court must

---

77. *See id.* at art. IV.
78. *In interest of* C.P., 533 A.2d 1001 (Pa. 1987).
79. *In re* D., 298 S.E.2d 243 (W.Va. 1982).
80. Interstate Compact on Juveniles, art. IV (1955).

determine whether the requisition is in order. If the court determines that the requisition is in order, the judge "shall deliver such delinquent juvenile" over to home state officials.[81] The mandatory nature of the return is clarified in the "rendition amendment," which requires that a juvenile charged as a delinquent for violating a criminal law "shall be returned to the requesting state[.]"[82] While the court may fix a time for the juvenile to contest the legality of the proceedings, the court does not make an inquiry into whether return of a juvenile delinquent is in the best interests of the juvenile. Courts have generally held that proceedings under Article V are mandatory and impose a ministerial duty.[83] Therefore, a court has no authority to make a determination concerning the best interest of a juvenile delinquent and must return the juvenile to the requesting state if the requisition is in order.[84] This position is not, however, universally held.[85] In conjunction with the "best interest" limitation for juvenile delinquents, authorities in the asylum state may not consider the potential punishment that the juvenile may receive in the home state. Courts in the asylum state may not refuse a requisition simply because the juvenile may be subject to the death penalty, which was not available in the asylum state.[86]The limited inquiry by the asylum state into the status of a juvenile is similar to, and essentially effectuates, safeguards available to adult criminals under the Extradition Clause.[87] However, a state may refuse to requisition a juvenile delinquent if the crime for which the juvenile is charged is not a crime in the asylum state, and the asylum state has, by statute enacted with the compact, reserved such discretion to itself.[88] Although courts appear to have implicitly recognized the right of a state to pass such a statute, the ultimate question of whether such an act is constitutional given the contractual nature of compacts has not been determined.

Moreover, transfer of a person is dependent upon their status in the requesting state, not the asylum state. Thus, an adult apprehended on a

---

81. *Id.* at art. V.
82. *Id.* at art. XVII.
83. *In re State*, 97 S.W.3d 746 (Tex. Ct. App. 2003).
84. *In re G.C.S.*, 360 A.2d 498 (D.C. 1976); *In re Teague*, 371 S.E.2d 510 (N.C. Ct. App. 1988); *In re Kallinger*, 392 A.2d 309, 310 (Pa. 1978); *In re R.H.*, 583 P.2d 936 (Colo. Ct. App. 1978).
85. *In re Schy*, 580 P.2d 1114 (Wash. Ct. App. 1978).
86. *In re O.M.*, 565 A.2d 573, 583 (D.C. 1989).
87. *Id.* at 583, *citing* Puerto Rico v. Branstad, 483 U.S. 219 (1987).
88. N.J. Rev. Stat. § 9:23-1.2 (2004).

warrant issued when he or she was a juvenile is subject to return under the ICP and is not subject to extradition considerations.[89] Similarly, where a juvenile would be considered an adult under the laws of the requesting state, the ICJ does not apply.[90] As part of its judicial review of the requisition request, a court may make a substantive determination that the juvenile appearing is the juvenile being sought by the requesting state.[91] Although juvenile delinquents may have a right to some due process considerations, juveniles delinquents are not entitled to the full panoply of constitutional rights that would otherwise be afforded a criminal defendant.[92] Consequently, there was no right to a jury trial under the ICJ because the proceedings under the compact do not adjudicate either rights or status.[93]

Because juvenile cases can involve overlapping jurisdictional considerations between states, the matter of determining which of the competing court orders is valid can be confusing. The potential interaction of the ICJ with the UCCJA, the Uniform Child Custody Jurisdiction and Enforcement Act (UCCJEA), and the Parental Kidnapping Prevention Act (PKPA) only adds to the confusion.[94] These other acts may be a factor in runaway and status offender cases, and in cases where abuse and neglect is an allegation; the ICJ would have only limited interaction with these other acts in purely juvenile delinquency cases. Generally, in circumstances involving runaway children, the claims of the custodial state are paramount to the concerns of the parental domicile state. A court of the state in which a juvenile is physically present has jurisdiction to detain a minor child, order appropriate detention and supervision, or consent to the child's return pursuant to a proper requisition issued by a court of competent jurisdiction in the state where the juvenile resided.[95] Under the UCCJA, a court has jurisdiction over a juvenile, including the jurisdiction in some circumstances to modify an out-of-state decree before entering a valid decree in that state.[96] A court may invoke jurisdiction over a child present in the state when it is necessary

---

89. State v. Cook, 64 P.3d 58 (Wash. Ct. App. 2003).

90. A Juvenile, 484 N.E.2d 995 (Mass. 1985).

91. *In re* Teague, 371 S.E.2d 510 (N.C. Ct. App. 1988).

92. Wood v. Benson, 740 P.2d 1196 (Okla. Ct. App. 1987).

93. Haskins v. Carter, 506 P.2d 1391 (Okla. Ct. App. 1973).

94. Some states have replaced the Uniform Child Custody Jurisdiction Act with the Uniform Child Custody Jurisdiction and Enforcement Act (U.C.C.J.E.A.). *See, e.g.,* CAL. FAM. CODE § 3400 (2004).

95. *In re* G., 539 S.W.2d 705 (Mo. Ct. App. 1976).

96. Wenz v. Schwartze, 598 P.2d 1086 (Mont. 1979).

to protect the child because of threatened mistreatment or abuse.[97] If there is no compliance with the notice requirements of the UCCJA by the state entering the initial decree, courts in the asylum state are not required to recognize and enforce an out-of-state decree.[98] Courts in the asylum state must, however, defer to the courts of a state that first grants a custody decree unless the originating state has lost jurisdiction under the UCCJA. The courts of one state are generally prohibited from conducting further proceedings until they have referred the case to the court that entered the original custody decree and obtained a response that it would not assume jurisdiction over the matter of custody.[99] It is possible, therefore, for the interaction of the ICJ and the UCCJA to place a court in the following situation: the court has the authority under the ICJ to deny a requisition ordering the return of a juvenile and arrange for the juvenile's custody; under the UCCJA, the court is not required to recognize or enforce the foreign state's decree, but the court is precluded from modifying the order.[100] Matters can also become complicated to the extent that the Parental Kidnapping Prevention Act (PKPA)[101] is a consideration in litigation involving the ICJ.

A practitioner should consider the application of other state and federal laws in cases brought under the ICJ. The subsequent adoption of the UCCJA and the UCCJEA by states that are members to the compact may constitute a "supplementary agreement" for purposes of Article X of the current compact. Consequently, ICJ cases do not stand alone, and the binding effect of the compact must be tempered by considerations for other laws. Whether the proposed ICJ will be more effective in addressing these interaction concerns remains to be determined. Because the proposed compact vests the interstate commission with authority to adopt rules that have the effect of statutory law in the member states, practitioners will have to pay particular attention to the interaction of the agreement and its rules with existing statutes addressing juvenile custody and procedural matters.

Like the ICPC, the ICJ has undergone major changes in recent years leading to a newer version of the agreement that is currently circulating in state legislatures and will replace the current ICJ upon obtaining the requisite approval of the states. The need for a revised compact was compelled

---

97. *In re* Pierce, 601 P.2d 1179 (Mont. 1979).
98. *Wenz*, 598 P.2d at 1096 (Mont. 1979).
99. E.P. v. Dist. Ct. of Garfield County, 696 P.2d 254 (Colo. 1985).
100. *In re* Pierce, 601 P.2d 1179, 1184 (Mont. 1979).
101. 28 U.S.C. § 1738A (2004).

by several considerations: (1) the lack of consistency between state versions of the existing agreement; (2) the failure of all member states to adopt various amendments to the agreement; (3) the lack of a coherent and acceptable administrative structure, including a defined commission with authority to adopt rules; and (4) the absence of enforcement mechanisms to ensure that state officials comply with the agreement. Additionally, there was a general consensus from many administrators that the 1955 version of the agreement did not reflect the changing nature of juvenile justice and was not sufficiently flexible to address future changes in the juvenile justice system.

In response to these concerns, the ICJ has been redrafted, largely mirroring many of the concepts and provisions of the Interstate Compact for Adult Offender Supervision. It should be noted that the ICJ has not yet been adopted by a sufficient number of states to become active. One point of interest is that the new ICJ specifically refers to the 1934 Crime Control Consent Act as giving advance congressional consent to the compact. As discussed, whether the ICJ actually requires congressional consent remains open to debate. And the mere fact that the ICJ contains references to congressional consent is not conclusive on whether consent is required given the nature of the agreement and its subject matter. In determining whether congressional consent is appropriate, one must look to the subject matter of the agreement and the impact the agreement has on federal interests. While the new ICJ radically departs from its predecessor by creating a governance structure rather than a purely regulatory scheme, the new ICJ continues to regulate a subject area that is no different than that covered by the old compact.

The most recent version of the ICJ creates a governance structure that is remarkably similar to the Interstate Commission for Adult Offender Supervision. Under Article VI of the new ICJ, management of the compact and its affairs is vested in a national commission that possesses formal rulemaking authority.[102] All rules adopted by the commission must substantially comply with the principles in the Model State Administrative Procedures Act[103] or such other administrative procedures as the commission deems appropriate.[104] Rules adopted by the commission have the "force and effect of statutory law in a compacting state."[105] In addition to its rulemaking

---

102. Interstate Compact on Juveniles, art. VI (Proposed Official Draft 2002).
103. UNIFORM LAWS ANN. 1981 ACT, vol. 15 (2001).
104. Interstate Compact on Juveniles, art. VI (B) (Proposed Official Draft 2002).
105. *Id.* at art. II (K).

authority, Article XI vests the new commission with broad enforcement authority to ensure that member states are complying with the terms and conditions of the agreement and any duly promulgated rules. The enforcement powers given to the commission include imposing technical assistance or remedial training; requiring participation in an alternative dispute resolution process; levying fines, fees, and costs in an amount determined appropriate by the commission; suspending or terminating a state's participation in the ICJ; or seeking judicial enforcement in the federal courts.[106] The propriety of this latter provision may be questionable given that courts have previously held that the ICJ does not need congressional consent and, therefore, is not federal law under the principle of *Cuyler v. Adams*. Outside of the Supreme Court's original jurisdiction, it has not been resolved whether the states can confer jurisdiction in the federal courts when the subject matter of the compact presents no question of federal interests. The mere conferring of federal jurisdiction by the states may, in and of itself, trigger the need for congressional consent.

9.1.5 National Crime Prevention and Privacy Compact (NCPPC)

The National Crime Prevention and Privacy Compact (NCPPC) authorizes and requires participating state criminal history repositories and the Federal Bureau of Investigation (FBI) to make unsealed criminal history records available for authorized requests (e.g., as employment background checks on those working with children or the elderly). The compact eliminates duplicate maintenance of criminal history records by the states and the FBI. The purpose of the NCPPC is to produce a uniform dissemination policy among states, while still ensuring that each state may apply its own laws within the state. Thus, the ultimate goal of the compact is to increase the completeness of records made available on an interstate basis for both criminal-justice and non-criminal-justice purposes, including the screening of firearms purchasers and child care providers, through the National Instant Criminal Background Check System (NICS). Participating state repositories will be authorized and required to make all unsealed criminal history records available in response to authorized non-criminal-justice requests. The compact was part of Senate Bill 2022, which was passed by Congress and signed into law by the president in October 1998.[107]

---

106. *See generally* Interstate Compact on Juveniles, art. XI (Proposed Official Draft 2002).
107. Crime Identification Technology Act of 1998; National Criminal History Access and Child Protection Act, 105 Pub. L. No. 251, 112 Stat. 1870 (1998). *See also In re* O.M., 565 A.2d 573, 583 (D.C. 1989).

States can participate in the "III-System" in two phases.[108] First, the state's central criminal history record repository must agree to make its III-System-indexed records available in response to requests from federal or out-of-state criminal justice agencies for criminal justice purposes. The FBI continues to maintain duplicate records of offenders in order to meet the needs of federal and out-of-state non-criminal-justice agencies that need the records for employment screening and other authorized non-criminal-justice purposes. Second, a state agrees to make its III-System records available on an interstate and federal-state basis for both criminal-justice and non-criminal-justice purposes. The NCPPC is privacy-neutral in that it respects the dissemination laws for each state. At the same time, it permits ratifying states with sufficient interstate record-dissemination authority to become full participants in the III-System.

When fully adopted, the NCPPC will bind the FBI and member states in a non-criminal-justice access program according to the compact and established system policies. Authorized users are the same as those now authorized to obtain records from the FBI's files. Non-criminal-justice access to the system will be through the FBI and state repositories. Requests must be fingerprint-supported to ensure positive identification, and the dissemination and use of records is governed by the receiving state's laws. Release and use of information obtained through the system for non-criminal-justice purposes will be governed by the laws of the receiving states, and the receiving repositories will be required to screen record responses and delete information that cannot be released legally within the state.

The compact establishes a compact council composed of 15 members representing federal and state officials and other user interests. Each member is appointed by the U.S. Attorney General and serves a three-year term. The council is charged with establishing operating policies for non-criminal-justice uses of the system and oversees the use of the III-System for such purposes. A majority of the members of the council must be state officials selected by the participating states. The council must publish any rules, procedures, or standards established by the Council in the *Federal Register*.[109] The NCPPC is unclear as to what process the council would employ in adopting rules and procedures. However, given the level of federal participation and the publication and notice requirements, one may presume that the federal Administrative Procedures Act would control the rulemaking process.

---

108. "III System" is shorthand for the interstate identification index, the cooperative state-federal system for exchange of criminal history records established under the NCPPC.

109. National Crime Prevention and Privacy Compact, art. VI (e) (1999).

The NCPPC contains a number of interesting governance provisions concerning the relationship between the compact, its council, and the federal government. The compact is housed within the FBI for administrative purposes, and the federal government is a signatory with the states. However, the compact is written to prevent compact considerations from trumping the operations of the FBI. For example, the compact provides:

> The Council may request from the FBI such reports, studies, statistics, or other information or materials as the Council determines to be necessary to enable the Council to perform its duties under this Compact. The FBI, to the extent authorized by law, may provide such assistance or information upon such a request.[110]

In effect, the FBI has some discretion over how much administrative support it will provide the council. Another provision in the compact limits the extent to which compact operations may impact FBI operations concerning data collection and dissemination. Article VIII(a) states:

> Administration of this Compact shall not interfere with the management and control of the Director of the FBI over the FBI's collection and dissemination of criminal history records and the advisory function of the FBI's Advisory Policy Board (APB) chartered under the Federal Advisory Committee Act (5 U.S.C. App.) for all purposes other than non-criminal justice.[111]

The compact provides for a dispute resolution process and vests that process in the council, subject to limitation of the subject matter. The council has initial authority to resolve disputes regarding (1) interpretation of the compact; (2) any rule or standard established by the council under Article V; and (3) any dispute or controversy between any parties to the compact.[112] The council is required to afford the parties a hearing, and any appeal from a council decision must be taken first to the U.S. Attorney General. Thereafter, an aggrieved party may file suit in the appropriate federal district court, which has original jurisdiction over all cases or controversies arising under the compact.[113] Any suit arising under the compact and initiated in a state

---

110. *Id.* at art. VI (e).
111. *Id.* at art. VIII (a).
112. *Id.* at art. VI (e).
113. *Id.*

court must be removed to the appropriate district court as provided in 28 U.S.C. § 1446, or other statutory authority.[114] This removal requirement is provided presumably to ensure that federal interests would not be subject to state court interpretation and adjudication.

The NCPPC is one of several examples of federal participation an interstate compact. While at first glance the compact would appear to have few general practice considerations and conclusions, there are aspects of the compact that should be of interest to those seeking background checks on individuals. Given its neutrality on privacy matters, the compact may open areas of litigation into the privacy interests of individuals and could raise matters for employers who rely upon criminal history to deny employment or take other actions. State officials involved in criminal history development, exchange, and dissemination may also be impacted by the compact, particularly to the extent that the council promulgates rules and policies affecting system requirements.

9.1.6 Driver License Compact (DLC)[115]

Like the Non-Resident Violator Compact (NRVC) discussed below, the Driver License Compact (DLC) was designed to enable states to exchange driver information and to create a mechanism to recognize and enforce out-of-state convictions—that is, convictions for serious traffic offenses that occur in a member state other than the state of the driver's residence. Where the NRVC is limited in scope, focusing on the resolution of out-of-state convictions, the DLC is directed at requiring states to report serious traffic violations to the home state in order to enable that state to take appropriate action pursuant to its laws. The DLC is primarily concerned with four classes of traffic offenses: (1) manslaughter or negligent homicide resulting from the operation of a motor vehicle; (2) driving a motor vehicle while under the influence of alcoholic beverages or a narcotic to a degree that renders the driver incapable of safely driving a motor vehicle; (3) any felony the commission of which involves a motor vehicle; or (d) failure to stop and render aid in the event of a motor vehicle accident resulting in the death or personal injury of another.[116] In a more general manner, the DLC covers other re-

---

114. *Id.*
115. *See* discussion, D.E. Evins, Annotation, *Validity, Construction, and Application of Provision for Revocation or Suspension of Driver's License Because of Conviction of Traffic Violation in Another State*, 87 A.L.R. 2d 1019 (1963).
116. Driver License Compact, art. IV (1)(a)-(d) (1994).

ported convictions requiring the home state to "give such effect to the conduct as is provided by the laws of the home state."[117] The terms of the compact become effective upon a state's entry into the agreement and cannot be applied retroactively.[118]

Under the DLC, the licensing authority of each member state is required to report each conviction of a driver from another party state to the licensing authority of the home state.[119] The report must identify the person convicted; describe the violation including the section of the statute, code, or ordinance violated; identify the court in which action was taken; indicate whether a plea of guilty or not guilty was entered or the conviction was a result of the forfeiture of bail, bond, or other security; and include any special findings made in connection with the case.[120] The compact addresses two classes of out-of-state offenses that can be used to suspend a license issued by the home state. This difference involves two different sets of considerations applicable to giving effect to an out-of-state conviction. First, upon receiving a report of conviction involving one of the four enumerated classes of offense, the licensing authority in the home state must give the same effect to the driver's conduct as if it had occurred in the home state.[121] For example, the DLC mandates that a conviction for driving while intoxicated in a party state must be given the same effect for purposes of license suspension as if the conduct had occurred in the home state. A driver whose license had been suspended based on an out-of-state drunk driving conviction is clearly "under suspension" within the meaning of a statute imposing penalties for driving with a suspended license.[122] Second, if the out-of-state conviction is for an offense that is not described in precisely the language of Article IV(a) of the compact, the home state can construe the out-of-state offense only if the foreign law at issue is "of a substantially similar nature."[123] Where underlying offenses are not "substantially similar in nature," the home state is not obligated to give effect to the out-of-state conviction.[124]

The DLC has its roots in the "Beamer Resolution" passed by Congress in 1958. This resolution encouraged states to enter into compacts to further high-

---

117. *Id.* at art. IV (2).
118. Snyder v. Dep't of Transp., 701 A.2d 286 (Pa. Commw. Ct. 1997).
119. Driver License Compact, art. III (1994).
120. *Id.*
121. *Id.* at art. IV (1).
122. State v. Cromwell, 477 A.2d 408 (N.J. Super. Ct. App. Div. 1984).
123. Walsh v. DOT, 47 Pa. D. & C.4th 370 (Common Pleas Court of Lackawanna Cty. 2000).
124. Tindal v. Commonwealth, 756 A.2d 724 (Pa. Commw. 2000).

way traffic safety by granting states advanced consent for such agreements.[125] With the assistance of organizations such as the Council of State Governments, state motor vehicle administrators, the International Association of Chiefs of Police, the American Association of Motor Vehicle Administrators, the Insurance Institute for Highway Safety, and other national safety organizations, the DLC became effective in 1962 when Mississippi became the second state to adopt the agreement. By 1966, 20 states were members of the compact.

Like many compacts, the DLC is entered through the adoption of reciprocal legislation by member states. Article VIII provides: "This compact shall enter into force and become effective as to any state when it has enacted the same into law." Unlike the NRVC, the DLC provides only one method by which it can become effective in a state. The compact cannot be entered into by administrative action or by delegation of legislative authority to an administrative agency.[126] One state court has held that the DLC did not have the effect of law because it was adopted through administrative action, and thus the state was without authority to suspend driver's licenses based on out-of-state convictions.[127] While the DLC was constitutional, its enactment by administrative agreement, though authorized by statute, was insufficient to bring the compact into force.[128]

Like other administrative compacts, the DLC is governed by a board. The compact provides: "The head of the licensing authority of each party state shall be the administrator of this compact for his state. The administrators, acting jointly, shall have the power to formulate all necessary and proper procedures for the exchange of information under this compact."[129] However, the compact does not spell out the exact parameters of the administrators' joint authority. The board has issued guidance to the states concerning their state-to-state procedures. Because of the broad and imprecise language of the compact, the extent of governance authority by joint action of the administrators has been more a function of default than legally defined parameters. The compact currently operates under the joint executive board that also manages the operations of the NRVC.[130]

---

125. Interstate Compacts for Highway Safety, Pub. L. No. 85-684, 72 Stat. 653 (1958), *amended by* Pub. L. No. 88-466, 78 Stat. 564 (1964).
126. Sullivan v. Dep't of Transp., 708 A.2d 481 (Pa. 1998).
127. Moreland v. Dep't of Transp., 701 A.2d 294 (Pa. Commw. Ct. 1997).
128. Whitlatch v. Dep't of Transp., 710 A.2d 604 (Pa. 1998).
129. Driver License Compact, art. VII (1) (1994).
130. Bylaws of the Driver License Compact and Nonresident Violator's Compact, art. I. & art. IV, § 3 (1994), *available at* http://www.aamva.org/Documents/drvCompactDLCProceduresManual.pdf.

The DLC is also managed within each state by an appropriate licensing authority that has, in many cases, issued its own administrative rules governing intrastate compact operations. These rules generally cover two matters: (1) application for new license, and (2) reportable offense of a resident of the home state. Most administrative rules provide that a state cannot issue a license to a new applicant who has had a driver's license suspended or revoked. Applicants are generally afforded an administrative hearing along with information for obtaining a letter of clearance from another state. At the hearing, the applicant is required to prove that: (1) at least one year has passed since the out-of-state license was suspended or revoked; (2) he or she has not driven since the imposition of a suspension or revocation; and (3) he or she is now a resident of the state. Rules may further provide that all offenses appearing on the out-of-state record may be viewed as if they had occurred in the state, and an analysis of the out-of-state record constitutes the investigation required in Article V of the DLC. The rules may further allocate other burdens of proof and describe the effects of reinstatement by other member states. Courts have generally acknowledged the appropriateness of state administrative rules and required the issuing state to comply fully with the literal meaning of the rules.[131]

The DLC is in effect in 45 states and the District of Columbia. Georgia, Massachusetts, Michigan, Tennessee, and Wisconsin are not members of the DLC. It should be noted that the DLC is currently being revised to incorporate several elements of the NRVC. The new agreement, titled the "Drivers License Agreement" (DLA), will replace both the NRVC and the DLC with a single integrated compact. Additionally, the new DLA will be expanded to address the issue of driver's license security in the post-September 11, 2001, era. The ultimate goal of the new DLA is to establish a "one driver/one record" system by a more efficient exchange of driver and conviction information between member states.

The DLC is similar to the NRVC in that it ensures that information concerning out-of-state traffic offenses is both transmitted to and given effect in the driver's home state. The DLC is dissimilar from the NRVC in that the former is directed to giving full effect to *convictions* of certain offenses while the later is intended to promote compliance with out-of-state driving citations. Thus, the DLC generally has effect after conviction, while the NRVC generally has effect prior to actual conviction. States that have enacted both compacts cover a range of driving offenses from citation to convictions. Some

---

131. Edge v. Dep't of Revenue, 53 P.3d 652 (Colo. Ct. App. 2001).

states operate exclusively under only one of the two compacts,[132] while two states have not enacted either compact.[133]

The constitutionality of the DLC has been upheld in the face of numerous challenges. Even before the adoption of the DLC, courts had upheld the constitutionality of a state statute directing the division of motor vehicles to suspend or revoke the license of any resident upon receiving notice of the conviction in another state for an offense that, if committed within the state, would be grounds for the suspension or revocation of the license. Such statutes do not violate the due process clause of the state constitution or the Fourteenth Amendment, since a license to operate a motor vehicle is not a contract or property right but a privilege dependent upon compliance with conditions and laws prescribed by the state.[134] There is nothing unconstitutional, illegal, or unfair in state legislature saying, in effect, "We have received notice of your conviction of a certain offense in another state, which indicates an abuse of your privilege to operate a motor vehicle. You have the opportunity to appear and deny that you were convicted of such offense. If you do not deny the conviction, we shall conclude our information is correct, and we shall suspend your privilege to operate."[135] Applying a similar analysis, one court has held that the DLC does not violate equal protection rights of a person whose driver's license was suspended pursuant to the compact for operating a motor vehicle while under the influence of alcohol, even though, had the motorist been arrested in the home state as a first-time offender, he or she could have had the charge dismissed with no suspension of license upon completion of an alcohol education program.[136] It may even be reversible error for a trial court to refuse to consider out-of-state convictions, since the legislative purpose of protecting the public from habitually imprudent drivers was better served by inclusion of foreign convictions.[137]

Given the constitutionality of the DLC, the compact nevertheless presents some practical challenges. First, while the substantive constitutionality of the DLC has been upheld, its implementation by the states has not always

---

132. States operating exclusively under the Non-Resident Violator Compact are Georgia, Massachusetts, and Tennessee. States operating exclusively under the DLC are Alaska, California, Montana, and Oregon.

133. States that are not members of either the Driver License Compact or the Non-Resident Violator Compact are Michigan and Wisconsin.

134. Goodwin v. Super. Ct. of Yavapai County, 201 P.2d 124 (Ariz. 1948).

135. Witsch Motor Vehicle Operator License Case, 168 A.2d 772 (Pa. Super. 1961).

136. Kostrzewski v. Comm'r of Motor Vehicles, 727 A.2d 233 (Conn. App. Ct. 1999).

137. State v. Peterson, 347 N.W.2d 398 (Iowa 1984).

been supported. The DLC merely provides a reporting scheme and requires a home state to take appropriate action based on a reported conviction.[138] Thus, like several other compacts, taken alone, the DLC does not affect substantive rights but merely creates a system by which states, through their own statutory schemes, can give effect to out-of-state behavior. For example, a state statute imposing a six-month suspension of drivers' licenses upon conviction in sister states for driving under the influence of alcohol could violate the Fourteenth Amendment if not read in conjunction with state statutes allowing for hardship relief, since the distinction between those convicted within and outside of the state lacks a rational basis.[139] Additionally, an administrative regulation that deferred state licensing decisions to an out-of-state licensing authority in contravention of the DLC, and merely required that the home state consider an out-of-state conviction as if it had occurred in-state in making licensing decisions, was invalid and unenforceable.[140] It is possible, therefore, for an out-of-state conviction to have only limited home-state effect based on the laws of the home state. One court has held that the DLC cannot provide a basis for revoking driving privileges such that the motorist was ineligible for a temporary restricted license under the state's drunk-driving statute; rather, information obtained from another state as a result of the compact was used by the state to pursue suspension or revocation under other applicable state statutes.[141] This illustrates some of the difficulties in implementing compacts like the DLC, given its deference to individual state application.

Because the DLC deals with the effect that out-of-state convictions are to be given in the home state, it is important to identify whether such a conviction must be reported and given effect. Forfeiture of a bond under the laws of the state in which a violation has occurred may be construed as a "conviction" for purposes of the DLC.[142] Courts have generally followed the rule that for an out-of-state offense to be treated as an in-state offense, the offense must (1) fall explicitly within those listed in Article IV(1)(a)-(d), or (2) be substantially similar to an offense in the home state such as to require reporting under Article IV(4). To constitute substantial similarity, the out-of-state stat-

---

138. The implementation of the DLC is governed by state law and is subject to state court interpretation.
139. Wright v. Ohio Bureau of Motor Vehicles, 644 N.E.2d 743 (Ohio Mun. Ct. 1994).
140. State v. Vargason, 607 N.W.2d 691 (Iowa 2000).
141. *Id.*
142. Strong v. Neth, 676 N.W.2d 15 (Neb. 2004).

ute forming the basis of the conviction must have elements similar to those in the home state, which does not require exact similarity or that two statutes precisely mirror one another for purposes of the DLC.[143] Thus, Montana authorities properly suspended the driving privilege of a motorist convicted of driving while impaired in New York, even though New York had a two-tier DUI statute (driving while impaired as lesser offense and driving while intoxicated or with per se blood alcohol level) and intoxication and impairment were not synonymous. Both New York's driving-while-impaired statute and Montana's DUI statute had similar elements.[144] Two drunk-driving statutes may be "substantially similar," even though one is broader so long as the conviction clearly relates to drunk driving, which would be an offense in the home state.[145] By contrast, a Utah offense of alcohol-related reckless driving was not substantially similar to a New Jersey offense of driving under the influence because the Utah offense merely required some consumption of alcohol in connection with reckless driving and did not require any impairment or showing that alcohol caused reckless driving.[146] Some courts apply the "functionally similar" test to determine whether an out-of-state conviction is to be given effect in the home state.[147]

Although the DLC requires the home state to give effect to an out-of-state conviction, the DLC has not been construed to limit the authority of a state to grant conditional driving privileges nor has it been construed in all cases as mandating suspension or revocation of privileges. The laws of the home state define the parameters of any suspension, revocation, or granting of conditional driving privileges. Thus, a person whose driver's license was suspended because of an out-of-state conviction for driving under the influence could petition for occupational driving privileges under the home state's applicable law.[148] Where state law mandates the revocation or suspension of driving privileges based on an out-of-state conviction, such laws are generally upheld.[149]

143. Lafferty v. Dep't of Transp., 735 A.2d 1289 (Pa. Commw. Ct. 1999), *appeal denied*, 757 A.2d 936 (2000).
144. Montanye v. State, 864 P.2d 1234 (Mont. 1993).
145. Draeger v. Reed, 69 Cal. App. 4th 1511 (Cal. Ct. App. 1999).
146. New Jersey Div. of Motor Vehicles v. Ripley, 835 A.2d 1252 (N.J. Super. Ct. App. Div. 2003).
147. Fetty v. Dep't of Transp., 784 A.2d 236 (Pa. Commw. Ct. 2001), *as amended* (Oct. 2, 2001).
148. Hughes v. Ohio Bureau of Motor Vehicles, 681 N.E.2d 430 (Ohio 1997).
149. State v. Cromwell, 477 A.2d 408 (N.J. Super. Ct. App. Div. 1984).

Once an out-of-state conviction is reported, the proceedings to revoke or suspend a license are civil, not criminal, in nature. A license revocation proceeding pursuant to a reported offense is remedial in nature and is not a punishment. Thus, the DLC and implementing state statutes do not violate a motorist's due process rights on grounds that it imposes sanctions for conduct occurring outside territorial borders of the home state.[150] A hearing on the question of suspension is not a criminal proceeding because the question is whether the operator could continue to exercise a privilege. Therefore, procedural and evidentiary burdens may be placed upon those seeking to exercise a privilege that could not be placed upon those charged with a crime, or even upon those defending property rights.[151] At least one court has held that a home state does not violate constitutional principles of fairness and due process when it imposes, without a hearing, a revocation or suspension based on an out-of-state conviction, finding that the operator, by pleading guilty to the offense, must accept all the burdens and disabilities that flow from an out-of-state judgment of conviction.[152] Nevertheless, it is generally held that the administrative agency has the burden of proving that the licensee has an out-of-state conviction.

The DLC illustrates the challenges of implementing an interstate compact at the state level, particularly when the implementation of the compact is controlled by each member states' laws. By requiring that out-of-state convictions be treated as if they occurred in the home state, the compact necessarily invokes the procedures and processes of the home state in effectuating the terms of the compact. This variance in approach can lead to significant confusion, as a driver must not only rely on the terms of the compact but also individual implementation according to their respective state's statutory schemes.

9.1.7   Nonresident Violator Compact (NRVC)

The purpose of the NRVC is to standardize procedures and protections various states employ to process nonresident violators—that is, persons who receive citations in a state other than their state of residence. The compact authorizes participating states to exchange information on nonresident violators, thereby enabling the home state to take appropriate action to secure

---

150. Correll v. Dep't of Transp., 726 A.2d 427 (Pa. Commw. Ct. 1999), *appeal granted, order aff'd,* 769 A.2d 442 (2001).
151. Witsch Motor Vehicle Operator's License Case, 168 A.2d 772 (Pa. Super. Ct. 1961).
152. Goodwin v. Super. Ct. of Yavapai County, 201 P.2d 124 (Ariz. 1948).

compliance with an out-of-state citation. The compact assures nonresident motorists who receive a citation for minor traffic offenses in a member state the same treatment the state would accord its own residents. Under the NRVC, a nonresident receiving a traffic citation in a member state must resolve the citation or face the possibility of license suspension in his or her home state. Suspensions generally last until the requirements of the citation are met and evidence of compliance is provided to the home state. Safeguards are built into the compact so that a nonresident driver receiving a citation has due process protections. The provisions of the NRVC do not apply to parking or standing violations, highway weight limit violations, and violations of laws governing the transportation of hazardous materials.[153] Moreover, the NRVC provides that the compact shall not be "construed to affect the right of any party jurisdiction to apply any of its other laws relating to license to drive to any person or circumstance, or to invalidate or prevent any driver license agreement or other cooperative arrangements between a party jurisdiction and a nonparty jurisdiction."[154]

The NRVC has its origins in several reciprocal agreements developed in the 1960s. In 1965, Maryland, Virginia, and the District of Columbia adopted an agreement entitled the Traffic Summons Reciprocal Agreement. This was followed in 1969 with New York, New Jersey, and a number of New England states adopting similar agreements. Each of these agreements were modeled after the suggested Traffic Violations Compact developed by the National Conference of Commissioners on Uniform State Laws. Jurisdictions participating in these reciprocal agreements would inform the motor vehicle administrations of other states that one of their residents refused to comply with a citation issued by a member jurisdiction. The motor vehicle administrator in the home state would then initiate proceedings to suspend a resident's driver's license until compliance. The limited nature of these early agreements produced decidedly non-uniform practices within the participating jurisdictions. As the need for greater uniformity arose, states began the process of developing a uniform interstate compact. This first effort produced the Nonresident Violators Compact of 1972. In 1976, the compact was redrafted in cooperation with the National Highway Transportation Safety Administration. The Nonresident Violators Compact of 1977 was the product of this effort. The compact has received congressional consent through the Interstate Compacts

---

153. Nonresident Violator Compact, art. VIII (1994).
154. *Id.* at art. V.

for Highway Safety Act.[155] However, at least one court has held that the NRVC does not require congressional consent, because it did not impermissibly enhance state power at the expense of the national government.[156]

Under the terms of the compact, entry into force is generally accomplished by resolution of ratification executed by an authorized official of the applying jurisdiction and submitted to the chairman of the board. Because the compact specifically authorizes entry into force through administrative action, such action does not constitute an impermissible delegation of legislative authority so long as the state legislature has authorized this mode of adoption.[157] However, states can also become members of the NRVC by (1) a state legislature authorizing a motor vehicle administrator to enter into a reciprocal agreement with other states, or (2) a state legislature adopting the full compact through legislation. A state may withdraw from the NRVC by giving official written notice to the other member jurisdictions directed to the compact administrator of each member jurisdiction. Withdrawal is not effective until 90 days after receipt of the written notice.[158]

The NRVC is governed by a board of compact administrators established by Article VI of the agreement.[159] Pursuant to an amendment to the bylaws of both the NRVC and the Driver License Compact (DLC), both agreements are overseen by a joint executive board comprised of representatives of states

---

155. Interstate Compacts for Highway Safety, Pub. L. No. 85-684, 72 Stat. 653 (1958), *as amended.*

Pub. L. No. 88-466, 78 Stat. 564 (1964), provides:

> That the consent of Congress is hereby given to any two or more of the several states, and one or more of the several states and the District of Columbia, to enter into agreements or compacts—(1) for cooperative effort and mutual assistance in the establishment and carrying out of traffic programs, including, but not limited to, the enactment of uniform traffic laws, driver education and training, coordination of traffic law enforcement, research into safe automobile and highway design and research programs of the human factors affecting traffic safety, and (2) for the establishment of such agencies, joint or otherwise, as they deem desirable for the establishment and carrying out of such traffic safety programs.

156. State v. Kurt, 802 S.W.2d 954 (Mo. 1991).

157. Whitlatch v. Dep't of Transp., 715 A.2d 387 (Pa. 1997).

158. Nonresident Violator Compact, art. VII(c) (1994).

159. *Id.* at art. VI.

that are members of both compacts.[160] Each party state's compact administrator is appointed by an executive authority and serves pursuant to applicable laws of the state the administrator represents. The compact allows the compact administrator to appoint an alternate, who may sit on the board as that state's representative. Each member of the board is entitled to one vote. No action of the board is binding unless it occurs in a meeting at which a majority of the party states is represented and a majority of the members present vote for the action. The board elects officers annually, which includes a chairperson and vice-chairperson.[161] The board is empowered to adopt bylaws for the conduct of its business that are not inconsistent with the provisions of the compact or the laws of a party jurisdiction.[162] Additionally, the board can formulate necessary procedures and develop uniform forms and documents for administering the provisions of the NRVC.[163] All procedures and forms adopted by the board must be contained in the compact manual. Currently, governance of the NRVC is managed by the board in cooperation with the American Association of Motor Vehicle Administrators (AAMVA). The National Highway Traffic Safety Administration also plays a key role. The AAMVA provides secretariat and technical services to the board.[164]

The NRVC is in effect in 44 states and the District of Columbia. Alaska, California, Montana, Oregon, Michigan, and Wisconsin are not members of the NRVC. Consequently, nonresident violators receiving citations in these states may be treated differently, within the bounds of due process and equal protection, than resident violators. Violations occurring in these states are generally not reported to other states unless done so pursuant to the Driver License Compact. A member state is not required to afford nonmember states the enforcement services allowed by the NRVC, including suspension for failure to appear or otherwise resolve a nonresident violation. As noted, the NRVC is currently being revised to incorporate several elements of the DLC. The new agreement, titled the Drivers License Agreement (DLA), discussed below, will replace both the NRVC and the DLC with a single integrated compact. Over the years, the constitutionality of the NRVC has been upheld by courts, and the binding

160. Bylaws of the Driver License Compact and Non-Resident Violator Compact, art. I & art. IV § 3 (1994), *available at* http://www.aamva.org/Documents/drvCompactsNRVCProceduresManual.pdf.
161. Non-Resident Violator Compact, art. VI (c) (1994).
162. *Id.* at art. VI (d).
163. *Id.* at art. VI (g).
164. *See generally* American Association of Motor Vehicle Administrators, *available at* http://www.aamva.org/.

nature of the agreement has been recognized notwithstanding questions regarding the need for congressional consent.[165]

The purpose of the NRVC has generally been twofold. First, the compact is intended to compel a nonresident violator to comply with an issuing jurisdiction by paying the fine or contesting the action to a final resolution.[166] Second, the compact is intended to provide equal application of the law to both resident and nonresident traffic violators of the party states.[167] Thus, for example, if a resident violator in a party state is only required to accept a citation and not post bond, other surety, or surrender a license to continue to a journey, the same process must be afforded a nonresident violator.[168] Upon receipt of a report of a failure to comply from the authority of the issuing state, the licensing authority of the home state must notify the motorist and initiate a suspension action according to the home state's procedures.[169] The suspension is valid until satisfactory evidence of compliance with the traffic citation is furnished to the home state's licensing authority. At least one state has held that the period of suspension in compact cases runs from the date of suspension until satisfactory evidence of compliance is presented and thus is generally not limited by other state statutes.[170] The burden is on the motorist to provide the evidence of compliance necessary to end a suspension. Filing a putative motion to dismiss an out-of-state citation does not comply with the NRVC.[171]

Although the NRVC mandates suspension of a driver's license for out-of-state violations, the compact does not provide the procedures by which the suspension is effectuated. Rather, Article IV(a) states the suspension occurs pursuant to the laws of the home state.[172] The only restriction on the suspension procedure is that the home state must safeguard due process. Whether a state's process has been appropriate provides the greatest source of litigation under the NRVC. Questions concerning the NRVC occur at the state level when licensing authorities initiate an enforcement action against a resident driver for failing to resolve an out-of-state citation or deny driving privileges. One state has held that out-of-state revocations and suspensions do not necessarily provide grounds for denial of driving privileges.[173] Under the home state law, a licensing author-

---

165. State v. Kurt, 802 S.W.2d 954 (Mo. 1991).

166. State v. Marshall, 845 P.2d 659 (Kan. 1993).

167. Non-Resident Violator Compact, art. I (a)(5), art. VI (c) (1994); United States v. Castro, 129 F.3d 752 (5th Cir. 1997).

168. Nonresident Violator Compact art. I (a)(5) & (b)(2), art. VI (c) (1994).

169. *Id.* at art. IV (a) & VI (c).

170. State v. Hudon, 763 P.2d 611 (Kan. 1988).

171. Davidson v. Dep't of Revenue, 981 P.2d 696 (Colo. Ct. App. 1999).

172. Non-Resident Violator Compact, art. IV (a) art. & VI (c) (1994).

173. State v. Vargaso, 607 N.W.2d 691, 696 (Iowa 2000).

ity could not issue a driver's license to any person whose driver's license or driving privilege is suspended or revoked, including based upon a driver's failure to pay a fine, penalty, surcharge, or court costs.[174]

Assuming the compact is in effect as between two states, the principal questions in NRVC cases are: (1) did the offender fail to resolve an outstanding citation in the issuing state; and (2) has the issuing state properly notified the home state? If these questions are affirmatively resolved, the NRVC requires the home state to initiate suspension proceedings according to its laws. Such proceedings are civil in nature and may be handled through administrative action. Because suspension proceedings are not criminal in nature, due process and equal protection concerns are substantially mitigated. The appropriateness of the administrative process is generally controlled by the Supreme Court's decision in *Mathews* v. *Eldridge*, which considers three distinct factors: (1) the private interest that will be affected by the official action; (2) the risk of an erroneous deprivation of such interest through the procedures used, and the probable value, if any, of additional or substitute procedural safeguards; and (3) the government's interest, including the function involved and the fiscal and administrative burdens that the additional or substitute procedural requirement would entail.[175] Applying this test, one court has held that the home state may provide a post-suspension hearing, as distinguished from a pre-suspension hearing, and still comply with due process requirements.[176] Thus, so long as a state affords a resident the opportunity to challenge a proposed suspension under the NRVC, and the administrative process meets the *Mathews* requirements, the violator has been afforded necessary due process protections.

9.1.8   Proposed Driver License Agreement (DLA)

No discussion concerning the Driver License Compact (DLC), the Non-Resident Violator Compact (NRVC) would be complete without reference to the proposed Driver License Agreement (DLA), a new interstate compact. This agreement, which is being proposed by the American Association of Motor Vehicle Administrators (AAMVA), would replace the current DLC and NRVC by combining many of their elements into a single agreement.[177]

---

174. Wood v. Iowa Dep't of Transp., 2003 Iowa App. LEXIS 796 (Iowa Ct. App. 2003).

175. Mathews v. Eldridge, 424 U.S. 319, 334-35 (1976).

176. Maumee v. Gabriel, 518 N.E.2d 558 (Ohio 1988).

177. Driver's License Agreement (Tentative Draft, February 2004). *See also* American Association of Motor Vehicle Administrators, Drivers License Agreement, *available at* http://www.aamva.org/drivers/drv_compactsDLA.asp.

The AAMVA, founded in 1933, is composed of administrators and public service executives who are responsible for motor vehicle administration, driver licensing issues, and the enforcement of state and national laws that govern the safe use of vehicles in the United States and Canada. The critical issues that the DLA seeks to address are to promote the "one license-one driver control record" concept and to provide for the fair and impartial treatment of all drivers operating in member jurisdictions. The DLA deals specifically with the issuance and retention of driver's licenses, the update and maintenance of driver records, compliance with the laws and regulations relating to highway safety and federal mandates, as well as the exchange of information between member jurisdictions.

The purposes of the DLA are:

(1) Each driver will have only one driver's license issued by a jurisdiction, which is recognized by all member jurisdictions, and will have only one driver control record;

(2) All efforts should be made to strengthen cooperation among member jurisdictions so that all drivers are required to answer charges of violation of motor vehicle and traffic laws, and to comply with the procedures for the disposition of such charges, regardless of the jurisdiction where any such violation occurs;

(3) Reciprocal recognition of drivers' licenses and of motor vehicle and traffic violations related to highway safety will be facilitated for the benefit of all member jurisdictions;

(4) Compliance by each driver with all provisions of law pertaining to the safe operation of a motor vehicle will be required as a condition of the issuance and retention of a driver's license;

(5) Conviction of a driver or owner for any motor vehicle and traffic violation related to highway safety in any jurisdiction will be treated as if the violation had occurred in the jurisdiction of record, for the purpose of maintaining the driver control record and of imposing administrative sanctions, as authorized by law; and

(6) All drivers will be allowed to proceed on their way and will not be required to appear in person before a court or other tribunal, regardless of their jurisdiction of record, after having been issued a citation for certain motor vehicle and traffic violations.[178]

Like the NRVC, a state may enter the DLA through administrative action by adopting a statute authorizing a state official to do so.

---

178. 2004 Conn. Pub. Acts 217 (2004).

9.2   CHILD WELFARE COMPACTS

This section surveys the following topics:

- General considerations in child welfare compacts
- The Interstate Compact on Child Placement
- The Interstate Compact on Adoption and Medical Assistance

9.2.1   General Considerations

Child welfare compacts pose particularly thorny issues because they must necessarily interact with other compacts, several uniform laws, and a host of other state and federal laws. This environment, overlaid with the inherent emotion of such cases and their great cost to state and federal budgets, creates issues experienced in no other compact realm, save perhaps those agreements dealing with environmental issues. These compacts also present unique issues with enforceability, choice of law, and the jurisdiction of various state and federal courts. Thus, child welfare compacts operate in an area that is dynamic, rapidly changing, and ever in flux. Where compacts in the area of crime control and education can be complex, they are not overlaid with the layers of confusing law that surround family and juvenile issues.

Part of the difficulty presented by child welfare compacts rests in the generally accepted principle that they do not require congressional consent because such agreements regulate in areas that have traditionally been within the general police powers of the states. These compacts neither create imbalances in the power distribution of the federal system nor are they deemed to intrude on the enumerated powers of Congress. As a result, short of invoking the original jurisdiction of the Supreme Court, the jurisdiction of federal courts as an enforcement mechanism is not available. For example, in *McComb v. Wambaugh*, the Court of Appeals for the Third Circuit noted that:

> The Interstate Compact on Placement of Children has not received Congressional consent. Rather than altering the balance of power between the states and the federal government, this Compact focuses wholly on adoption and foster care of children—areas of jurisdiction historically retained by the states. Congressional consent, therefore, was not necessary for the Compact's legitimacy. Because Congressional consent was neither given nor required, the Compact does not express federal law. Consequently, this Compact must be construed as state law.[179]

---

179. McComb v. Wambaugh, 934 F.2d 474, 479 (3d Cir. 1991).

Thus, child welfare compacts illustrate and reinforce the principle that compacts between states can legitimately regulate interstate matters that are traditionally of state concern and may do so without the need for congressional consent. However, because of the absence of congressional consent, these compacts do not function as federal law under the principles articulated in *Cuyler v. Adams* and its progeny. Such compacts, though enforceable agreements, also demonstrate the difficulty with state-to-state compacts. The very fact that such compacts are, in the words of *McComb v. Wambaugh*, state agreements that "must be construed as state law," has left child welfare compacts hostage to wildly varying state court interpretation, application, and compliance. In the context of the Interstate Compact on the Placement of Children (ICPC), it is not unusual for families involved in interstate cases to be subject to contradictory orders issued by the state courts involved with interstate placements. This fact alone has led to calls to rewrite and "federalize" the ICPC.[180]

An additional difficulty facing many child welfare compacts rests in the relationship these agreements have with other child welfare laws. This interaction can also produce confusing results in individual cases with uniform laws influencing the outcome of particular cases that also are arguably controlled by existing compacts. For example, a single juvenile case involving interstate matters may involve attributes of the ICPC, the Interstate Juvenile Compact (ICJ), the Uniform Child Custody Jurisdiction Act (UCCJA) or its replacement the Uniform Child Custody Jurisdiction and Enforcement Act (UCCJEA), the Adoption and Safe Family Act (ASFA), and the Parental Kidnapping Prevention Act (PKPA). Each of these uniform acts and federal laws can impact jurisdiction and other matters presented by a single interstate case with different courts applying different aspects of each law. Consequently, knowing what law to apply in what circumstances is more an art than science, the result being a labyrinth of confusion between intertwining federal laws, uniform laws, and interstate compacts. And because these compacts do not require congressional consent with its resulting "federalization," it is difficult at times to identify the controlling law in a case because each state has a certain freedom to apply its "state law"; that is, its interpretation of the compact and competing laws.

Currently, there are several child welfare compacts in effect nationally, most having been adopted by all 50 states. Two compacts, the ICPC and the Interstate Compact on Adoption and Medical Assistance Compact (ICAMA), deserve special attention. These agreements illustrate both the possibilities and the problems of using interstate compacts to regulate, across state bor-

---

180. Francis J. Foley, *An Opinion: Federalize the ICPC*, 50 Juv. & Fam. Ct. J. 65 (1999).

ders, matters that most state officials deem critical to the exercise of their inherent police powers—the protection of children. These two compacts also provide excellent insights into (1) how compacts do or do not function well in an environment of overlapping jurisdiction and laws, and (2) what happens when the interpretation and enforcement of an interstate compact is ultimately left to the vagaries of the many state courts.

9.2.2   Interstate Compact on the Placement of Children (ICPC)

Although the Interstate Compact on the Placement of Children (ICPC) is undergoing a major redrafting, the agreement is one of the most far reaching and complicated compacts currently affecting interstate child welfare concerns. The ICPC, effective in 52 jurisdictions, seeks to establish a uniform legal and administrative structure for governing the interstate placement of children.[181] The need for the compact was recognized in the 1950s when problems were identified with the movement of children between states for adoption or placement in foster care. Among the most serious problems identified were those concerned with the ability of then-existing state laws to provide adequate protection for children moving between states and the patchwork of regulation created by individual state action. Because state jurisdiction is inherently geography-based and ends at the border, there was little ability to compel agencies or persons charged with child protection to comply with foreign state court orders regarding placement or to assist in making sure that the placement was safe and suitable for a child. Although some public child welfare agencies provided "courtesy supervision," children were not entitled to protection or services in another state as a matter of right when placed across state lines. As a result, the ICPC was drafted and was first enacted by New York in 1960.

The compact is generally applied in four situations: (1) placement preliminary to adoption; (2) placement into foster care, including foster homes, group homes, residential treatment facilities, and institutions; (3) placement with a parent or relative when a parent or relative is not making the placement; and (4) placement of adjudicated delinquents in out-of-state institutions. While these are the generally accepted categories of cases covered by the compact, the practical application of the compact has been anything but clear. With regards to delinquents, the Interstate Compact on Juveniles (ICJ) may also be involved, complicating matters. The ICPC gen-

---

181. For additional resources, *see* Association of Administrators of the Interstate Compact on the Placement of Children, *available at* http://icpc.aphsa.org/documents.asp.

erally does not apply when placing a child in a medical facility or mental health facility, or when placing a child in a boarding school or an institution primarily educational in nature.[182] The ICPC also does not apply when the placement is made by a parent, stepparent, grandparent, adult brother or sister, adult uncle or aunt, or a child's legal guardian.[183] Thus, the compact would not apply when a child is being placed with a biological parent in another state.[184] It is important to note that the ICPC applies to both public and private interstate placements[185] and applies to private interstate adoptions.[186] Unlike the ICJ, which applies to juvenile offenders and is, therefore, a compact controlling intergovernmental action, the ICPC has much broader reach, impacting private interests as well.

Under Article VII of the ICPC, governance of the agreement is vested in a group of state officials who may, acting jointly, promulgate rules to effectuate the goals of the compact. In addition to promulgating rules, under the compact, the state official appointed by the executive head of each state is the general coordinator of activities for that state.[187] To aid in the management of the compact, the Association of Administrators of the Interstate Compact on the Placement of Children (AAICPC) was established in 1974. Although the AAICPC claims to have authority under ICPC to "promulgate rules and regulations to carry out more effectively the terms and provisions of this compact," nothing in the compact specifically recognizes the AAICPC as the agency of "joint officers" required by the agreement. The AAICPC is a de facto, not necessarily de jure, interstate commission for the ICPC. The AAICPC obtains its secretariat services as an affiliate of the American Public Human Services Association (APHSA). The secretariat to AAICPC provides ongoing administrative, legal, and technical assistance to the member states. Under the auspices of the AAICPC, the secretariat also provides resources for the purpose of resolving problems and formulating policies, practices, and goals. The secretariat issues opinions on the application of the ICPC in particular cases or circumstances. These opinions are advisory in nature and have no legal or controlling

---

182. Interstate Compact on the Placement of Children, art. II (d) (1960).
183. *Id.* at art. VIII (a).
184. McComb v. Wambaugh, 934 F.2d 474 (3d Cir. 1991); *In re* Johnny S., 40 Cal. App. 4th 969 (Cal. Ct. App. 1995).
185. Interstate Compact on the Placement of Children, art. II (1960); State Dep't of Econ. Sec. v. Leonardo, 22 P.3d 513 (Ariz. Ct. App. 2001).
186. Matter of Adoption of Baby "E," 427 N.Y.S.2d 705 (N.Y. Fam. Ct. 1980).
187. *Id.* at art. VII.

force on the operations of the compact.[188] Such opinions can, undoubtedly, be highly persuasive notwithstanding their advisory nature.

Pursuant to the ICPC, the AAICPC has issued rules. Rules cover such matters as forms, conversion of an intrastate placement into an interstate placement, placements with parents, relatives, and in nonguardian or non-family settings, residential placement, permission to place a child, time limitations and reapplication, priority placements, change of placement, visits that do not constitute placements, and guardians.[189] However, while the ICPC clearly allows for the promulgation of rules and regulations, the compact does not give unlimited authority to promulgate any rule that might involve child placement. The rules promulgated by the AAICPC cannot expand the operational role of the ICPC beyond its statutory mandate. At least one court has determined that the AAICPC Regulation 3, governing placement, was contrary to the expressed terms of Article III of the compact and, further, would produce the anomalous situation of imposing a financial obligation upon a sending state that supersedes parents' duty to support their children and, therefore, could not be sustained.[190] Other courts have shared a similar view that regulations promulgated by a compact commission must conform to the terms of the compact and cannot expand regulatory authority beyond the compact or reduce the regulatory power of the agreement beyond that contemplated by a clear reading of the compact as a statute.[191] The AAICPC could not, by rule, expand the coverage of the compact to include placements with parents.[192]

Currently, the ICPC is being redrafted in response to concerns that have arisen over the years with its inconsistent application and lack of enforceability. Concerns have been expressed with the timeliness of its procedures, the lack of state resources contributing to long delays in cross-state placements, and the overly broad application of the compact due, in part, to its non-restrictive language. Added to the language and implementation problems of the compact is the confusion produced by the interaction of the compact with

---

188. Although not published on the Internet, secretariat opinions are available through the American Public Human Services Association *at* http://www.aphsa.org.
189. Interstate Compact on the Placement of Children, Reg. No. 0.01; Reg. No. 1; Reg. No. 3; Reg. No. 4; Reg. No. 6; Reg. No. 7; Reg. No. 8; Reg. No. 9; Reg. No. 10 (2002).
190. McComb v. Wambaugh, 934 F.2d 474 (3d Cir. 1991).
191. Ark. Dep't of Human Servs. v. Huff, 65 S.W.3d 880 (Ark. 2002).
192. *In re* Johnny S., 47 Cal. Rptr. 2d 94 (Cal. Ct. App. 1995).

several uniform and federal laws. Consequently, suggestions have been made to redraft the ICPC and make its application significantly narrower. For example, the current ICPC applies to a host of placement decisions including private and public adoptions, foster care placements, and placements in residential treatment centers. A task force has made several recommendations including limiting the process required for independent and private adoptions and intercountry adoptions, applying less restrictive standards of oversight to placements in residential treatment centers, and giving sending agencies greater flexibility to make placements with a nonoffending custodial parent. It is the intention of the AAICPC and the APHSA to propose a new ICPC in 2005.[193]

The ICPC has been a source of confusion in its interpretation and application.[194] The confusion is heightened by a number of other laws—such as the Uniform Child Custody Jurisdiction Act (UCCJA),[195] Uniform Child Custody Jurisdiction Enforcement Act[196] (UCCJEA), the Parental Kidnapping Prevention Act[197] (PKPA), and the ICJ—that interface with and may at times lead to contradictions with the ICPC. Part of the difficulty with the ICPC may also rest in Article VIII (b) of the compact.[198] This provision states that the ICPC does not apply to "[a]ny placement, sending or bringing of a child into a receiving state pursuant to any other interstate compact to which both the state from which the child is sent or brought and the receiving state are party, or to any other agreement between said states which has the force of law." This provision essentially authorizes side agreements between states and arguably could allow those agreements to exclude the ICPC as a consideration in the placement of a child. As a result, compliance with the ICPC can be described as sometimes difficult, partly the result of outside agreements and laws, partly the result of the unclear reach of the ICPC, and partly the result of limited resources. The lack of understanding regarding the legal

---

193. Congress has also taken a keen interest in the ICPC. *See* Safe and Timely Interstate Placement of Foster Children Act of 2004, H.R. 4504, 108th Cong. (2004); Orderly and Timely Interstate Placement of Foster Children Act of 2004, S. 2779, 108th Cong. (2004).

194. Though beyond the scope of this publication, one additional area of potential confusion involves application of the Indian Child Welfare Act (ICWA) to cases that might also be subject to the ICPC. 25 U.S.C. § 1901 (2004). For a discussion on the interaction of ICWA and the ICPC, *see* In the Matter of the Adoption of J.H.G., 869 P.2d 640 (Kan. 1994).

195. Uniform Child Custody Jurisdiction Act (1968).

196. Uniform Child Custory Jurisdiction Enforcement Act (1997).

197. 28 U.S.C. § 1738A (2004).

198. Interstate Compact on the Placement of Children, art. VIII(b) (1960).

standing and role of interstate compacts and their interaction with various state and federal laws may also contribute to problems with the administration of the ICPC.

The ICPC provides a sending state with the opportunity to have placement recipients and the placement environment evaluated to ensure that it "does not appear contrary to the interests of the child." The standard is not as high as the "best interest" of the child standard applied by courts in many other child welfare contexts. Under the ICPC, the laws of the receiving state govern the procedures regarding the assessment of the prospective family, their eligibility, and many other issues related to child placement. Additionally, the ICPC protects the legal, administrative, and financial interests of the child by allocating responsibility between the sending agency, receiving state, and individual. The ICPC requires that no child can be sent to another state for foster care until the sending state has furnished public authorities in the receiving state with written notice of the planned placement and the reasons for the placement.[199] A child may not be sent to a receiving state until the sending state has received approval in the form of a written notice that the placement does not appear to be contrary to the interests of the child.[200] The receiving state's laws determine whether a proposed family is suitable for adoption or to provide foster care. The ICPC provides that no child can be sent out-of-state unless the sending agency has complied with the requirements in Article III.[201] It is unlawful to leave the sending state or enter the receiving state without ICPC approval.

The ICPC applies to both public and private interstate placements and to certain private interstate adoptions.[202] Thus, as previously noted, the compact controls both governmental action and private rights. In the context of adoptions, the compact requires that the state where the child and birth mother reside and the state where the adoptive parents reside both agree that the child can come to live with the adoptive parents. The sending state must ensure that the legal rights of birth parents have been lawfully terminated either through a court proceeding or by consent. A child is permitted to leave a state once all documentation is received by the sending state and approval is obtained.

---

199. Interstate Compact on the Placement of Children, art. III (b) (1960).
200. *Id.* at art. III (d).
201. *Id.* at art. III (a). *See also* Templeton v. Witham, 595 F. Supp. 770 (S.D. Cal. 1984).
202. Interstate Compact on the Placement of Children, art. II (1960). *See* State Dep't of Econ. Sec. v. Leonardo, 22 P.3d 513 (Ariz. C.A. 2001); Matter of Adoption of Baby "E," 427 N.Y.S.2d 705 (N.Y. Fam. Ct. 1980).

Officials in the receiving state may (and generally will) require a home study of the adoptive family to ensure a suitable home for the child and to make certain that the child will receive appropriate care. The placement of a child in another state does not automatically deprive the sending agency of jurisdiction. A sending state retains jurisdiction over the child "sufficient to determine all matters in relation to the custody, supervision, care, and disposition of the child which it would have had if the child remained in the sending agency's state, until the child is adopted, reaches majority, becomes self-supporting or is discharged with the concurrence of the appropriate authority in the receiving state."[203] This provision has been problematic because competing court orders are possible given overlapping jurisdiction under various state laws and other compacts. The ICPC provides that the sending agency can obtain supervision and regular reports on the progress of the placement from the receiving state.

The failure to comply with the requirements of the ICPC may invoke Article IV penalties, which allow both the sending and receiving states to impose penalties authorized by their respective laws. Sending a child to the receiving state before complying with the terms of the compact is in an illegal act.[204] Some states have held that violations of the ICPC, even in circumstances involving adoptions by private parties, may warrant dismissal of the adoption action[205] or return of a child to its biological parents.[206] However, most courts appear reluctant to vacate an adoption even when there is a claim by a biological parent that violation of ICPC justify revoking the parent's consent to the adoption. In cases of intentional violations of the ICPC, courts generally strictly apply the agreement even to the extent of forgoing considerations for the best interests of the child.[207] Not all courts agree with this position, some holding that the best interest of the child is the critical consideration in imposing a penalty even in cases of willful violations of the ICPC.[208] At least one court has held that dismissal of an action or vacation of an adoption order is not warranted when a violation of the ICPC was unintentional.[209] In other circumstances, courts exercise discretion in determining the

203. Interstate Compact on the Placement of Children, art. V (a) (1960).
204. H.P. v. Dep't of Children & Families, 838 So. 2d 583 (Fla. Dist. Ct. App. 2003).
205. *In re* Adoption of T.M.M., 608 P.2d 130, 133 (Mont. 1980).
206. *In re* Adoption/Guardianship No. 3598, 675 A.2d 170 (Md. Ct. Spec. App. 1996).
207. *Id.* at 187.
208. *In re* Calynn M. G., 523 N.Y.S.2d 729 (N.Y. Surrogate Ct. 1987).
209. *In re* C.M.A., 557 N.W.2d 353 (Minn. Ct. App. 1996).

appropriate sanction for violations of the ICPC.[210] Other penalties provided in Article V include "suspension or revocation of a license, permit, or other legal authorization held by the sending agency which empowers or allows the sending agency to place or care for children."[211] An attorney's license can be suspended or even revoked for failing to comply with the ICPC.[212] A state may also impose criminal penalties on those who violate the ICPC.[213] A court's failure to comply with the ICPC may be deemed an extrajurisdictional act requiring relief from an order placing a child out of state.[214]

Several areas of the current ICPC raise concerns precisely because the exact boundaries of the compact are unclear, leading to inconsistent court decisions and significant departures of interpretation between state courts. For example, unless jurisdiction is properly terminated under the ICPC, the compact requires that a sending state retain jurisdiction over the child being placed regardless of the jurisdictional interests of the receiving state. Jurisdiction in an ICPC case can only be terminated when the child is adopted, reaches majority, becomes self-supporting, or is discharged in conjunction with the appropriate authorities in a receiving state.[215] While some courts have applied this standard strictly,[216] other courts—particularly those in receiving states—have been less willing to concede that jurisdiction remains in the sending state regardless of the underlying situation.[217] Courts have found a variety of grounds to override the ICPC jurisdictional features, including considerations for the best interest of the child and the failure of a sending state to abide by its obligations.[218] Although the compact's language on jurisdiction is clear, its application to specific cases has been divergent.

One factor that is critical to determining whether the ICPC applies and, if so, which state has jurisdiction, is defining what constitutes a "sending agency." This is a critical consideration because defining the sending agency

---

210. *In re* Baby Girl, 850 S.W.2d 64 (Mo. 1993).
211. Interstate Compact on the Placement of Children, art. IV (1960).
212. State *ex rel.* Okla. Bar Ass'n v. Johnson, 863 P.2d 1136 (Okla. 1993); Iowa Sup. Ct. Bd. of Prof'l Ethics & Conduct v. Hill, 576 N.W.2d 91 (Iowa 1998).
213. *In re* Jon K., 535 N.Y.S.2d 660 (N.Y. Fam. Ct. 1988).
214. Pima County Juvenile Action No. 18635 v. Fisher, 610 P.2d 64 (Ariz. 1980).
215. Interstate Compact on the Placement of Children, art. V (1960).
216. Williams v. Glass, 664 N.Y.S.2d 792 (N.Y. App. Div.1997).
217. Fla. Dep't of Health & Rehab. Servs. v. Thornton, 396 S.E.2d 475 (W.Va. 1990).
218. In the Matter of Shakiba P., 586 N.Y.S.2d 300 (N.Y. App. Div. 1992); Templeton v. Witham, 595 F. Supp. 770 (S.D. Cal. 1984).

not only determines its obligations under the ICPC but can also expose the agency to liability for its actions. A contract between a private placement agency and adoptive parents in another state implicates the ICPC, which can then be a predicate for imposing long arm jurisdiction over out-of-state agencies involved in civil suits.[219] Article X of the ICPC requires that the term "sending agency" be interpreted broadly. A sending agency can be a party state and its political subdivisions, including all officials and employees, a court of a party state, or "a person, corporation, association, charitable agency or other entity which sends, brings, or causes to be sent or brought any child to another party state."[220] What constitutes a sending agency is usually not at issue with foster care placements, public agency adoptions, or public agencies having custody of a child. The matter becomes complicated and confusing with regard to independent and private adoptions because it may be unclear which of the parties is the "sending agency." A parent is not a "sending agency" when the parent uses an agency to effectuate an out-of-state adoption.[221] However, when a birth parent acts as a sending agency, a different set of problems may be generated. It has been held that a birth parent who acts as a sending agency under the ICPC relinquishes an absolute right to seek return of a child because jurisdictional authority has been transferred to the receiving state by the consent to adopt.[222] The provisions in Article V related to retention of jurisdiction do not include "the absolute right to regain custody of a child that the mother, acting as a sending agency, has placed in another state for adoption."[223]

Most state courts have held that the ICPC applies to independent and private adoptions—that is, those adoptions that ordinarily do not occur under the auspices of a state child welfare agency. Unless the parties are exempt from compliance as "non-agency guardians," the requirements of the ICPC must be followed.[224] At least one court, however, has applied a less restrict standard holding that the ICPC does not apply in private placement adoptions or so-called independent adoptions—that is, those not involving a government or private agency.[225] To qualify as a "non-agency guardian," courts require that

219. Prince v. Illien Adoptions Int'l, Ltd., 806 F. Supp. 1225 (D. Md. 1992).
220. Interstate Compact on the Placement of Children, art. II (1960).
221. Matter of Male Child Born July 15, 1985 to L.C., 718 P.2d 660 (Mont. 1986).
222. Matter of Jarrett, 660 N.Y.S.2d 916 (N.Y. App. Div. 1997).
223. Broyles v. Ashworth, 782 S.W.2d 31 (Tex. App. 1989).
224. *In re* Adoption of T.M.M., 608 P.2d 130 (Mont. 1980).
225. *In re* Adoption of M.M., 652 P.2d 974 (Wyo. 1982).

the person receiving the child meet the same standards as the person who places the child to ensure that "only one whose legal relationship toward the child has been independently and legitimately established will have the right to effect such a drastic change as an interstate placement without the oversight and supervision of the contracting states."[226] It is important to note that the placement of a child preliminary to adoption is the triggering event for the ICPC, not the date on which the biological parents consent to the adoption.[227]

While courts generally defer to a sending state's jurisdiction in public agency adoptions, courts are less likely to defer to jurisdiction in the context of private adoptions. Courts have found that in private adoptions, jurisdiction under the ICPC should not be determined by which state possesses jurisdiction but rather by which party has responsibility for the child's welfare.[228] Courts also consider the impact of the UCCJA and PKPA in determining jurisdiction, even to the apparent exclusion for the jurisdictional mandates of the ICPC.[229] One court has held that the UCCJA requires that the receiving state exercise jurisdiction in the context of private adoptions where a child's contacts with a sending state are minimal.[230] Article V(a) of the ICPC does not preclude the sending agency from transferring its responsibility to another entity in the receiving state, including the prospective adoptive parents. Nor does the ICPC empower the courts of the sending state to exercise jurisdiction over an adoption proceeding; the validity of a court's jurisdiction depends on the UCCJA and the PKPA, not the ICPC.[231]

Jurisdictional issues with the ICPC continue to present significant problems for private agencies and attorneys, particularly in light of other legislative acts. Generally, the ICPC places jurisdiction in the sending state. That jurisdiction can only be terminated for the reasons listed in Article V, and any other termination is a violation of the ICPC.[232] However, the ICPC may, at times, work in conjunction with the UCCJA, UCCJEA, or the PKPA, each of which may have a different standard for determining jurisdiction. The ICPC governs all out-of-state placements that are foster care in nature or are preliminary to adoption. This has been interpreted as applying to placements with residential treatment centers, relatives, and biological parents. However,

---

226. In the Matter of Baby "E," 427 N.Y.S.2d 705 (N.Y. Fam. Ct. 1980).
227. *In re* Adoption of A.M.M., 949 P.2d 1155 (Kan. Ct. App. 1997).
228. *In re* Ascente, 1999 Ohio App. LEXIS 5101 (Ohio Ct. App. 11 Dist. 1999).
229. McCulley v. Bone, 979 P.2d 779 (Or. Ct. App. 1999).
230. *In re* Lamber, 993 S.W.2d 123 (Tex. Ct. App. 1999).
231. J.D.S. v. Franks, 893 P.2d 732 (Ariz. 1995).
232. Matter of Shaida W., 626 N.Y.S.2d 35 (N.Y. 1995).

the UCCJA provides that jurisdiction can shift to another state when the basis of jurisdiction ceases, and states can assume equal jurisdiction in emergency circumstances. By contrast, the UCCJEA provides that a state retains jurisdiction so long as it maintains significant contacts with the participants or until the participants move to another jurisdiction. The UCCJEA specifically exempts adoption proceedings from its coverage. And the PKPA limits conflicting state court orders by imposing certain jurisdictional considerations including whether the state is the home state, whether it has significant connections to the participants, whether it is acting in an emergency, or whether it has been granted jurisdiction by default. The overall intent of the statutes is to prevent conflicting child custody orders by preventing forum shopping.

These statutes, when interacting with the ICPC, can produce conflicts. Which court properly has jurisdiction over an interstate custody dispute may require an analysis of three separate statutes: the ICPC, the UCCJA, or its revised counterpart the UCCJEA where adopted, and the PKPA. It has been held that a receiving state cannot exercise jurisdiction under the UCCJA because the sending state retained jurisdiction under both the ICPC and the UCCJA.[233] Likewise, the ICPC and UCCJA prohibit a receiving state from modifying a sending state's custody orders.[234] Yet it has also been held that the UCCJA and the "best interest of the child" standard enable a court to exercise jurisdiction over foster children that have been residing in the receiving state, notwithstanding transfer under the ICPC.[235] One court has held that nowhere does the ICPC allow a compact administrator in either the sending state or the receiving state to ignore or contradict preexisting court orders concerning the custody and placement of children finding that it would be counterproductive to interpret the ICPC as negating the jurisdictional provisions of the UCCJA.[236] And still another state court has determined that the ICPC must yield to the UCCJA and the PKPA concerning a child's "home state" or the state that has a "significant connection" to and "substantial evidence" about the child.[237] A state may even lose jurisdiction under the PKPA when certain officials fail to comply with the ICPC.[238] In effect, practitioners involved in interstate adoptions or foster care cases must be cognizant of the interaction that uniform and federal laws have with the compact.

---

233. Matter of C.B., 616 N.E.2d 763 (Ind. Ct. App. 1993).
234. Squires v. Squires, 468 N.E.2d 73 (Ohio Ct. App. 1983).
235. *In re* Marriage of Slate, 536 N.E.2d 894 (Ill. App. Ct. 1989).
236. *In re* D.N., 858 So. 2d 1087 (Fla. Dist. Ct. App. 2003).
237. Sturgill v. Super. Ct. of Ariz., 893 P.2d 749 (Ariz. Ct. App., 1994).
238. Templeton v. Witham, 595 F. Supp. 770 (S.D. Cal. 1984).

The time delays with, and confusion over, the application of the ICPC have led to calls for redrafting the agreement to clarify its parameters. No doubt, the interaction of the compact with other state and federal laws is compelling reconsideration of the agreement. Perhaps the current confusion over the ICPC and other related statutes portray the difficulty of drafting an interstate compact in the area of child welfare, an area that is constantly changing and charged with highly emotional considerations. Even a redrafted ICPC will likely not solve the myriad of jurisdictional problems associated with interstate child placement, the responsibilities of the states, and the procedures applicable to interstate cases.

9.2.3   Interstate Compact on Adoption and Medical Assistance (ICAMA)

The purpose of the Interstate Compact on Adoption and Medical Assistance (ICAMA) is to provide interstate services, protections, and guarantees for children with special needs receiving adoption assistance when they move with their adoptive families across state lines or are initially placed for adoption in another state.[239] The compact is designed to (1) strengthen protections for the interests of children with special needs on behalf of whom adoption assistance is to be paid, and (2) provide substantive assurances and operating procedures to promote the delivery of medical and other services to children on an interstate basis through programs of adoption assistance established by the laws of the member states.[240] Under the agreement, member states have agreed to provide medical assistance to children subject to Title IV-E adoption assistance agreements in another state and, in many states, for children receiving state-funded adoption assistance.[241] Moreover, each member state acknowledges that the assistance outlined in an adoption assistance agreement "is for the benefit of the child, the adoptive parents and the state and that it is enforceable by any or all of them[.]"[242] Thus, ICAMA may create a private right of action to enforce the mandated provision of services as outlined in an adoption assistance agreement.

In effect, ICAMA ensures that a receiving state will not be saddled with the expenses of providing adoption assistance payments to adopted children with special needs, and that Title IV-E eligible children will continue to

---

239. Interstate Compact on Adoption and Medical Assistance, art. I (1984).
240. *Id.* at art II.
241. *Id.* at art. IV.
242. *Id.* at art. IV (c)(4).

receive medical and other services when they move or are placed across state lines. ICAMA applies to children with special needs who are adopted under an adoption assistance agreement. The individual adoption assistance agreement is, therefore, a crucial element in ICAMA cases and can drive many considerations of the placement and subsequent services. The compact applies when (1) a special needs child is adopted by a family in another state, or (2) the adoptive family moves from one state to another. Benefits coordinated under ICAMA include Medicaid, Title IV-E and Title XX payments, and state subsidies.[243] In practice, states provide services under the Title XX program and other post-placement and post-adoption support services. Member states are supposed to make arrangements to ensure the continuation of benefits and services even when the child has relocated to another state. For children covered by Medicaid, the receiving state may issue a new Medicaid card to the child.

ICAMA has its roots in the Adoption Assistance and Child Welfare Act of 1980.[244] As such, ICAMA is an example of Congress using its advance consent powers to encourage states to enact interstate compacts for a specific purpose. The act encourages the Secretary of Health and Human Services to:

> [T]ake all possible steps to encourage and assist the various States to enter into interstate compacts (which are hereby approved by the Congress) under which the interests of any adopted child with respect to whom an adoption assistance agreement has been entered into by a State under section 673 of this title will be adequately protected, on a reasonable and equitable basis which is approved by the Secretary, if and when the child and his or her adoptive parent (or parents) move to another State.[245]

The mandate comes from the definition section in Section 675(3)(b), which states that "[t]he agreement shall contain provision for the protection (under an interstate compact approved by the Secretary or otherwise) of the interests of the child in cases where the adoptive parents and child move to another State while the agreement is effective."[246] Suggested language for ICAMA was developed by the American Public Welfare Association in 1983. Unlike many compacts, ICAMA specifically authorizes states to enter into

---

243. 42 C.F.R. § 435.227 (2004).
244. 42 U.S.C. § 673a (2004).
245. *Id.*
246. 42 U.S.C. § 675(3)(b) (2004).

supplementary agreements to provide for additional medical benefits for children with special needs and for delivery of interstate services such as education, mental health, and rehabilitation.[247] The agreements must be consistent with the purposes of the compact and may not relieve a party state of any obligation to provide adoption and medical assistance.[248]

The compact may be executed either by explicit adoption or through legislative delegation. However, the agreement specifically provides that regardless of the manner of execution, "each party state shall cause the full text of the Compact and notice of its execution to be published in his or her state."[249] A state may withdraw from ICAMA upon written notice sent by the authority that executed the agreement, but no withdrawal will take effect until one year after notice has been given.[250] A state's decision to withdraw from the agreement does not relieve it of its obligations to abide by any adoption assistance agreements in effect at that time. The compact specifically provides that such agreements only terminate upon expiration or according to their terms and "the withdrawing state shall continue to administer the Compact to the extent necessary to accord and implement fully the rights and protections preserved hereby."[251] Thus, a state may be required to abide by the terms and conditions of the agreement for periods substantially longer than one year after notice of withdrawal to the extent that adoption assistance agreements remain in effect.

Nationally, ICAMA is governed by joint action of each member state's compact administrator appointed as required by the agreement.[252] Each state must also appoint a deputy compact administrator.[253] Individual compact administrators are charged with coordinating activities with other member states and acting as the principal contact both in-state and out-of-state for all matters related to the purposes and activities of the agreement.[254] The compact administrators, acting jointly, have the authority to promulgate uniform forms and administrative procedures for the interstate delivery of adoption and medical assistance.[255] The compact is overseen by the Association of Administrators of the Interstate Compact on Adoption and Medical Assistance (AAICAMA),

---

247. Interstate Compact on Adoption and Medical Assistance, art. VI (c)(1) (1984).
248. *Id.*
249. *Id.* at art. VII (b).
250. *Id.* at art. VII (c).
251. *Id.* at art. VII (d).
252. *Id.* at art. VI.
253. *Id.* at art. VI (a).
254. *Id.*
255. *Id.* at art. VI (b).

a nonprofit corporation established in 1986 to facilitate the administration of the compact.[256] The American Public Human Services Association (APHSA) provides secretariat services to the association. The APHSA staff also provides member states with technical assistance and support in administering the compact and assists them in improving professional practices pertaining to the interstate aspect of adoption assistance programs. In addition, the secretariat facilitates the collaboration of activities and exchange of information among compact administrators, private adoption agency representatives, and others concerned with special-needs adoptions to improve services for special-needs children and their families. This Compact Administrators Association is similar to the Compact Administrators for the Interstate Compact on the Placement of Children (ICPC), and the ICAMA secretariat is largely patterned after the secretariat services provided to the ICPC, with a similar legal basis and similar functions. Unlike in the context of the ICPC, the ICAMA secretariat has not engaged in providing "Secretariat Opinions," and the provisions of ICAMA do not confer upon the secretariat the power do so. Therefore, any opinions rendered by the secretariat would be advisory in nature and, therefore, not legally binding on the member states.

It should be noted that ICAMA does not deal directly with intrastate administration of the agreement and has no provisions relating to that subject. Thus, intrastate administration of the compact is left to the discretion of each member state in regard to both structure and intrastate procedures. ICAMA does not specially provide for resolution of disputes between member states. Generally a state's children's services agency and its Medicaid agency must perform their respective functions under an adoption assistance agreement and ICAMA. ICAMA has been adopted in 44 states and the District of Columbia. The states of Michigan, New Jersey, New York, Tennessee, Vermont, and Wyoming are not members of the compact.

Because of the relative newness and limited scope of ICAMA, there is little to no judicial interpretation of the agreement. With limited exception, it is highly unlikely that courts will have an opportunity to rule upon or comment on ICAMA. Judicial interpretation of ICAMA may occur in those cases where a state has refused to comply with an adoption assistance agreement or where a dispute would arise between two member states. Such cases would not be based on ICAMA per se, but rather upon a state's failure to comply with an adoption assistance agreement. However, notwithstanding the lack of

---

256. *See generally* Association of Administrators of the Interstate Compact on Adoption and Medical Assistance, *available at* http://aaicama. aphsa.org.

judicial interpretation of ICAMA, two jurisdictional comments must be mentioned. First, as Congress has granted its explicit consent to ICAMA-like agreements, the compact constitutes a "law of the union" enforceable as federal law under the *Cuyler* doctrine. Therefore, the likely venue for state-to-state disputes will be the federal courts. ICAMA is silent on which federal court will exercise jurisdiction over any such disputes, and therefore, presumably, any federal district court could entertain an action. Second, although ICAMA is federalized by congressional consent, state courts may become involved in ICAMA-related cases by virtue of the fact that adoption—even interstate adoption—is generally considered a state matter. Therefore, to the extent that an adopted child or adoptive parents encounter problems with state administration of benefit programs, an action to enforce compliance with the adoption assistance agreement would likely be brought in state court against a state administrative agency based on a state administrative determination. In this context, the state court is required by the Supremacy Clause to give full effect to the agreement. Thus, for example, to the extent that a state fails to pay for assistance mandated by the compact or an adoption assistance agreement as required by Article IV (c)(1), it is conceivable that a state court would entertain an action to compel compliance.

Most adoption assistance agreements have provisions giving the adoptive parents rights to appeal a state's decision regarding the level of assistance and payment for services. Such appeals are generally administrative in nature and take place within the administrative procedures of the agency providing assistance. Judicial review of an agency determination is, therefore, an intrastate matter controlled by the state law applicable to administrative appeals, which may include deference to an agency's determination when it is supported by substantive evidence.[257] Finally, because each member state of ICAMA determines the amount of assistance to be provided to adoptive children and their parents, venue for an appeal of a state agency's administrative action or omission is in the state where the action was taken or omitted.[258] Therefore, venue may rest in either the sending or receiving state depending on the nature of the dispute and the services or payments in dispute. For example, in some instances, the administrative act forming the basis of a complaint may have occurred in the sending state. In other instances, the administrative act or omission may have occurred in the receiving state. Where a complaint is against an act or omission of the adoption assistance state, adoptive parents may have to travel to the adoption assistance state to effectuate an appeal.

---

257. *Cf.*, Spiegler v. Dist. of Columbia, 866 F.2d 461 (D.C. Cir. 1989).
258. Interstate Compact on Adoption and Medical Assistance, art. IV (a) (1984).

For practitioners or those involved with the interstate adoption of children with special needs, several additional observations are warranted. First, it is important that any adoption assistance agreements refer to ICAMA, if only to clarify and emphasize to adoptive parents the relationship between ICAMA requirements and the benefits and obligations they have under their agreement. This will also ensure that a state can demonstrate it is meeting federal requirements related to the protection of interstate interests by compacts. Second, adoption assistance agreements may vary widely. It is important, however, that such agreements recite that adoptive parents understand the extent to which Title XIX, Medicaid, and Title XX, Social Services, will be provided by the residence state.[259] Third, some adoption assistance agreements provide specific evidence that a child is not adoptable without state subsidy in an effort to ensure that the definition of "child with special needs" complies with both federal law and ICAMA. The secretariat suggests that after reciting the conditions that cause a child to be designated as having special needs, the agreement recite Article III of the compact, which states "because of which it is reasonable to conclude that such child cannot be placed with adoptive parents without providing adoption assistance."[260]

9.3. HEALTH COMPACTS GENERALLY

This section discusses the Interstate Compact on Mental Health.

9.3.1   Interstate Compact on Mental Health (ICMH)

The Interstate Compact on Mental Health (ICMH) is designed to ensure that mental health services are available to individuals regardless of their state of residency. The compact consists of 14 articles governing a broad range of issues including the provision of mental health services (including aftercare services), the transfer of patients to other states for treatment, the return of patients, and the process for dealing with patients who have escaped and who pose a public safety risk. The ICMH recognizes that an individual who is mentally ill and in need of treatment should receive such treatment from the jurisdiction in which he or she is physically present, without regard to legal concerns for residency. The ICMH authorizes party states to give such care and treatment to the mentally ill and mentally disabled as is neces-

---

259. American Public Human Services Association, Issue Brief III: Federal Law, the Compact, and State Adoption Assistance Agreements (December 1988), *available at* http://aaicama.aphsa.org/IssueBriefs/IB%20HTML/ 03BRIEF.html.

260. *Id.*

sary and desirable regardless of the residence or citizenship, the controlling
factors being community safety and humanitarianism.

The compact arose out of concern that states were limiting treatment
services to mentally ill individuals based on jurisdictional concerns and not
treatment needs. As one court observed, in *Clark v. Settle*, through the compact "enlightened States have recognized that 'proper and expeditious treatment of the mentally ill and mentally deficient can be facilitated by cooperative
action' and that such care and treatment bears no primary relation to the
residence or citizenship of the patient.'"[261] The public policy of many states
prior to the adoption of the ICMH was to limit access to mental health services to bona fide residents of the state and to limit out-of-state residents to
only those services necessary pending return to their state of residency.[262] The
adoption of the ICMH represented a total change in the policy of many states
regarding providing mental health services to nonresidents. For example, the
ICMH largely rendered the Uniform Act for the Extradition of Persons of
Unsound Mind obsolete, although various aspects of that act are still in effect
in several states.[263] Although these two pieces of legislation stand independently, at least one court has considered how to reconcile the requirements of
the ICMH with the Uniform Act in those states maintaining both provisions.[264]
The ICMH makes no distinction between voluntary and involuntary commitments and, therefore, is applicable and controlling in both settings so long as
a state can establish its authority over a patient.[265] As an interstate compact,
the ICMH confers no special status upon the public nor does it give rise to a
special relationship such that state officials are liable for the injurious acts of
an escapee, notwithstanding the state's failure to comply with provisions of
the compact.[266]

One feature of the compact that is somewhat unusual and similar to the
Interstate Compact on the Placement of Children is the ability of member
states to enter into supplementary agreements. Article XI provides that the
compact administrators of any two or more states can negotiate supplementary or so-called "side" agreements.[267] These agreements are limited to providing services or facilities, or for the maintenance of an institution.[268]

261. Clark v. Settle, 206 F. Supp. 74, 76 n.2 (W.D. Mo. 1962).
262. 1979-80 Op. Att'y Gen. Mich. 969 (1980).
263. ALASKA STAT. § 47.30.410 (2004).
264. State *ex rel.* Melentowich v. Klink, 321 N.W.2d 272 (Wis. 1982).
265. *In re* M.D., 655 A.2d 723, 725 (Vt. 1994).
266. Amadon v. New York, 565 N.Y.S.2d 677 (N.Y. Ct. Cl. 1990).
267. *See, e.g.,* Interstate Compact on Mental Health, art. XI (2003).
268. *Id.*

Consequently, two states could negotiate a side agreement distributing the expenses of institutional improvements. Notwithstanding the ability of states to enter into supplementary agreements, such agreements may not relieve any member state of any obligation that it otherwise has incurred by joining the ICMH.[269] The number and extent of such supplementary agreements is unknown. The ICMH does allow states to withdraw from the agreement by enacting legislation repealing the ICMH. However, the withdrawal does not take effect until one year after notice has been sent to the governors and compact administrators of the member states.[270] A state withdrawing from the compact cannot change the status of any patient transferred under the agreement.

The ICMH requires each state to appoint a compact administrator who "shall act as general coordinator of activities under the compact."[271] The compact administrator or designee "shall be the official with whom other party States shall deal in any matter relating to the compact or any patient processed thereunder."[272] The compact administrators, acting jointly, have power to promulgate reasonable rules and regulations to carry out the terms of the agreement. However, like many other compacts, the ICMH does not create an identifiable body or commission nor does it provide any guidance for a rulemaking process. Although authorized to do so, the compact administrators have not promulgated uniform rules and, as a result, the administration of the compact is generally handled on a state-by-state basis and under state promulgated administrative rules.[273] Currently, 45 states and the District of Columbia are members of the ICMH. The federal government is not a member of the ICMH.

The following types of cases must be processed through the ICMH: (1) a request to transfer an out-of-state resident to another state for inpatient or aftercare treatment; and (2) a request from a state for the return of a patient who is absent without leave from a state facility. The compact also governs the return of dangerous or potentially dangerous persons who have escaped from a facility. However, the ICMH makes no provision for the transfer of

---

269. *Id.*
270. *Id.* at art. XIII.
271. *Id.* at art. X (a).
272. *Id.*
273. *See, e.g.*, Minnesota Department of Human Services, *Social Services Manual*, Interstate Compact on Mental Health XI-3000 (June 4, 1999), *available at* http://www.dhs.state.mn.us/main/groups/county_access/documents/pub/dhs_id_018628.pdf.

inmates from penal institutions and has been read to be inapplicable in the context of the interstate transferring of criminal offenders sentenced to a mental health facility in lieu of incarceration at a state penal institution.[274] However, Article V has been read to have limited application to a criminal offender who escaped from a mental health facility.[275] The compact would not apply in cases involving juveniles who might otherwise be covered by the Interstate Compact on Juveniles nor would it apply in those cases involving the transfer of children under the Interstate Compact on the Placement of Children.

Article III(a) of the compact provides that whenever a person physically present in any party state is in need of institutionalization by reason of mental illness or mental deficiency, he or she is eligible for care and treatment in an institution in that state irrespective of his or her residence, settlement, or citizenship qualifications.[276] Additionally, the ICMH provides that a patient may be transferred to an institution in another member state based on a clinical determination indicating that care and treatment would be improved by such a transfer.[277] However, before a patient can be transferred to a facility in another state, officials in the receiving state must be provided the opportunity to review the patient's records and consent to the transfer.[278] A person may be a patient of only one institution at a time under the compact; therefore, the patient becomes a patient of the institution in the receiving state upon consent to the transfer.[279] The costs of maintaining a person transferred under the compact become the responsibility of the receiving state upon consenting to the transfer.[280] Thus, a state department of mental health would not continue to have an obligation to provide care and treatment after the patient is transferred under the compact.[281] Other than the transfer of a patient under the interstate compact, there is no authority for a placement or a transfer of a patient to or in another state. Once the transfer of an out-of-state patient is completed, the receiving state must provide that level of mental health care that it would otherwise afford a resident of its state.[282]

---

274. Coffee v. O'Keefe, 1999 Minn. App. LEXIS 1110 (Minn. Ct. App. 1999).
275. *In re* Ricardo Montes, 1996 Mass. Super. LEXIS 184 (Super. Ct. Middlesex 1996).
276. *See* Interstate Compact on Mental Health, art. III (a) (2003).
277. *See id.* at art. III (b).
278. *See id.* at art. III (c).
279. Op. Mo. Atty. Gen. 79-17 (1979).
280. *See* Interstate Compact on Mental Health, art. VII (a) (2003).
281. Op. Wis. Atty. Gen. 12-89 (1989).
282. *See* Interstate Compact on Mental Health, art. IV (c) (2003).

Two areas of the ICMH have presented limited problems to courts and practitioners. First, courts are not united in the extent of due process protections that apply when an escaped patient is being returned nor is there universal consistency on the extent to which consent is required for transfers. The ICMH contains a general provision for the apprehension and return of patients who escape from a mental health facility or program. Article V requires that upon learning of an escape, officials shall notify all appropriate authorities within and outside the jurisdiction "in a manner reasonably calculated to facilitate the speedy apprehension of the escapee."[283] Upon apprehension, the state having custody of the escapee must detain the person until the detention is resolved according to law. Presumably "according to law" means according to the law of the state in which the escapee is being held. This may trigger the due process standards of that state, which may be different than those accorded a criminal defendant.[284] Courts addressing the due process issue have generally concluded that an escaped patient is entitled to be informed of the reasons for the detention, must be granted a hearing to determine his or her identification, and must have access to counsel.[285] One court has held that an escapee is entitled to be provided that level of due process otherwise accorded someone subject to extradition under a governor's warrant. Once a governor in an asylum state is satisfied that a demand for return conforms to the law, the governor must issue a warrant for the apprehension of the escapee. The issuance of a governor's warrant is a summary executive proceeding and constitutes prima facie evidence that all applicable statutory requirements have been met. A court is generally limited to deciding whether the extradition documents on their face are in order, whether the petitioner is the person charged in the documents, and whether the person is a fugitive.[286] Extradition proceedings, under the ICMH, can only be attacked in the asylum state, and after an alleged fugitive has been delivered to the demanding state. Such proceedings cannot be questioned on habeas corpus.[287] However, apparently a person held or transferred pursuant to the compact can challenge its constitutionality in a 42 U.S.C. Section 1983 action, notwithstanding the fact that only his or her actual detention can be challenged through habeas corpus.[288]

---

283. *Id.* at art. V.
284. State *ex rel.* White v. Todt, 475 S.E.2d 426 (W. Va. 1996).
285. *Id.*
286. *In re* Ricardo Montes, 1996 Mass. Super. LEXIS 184 (Super. Ct. Middlesex 1996).
287. Lyons v. Thomas, 378 S.W.2d 798 (Ky. Ct. App. 1964).
288. Hartman v. Scott, 488 F.2d 1215 (8th Cir. 1973).

Second, the payment of expenses associated with out-of-state placements has given rise to some controversy. Although the ICMH generally requires that the costs associated with institutionalization be borne by the state having custody of the person, some courts have held that that the sending jurisdiction may be liable for the out-of-state treatment costs of those under its care and custody. Thus, for example, in *In re Michael Myrick*, the Court of Appeals for the District of Columbia upheld a trial court decision mandating out-of-state mental health treatment for a nonresident and requiring the district to pay for that treatment.[289] The court reasoned that the district's Ervin Act guaranteed adequate treatment of all persons within the district.[290] The fact that Myrick was not a resident did not relieve the district of its obligations to care for him. This obligation extended to providing the most appropriate care, even if that care was in another state. The district could not evade its obligations—either treatment or financial—by transferring a mentally ill patient to a program in another state.[291] However, the holding in *In re Michael Myrick* may be unique given the particular circumstances of the case and the unique position of the District of Columbia.

The ICMH represents the use of compacts to manage interstate health matters. Examples of other health compacts include the New England Radiological Health Compact and the Nurse Licensure Compact. At least one other health compact is being promoted to allow out-of-state physicians to practice in the event of an emergency. The proposed compact is in reaction to the events of September 11, 2001, and is intended to provide more rapid delivery of medical services in the event of a natural disaster or terrorist attack.[292] However, the use of interstate compacts to regulate health matters—as distinguished from environmental matters—has been quite modest and limited. Although health matters clearly transcend state boundaries, states appear to have resisted the temptation to use the device as a cross-border management tool. Rather, health and health-related matters have generally been left to the individual states, and there appears little likelihood that the number and breadth of health compacts will ever rise to levels seen in other topical areas.

---

289. *In re* Myrick, 624 A.2d 1222 (D.C. 1987).

290. D.C. CODE ANN. § 21-501 (2003).

291. *Id.*

292. *States Seek Emergency Medical Compacts*, STATELINE.ORG (Sept. 7, 2004), *available at* http://stateline.org/stateline/?pa=story&sa=showStoryInfo&id=396890.

9.4 ENVIRONMENTAL AND NATURAL RESOURCE COMPACTS

This section surveys the following topics:

- General Considerations
- Interstate Compacts Concerning Waters within the United States
- Low-level Radioactive Waste Disposal Compacts
- Solid/Hazardous Waste Compacts
- Air Quality/Air Pollution Compacts
- Natural Resource Protection Compacts
- Conclusions

9.4.1 General Considerations

Interstate compacts involving environmental and natural resource matters[293] follow the same principles discussed in this text for other types of compacts. Many interstate compacts in the area of environmental regulation have the potential to infringe on federal power thus necessitating congressional approval, and in that manner become federal law for the limited purposes of interpretation and enforcement. Interstate compacts in the field of environmental and natural resource administration, however, provide states flexibility to design and implement management of the environment and natural resources. They provide a level of control beyond that available to the states acting individually, permitting state control on an interstate or regional level without the impositions that accompany federal laws.

This is particularly important given that most environmental issues—ranging from water resource allocation to pollution control to resources protection—clearly ignore state geographical boundaries. This is not to say that interstate compacts are a panacea. Criticism surrounding the use of compacts concern their potential to infringe on fundamental democratic rights.[294] Other critics raise concerns that the use of interstate compacts to address water pollution issues "more often than not" is simply "a smoke screen to ward off overdue action by the Federal government, rather than as a means of solving the prob-

---

293. For purposes of this publication, "environmental" refers to matters that involve actions of man that result in pollution of environmental media, e.g., of air, land, and water. "Natural resources" refers to those resources that are sought to be used by man, e.g., fisheries, timber, water.

294. *See* Jill Elaine Hasday, *Interstate Compacts in a Democratic Society: The Problem of Permanency,* 49 FLA. L. REV. 1 (1997).

lems over which they are given jurisdiction."[295] Enforcement of provisions of interstate compacts presents its own unique set of problems.[296] For example, commissions formed under congressionally approved compacts do not necessarily enjoy the protection from suit provided by the Eleventh Amendment.[297]

Notwithstanding these concerns, interstate compacts in the natural resource area are as old as the nation. One of the earliest environmental compacts addressed disputes over the use and allocation of waters of the Potomac River.[298] The 1785 compact between Virginia and Maryland demarcated each state's boundaries along the Potomac River. Because this agreement preceded the formation of Congress, the Supreme Court subsequently held that when Congress approved a later agreement between these two states—the Black-Jenkins Award—it implicitly consented to the 1785 compact.[299] Later disputes between the states resulted in a new compact that superseded the 1785 compact, but specifically preserved the rights delineated in Article VII of the 1785 compact, which provides: "The citizens of each state . . . shall have full property in the shores of Potowmack river adjoining their lands, with all emoluments and advantages thereunto belonging, and the privilege of making and carrying out wharves and other improvements, so as not to obstruct or injure the navigation of the river."[300] The significance of this very early

---

295. Oliver A. Houck, *TMDLs: The Resurrection of Water Quality Standards-Based Regulation Under the Clean Water Act*, 27 ENVTL. L. REP. 10,329 (July 1997), quoting Weldon Barton, Assistant Director of Legislative Services, National Farmers' Union, House Hearings II, Water Pollution Control Legislation—1971: Hearings on H.R. 11896, H.R. 11895 before the Committee on Public Works, 92d Cong., 1st Sess. 695, 698 (1971).

296. Kansas v. Colorado, 533 U.S. 1, 8 (2001) (noting that recovery of monetary damages, as opposed to injunctive relief, may be proper).

297. *See* Hess v. Port Auth. Trans-Hudson Corp., 513 U.S. 30 (1994) (bi-state railway created pursuant to Constitution's Interstate Compact Clause did not enjoy the states' Eleventh Amendment immunity from federal claim); Lake Country Estates, Inc. v. Tahoe Reg'l Planning Agency, 440 U.S. 391 (1979) (authority does not enjoy 11th Amendment immunity); Byram River v. Village of Port Chester, 394 F. Supp. 618, 626-28 (S.D. N.Y. 1975) (holding that the Interstate Commission is not an "alter ego" of the state such that it enjoys 11th Amendment immunity).

298. *See* Virginia v. Maryland, 504 U.S. 56 (2003).

299. *Id.* at 603 n.3, *citing* Wharton v. Wise, 153 U.S. 155, 165-73 (1894) (noting that the 1785 Compact was before the Constitution and thus not previously approved).

300. *See* Potomac River Compact (1958). A history of the compact can be found in Dutton v. Tawes, 171 A.2d 688 (Md. 1961); Barnes v. State, 47 A.2d 50 (Md. 1946).

interstate compact is still evident today in Supreme Court decisions interpreting the terms of the 1785 compact as relevant to current disputes between Virginia and Maryland over the use and jurisdiction of the river.[301]

Various types of interstate compacts fall within the broad scope of environmental compacts; e.g. compacts governing conservation, development of natural resources, fisheries, low-level radioactive waste, mining, parks and recreation, water allocation, and water or air pollution. These compacts also address broader disputes between states such as use of oil and gas resources, delineation of boundaries, forest fire management, flood control, and sanitation. This section provides a general overview of some of the types of agreements states have and continue to use to address a broad array of environmental matters.

It must be noted that while the use of the compact device to govern environmental matters is very old, the environmental compacts actually came into broad use in the late 1960s and throughout the 1970s. Federal involvement in environmental and natural resource issues began in earnest in the 1970s with the passage of numerous federal laws governing issues such as water, air, endangered species, waste disposal, and the requirement to consider environmental issues in federal decision making. Interstate compacts that address issues such as apportionment of water, trans-boundary pollution, and the management of various resources may be limited or qualified by these federal environmental and natural resource laws.

9.4.2 Interstate Compacts Concerning Waters Within the United States

Historically, federal common law has governed interstate bodies of water. This common law ensures that, as between states that rely on a source of water for its citizens, the water is equitably apportioned, and neither state may harm another's interest in the water.[302] Today, interstate compacts are a

---

301. *See* Virginia v. Maryland, 504 U.S. 56, 57 (2003) (Article VII one of the terms governing the dispute).
302. Kansas v. Colorado, 206 U.S. 46, 98 (1907). *See also* Colorado v. New Mexico, 459 U.S. 176 (1982) (equitable apportionment is the doctrine of federal common law that governs the disputes between states concerning their rights to use the water of an interstate stream. Factors relevant in determining equitable apportionment include prior apportionment, protecting an existing economy, physical and climatic conditions, consumptive use of water, the character and rate of return flows, the established uses and availability of storage water, the practical effect of wasteful uses on downstream areas, and

common method to allocate water between and among states bordering on water supplies including rivers, lakes, and bays. Indeed, the Supreme Court has expressly encouraged states to resolve water disputes through interstate compacts rather than by equitable apportionment adjudication.[303]

Compacts that affect interstate waters require congressional approval given Congress's authority to regulate navigable waters under its Commerce Clause powers.[304] The use of interstate compacts permits allocation or apportionment of water based on equitable principles but also allows flexibility to consider all possible uses of the water and to allocate on a basis other than simple equitable distribution.[305] Usually, compacts involving interstate waters include more than simply the allocation of a water supply. Some compacts address concerns such as pollution and flood control,[306] natural resource management, such as fisheries and protection of aquatic resources,[307] as well

---

the damage to upstream areas as compared to the benefits to downstream areas.). *See also* Nebraska v. Wyoming, 325 U.S. 589, 618 (1945) (noting these factors are not exclusive but representative of "the nature of the problem of apportionment and the delicate adjustment of interests which must be made").

303. *See* Sporhase v. Nebraska, 458 U.S. 941, 960 n.20 (1982), *citing* Colorado v. Kansas, 320 U.S. 383, 392 (1943).

304. *See* First Iowa Hydro-Elec. Co-op. v. Fed. Power Comm'n, 328 U.S. 152, 173 (1946) (Commerce Clause "lift[s] navigable waters of the United States out of local controls and into the domain of federal control").

305. For examples of interstate compacts concerning allocation of water, *see* Pecos River Compact (1949); Arkansas River Basin Compact of 1970 (1973); Arkansas River Compact of 1949 (1949); Bear River Compact (1958). For additional information on apportionment and water compacts, *see* United States Fish and Wildlife Service, *available at* http://laws.fws.gov/lawsdigest/compact.html#list; Council of State Governments, *available at* http://ssl.csg.org/compactlaws/comlistlinks.html.

306. *See, e.g.,* Wheeling Creek Watershed Protection and Flood Prevention Compact (1967); Connecticut River Flood Control Compact (1953); Merrimack River Flood Control Compact (1957); Interstate Water Pollution Control Compact, ME. REV. STAT. ANN. tit. 38, § 491 (2004). *See also* 33 U.S.C. § 1154 (2004).

307. *See, e.g.,* Article VII of the proposed Apalachicola-Chattahoochie-Flint River Basin Compact, GA. CODE ANN. § 12-10-100 (2004), which provides for a subsequent equitable apportionment of the basin by an interstate commission, subject to federal approval, "while protecting water quality, ecology, and biodiversity of the ACF" as provided by the Clean Water Act, the Endangered Species Act, the National Environmental Policy Act, and the Rivers and

as economic uses of the river,[308] including basin planning.[309] Many compacts include more than one of these areas.[310] Further, these compacts often raise additional issues that are also subsequently addressed by additional compacts concerning such things as jurisdiction on the river.[311] States usually enter numerous compacts to apportion the waters of the various rivers or tributaries within or bordering the state. For example, Colorado has enacted nine interstate compacts to apportion interstate rivers,[312] and Texas is a member of at least five different apportionment compacts.[313]

Compacts involving the use and allocation of interstate waters are probably the oldest in the nation. Beginning as early as 1785, Virginia and Maryland were using a compact to manage allocation and natural resources issues of the shared Potomac River.[314] As recently as 2003, the Supreme Court interpreted the 1785 compact and subsequent agreements[315] to determine that

---

Harbors Act of 1899. Article VII of the Alabama-Coosa-Tallapoosa River Basin Compact, GA. CODE ANN. § 12-10-110 (2004), is identical. *See also* Connecticut River Atlantic Salmon Compact (1983); Oregon-Washington Columbia River Fish Compact, Pub. L. No. 65-123, 40 Stat. 515 (1918).

308. *See* Missouri River Barge Traffic Compact (1984).

309. *See, e.g.,* New Hampshire-Vermont Interstate Public Water Supply Compact (1996). The 1921 Port Compact created the Port Authority of New York and New Jersey, which has responsibility for purchasing, constructing, leasing, and operating terminal, transportation, and facilities of commerce of the Port of New York and the adjacent area. 42 Stat. 174 (1921). The 1921 Port Compact is discussed in more detail in this treatise.

310. A list and link to compacts concerning apportionment, pollution, and resources and flood control can be found on the U.S. Fish and Wildlife Web site, *at* http://laws.fws.gov/lawsdigest/compact.html.

311. *See, e.g.,* Interstate Compact for Jurisdiction on the Colorado River (2003).

312. *See* COLO. REV. STAT. §§ 37-61-101 to 37-69-101 (2001).

313. *See* Paul Elliott, *Texas' Interstate Water Compacts*, 17 ST. MARY'S L.J. 1241 (1986).

314. For a discussion of the history of this compact and its ongoing disputes, *see* Virginia v. Maryland, 540 U.S. 56, 63 (2003).

315. The 1785 Compact resolved disputes as to the use by each state of the water of the Potomac River but did not resolve the boundary dispute. The boundary dispute was not resolved until the 1874 Black-Jenkins Award. Maryland and Virginia each ratified the Black-Jenkins Award. *See* 1878 Md. Laws 274; 1878 Va. Acts ch. 246. Congress approved the Award pursuant to the Compact Clause. *See* Act of Mar. 3, 1879, 20 Stat. 481 (1879). *See also* Wharton v. Wise, 153 U.S. 155, 173 (1894). There is a later compact between Virginia and

Virginia has the right to construct improvements and remove waters of the Potomac, without regulatory oversight by Maryland, provided Virginia "did not interfere with the 'proper use of' the river" by Maryland.[316] The 1785 compact also regulated fishing in the Potomac by citizens of Maryland and Virginia.[317] The ongoing dispute between Virginia and Maryland and the use of an interstate compact is reflective of environmental and natural resource interstate compact issues throughout the country.

9.4.2.1 *Allocation and Apportionment Compacts*

Allocation issues arise among states for a variety of reasons: increases in population with demands for drinking water, sewage, and day-to-day activities; agriculture and irrigation demands; demands of commercial and industrial businesses; requirements for recreation; preservation of natural resources, aquatic or terrestrial; Indian Reserved Water Rights;[318] the ubiquitous and never-resolved issue of climate change on the availability of natural water supplies,[319] as well as the fact that information on flow rates has changed over the years, and some compacts overestimated the average flow to be allocated among the various interests.[320] An issue not addressed by interstate compacts, but that has

---

Maryland concerning the Potomac River. However, the later compact preserves some of the right delineated in the 1785 Compact. *See* Potomac River Compact of 1958. *See generally* Virginia v. Maryland, 540 U.S. 56, 57 (2003).

316. *Id.*
317. The Potomac River Fisheries Commission and the 1958 Compact are discussed in more detail under the *Fishery Resource Management* section of this chapter.
318. *See* Winters v. United States, 207 U.S. 564 (1908).
319. *See, e.g.,* U.S. Environmental Protection Agency, Clean Water After Climate Change, Inside the Greenhouse, EPA-430-N-01-005 (2001), *available at* http://www.epa.gov/globalwarming/greenhouse/greenhouse15/water.html, which compares and contrasts the effect on a national versus local level. *See also* Ludwik A. Teclaff, *The River Basin Concept and Global Climate Change*, 8 PACE ENVTL. L. REV. 355 (1991); David Getches, *Water Wrongs: Why Can't We Get It Right the First Time?*, 34 ENVTL. L. 1, 10 (2004).
320. *See, e.g.,* Douglas L. Grant, *Interstate Water Allocation Compacts: When the Virtue of Permanence Becomes the Vice of Inflexibility*, 74 U. COLO. L. REV. 105, 117-18 (2003) (discussing overestimates of the Colorado River's annual average flow). *See also* Texas v. New Mexico, 462 U.S. 554 (1983).

become of increasing concern, is the availability and quality of transboundary rivers, such as those that flow from the U.S. to Mexico.[321]

There are several benefits to the use of interstate compacts as a means to allocate interstate waters. As recognized by Justice Felix Frankfurter and James Landis in their seminal article on the Compact Clause, compact negotiation, freed from strict legal rules, allows the parties to reach "sensible compromise" without the adversarial environment of court.[322] Another benefit of developing allocation methods using compacts is that the flexibility of compacts permits more ready adjustments to changing circumstances, for example, through the use of a compact commission to implement the agreement, in contrast to judicial determinations allocating water rights.[323] A third benefit is that those relying on access to the water have more security knowing the quantities available, which reduces the risk of investments and enables states to obtain federal funding for development projects on the river.[324]

Notwithstanding these benefits, there are increasing conflicts over the use of interstate compacts to allocate waters, especially in western states that are the main signatories of water allocation compacts. Concerns with the allocation compacts, as evidenced by the litigation involving these compacts, stems at least in part from the fact that many of these compacts were negotiated and approved by Congress during very different economic and social

---

321. Treaties have been used to address some of these issues. *See, e.g.,* Water Treaty of 1944, 59 Stat. 1219 (1944); Convention-Mexico, May 21, 1906, United States-Mexico, art. I, 34 Stat. 2953, 2954 (1906) (60,000 acre-feet annually at the Old Mexican Canal above Juarez); Treaty between the United States of America and Mexico Respecting Utilization of Waters of the Colorado and Tijuana Rivers and of the RioGrande, Feb. 3, 1944, U.S.-Mex., 59 Stat. 1219 (1944). From an environmental standpoint, these treaties do little to resolve the ongoing water shortage problems and inherent environmental problems that arise because of the shortages. *See* David H. Getches, *Water Management in the United States and the Fate of the Colorado River Delta in Mexico*, 11 U.S.-MEX. L.J. 107 (2003).
322. Felix Frankfurter & James M. Landis, *The Compact Clause of the Constitution—A Study in Interstate Adjustments*, 34 YALE L.J. 685, 706-07 (1925).
323. *Id.* at n.364.
324. *See* Charles J. Meyers, *The Colorado River*, 19 STAN. L. REV.1, 48 (1966) (suggesting that "[m]ost compacts" were negotiated in an effort to obtain "federal benefits . . . contingent upon agreement being reached" citing the Colorado River Compact and the Upper Colorado River Compact as examples).

eras.[325] Population surges in western states, the agricultural explosion, and industrial development often collide with quality of life, human health, recreational and ecological concerns, which are increasingly drawing attention.[326] Managing these competing and developing interests presents ongoing challenges to compact commissions and to states that must defend suits concerning apportionment agreements. The compacts discussed below are only a few of those with ongoing management issues.[327]

Water compacts vary in the methods for apportioning the quantity of water to each signatory state as well as other interested parties (e.g., Indian tribes). Some compacts allocate water based on an "acre foot" that refers to the quantity of water covering an acre of land to a depth of one foot.[328] Other compacts rely on determinations, such as a percentage allocation of the waters of designated streams,[329] a mean daily flow of the river,[330] a precompact baseline,[331] or a provision allowing signatory states to demand releases at times and rates specified in the compact.[332] Other compacts leave apportion-

---

325. *See* Douglas L. Grant, *Interstate Water Allocation Compacts: When the Virtue of Permanence Becomes the Vice of Inflexibility*, 74 U. Colo. L. Rev. 105 (2003).

326. For further discussion of allocation compact issues, *see id.* at 105 n.368 (2003). *See also* Paul Elliott, *Texas' Interstate Water Compacts*, 17 St. Mary's L.J. 1241 (1986).

327. Other compacts that address water apportionment issues are catalogued by the U.S. Fish and Wildlife Service, *available at* http://laws.fws.gov/lawsdigest/compact.html#list).

328. An acre-foot is equivalent to 325,900 gallons of water. Kansas v. Colorado, 514 U.S. 673, 677 n.1 (1995). *See* Wyoming v. Colorado, 259 U.S. 419 (1922), *decree vacated by joint motion of parties*, 353 U.S. 953 (1957). The allocations of the Lower Colorado River Basin through the Boulder Canyon Project Act are an example of allocation by acre-feet. *See* 43 U.S.C. § 617 (2004). *See also* Arizona v. Morton, 549 F.2d 1231, 1235 (9th Cir. 1977). Under the 1922 Colorado River Compact, the Upper Basin states agreed to deliver 7.5 million acre-feet annually to the Lower Basin states. Pub. L. No. 70-642, 45 Stat. 1057 (1928); 46 Stat. 3000 (June 25, 1929).

329. *See, e.g.,* Yellowstone River Compact, art. V (1951).

330. *See* Hinderlider v. La Plata River & Cherry Creek Ditch Co., 304 U.S. 92 (1938).

331. Pecos River Compact, art. III (1949).

332. Arkansas River Compact (1949). For a detailed discussion of this compact, *see* David W. Robbins & Dennis M. Montgomery, *The Arkansas River Compact*, 5 U. Denv. Water L. Rev. 58 (2001).

ment determinations to a compact commission.[333]

The Supreme Court expressly advocates developing apportionment methods for interstate waters through interstate compacts and agreements. The Court has stated that disputes between states concerning allocation of riverine waters "is not to be determined as if it were one between two private riparian proprietors or appropriators."[334] Further, the downstream state "is not entitled to have the stream flow as it would in nature regardless of need or use. If . . . [the upstream state] is devoting the water to a beneficial use, the question to be decided, in the light of existing conditions in both states, is whether, and to what extent, her action injures the lower state and her citizens by depriving them of a like, or an equally valuable, beneficial use."[335] The Court had previously determined where there are "equitable division[s] of benefits" between the uses each state makes of the water, the Court will not intervene in the dispute.[336] When subsequently asked to intervene, the Court stated:

---

333. *See, e.g.*, The Alabama-Coosa-Tallapoosa River Basin (ACT) Compact (1997), and the Apalachicola-Chattahoochee-Flint River Basin (ACF) Compact (1997). The bill enacting these compacts specifically provides:

> The Acts do not provide specific percentages or formulas under which the surface waters will be allocated among the states. Instead, the Acts provide for the formation of a Commission for each Compact. Each Commission will consist of the Governors of each state and a federal Commissioner appointed by the President. Each Commission, by unanimous vote, will approve an allocation formula for dividing surface waters in the two basins among the three states. However, the federal Commissioner's concurrence in the allocation formulas can be overridden by the remaining Commission members. The Acts provide that the allocation formulas will protect water quality, ecology, and biodiversity within the meaning of federal environmental protection legislation.

1997 Ga. Laws 15, 29. For a discussion of these compacts, *see* Mary R. Hawk, *Interstate Compacts: Allocate Surface Water Resources From the Alabama-Coosa-Tallapoosa River Basin Between Georgia and Alabama; Allocate Surface Water Resources From the Apalachicola-Chattahoochee-Flint River Basin Among Alabama, Florida, and Georgia*, 14 GA. ST. U. L. REV. 47 (1997).

334. Colorado v. Kansas, 320 U.S. 383, 393 (1943).

335. *Id.*

336. Kansas v. Colorado, 206 U.S. 46 (1907).

[S]uch controversies may appropriately be composed by negotiation
and agreement, pursuant to the compact clause of the Federal constitution. We say of this case, as the court has said of interstate differences of like nature, that such mutual accommodation and agreement
should, if possible, be the medium of settlement, instead of invoca-
tion of our adjudicatory power.[337]

Nonetheless, where efforts to use interstate negotiation and compacts to
settle allocation disputes between or among states are unsuccessful, and when
a genuine controversy exists, the Court will use its powers to resolve the
matter.[338]

While equitable apportionment may be imposed by the Court or Congress, states consistently use interstate compacts as a means to address allocation issues as well as to resolve other disputes that involve the use or availability
of waters between or among states. This is not to say that litigation over
allocation and other water use issues is nonexistent. However, the litigation
often centers on the implementation and enforcement of the compacts negotiated to address water use and allocation rather than asking the courts to
specifically designate flow rates or apportion allocation.[339]

9.4.2.1.1   *Arkansas River Compact*

The Arkansas River begins in the mountains of Colorado just east of the
Continental Divide, descends for about 280 miles to the Kansas border, flows
through that state, meanders through Oklahoma and Arkansas, eventually
emptying into the Mississippi River. The dispute between Colorado and Kansas concerning the use of water from the Arkansas River is over a century old.
The Supreme Court in 1907 applied the doctrine of "equitable apportionment" in the case brought by Kansas against Colorado alleging that Colorado
was removing more than its share of water from the Arkansas. While the
Court dismissed the Kansas complaint, it did so without prejudice and with
the recognition that if, in the future, Colorado did increase its water usage
resulting in inequitable distribution of benefits from the river water, then

---

337. Colorado v. Kansas, 320 U.S. 383, 392 (1943).
338. *See, e.g.,* Nebraska v. Wyoming, 325 U.S. 589, 616 (1945).
339. *See, e.g.,* Kansas v. Nebraska, 525 U.S. 1101 (1999) (Republican River
      Compact); Oklahoma v. New Mexico, 484 U.S. 808 (1987) (Canadian River
      Compact); Kansas v. Colorado, 475 U.S. 1079 (1986) (Arkansas River Com-
      pact); Texas v. New Mexico, 343 U.S. 932 (1952); Texas v. New Mexico,
      353 U.S. 991 (1957).

Kansas could seek relief.[340] Between 1907 and 1943, there were ongoing disputes between these two states that resulted in the Supreme Court again considering allocation issues.[341] This time, although the Court acknowledged that Colorado diversions had continued, it refused to grant relief to Kansas, instead recommending that such matters are better resolved through the negotiation and execution of compacts between the states.[342]

As a result of this case and other efforts to allocate the waters of the Arkansas River, Colorado and Kansas negotiated the Arkansas River Compact.[343] The compact's stated purpose is to "[s]ettle existing disputes and remove causes of future controversy" between the two states and their citizens concerning the use and control of waters of the Arkansas River and to "[e]quitably divide and apportion" the waters and the benefits arising from construction and operation of the federal "John Martin Reservoir" water conservation project.[344] The reservoir is a key element to cooperation between Kansas and Colorado concerning the river waters. Both Kansas and Colorado place high importance on the operation of the reservoir because the water it stores is indispensable to efficient management of the river, which is "central to the Arkansas River Compact, the [administration of] that Compact, the interests of Colorado and Kansas, and resoltion of" the disputes between these states.[345]

The compact created the Arkansas River Compact Administration (ARCA). While the Army Corps of Engineers operates the John Martin Reservoir, the ARCA plays a key role in administration and management of the reservoir.[346] The ARCA's 1980 Operating Plan (amended in 1984) is designed to provide greater reliability in the use of the reservoir's water by designating allocations of water within the reservoir's conservation pool, thus ensuring each state a percentage of the reservoir pool waters.[347] Courts have upheld the ARCA's actions with respect to management and administration of the reservoir where those actions advance the terms of the compact and do not conflict materially with them and have deferred to decisions of the ARCA that are mutually beneficial to the states.[348] Enforcement under the compact occurs

---

340. Kansas v. Colorado, 206 U.S. 46 (1907).

341. *See* Colorado v. Kansas, 320 U.S. 383 (1943).

342. *Id.* at 392.

343. Congress consented to the compact in 1949. *See* Pub. L. No. 81-82, 63 Stat. 145 (1949).

344. Arkansas River Compact, art. I (1949).

345. Simpson v. Highland, 917 P.2d 1242, 1249 (Colo. 1996).

346. Arkansas River Compact, art. VIII, § G (1949).

347. *See* Simpson v. Highland, 917 P.2d 1242, 1245 (Colo. 1996).

348. *Id.* at 1249.

through state agencies charged with administering water rights in each state.[349]

While the compact attempted to resolve the then-ongoing disputes as to appropriation of water from the Arkansas River, the disputes continue. As recently as 2001, the Supreme Court again considered a Kansas claim that Colorado's use of the Arkansas waters violated the compact, specifically Article IV-D that provided, among other things, that future development or construction within the river basin would not materially deplete in quantity or availability water available to users in Colorado and Kansas.[350] Adopting most of a Special Master's report, the Court held that Colorado's postcompact increases in groundwater well pumping had materially depleted the waters in violation of Article IV-D and awarded monetary damages, not water, to Kansas.[351]

Notwithstanding the difficulty in ascertaining the damages accruing from a violation of the compact, the Court awarded monetary damages to Kansas, rejecting Colorado's contention that such an award violated the Eleventh Amendment, since individual water users were the parties hurt by any violation of the compact.[352] This is not the first time the Court has allowed recovery of monetary damages for violations of interstate compacts. In 1987, the Court decided *Texas v. New Mexico*, another case involving a violation of an interstate compact apportioning stream flow.[353] In *Texas v. New Mexico*, the Court allowed a state to recover monetary damages for another state's violation of an interstate compact apportioning the flow of an interstate stream finding that recovery of money damages can be within a state's proper pursuit of the "general public interest" in an original action.[354] Interestingly, the Court permitted Texas to recover monetary damages at the behest of New Mexico, the breaching state.[355]

While Kansas may receive a significant monetary award as a result of Colorado's breach of the compact, given the need for additional irrigation water, it is unclear that such a resolution serves the state's ongoing interest to ensure adequate quantity and availability of water from the river. Despite that interstate compacts are contracts, it can be questioned whether monetary

---

349. Arkansas River Compact, art.VIII, § H (1949).
350. Kansas v. Colorado, 533 U.S. 1, 5 (2001).
351. *Id.*
352. *Id.* at 8 (Kansas is a real party in interest and not simply a nominal defendant for water users in Kansas.).
353. Texas v. New Mexico, 482 U.S. 124 (1987).
354. *Id.* at 132 n.7.
355. *Id.* at 129-32.

awards, as traditional remedies for breach of contract, are an acceptable substitute for the water that should have flowed into the state.[356]

In addition to an award of monetary damages, the Court in *Kansas v. Colorado* also held that the unliquidated nature of Kansas's money damages did not bar an award of prejudgment interest, although it did find that accrual of the interest began at a later date than that sought by Kansas.[357] The Court permitted prejudgment interest despite the fact that at the time Colorado and Kansas entered into their agreement, the state of the law "regarding awards of prejudgment interest for unliquidated claims was uncertain at best."[358] Thus, according to the dissent in that case, interest would not have been contemplated by the parties while negotiating the terms of the compact.[359] Permitting recovery of interest as a part of the remedy for violation of an interstate compact significantly increases the potential liability of a state found in violation of a compact, particularly if it is determined that the violation has occurred over a number of years. The Court in *Kansas v. Colorado* determined that interest should accrue from the date Colorado "knew or should have known" it was violating the compact and, in this case, determined that this was the date on which Kansas filed its complaint.[360] This date, however, was agreed to as a compromise between the majority justices who apparently disagreed as to the date on which Colorado "knew or should have known."[361] Thus, in future compact disputes, the date of the filing of the complaint may not necessarily be determinative of when a state "knew or should have known" it was in violation of its obligations under an interstate compact.

---

356. *See* Joseph W. Girardot, *Toward a Rational Scheme of Interstate Water Compact Adjudication*, 23 U. MICH. J.L. REFORM 151, 164 (1989) ("A remedy that substitutes money for water clearly frustrates congressional intent, for Congress has stated that it intends [interstate water compacts] to provide for the equitable distribution of the present available water supply.") *See also* David H. Gold, *Supreme Court Struggles With Damage Assessment in Water Dispute as Interstate Compact Breaks Down*, 29 ECOLOGY L.Q. 427, 429-30 (2002).

357. Kansas v. Colorado, 533 U.S. 1, 16 (2001).

358. *Id.* at 21 (O'Connor, J., dissenting in part).

359. *Id.* at 20-21 (O'Connor, J., dissenting in part).

360. *Id.* at 15.

361. *Id.* at 15 n.5.

9.4.2.1.2   *Colorado River Compact*

Allocation issues are also pressing for states using water from the Colorado River.[362] The Colorado River flows through seven states.[363] In addition, there have been attempts to divert basin water to areas outside of the watershed (e.g., to the city of Denver).[364] Allocation issues arose in the early twentieth century; they were then and continue to be contentious.[365] The Colorado River Compact took years to negotiate[366] and is the source of ongoing litigation.[367] This compact, in contrast to some other water allocation compacts, does not allocate a specific amount of water to each state.[368] The compact divides the Colorado

---

362. For a historical and current-day perspective on Colorado River Basin issues, *see* Charles J. Meyers, *The Colorado River*, 19 STAN. L REV. 1 (1966).

363. The states through which the river flows are Colorado, Utah, Arizona, Nevada, and California, and tributaries entering from New Mexico and Wyoming.

364. The Homestake II project would have diverted water out of basin to Denver and Colorado Springs. The project did not go forward, however. *See* Geoffrey M. Craig, *House Bill 1041 and Transbasin Water Diversions: Equity to the Western Slope or Undue Power to Local Government?*, 66 U. COLO. L. REV. 791, 798-99 (1995). *See also* 6 WATERS AND WATER RIGHTS § 50 (Robert E. Beck ed., 1991) (predicting that "substantial additional development in the Upper Basin is unlikely unless endangered species problems are successfully addressed").

365. For a history of the Colorado River and its development, *see* Arizona v. California, 373 U.S. 546 (1963), *abrogated by* California v. United States, 438 U.S. 645 (1978). *See also* Arizona v. California, 530 U.S. 392 (2000).

366. For a history of the Colorado River Compact, *see* Daniel Tyler, *Delphus Emory Carpenter and the Colorado River Compact of 1922*, 1 U. DENV. WATER L. REV. 228 (1998).

367. *See* 42 Stat. 171 (1921) & 46 Stat. 20 (1929). Other federal controls over the flow of the river are provided by the Mexican Water Treaty, T.S. 994, 59 Stat. 1219; the Colorado River Storage Project Act, 43 U.S.C. §§ 620-20o (1970); and the Colorado River Basin Project Act, 43 U.S.C. §§ 1501-56 (1970). For a history and discussion of the Colorado River legislation, *see* H.R. REP. NO. 1312 (1968) (Interior and Insular Affairs Committee), *reprinted in* 1968 U.S.C.C.A.N. 3672-86.

368. The Colorado River Compact did not create a commission because the compact provides for water to be apportioned "in perpetuity." *See* 42 Stat. 171 (1921); 46 Stat. 20 (1929); Colorado River Compact, art. III (1922). When disputes arise, the governors of the compact states appoint commissioners who then have authority to resolve the disputes, subject to approval of the respective state legislatures. Colorado River Compact, art. VI (1922).

River between the upper and lower basins of the river.[369] Within each basin, the river is then apportioned among Upper Basin states[370] by the Upper Basin Compact.[371] The Upper Colorado River Basin Compact enacted in 1948 by Arizona, Colorado, New Mexico, Utah, and Wyoming divides the Upper Basin's share of water.[372] This compact obligates member states to maintain certain water flows up river to ensure that the obligations under the Colorado River Compact, approved by Congress in 1928, can be met.

The water is apportioned among the Lower Basin states[373] by the Boulder Canyon Project Act.[374] In contrast to the Upper Colorado River Basin Compact's commission, the Boulder Canyon Project Act designates the Secretary of the Interior as responsible for delivery of water to the Lower Basin states, which occurs from federal reservoirs.[375]

---

369. Congress consented to negotiation of the Colorado River Compact in 1921. The compact was signed Nov. 24, 1922. The text of the compact can be found at 70 CONG. REC. 324 (1928). The river is divided into the upper and lower basins at Lee's Ferry, Arizona. Colorado River Compact, art. I & art. II (e)-(g). A total of seven states are members of the Colorado River Compact, but the allocation of water is by basin, not by individual state. Colorado River Compact, art. I (1922).
370. Upper Basin states are Utah, Colorado, Wyoming and New Mexico. *See* Arizona v. California, 283 U.S. 423, 462 n.13 (1931). Colorado River Compact, art. II (1922).
371. Upper Colorado River Basin Compact (1949).
372. Approved by Congress, 63 Stat. 31 (1949). *See also* COLO. REV. STAT. ANN. § 37-62-101 (2004).
373. Lower Basin states are Arizona and parts of Nevada and California. Arizona v. California, 283 U.S. 423, 462 n.13 (1931). Colorado River Compact, art. II (1928).
374. Boulder Canyon Project Act of 1928, 43 U.S.C. § 617 (2004). *See* Arizona v. California, 373 U.S. 546 (1963), *abrogated by* California v. United States, 438 U.S. 645 (1978).
375. *See* Arizona v. California, 373 U.S. 546, 580 (1963) ("Congress intended the Secretary of the Interior, through his section 5 contracts, both to carry out the allocation of the waters of the main Colorado River among the Lower Basin States and to decide which users within each State would get water," interpreting the Boulder Canyon Act, 43 U.S.C. §§ 617-617t (1928)), *abrogated on other grounds,* California v. United States, 438 U.S. 645 (1978). *See also* Colorado River Interim Surplus Guidelines, 66 Fed. Reg. 7772 (Jan. 25, 2001). On October 16, 2003, Secretary of the Interior Gale Norton signed the Colorado River Delivery Agreement, *available at* http://www.doi.gov/issues/colorado.html.

The majority of states through which the Colorado flows or borders ratified the Colorado River Basin Compact that was approved by Congress when it passed the Boulder Canyon Act of 1928.[376] Arizona was the only state through which the river system extends that did not originally ratify the Colorado River Basin Compact.[377] The state of Arizona petitioned the Supreme Court to find the Colorado River Compact and the Boulder Canyon Act null and void and to enjoin construction of the Boulder Canyon Dam.[378] The Supreme Court dismissed Arizona's petition, upheld the Boulder Canyon Act, and determined that no present right of Arizona to divert and use unappropriated water had been infringed.[379]

Since the 1931 decision, the Supreme Court has addressed various issues involving the Colorado River Compact; the debate focuses on how much water each state has a legal right to use out of the waters of the Colorado River and its tributaries.[380] The basic underlying reason for the contentious nature of apportionment of the Colorado River is that at the time initial allocations were made, the assumptions of flow in the Colorado River were based on incomplete infor-

---

376. The Boulder Canyon Project Act approved the Colorado River Compact subject to certain limitations and conditions. Congressional approval was effective when California and at least five of the six other states ratified the compact, as modified. The legislatures of all these states, except Arizona, ratified the modified compact. *See* Arizona v. California, 283 U.S. 423, 449 (1931). Arizona ratified the compact at a later date. *See* Arizona v. California, 373 U.S. 546, 558 n.24 (1963) and H.R. Rep. No. 1312 (Interior and Insular Affairs Committee, Apr. 24, 1968), *reprinted in* 1968 U.S.C.C.A.N. at 3676.

377. Of the Colorado River's 1,293 miles, over half, 688 miles, flows in Arizona or along the state's border. Arizona ratified the compact in 1944.

378. *See* Arizona v. California, 283 U.S. 423 (1931).

379. *Id.* at 464.

380. *See, e.g., id. See also* Arizona v. California, 292 U.S. 341 (1934); Arizona v. California, 298 U.S. 558 (1936). *See also* United States v. Arizona, 295 U.S. 174 (1935); Arizona v. California, 373 U.S. 546 (1963); Arizona v. California, 376 U.S. 340 (1963) (decree carrying into effect Court's order entered in 373 U.S. 546); Arizona v. California, 383 U.S. 268 (1966) (amended decree entered); Arizona v. California, 444 U.S. 1009 (1980) (Memorandum and Report of the Special Master on preliminary issues received and ordered filed); Arizona v. California, 456 U.S. 912 (1982); Arizona v. California, 460 U.S. 605 (1983); Arizona v. California, 466 U.S. 144 (1984); Arizona v. California, 493 U.S. 886 (1989); Arizona v. California, 530 U.S. 392 (2000).

mation and significantly overestimated (and thus overallocated) the available water. The result, of course, is a consistent tension among all users.[381] These issues as to the quantity of water and the amounts allocated have never ceased to exist; they commenced as soon as the compact was ratified.[382]

Because the Colorado River is one of the most regulated rivers in the world, other factors complicate apportionment of the river waters, including the management of dams built to create storage reservoirs, as well as management through public laws and international treaties.[383] The river's reservoirs provide a storage capacity of more than 60 million acre-feet, a four- to five-year supply. There are more than 20 major dams along the Colorado River and its various tributaries operated by not only the Bureau of Reclamation but also other agencies. Thus, resolving issues involving apportionment necessarily involves not only the signatory states to the compact but also the mandates and contract obligations of other entities. Resolving these disputes inevitably results in litigation that further refines the interpretation and implementation of applicable law such as the Boulder Canyon Act. For example, in *Bryant v. Yellen*,[384] the Supreme Court held that the general rule under federal reclamation law, which limits a single owner to irrigation waters for no more than 160 acres of land,[385] did not apply to lands in California's Imperial Valley that were already privately irrigated in 1929 when Congress passed the Boulder Canyon Act.[386]

Another complicating factor is that the Colorado River flows from the United States into Mexico; yet at the time the states ratified and Congress approved the 1922 compact, no consideration was given to Mexico's economic or environmental reliance on waters from the river.[387] While a 1944

---

381. *See, e.g.,* David Getches, *Water Wrongs: Why Can't We Get It Right the First Time?*, 34 ENVTL. L. 1 (2004).

382. *See* Daniel Tyler, *Delphus Emory Carpenter and the Colorado River Compact of 1922*, 1 U. DENV. WATER L. REV. 228 (1998).

383. *See* http://www.crwua.com/colorado_river/reclamation.htm.

384. Bryant v. Yellen, 447 U.S. 352 (1980).

385. The general rule under federal reclamation law limits delivery of irrigation water from reclamation projects to 160 acres under single ownership. Reclamation Act of 1902, § 5, 43 U.S.C. § 431 (2003). *See* Bryant v. Yellen, 447 U.S. 352, 369 n.19 (1980), *citing* Ivanhoe Irrigation Dist. v. McCracken, 357 U.S. 375 (1958).

386. Bryant v. Yellen, 447 U.S. 352, 368-69 (1980).

387. For an excellent overview of this issue, *see* David H. Getches, *Water Management in the United States and the Fate of the Colorado River Delta in Mexico*, 11 U.S.-MEX. L.J. 107 (2003).

treaty subsequently allocated over a million acre-feet of water to Mexico, the treaty addressed only a quantity of water allocated, not its quality.[388] As a result, the treaty was later amended to address excessive salinity problems.[389] Outstanding issues that will eventually need to be addressed between the two countries are the environmental, natural resource, and economic effect the draining of the Colorado has had on indigenous people relying on the river delta for their livelihood.[390] The United States is already addressing these issues within the Colorado River Basin itself.[391] Some of these issues are discussed in more detail below.

9.4.2.1.3 Proposed Great Lakes Basin Water Resources Compact

Allocation of water from the Great Lakes has historically presented national and international issues.[392] In the mid-1980s, allocation of water occurred through nonbinding agreements and federal legislation under the 1986 Water Resources Development Act.[393] Neither of these solved the problems surrounding diversions of waters[394] and withdrawal of waters from the Great Lakes.

In 2001, the governors of the eight states and the premiers of the Canadian provinces signed a nonbinding Annex to the Great Lakes Charter (known as "Annex 2001"). In the Annex 2001, the heads of these governments agreed to fundamental principles for managing the Great Lakes water and, significantly, agreed to develop a binding agreement to address new or increased diversions and consumptive uses for the Great Lakes Basins.[395] In December

---

388. *See id.*
389. *See* David Getches, *Water Wrongs: Why Can't We Get It Right the First Time?*, 34 ENVTL. L. 1 (2004).
390. *See* David Getches, *supra* note 386 at 107 (Spring 2003).
391. *See, e.g.,* Colorado River Water Pact, *available at* http://www.doi.gov/issues/colorado.html. This agreement is intended to restore wildlife habitat and protect endangered species along the lower Colorado River.
392. Eight states and two Canadian provinces share water from the lakes: Michigan, Wisconsin, Ohio, New York, Indiana, Illinois, Minnesota, and Pennsylvania; and the provinces of Ontario and Quebec.
393. 42 U.S.C. § 1962d (2003).
394. Because of growing demand nationally and worldwide, there has been pressure to export water to Asia as well as to areas within the states outside of the Great Lakes watershed. *See* Noah D. Hall, *Great Lakes governors propose historic water resources compact,* TRENDS (ABA Environment, Energy and Resources Newsletter), Nov./Dec. 2004. at 4-5.
395. These include tributary surface water and groundwater.

2005, the governors of the eight Great Lake states and the Premiers of Ontario and Quebec signed the Great Lakes-St. Lawrence River Basin Sustainable Water Resources Agreement and the Great Lakes-St. Lawrence River Basin Water Resources Compact.[396] Significantly, these agreements ban new diversions of water outside the Basin, with the few exceptions to the ban being strictly regulated, and are designed to improve and protect the health and economic vitality of the Great Lakes region. They detail how the States and Provinces will manage and protect the Great Lakes-St. Lawrence River Basin and will provide a framework for each State and Province to enact laws protecting the Basin. For example, the States and Canadian Provinces will use a consistent standard to review proposed uses of Great Lakes' water, and they will share technical data and information among themselves to help improve decision making. Each State and Province will develop and implement individual water conservation and efficiency programs based on regional goals and objectives that will be jointly developed. The agreements balance economic development with sustainable water use, recognizing that the Basin is a "shared public treasure"[397] that requires protecting "the long-term health of the Great Lakes-St. Lawrence River Basin and the availability of that water in the future."[398]

9.4.2.1.4   *Issues That Affect Compacts Apportioning Interstate Water*

As discussed throughout this work, there are numerous laws, regulations, legal principles, and policies that may influence or affect how interstate compacts are implemented. Briefly discussed below are issues involving the Endangered Species Act, states rights, and modification of compacts involving interstate water. Other issues that directly and indirectly affect apportionment of water under interstate compacts include the Fifth Amendment takings doctrine,[399] and

---

396. A copy of these agreements is available at: http: Www.cglg.org.projects. water.annex2001Implementing.asp. This compact is subject to Congressional approval.

397. Water within the Great Lakes accounts for almost 20% of the world's available fresh water and 95% of the fresh water in the United States.

398. *See* www.cglg.org.projects.water.annex2001Implementing.asp.

399. *See, e.g.,* Maricopa-Stanfield Irrigation and Drainage Dist. v. United States, 158 F.3d 428, 431 (9th Cir. 1998) (involving a Fifth Amendment taking claim by irrigation districts asserting a right to excess stored water. The court held there was no taking under the Fifth Amendment.). *See also* Tulare Lake Basin Water Storage Dist. v. United States, 49 Fed. Cl. 313 (Fed. Cl. 2001) and Tulare Lake Basin Water Storage Dist. v. United States, 59 Fed. Cl. 246 (Fed.

the Clean Water Act[400] programs, such as the Section 404 permitting[401] and the Total Maximum Daily Loads (TMDLs).[402] These issues may apply to imple-

Cl. 2003) (finding water restrictions imposed under the Endangered Species Act effected a Fifth Amendment taking of contractually conferred rights to use water and determining damages due).

400. 33 U.S.C. § 1251 *et seq.* (2004).

401. *See* Clean Water Act, § 404, 33 U.S.C. § 1344 (2004) (requiring a party to obtain permits from the Army Corp of Engineers for discharge of dredge or fill material into navigable waterways. This arises often in the context of draining wetlands for various projects.). *See, e.g.,* Riverside Irrigation Dist. v. Andrews, 758 F.2d 508, 513, 514 (10th Cir. 1985) (The irrigation district argued that denial of the section 404 permit would prevent Colorado from diverting and using the water allocated to it under the South Platte River Compact.). While the district court held that Congress had the power to enact legislation that conflicts with and overrides a prior compact, even if its effect is to alter interstate water compact allocations, (Riverside Irrigation Dist. v. Andrews, 568 F. Supp. 583, 589-90 (D. Colo. 1983)), the appeals court refused to address the question of compact preemption and found for the Corps on other grounds, noting that "a decision on the question of the impact of the interstate compact would be premature." Riverside Irrigation Dist. v. Andrews, 758 F.2d at 514.

402. 33 U.S.C. § 1313 (d) (2004). The requirement to establish a total maximum daily load (TMDL) is triggered when a body of water or a segment of water is impaired by one or more pollutants and placed on the Clean Water Act list. The appropriate state, territory, or authorized tribe must develop a strategy to meet Water Quality Standards. *Id.* Water quality standards (WQSs) are the foundation of the water quality-based control program mandated by the Clean Water Act. WQSs define the goals for a waterbody by designating its uses, setting criteria to protect those uses, and establishing provisions to protect water quality from pollutants. Water quality standards are set by states, territories, and tribes. They identify the uses for each waterbody, for example, drinking water supply, contact recreation (swimming), aquatic life support (fishing), and the scientific criteria to support that use. A TMDL is the sum of the allowable loads of a single pollutant from all contributing point and non-point sources. The calculation must include a margin of safety to ensure that the waterbody can be used for the purposes the state has designated and account for seasonal variation in water quality. For a review of the law, *see generally* Oliver A. Houck, *TMDLs: The Resurrection of Water Quality Standards-Based Regulation Under the Clean Water Act,* 27 ENVTL. L. REP. 10,329 (1997); Oliver A. Houck, *TMDLs, Are We There Yet? The Long Road Toward Water Quality-Based Regulation Under the Clean Water Act,* 27 ENVTL. L. REP. 10,391 (1997); Oliver A. Houck, *TMDLs III: A*

mentation of other compacts, with their impact varying depending on the facts at issue and the provisions of the individual compact at issue. Because of the survey format of this book, it is not possible to discuss all external influences on compacts; it is helpful, however, to highlight a few of them. The topics discussed below are by no means the only influences on compacts, and it can be debated whether these or others are more important or influential. The following discussion is meant to raise some issues that practitioners need to consider and provide a stepping-stone for discussing other issues.

9.4.2.1.5   Endangered Species Act

Many water allocation compacts were negotiated, ratified by the states, and approved by Congress long before the 1980s when many federal environmental laws were enacted.[403] These subsequently enacted environmental and natural resource laws may directly and indirectly affect implementation of the compacts.[404] When determining apportionment issues, compact commissions and state and federal governments that seek to enforce such laws to protect habitat and species must respond to various issues that involve not only legal factors but also social attitudes as well as the interests of other groups, such as developers and agricultural interests.[405]

New Framework for the Clean Water Act's Ambient Standards Program, 28 ENVTL. L. REP. 10,415 (1998); Oliver A. Houck, *TMDLs IV: The Final Frontier,* 29 ENVTL. L. REP. 10,469 (1999). Oliver A. Houck, *The Clean Water Act TMDL Program V: Aftershock and Prelude,* 32 ENVTL. L. REP. 10,385 (2002).

403. For a discussion of the permanency of interstate water allocation compacts in light of laws such as the Endangered Species Act and other changes that affect water usage and allocation, *see* Douglas L. Grant, *Interstate Water Allocation Compacts: When the Virtue of Permanence Becomes the Vice of Inflexibility,* 74 U. COLO. L. REV. 105 (2003).

404. *See, e.g.,* Riverside Irrigation Dist. v. Andrews, 568 F. Supp. 583 (D. Col. 1983) (approval of compact did not limit congressional authority to subsequently enact the Clean Water Act, even though the act affected state water rights in a manner inconsistent with the compact); Rio Grande Silvery Minnow v. Keys, 333 F.3d 1109 (10th Cir. 2003), *vacated,* 355 F.3d 1215 (10th Cir. 2004).

405. For an excellent discussion on some of these issues, *see* Joseph L. Sax, *Environmental Law at the Turn of the Century: A Reportorial Fragment of Contemporary History,* 88 CAL. L. REV. 2375, 2377-78 (2000) (identifying three stages in the development of twentieth-century environmental law and how with the third stage, biodiversity protection and restoration, many of these issues arise in situations involving apportionment of river waters).

The Endangered Species Act (ESA)[406] may affect the allocation process and obligations under interstate compacts. As of October 2004, within Fish and Wildlife Service Regions 1, 2, 6 and 7,[407] more than 80 fish species are listed as threatened or endangered.[408] Of course, this represents only a fraction of the endangered or threatened water-dependent species (animal or plant) listed under the ESA for those regions.[409] Thus, listing under ESA and designation of critical habitat imposes limitations on the availability and use of waters on which the listed species are dependent.

For example, imposition of ESA terms on the Colorado River Basin will likely only exacerbate the dire conditions discussed above for apportionment within the Colorado River Basin. At this time, the Upper Basin states have developed a recovery program for several species listed as endangered, which includes preservation and augmentation of in-stream flows, habitat restoration, restocking native fish, and management of non-native fish species.[410] Balanced with these ecosystem concerns is an effort to avoid restricting the Upper Basin states from developing their remaining water rights under the Colorado River Compact. Clearly, a difficult balance, and the effectiveness of the program is certainly open to debate. Critics note that although the Upper Colorado River Basin program addressing ESA issues has been in place for over 15 years, many of the species of concern are still in trouble.[411]

---

406. 16 U.S.C. §§ 1531-1544 (1994).
407. The Fish and Wildlife Service Regions include the Pacific states and U.S. territories, Southwest states, Mountain-Prairie states, and Alaska. *See generally* http://www.fws.gov/.
408. Threatened and Endangered Species System (TESS) Detailed Species Ad hoc Report, *available at* http://ecos.fws.gov/tess_public/servlet/gov.doi.tess_public.servlets.EntryPage.
409. It also does not include those species proposed as candidates for listing under the Endangered Species Act. For additional listed water-dependent species (e.g., amphibians, reptiles, birds, plants), *see* USFWS Threatened and Endangered Species System (TESS), *available at* http://ecos.fws.gov/tess_public/.
410. For a discussion of these programs, *see* Mary Christina Wood, *Reclaiming the Natural Rivers: The Endangered Species Act as Applied to Endangered River Ecosystems*, 40 Ariz. L. Rev. 197, 229-30 (1998). *See also* Douglas L. Grant, *Interstate Water Allocation Compacts: When the Virtue of Permanence Becomes the Vice of Inflexibility*, 74 U. Colo. L. Rev. 105, 113-14 (2003).
411. *See* Sarah B. Wetering & Robert W. Adler, *New Directions in Western Water Law: Conflict or Collaboration?*, 20 J. Land Resources & Envtl. L. 15, 26-27 (2000).

In contrast to the program developed in the 1980s for the Upper Colorado River Basin, the Lower Basin states are now in the process of developing a multispecies conservation program in anticipation of possibility of listings.[412]

New Mexico has faced allocation issues under the Pecos River Compact and the Rio Grande River Compact as a result of listing by the U.S. Fish and Wildlife Service (USFWS) of two small fish found in those rivers.[413] Under the Pecos River Compact, New Mexico is obligated to deliver water to Texas. New Mexico's failure to meet this obligation resulted in a determination that New Mexico violated the compact, and the state was ordered to pay millions to Texas in settlement.[414] As a result, New Mexico has already spent many millions more to ensure it is not in violation of the compact in the future.[415] Requirements under the ESA complicated New Mexico's water delivery obligations when the USFWS listed the Pecos bluntnose shiner as threatened[416] and designated its critical habitat.[417] The result of the listing is that New Mexico must maintain a minimal flow in a river that runs through an arid area resulting in evaporative losses.[418] At this point, the federal government has assisted the state to recover some water loss, and New Mexico has several options, such as instituting conservation programs or terminating water rights

---

412. *See* Douglas L. Grant, *Interstate Water Allocation Compacts: When the Virtue of Permanence Becomes the Vice of Inflexibility*, 74 U. Colo. L. Rev. 105, 113-14 (2003).

413. *Id.*

414. Texas v. New Mexico, 482 U.S. 124 (1987) (Court determined New Mexico failed to deliver, as obligated, water to Texas for a period of 35 years.). New Mexico and Texas settled the suit for $14 million. Texas v. New Mexico, 494 U.S. 111 (1990).

415. Douglas L. Grant, *Interstate Water Allocation Compacts: When the Virtue of Permanence Becomes the Vice of Inflexibility*, 74 U. Colo. L. Rev. 105, 110 (2003).

416. Listing for *Notropis simus pecosensis* (Pecos Bluntnose Shiner), 52 Fed. Reg. 5295 (Feb. 20, 1987). See also 70 Fed. Reg. 2121 (Sept. 1, 2005) (Draft EIS).

417. Designation of Critical Habitat for Notropis simus pecosensis (Pecos Bluntnose Shiner), 52 Fed. Reg. 5295 (Feb. 20, 1987).

418. Douglas L Grant, *Interstate Water Allocation Compacts: When the Virtue of Permanence Becomes the Vice of Inflexibility*, 74 U. Colo. L. Rev. 105, 110 (Winter 2003). *See also Hearing on H.R. 3160, To Reauthorize and Amend the Endangered Species Act of 1973, "Common Sense Protections for Endangered Species Act," before the House Comm. on Resources,* 106th Cong. 68 (2000) (statement of Bennett W. Raley, National Water Resources Association).

under the prior appropriation doctrine, both of which have financial and economic implications.[419] Another option that has been proposed is modifying New Mexico's obligation under the Compact to require that Texas also share the burdens imposed by the federal laws and regulations.

In *Rio Grande Silvery Minnow,* the issue was whether the Bureau of Reclamation (BOR) had discretion to reduce deliveries of available water under its contracts with irrigation districts and cities to comply with the ESA.[420] The court noted the applicability of the unmistakable terms doctrine but further noted that neither party raised it.[421] The concurring opinion specifically addressed the applicability of this doctrine.[422] Because this opinion was subsequently vacated by the court, noting that Congress had specifically precluded the Secretary of the Interior from using funds to reduce delivery of water in New Mexico to meet ESA requirements, this case does not provide any clear direction on the applicability of the ESA in these complicated scenarios. [423]

Additional confusion concerning water allocation issues arises because the requirements under the ESA often run headlong into the Reclamation Act of 1902 and its amendments.[424] The Reclamation Act itself requires that ques-

---

419. Douglas L. Grant, *Interstate Water Allocation Compacts: When the Virtue of Permanence Becomes the Vice of Inflexibility,* 74 U. COLO. L. REV. 105, 111 (2003).
420. Rio Grande Silvery Minnow v. Keys, 333 F.3d 1109 (10th Cir. 2003), *vacated,* 355 F.3d 1215 (10th Cir. 2004).
421. The "unmistakable terms" doctrine is outlined in *United States v. Winstar Corp.,* 518 U.S. 839, 877-78 (1996). It is discussed *infra.*
422. Rio Grande Silvery Minnow v. Keys, 333 F.3d at 1139, *vacated,* 355 F.3d 1215 (10th Cir. 2004).
423. *Id.* at 1221 n.1. The New Mexico congressional delegation introduced legislation to void the panel opinion. Subsequent passage of the Energy and Water Development Appropriations Act of 2004, Pub. L. No. 108-137 § 208 (a), 117 Stat. 1827 (Dec. 1, 2003) mooted the appeal of the panel opinion. This Act prohibits the Secretary of the Interior from using any funds appropriated for the current fiscal year to "restrict, reduce or reallocate any water stored in Heron Reservoir or delivered pursuant to San Juan-Chama Project contracts . . . to meet the requirements of the Endangered Species Act." Energy and Water Development Appropriations Act of 2004, Pub. L. No. 108-137 § 208 (a), 117 Stat. 1827 (Dec. 1, 2003).
424. *See* Reclamation Act of 1902, 32 Stat. 388 (codified at 43 U.S.C. § 371, et seq. (2004)), and the Act of Feb. 9, 1905, 33 Stat. 714 (1905).

tions of water rights arising in relation to federal projects are determined according to state law,[425] except where there is "clear congressional directive" to the contrary.[426] As commentators have recognized:

> A compact is more than a contract among states. It is a contract that furthers a federal interest: interstate cooperation. Thus, state interests recognized in a compact may be subject to federal policies articulated after the compact was negotiated. The federal government has the power to apportion interstate waters, and therefore no state rights are vested against federal apportionment. Any state water rights, be they based on state law or an interstate compact, therefore remain subject to subsequent diminution by Congress, if Congress decides to use this power.[427]

The Supreme Court's decision in *Bennett v. Spear*,[428] gives rise to additional challenges. In *Bennett*, the Court held that plaintiffs who have purely

---

425. Sporhase v. Nebraska, 458 U.S. 941, 959 (1982) (Reclamation Act of 1902 "mandates that questions of water rights that arise in relation to a federal project are to be determined in accordance with state law[.]").

426. *See* S. Delta Water Agency v. United States, 767 F.2d 531, 538 (9th Cir. 1985); Westlands Water Dist. v. Dep't of Interior (Westlands I), 805 F. Supp. 1503, 1509 (E.D. Cal. 1992) ("Under Section 8 of the 1902 Reclamation Act, federal reclamation projects must be operated in accordance with state water law, when not inconsistent with congressional directives."). The Ninth Circuit interprets the term "congressional directive" as "a preemptive federal statute." *See* Natural Res. Def. Council v. Houston, 146 F.3d 1118, 1132 (9th Cir. 1998), *citing* United States v. California, 694 F.2d 1171, 1176-77 (9th Cir.1982). *See also* Concerned Irrigators v. Belle Fourche Irrigation Dist., 235 F.3d 1139, 1143 n.3 (8th Cir. 2001), *citing* California v. United States, 438 U.S. 645, 670-79 (1978) ("Reclamation projects are . . . subject to state law, so long as that law is not inconsistent with federal law."); Westlands Water Dist. v. Dep't of Interior, 153 F. Supp.2d 1133 (E.D. Cal. 2001).

427. A. Dan Tarlock, *The Endangered Species Act and Western Water Rights*, 20 LAND & WATER L. REV. 1, 25 (1985). *See also* Riverside Irrigation Dist. v. Andrews, 568 F. Supp. 583 (D. Colo. 1983) (finding that approval of compact did not limit congressional authority to subsequently enact the Clean Water Act, despite the fact that the Act affected state water rights in a manner inconsistent with the compact.)

428. Bennett v. Spear, 520 U.S. 154 (1997).

economic interests have standing to sue under the citizen-suit provision of the ESA to challenge implementation of the statute.[429] Thus, ranchers, irrigation districts, and others, such as those with recreational or commercial interests who meet Article III standing requirements, may bring a civil action to enforce the ESA even if such parties seek to prevent application of the ESA provisions that would protect endangered or threatened species.[430] While litigation brought by such parties may limit application of the ESA, and thus eliminate an additional draw on already overtaxed allocation systems, it is likely that the litigation will heighten the contentious nature of water allocation, further polarizing interests, making it more difficult to reach resolution.

9.4.2.1.6   *Unmistakable Terms Doctrine*

As described by the Supreme Court, the doctrine of unmistakable terms posits that absent an unmistakable provision to the contrary, contractual arrangements, including those to which a sovereign itself is a party, remain subject to subsequent legislation enacted by the sovereign.[431] Given that none of the opinions in *United States v. Winstar Corporation* commanded a majority, there is uncertainty as to its applicability in specific situations.[432] A few courts have had an opportunity to discuss the doctrine's applicability in the context of water storage projects that store water for various users including municipalities, agricultural operations, and developers.[433] While many of these

---

429. *Id.* at 166.
430. *Id.*
431. United States v. Winstar Corp., 518 U.S. 839, 877-78 (1996), *citing* Bowen v. Pub. Agencies Opposed to Social Security Entrapment, 477 U.S. 41, 52 (1986).
432. *See* Yankee Atomic Elec. Co. v. United States, 112 F.3d 1569, 1578-79 (Fed. Cir. 1997); Joan E. Drake, *Contractual Discretion and the Endangered Species Act: Can the Bureau of Reclamation Reallocate Federal Project Water for Endangered Species in the Middle Rio Grande?*, 41 Nat. Resources J. 487, 523 (2001) ("In sum, the fractured *Winstar* decision leaves us with some uncertainty regarding the extent and applicability of the unmistakable terms doctrine in specific situations.").
433. Various agencies and authorities within the federal government are responsible for water storage projects. For example, some of these projects are managed through the Bureau of Reclamation under the Reclamation Act of 1902 and its amendments. 43 U.S.C. § 371 et seq. (2004). Other projects, such as the Colorado Basin Project Act of 1968, authorize the Secretary of the Interior to build, operate, and maintain the Central Arizona Project to allocate Arizona's share of the Colorado River. 43 U.S.C. § 1501 et seq. (2004). The state receives water through the Colorado River Compact and the Boulder Canyon Project Act of 1928. *See* 42 U.S.C. § 1521 (2004).

cases do not directly affect actions under interstate compacts, because water storage projects work in concert with interstate compacts to provide water, limitations on the availability of water in such storage projects can affect the availability of water through interstate compacts.[434]

Under the unmistakable terms doctrine, these contracts between private parties and public entities or entities of the federal government, such as the Bureau of Reclamation or the Secretary of the Interior, are still subject to subsequent legislation, unless the contracts expressly provide in unmistakable terms that such subsequent laws do not apply—an unlikely scenario.[435]

9.4.2.1.7   State Water Rights

In addition to the unmistakable terms doctrine, state water rights, including minimum flow laws, are matters that may arise in apportionment situations.[436] Courts have recognized that absent a reservation by states to require application of state laws in interstate compacts, states have no right to impose state requirements.[437] Further, state water rights holders are sub-

---

434. *See, e.g.,* Maricopa-Stanfield Irrigation & Drainage Dist. v. United States, 158 F.3d 428, 431 (9th Cir. 1998).

435. *See, e.g., id.* at 439. The court addressed a Fifth Amendment takings claim by irrigation districts that subsequent federal law deprived them of a property right to water held in the Central Arizona Project. The court held that there was no Fifth Amendment taking, as the irrigation districts had no property right to excess water, as claimed. The court analyzed, among other things, the applicability of the "unmistakability doctrine," finding there was no evidence that Congress had relinquished its own prerogative to use subsequent legislation to reallocate water available in the project. *Id.* at 438-39. *See also* O'Neill v. United States, 50 F.3d 677, 686 (9th Cir. 1995) (Even if water supply contract did obligate federal government to supply specified amount of water without exception, under the "unmistakable terms" doctrine, the contract was subject to any subsequently enacted statutes.).

436. *See, e.g.,* United States v. Glenn-Colusa Irrigation Dist., 788 F. Supp. 1126, 1134 (E.D. Cal. 1992) (rejecting an argument that state water law rights should prevail over Endangered Species Act requirements).

437. Seattle Master Builders Ass'n v. Pac. N.W. Elec. Power & Conservation Planning Council, 786 F.2d 1359, 1371 (9th Cir. 1986) ("A state can impose state law on a compact organization only if the compact specifically reserves its right to do so."); California Dep't of Transp. v. South Lake Tahoe, 466 F. Supp. 527, 537 (1978) (Although not expressly provided for in the compact, the provisions of the California Environmental Quality Act apply to the Tahoe

ordinate to allocations made pursuant to an interstate compact.[438] These principles, in conjunction with the prohibition that states cannot unilaterally refuse to comply with terms of an interstate compact, may conflict with the reserved powers doctrine.[439]

While the state may reserve the right to impose state laws on interstate contracts, this principle permits neither anticipatory limitation nor barring exports of water to meet anticipated future needs within a state; limitations on water exports as to time and place that do not unreasonably burden interstate commerce may be permitted.[440] "[I]t would be unreasonable to require a state to wait until it is in the midst of a dire shortage before it can prefer its own citizens' use of the available water over out-of-state usage."[441]

Courts have also been called on to determine how the "prior appropriation doctrine may be reconciled with the equitable apportionment of water under federal law."[442] State water law issues also arise in the context of reclamation projects. The Supreme Court has held that Section 8 of the 1902 Reclamation Act subjected the distribution of water to state law unless that

Regional Planning Authority under article of compact creating the authority.). *See also* JAMES T. O'REILLY & CAROLINE BUENGER, RCRA AND SUPERFUND: A PRACTICE GUIDE WITH FORMS § 43.52A.010 (3d ed. West 2003).

438. Hinderlider v. La Plata River & Cherry Creek Ditch Co., 304 U.S. 92, 106 (1938); Frontier Ditch Co. v. Southeastern Colo. Water Conservancy Dist., 761 P.2d 1117, 1123 (Colo. 1988) (reaffirming that entry into a compact is a surrender of state sovereignty and, thus, conflicting state laws are preempted); Badgley v. City of New York, 606 F.2d 358 (2d Cir. 1979) (riparians in downstream states injured by reduced flows have no right to damages against upstream state which makes an authorized compact withdrawal).

439. United States Trust Co., 431 U.S. 1, 23 (1977) (While the Contract Clause limits the power of a state to modify its own contracts, it does not require a state "to adhere to a contract that surrenders an essential attribute of its sovereignty."). *See also* Douglas L. Grant, *Interstate Water Allocation Compacts: When the Virtue of Permanence Becomes the Vice of Inflexibility*, 74 U. COLO. L. REV. 105 (2003).

440. City of El Paso v. Reynolds, 597 F. Supp. 694, 701 (D. N.M. 1984).

441. *Id.*

442. Matter of Rules and Regulations Governing Use, Control, and Protection of Water Rights for Both Surface and Underground Water Located in Rio Grande and Conejos River Basins and Their Tributaries, 674 P.2d 914, 923 (Colo. 1984).

state law is inconsistent with congressional directives.[443] This issue has been directly addressed several times by the Supreme Court concerning the Colorado River and distributions from the Boulder Canyon Project.[444]

9.4.2.1.8 Modification of Interstate Compacts to Address Current and Future Water Needs

When interstate compacts allocating water become outdated, there are several methods to revise the allocated amounts. The states can petition the Supreme Court to allocate water, Congress may, in some instances, legislate apportionment, or the states themselves can resolve the dispute through modification of the compact provisions, which may require approval of Congress if the modification exceeds the prior consent.[445] If the Supreme Court chooses to step in, the Court has historically applied federal common law and the equitable apportionment doctrine. However, the Court has also declined to intervene in these disputes recognizing that the interstate compact process is better suited to resolving these types of disputes.[446] Congress has been reluctant to intervene in water allocation disputes and, in fact, has only legislated allocation in a few instances.[447] Commissions and states will continue to grapple

---

443. California v. United States, 438 U.S. 645, 674-75 (1978) (clear language of section 8 of the 1902 Reclamation Act permits a state to impose any condition on "control, appropriation, use or distribution of water" in a federal reclamation project provided that the state's conditions are not inconsistent with clear congressional directives respecting the project). *See also* California v. FERC, 495 U.S. 490, 502-04 (1990).

444. *See* Arizona v. California, 373 U.S. 546, 586 (1963) (holding "that the Secretary in choosing between users within each State and in settling the terms of his contracts is not bound by these sections to follow state law"), *disavowed*, California v. United States, 438 U.S. at 674-75 (The clear language of section 8 of the 1902 Reclamation Act permits a state to impose any condition on "control, appropriation, use or distribution of water" in a federal reclamation project provided that the state's conditions are not inconsistent with clear congressional directives respecting the project.). For a history of litigation at the Supreme Court involving the Colorado River, *see* Arizona v. California, 530 U.S. 392 (2000).

445. *See* Douglas L. Grant, *Interstate Water Allocation Compacts: When the Virtue of Permanence Becomes the Vice of Inflexibility*, 74 U. Colo. L. Rev. 105, 173-75 (2003).

446. *See, e.g.,* Colorado v. Kansas, 320 U.S. 383, 392 (1943); Kansas v. Colorado, 206 U.S. 46 (1907).

447. *See* Arizona v. California, 373 U.S. 546 (1963) (recognizing that Congress had allocated waters of the lower Colorado River when it enacted the Boul-

with questions of how to adapt compacts to address subsequent changes in social attitudes toward environmental and natural resource issues that directly affect water usage and availability[448] as well as legal obligations that arise subsequent to ratification and approval of the compacts or related contracts that affect allocations made under those compacts.

9.4.2.2   *Water Pollution and Water Quality*

The use of interstate compacts to tackle water quality issues highlights the tensions between permitting development and protecting natural resources that each state faces. Pollution and planning have outgrown an individual state's boundaries and concerns. Such issues must be addressed at least regionally to encompass the area that will be affected by activities taken by each state.[449] "[T]he handling of water quality regulation on a regional basis [, thus,] is so sensible that it is nearly inescapable."[450] Notwithstanding this view, critics of the use of interstate compacts to address regional water pollution issues have noted that "more often than not [the compacts] have been used as a smoke screen to ward off overdue action by the Federal government, rather than as a means of solving the problems over which they are given jurisdiction."[451]

der Canyon Project Act); Congress also allocated water in the Truckee-Carson-Pyramid Lake Water Rights Settlement Act of 1990, Title II of the Act of Oct. 27, 1990, Pub. L. No. 101-618, 104 Stat. 3289 (1990). For further discussion, *see* Douglas L. Grant, *Interstate Water Allocation Compacts: When the Virtue of Permanence Becomes the Vice of Inflexibility*, 74 U. Colo. L. Rev. 105, 171-76 (2003).

448. Societal attitudes that emphasize biodiversity, ecosystem management, and recreational values are evidenced by federal and state laws promoting protection of endangered species and imposition of state minimum stream flow laws. *See, e.g.,* Idaho Code §§ 42-1501 to 42-1505 (1990 & Supp. 2001); Or. Rev. Stat. §§ 537.332 to 537.360 (1999); Wyo. Stat. Ann. §§ 41-3-1001 to 41-3-1010 (2001). *See also* Robert E. Beck, *Use Preferences for Water,* 76 N.D. L. Rev. 753, 784 (2000).

449. *See* West Virginia *ex rel.* Dyer v. Sims, 341 U.S. 22, 27-28 (1951). *See also* J.B. Ruhl, *Interstate Pollution Control and Resource Development Planning: Outmoded Approaches or Outmoded Politics?,* 28 Nat. Resources J. 293, 294-95 (1988).

450. N. William Hines, *Nor Any Drop to Drink: Public Regulation of Water Quality—Part II: Interstate Arrangements for Pollution Control,* 52 Iowa L. Rev. 432, 457 (1966).

451. Oliver A. Houck, *TMDLs: The Resurrection of Water Quality Standards-Based Regulation Under the Clean Water Act,* 27 Envtl. L. Rep. 10,329 (July, 1997).

Notwithstanding concerns about leaving water quality issues to the states, interstate compacts and other interstate agreements involving pollution control seek to address issues of sewage and waste disposal as well as manage pollution in interstate streams, ponds, and lakes.[452] The sewage and waste disposal compacts are beneficial to smaller states to "avoid duplication of cost and effort, and in order to take advantage of economies of scale" by cooperating to establish joint sewage and waste disposal facilities.[453] Compacts concerning discharge of pollutants into waterways were the first step to addressing increasing water pollution and water quality concerns. The existence of interstate compacts to manage water pollution issues, however, did not preclude Congress from enacting the Clean Water Act (CWA),[454] even though provisions of the CWA conflict with those of a preexisting compact.[455] In fact, Congress recognized the benefits of such compacts and pro-

---

452. *See, e.g.,* New Hampshire-Vermont Interstate Sewage and Waste Disposal Facilities Compact (1976); New Hampshire-Massachusetts Interstate Sewage and Waste Disposal Facilities Compact (codified at N.H. Rev. Stat. Ann. § 149-J (2004)). Massachusetts has not adopted this compact. E-mail from Massachusetts Department of Environmental Protection (Sept. 24, 2004) (on file with authors). For the text of these compacts, *see* Council of State Governments, Suggested State Legislation, Interstate Compacts—Information and Directories, *available at* http://ssl.csg.org/compactlaws/comlistlinks.html. *See also* New England Interstate Water Pollution Control Compact (1947).

453. *See* New Hampshire-Massachusetts Interstate Sewage and Waste Disposal Facilities Compact, art. I (2004). This compact was not enacted by Massachusetts. E-mail from Massachusetts Department of Environmental Protection (Sept. 24, 2004) (on file with authors). *See also* New Hampshire-Vermont Interstate Sewage and Waste Disposal Facilities Compact (1976).

454. 33 U.S.C. § 1251 (2004). An in-depth discussion of the Clean Water Act and its provisions is beyond the scope of this chapter. For an excellent resource on the Clean Water Act, *see* Mark A. Ryan, The Clean Water Act Handbook (American Bar Ass'n, 2d ed. 2003). *See also* Riverside Irrigation Dist. v. Andrews, 568 F. Supp. 583, 589-90 (D. Colo. 1983) (Congress cannot unilaterally amend or repeal an interstate compact, but approval of an interstate compact does not limit congressional authority to later enact federal laws affecting rights or obligations under a compact; a "subsequent federal law of nationwide applicability will therefore be enforceable even if it affects a prior compact."), *aff'd,* Riverside Irrigation Dist. v. Andrews, 758 F.2d 508 (10th Cir. 1985).

455. Riverside Irrigation Dist., 568 F. Supp. at 590, *quoting* Pennsylvania v. Wheeling & Belmont Bridge Co., 59 U.S. 421 (1856) ("The question here is, whether

vided that states wanting to administer their own permit program under the CWA, in lieu of the federal program, may establish and administer such a program through interstate compacts.[456] Interstate compact commissions also submit water quality reports to EPA pursuant to CWA requirements.[457]

9.4.2.2.1   New England Interstate Water Pollution Control Compact

Interstate water pollution control compacts strive for a "cooperative approach to the abatement and control of water pollution."[458] After World War II, the industrial revolution brought changes to agriculture and increases in population concentrations as well as recreational and other uses that altered the demands placed on water systems. Governments, state and federal, realized the need to protect the quality of interstate surface waters.[459] In 1947, Congress authorized the New England states, through the New England Interstate Water Pollution Control Compact, to form a commission to respond to the unchecked flow of pollutants into lakes, rivers, and coastal waters.[460] While the New England Interstate Water Pollution Control Commission (NEIWPCC) initially focused on wastewater treatment issues affecting surface waters, the NEIWPCC's role has expanded in the intervening years to address wetlands restoration, nonpoint source pollution, source-water protection, wastewater treatment plant security, water allocation, and underground storage tanks, as well as becoming involved in policy and advocacy for the member states.[461]

9.4.2.2.2   Tri-State Compact of 1935

Other interstate commissions have experienced similar expansion of their role and responsibilities for member states. In October 2000, the Interstate

---

or not the compact can operate as a restriction upon the power of Congress under the Constitution to regulate commerce among the several states? Clearly not. Otherwise Congress and two States would possess the power to modify and alter the Constitution itself.").

456. See Clean Water Act § 103, 33 U.S.C. § 1253 (2004); Clean Water Act § 402 (b), 33 U.S.C. § 1342 (b) (2004).

457. See Clean Water Act § 305, 33 U.S.C. § 1315 (2004). See also National Water Quality Inventory: 1996 Report to Congress, U.S. Environmental Protection Agency, available at http://www.epa.gov/owow/305b/96report/commissions.pdf.

458. New England Interstate Water Pollution Control Compact (1947).

459. See generally History, New England Interstate Water Pollution Control Commission (NEIWPCC), available at http://www.neiwpcc.org/.

460. Id.

461. Id.

Sanitation Commission (ISC), formed through an interstate compact ratified by New Jersey, New York and Connecticut,[462] changed its name to the Interstate Environmental Commission (IEC)[463] to "more accurately reflect the nature of the Commission's mandates, mission and responsibilities that embrace a broad range of programs and activities."[464] The interstate compact that created the ISC was one of the first regional compacts formed to address water pollution of interstate waters. The Tri-State Compact of 1935[465] addressed pollution of coastal, estuarial, and tidal waters, and New York and New Jersey were initial members of the compact with Connecticut joining in 1941.[466] To address water quality and water pollution issues, the ISC, through its authority from the Tri-State Compact, issued regulations setting effluent limits for certain pollutants.[467] Despite the fact that the ISC regulations are not federal standards, courts have enforced the regulations through the CWA in the same manner as federal standards because the ISC standards are included within the National Pollutant Discharge Elimination System (NPDES) permits issued by the state of New Jersey, the designated permit authority.[468] "Such permits make the ISC's standards enforceable NPDES restrictions, and a violation of the standards constitutes a violation" of the CWA.[469]

9.4.2.2.3   Ohio Valley River Sanitation Compact

The Ohio River Valley Water Sanitation Commission (ORSANCO),[470] established through the Ohio River Valley Water Sanitation Compact, represents eight states and the federal government to improve water quality in the

---

462. *See* N.J. STAT. ANN. § 32:18-1 (2003); N.Y. ENVTL. CONSERV. LAW § 21-0501 (2004); CONN. GEN. STAT. ANN. § 22a-294 (2003).

463. Redesignated as the Interstate Environmental Commission pursuant to the Energy and Water Development Appropriations Act, Pub. L. No. 106-377, 114 Stat. 1441B-27 (2000).

464. *See generally* About Us, Interstate Environmental Commission *at* http://www.iec-nynjct.org/.

465. Tri-State Sanitation Compact (1937).

466. *See generally* Interstate Environmental Commission, http://www.iec-nynjct.org/.

467. United States v. City of Hoboken, 675 F. Supp. 189, 196 (D. N.J. 1987).

468. *Id.* at 196, *citing* 33 U.S.C. §§ 1311(b)(1)(C) & 1342. *See also* U.S. Steel Corp. v. Train, 556 F.2d 822, 830, 837-38 (7th Cir.1977).

469. *City of Hoboken*, 675 F. Supp. at 196, *citing* 33 U.S.C. § 1342 (2003).

470. Ohio River Valley Water Sanitation Compact, art. III (1940). For additional information, *see* The Ohio River Valley Water Sanitation Commission, *at* http://www.orsanco.org/.

Ohio River Basin by controlling pollution. The commission operates monitoring programs with the goal of using the river basin for drinking water, industrial supplies, and recreational purposes, as well as maintaining a robust riverine ecosystem within the basin.[471] ORSANCO was approved by Congress prior to passage of federal water pollution control statutes; thus ORSANCO, working through state and local statutes, addressed issues involving water quality and supply prior to federal regulation in that area.

ORSANCO's authority includes establishing pollution control standards for discharges into the Ohio River Basin. The purpose of these standards is:

> [T]o ensure that the water quality of the river is suitable for the uses designated by the Compact; public and industrial water supply (after reasonable treatment), recreational use, and warm water aquatic habitat, as well as other legitimate uses. The standards recommend stream criteria to assure that these uses will be achieved, and set waste water discharge requirements to attain these criteria.[472]

The ORSANCO pollution standards are incorporated into the permits issued dischargers under the National Pollution Discharge Elimination System (NPDES).[473] These standards apply to all direct dischargers into the Ohio River, although each state may adopt more stringent regulations.[474] ORSANCO, in an effort to address different regulations among the various Ohio River Basin states (e.g., differences in water quality standards, mixing zone policies, cancer risk level, terminology used in NPDES permits), has developed a protocol to alleviate perceived or actual inequities among river users.[475] Similar to other interstate water compacts, the federal government participates in ORSANCO.[476]

---

471. West Virginia *ex rel.* Dyer v. Sims, 341 U.S. 22 (1951).
472. *See* Ohio River Valley Water Sanitation Commission, FAQs, *available at* http://www.orsanco.org/watqual/standards/faqs.htm.
473. *Id.* The NPDES is found at 33 U.S.C. § 1342 (2004).
474. Thus, "the ORSANCO standards provide a minimum level of protection for the water quality of the river by which all the Compact states must abide." Ohio River Valley Water Sanitation Commission, FAQs, *available at* http://www.orsanco.org/watqual/standards/faqs.htm.
475. *See* Ohio River Valley Water Sanitation Commission, Protocol for Addressing Interstate Inconsistencies, *available at* http://www.orsanco.org/watqual/protocol.htm.
476. Other examples of federal-interstate water compacts include the Delaware River Basin Compact (1961), the Upper Colorado River Basin Compact (1941), the Susquehanna River Basin Compact (1970), and the Potomac River Basin Compact (1940). For discussion of federal involvement in interstate water compacts, *see* Frank P. Grad, *Federal-State Compact: A New*

Other compacts involving water pollution control include: Bi-State Metropolitan Development District Compact (Illinois and Missouri), New Hampshire-Vermont Interstate Sewage and Waste Disposal Facilities Compact, Red River Compact, and Tennessee River Basin Water Pollution Control Compact, just to name a few. In addition, there is the Association of State and Interstate Water Pollution Control Administrators (ASIWPCA).[477] This association acts as liaison among state, interstate and territorial officials responsible for implementing surface water programs; promotes public education and interaction with federal agencies; and serves as a clearing house for technical information and innovative tools.

9.4.3 Low-Level Radioactive Waste Compacts

9.4.3.1 Background

Management and disposal of low-level radioactive waste (LLRW) presents not a small problem. The waste is generated from numerous sources including the government, medical and research facilities, schools, and industry. It includes contaminated industrial or research waste such as paper, needles, test tubes, laboratory animal carcasses and tissues, plastic bags, protective clothing, packing materials, fluids, and water-treatment residues. Its classification is based on the source, and does not depend directly on the wastes level of radioactivity.[478]

Experiment in Co-operative Federalism, 63 COLUM. L. REV. 825 (1963); Leonard J. Feldman, *The Interstate Compact: A Cooperative Solution to Complex Litigation in State Courts*, 12 REV. LITIG. 137, 164 (1992).

477. *See* Association of State and Interstate Water Pollution Control Administrators, *at* http://www.asiwpca.org/links/interagencies.htm.

478. *See* U.S. Environmental Protection Agency, Radiation Publications, *available at* http://www.epa.gov/radiation/pubs.htm#radioactive_materials_ waste. *See also* Nuclear Regulatory Comm'n Web site, *at* http://www.nrc.gov/ waste/low-level-waste.html. According to the EPA, radioactive waste is divided into five categories: "(1) spent nuclear fuel from nuclear reactors and high-level waste from the reprocessing of spent nuclear fuel, (2) transuranic waste mainly from defense programs, (3) uranium mill tailings from the mining and milling of uranium ore, (4) low-level waste, and (5) naturally occurring and accelerator-produced radioactive materials. Radioactive waste is categorized according to its origin and not necessarily according to its level of radioactivity. For example, some low-level waste has the same level of radioactivity as some high-level waste." *See* U.S. Environmental Protection Agency, Radioactive Waste Disposal: An Environmental Perspective, *available at* http://www.epa.gov/radiation/docs/radwaste/index.html.

The amount of LLRW generated has increased significantly over the past
several years, which creates substantial concerns over the continuing availability of disposal sites. The Supreme Court has recognized the monumental
and pervasive disposal concerns surrounding these wastes.[479] Because of the
dire disposal situation in the late 1970s, specifically that the closure of two
other disposal sites left South Carolina as the only site for disposal of LLRWs,
Congress enacted the Low-Level Radioactive Waste Policy Act of 1980.[480]

The stated policy of the Act was to hold each state "responsible for
providing for the availability of capacity either within or outside the State
for the disposal of low-level radioactive waste generated within its borders," finding that regional disposal of this waste was the safest and most
efficient means of disposal.[481] The mechanism Congress devised was to ensure that waste from distant parts of the country would not, as then existed,
be shipped solely to one state, such as South Carolina. Thus, "the 1980 Act
authorized States to enter into regional compacts that, once ratified by Congress, would have the authority beginning in 1986 to restrict the use of
their disposal facilities to waste generated within member States."[482] Incentives were provided to states that joined a compact (e.g., states with an
existing waste disposal site could refuse to accept waste from any states that
had not entered a compact by January 1, 1986, and obtained congressional
approval).[483] Despite the incentives, however, few states entered into compacts. Only three regional compacts were formed, and these involved the
three states that had last operated low-level radioactive waste disposal facilities: Washington, Nevada, and South Carolina.[484]

With the impending possibility that these three states would refuse to
accept waste from the remaining states not within a compact, Congress
amended the 1980 Act with the Low-Level Radioactive Waste Policy Amendments Act of 1985.[485] The 1985 Amendments provided for a seven-year

---

479. New York v. United States, 505 U.S. 144, 149-50 (1992).
480. Pub. L. No. 96-573, 94 Stat. 3347 (1980), *repealed by* Pub. L. No. 99-241, 99
     Stat. 184 (1986). *See also* 42 U.S.C. § 2021b (2003) (Low-Level Radioactive
     Waste Amendment Act of 1985).
481. 42 U.S.C. § 2021d (a)(1) (2003).
482. New York v. United States, 505 U.S. 144, 150 (1992), *citing* Pub. L. No. 96-
     573, § 4(a)(2)(B), 94 Stat. 3347 (1980).
483. Pub. L. No. 96-573, § 4(a)(2)(B), 94 Stat. 3347 (1980) (codified at 42 U.S.C. §
     2021d (c) (2003)).
484. New York v. United States, 505 U.S. 144, 150 (1992).
485. Pub. L. No. 99-240, 99 Stat. 1842 (1986) (codified at 42 U.S.C. § 2021c
     (2003)).

transition during which time those states not within a compact could continue to dispose of wastes in Washington, Nevada, and South Carolina, provided the noncompacting state was actively developing its own site for disposal.[486] States needed to demonstrate that they had joined a compact, completed a detailed plan for a new facility, and submitted an application for a license from the Nuclear Regulatory Commission.[487]

While the Supreme Court has upheld Congress's authority under the Commerce Clause to regulate the interstate market in radioactive waste disposal,[488] it has considered and struck one of the three incentives established under the 1985 Amendments.[489] The 1985 Amendments established monetary incentives, access incentives, and a "take title" provision.[490] The Court found it permissible under the Tenth Amendment for Congress to provide states monetary incentives[491] and access incentives[492] to encourage states to provide LLRW disposal facilities. The Court, however, struck the third incentive, holding that an incentive that required states to "take-title" to waste or be liable to a generator/owner for any failure to take title was unconstitutional under the Tenth Amendment.[493]

9.4.3.2 Current Status

There are currently 10 Low-Level Radioactive Waste Regional Compacts involving 43 states: Appalachian Compact (Delaware, Maryland, Pennsylvania, West Virginia); Central Interstate Compact (Arkansas, Kansas, Louisiana, Oklahoma); Central-Midwest Compact (Illinois, Kentucky); Midwest Compact (Indiana, Iowa, Minnesota, Missouri, Ohio, Wisconsin); Atlantic Interstate Compact (Connecticut, New Jersey, South Carolina); Northwest Compact (Alaska, Hawaii, Idaho, Montana, Oregon, Utah, Washington, Wyoming); Rocky Mountain Compact (Colorado, Nevada, New Mexico); Southeast Compact (Alabama, Florida, Georgia, Mississippi, Tennessee, Virginia);

---

486. 42 U.S.C. § 2021e (2003).

487. 42 U.S.C. § 2021e(e)(1) (2003).

488. For a history of the Low-Level Radioactive Waste Policy Act and amendments, *see* New York v. United States, 505 U.S. 144, 160 (1992).

489. 42 U.S.C. § 2021b (2003).

490. 42 U.S.C. § 2021e(e)(1) (2003).

491. The incentives were payments made to states that had complied with statutory deadlines. *New York*, 505 U.S. at 152, *citing* 42 U.S.C. § 2021e (1992).

492. The incentives imposed surcharges on waste disposed by states that had not complied with certain deadlines and could result in a denial of access to disposal sites after a certain period. *Id.*

493. *Id.*

Southwestern Compact (Arizona, California, North Dakota, South Dakota) and the Texas Compact (Texas, Vermont).[494]

Nonetheless, despite the fact that most states have entered into these compacts, the goal of the Act—that disposal occur within a region—has not been achieved, as no new disposal facilities have been built. Waste is still sent to the South Carolina Barnwell facility, the Envirocare facility in Utah that accepts certain mixed wastes, and in certain instances, a commercial facility in Richland, Washington.[495] Seven states, Puerto Rico, and the District of Columbia are not affiliated with any compact.[496] Low-level radioactive waste from these six states and the District of Columbia may be shipped to the facility operating in South Carolina, at least until mid-2008.[497]

494. *See generally* U.S. Nuclear Regulatory Commission, Low-Level Waste Compacts, *at* http://www.nrc.gov/waste/llw-disposal/compacts.html. Regarding the Central Interstate Low-Level Radioactive Waste Compact, *see* Central Interstate Low-Level Radioactive Waste Commission, *at* http://www.cillrwcc. org/. Regarding the Southeast Radioactive Waste Disposal Compact, *see* Southeast Compact Commission for Low-Level Radioactive Waste Management, *at* http://www.secompact.org. Regarding the Southwest Radioactive Waste Disposal Compact, *see* Southwestern Low-Level Radioactive Waste Commission, *at* http://www.swllrwcc.org. For contact persons for other radioactive waste disposal compacts, *see* LLW Forum, *at* http://www.llwforum.org/membership.htm. It should be noted that the makeup of the specific compacts has changed over time.
495. *See generally* U.S. Nuclear Regulatory Commission, Low-Level Waste Disposal, What We Regulate, *available at* http://www.nrc.gov/waste/llw-disposal.html. Waste from the Northwest Compact and Rocky Mountain Compact is disposed of at a commercial disposal facility in Hanford, Washington. *See* U.S. Army Corps of Engineers, HTRW Center of Expertise Information—TSDF, Overview of Regional Interstate Compacts, *available at* http://www.environmental.usace.army.mil/library/pubs/tsdf/sec9-2/sec9-2.html. The Beatty, Nevada, facility was used by the Rocky Mountain Compact Commission until it closed on December 31, 1992. *See* Appalachian States Low-Level Radioactive Waste Comm'n v. O'Leary, 93 F.3d 103, 107 (3d Cir. 1996). For a discussion of the three sites, *see* U.S. General Accounting Office, Low-Level Radioactive Waste, Disposal Availability Adequate in the Short Term, but Oversight Needed to Identify Any Future Shortfalls, GAO-04-604 (June 2004), *available at* http://www.gao.gov/new.items/d04604.pdf.
496. The states are Maine, Massachusetts, Michigan, New York, North Carolina, New Hampshire, and Rhode Island.
497. For a discussion of Low-Level Radioactive Waste Regional Compacts, *see* U.S. Army Corps of Engineers, HTRW Center of Expertise Information—

Developing disposal sites for LLRW poses many difficulties, not the least of which are the NIMBY[498] or LULU[499] syndromes. Commercial sites accepting LLRW must be licensed by the Nuclear Regulatory Commission (NRC) or Agreement states.[500] The licensure imposes design, construction, and operational safety standards on waste facilities.[501] But even states that have joined a compact and have been selected by the compact commissions to be the host state for receiving LLRW have fought strenuously to avoid becoming a repository.[502] A recent example involves the state of Nebraska and the Central Low-Level Radioactive Waste Compact. Years of litigation resulted in a judgment against Nebraska and a finding that the former governor engaged in a politically motivated plot to keep the regional dump from being built in Nebraska.

TSDF, Overview of Regional Interstate Compacts, *available at* http://www.environmental.usace.army.mil/library/pubs/tsdf/sec9-2/sec9-2.html. *See also* U.S. General Accounting Office, Low-Level Radioactive Waste, Disposal Availability Adequate in the Short Term, But Oversight Needed to Identify Any Future Shortfalls, GAO-04-604 (June 2004), *available at* http://www.gao.gov/new.items/d04604.pdf.

498. "Not in My Backyard."

499. "Locally Undesirable Land Use."

500. States assume NRC regulatory authority pursuant to the Atomic Energy Act of 1954, § 274, Pub. L. No. 83-703, 68 Stat. 919 (1954). *See* discussion, U.S. Nuclear Regulatory Commission, Agreement State Program, *at* http://www.nrc.gov/what-we-do/state-tribal/agreement-states.html. Approximately 33 states have assumed NRC regulatory authority under section 274.

501. *See* U.S. Nuclear Regulatory Commission, Low-Level Waste Disposal, What We Regulate, *available at* http://www.nrc.gov/waste/llw-disposal.html.

502. For a discussion on the seemingly interminable litigation involving the siting and licensing of a facility in Nebraska, *see* Concerned Citizens of Nebraska v. U.S. Nuclear Regulatory Comm'n, 970 F.2d 421, 426-27 (8th Cir. 1992); Nebraska v. Central Interstate Low-Level Radioactive Waste Comm'n, 26 F.3d 77 (8th Cir.1994); Burton v. Central Interstate Low-Level Radioactive Waste Comm'n, 23 F.3d 208 (8th Cir.1994); County of Boyd v. United States Ecology, Inc., 48 F.3d 359 (8th Cir.1995); Nebraska v. Central Interstate Low-Level Radioactive Waste Compact Commission, 187 F.3d 982, 986 (8th Cir. 1999); Nebraska v. Central Interstate Low-Level Radioactive Waste Comm'n, 207 F.3d 1021 (8th Cir. 2000); Entergy, Arkansas, Inc. v. Nebraska, 241 F.3d 979, 990 (8th Cir. 2001); Entergy, Arkansas, Inc. v. Nebraska, 210 F.3d 887, 888 (8th Cir. 2000); Entergy, Arkansas, Inc. v. Nebraska, 358 F.3d 528, 547 (8th Cir. 2004), *reh'g denied, en banc,* 366 F.3d 688 (8th Cir. 2004), *cert. dismissed,* 125 S. Ct. 22 (Aug. 23, 2004). *See also* Thomas O. Kelly, Note, *Nebraska's $160 Million Liability?—Entergy, Arkansas, Inc. v. Nebraska, 241 F.3d 979 (8th Cir. 2001)*, 80 Neb. L. Rev. 574 (2001).

The settlement required Nebraska to pay $141 million plus interest for blocking efforts to build a low-level radioactive waste dump, but permitted the state to continue to oppose locating the dump in the state.[503] Kansas, a member of the compact, voted against the settlement, stating, through their commission representative, "It means that a state can conduct . . . what amounts to a sham review of a license application, do so at an exorbitant cost, and then, when eventually being caught at it, can absolve itself by refunding the money."[504] Notwithstanding Kansas's opposition, the settlement was finalized and even provides for Nebraska to rejoin the compact upon meeting certain conditions.

LLRW compacts circumscribe the ability of a host state (i.e., a state selected to construct and approve a disposal facility) to dictate how licensing and acceptance of the waste will proceed in a host state. For example, the compact commission may impose reasonable deadlines on a host state for processing of a waste facility license application.[505] A host state for a LLRW disposal facility has no right to veto permits to export waste from the compact region where the export permits are approved by a majority of the compact commission.[506] Given the fact that courts interpret compacts as they would any contract, states entering into compacts must exercise care in drafting, knowing they will be held accountable for their agreements.

The litigation that has resulted from the efforts of states to avoid becoming a repository for LLRW provides a perspective on how the courts will interpret and enforce the LLRW compacts. For example, states that enter LLRW compacts approved by Congress have waived their Eleventh Amendment right to immunity from suit in federal court. Thus, the compact commission may sue states that are a party to the compact.[507] Further, because the

---

503. As of July 2004, Nebraska is no longer a member of the Central Interstate Low-Level Radioactive Waste Compact.

504. Statement of Jim O'Connell, Kansas's representative on the Commission, concerning why he voted against the settlement. Kevin O'Hanlon, Associated Press, Aug. 10, 2004. Interestingly, the Ponca Tribe of Nebraska offered to host the facility on tribal land. *See* Don Walton, *Tribe had offered land for nuke waste facility,* LINCOLN JOURNAL STAR, Aug. 11, 2004, *available at* http://www.journalstar.com/articles/2004/08/10/local/10053512.txt.

505. *See* Nebraska v. Central Interstate Low-Level Radioactive Waste Compact Comm'n, 187 F.3d 982, 986 (8th Cir. 1999).

506. Nebraska v. Central Interstate Low-Level Radioactive Waste Compact Comm'n, 207 F.3d 1021, 1026 (8th Cir. 2000).

507. Entergy, Arkansas, Inc. v. Nebraska, 210 F.3d 887, 888 (8th Cir. 2000). *But see* Kansas v. Colorado, 533 U.S. 1, 7 (2001) ("It is firmly established, and undisputed in this litigation, that the text of the Eleventh Amendment would bar a direct action against Colorado by citizens of Kansas.").

LLRW compact is a federal law, it is congressionally sanctioned within the Compact Clause; a party "may sue a state officer for prospective relief in order to stop an ongoing violation of a federal right."[508] For example, in *Entergy, Arkansas, Inc. v. Nebraska,* the Central Interstate Low-Level Radioactive Waste Commission was authorized and required to sue Nebraska to prevent it from conducting further administrative proceedings concerning the state's denial of a license application for a LLRW disposal facility where the compact commission was seeking to enforce Nebraska's obligations under the compact.[509]

Under the LLRW compact, the state selected by the commission to host the disposal facility also must "process all applications for permits and licenses required for the development and operation of any regional facility or facilities within a reasonable period from the time that a completed application is submitted."[510] In cases involving an alleged breach of the covenant of good faith under the LLRW compact, which provides that "[e]ach *party state* has the right to rely on the good faith performance of each other *party state*,"[511] a court has rejected an argument that the applicant for a license to operate a disposal facility has the right to bring a claim against a compact state to enforce the good faith provision under the compact.[512]

In contrast, courts have permitted state entities other than the boards or commissions formed under the LLRW compacts to seek relief to enforce violations of a compact. In *Colorado Department of Public Health and Environment v. Caulk,*[513] the state sued a hazardous waste recycler for alleged violations of hazardous waste laws and the low-level radioactive waste compact. The defendant challenged whether the department had standing to seek an injunction for alleged violations of the Rocky Mountain Low-Level Radioactive Waste Compact. Finding that it had subject matter jurisdiction, the court determined that the Rocky Mountain Low-Level Radioactive Waste Board did not have exclusive authority to enforce violations of the com-

---

508. Entergy, Arkansas, Inc. v. Nebraska, 210 F.3d 887, 888 (8th Cir. 2000).
509. *Id.* at 897.
510. Central Interstate Low-Level Radioactive Waste Compact, art. V(e)(2) (1986). *See also* NEB. REV. STAT. § 71-3522 (2003); Omnibus Low-Level Radioactive Waste Interstate Compact Consent Act, Pub. L. No. 99-240, 99 Stat. 1859 (1986).
511. Central Interstate Low-Level Radioactive Waste Compact, art. III (f).
512. Entergy, Arkansas, Inc. v. Nebraska, 241 F.3d 979, 990 (8th Cir. 2001).
513. Colorado Dep't of Pub. Health & Env't v. Caulk, 969 P.2d 804 (Colo. Ct. App. 1998).

pact.[514] The language of the compact provided for intervention by the board in "any administrative or judicial proceeding involving low-level waste" and contemplated that other entities may enforce the compact—in this instance the department, which had responsibility for administration of the compact on behalf of the state.[515]

When a state breaches its "good faith" obligations compact, the appropriate relief is monetary relief, and not to remand to state agencies that administered the licensing process; the commission was not challenging the particular action in delaying and denying the permit application.[516] Further, where a state has waived its sovereign immunity from an award of damages, it has also waived immunity from the assessment of interest and, in this case, the court correctly calculated the amount of interest due.[517] There is no right to jury trial under the Seventh Amendment in cases brought by a LLRW commission seeking to enforce a compact state's obligations to process promptly a license for a proposed LLRW disposal facility.[518]

The Eighth Circuit has also considered the rights of the compact state's citizens in terms of the location of LLRW facilities. The court determined that there is no fundamental constitutional right to an environment free from radioactive contamination, and thus citizens could not challenge NRC performance standards for facilities accepting LLRW.[519] The citizens had argued that the Ninth Amendment, which provides that the "enumeration in the Constitution, of certain rights, shall not be construed to deny or disparage others retained by the people," protects fundamental unenumerated rights, including the right to be free from non-natural radiation, such as that resulting from a disposal facility for LLRW.[520]

---

514. *Id.* at 808.
515. *Id.*
516. Entergy, Arkansas, Inc. v. Nebraska, 358 F.3d 528, 544 (8th Cir. 2004), *reh'g denied en banc,* 366 F.3d 688 (8th Cir. 2004), *cert. dismissed,* 125 S. Ct. 22 (2004). *See also* Entergy, Arkansas, Inc. v. Nebraska, 241 F.3d 979, 988 (8th Cir. 2001); Kansas v. Colorado, 533 U.S. 1, 7 (2001) (awarding monetary relief for violations of interstate compact).
517. Entergy, Arkansas, Inc. v. Nebraska, 358 F.3d 528, 556 (8th Cir. 2004). *See also* Kansas v. Colorado, 533 U.S. 1, 11 (2001) ("Our cases since 1933 have consistently acknowledged that a monetary award does not fully compensate for an injury unless it includes an interest component.").
518. *Entergy, Arkansas, Inc.,* 358 F.3d 528, 547 (8th Cir. 2004).
519. Concerned Citizens of Nebraska v. U.S. Nuclear Regulatory Comm'n, 970 F.2d 421, 426-27 (8th Cir. 1992).
520. *Id.* at 426-27.

Despite the fact that there may be negative economic ramifications from a state's announcement that certain property is under consideration for locating a LLRW disposal facility, where the claim is based on preliminary, precondemnation activities by the state, there is no Fifth Amendment taking claim.[521] Another court rejected a Tucker Act claim, in which the plaintiff alleged that by its status, it was a third-party beneficiary of a contract between the United States and the state for the sale of land to the state for use as a low-level radioactive waste facility. In *U.S. Ecology, Inc. v. United States*,[522] the court determined that the federal government, by working with the plaintiff as licensee-designee for operation of the facility, did not intend to confer a benefit on any third party.[523] Further, even assuming there was such intent, the court determined that the plaintiff could not be a third-party beneficiary when it had not been licensed by the state prior to the federal government's alleged breach, and the state was not obligated to issue a license solely to plaintiff.[524]

A state voter initiative that seeks to preclude importation of LLRW into the state violates the Supremacy Clause because it seeks to "regulate legitimate federal activity and to avoid the preemption of the Atomic Energy Act" and violates the Commerce Clause because it attempts to stifle the "free flow of interstate commerce."[525]

9.4.3.3 Conclusion

A recent Government Accountability Office (GAO) report concludes that availability of disposal sites is adequate in the short term but that oversight is necessary to determine future needs.[526] The GAO report also notes that several changes since its 1999 report may have long-term implications that affect disposal availability and federal oversight. These include, "South Carolina's decision to close the Barnwell disposal facility to non-compact states by mid-2008, issuance of a license to Envirocare to accept class B and C wastes

---

521. Santini v. Connecticut Hazardous Waste Mgmt. Serv., 342 F.3d 118, 132 (2d Cir. 2003).

522. U.S. Ecology, Inc. v. United States, 245 F.3d 1352 (Fed. Cir. 2001).

523. *Id.* at 1356.

524. *Id.*

525. Washington State Bldg. & Constr. Trades Council v. Spellman, 684 F.2d 627, 630 (9th Cir. 1982).

526. U.S. General Accounting Office, Low-Level Radioactive Waste, Disposal Availability Adequate in the Short Term, but Oversight Needed to Identify Any Future Shortfalls, GAO-04-604 (June 2004), *available at* http://www.gao.gov/new.items/d04604.pdf.

pending approval by the Utah legislature and governor, and Texas legislation
to allow the licensing of a new disposal facility in that state."[527] At the time of
the report, the settlement agreement involving Nebraska and the Central Interstate Low-Level Radioactive Waste Commission had not been concluded,
so it is unclear what impact, if any, that settlement may have on the conclusions in the report. In addition, the report noted that federal changes, including changes in the Department of Energy's involvement in the National
Low-Level Waste Management Program and a decrease in the NRC's direct
involvement in LLRW management since the late 1990s,[528] could affect long-
term management; yet the report recommends continued federal oversight of
the management and disposal situation.[529]

9.4.4   Solid Waste/Hazardous Waste Compacts

There is no federal statute similar to the Low-Level Radioactive Waste
Amendment Act[530] for authorizing or requiring interstate compacts for management and disposal of solid[531] or hazardous[532] waste. The Resource Conser-

---

527. *Id.*
528. *Id.*
529. *Id.*
530. Low-Level Radioactive Waste Amendment Act, Pub. L. No. 96-573, 94 Stat.
     3347 (1980) (codified at 42 U.S.C. § 2021d (2004)).
531. Under the Resource Conservation and Recovery Act (RCRA), solid waste is
     defined as "[A]ny garbage, refuse, sludge from a waste treatment plant,
     water supply treatment plant, or air pollution control facility and other
     discarded material, including solid, liquid, semisolid, or contained gas-
     eous material resulting from industrial, commercial, mining, and agricul-
     tural operations, and from community activities, but does not include solid
     or dissolved material in domestic sewage, or solid or dissolved materials in
     irrigation return flows or industrial discharges which are point sources sub-
     ject to permits under section 1342 of title 33 [Clean Water Act], or source,
     special nuclear, or byproduct material as defined by the Atomic Energy Act
     of 1954, as amended (68 Stat. 923)." Resource Conservation and Recovery
     Act § 1004 (27), 42 U.S.C. § 6903 (27) (2004).
532. Hazardous waste is a subset of solid waste and is defined as "[A] solid waste,
     or combination of solid wastes, which because of its quantity, concentration,
     or physical, chemical or infectious characteristics may—(A) cause, or signifi-
     cantly contribute to an increase in mortality or an increase in serious irrevers-
     ible, or incapacitating reversible, illness; or (B) pose a substantial present or
     potential hazard to human health or the environment when improperly treated,
     stored, transported, or disposed of, or otherwise managed." Resource Conser-
     vation and Recovery Act § 1004 (5), 42 U.S.C. § 6903 (5) (2004).

vation and Recovery Act (RCRA)[533] provides for states to enter agreements or compacts for management and disposal of solid and hazardous waste. Similarly, the Comprehensive Environmental Response Compensation and Liability Act (CERCLA),[534] also called Superfund, provides for interstate agreements to ensure adequate capacity for handling cleanup of hazardous wastes. These provisions, however, are less comprehensive than that provided in the Low-Level Radioactive Waste Amendment Act and have had limited application. Further, state attempts to employ interstate agreements for management and cleanup of waste have been fraught with difficulties. At times, efforts in using or requiring interstate agreements have run afoul of Commerce Clause issues; at other times, economic burdens have plagued the waste management arrangements.

Similar to the increasing problems posed by the disposal of low-level radioactive waste (LLRW), the volumes of solid and hazardous wastes have increased dramatically in past years.[535] Although solid and hazardous waste disposal facilities are not in as short supply as are LLRW disposal sites, states nonetheless are concerned with the increasing volumes of waste crossing state lines for disposal. Despite the fact that the EPA encourages source reduction, reuse and recycling of solid and hazardous waste,[536] combustion and land

---

533. 42 U.S.C. § 6901 (2004).
534. 42 U.S.C. § 9601 et seq. (2004).
535. It is estimated that the United States produced about 230 million tons of municipal solid waste in 2001. While this is slightly down from 2000 levels, it still represents a drastic increase in the amount of municipal solid waste disposed of when compared with 88 million tons in 1960. This reflects an increase, per person per day, from 2.7 pounds to 4.4 pounds. *See* U.S. Environmental Protection Agency, Municipal Solid Waste in the U.S.: 2003 Facts and Figures, Executive Summary (2003), *available at* http://www.epa.gov/msw/msw99.htm.
536. In fact, RCRA promotes developing methods of solid waste disposal that are "environmentally sound" and that maximize reuse of valuable resources such as energy and materials. Resource Conservation and Recovery Act § 4001, 42 U.S.C. § 6941 (2004). In terms of hazardous waste management, the land disposal restrictions are also intended to promote management of hazardous waste in a manner other than disposal land. Resource Conservation and Recovery Act § 3004 (c) & (d), 42 U.S.C. § 6924 (c) & (d) (2004). *See also* 1984 Hazardous and Solid Waste Amendments to RCRA, in which Congress expressed a clear preference for reducing or eliminating the generation of hazardous waste over managing such waste at treatment, storage, or disposal facilities. "The Congress hereby declares it to be the national policy of the

disposal still accounted for the management of over 70 percent of municipal solid waste (MSW)[537] in the United States as of 2001.[538] Given these figures, states and communities must determine how to manage huge volumes of MSW each year.

9.4.4.1 Solid and Hazardous Waste Under RCRA

To assist states with the management of solid and hazardous waste, RCRA Section 1005 provides that states may negotiate interstate agreements or compacts for management of solid or hazardous waste, or both.[539] These agreements or compacts require approval of Congress as well as the EPA administrator.[540] One example of efforts by states to employ interstate compacts to address solid waste management issues is the Vermont and New Hampshire Compact ratified by Congress in 1982.[541] This compact authorized the New Hampshire-Vermont Solid Waste Project, a regional cooperative that manages MSW with the goal of providing economic benefits through re-

---

United States that, wherever feasible, the generation of hazardous waste is to be reduced or eliminated as expeditiously as possible. Waste that is nevertheless generated should be treated, stored, or disposed of so as to minimize the present and future threat to human health and the environment." Resource Conservation and Recovery Act § 1003(b), 42 U.S.C. § 6902(b) (2004).

537. Municipal solid waste is defined in the Comprehensive Environmental Response Compensation and Liability Act (CERCLA) to include waste generated by a household and certain materials generated by commercial, industrial or institutional entities; it includes food and yard waste, paper, clothing, consumer product packaging, office supplies, cosmetics, school science laboratory waste, and household hazardous waste. CERCLA § 107(p)(4), 42 U.S.C. § 9607(p)(4) (2004). There are certain exclusions from this definition. *See* CERCLA § 107(p)(4)(C), 42 U.S.C. § 9607(p)(4)(C) (2004).

538. The Environmental Protection Agency reports that 55.7% of municipal solid waste was disposed of in landfills in 2001, which actually represents a decrease since 1960. About 14.7% of municipal solid waste is combusted, with 29.7% sent for recovery. *See* U.S. Environmental Protection Agency, Municipal Solid Waste in the U.S.: 2003 Facts and Figures (2003), *available at* http://www.epa.gov/msw/msw99.htm.

539. 42 U.S.C. § 6904 (2004).

540. Resource Conservation and Recovery Act § 1005(b), 42 U.S.C. § 6904(b) (2004).

541. *See* New Hampshire-Vermont Solid Waste Compact (1982).

duced solid waste disposal costs and helping to maintain a safe and healthy environment.[542] Despite the innovative efforts of Vermont and New Hampshire to address waste management issues that arise in small, more remote states, this cooperative has had to deal with numerous environmental and economic issues, including filing, unsuccessfully, for bankruptcy protection.[543]

9.4.4.2 Hazardous Waste Disposal Under CERCLA

States have also faced challenges complying with the requirements under CERCLA to demonstrate adequate capacity for disposal of hazardous waste generated in that state. CERCLA Section 104(c)(9) requires that states provide a "capacity assurance" (i.e., to demonstrate the availability of hazardous waste treatment or disposal facilities or risk the loss of federal assistance with remediation of hazardous waste sites).[544] States can demonstrate the availability of adequate treatment and disposal capacity through an interstate agreement,[545] which includes the use of an interstate compact.[546] The purpose of the capacity assurance requirements under CERCLA is to ensure that states

---

542. *See In re* Sullivan County Reg'l Refuse Disposal Dist., 165 B.R. 60, 64 n.4 (Bankr. D. N.H. 1994); New Hampshire-Vermont Solid Waste Compact (1982). As a result of its structure, there is no commission that oversees the regulation or enforcement of the compact.

543. *See In re* Sullivan County Reg'l Refuse Disposal Dist., 165 B.R. 60 (Bankr. D. N.H. 1994) (dismissing Chapter 9 bankruptcy petitions for failure of the municipalities to file the petitions in good faith).

544. *See* Comprehensive Environmental Response Compensation and Liability Act § 104(c)(9), 42 U.S.C. § 9604(c)(9) (2004).

545. CERCLA uses the term "interstate agreements or regional agreement." *See* CERCLA § 104(c)(9)(B), 42 U.S.C. § 9604(c)(9)(B) (2004). The EPA has interpreted this to include various types of agreement, not limited to interstate compacts. *See* U.S. Environmental Protection Agency, Guidance for Capacity Assurance Planning Capacity Planning Pursuant to CERCLA § 104(c)(9) EPA530-R-95-016 (May 1993), *available at* http://www.epa.gov/epaoswer/hazwaste/tsds/capacity/cap_rpt.txt.

546. CERCLA § 104(c)(9), 42 U.S.C. § 9604(c)(9) (2004). Not limited to an interstate compact, a state can meet the capacity assurance requirements by any combination of three measures: (1) creating new disposal capacity within the state, (2) entering into interstate or regional agreements allowing use of capacity located in other states, and (3) contracting with private waste management facilities. *See* Nat'l Solid Waste Mgmt. Ass'n v. Ala. Dep't of Envtl. Mgmt., 910 F.2d 713, 717 (11th Cir.1990), *modified*, 924 F.2d 1001 (11th Cir. 1991).

Chapter 9

accept responsibility for hazardous waste generated within their borders.[547]
CERCLA Section 104(c)(9), however, has not yet met this objective.[548] What
has occurred is that states appear to be talking more seriously among themselves about the need for interstate cooperation to manage solid and hazardous waste disposal issues.[549]

---

547. *See* U.S. Environmental Protection Agency, National Capacity Assessment
Report, Capacity Planning Pursuant to CERCLA Section 104(c)(9), EPA530-
R-95-016 (May 1993), a*vailable at* http://www.epa.gov/epaoswer/hazwaste/
tsds/capacity/cap_rpt.txt. *See also* CERCLA § 104(c)(3), 42 U.S.C. §
9604(c)(3) (2004).

548. States were to file the required capacity assurance plans (CAPs) with the
Environmental Protection Agency (EPA) by October 1989. The adequacy
with which states met this requirement has been disputed and resulted in
litigation seeking to require the EPA to conduct a "meaningful review" of
the state CAPs. *See* B.J. Wynne III & Terri Hamby, *Interstate Waste: A Key
Issue in Resolving the National Hazardous Waste Capacity Crisis,* 32 S.
Tex. L. Rev. 601, 627 (1991). *See also* New York v. Reilly, 143 F.R.D. 487
(N.D. N.Y. 1992) (granting standing to plaintiffs and intervenors, finding
that their allegations were sufficient to state claim against the EPA based on
its failure to withhold Superfund monies from states that did not ensure
adequate hazardous waste disposal capacity).

Notwithstanding these disputes, the EPA has not withheld Superfund
monies from any state based on its failure to meet the CERCLA § 104(c)(9)
requirements. In fact, EPA's National Capacity Assessment Report stated
that the EPA "has determined . . . that there exists adequate *national* capacity" through 2013. *See* U.S. Environmental Protection Agency, National
Capacity Assessment Report, Capacity Planning Pursuant to CERCLA Section 104(c)(9) EPA530-R-95-016 (May 1993), *available at* http://
www.epa.gov/epaoswer/hazwaste/tsds/capacity/cap_rpt.txt.

549. Some commentators have seen several beneficial aspects of the CAP program. The former chairman of the Texas Water Commission noted:

> For the first time, many states developed an understanding of their
> industry's waste generation, how wastes are managed, and the in-
> state needs for capacity. Additionally, states and regions began to
> talk seriously to each other about waste management capacity and
> interstate shipment. Finally, for some states, preparation of a CAP
> centered public interest on state waste-minimization programs.

See B.J. Wynne III & Terri Hamby, *Interstate Waste: A Key Issue in Resolving the National Hazardous Waste Capacity Crisis,* 32 S. Tex. L. Rev. 601,
629 (1991).

Notwithstanding the increased attention states are giving to interstate waste management issues, states that have attempted to use interstate agreements to meet the CERCLA Section 104(c)(9) requirement have been successfully challenged for violating the Commerce Clause.[550] South Carolina attempted to blacklist certain hazardous waste from disposal in that state by prohibiting waste treatment facilities in the state from accepting "any hazardous waste generated in any jurisdiction . . . which has not entered into an interstate or regional agreement for the safe treatment of hazardous waste pursuant to the federal [CERCLA]."[551] As has been repeatedly recognized by the Supreme Court, it is one thing for Congress to regulate interstate movement of wastes, but providing for state authority over waste management "is in no sense an affirmative grant of power to the state to burden interstate commerce."[552] The Superfund Amendment and Reauthorization Act,[553] by providing for the use of interstate agreements, including interstate compacts,

---

550. *See, e.g.,* Hazardous Waste Treatment Council v. South Carolina, 945 F.2d 781 (4th Cir. 1991) (South Carolina statutes, regulations, and orders limiting disposal in state of hazardous waste generated outside of the state violated the Commerce Clause.). *See also* Envtl. Tech. Council v. Sierra Club, 98 F.3d 774 (4th Cir. 1996); Chem. Waste Mgmt., Inc. v. Hunt, 504 U.S. 334 (1992) (Alabama statute imposing additional fee on all hazardous waste generated out of state and disposed of within state); Nat'l Solid Wastes Mgmt. Ass'n v. Ala. Dep't of Envtl. Mgmt., 910 F.2d 713 (11th Cir. 1990), *as modified upon denial of reh'g,* 924 F. 2d 1001 (11th Cir. 1991), *cert. denied,* 501 U.S. 1206 (1991) (Alabama statute blacklisting certain hazardous wastes generated out of state violated the Commerce Clause); *In re* S.E. Ark. Landfill v. Ark. Dep't of Pollution Control & Ecology, 981 F.2d 372 (8th Cir. 1992) (Resource Conservation and Recovery Act (RCRA), by mandating system of regional solid waste planning by states, does not authorize states to treat out-of-state waste differently from in-state waste.).

551. *See* Envtl. Tech. Council v. Sierra Club, 98 F.3d 774, 780 (4th Cir. 1996).

552. *See* New England Power Co. v. New Hampshire, 455 U.S. 331, 341 (1982); Philadelphia v. New Jersey, 437 U.S. 617, 622-23 (1978) ("Just as Congress has power to regulate the interstate movement of these wastes, States are not free from constitutional scrutiny when they restrict that movement.").

553. The Comprehensive Environmental Response, Compensation, and Liability Act of 1980, commonly known as CERCLA or Superfund, was enacted in 1980 and substantially amended by the Superfund Amendments and Reauthorization Act (SARA) of 1986, Pub. L. No. 99-499, 100 Stat. 1613 (1986).

did not authorize protectionist measures by states to exclude hazardous waste, which is an object of commerce.[554]

In another instance, when North Carolina failed to comply with the terms of the regional agreement it had signed with several other states,[555] those states sued the EPA seeking to have Superfund monies cut off to North Carolina.[556] The complaint was dismissed for failure to state a claim;[557] the EPA did not use its discretionary authority to cut off Superfund monies to North Carolina.

9.4.4.3 Conclusion

The use of interstate compacts as a means to manage waste disposal and cleanup offers possibilities to states to avoid duplication of costs and to take advantage of economies of scale. However, courts are clear that when states enter agreements with private industry through the use of such interstate agreements, they are expected to fulfill their obligations under the agreement as any other party would.[558] Further, Congress's encouragement that states manage waste through interstate agreements does not unmistakably or clearly evidence the requisite congressional intent to permit states to burden interstate commerce.[559] Thus, Congress did not authorize discrimination by one state against another's hazardous wastes, in order to assure capacity for instate waste and to fulfill interregional agreements, by delegating authorization of state RCRA programs to the EPA or through CERCLA's requirement of a capacity assurance plan.[560] As such, interstate agreements, including in-

---

554. Nat'l Solid Wastes Mgmt. Ass'n v. Ala. Dep't of Envtl. Mgmt., 910 F.2d 713 (11th Cir. 1990), *as modified upon denial of reh'g*, 924 F. 2d 1001 (11th Cir. 1991) (Alabama statute blacklisting certain hazardous wastes generated out of state violated the Commerce Clause.).

555. On October 17, 1989, the governors of Alabama, South Carolina, Tennessee, and Kentucky entered into an interstate agreement titled "SARA Capacity Assurance Agreement." The Environmental Protection Agency approved the CAP May 10, 1990. *See* Hazardous Waste Treatment Council v. South Carolina, 945 F.2d 781, 786 (4th Cir. 1991).

556. *See* South Carolina v. Reilly, 1992 WL 409971 (D. D.C. 1992) (North Carolina joined the Agreement; however, that state's participation depended on the construction or permitting of certain new facilities.).

557. *Id.*

558. *See, e.g., In re* Sullivan County Reg'l Refuse Disposal Dist., 165 B.R. 60 (Bankr. D. N.H. 1994).

559. Envtl. Tech. Council v. Sierra Club, 98 F.3d 774, 782-83 (4th Cir. 1996).

560. *Id.*

terstate compacts, may provide a means to avoid cost duplication, but they may not meet the goal to encourage states to build needed waste management facilities in-state. States are assured of some location available in other states for disposal of their waste.

9.4.5   Air Quality and Air Pollution Compacts

Air pollution can be transported hundreds of miles away from its emission source, even crossing state borders. As a result, individual state corrective efforts to deal with air pollution are bound to be ineffective if they are not accompanied by similar efforts from neighboring states. A shared vision and commitment to solve the problems of air pollution is necessary in order to achieve significant progress. However, a consensus on the necessity to do something is not easily reached, as pollution, carried by the winds, does not affect all states equally.[561]

Several states have codified interstate compacts. For example, Missouri codified the Kansas-Missouri Air Quality Compact in 1967.[562] However, it did not become effective because Kansas never enacted this compact.[563] Nonetheless, the provisions as codified in Missouri reflect a recognition in the late 1960s of the need to address interstate movement of air pollutants and to work cooperatively with other states to protect air quality, public health, welfare, and property.[564] Kentucky codified the Interstate Compact on Air Pollution, but no other state passed a similar law so this compact is not in use.[565] The situation is similar with the Mid-Atlantic States Air Pollution Control Compact.[566] These are older laws that are dormant at this point. With the passage of the 1970 federal Clean Air Act (CAA) and its all-encompassing

---

561. Ophelia Eglene, *Transboundary Air Pollution: Regulatory Schemes & Interstate Cooperation*, 7 ALB. L. ENVTL. OUTLOOK J. 129, 131 (2002).

562. Mo. REV. STAT. § 643.600 (1986).

563. Status of Kansas compact confirmed by E-mail, Missouri Dep't of Natural Resources, April 14, 2004 (on file with authors).

564. *See, e.g.,* Kansas-Missouri Air Quality Compact, art. III, Purpose, *at* Mo. REV. STAT. § 643.600 (2004).

565. KY. REV. STAT. ANN. § 224.18 (2004).

566. *See, e.g.,* CONN. GEN. STAT. ANN. § 22a-166 (2003). In addition, Illinois and Indiana created an Air Pollution Control Commission that failed due in large measure to a lack of enforcement powers. *See* Comment, *The Limits of Devolution in Environmental Law: A Comparison of Regional and State-wide Ambient Air Quality Planning in The United States and Germany*, 1997 U. CHI. LEGAL F. 527 (1997), *citing* DAVID P. CURRIE, AIR POLLUTION: FEDERAL LAW AND ANALYSIS § 1.10 at 10-12 (Callaghan 1981 & Supp. 1991).

framework for management of air pollution and air quality nationwide, they are not likely to be implemented by the states, but these compacts are still on the books and remain available should states choose to use a compact to comply with the provisions of the CAA.

"Significant progress" to solve the air pollution problems plaguing the United States was the goal of the CAA as reinforced by its amendments. The CAA developed from 10 separate Acts of Congress. The CAA was originally designed to deal with ambient air surrounding regions where pollution originated. It was less effective at addressing transboundary pollution.[567] Congress attempted to correct this with the 1990 Clean Air Act Amendments.[568] The 1990 CAA Amendments are known for their complexity, encompassing 313 pages in the Statutes at Large, requiring in excess of 175 new regulations, 30 guidance documents, and significant numbers of studies, reports, and research and investigation initiatives.[569] Given the unwieldiness of this law and

---

567. *See* Geoffery L. Wilcox, *New England and the Challenge of Interstate Ozone Pollution Under the Clean Air Act Of 1990*, 24 B.C. ENVTL. AFF. L. REV. 1, 13-14 (1996) (before 1970 Clean Air Act, Congress promoted the use of interstate conferences to address issues of transboundary pollution, which were ineffective). With adoption of the 1970 Clean Air Act, the U.S. EPA was given a more active role in addressing interstate pollution issues. *See generally* 42 U.S.C. 7410 (2003).

568. *See, e.g.,* Clean Air Act § 176A, 42 U.S.C. § 7506a (2003) (interstate transport commissions); Clean Air Act § 182 (j), 42 U.S.C. § 7511a (j) (2003) (state coordination—ozone non-attainment area); Clean Air Act § 184, 42 U.S.C. § 7511c (2003) (interstate ozone control); Clean Air Act § 187(e), 42 U.S.C. § 7512a(e) (2003) (multistate carbon monoxide non-attainment areas). *See also* Theodore L. Garrett & Sonya D. Winner, *A Clean Air Act Primer: Part I*, 22 ENVTL. L. REP. 10,159 (March 1992).

569. WILLIAM A. RODGERS, 1 ENVIRONMENTAL LAW, CLEAN AIR ACT AMENDMENTS OF 1990: INTRODUCTION, PERSPECTIVE, AND TECHNIQUES § 3.1A (1986) (see this treatise for an extensive discussion of other firsts and requirements of these amendments). *See also* Motor Vehicle Mfrs. Ass'n, Inc. v. New York Dep't of Envtl. Conservation, 17 F.3d 521, 525 (2d Cir. 1994) ("The *amicus* brief of the United States describes the Clean Air Act as an extremely complex law and tells us that the 'enormity of the 1990 amendments beggars description.' Congress, *amicus* informs us, took what was widely perceived as an 'unapproachable piece of legislation' and tripled the Act's length and 'geometrically increased its complexity.' After reviewing the Clean Air Act and the voluminous record pertaining to the Act submitted on this appeal, we have no reason to doubt the validity of the government's description of it.").

the indisputable transboundary or interstate nature of many pollutants caus-ing regional air pollution problems, this area of environmental law would seem to be a model for implementation of interstate compacts and, in fact, the CAA recognizes interstate compacts as a tool to help resolve the interstate nature of air pollution.[570]

The CAA, through the National Ambient Air Quality Standards (NAAQS)[571] and the State Implementation Plans (SIPs) creates a federal-state arrangement for management of air pollution.[572] The CAA also ex-pressly provides for the use of interstate compacts, agreements, or the establishment of interstate commissions.[573] However, compacts to address air pollution problems are not as common as other interstate agreements or com-missions,[574] and even the use of interstate agreements or commissions to ad-dress air pollution issues have their own limitations.

---

570. *See* U.S. Environmental Protection Agency, The Plain English Guide to the Clean Air Act, EPA-400-K-93-001 (1993), *available at* http://www.epa.gov/oar/oaqps/peg_caa/pegcaain.html ("Air pollution often travels from its source in one state to another state. In many metropolitan areas, people live in one state and work or shop in another; air pollution from cars and trucks may spread throughout the interstate area."). *See, e.g.,* Clean Air Act § 101, 42 U.S.C. § 7401 (2004) (recognizing the interstate nature of urbanization and the increasing use of motor vehicles among and through various juris-dictions); Clean Air Act § 102, 42 U.S.C. § 7402 (2004) (encouraging coop-eration between and among states and providing advance consent of Congress for states to enter into compacts or other binding agreements); Clean Air Act § 184, 42 U.S.C. § 7511c (2004) (requiring certain states to cooperate regionally).

571. Clean Air Act § 109, 42 U.S.C. § 7409 (2004).

572. Clean Air Act § 110, 42 U.S.C. § 7410 (2004). The State Implementation Plan (SIP) program requires each state to generate an implementation plan that specifies the enforceable pollution control measures it will undertake to reduce emissions and comply with the National Ambient Air Quality Standard (NAAQS). 42 U.S.C. § 7409 (2004).

573. *See, e.g.,* Clean Air Act § 102 (a) & (c), 42 U.S.C. § 7402 (a) & (c) (2004); Clean Air Act § 106, 42 U.S.C. § 7406 (2004); Clean Air Act § 174 (c), 42 U.S.C. § 7504 (c) (2004); Clean Air Act § 176A, 42 U.S.C. § 7506a (2004); Clean Air Act § 184, 42 U.S.C. § 7511c; Clean Air Act § 502, 42 U.S.C. § 7661a (2004).

574. There are historic attempts at using interstate compacts for management of air quality issues. *See, e.g.,* the Kansas-Missouri Air Quality Compact, Mo. Rev. Stat. § 643.600 (2004) (defunct though still codified in Missouri); the Mid-Atlantic States Air Pollution Control Compact, N.Y. Envtl. Conserv. Law § 21-

The CAA expressly provides for the creation of state compacts as a means to "encourage cooperative activities" among states to prevent and control air pollution.[575] Congress gives its consent for the formation of interstate agreements or compacts under this section.[576] In addition, as part of the SIP program, Congress required that a state SIP must include adequate provisions that prohibit sources within that state from emitting pollutants in amounts that will "contribute significantly to nonattainment" of air quality standards in any other state.[577] But the EPA's interpretation of earlier versions of this provision fell short of requiring any sort of interstate compact, relying instead on an exchange of information between states.[578] The courts agreed with the EPA's interpretation that the CAA did not require any "binding enforcement agreement" to demonstrate "intergovernmental cooperation."[579] Finally, the use of interstate compacts is also recognized in the CAA permit program.[580] Although EPA regulations detail the minimum requirements for

---

    1501 (McKinney 1967) (did not take effect for lack of congressional consent); West Virginia, Interstate Compact on Air Pollution, W. Va. Code §§ 29-1G-1 to 29-1G-5 (2004), *repealed,* 1979 W. Va. Acts 3.

575. Clean Air Act § 102 (a), 42 U.S.C. § 7402(a) (2004).

576. 42 U.S.C. § 7402 (c) (2004).

577. 42 U.S.C. § 7410 (a)(2)(D) (2004).

578. *See* 40 C.F.R. § 51.21c (1977).

579. Natural Res. Def. Council v. EPA, 483 F.2d 690, 691-92 (8th Cir. 1973) (upholding EPA's regulations, interpreting the 1970 Clean Air Act to only require upwind states to inform downwind state of actions that might significantly affect air quality). The Clean Air Act required the SIP to contain "adequate provisions for intergovernmental cooperation, including measures necessary to insure that emissions of air pollutants from sources located in any air quality control region will not interfere with the attainment or maintenance of such primary or secondary standard in any portion of such region outside of such State or in any other air quality control region." *See* 42 U.S.C. § 7410 (a)(2)(E) (1970). This language was changed with the 1977 Clean Air Act amendments, and the current language is now found in Clean Air Act § 110 (a)(2)(D), 42 U.S.C. § 7410 (a)(2)(D) (2004), which does not use the term "intergovernmental cooperation." *See* Pub. L. No. 95-95, § 108 (a)(4), 91 Stat. 685 (1977).

580. Clean Air Act § 502, 42 U.S.C. § 7661a (2004) established a permit program for various "sources" as defined in the CAA, which makes it unlawful to construct, modify or operate a "source" without a permit.

the permit program, the states themselves develop the permit program under state or local law "or under an interstate compact."[581]

Notwithstanding the option to use interstate compacts to address interstate air pollution issues, the CAA and states, particularly those of the northeast, use various other methods of interstate cooperation[582] including commissions,[583] temporary advisory groups,[584] independent lobbying groups,[585] and states peti-

---

581. *See* 42 U.S.C. § 7661a (b) & (d) (2004).
582. For a discussion of these various mechanisms, *see* Ophelia Eglene, *Transboundary Air Pollution: Regulatory Schemes & Interstate Cooperation,* 7 ALBANY L. ENVTL. OUTLOOK J. 129, 147 (2002).
583. *See, e.g.,* 42 U.S.C. § 7506a (b) (providing for interstate transport commissions to make recommendations to the Environmental Protection Agency about measures to achieve compliance with Clean Air Act § 110 (a)(2)(D), 42 U.S.C. § 7410 (a)(2)(D)); 42 U.S.C. § 7511c (creating special interstate air commission for ozone comprising states in northeastern United States); and 42 U.S.C. § 7492 (c) (providing for interstate transport commissions to address degradation of visibility in pristine areas).
584. The Ozone Transport Assessment Group (OTAG) was a partnership between the U.S. Environmental Protection Agency, the Environmental Council of the States (ECOS), and various industry and environmental groups. The ECOS is a national organization of environmental commissioners with members from 50 states and territories. *See generally* Environmental Council of the States, *at* http://www.ecos.org/. The OTAG began in 1995 and concluded in 1997. *See generally* U.S. Environmental Protection Agency, Technology Transfer Network Ozone Implementation, *available at* http://www.epa.gov/ttn/naaqs/ ozone/rto/otag/index.html. The goal of OTAG was to develop an assessment and a consensus agreement for reducing ground-level ozone and the pollutants that cause it, specifically the ozone transport issues over the eastern United States. Recognizing that no one state or regional jurisdiction could completely assess or resolve all the issues associated with long-range transport of ground-level ozone, OTAG sought consensus solutions by bringing together interested stakeholders, such as states, industry, and environmental groups. "OTAG's primary objective is to collectively assess ozone transport and to develop a strategy for reducing ozone pollution on a regional scale." *See* U.S. Environmental Protection Agency, Ozone Implementation, FAQs, *available at* http://www.epa.gov/ttn/naaqs/ozone/rto/otag/faq.html. OTAG's final report determined that the NOx emissions from over 20 states significantly contribute to achieving NAAQS in the eastern United States. *See* U.S. Environmental Protection Agency, Ozone Technical Assistance Group, Technical Supporting Document, *available at* http://www.epa.gov/ttn/naaqs/ ozone/rto/otag/finalrpt. As a result of these findings, the EPA required "under

tioning EPA for relief or suing other states.[586] For example, to address directly
issues of interstate air pollution, the CAA authorizes the EPA to pay the initial
costs of the air quality planning program costs of a commission established to
control interstate air pollution or interstate ozone pollution, and provides for an
ongoing reduced level of funding.[587] One such commission is the Ozone Transport Commission (OTC).[588] The OTC is a multistate organization comprised of

---

Clean Air Act section 110 (a)(1) and 110 (k)(5), that the 23 jurisdictions
adopt and submit SIP revisions that, in order to assure that their SIPs meet
the requirements of section 110 (a)(2)(D)(i)(I), contain provisions adequate
to prohibit sources in those States from emitting NO subX in amounts that
'contribute significantly to nonattainment in, or interfere with maintenance
by,' a downwind State." *See* Finding of Significant Contribution and
Rulemaking for Certain States in the Ozone Transport Assessment Group
Region for Purposes of Reducing Regional Transport of Ozone, 63 Fed.
Reg. 57,356 (Oct. 27, 1998).

585. For example, the Northeast States for Coordinated Air Use Management
(NESCAUM) was originally formed in 1967 by six New England states:
Maine, Vermont, New Hampshire, Connecticut, Rhode Island, and Massachusetts. New York and New Jersey joined later. The organization's purpose
is to "exchange technical information, and to promote cooperation and
coordination of technical and policy issues regarding air quality control
among the member states." Technical committees of the group work with
the Environmental Protection Agency to address specific areas of concern.
While originally formed to address problems associated with emissions
from large power plants in nearby states, the organization has expanded its
focus to address acid rain, ozone, wood stove emissions, and training issues. *See generally* Northeast States for Coordinated Air Use Management,
About NESCAUM, *at* http://www.nescaum.org/about.html.

587. *See* Clean Air Act § 126, 42 U.S.C. § 7426 (2004), permitting states to
petition the Environmental Protection Agency for a finding that a source in
one state emits or would emit air pollutants in violation of the Clean Air Act
and providing for an enforcement order from the Environmental Protection
Agency for such violations.

587. Clean Air Act § 106, 42 U.S.C. § 7406 (2003). Formation of these commissions is provided for in Clean Air Act § 176A. *See* 42 U.S.C. § 7506a (2004).
See also Clean Air Act § 184, 42 U.S.C. § 7511c (2004) (interstate ozone
control).

588. The Ozone Transport Commission is created under Clean Air Act § 184, 42
U.S.C. § 7511c (2004). Clean Air Act § 176A allows the Environmental Protection Agency or states to establish interstate transport regions elsewhere in
the country. *See* 42 U.S.C. § 7506a (2003). These regions may recommend

the governors of 12 northeastern states[589] and the Mayor of Washington, D.C. (or their delegates), whose main focus is to develop regional solutions to the ground-level ozone problem[590] in the mid-Atlantic and northeast region of the United States.[591] The OTC is empowered to make recommendations to the EPA about how to achieve this goal.[592] The EPA then has a timeframe within which to approve or disapprove, in whole or part, the recommendation.[593] Should the EPA approve the recommendation, it must declare each state's SIP inadequate and order the states to include the approved control measures in their revised

---

strategies and plans to the Environmental Protection Agency and "may request" that agency to issue findings that a member state's implementation plan is substantially inadequate. *See* Clean Air Act § 176A (a) & (b)(2), 42 U.S.C. § 7506a (a) & (b)(2) (2004). An individual state, or the subdivision of a state, may petition the Environmental Protection Agency with respect to the State Plan of a neighboring state. *See* Clean Air Act § 126(b), 42 U.S.C. § 7426(b) (2004).

589. States in the Northeast Ozone Transport Region are: Connecticut, Delaware, Maine, Maryland, Massachusetts, New Hampshire, New Jersey, New York, Pennsylvania, Rhode Island, Virginia, and Vermont. *See* 42 U.S.C. § 7511c (a) (2004). Virginia is included to the extent that its geographic region is within the Washington, D.C. metropolitan area. *See* Virginia v. EPA, 108 F.3d 1397, 1401 n.2 (D.C. Cir. 1997).

590. Ground-level ozone is a major constituent of smog, in contrast to ozone found higher in the atmosphere that absorbs harmful ultraviolet radiation. The mechanisms that create ground-level ozone are complicated but are generally believed to result from the chemical interactions of volatile organic compounds (VOCs) and nitrous oxides (NOx), which then react with sunlight. VOCs and NOx are air pollution emissions resulting from automobiles and industry. For a simplified discussion, *see id.* at 1399-1400. *See also* U.S. Environmental Protection Agency, Ozone (O_3)—Plain Language Information About Pollutants, *available at* http://www.epa.gov/ttn/naaqs/standards/ozone/s_o3_plain.html.

591. For information on the Ozone Transport Commission (OTC), *see* Ozone Transport Commission, What Is the Ozone Transport Commission?, *at* http://www.otcair.org. The OTC has designed an emissions-trading program for NOx emissions similar to that created under EPA's Acid Rain program. The NOx program is called the "NOx Budget Program" and permits states to allocate allowances to their industries. *See* U.S. Environmental Protection Agency, Overview of NOx Trading Programs, *available at* http://www.epa.gov/airmarkets/progsregs/noxview.html#overview.

592. Clean Air Act § 184 (c)(1), 42 U.S.C. § 7511c (c)(1) (2004).

593. Clean Air Act § 184 (c)(4), 42 U.S.C. § 7511c (c)(4) (2004).

plans.[594] "Failure to heed EPA's order unleashes a panoply of sanctions upon the noncomplying state."[595]

Despite the express language of CAA Section 184 requiring the EPA to impose the approved recommendation on states through the SIP process, courts have imposed limits on the use of the OTC recommendations to address interstate ozone problems. In *Virginia v. Environmental Protection Agency*,[596] the court of appeals invalidated the EPA's final rule for controlling ground-level ozone in the northeastern United States to the extent that it required the states to adopt the EPA-selected vehicle emission standards.[597] The EPA's final rule would have required twelve states in the region, as well as Washington, D.C., to adopt what was essentially California's vehicle emission program.[598] The final rule resulted from a recommendation of a majority of the OTC.[599] The court determined that while CAA Section 184 gives the EPA authority to condition approval of a state's implementation plan on adoption of particular control measures, other provisions of the CAA[600] precluded the EPA from selecting the means for the states to achieve the air pollutant reductions.[601] The court noted that although the EPA could impose the ends (i.e., "the standards of air quality)," the CAA gives states the authority to determine the means.[602] Thus, while the use of interstate commissions may assist in addressing interstate air pollution issues,[603] there are limits to the reach and authority of the commission.

594. Clean Air Act § 184 (c)(5), 42 U.S.C. § 7511c (c)(5) (2004).
595. Virginia v. EPA, 108 F.3d 1397, 1402 (D.C. Cir. 1997), *modified by* Virginia v. EPA, 116 F.3d 499 (D.C. Cir.1997).
596. *Id.*
597. Although challenged on several constitutional grounds, including that Clean Air Act § 184 violated the Compact Clause, the court did not address the constitutional issues but decided the case based on the language of the Clean Air Act itself. *Id.*
598. *Id. at* 1397.
599. *Id.* at 1402, *citing* Clean Air Act § 184, 42 U.S.C. § 7511c (1997).
600. Specifically, Clean Air Act § 177 and § 202 imposed limits on the Environmental Protection Agency's authority. *Id.* at 1411-14.
601. *Id.* at 1410.
602. *Id.* at 1408.
603. For a discussion of Ozone Transport Commission and trading program for NOx, commonly referred to as the "NOx Budget Trading Program," which is designed to reduce NOx emissions from power plants and other large combustion sources in the Northeast, *see* Environmental Protection Agency, OTC 1999-2002 Progress Report (March 2003), *available at* http:// www.epa.gov/ airmarkets/otc/otcreport.pdf. *See also* Environmental Protection Agency In-

According to the EPA, in addition to supporting the OTC and the Northeast States for Coordinated Air Use Management, there are five regional planning organizations (RPOs) developing technical information for their state and tribes to use for their Regional Haze State/Tribal implementation plans.[604] The RPOs will evaluate this technical information to understand the impact of the member states and tribes on air quality in national park and wilderness areas and to assist in developing regional strategies to reduce emissions of particulate matter and other pollutants leading to regional haze.[605]

Another mechanism to address air quality issues is oversight, monitoring, or regulation by compact commissions, which have broad authority over a wide range of environmental quality and natural resource issues for an area. The Great Lakes Commission, created under the Great Lakes Compact, is involved with air issues within the region.[606] Also, the 1980 modification of the Tahoe Regional Planning Compact,[607] among other things, directs the Tahoe Regional Planning Authority (TRPA) to develop regional "environmental threshold carrying capacities," which includes setting standards for "air quality, water quality, soil conservation, vegetation preservation and noise."[608] Although tardy, the TRPA adopted Resolution 82-11, which establishes environmental thresholds for air quality, in addition to thresholds for water quality, soil conservation, vegetation preservation, wildlife, fisheries, noise, recreation, and scenic resources.[609] This resolution has since been incorporated in planning documents for the region.[610]

---

terstate Air Quality Rule, 69 Fed. Reg. 4566 (Jan. 30, 2004) (proposed rule), which is fashioned after the NOx Budget Trading Program.

604. E-mail from Stephen D. Page, Director, Office of Air Quality Planning and Standards (Apr. 30, 2004) (on file with authors). The Environmental Protection Agency's Office of Air Quality Planning and Standards, part of the Office of Air and Radiation, manages the RPO project to facilitate interaction on a national level to ensure consistency, and the Environmental Protection Agency Regional offices manage the specific grants for RPOs in their region.

605. *Id.*

606. *See* discussion, *infra* § 9.4.6.2.5.

607. The 1980 Tahoe Regional Planning Compact, App. 37, 94 Stat. 3235-3238. The Tahoe Regional Planning Compact is discussed *infra*.

608. 94 Stat. 3235, 3239.

609. Tahoe-Sierra Preservation Council, Inc. v. Tahoe Reg'l Planning Agency, 535 U.S. 302, 310, 122 S. Ct. 1465, 1472 (2002).

610. *See* TRPA Code of Ordinances, Section XI, *available at* the TRPA Web site, www.trpa.org.

Another commission with authority over air quality is the Columbia River Gorge Commission. A recent amendment to the Management Plan for the Columbia River Gorge National Scenic Area provides for states and the Forest Service to monitor air quality in the Gorge and identify emissions sources contributing to air pollution. Based on analysis of the emissions data, the states are then directed to develop and implement a regional air quality strategy consistent with the purposes of the Scenic Area and in consultation with the Forest Service, the Southwest Air Pollution Control Authority, and affected stakeholders. The states and the Forest Service must submit annual reports to the commission on progress made in implementing the strategy, including a work plan and time line for gathering and analyzing data and implementing the strategy. The commission must approve the work plan and strategy. The commission's authority to develop and implement air quality strategies is tied to the issues of visibility and natural resource issues, which the commission expressly regulates under the compact.[611]

9.4.6   Natural Resource Protection Compacts

There are numerous examples of interstate compacts that address issues involving natural resources. These compacts tackle topics as diverse as forest fire protection, management of scenic areas, management and regulation of wildlife, and fishery resource management.[612] The compacts and issues discussed below are merely an introduction to the numerous and complex issues that arise in the context of such compacts.

---

611. Management Plan for the Columbia River Gorge National Scenic Area, SMA Natural Resource Policy No. 12 at 1-123 (Plan Amendment No. PA-00-05 (May 11, 2000)). The Columbia River Gorge Compact and Commission are discussed in more detail below.

612. *See, e.g.*, Northeastern Interstate Forest Fire Protection Compact (1952); Interstate Forest Fire Suppression Compact (1956); Southeastern Interstate Forest Fire Protection Compact (1954); Middle Atlantic Interstate Forest Fire Protection Compact (1956). In addition to the Columbia River Gorge National Scenic Area Act and associated compact, other scenic area compacts include Tahoe Regional Planning Compact, Pub. L. No. 91-148, 83 Stat. 360 (1969), *amended by* Pub. L. No. 96-551, 94 Stat. 3233 (1980). *See also* Palisades Interstate Park Comm'n, 75 Pub. Res. 65, 50 Stat. 719 (1937).

9.4.6.1 Scenic Areas and Wildlife Management

9.4.6.1.1   Columbia River Gorge Compact

The Columbia River Gorge National Scenic Area Act of 1986[613] (Gorge Act or Act) exemplifies the benefits that interstate compacts offer in the management of natural resources. Not without its detractors and only passed after years of negotiations, the Gorge Act is federal legislation that establishes legal management standards for the Columbia River Gorge National Scenic Area. This area straddles several counties along the Washington/Oregon state line created by the Columbia River.[614] Through the Act, Congress consented in advance to an agreement between Washington and Oregon that would incorporate the provisions of the Act and create a commission to carry out the functions detailed in the Act.[615] Congress conditioned approval of the interstate agreement on compliance with these specific details.[616] In 1987, Oregon and Washington adopted the Columbia River Gorge Compact, incorporating the Gorge Act and establishing the Gorge Commission in accordance with the Act.[617]

---

613. 16 U.S.C. §§ 544-544p, Pub. L. No. 99-663, 100 Stat. 4274 (1986).

614. For an explanation of the development of the Columbia River Gorge National Scenic Act and its components, *see* Bowen Blair, Jr., *The Columbia River Gorge National Scenic Area: The Act, Its Genesis And Legislative History*, 17 ENVTL. L. 863 (1987). The standards for the Scenic Area Management Plan are found in 16 U.S.C. § 544d (2003). The Scenic Area is defined in 16 U.S.C. § 544b (2003). The area consists of land in six counties in the Columbia River Gorge. Three of the counties are in Washington (Clark, Klickitat, and Skamania), and three are in Oregon (Hood River, Multnomah, and Wasco). For a map of the area, *see* U.S. Dep't of Agric., Forest Service, Map of the Columbia River Gorge National Scenic Area, *available at* http://www.fs.fed.us/r6/columbia/maps/map.htm.

615. 16 U.S.C. § 544c (2003). The Gorge Commission has 12 voting members and one ex officio nonvoting member. The governors of Washington and Oregon each appoint three members, who must be residents of their respective states. At least one of each governor's appointees must be a resident of the Scenic Area. The governing body of each of the six counties in the Scenic Area appoints one of its residents to the Commission. The Secretary of the Department of Agriculture appoints the ex officio nonvoting member, who must be an employee of the U.S. Forest Service. *Id.* The Columbia River Gorge Commission's Web site is *at* http://www.gorgecommission.org/.

616. 16 U.S.C. § 544c (2004).

617. OR. REV. STAT. §196.150 (1991); WASH. REV. CODE ANN. § 43.97.105 (1992); 16 U.S.C. § 544.

The Gorge Act's purposes are to protect and enhance the scenic, cultural, recreational, and natural resources of the Columbia River Gorge and to protect and support the economy of the area by allowing economic development consistent with the first purpose.[618] It is designed to achieve these purposes through a balance between federal, state, and local management. The Act divides the Scenic Area into three management units: (1) the Special Management Areas (SMAs), federal land that is planned for and managed by the U.S. Forest Service and nonfederal land that is planned for by the Forest Service, but managed by the Columbia River Gorge Commission;[619] (2) the General Management Areas (GMAs), nonfederal public and private lands within the Scenic Area managed by the Columbia River Gorge Commission;[620] and (3) the Urban Areas (UAs), which include 13 towns and cities that are exempt from the Management Plan requirements, but enjoy some of the benefits of the Act.[621]

The Act requires the commission, working with the U.S. Forest Service, to establish a "Management Plan" for the Scenic Area that details management of federal lands (the SMAs) as well as administration of nonfederal lands (GMAs) within the area.[622] The Management Plan is subject to approval by the Secretary of Agriculture [623] and must be reviewed at least every 10

---

618. 16 U.S.C. § 544a (2004).
619. 16 U.S.C. § 544b (b) & § 544f (2004). SMAs are those areas with significant scenic, natural, recreational or cultural value and have often been subject to development. *See* Bowen Blair, Jr., *The Columbia River Gorge National Scenic Area: The Act, Its Genesis and Legislative History*, 17 ENVTL. L. 863, 934 (1987).
620. 16 U.S.C. § 544d (b) & § 544e (a) (2004). Land within the GMAs may also have scenic, natural, recreational or cultural value but is not seen as having the significance of the SMAs. *See* Bowen Blair, Jr., *The Columbia River Gorge National Scenic Area: The Act, Its Genesis and Legislative History*, 17 ENVTL. L. 863, 935 (1987).
621. 16 U.S.C. § 544d (c)(5)(B) & § 544b (e) (2004). This discussion will focus on the role of the Gorge Commission, with recognition that the U.S. Forest Service has specific and complementary responsibilities for the SMAs.
622. 16 U.S.C. § 544d (2003). The U.S. Forest Service develops management plans for the SMAs. *See* 16 U.S.C. § 544d (c) & § 544f (2003). For a detailed discussion of the development of the Management Plan, *see* Bowen Blair, Jr., *The Columbia River Gorge National Scenic Area: The Act, Its Genesis and Legislative History*, 17 ENVTL. L. 863, 937-50 (1987).
623. 16 U.S.C. § 544d (f) (2004).

years to determine needed revisions.[624] The six counties within the Scenic Area (three in Oregon and three in Washington) are responsible for implementing the Management Plan through adoption of local ordinances.[625] The counties' plans are subject to approval by the commission, and, for those areas within the SMAs, subject to approval by the Secretary of Agriculture.[626] At each step of the approval process, the county can be required to modify or revise their ordinances to make them consistent with the regional Management Plan.[627]

When a local ordinance is approved by the commission, that county is responsible for enforcing the ordinance with oversight by the commission, which also serves in an appellate administrative capacity.[628] If a county does not submit an ordinance or chooses not to revise it, the commission must adopt and administer an ordinance for Scenic Area lands in that county.[629] In addition to its authority in approving county ordinances to ensure consistency with the Management Plan, the commission has land use regulatory powers permitting it to designate and restrict the use of private and public property. This includes, prior to the adoption of land use ordinances for each county, the power to review all proposals for major development actions and new residential development in each county in the Scenic Area, except urban areas, and the power to disapprove such development if the commission finds the development inconsistent with the purposes of the Gorge Act.[630]

---

624. 16 U.S.C. § 544d (g) (2004).
625. 16 U.S.C. § 544e (b) (2004). The local land use ordinances must be consistent with the management plan and are subject to approval by the Gorge Commission and Secretary of Agriculture. 16 U.S.C. § 544e & § 544f (2003). The process of approval of local ordinances differs between the GMAs and the SMAs because of concern with the federal oversight of local zoning issues in the SMAs. *Compare* 16 U.S.C. § 544e (b)-(c) *with* § 544f (h)-(j). *See also* Bowen Blair, Jr., *The Columbia River Gorge National Scenic Area: The Act, Its Genesis and Legislative History*, 17 ENVTL. L. 863. 944 (1987).
626. 16 U.S.C. §§ 544e (b) & 544f (h)-(n) (2004).
627. 16 U.S.C. §§ 544e (b) & 544f (i) (2004). The Commission does have a veto override authority if it does not agree with the Secretary's denial of approval. 16 U.S.C. § 544f (j)-(l) (2004).
628. 16 U.S.C. § 544m (2003). Denial of an ordinance carries penalties for the county; *see* 16 U.S.C. § 544n (c) (2004).
629. 16 U.S.C. §§ 544e (b)–(c) & 544f (i)-(l) (2004). Any ordinance adopted by the Commission for SMAs is subject to approval by the Secretary.
630. WASH. REV. CODE § 43.97.015 (a)(4) (2004), *citing* Pub. L. No. 99-663 § 10 (c), 16 U.S.C. § 544h (c). *See also* Murray v. C.R.G.C., 891 P.2d 1380, 1382 n.2 (Or. Ct. App. 1995).

These provisions of the Gorge Act directly impact county governments. A county's failure to submit, revise, or obtain approval of its ordinances results in the Gorge Commission assuming responsibility for land use decisions within that county's geographic region of the Scenic Area. In adopting an ordinance consistent with the commission's overall management plan, however, local governments that plan land use for areas outside the Scenic Area may be creating conflicts between local land use ordinances and those of the Scenic Area.[631]

As a result of the Gorge Act's management design, the Scenic Area within the Columbia River Gorge is administered through a complex set of standards that involve the federal government, Washington, and Oregon through the commission, six counties within those states,[632] and four Indian tribes.[633] This combination of governmental and management entities interacting to implement the Gorge Act and the compact provides a novel means to protect an area rich in cultural history, scenic beauty, and economic opportunity that does not rely solely on federal laws and enforcement. Nor does it leave management to the, at times, conflicting and often short-sighted management of local, regional, or state bodies.

Since its inception, the commission's implementation of the Gorge Act has been subject to extensive litigation that provides some insight into how interstate compacts fit into management of natural resources.[634] The Ninth Circuit has considered constitutional and federalism issues surrounding the use of interstate compacts to address regional issues involving natural resources, upholding the constitutionality of the Gorge Act and the compact in *Columbia Gorge United v. Yuetter.*[635]

In that case, Columbia Gorge United (CGU), an organization and group of individuals that own land within the Scenic Area, sued the Gorge Commis-

---

631. Critical Areas Regulation, ALI-ABA Course of Study—Land Use Institute: Planning, Regulation, Litigation, Eminent Domain, and Compensation, C851 ALI-ABA 961, 968 (Aug. 18, 1993).

632. Three of these counties, Hood River, Multnomah, and Wasco, are in Oregon. The three others, Clark, Klickitat, and Skamania, are in Washington. 16 U.S.C. § 544 (d) (2003).

633. 16 U.S.C. § 544 (g) & § 544d (e) (2003). The tribes are the Nez Perce, the Yakima Indian Nation, the Warm Springs Tribes, and the Umatilla Tribes.

634. *See generally* Columbia Gorge Legal and Conservation Links, *available at* http://www.nathanjbaker.com. The links at this site include many that discuss legal issues beyond those involving interstate compacts.

635. Columbia Gorge United—Protecting People & Property v. Yeutter, 960 F.2d 110 (9th Cir. 1992).

sion and the Secretary of Agriculture,[636] challenging the constitutionality of the Gorge Act. Plaintiffs contended, among other arguments, that the Gorge Act exceeded congressional authority, violated the Commerce Clause, the Property Clause, and the Compact Clause and that denial of their application to develop their properties resulted in a taking in violation of the Fifth Amendment. The district court found for the defendants on all claims.[637] CGU appealed the decision. The Ninth Circuit upheld the constitutionality of the Gorge Act, finding Congress did not exceed its authority because the Act is valid under the Commerce Clause, and, as such, does not violate the Tenth Amendment.[638] The court also held that the interstate compact between Washington and Oregon, and approved by Congress, was valid under the Compact Clause finding the compact "an innovative solution to a difficult interstate land preservation problem."[639]

The district court and the Ninth Circuit both rejected the CGU's contention that the compact was invalid because Washington and Oregon were "coerced" by Congress to enter into the compact. CGU claimed that Congress created the elaborate scheme that the states were forced to accept.[640] In fact, the court noted, the states' attorneys general argued that "the Act and the Compact were a product of mutual cooperation between federal and state governments to achieve a result satisfactory to both states."[641] Further, the court determined that the Gorge Act did not compel a compact between the states, and the states could have rejected the conditions of the compact.[642]

---

636. A summary of the roles of the Commission and the Secretary of Agriculture is found in Bowen Blair, Jr., *The Columbia River Gorge National Scenic Area: The Act, Its Genesis and Legislative History*, 17 ENVTL. L. 863 (1987).

637. Columbia Gorge United—Protecting People & Property v. Yeutter, 1990 WL 357613, CV No. 88-1319-PA (D. Or. May 23, 1990).

638. Columbia Gorge United—Protecting People & Property v. Yeutter, 960 F.2d 110, 113-114 (9th Cir. 1992). The court also rejected an equal protection challenge. *Id.* at 115.

639. *Id.* at 114–15.

640. *Id.*; Columbia Gorge United—Protecting People & Property v. Yeutter, 1990 WL 357613, 8, CV No. 88-1319-PA (D. Or. May 23, 1990).

641. Columbia Gorge United—Protecting People & Property v. Yeutter, 960 F.2d 110, 112 (9th Cir. 1992).

642. Columbia Gorge United—Protecting People & Property v. Yeutter, 1990 WL 357613, 8, CV No. 88-1319-PA (D. Or. May 23, 1990).

Thus, Congress can consent to a compact prior to states agreeing and can even make approval contingent on incorporation of specific conditions.[643]

The determination of the constitutionality of the Gorge Act provides a means to protect a scenic area that was historically rife with management disputes. The Scenic Area lies within two states having significantly different land management policies.[644] An even more serious impact on the Scenic Area was from local pressures—in particular, residential development by individual landowners outside the urban areas. Because the Scenic Area lies within six different counties of the two states, decisions concerning land use for the area usually fell to local decision makers, resulting in conflicting management objectives and approaches.[645]

The Gorge Act does not resolve these issues completely. To some, it simply shifts the approaches and focuses. Local governments have raised concerns regarding the infringement by the Act, the compact, and commission into local issues of zoning and development. In fact, local governments fairly bristle at the authority vested in the Gorge Commission to manage the areas within its jurisdiction at the expense of local control.[646] As discussed above, Congress designed the Act to invest the commission and Secretary with significant authority to decrease potential local decision making that

---

643. *Id.*, *citing* Petty v. Tenn.-Mo. Bridge Comm'n, 359 U.S. 275, 281-82 (1959); Seattle Master Builders Ass'n v. Pac. N.W. Elec. Power & Conservation Planning Council, 786 F.2d 1359, 1374 (9th Cir.1986).

644. Bowen Blair, Jr., *The Columbia River Gorge National Scenic Area: The Act, Its Genesis and Legislative History*, 17 Envtl. L. 863, 872-73 (Summer 1987), noting that, at the time, Oregon had a statewide land use program imposing on counties significant responsibility for zoning matters; Washington did not. Washington, however, had a State Environmental Policy Act similar to the federal National Environmental Policy Act, and a Shoreline Management Act. Washington now has a Growth Management Act, RCW 36.70.

645. Bowen Blair, Jr., *The Columbia River Gorge National Scenic Area: The Act, Its Genesis and Legislative History*, 17 Envtl. L. 863, 873 (Summer 1987).

646. P. Stephen DiJulio & Thomas M. Pors, *Reflections on the First Five Years Under the Columbia River Gorge Scenic Area Act: Local Government Perspective*, Critical Areas Regulation, ALI-ABA Course of Study—Land Use Institute: Planning, Regulation, Litigation, Eminent Domain, and Compensation, C851 ALI-ABA 961 (Exhibit 3) (Aug. 18, 1993) (This article was presented at the Environmental and Land Use Section Midyear Meeting of the Washington State Bar Association and concerns the author's representation of Klickitat County and its challenge of the Scenic Area Act's abrogation of local land use authority.).

may defeat the purposes of the Act. Certainly, the Gorge Act was designed to subordinate local land use decisions to the broader purpose of the Act—protecting and providing "for the enhancement of the scenic, cultural, recreational and natural resources of the Columbia River Gorge."[647]

Notwithstanding the commission's extensive authority with respect to land use issues in the Scenic Area, the courts have expressed an expectation that the commission will, within its authority and responsibilities, work with counties. In this regard, the Washington Supreme Court rejected the commission's interpretation of the Act, which would have permitted the commission to ignore time periods within which appeals to county land use decisions could be filed.[648] The court noted, among other things, that "the Gorge Commission's interpretation of the Act removes any incentive for the Gorge Commission to work together with the Scenic Area counties to engage in early and thorough review of proposed developments."[649] While the concurrence to this opinion reiterates some of the concerns raised by the commission, it is clear that a balance must be struck between the role of the commission and that of the counties to ensure that the best possible decisions are made concerning land use and development in the Scenic Area.

In addition to issues involving local governments, courts have addressed issues concerning the interplay of state and federal laws and the structure created by the Gorge Act for management of the Scenic Area. One such issue involves whether actions by the commission under the Gorge Act effect a taking of property requiring compensation. Property owners within the Scenic Area have argued that the level of jurisdiction and control provided to the commission does just that.[650] Courts have rejected this argument.[651]

---

647. 16 U.S.C. § 544a (2003).
648. Skamania County v. Columbia River Gorge Comm'n, 26 P.3d 241, 251 (Wash. 2001).
649. *Id.* at 251.
650. Critical Areas Regulation, ALI-ABA Course of Study—Land Use Institute: Planning, Regulation, Litigation, Eminent Domain, and Compensation, C851 ALI-ABA 961, 968 (Aug. 18, 1993).
651. Murray v. Columbia River Gorge Comm'n, 865 P.2d 1319, 1320 (Or. Ct. App. 1993) (court rejected an argument that the Commission's rejection of application to subdivide agricultural land for residential purposes constituted an uncompensated taking under the Constitution because the Commission's action did not deprive plaintiff of "all economically viable or beneficial use of his property"); Miller v. Columbia River Gorge Comm'n, 848 P.2d 629 (Or. App. 1993).

Another issue courts have considered involves the concerns raised by some counties that by entering into the compact, the state has imposed on the counties an impermissible unfunded mandate to comply with the provisions of the compact.[652] One county sought compensation from the state for increased costs incurred to adopt, implement, and administer the ordinances and programs created under the management plan.[653] The Washington Court of Appeals rejected this position, finding the state not liable and without a duty to indemnify the county for such costs.[654] The court determined that the state agreeing to the Gorge Compact did not violate state law precluding imposition of unfunded mandates. The "land use requirements [under the Gorge Act] . . . are not a state program" within the relevant state law. Congressional consent to the Gorge Compact "transforms the States' agreement into federal law under the Compact Clause."[655] Recognizing that the Gorge Commission is a creature of federal law, the Washington Court of Appeals also rejected an argument that the state would be responsible for paying and defending inverse condemnation actions brought by private landowners affected by land use regulations adopted by the county under the Management Plan.[656] While the courts have found the commission a "creature of federal law," the Act expressly provides that it is not a federal agency or instrumentality.[657] Thus, the commission "is acting under authority of state law even though its authority extends beyond our state's borders by virtue of the interstate compact."[658]

The concern with the potential conflict between interstate compacts and state law is also exemplified in several cases. The first case sought to force the Gorge Commission to comply with Washington's State Environmental Policy Act (SEPA).[659] Another case argued that the Gorge Commission's adop-

---

652. *See, e.g.,* Klickitat County v. Washington, 862 P.2d 629 (Wash. Ct. App. 1993).

653. *Id.*

654. *Id.* at 631.

655. *Id.* at 633, *quoting* Cuyler v. Adams, 449 U.S. 433, 440 (1981).

656. *Id.* at 634.

657. 16 U.S.C. § 544c (a)(1)(A) (2003).

658. Tucker v. Columbia River Gorge Comm'n, 867 P.2d 686, 688 (Wash. Ct. App. 1994).

659. Klickitat County v. Columbia River Gorge Comm'n, 770 F. Supp. 1419, 1429 (E.D. Wash. 1991) (Commission is not required to comply with state requirement to prepare EIS). The Gorge Act expressly exempts the U.S. Forest Service from compliance with EIS requirements under the National Environmental Policy Act. *See* 16 U.S.C. § 544o (f)(1) (2003). The Forest Service is also exempt from the planning regulations under the National Forest Management Act. Klickitat County, 770 F. Supp. at 1432.

tion of regulations concerning lot size was not in accordance with the procedures set forth in the Washington Administrative Procedure Act, RCW 34.05.[660] In upholding the actions of the commission in both of these cases, the courts relied on the Act and its legislative history to note that Congress required the Gorge Commission to "adopt a uniform set of laws relating to administrative procedure and the functioning of the Commission" and "to ensure that the Commission members are following the laws of his or her own state, the commission [was] directed to adopt the law of either Washington or Oregon, whichever [was] more restrictive in scope."[661]

Jurisdictional issues have also been litigated. The court in *Broughton Lumber Co. v. Columbia River Gorge Commission*[662] determined it had no jurisdiction over a landowner's declaratory judgment action against the Columbia River Gorge Commission because the Act did not provide that the states joining the compact under the Act waive their immunity from suit in federal court.[663] Similarly, the commission had not expressly waived its sovereign immunity to suit in federal court and the waiver of sovereign immunity in the state courts does not act as a waiver of Eleventh Amendment immunity in the federal courts.[664] Further, the court held that federal courts lack jurisdiction over the commission, as Section 544m(b) "confers mandatory jurisdiction upon the state courts for actions involving the Commission."[665] The court also affirmed that because the Gorge Act did not provide for state court jurisdiction over the Gorge Commission in this matter,[666] it lacked subject matter jurisdiction to enjoin the commission from adopting and implementing land use regulations under the Management Plan.[667]

---

660. Tucker v. Columbia River Gorge Comm'n, 867 P.2d 686, 689 (Wash. Ct. App. 1994).

661. Klickitat County v. Columbia River Gorge Comm'n, 770 F. Supp. 1419, 1428-29 (E.D. Wash. 1991), *quoting* 132 CONG. REC. 15628 (emphasis omitted); Tucker v. Columbia River Gorge Comm'n, 867 P.2d 686, 689 (Wash. Ct. App. 1994), *quoting* 16 U.S.C. § 544c(b) and 132 CONG. REC. 15627.

662. Broughton Lumber Co. v. Columbia River Gorge Comm'n, 975 F.2d 616, 619 (9th Cir. 1994).

663. *Id.* at 621.

664. *Id.* at 620, *citing* 16 U.S.C. § 544m (b).

665. *Id.* at 620.

666. The Gorge Act does provide for state court jurisdiction over civil actions brought against the Commission by persons or entities "adversely affected" for violations of or the failure to perform a duty under the Act. 16 U.S.C. § 544m (b)(6) (2004).

667. Klickitat County v. Washington 862 P.2d 629, 632 (Wash. Ct. App. 1993).

While the local governments in Washington and Oregon face numerous challenges in implementing their responsibilities consistent with the dictates of the Gorge Act and compact, the Gorge Commission faces its own challenges to fulfill its mandate. In contrast to cases challenging the extent of the commission's authority to reject land use applications, the commission itself has been subject to litigation concerning its decisions to permit certain developments. Courts have recognized the right of the commission to permit development within the Gorge Area. An environmental group seeking review of the commission's decision to permit installation of an explosive storage facility on national forest land was rejected; the court found that the decision did not contravene the Gorge Act or the commission's final interim land use guidelines.[668]

Courts have also addressed the question of what law the commission applies in its determinations under the management plan. Usually, after approval by states and ultimately Congress, the courts look to the interstate compact to determine applicable law. The Gorge Compact and the Gorge Act dictate the operations of the Gorge Commission and provide for a uniform system of laws applicable to the commission and that govern administrative procedures, contracting, conflicts of interest, financial disclosure, open meetings, and information disclosure.[669] This uniform system is to be consistent with the more restrictive state's laws.[670] Nonetheless, in a case involving local zoning issues, the court determined that the state law of Washington should have been applied by the commission. In *Skamania County v. Woodall*,[671] the court determined that neither the Act nor the compact resolved whether state or federal law applied to a case involving whether a nonconforming use had been discontinued. The Skamania County planning department approved an application to operate a mobile home park in a Special Management Area of the Gorge, determining that because, prior to the new zoning rules, the area had previously been a mobile home park, it was a valid nonconforming use. A neighboring mobile home park owner appealed this decision to the Skamania County Board of Adjustment, which upheld the approval, applying Washington law.[672] The appellant appealed the decision of the Board of Adjustment to

---

668. Friends of the Columbia Gorge v. Columbia River Gorge Comm'n, 889 P.2d 1303 (Or. Ct. App. 1995).
669. 16 U.S.C. § 544c (b) (2003).
670. *Id.*
671. Skamania County v. Woodall, 16 P.3d 701 (Wash. Ct. App. 2001); *rev. denied*, 34 P.3d 1232 (2001) (in applying Washington law, the court noted that the only other option was to apply Oregon law, and neither party argued that it applied).
672. *Woodall*, 16 P.3d at 704.

the Gorge Commission, which reversed the Board of Adjustment, finding it wrongly applied state law, rather than the commission's prior interpretation of the relevant provision.[673] Emphasizing that its interpretation of the legal standard to be applied was consistent with the purposes of the Gorge Act and with uniform enforcement, the commission asserted that as an entity created by the interstate compact, its interpretation of the law preempted state law interpretations.[674]

The Washington Court of Appeals disagreed. It analyzed at least seven justifications for determining that neither federal law nor the commission's interpretation of the law applied to this case and why Washington state law as interpreted by Washington courts did apply. These reasons included that Congress gave state courts almost exclusive jurisdiction (and federal courts have no concurrent jurisdiction) over appeals from the commission;[675] the legislative history indicates that Congress did not want federal law applied to local zoning issues;[676] Congress approved the compact, which provided that "the provisions of [the Columbia River Gorge Compact] hereby are declared to be the law of this state;"[677] Congress knew, absent an express requirement to apply federal law, that state courts are required to apply state law;[678] contrary to requiring that state courts ignore state law, the compact reserves to counties a significant role in drafting, implementing, and enforcing land use requirements;[679] and the commission's management plan indicates that as to vested rights issues, state law applies.[680] Both the Washington Supreme Court and the U.S. Supreme Court denied review of this case.

The complexity that this raises, of course, is that it may force the commission to issue inconsistent rulings depending on the state or county within which the parties bring suit.[681] Despite the continued disputes, which are

---

673. *Id.*
674. *Id.*
675. *Id.* at 706, *citing* 16 U.S.C. § 544m (b)(6), and Broughton Lumber Co. v. Columbia River Gorge Comm'n, 975 F.2d 616, 621 (9th Cir. 1992).
676. *Id.* at 706.
677. *Id.* at 706, *quoting* WASH. REV. CODE § 43.97.015.
678. *Id.*
679. *Id.* at 706-07.
680. *Id.* at 705-09. *See also* Tucker v. Columbia River Gorge Comm'n, 867 P.2d 686 (Wash. Ct. App. 1994) (state zoning standards of review applied to a review of Commission actions).
681. The concern over inconsistent application of the rules was raised by the state of Oregon in its amicus curiae brief in support of the petitioner's request for a writ of certiorari from the U.S. Supreme Court in *Woodall v. Skamania County*, 535 U.S. 980 (2002). *See* Brief of the State of Oregon as Amicus Curiae

inevitable, the Gorge Act and associated compact do provide an alternative means to manage natural resources that have inherent transboundary issues between states and communities.

9.4.6.1.2 *Tahoe Regional Planning Compact (TRPC)*

The Tahoe Regional Planning Compact (TRPC) was developed in the 1960s out of concern over increased development in the Lake Tahoe Basin and the impact that development was having on the lake and the surrounding ecosystem. Recognizing the bi-state nature of an area involving significant land in California and Nevada, conservationists initially sought to create national protections for the Basin. However, this approach generally failed, in large measure because much of the land desired for protection was already privately owned and subject to ongoing logging or other development. The desire for protecting the Basin against overdevelopment nevertheless continued, and the need to maintain the water quality of the lake compelled further consideration of regulatory schemes. It was out of this background that the Tahoe Regional Planning Compact emerged in 1968.

The compact created the Tahoe Regional Planning Agency (TRPA), a bi-state regional planning commission comprised of representatives from both California and Nevada and reaching all levels of government.[682] The TRPA was charged with planning and oversight of land use in the Lake Tahoe Basin and the surrounding environment, encompassing some 501 square miles. The compact was amended in 1980, in response to criticism that the original commission was dominated by local government leading to land use decisions that were overtly pro-development and parochial in nature. One observer noted that the TRPA under the original compact "achieved national

---

Supporting Petitioner, 2001 U.S. Briefs 958 (March 1, 2002) ("Short of this Court's intervention, Washington state courts will pursue their own interpretation of the Gorge Commission's authority concerning county ordinances on the Washington side of the river. Were Oregon courts to follow suit, they would pursue their own interpretation of county ordinances on the Oregon side. Even if Oregon courts agreed with the Gorge Commission that county ordinances must be interpreted to be consistent with the Management Plan, the result would be non-uniformity of land use planning in the Columbia River Gorge area. That is the antithesis of what Congress, Washington and Oregon intended in creating the Columbia River Gorge Commission as the steward for the National Scenic Area.").

682. Tahoe Regional Planning Compact, art. III (a) (1980). The compact received congressional consent in 1969. *See* Pub. L. No. 91-148, 83 Stat. 360 (1969).

recognition as a failure."[683] The 1980 revision to the compact gave the states greater representation on the commission. The revision also changed the conditions under which development permits were granted by eliminating an earlier requirement that deemed proposals approved if the TRPA failed to deny a permit within 60 days of application and replacing it with a requirement that all permits either be denied or approved.

The TRPC is important for several reasons. First, the TRPC is the first use of a compact to promote environmental and land use regulation on a broad scale by creating the first bi-state regional environmental planning agency in the country. Prior to the TRPC, land-use compacts were generally directed at promoting development—primarily in large urban metropolitan areas—not controlling development based on environmental concerns. The TRPC marks an important shift in land use compacts away from development and toward ecological preservation through restricting land use. Today, regulation of land use and development has become an appropriate subject for interstate compacts as evidenced by the Columbia River Gorge National Scenic Area Act, which created the Columbia River Gorge Commission and charged that commission with duties similar to the TRPA.[684]

Second, the TRPC has been the source of several celebrated court cases concerning the powers of interstate compact commissions, their status in the federal system of government, and the extent of their liability under the Eleventh Amendment. Several cases have also addressed the rulemaking process used by such entities. Many of these cases stem from revisions to the compact in 1980 that gave the TRPA the authority to adopt environmental quality standards called "thresholds," and to enforce ordinances designed to achieve those thresholds. One court has described the TRPA as having "broad powers to make and enforce a regional plan of an unusually comprehensive scope."[685] The TRPA adopted the thresholds in 1982.[686] In 1984 it adopted a long-range regional plan that resulted in a moratorium on development in the Lake Tahoe Basin. These actions spurred numerous lawsuits, some reaching the U.S. Supreme Court, challenging various aspects of the TRPA rules as, in effect, constituting impermissible "takings." In the end, however, the author-

---

683. Bowen Blair, Jr., *The Columbia River Gorge National Scenic Area: The Act, Its Genesis and Legislative History*, 17 ENVTL. L. 863, 892 (1987).

684. *See* Columbia River Gorge National Scenic Area Act, 16 U.S.C.S. §§ 544-544p (2004).

685. People v. County of El Dorado, 487 P.2d 1193, 1196 (Cal. 1971).

686. Tahoe Regional Planning Agency Governing Board, Resolution No. 82-11 (Aug. 26, 1982).

ity of the TRPA and its rules has generally been upheld by the courts, with the U.S. Supreme Court holding in one case that mere enactment of regulations implementing a 32-month moratorium on development in the Basin did not constitute a per se taking of the landowners' property.[687] The Court reasoned that whether a taking occurred depended upon the considerations of the landowners' expectations, actual impact, public interest, and reasons for the moratorium, not the mere adoption of regulations imposing the moratorium.[688]

Finally, through its Code of Ordinances, the TRPA has created an extensive land use regulatory system.[689] The Code sets minimum standards applicable throughout the Lake Tahoe Basin and regulates land use, density, rate of growth, land coverage, excavation, and scenic impacts. While political subdivisions may adopt higher standards, they cannot adopt lower standards.[690] For example, under Chapter 3 of the Code, the TRPA regulates the construction of foundations for single family homes.[691] The TRPA requires that certain projects be approved by the governing board or a hearing officer, including substantial harvesting or tree removal plans, historic resource determinations, special uses, variances for building height, tourist accommodation projects, and shorezone projects.[692]

Management of the TRPC is vested in a governing board composed of delegations from California and Nevada representing state, county, and local interests.[693] With limited exception, members of the governing board serve at the pleasure of the appointing authority.[694] Additionally, the compact calls for

---

687. Tahoe-Sierra Preservation Council v. Tahoe Reg'l Planning Agency, 535 U.S. 302 (2002).

688. *Id.*

689. *See* Tahoe Regional Planning Agency, Code of Ordinances, *available at* http://www.trpa.org/Ordinances/Code.html.

690. *See* Tahoe Regional Planning Agency, Code of Ordinances, ch. 1, § 1.1 (2004), *available at* http://www.trpa.org/documents/docdwnlds/ordinances/code1.pdf. This provision states, "The Code establishes the minimum standards applicable throughout the Tahoe Region. Any political subdivision or public agency may adopt and enforce an equal or higher requirement applicable to the same subject or regulation in its territory. All projects and activities shall comply with the provisions of the Code."

691. *See* Tahoe Regional Planning Agency, Code of Ordinances, ch. 3, § 3.3 (2004), *available at* http://www.trpa.org/documents/docdwnlds/ordinances/code3.pdf.

692. *See* Tahoe Regional Planning Agency, Code of Ordinances, ch. 4 (2004), *available at* http://www.trpa.org/Ordinances/pdffiles/Code4A.pdf.

693. Tahoe Regional Planning Compact, art. III (1980).

694. *Id.* at art. III (c).

the creation of an advisory planning commission comprised of various representatives of state, county, and local government along with the administrator of the Lake Tahoe Management Unit of the U.S. Forest Service.[695] The governing body is empowered to hire staff, fix salaries, establish an office, and set personnel policies and standards that substantially conform to the civil service requirements of California or Nevada.[696] The staff of the TRPA is overseen by an executive director. In carrying out its functions, the governing board is, arguably, both quasi-legislative and administrative in nature; adopting regulations and enforceable ordinances to effectuate the regional planning mandated by the compact while also providing for administrative enforcement of its regulations and ordinances.[697] The TRPA is financed through an apportionment formula divided across the local governments within the region and with additional unspecified contributions by state governments based on an apportionment formula.

　　Management of compact affairs at the staff level occurs through various operational units.[698] Additionally, the governing board is aided by an agency legal counsel and the advisory planning commission established by Article III(h).[699] TRPA has established working groups to aid in various aspects of management and coordination of services. For example, the Motorized Watercraft Technical Advisory Committee is a working group formed to address the issue of boating-related pollution in Lake Tahoe. It is composed of water quality experts from agencies and universities, and representatives from the engine manufacturing industry. The group researched the issue and recommended a ban on certain types of two-stroke engines on Lake Tahoe.[700] Other examples of working groups include the Science Advisory Group, the Bio-

---

695. *Id.* at art. III (h).

696. *Id.* at art. III (i) & art. IV.

697. *Id.* at art. VI (a). Among its enforcement tools are the authority to issue corrective notices, cease and desist orders, suspension or revocation of permits, and imposition of monetary penalties. *See* Tahoe Regional Planning Agency, Code of Ordinances §§ 8.3–8.5 (2004), *available at* http://www.trpa.org/documents/docdwnlds/ordinances/code3.pdf.

768. The current units are: environmental compliance, environmental improvement program (EIP), finance, human relations, long-range planning, management support, public affairs, project review, transportation, and special programs administration

699. Tahoe Regional Planning Compact, at art. III (h) (1980).

700. *See* Tahoe Regional Planning Agency, What Is a Working Group, *at* http://www.trpa.org/wrkgrp.html.

logical Advisory Group, and the Lake Tahoe Source Water Group. In all, the TRPA relies on some 30 working groups that assist its work.

The regulatory scope of the TRPA is, like all compact agencies, defined by the terms and conditions of the underlying compact. The primary responsibility of the TRPA is to develop and implement an environmental and land use plan that is specifically directed at preserving the natural quality of the Lake Tahoe Basin. The compact requires the TRPA to adopt a plan prohibiting development that exceeds specific "environmental threshold carrying capacities," which are defined as an environmental standard necessary to maintain a significant scenic, recreational, educational, scientific, or natural value of the region, or to maintain public health and safety within the region. Such standards must include standards for air quality, water quality, soil conservation, vegetation, preservation, and noise.[701] The TRPC vests the governing board with the power to "adopt all necessary ordinances, rules, and regulations to effectuate the adopted regional plan."[702] The regulations and ordinances adopted by the TRPA set minimum standards for such diverse matters as water purity and clarity, subdivision, zoning, tree removal, solid waste disposal, sewage disposal, land fills, excavation, cuts and grading, piers, harbors, breakwaters, channels, shoreline development, mobile home parks, house relocation, outdoor advertising, soil and sediment control, air quality, and watershed protection.[703] Like other compact agencies, as long as the TRPA operates within its mandate, it has authority to issue rules and regulations. Judicial inquiry into an agency's actions is limited to determining whether an act or decision was arbitrary, capricious, lacked substantial evidentiary support, or the agency failed to proceed in a manner required by law.[704] Much of the work of the TRPA centers on implementing a series of regional plans developed by the planning commission and approved by the governing board. The plan proposed by the commission and adopted by the governing board is intended to be a single enforceable regional plan.[705]

---

701. For example, the 2001 Threshold Evaluation Report evaluates regional air quality matters within the context of regional transportation needs. *See* Tahoe Regional Planning Agency, 2001 Threshold Evaluation Report (July 2002), *available at* http://www.trpa.org/default.aspx?tabindex=1&tabid=174.
702. Tahoe Regional Planning Compact, art. VI (a) (1980).
703. *Id.*
704. Comm. for Reasonable Regulation of Lake Tahoe v. Tahoe Reg'l Planning Agency, 311 F. Supp. 2d 972 (D. Nev. 2004).
705. Tahoe Regional Planning Compact, art. V (c)(1)-(5) (1980).

The specific powers of the TRPA are outlined in Article VI of the compact, including the power to make rules.[706] The TRPA is mandated to adopt all rules and ordinances necessary to effectuate the regional plan approved by the governing body. It is important to note that in the rulemaking context the governing board and the TRPA are synonymous; that is, the rules issued by the TRPA are those approved by the governing board in furtherance of the approved regional plan. The TRPA has the authority to both exempt certain activities from its regulatory mandate and to include other activities within its regulatory scope by function of their impact on the land, water, air, space, or natural resources of the Basin. With limited exception, no development project in the Basin can proceed without the approval of the TRPA, and no project can be approved unless it complies with the approved regional plan and the ordinances adopted in pursuit of that plan.[707]

The broad authority given the TRPA in land use and planning matters has led to much litigation and several important court cases concerning the powers of compact-created agencies charged with land use and development regulation. The most important of these cases tend to center on two topical areas: (1) the immunity of compact agencies under the Eleventh Amendment; and (2) the implications of agency-created regulations on the private property interests of citizens. Several cases deserve special note because they have wide implications not only for the TRPA but for like agencies of government, whether compact-created or not.

The Tahoe Regional Planning Compact has raised questions regarding the application of Eleventh Amendment immunity of compact-created agencies. In *Lake Country Estates, Inc. v Tahoe Regional Planning Agency*, the U.S. Supreme Court held that a compact-created agency could not claim Eleventh Amendment immunity because such immunity was available only to one of the United States.[708] The Court noted that while agencies exercising state power could invoke Eleventh Amendment immunity to protect the state treasury, the Eleventh Amendment did not afford protection to political subdivisions, such as counties and municipalities, even though such entities exercised "state" power. Likewise, the Eleventh Amendment does not immunize a compact-created agency unless the member states structured it to enjoy the special constitutional protection of the states themselves, and Congress con-

---

706. *Id.* at art. VI (a) (1980).
707. *Id.* at art. VI (b) (1980). *But see id.* at art. VI (d), (e), (f) & (g) (1980), listing certain exceptions to TRPA's broad regulatory authority relative to certain projects initiated before May 4, 1979.
708. Lake Country Estates, Inc. v. Tahoe Reg'l Planning Agency, 440 U.S. 391 (1979).

curred in that purpose.[709] Other courts have reached similar conclusions hold-ing that, for example, an interstate park commission does not enjoy Eleventh Amendment immunity because language in a compact authorizing the agency to "sue and be sued" evidenced that the member states intended to waive immunity considerations.[710] The question of whether a compact-created agency is entitled to Eleventh Amendment immunity turns on whether the agency is an instrumentality of the signatory parties and an arm of the state, not a mere "political subdivision" of the member states similar to a county or municipal-ity.[711] Thus, where the states have disclaimed any intent to confer immunity on the agency, the agency cannot on its own claim such immunity. In the end, federal law determines whether an interstate compact embodies a waiver of the member states' immunity from suit, not the states' construction of the agreement.[712]

The second area of concern regarding regulated use of private property has produced a more robust debate. In the mid-1980s, the TRPA imposed a moratorium on development in the Tahoe Basin to enable it to develop its regional plan. The moratorium was intended to freeze development so that the regional plan, mandated by the compact, could evolve without concern for continued development. The moratoria, which occurred on two separate cycles, resulted in a 32-month ban on development and led to numerous lawsuits claiming that it constituted a government taking without compensa-tion in violation of the Fifth Amendment. Two cases that reached the U.S. Supreme Court are particularly noteworthy because they generally define the circumstances under which government land regulations rise to the level of a taking without compensation. In *Suitum v. Tahoe Regional Planning Agency*, the Court held that a government regulation does not constitute a per se categorical taking of property where a regulation merely bans certain private uses of a portion of an owner's property.[713] Moreover, a party must demon-strate that they have both received a final decision regarding the application of the challenged regulations from the agency charged with implementing

---

709. *Id.*
710. Interstate Wrecking Co. v. Palisades Interstate Park Comm'n, 262 A.2d 710 (N.J. Super. 1970).
711. Sanders v. Wash. Metro. Area Transit Auth., 652 F. Supp. 765 (D. D.C. 1986). *But see* Broughton Lumber Co. v. Columbia River Gorge Comm'n, 975 F.2d 616 (9th Cir. 1992). For further discussion, *see* Chapter 7.
712. Parden v. Terminal Railway of Ala. State Docks Dep't, 377 U.S. 184, 196 (1964).
713. Suitum v. Tahoe Reg'l Planning Agency, 520 U.S. 725 (1997).

the regulations and sought compensation through the procedures provided for doing so.[714] Where a regulatory regime offers the possibility of a variance from its facial requirements, a landowner must go beyond submitting a plan for development and actually seek such a variance to ripen a claim.[715]

While *Suitum v. Tahoe Regional Planning Agency* generally addressed the procedural circumstances under which a landowner could seek compensation, *Tahoe-Sierra Preservation Council, Inc. v Tahoe Regional Planning Agency* presented the Court with an opportunity to define under what conditions government land use regulations actually constitute a taking.[716] The petitioners challenged the two moratoria imposed before 1984 as regulatory takings. The Court held that regulatory takings cases were generally decided on a case-by-case basis while physical takings required compensation because of their nature. Compensation is required only when a regulation deprives an owner of all economically beneficial use of land.[717] Whether a taking occurs within the context of a development moratorium depends upon consideration of a landowner's investment-backed expectations, the impact of the regulation, the importance of the public interest involved, and the reasons for imposing the temporary restriction. The Court concluded that to find a "categorical taking" occurs whenever government regulation deprives an owner of all economic use, no matter how brief, would impose unreasonable financial obligations on governments for the normal delays involved in processing land use applications, and would improperly encourage hasty decision making.[718]

Although, with limited exception, the courts have not generally addressed the parameters of the TRPC and similar counterparts, the cases surrounding the compact are instructive. By upholding the broad authority of the TRPA, the courts have signaled an understanding that states and Congress can create compact agencies with extraordinarily broad regulatory authority. However, by severely restricting the application of Eleventh Amendment immunity, the courts have also signaled an unwillingness to allow compact-created regulatory agencies to escape the consequences of their actions. In effect, the courts have affirmed the principle that the states and Congress, in the exercise of their political power, have broad ability to fashion unique regulatory schemes to meet the challenges of governing across state lines, implicitly recognizing the importance and standing of compact-created agencies. However, the courts

---

714. *Id.* at 734.
715. *Id.* at 737.
716. Tahoe-Sierra Pres. Council, Inc. v. Tahoe Reg'l Planning Agency, 535 U.S. 302 (2002).
717. *Id.* at 329-30.
718. *Id.* at 339.

have also, in effect, stated that regardless of the nature of the scheme created by the states and Congress, states are still states holding a unique position within the federal structure for which there is no substitute. In the absence of language to the contrary in the enabling compact, a compact-created agency cannot hide behind the fact that it is a creation of the states for protection from its actions.

9.4.6.1.3   *Interstate Wildlife Violator Compact*

Wildlife is held in trust by states for the public.[719] Thus, much of the regulation and management of wildlife is controlled by state laws and regulations. To facilitate state enforcement, many states have entered into the Interstate Wildlife Violator Compact that enables them to coordinate and complement enforcement against those violating state wildlife laws.

The genesis of the Wildlife Violator Compact was in the 1980s when members of the Western Association of Fish and Wildlife Agencies began discussing alternatives to handling poachers in various states.[720] What emerged has expanded well beyond the initial two or three states that developed the idea of a compact modeled after compacts that were already in place to deal with motor vehicle violators. [721] Since 1989 when Colorado, Oregon, and Nevada passed legislation entitled the Wildlife Violators Compact, the number of states has increased to over 20, with several introducing legislation in 2004 to adopt the compact.[722]

The Interstate Wildlife Violator Compact differs from other interstate compacts involving natural resources because it has not been, and need not be, approved by Congress to become effective.[723] Because the compact is not approved by Congress, it is more flexible than other compacts in that it can

---

719. The parameters of the public trust doctrine have not been clearly delineated. *See, e.g.,* Joseph L. Sax, *The Public Trust Doctrine in Natural Resource Law: Effective Judicial Intervention,* 68 MICH. L. REV. 471 (1970); Joseph L. Sax, *Liberating the Public Trust Doctrine From Its Historical Shackles,* 14 U.C. DAVIS L. REV. 185, 188 (1980); Ralph W. Johnson & William C. Galloway, *Protection of Biodiversity Under the Public Trust Doctrine,* 8 TULANE ENVT'L L.J. 21 (1994).
720. *See* Nevada Dep't of Wildlife, What Is the Wildlife Violator Compact, *available at* http://www.stoppoaching.org/laws/wvc_index.shtm. *See also* Wildlife Violator Compact Operations Manual 1—Background.
721. *Id.*
722. For a list of states within the compact, *see* Nevada Dep't of Wildlife, Wildlife Violator Compact, *available at* http://www.stoppoaching.org/laws/wvc_index.shtm.
723. Congressional approval of interstate compacts is discussed in Chapter 2.

be amended by participating states as provided in the compact without the need for congressional affirmation of any amendments. Thus, agreements of prior state legislators do not bind subsequent ones as rigidly as with compacts operated under the Compact Clause of the Constitution, which may help alleviate concerns raised by at least one commentator concerning the constraints imposed by interstate compacts on our democratic system.[724] Nevertheless, all member state legislatures are bound by the contract principle that a compact cannot be unilaterally changed by any one member, even if congressional consent is inapplicable.

The Wildlife Violator Compact recognizes that "[w]ildlife resources are valuable without regard to political boundaries, [and it requires that] all persons . . . comply with wildlife preservation, protection, management and restoration laws, ordinances and administrative rules and regulations of all party states as a condition precedent to the continuance or issuance of any license to hunt, fish, trap or possess wildlife."[725]

Although states have primary responsibility for management of wildlife and enforcement of state wildlife laws, there are some federal laws that regulate wildlife that moves interstate or that protects endangered or threatened wildlife (e.g., the Lacey Act,[726] the Migratory Bird Treaty Act,[727] the Bald and Golden Eagle Protection Acts,[728] and the Endangered Species Act).[729] These Acts, however, tend to work in conjunction with and supplement the control over wildlife by states.[730] Thus, for example, violations of the Lacey

---

724. *See, e.g.*, Jill Elaine Hasday, *Interstate Compacts in a Democratic Society: The Problem of Permanency*, 49 FLA. L. REV. 1 (1997).
725. *See, e.g.*, OR. REV. STAT. § 496.750 (2004); COLO. REV. STAT. § 24-60-2602 (2004). *See also States Share Info on Wildlife Violators*, THE CHATTANOOGAN.COM, May 31, 2002, *available at* http://www.chattanoogan.com/articles/article_22563.asp.
726. 16 U.S.C. §§ 701, 3371-3378 & 18 U.S.C. § 42 (2004) (federal offense to transport or ship illegally taken or possessed wildlife or fish into interstate commerce; violations can result in civil or criminal penalties).
727. 16 U.S.C. § 703 (2004) (establishes hunting seasons for migratory birds; mandates cooperation between federal and state governments that results in determining the length of the hunting seasons and the bag limits.).
728. 16 U.S.C. §§ 668-668d (2004).
729. 16 U.S.C. §§ 1531-1544 (2004).
730. *See, e.g.*, The Lacey Act Amendments of 1981, 16 U.S.C. §§ 3371-3378 (1981), which specifically provides that the Act does not "preempt[ ] or supersede[ ] the authority of a State to regulate wildlife species within that State." 16 U.S.C. § 3372 (e)(4) (2004). *See also* Fish and Wildlife Coordination Act, 16

Act may result in fines or penalties based on the federal law. In addition, if the states within which the Lacey Act violations occurred are members of the Interstate Wildlife Violator Compact, the violator may face suspension of licenses in those states.[731]

To become a part of the Wildlife Violator Compact, a state must pass legislation in substantially the same form as other states within the compact, or the state legislature may authorize and direct the state's wildlife agency to enter into the compact.[732] The state must then submit a resolution of ratification and an application to the board of compact administrators for approval.[733]

The Wildlife Violator Compact assures that when a nonresident violates wildlife laws in a participating state, that nonresident is afforded the same treatment as residents of that state who are in violation.[734] Then, through a central Interstate Wildlife Violator Compact database,[735] the state of the nonresident violator may enforce against their resident as if the violation oc-

---

U.S.C. §§ 661-666c (2004) ("Cooperation of the various states in the management of wildlife and wildlife habitat on lands acquired by the federal Government and administered by its agencies is authorized."). United States v. 67.59 Acres of Land, More or Less, in Huntingdon County, 415 F. Supp. 544 (M.D. Pa. 1976).

731. The Lacey Act, when passed in 1900, was viewed "not as increasing the Federal role in managing wildlife, but as a federal tool to aid states in enforcing their own laws concerning wildlife." S. Rep. No. 97-123, 97th Cong., 1st Sess., at 2 (1981), *reprinted in* 1981 U.S.C.C.A.N. 1749. The 1981 amendments to the Act were "to provide comprehensive enforcement of wildlife laws and regulations established by state and local entities." United States v. Big Eagle, 881 F.2d 539, 540-41 (8th Cir. 1989).

732. Missouri is, however, an example of a state in which the legislature authorized the state's Conservation Commission, a constitutional body in Missouri, to enter into the compact. *See* Mo. Rev. Stat. § 252.247 (2004).

733. Wildlife Violator Compact Operations Manual 20—Administrative Matters (2003).

734. *Id.* at 11—Procedural Matters.

735. This database is contained within the Utah Law Enforcement Information Network (ULEIN) and grants access to all member states. Each member state can enter individual suspension information that is then accessible by member states. Quarterly reports are also sent to each state concerning suspensions. Wildlife Violator Compact Operations Manual 18—Compact Process (2003). *See also* Colorado Division of Wildlife, Annual Law Enforcement and Violations Report (May 1, 2003), *available at* http://wildlife.state.co.us/about/LawEnforcement/2003/2003_law_enforcement.pdf.

curred in the home state. [736] In effect, when a person is suspended in one of the compact states through the legal process where the violation occurred, the suspension is recognized by all the compact member states.[737]

One of the recognized benefits of this compact for those regulated under wildlife laws is that delays or inconvenience associated with processing violations of those laws are comparable for residents and nonresidents. In addition, personal recognizance is permitted in many cases involving such violations.[738] Benefits for the agency include fostering better communication among enforcement officers in different states and deterring poaching operations within member states and across state borders.[739] In addition, wildlife law enforcement officers devote more time to patrol and apprehension of violators, and less to paperwork processing. Court and jail facilities are less burdened, and the number of "failure to appear" cases is reduced because nonresidents cannot ignore a citation from a participating state without facing suspension of license privileges in their home states.[740] The compact also ensures uniformity in the management and enforcement of persons that violate wildlife laws or regulations that may affect more than one state, while not limiting a member state's enforcement of its own laws.

Because most of the actions taken regarding violations of state wildlife codes are administrative actions involving suspension of licenses,[741] there is little reported case law involving the Wildlife Violator Compact. In Arizona, a court held that the Wildlife Violator Compact's mandatory requirement that

---

736. The process for complying with the compact are detailed in the Wildlife Violator Compact Operations Manual, § IV. *See, e.g.,* OR. REV. STAT. § 496.750 (art. I (b) (4)-(5) & art. V) (2004); COLO. REV. STAT. § 24-60-2602 (art. I (b) (4)-(5) & art. V) (2004). *See also* Nevada Dep't of Wildlife, What Is the Wildlife Violator Compact?, *available at* http://www.stoppoaching.org/laws/wvc_index.shtm.

737. WILDLIFE VIOLATOR COMPACT OPERATIONS MANUAL, § IV (2003). *See also* Colorado Division of Wildlife, Annual Law Enforcement and Violations Report (May 1, 2003), *available at* http://wildlife.state.co.us/about/LawEnforcement/2003/2003_law_enforcement.pdf.

738. WILDLIFE VIOLATOR COMPACT OPERATIONS MANUAL 1—BACKGROUND (2003).

739. Ruth S. Musgrave, Sara Parker & Miriam Wolok, *The Status of Poaching in the United States—Are We Protecting Our Wildlife?*, 33 NAT. RESOURCES J. 977, 999-1000 (1993).

740. WILDLIFE VIOLATOR COMPACT OPERATIONS MANUAL 1-2—BACKGROUND (2003).

741. WILDLIFE VIOLATOR COMPACT OPERATIONS MANUAL 11—PROCEDURAL MATTERS (compact is not a device to secure court appearance, to ensure collecting of unpaid portions of fines, or a punitive device).

a participating state recognize license suspensions in another state supersedes that state's requirement for notice prior to suspending a license.[742] The court noted that the statutory requirement that the Game and Fish Commission give notice that it will suspend a hunting license within 180 days of a conviction applies only to discretionary suspensions, and does not apply to the mandatory suspension proceedings under the Wildlife Violator Compact, which requires participating states to recognize a suspension in another participating state.[743] Given that the states entering the Wildlife Violator Compact adopt the same or substantially similar language, it is likely that other states may also determine that the mandatory requirements of the compact control over discretionary provisions of the state's laws.

9.4.6.1.4   *Fishery Resource Management*

Interstate compacts addressing fisheries management usually are broad in scope and, of necessity, may also address other species and marine or fresh water ecosystems critical to management and sustainability of the fisheries. Some fisheries compacts address concerns with the depletion and threatened extinction of anadromous fish,[744] such as the Atlantic and Pacific salmon. Other compacts address depleted stock, such as the fishery resources in the Great Lakes states. However, management of the Great Lakes fishery resources occurs not simply through an interstate compact,[745] but also through a joint commission and a 1955 convention between Canada and the United States.[746] Compacts are also used to manage marine fishery resources and ecosystems that support those species. These compacts include the Atlantic Interstate Fisheries Compact,[747] the Pacific States Fisheries Compact,[748] and the Gulf States Marine Fisheries Compact.[749] These three marine fishery compacts are similar in that they all were entered into in the 1940s with the recognition that fishery resources move between and among various political boundaries. They differ, however, in the approaches their respective commissions take to the management of the fishery resources under their jurisdictions.

---

742. *See* Stapley v. State, 966 P.2d 1031 (Ariz. Ct. App. 1998).
743. *Id.* at 1034.
744. Anadromous fish breed in freshwater and live in salt water.
745. *See* discussion in this chapter under "Water Resources and Flood Control."
746. *See generally* The Great Lakes Fishery Commission, *at* http://www.glfc.org/ aboutus/index.php. *See also* The Great Lakes Fishery Commission, Fact Sheet 1, *available at* http://www.glfc.org/pubs/FACT_1.pdf.
747. Atlantic States Marine Fisheries Compact (1942).
748. Pacific Marine Fisheries Compact (1947).
749. Gulf States Marine Fisheries Compact (1949).

What is important to recognize is that although the compacts are each discussed separately, the commissions of the various compacts must work cooperatively and closely with one another and with other stakeholders and interest groups in order to ensure that the commissions can comply with their mandates and that the ecosystems and resources of concern are not subject to conflicting or contradictory requirements or regulations.

9.4.6.1.5   *Connecticut River Atlantic Salmon Compact*

The Connecticut River Atlantic Salmon Compact[750] is one example of an interstate compact that addresses concerns of anadromous fish. This compact developed from concern about the decline in Atlantic salmon due to damming of the Connecticut River and its tributaries. The purpose in developing the compact was to protect, manage, research, and regulate the Atlantic salmon population in the Connecticut River to return the "salmon to the Connecticut River in numbers as near as possible to their historical abundance."[751] The compact created a federal-state commission comprised of Vermont, Connecticut, Massachusetts, New Hampshire, the U.S. Fish and Wildlife Service, and the National Marine Fisheries Service, as well as public-sector representatives, which are all involved with restoration of Atlantic salmon and other migratory species.[752]

As mandated by the compact, the commission develops regulations that govern Atlantic salmon fishing in the mainstream of the Connecticut River and reviews and comments on regulations developed within each of the signatory states for salmon fishing in tributary streams. The commission also has licensing and enforcement authority within the Connecticut River Basin. The commission has succeeded in building fish ladders to assist salmon and shad populations with up-river runs over the dams, which has increased the annual run of salmon.[753]

---

750. Connecticut River Basin Atlantic Salmon Compact (1983). Originally, the compact had a duration of 20 years. However, the compact was reauthorized by Congress in 2002 for another 20 years, thus remaining in place through October 28, 2023. *See* Farm Security & Rural Investment Act of 2002, Pub. L. No. 107-171, 116 Stat. 134 (2002), *amending* Pub. L. No. 98-138 § 3 (2), 97 Stat. 870 (1983).

751. Pub. L. No. 98-138, 97 Stat. 866 (1983).

752. *See generally* U.S. Fish & Wildlife Service, Connecticut River Coordinator's Office, Connecticut River Atlantic Salmon Commission, *at* http://www.fws.gov/r5crc/who/crasc.html.

753. E-mail from Janice Rowan, U.S. Fish & Wildlife Service (June 2004) (on file with authors). For additional information, *see* U.S. Fish & Wildlife Service, Connecticut River Coordinator's Office, *at* http://www.fws.gov/r5crc.

9.4.6.1.6   *Oregon-Washington Columbia River Fish Compact*

In the Northwest, numerous federal, state, and regional organizations manage the regional fishery resources. Regulation of salmon and steelhead harvests from the Columbia River, for example, requires a "complex judicial and administrative scheme" that requires ongoing oversight by the courts to regulate and manage the fishery resources.[754] The Oregon-Washington Columbia River Fish Compact[755] was intended to provide uniformity in regulation of the fish resources on the interstate portion of the Columbia River's mainstream.[756] The original 1918 compact was amended to provide that the signatory state fish and wildlife commissions could enter into agreements to adopt seasons and rules for commercial fishing within the Columbia River

---

754. *See* United States v. Oregon, 913 F.2d 576, 579 (9th Cir. 1990). *See also* United States v. Oregon, 657 F.2d 1009, 1016 (9th Cir. 1982) (plan expressly states that it does not govern all fishing rights, but provides that "significant management problems" are handled by the district court; "[i]n any event," the district court retains jurisdiction over the case; provisions point to judicial resolution of unsettled questions). *See also* Comment, *Sohappy v. Smith: Eight Years of Litigation over Indian Fishing Rights,* 56 Or. L. Rev. 680 (1977); Sohappy v. Smith, 302 F. Supp. 899 (D. Or. 1969); United States v. Oregon, 529 F.2d 570 (9th Cir. 1976); United States v. Oregon, 718 F.2d 299 (9th Cir. 1983); United States v. Oregon, 769 F.2d 1410 (9th Cir. 1985); United States v. Oregon, 666 F. Supp. 1461 (D. Or. 1987); United States v. Oregon, 699 F. Supp. 1456 (D. Or. 1988), *aff'd,* United States v. Oregon, 913 F.2d 576 (9th Cir. 1990); United States v. Oregon, 1992 WL 613238, 1, Civ. No. 68-513-MA (D. Or. Feb. 29, 1992).

755. The compact was created by federal statute in 1918 and is a coordination compact relating to anadromous fish management between the states of Oregon and Washington. *See* Pub. L. No. 65-123, 40 Stat. 515 (1918). *See also* Or. Rev. Stat. § 507.010 (2003) and Wash. Rev. Code § 77.75.010 (2004) (requiring the two states' consent for all laws "regulating, protecting or preserving fish in the waters of the Columbia River, or its tributaries, over which the states of Washington and Oregon have concurrent jurisdiction"). Although the state of Idaho has sought to join the compact, it is not a party to the compact at this time. *See* Idaho *ex rel.* Evans v. Oregon, 444 U.S. 380, 384 (1980).

756. The waters over which Oregon and Washington have concurrent jurisdiction are "the waters of the Columbia River and its tributaries, within the confines of the States of Oregon and Washington, where such waters are state boundaries." *See, e.g.,* Or. Rev. Stat. § 507.020 (2003).

and its tributaries.[757] The compact imposes on Oregon and Washington "an affirmative duty under the doctrine of equitable apportionment to take reasonable steps to conserve and even augment the natural resources within their borders for the benefit of other states."[758]

Although Oregon and Washington, as the compact signatories, are intimately involved with management of Columbia River fishery resources, they are only a small piece of a much larger, more complex management regime. The Columbia River Fish Management Plan, as amended, is a court-approved management plan[759] developed by not only Oregon and Washington, the only voting members of the compact, but also several interested Indian Tribes and the United States.[760] The 1988 Management Plan for the Columbia River developed from numerous negotiations and years of litigation. In 1977, a five-year plan entitled "A Plan for Managing Fisheries on Stocks Originating from the Columbia River and its Tributaries above Bonneville Dam" set conservation goals for each fish species, established fishing regulations, and provided for the establishment of future management techniques, but did not establish locations, times, or quotas for fish harvests.[761] The district court overseeing management of the Columbia River fish resources recognized that these "details are regulated through the Columbia River Compact . . . Under the Compact, the Columbia River is divided into six commercial fishery zones, and annually it estimates the size of the runs and determines the length of fishing seasons that the runs can support."[762] In 1983, the district court found that changed circumstances of law and fact made the original 1977 plan subject to revision or modification and ordered the parties to attempt to agree upon a revised or modified agreement. Through subsequent negotiation and litigation, the 1988 Columbia River Fish Management Plan was developed, although not with unanimous consent of the various parties involved, and approved.[763]

---

757. *See, e.g.,* OR. REV. STAT. § 507.030 (2003). *See also* Columbia River Compact (1918).

758. Idaho *ex rel.* Evans v. Oregon, 462 U.S. 1017, 1025 (1983).

759. *See* United States v. Oregon, 699 F. Supp. 1456 (D. Or. 1988), *aff'd,* United States v. Oregon, 913 F. 2d 576 (9th Cir. 1990).

760. *Id. See also* United States v. Oregon, 1992 WL 613238, 1, Civ. No. 68-513-MA (D. Or. Feb 29, 1992).

761. For a history of the development of the Management Plans, *see* United States v. Oregon, 699 F. Supp. 1456, 1459-60 (D. Or. 1988).

762. *Id.* at 1459.

763. *Id.* at 1459-60.

Courts have described the Columbia River Fish Management Plan as "a delicate, but effective structure for allocating and planning harvest activities."[764] The Management Plan ultimately determines when each fishing season will occur. While the compacting states meet to decide on yearly regulations for Columbia River fisheries management, those regulations must be consistent with the court-approved Columbia River Fish Management Plan.[765] To manage fishery resources, Oregon and Washington set harvest quotas after negotiating with other interested parties.[766] Because of the significant fishery resources within the Columbia River and the multitude of competing interests, the mandate under the compact has become increasingly difficult and requires coordination by numerous parties.

The Management Plan allocates harvests between Indians who have treaty rights to the fish and to the non-Indian fisheries, but this also includes consideration of federal interests such as the National Marine Fisheries Service (NMFS), which participates through the Management Plan's Technical Advisory Committee.[767] Other interested parties include representatives of the Oregon Fish and Wildlife Commission (OFWC) and the Washington Fish and Wildlife Commission (WFWC), as well as the Columbia River Inter-Tribal Fish Commission (CRITFC),[768] which has authority to regulate treaty

---

764. Pac. N.W. Generating Coop. v. Brown, 822 F. Supp. 1479, 1486 (D. Or. 1993), *aff'd,* Pac. N.W. Generating Coop. v. Brown, 38 F.3d 1058 (9th Cir. 1994). *See also* United States v. Oregon, 913 F.2d 576 (9th Cir. 1990).

765. United States v. Oregon, 1992 WL 613238, 1, Civ. No. 68-513-MA (D. Or. Feb 29, 1992). Signatories to the plan include the United States, the Nez Perce Tribe, the Confederated Tribes of the Umatilla Indian Reservation, the Confederated Tribes of the Warm Springs Reservation, the Confederated Tribes of the Yakima Indian Nation, the states of Oregon, Washington, and Idaho, and, subject to certain defined limitations, the Shoshone-Bannock Tribe. *See* Pac. N.W. Generating Coop. v. Brown, 822 F. Supp. 1479, 1486 n.13 (D. Or. 1993), *aff'd,* Pac. N.W. Generating Coop. v. Brown, 38 F.3d 1058 (9th Cir. 1994).

766. *See* United States v. Oregon, 699 F. Supp. 1456 (D. Or. 1988) (retaining jurisdiction over allocations of fish entering Columbia River system); United States v. Washington, 384 F. Supp. 312 (W.D. Wash. 1974), *aff'd,* 520 F.2d 676 (9th Cir. 1975).

767. Pac. N.W. Generating Coop. v. Brown, 822 F. Supp. 1479, 1486 (D. Or. 1993), *aff'd,* Pac. N.W. Generating Coop. v. Brown, 38 F.3d 1058 (9th Cir. 1994).

768. The CRITFC is a coordinating agency for fishery management policies of the four Columbia River treaty tribes. Membership includes the fish and wildlife

Indian fisheries.[769] After negotiating a fish management plan, the plan must be approved by the courts retaining jurisdiction over the disputes as to allocation of fishery resources.[770] The final plans are characterized as consent decrees and, on appeal, the courts review approval of the decrees using an abuse of discretion standard.[771] Parties, such as the state of Idaho and Indian tribes, have been permitted to intervene[772] and to challenge these management plans, but their burden is heavy once a plan is approved, and the challenges are often unsuccessful.[773] In addition, while the Oregon-Washington Compact Commission cannot directly regulate sport fishing seasons or rules, it must

------

committees of these tribes. *See* Columbia River Inter-Tribal Fish Commission, What Is CRITFC?, *available at* http://www.critfc.org/text/work.html. For involvement of the tribes, *see* Sohappy v. Smith, 302 F. Supp. 899 (D.Or. 1969), *aff'd,* 529 F.2d 570 (9th Cir. 1970). *See also* Idaho *ex rel.* Evans v. Oregon, 444 U.S. 380, 384-85 (1980).

769. The Columbia River Basin Fish and Wildlife Authority facilitates management of the Columbia River Basin. The Authority consists of the four state and two federal fish and wildlife management entities and 13 Indian tribes of the Columbia River Basin that are the legally recognized managers of the fish and wildlife resources. *See generally* Columbia Basin Fish & Wildlife Authority, *at* http://www.cbfwa.org/default.cfm.

770. *See* United States v. Oregon, 699 F. Supp. 1456 (D. Or. 1988) (retaining jurisdiction over allocations of fish entering Columbia River system); United States v. Washington, 384 F. Supp. 312 (W.D. Wash. 1974), *aff'd,* 520 F.2d 676 (9th Cir. 1975) (retaining jurisdiction over allocation of fish rights within Washington state and three miles out to sea). *See also* United States v. Oregon, 913 F. 2d 576, 579 (9th Cir. 1990) (stating the courts of Washington and Oregon have continuing jurisdiction to ensure harvesting of fish and protection of Indian treaty rights). The Oregon District Court has had jurisdiction over the case since 1969. Some of the disputes were settled when the district court approved the parties' 1988 Columbia River Management Plan.

771. United States v. Oregon, 913 F. 2d 576, 580 (9th Cir. 1990).

772. *See, e.g.,* United States v. Oregon, 745 F.2d 550, 553 (9th Cir. 1984) (permitting Idaho to intervene to challenge a fishery management plan for the river); United States v. Oregon, 913 F.2d 576, 588 (9th Cir. 1990) (recognizing that Indian tribes have been permitted to intervene but affirming denial of the Makah Indian Tribe right to intervene).

773. *See* United States v. Oregon, 699 F. Supp. 1456 (D. Or. 1988) (approving management plan over objections); United States v. Oregon, 913 F.2d 576, 580-81 (9th Cir. 1990) (affirming plan over state and tribal objections).

consider the sport fishery demands when allocating the limited fishery resources among users.[774]

In addition to addressing concerns of multiple constituents, the Columbia River Compact commission must consider the quota impacts on species listed under the Endangered Species Act (ESA).[775] The ESA issues involved with the management of salmon harvests in the Columbia River imposes another level of increasing complexity on already difficult management issues where managers of the salmon resources, "by virtue of their numbers and their unwieldiness, [have] become an additional threat."[776] Also, because federal agencies are involved with management of fish stock in the Columbia River system, the National Environmental Policy Act of 1969 (NEPA) applies to major federal actions involving such management.[777] Other federal laws that indirectly affect management of the Columbia River fishery resources include the Fishery Conservation and Management Act of 1976.[778] This law created other management bodies such as the Pacific Fishery Management Council that manages areas seaward of the boundaries of Washington, Oregon, and California.[779] Because salmon and other anadromous fish

---

774. *See generally* Washington Dep't of Fish & Wildlife, *at* http://wdfw.wa.gov/fish/crc/crcindex.htm.

775. *See, e.g.,* Ramsey v. Kantor, 96 F.3d 434 (9th Cir. 1996) (finding state salmon fishing regulations did not violate the ESA); Idaho Dep't of Fish & Game v. Nat'l Marine Fisheries Serv., 850 F. Supp. 886 (D. Or. 1994) (remanded with instructions to vacate judgment and dismiss). *See* Idaho Dep't of Fish & Game v. Nat'l Marine Fisheries Serv., 56 F.3d 1071 (9th Cir. 1995).

776. Pac. N.W. Generating Coop. v. Brown, 822 F. Supp. 1479, 1487 n.15 (D. Or. 1993), *aff'd,* Pac. N.W. Generating Coop. v. Brown, 38 F.3d 1058 (9th Cir. 1994).

777. *See* Ramsey v. Kantor, 96 F.3d 434, 444 (9th Cir. 1996) (issuance of an incidental take statement in relation to Columbia River Fish Management Plan is a "major federal action" requiring compliance with NEPA before statement is issued).

778. *See* 16 U.S.C. § 1801 (Supp. V, 1985) (also known as the Magnuson-Stevens Fishery Conservation and Management Act, or Magnuson Act). The Magnuson Act provides for exclusive fishery management over all fish in a zone extending 200 miles seaward from a state's boundary. *See also* Executive Order No. 13,158—Marine Protected Areas, 36 Weekly Comp. Pres. Doc. 1230 (May 26, 2000). *See generally* Pacific Fisheries Management Council, *at* http://www.pcouncil.org/.

779. 16 U.S.C. § 1852 (a)(6) (2003); 16 U.S.C. § 1853 (a)-(c) (2003). The Pacific Fisheries Management Council is composed of representatives from Wash-

leave the Columbia River for the sea and then later return to the river to spawn, management of such fish requires coordination with organizations such as the Pacific Fishery Management Council.

This very brief overview of management of salmon within the Columbia River only begins to address the complexity of the management that necessarily involves state and federal laws, as well as numerous governmental and tribal agencies, voluntary consensus building organizations, and statutorily created management organizations, commercial interests, environmental groups, and individual citizens. Further, salmon and other anadromous fish are only some of the various species of fish that share the Columbia River and are regulated for harvests, conservation, and preservation. These issues must be coordinated with other interests that include habitat management, hydropower demands, and hatchery issues.[780]

9.4.6.1.7 *Atlantic Interstate Fisheries Compact; Maryland and Virginia Potomac River Compact of 1958*

Fifteen coastal states comprise the Atlantic States Marine Fisheries Commission (ASMFC) created under the Atlantic Interstate Fisheries Compact.[781] The ASMFC coordinates and manages sustainable use of "shared near shore fishery resources—marine, shell, and anadromous."[782] The commission is composed of three commissioners from each state whose responsibilities include interstate fisheries management, research and statistics, fisheries science, habi-

---

ington, Oregon, California, and Idaho; eight members appointed by the Secretary of Commerce; and the regional director of the National Marine Fisheries Service. *See generally* Pacific Fisheries Management Council, Navigating the Council Process, *available at* http://www.pcouncil.org/guide/Guide-part1.html.

780. *See, e.g.,* The Pacific Northwest Electric Power Planning and Conservation Act of 1980, 16 U.S.C. § 839 (2003).

The Northwest Electric Power and Conservation Planning Council was created to give the region an opportunity to design and implement a program for protection of anadromous and resident fish and wildlife in the Columbia Basin, rather than having narrowly focused recovery programs developed in Washington, D.C., or in federal court. *See also* Pac. N.W. Generating Coop. v. Brown, 822 F. Supp. 1479 (D. Or.1993), *aff'd,* Pac. N.W. Generating Coop. v. Brown, 38 F.3d 1058 (9th Cir. 1994).

781. Atlantic Interstate Fisheries Compact (1942), creating the Atlantic States Marine Fisheries Commission (ASMFC). The compact was amended by repealing limitation on life of the compact. Some states refer to the compact as the Atlantic States Marine Fisheries Compact.

tat conservation, and law enforcement. The ASMFC strives to better use the
fisheries resources of the Atlantic seaboard through joint programs.[782] To
achieve this goal, the ASFMC also cooperates with federal agencies, such as
the National Marine Fisheries Service and the U.S. Fish and Wildlife Service, as well as other compact commissions.[784] This cooperative approach
developed from other multijurisdictional efforts, including cooperative efforts at fishery resource management developed under the federal Magnuson-
Stevens Fishery Conservation and Management Act.[785] In addition to the
Magnuson Act, other federal laws promote cooperative management of the
Atlantic Coast fishery resources.[786]

Of necessity, other entities also have overlapping responsibility and authority for fishery resources managed by the Atlantic States Marine Fisheries
Commission (ASMFC). One of these is the Potomac River Fisheries Com-
mission (PRFC) created by Article I of the 1958 Potomac River Compact,
which still actively manages the fishery resources of the Potomac River.[787]
The PRFC's authority encompasses all recreational and commercial fishing,
crabbing, oystering, and clamming in "the main stem of the tidal Potomac
River from the Maryland/Washington, D.C. boundary line (near the Woodrow
Wilson Bridge), to the mouth of the river at Point Lookout, MD and Smith
Point, VA."[788] The PRFC has the authority to issue licenses for those activi-
ties, and "coordinates regulations with the Maryland Department of Natural
Resources (DNR), the Virginia Marine Resources Commission (VMRC) and

---

782. *See* Atlantic States Marine Fisheries Commission, About Us, *available at*
     http://www.asmfc.org/.
783. *Id.*
784. For the involvement of the National Marine Fisheries Service, *see generally*
     National Oceanographic & Atmospheric Administration, National Marine
     Fisheries Service (NOAA Fisheries), *available at* http://www.nmfs.noaa.gov/
     sfa/state_federal/state_federal.htm. For a discussion of the Interstate Fish-
     eries Management Program, *see* Atlantic States Marine Fisheries Commis-
     sion, *at* http://www.asmfc.org/interstate.htm/.
785. *See* 16 U.S.C. § 1801 (2003).
786. *See, e.g.,* Atlantic Striped Bass Conservation Act, 16 U.S.C. § 5151 (2004).
     See also Atlantic Coastal Fisheries Cooperative Management Act, 16 U.S.C.
     § 5101 (b) (2004).
787. *See generally* Potomac River Fisheries Commission, *at* http://
     www.prfc.state.va.us/.
788. *See* Potomac River Fisheries Commission, History and Mission Statement
     of the PRFC, *available at* http://www.prfc.state.va.us/.

the Department of Game and Inland Fisheries, (DGIF), and with the other Atlantic coastal states" through the ASMFC.[789]

Courts have recognized the authority of the PRFC within its jurisdiction to preempt state laws conflicting with the PRFC's regulations. For example, an individual that obtains a license issued by the Potomac River Fisheries commission and who fishes in compliance with the regulations promulgated by the commission has the right to fish the Potomac River waters within the commission's jurisdiction despite contrary state laws.[790] As the Maryland courts recognized, if state laws superseded the commission's regulations within the fishery areas of the commission's jurisdiction, "the Commission regulations would be quite limited in scope" and licenses issued by the commission would be of little value because activities in the waters governed by the license could be "preempted by the riparian owners."[791]

9.4.6.1.8   *Pacific Marine Fisheries Compact*

The 1947 Pacific Marine Fisheries Compact includes the states of Alaska, California, Idaho, Washington, and Oregon, and created the Pacific States Marine Fisheries Commission (PSMFC).[792] The PSMFC's goal is to "promote and support policies and actions directed at the conservation, development and management of fishery resources of mutual concern to member states through a coordinated regional approach to research, monitoring and utilization."[793] In contrast to the Atlantic States Marine Fisheries Commission (ASMFC), the PSMFC has no regulatory or management authority but serves as a consensus-building forum to better manage coastal resources.[794]

The PSMFC does recommend legislation and regulations for the compacting states to enact; however, no state is obligated to act on these recommendations, and "[n]othing in this compact shall be construed to limit the powers of any state or to repeal or prevent the enactment of legislation or the enforcement of any requirement by any state imposing additional conditions and restrictions to conserve its fisheries."[795] Thus, because Alaskan salmon

---

789. *Id.*
790. *See* Brown v. Bowles, 254 A.2d 696, 700 (Md. 1969).
791. *Id.* at 700.
792. Pacific Marine Fisheries Compact (1947). *See also* Pacific Marine Fisheries Commission, *at* http://www.psmfc.org/.
793. The Pacific Marine Fisheries Compact, art. IV (1947). *See also* Pacific Marine Fisheries Commission, *at* http://www.psmfc.org/.
794. *Id.*
795. Pacific Marine Fisheries Compact, art. IV & art. VIII (1947).

waste law is "both more recent and more specific to the salmon resource" than the Pacific Marine Fisheries Compact, its provisions or regulations control to the extent there is a conflict.[796] To foster conservation of marine resources, the compact does provide that the state fishery research agencies will work cooperatively as the official research agency of the PSMFC.[797] Citizen and commercial interests have an advisory role as to recommendations for the PSMFC.[798]

9.4.6.1.9   *Gulf States Marine Fisheries Compact*

The goal of the Gulf States Marine Fisheries Compact is to conserve and prevent waste of fisheries, marine, shell, and anadromous fish, and to develop and make full use of the Gulf of Mexico's fishery resources.[799] The compact authorizes the Gulf States Marine Fisheries Commission (GSMFC) to draft and recommend to the compact states legislation to conserve and prevent the depletion and physical waste of the marine, shell, and anadromous fisheries of the Gulf Coast.[800] The GSMFC is composed of 15 commissioners, three each from Louisiana, Texas, Mississippi, Alabama, and Florida, the five states that are members of the compact. The commission works on national fisheries issues in conjunction with both the Atlantic States Marine Fisheries Commission and the Pacific States Marine Fisheries Commission to promote coastal fisheries issues.[801]

The GSMFC designates the U.S. Fish and Wildlife Service as primary research agency of the commission to cooperate with state research agencies.[802] The commission also helps coordinate and administer various state and federal marine fisheries programs, including the Southeast Area Monitoring and Assessment Program that collects and disseminates fishery data for the southeastern United States, a sport fish restoration program, and a habitat program that works cooperatively with Mexican fishery agencies, as well as the interjurisdictional fishery program that manages fishery resources that migrate through state and federal jurisdictional waters.[803] Congress has rec-

---

796. O'Callaghan v. Rue, 996 P.2d 88, 99 (Alaska 2000).
797. Pacific Marine Fisheries Compact, art. VII (1947).
798. *Id.*
799. Gulf States Marine Fisheries Compact, art. I (1949).
800. Gulf States Marine Fisheries Compact, art. IV (1949). *See generally* Gulf States Marine Fisheries Commission, *at* http://www.gsmfc.org.
801. *See* Gulf States Marine Fisheries Commission, *at* http://www.gsmfc.org.
802. Gulf States Marine Fisheries Compact, art. VII (1949).
803. *See* Gulf States Marine Fisheries Commission, *at* http://www.gsmfc.org.

ognized the importance of interjurisdictional management of certain fishery resources and has provided funding to support state activities that facilitate management of these interjurisdictional resources.[804]

9.4.6.2   River Basin and Watershed Resources Compacts

Management, preservation, development, and protection for watersheds or water basins has historically been complex and has fluctuated from an effort for comprehensive, integrated management to one focusing on water use and development for human benefit. It now appears to be swinging back to a more integrated planning approach.[805] An in-depth discussion of these historical beginnings and trends is beyond the scope of this text and is comprehensively discussed in other material.[806] This section provides an introduction to the concerns historically addressed and a survey of the interstate compacts to manage watershed issues, only one of several management tools.

9.4.6.2.1   Background

Although federal recognition of the need for integrated policies for management of watersheds began in the early twentieth century, federal involvement devolved to individual federal agencies, with an emphasis on use and development by humans as opposed to addressing broader ecosystem or land resource issues.[807] The New Deal Era brought a renewed effort for a "comprehensive approach integrating all resources into a unified, balanced program," but in the end continued to focus on individual projects. [808]

Finally, in the 1960s, Congress acknowledged the benefit of management of river basin[809] resources, including coordination of federal programs

---

804. *See* Interjurisdictional Fisheries Act of 1986, Pub. L. No. 99-659, 100 Stat. 3706 (1986) (codified at 16 U.S.C. § 4101 (1986)).

805. For historical discussion of watershed planning, *see* Robert W. Adler, *Addressing Barriers to Watershed Protection*, 25 ENVTL. L. 973 (1995)

806. *Id.*

807. *Id.*

808. *Id.* at 1007.

809. River basins are defined as "the area or basin drained by a river and its tributaries." WEBSTER'S NEW UNIVERSAL UNABRIDGED DICTIONARY 1566 (2d ed.). Many of the river basin compacts define the "basin" areas similarly. *See, e.g.,* Delaware River Basin Compact (1961) ("'Basin' shall mean the area of drainage into the Delaware River and its tributaries, including Delaware Bay."); Susquehanna River Basin Compact (1970) ("'Basin' shall mean the area of drainage of the Susquehanna River and its tributaries"); Potomac River Basin Compact Amendments (1970).

and water quality/quantity issues, in 1965, when it passed the Water Resources Planning Act.[810] The Act was to "encourage the conservation, development and utilization of water and related land resources . . . on a comprehensive and coordinated basis by the Federal Government, States, localities, and private enterprises" although the "development" aspect was distinctly favored.[811] This Act provided for the president to designate river basin commissions composed of state, federal, and international representatives as well as representatives of agencies created by interstate compacts with jurisdiction over waters of the area or river basins.[812] These commissions developed comprehensive regional river basin plans.[813] Between 1965

---

810. Water Resources Planning Act of 1965, 42 U.S.C. § 1962 to 1962d-20 (2004).
811. *See* Water Resources Planning Act, 42 U.S.C. § 1962 to 1962d-20 (2004), noting the Act cannot supersede, modify, or repeal any existing law applicable to federal agencies authorized to develop or participate in development of water and related land resources. The Act was intended to provide for the optimum development of the nation's natural resources through the coordinated planning of water and related land resources. The plans themselves, however, were to achieve "optimum development of water and related land resources." *See* 42 U.S.C. § 1962b(b)(2) (2004). Also, the Water Resource Commission was to review each plan "with special regard to" the development goal and to evaluate the effect of the plan on "other programs for the development" of national resources. *See* 42 U.S.C. § 1962a-3 (2004). For a discussion of the Act, *see* Robert W. Adler, *Addressing Barriers to Watershed Protection*, 25 ENVTL. L. 973, 1009 (1995).
812. Water Resources Planning Act, § 202, Pub. L. No. 89-80, 79 Stat. 244 (1965). Notwithstanding the composition of the commissions, the federal focus of the Act clearly dominated. *See* discussion, Robert W. Adler, *Addressing Barriers to Watershed Protection*, 25 ENVTL. L. 973, 1011 (1995).
813. Water Resources Planning Act, § 201(b), Pub. L. No. 89-80, 79 Stat. 244 (1965).
814 *See* Establishment of the Pacific Northwest River Basins Commission, Exec. Order No. 11,331, 32 Fed. Reg. 3875 (Mar. 6, 1967); Establishment of the Great Lakes Basin Commission, Exec. Order No. 11,345, 32 Fed. Reg. 6329 (Apr. 20, 1967); Establishment of the Souris-Red-Rainy River Basins Commission, Exec. Order No. 11,359, 32 Fed. Reg. 8851 (June 20, 1967); Establishment of the New England River Basins Commission, Exec. Order No. 11,371, 32 Fed. Reg. 12,903 (Sept. 6, 1967); Establishment of the Ohio River Basin Commission, Exec. Order No. 11,578, 36 Fed. Reg. 683 (Jan. 13, 1971); Establishment of the Upper Mississippi River Basin Commission, Exec. Order No. 11,659, 37 Fed. Reg. 6047 (Mar. 22, 1972); Establishment of the Missouri River Basin Commission, Exec. Order No. 11,658, 37 Fed. Reg. 6045 (Mar. 22, 1972).

and 1980, seven river basin commissions were created by executive order.[814] In addition to creating the basin commissions, the Act created a federal inter-agency Water Resources Council (WRC) whose responsibilities included assessing adequacy of water supplies for each region of the country, studying the relationship of regional or river basin plans in relation to the requirements of larger regions of the nation, and evaluating the adequacy of coordinating water and related land resource programs of federal agencies.[815] The WRC was also required to establish standards and procedures for federal participation in development of comprehensive basin plans to formulate and evaluate water and land resource projects.[816]

The federal government's efforts at basin management ended in 1981 when President Reagan terminated six of the basin commissions.[817] Criticism of the river basin commissions and the WRC was heard from all sides. Explanations for termination of the commissions and the Water Resources Council vary and are attributed to the fiscal conservatism of the Reagan administration; criticism by environmental groups of the emphasis by water resource management on hydroelectric plants, irrigation and flood control projects, and the ecological impacts of this focus; states' abilities to manage their own water resources notwithstanding the interstate nature of most waters, which needed federal/state coordination to take place as necessary, and that the in-

---

815. The Water Resources Commission is now composed of the secretaries of Agriculture, Army, Commerce, Energy, Interior, and Housing and Urban Development, and the administrator of the Environmental Protection Agency. *See* 42 U.S.C. § 1962a (2004). When created in 1965, the Water Resources Commission included the secretaries of the Interior; Agriculture; Army; Health, Education and Welfare; and the chairman of the Federal Power Commission. *See* Water Resources Planning Act, §§ 101(b) & 102(b), Pub. L. No. 89-80, 79 Stat. 244 (1965).

816. Water Resources Planning Act of 1965, § 103, Pub. L. No. 89-80, 79 Stat. 244 (1965).

817. Six of the river basin commissions were terminated in 1981. *See* Exec. Order No. 12,319, 46 Fed. Reg. 45,591 (Sept. 9, 1981). The seventh commission, the Souris-Red-Rainy River Basins Commission, was terminated in 1973. *See* Exec. Order No. 11,635, 36 Fed. Reg. 23,615 (Dec. 9, 1971). Subsequently, the portions of the states of Minnesota and North Dakota that are drained by the Souris-Red-Rainy Rivers system were added to the Upper Mississippi River Basin Commission. *See* Exec. Order No. 11,737, 38 Fed. Reg. 24,883 (Sept. 7, 1973). The Upper Mississippi River Basin Commission is one of the six terminated in 1981.

struments of the Water Resources Planning Act were ineffective; and the fact that federal financing was on the wane.[818] Probably all these factors contributed to termination of the commissions and the WRC.

Notwithstanding the termination of the commissions and the WRC by the Reagan administration, the Water Resources Planning Act was never repealed.[819] Water resource planning remains a congressional policy and is supported by declarations that congressional authority to manage interstate waterways falls within the Commerce Clause powers.[820] Further, although the river basin commissions under the Water Resource Planning Act no longer function, the federal government is still active in river basin management. Much of the federal government's involvement is mission oriented. [821] Even though federal agency involvement has a narrow focus, many of the states have entered into federal-interstate compacts[822] that provide for interstate

---

818. *See generally* Robert W. Adler, *Addressing Barriers to Watershed Protection*, 25 Envtl. L. 973, 1009-13 (1995); William Goldfarb, W*atershed Management: Slogan or Solution?*, 21 B.C. Envtl. Aff. L. R. 483, 488 (1994); Jayne E. Daly, *From Divining Rods to Dams: Creating a Comprehensive Water Resource Management Strategy for New York*, 1995 Pace L. Rev. 105 (Commemorative ed. 1995); Leonard B. Dworsky, David J. Allee & Ronald M. North, *Water Resources Planning and Management in the United States Federal System: Long-Term Assessment and Intergovernmental Issues*, 31 Nat. Resources J. 475, 480 (1991).

819. *See* 42 U.S.C. § 1962 (2004).

820. *See* Water Resources Development Act, 33 U.S.C. § 2201 (2004). The focus of the Act is to enhance national economic development through water resources planning using a cost-benefit analysis to determine the viability of the projects. In addition, water planning falls under the Clean Water Act, 33 U.S.C. §§ 1251-1387 (2003). Water quality control and management on a basin-wide level is found at 33 U.S.C. § 1289. Water planning at the basin level is eligible for grants.

821. *See* Reclamation Act of June 17, 1902, Pub. L. No. 57-161, 32 Stat. 388 (1902); Federal Power Act of 1920, Pub. L. No. 66-280, 41 Stat. 1063 (1920); Flood Control Act of 1958, Pub. L. No. 85-500, 72 Stat. 297 (1958). The Federal Power Act was originally entitled the Federal Water Power Act. *See* 16 U.S.C. § 791a. This Act created the Federal Power Commission, now known as the Federal Energy Regulatory Commission (FERC). *See* Department of Energy Organization Act, 42 U.S.C. § 7172(a) (1988). The purpose of the Federal Power Act was to centralize licensing for water projects to facilitate hydroelectric power and navigation.

822. A significant feature of federal-interstate compacts is that courts have upheld the subordination of federal interests to those of the regional compact. *See*

commissions with functions similar to that of the terminated Water Resources Planning Act commissions, although the commissions under the compacts address and consider concerns broader than simply development of the watersheds.

9.4.6.2.2   *Survey of Interstate Compacts Addressing Water Basins*

As with many interstate compacts involving natural resources, compacts involving management of water resources within a river basin or watershed are not limited to a single issue but address multiple concerns. River basin interstate compacts address not only water quality and supply, but also flood control, conservation, and development of river basins.[823]

9.4.6.2.3   *Susquehanna River Basin Compact*

The Susquehanna River Basin Commission is an example of a federal-interstate compact commission formed to address water usage and conservation matters within the Susquehanna River Basin. Congress approved the Susquehanna River Basin Compact, which was ratified by New York, Pennsylvania, and Maryland, and created the Susquehanna River Basin Commission (SRBC).[824] In addition to representatives of the signatory states, a representative of the federal government is also an SRBC member.[825] The SRBC's responsibilities include development of a comprehensive plan for immediate and long-term development and use of water resources including allocation, conservation, and management.[826] The SRBC uses a variety of methods to achieve this mission including flood control programs, reasonable and sustained development addressing municipal, agricultural, recreational, commercial, and industrial water needs, fisheries, wetland, and aquatic habitat management, as well as water quality and usage.[827]

The SRBC's focus as a federal-interstate compact commission is on regional river basin issues, not simply individual state concerns. In this way, it

Seattle Master Builders Ass'n. v. Pac. N.W. Elec. Power & Conservation Planning Council, 786 F.2d 1359 (9th Cir. 1986).

823. *See generally* Jerome C. Muys, *Interstate Compacts and Regional Water Resources Planning and Management*, 6 Nat. Resources L. 153 (1973).

824. Pub. L. No. 91-575, 84 Stat. 1509 (1970). *See also* Susquehanna River Basin Compact, art. II (1970).

825. *See* Susquehanna River Basin Compact, art. II § 2.2 (1970).

826. *Id.* at art. III (1970).

827. *See generally* Susquehanna River Basin Commission, *at* http://www.srbc.net/.

coordinates among its member states and the federal government to resolve water issues within the basin.[828] The SRBC developed a Comprehensive Plan for the Management and Development of the Water Resources of the Susquehanna Basin that includes: flood plain management and protection; water supply; water quality; watershed protection and management; recreation, fish wildlife management, and cultural, visual, and other amenities.[829]

One interesting aspect of the SRBC is that the compact authorizes the commission to enact rules that become, after notice and comment, federally enforceable rules.[830] Although the commission is not subject to the federal Administrative Procedures Act, and is not legally obligated to proceed through notice and comment rulemaking, it chooses to do so because the commission believes that uniformity is important for the three jurisdictions that the commission serves.[831] The SRBC has also developed an extensive set of policies for management of the river basin.[832]

9.4.6.2.4   *Potomac River Basin Interstate Compact*

One of the oldest interstate river basin commissions in the nation is the Interstate Commission on the Potomac River Basin (ICPRB).[833] Its concerns include living resources within the river basin, water quality, and supply, as well as involvement with education and outreach. In 1970, Congress amended the Potomac River Basin Interstate Compact[834] to provide for the creation of

---

828. *Id.*
829. *See* Susquehanna River Basin Commission, Overview, *available at* http://www.srbc.net/geninfo.htm.
830. 18 C.F.R. §§ 803 to 805 (1998).
831. E-mail from Rich Cairo, SRBC Commission Counsel (May 27, 2004) (on file with authors). Mr. Cairo also noted that having the regulations in one convenient place makes it easier for each of the jurisdictions to locate them.
832. *See* Susquehanna River Basin Commission, Guidelines for Using and Determining Passby Flows and Conservation Releases for Surface-Water and Ground-Water Withdrawal Approvals, Policy No. 2003-01 (Nov. 8, 2002), *available at* http://www.srbc.net/docs/Policy%202003_01.pdf.
833. *See generally* Interstate Commission on the Potomac River Basin, *at* http://www.potomacriver.org/.
834. *See* Pub. L. No. 91-407, 84 Stat. 856 (1970). Congress granted consent to the signatory states to create the Potomac Valley Conservancy District as an interstate commission. The act of consent provided "[t]hat nothing contained in such compact shall be construed as impairing or in any manner affecting any right or jurisdiction of the United States in and over the region which forms the subject of this compact." Potomac River Basin Compact, art. VII (1970).

the ICPRB with the purpose of "cooperatively address[ing] water quality and related resource problems in the Potomac watershed."[835] In contrast to the Susquehanna River Basin Commission, the ICPRBC is an advisory body that has no regulatory power; relying instead on "cooperation, rather than regulation [as] the appropriate method of achieving its goals."[836] In fact, the ICPRB prides itself that "for more than 60 years [it has sought] to build partnerships between governments, businesses, non-profits, and concerned citizens in order to increase efficiency, reduce duplication of efforts, and leverage resources to address Potomac water quality."[837]

9.4.6.2.5 *Great Lakes Compact*

The Great Lakes Compact is another example of an interstate compact that addresses multiple environmental, economic, and natural resource issues.[838] The Great Lakes Commission, formed by the compact is an advisory body that represents the eight Great Lakes states on various environmental and economic issues.[839] In addition, in 1999, the Great Lakes Commission entered into a Declaration of Partnership establishing associate membership for the two Canadian provinces of Ontario and Quebec.[840] Thus, while the Great Lakes Compact is a multistate compact, the Declaration of Partnership actually makes the Great Lakes Commission a unique bi-national public agency to address water resource issues involving the Great Lakes and the St. Lawrence River system.

The commission's focus is on sustainable environment and resource management as well as transportation and economic development within the Great Lakes-St. Lawrence system.[841] Programs implemented by the commission include: administration, communication and Internet technology, data manage-

---

835. *See* Interstate Commission on the Potomac River Basin, Frequently Asked Questions, *available at* http://www.potomacriver.org/about_ICPRB/faqs.htm.

836. *Id.*

837. *Id.*

838. Great Lakes Compact (1968). This compact is not strictly a federal-interstate compact, although it does provide a unique multinational approach to management of water basins. *Available at* http://www.glc.org./about/glbc.htm.

839. The member states are Illinois, Indiana, Michigan, Minnesota, New York, Ohio, Pennsylvania, the United States, and Wisconsin.

840. *See* Great Lakes Basin Commission, Declaration of Partnership, *available at* http://www.glc.org/about/pdf/declarations.pdf.

841. *See* Great Lakes Basin Commission, About the Great Lakes Commission, *at* http://www.glc.org/about/.

ment, environmental quality, regional coordination, resource management, transportation, and sustainable development.[842] In contrast to some interstate commissions that issue regulations for management of river basin resources, the Great Lakes Commission has no regulatory authority. It does, however, provide information on public policy issues and is a "forum for developing and coordinating public policy; and a unified, system-wide voice to advocate member interests."[843] Interestingly, while the commission's initial focus was the water resources of the Great Lakes, its involvement has expanded to include land and soil issues as well as air issues within the region.[844] The commission is experienced in developing regional air toxics inventory comprising statewide inventories. Thus, while not a regulatory body, the commission is effective at coordinating the multitude of environmental and economic interests that compete for the resources within the Great Lakes and St. Lawrence Basin.[845] For example, the commission has recently revised *The Great Lakes Program to Ensure Environmental and Economic Prosperity*, a policy document that compiles "federal legislative and appropriations priorities that would help secure a clean environment, strong economy and high quality of life for residents of the eight-state Great Lakes region."[846]

9.4.6.2.6   *Delaware River Basin Compact*

The Delaware River Basin Compact addresses regional issues involving the water quality of the Delaware River and its tributaries through the Dela-

---

842. *See* Great Lakes Basin Commission, Commission Programs, *available at* http://www.glc.org/about/programs/.

843. *See* Great Lakes Basin Commission, About the Great Lakes Commission, *at* http://www.glc.org/about/.

844. *See, e.g.,* Great Lakes Basin Commission, Land & Soil Management, *at* http://www.glc.org/landsoil.html. *See also* Great Lakes Basin Commission, Air & Water Quality, *at* http://www.glc.org/airwater.html. Water resource issues include water quality, navigation and port facilities, fisheries, and wetland and flood-plain protection, as well as zoning and hydroelectric power. *See* Matthew Sundeen & L. Cheryl Runyon, *Interstate Compacts and Administrative Agreements*, 23 STATE LEGIS. REP. (March 1998), *available at* http://www.ncsl.org/.

845. For policy positions adopted by the Commission to guide use and development of the basin, *See* Great Lakes Basin Commission, Policy Positions, *available at* http://www.glc.org/policy/.

846. *See id.*

ware River Basin Commission (DRBC), formed under the compact.[847] Parties signatory to this federal-interstate compact include the states of Delaware, New Jersey, New York, and Pennsylvania, as well as the federal government.[848] In addition to representatives of these states, a representative of the federal government is also a voting member of the DRBC.[849]

Significant for management from an ecosystem perspective, the compact addresses a variety of issues other than simply water quality within the Basin, including hydroelectric power, recreational development, conservation, flood protection, and drought management programs, as well as water supply and diversion issues.[850] To ensure management of all these issues, the compact requires the DRBC to prepare *and* to review and revise a Comprehensive Plan for the Basin.[851] In other words, the compact requires the commission to undertake an ongoing monitoring and study of the water resources and the Basin. The purpose of the Comprehensive Plan is to address immediate and long-range development and use of water resources (surface and ground water) within the Basin. Noteworthy from a management standpoint is that concurrence by the DRBC's federal representative to any revision of the Comprehensive Plan precludes actions by other federal agencies that conflict with the management of the water resources or related land resources under the Comprehensive Plan.[852]

As part of the DRBC's duties, the commission has regulatory review authority involving permitting as well as responsibility for developing water quality standards and regulations for the Basin.[853] The DRBC can finance and

---

847. Delaware River Basin Compact (1961). The member states are Delaware, New Jersey, NewYork, and Pennsylvania. *See* Delaware River Basin Commission, *at* http://www.state.nj.us/drbc/over.htm.

848. The involvement of the federal government in the Delaware River Basin Compact is subject to conditions and reservations. *See* Delaware River Basin Compact (1961). Among the reservations are conditions on project development and financing, the exercise of executive powers in the event of an emergency, and application of federal contracting law to commission activities.

849. *See* Delaware River Basin Compact, art. 2 (1961).

850. *See id.* at art. 3 (1961).

851. *See id.* at art. 3, § 3.2 & art. 13, § 13.1 (1961).

852. *See id.* at art. 15, § 15.1(s)(1) (1961).

853. *See generally* Delaware River Basis Commission, *at* http://www.state.nj.us/drbc/over.htm. *See also* Delaware River Basin Commission, Administrative Manual—Part III, Water Quality Regulations, *available at* http://www.state.nj.us/drbc/regs/wq-regs.pdf.

construct capital improvements within the Basin.[854] It can also assess fees for use of its facilities.[855] The DRBC also determines the amount of water communities may divert from the river.[856] This power is circumscribed by the U.S. Supreme Court decree in *New Jersey v. New York* that authorizes certain diversions of water from the Delaware River watershed, which predate the compact.[857] Signatory states to the compact have agreed not to seek modification of the 1954 Supreme Court decree to increase or decrease diversions from the river.[858]

The DRBC has published an Administrative Manual of Rules of Practice and Procedures.[859] The Manual guides the DRBC's duties under the compact to formulate and adopt various programs including the Comprehensive Plan and Water Resources Program. For example, under the compact, the DRBC is required to review, against the Comprehensive Plan, any project that has a substantial affect on the water resources of the Basin.[860] This responsibility includes plans that require review under the National Environmental Policy Act (NEPA).[861] Courts are divided as to the DRBC's role in reviewing and preparing Environmental Impact Statements (EIS) under NEPA for projects affecting the Delaware River Basin.[862] Nonetheless, courts that have consid-

---

854. *See* Delaware River Basin Compact, art. 3 (1961).
855. *See id.* at art. 3, § 3.7 (1961). *See also* Borough of Morrisville v. Delaware River Basin Comm'n, 399 F. Supp. 469 (E.D. Pa. 1975).
856. *See* Delaware River Basin Compact, art. 3, § 3.3 (1961).
857. New Jersey v. New York, 347 U.S. 995 (1954). *See also* Delaware River Basin Compact, art. 3, § 3.5 (1961).
858. *See* Delaware River Basin Compact, art. 3, § 3.4 (1961).
859. *See* Delaware River Basin Commission, Administrative Manual, Rules of Practice and Procedures (2002), *available at* http://www.state.nj.us/drbc/regs/rules.pdf.
860. *See* Delaware River Basin Compact, art. 3, § 3.8 (1961).
861. National Environmental Policy Act of 1969, 42 U.S.C. § 4332 (2004). Federal agencies are required to prepare an Environmental Impact Statement (EIS) on all major federal actions affecting the environment. 42 U.S.C. § 4332(2)(C) (2004).
862. *Compare* Bucks County Bd. of Comm'rs v. Interstate Energy Co., 403 F. Supp. 805, 808 (E.D. Pa. 1975) (the DRBC as the designated federal agency to prepare and review an EIS) *with* Delaware Water Emergency Group v. Hansler, 536 F. Supp. 26, 35 (E.D. Pa. 1981) (it is "very doubtful" the DRBC is a federal agency for purposes of NEPA, but not deciding the issue in this case). *See also* Borough of Morrisville v. Delaware River Basin Comm'n, 399 F. Supp. 469, 479 n.7 (E.D. Pa. 1975) (DRBC conceded it was a federal agency

ered the DRBC's role involving projects falling under NEPA have upheld the DRBC's decision not to prepare an EIS in a case in which the DRBC approved an application to construct a water diversion project in the Basin.[863] An earlier court upheld the DRBC's preparation and review of an EIS and also determined that neither NEPA nor the DRBC's Rules of Practice required an adversary hearing concerning objections to the EIS; in both instances, such hearings were discretionary.[864] With regard to the DRBC's Rules of Practice, the court found that the executive director of the DRBC had the discretion, which was exercised in this case, to deny an adversary hearing because it was determined that the objections to the project were not sufficiently substantial.[865]

Given the breadth of responsibility, power, and independence granted the DRBC under the compact, the role of the DRBC and its responsibilities under the compact provide an interesting study in the ability of an interstate commission to manage and implement an ecosystem approach to water basin management.

9.4.7   Conclusion

Interstate compacts involving environmental and natural resource matters are varied and complex. Some require federal approval under the Compact Clause of the Constitution, others are agreements that do not interfere with federal authority and thus do not require congressional consent. All attempt to resolve multistate and regional issues that arise outside the authority of individual states.

---

for purposes of NEPA). Other courts have held that in the context of interstate compacts in which the federal government does not have a voting member, such interstate commissions are not federal agencies subject to NEPA. *See, e.g.*, Cal. Dep't of Transp. v. City of S. Lake Tahoe, 466 F. Supp. 527, 534-36 (D.C. Cal. 1978) (bi-state planning organization formed by interstate compact was not a federal agency and, thus, was not subject to NEPA).

863. Delaware Water Emergency Group v. Hansler, 536 F. Supp. 26, 36 (E.D. Pa. 1981), *aff'd,* 681 F.2d 805 (3d Cir. 1982) (the "DRBC regulations in substance adopt all NEPA requirements, and possibly some additional procedural steps," so that determining applicability of NEPA to the DRBC need not be decided here).

864. Bucks County Bd. of Comm'rs v. Interstate Energy Co., 403 F. Supp. 805, 817-18 (E.D. Pa. 1975).

865. *Id.* at 820.

While authorities debate the effectiveness of such interstate compacts, they are a viable alternative to no regulation or to the imposition of federal authority over interstate matters, which may need a more regional focus. Environmental and natural resource interstate compacts have been used to resolve disputes since before the founding of the nation and have become an integral part of management of the country's natural resources.

9.5   REGIONAL ECONOMIC DEVELOPMENT AND TRANSPORTATION COMPACTS

This section surveys the following topics:

* General Considerations
* New York–New Jersey Port Authority Compact
* Bi-State Development Compact
* Washington Metropolitan Area Transportation Compacts

9.5.1   Generally

Regional economic, planning, and development compacts find their roots in the twentieth century and were generally adopted by the states in response to growing metropolitan areas or increased urbanization. Thus, regional economic and development compacts represent, at their core, an effort by states to confront regional issues caused by the development of large metropolitan areas that jump state boundaries. These agreements have resulted in some of the most powerful and far reaching regional agencies in the nation. Although the New York–New Jersey Port Authority compact represents the first effort by states to create regional governance through the compact instrument, this compact is not the sole example of regionalizing issues through an interstate agreement. While clearly the New York–New Jersey Port Authority Compact is the most famous of the agreements, other agreements evidence the wide use of interstate compacts for these purposes. For example, port facilities and high-speed transportation systems in the Philadelphia metropolitan area are managed by the Delaware River Port Authority (DRPA). Bridges and transportation systems between New Jersey and Delaware are managed under the auspices of the Delaware River and Bay Authority (DRBA). Today, regionalization through compacts is illustrated by agreements creating such diverse entities as the Washington Metropolitan Area Transit Authority, the Bi-State Development Agency, and the Chickasaw Trail Economic Development Compact. Each of these agreements—and many others—exists for the sole purpose of promoting regional development, regional planning, or regional transportation development across state boundaries.

Perhaps what is most interesting about the use of interstate compacts to promote the principle of regional governing is that their use has been largely topic driven—that is, limited to specific issues of regional interest. No interstate compact has been developed and adopted that recognizes the regional nature of many multistate metropolitan areas and truly promotes regional governing on a broad scale. Thus, states have adopted compacts such as the Kansas City Metropolitan Culture District and the Bi-State Tax in Kansas and Missouri. Compacts have been written to promote regional transportation solutions and manage specific economic concerns as illustrated by the Washington Metropolitan Area Transportation Compact, all of which create commissions with authority to manage and regulate particular aspects of public and commercial transportation in the Washington, D.C. metropolitan area, including in the case of the Washington Metropolitan Area Transit Commission to regulate interstate taxi rates and insurance standards.[866]

The use of compacts to govern regional issues is not, of course, the only path available to government officials. Informal interstate cooperation exists in many metropolitan regions, compelled by the simple reality that many issues ignore state boundaries. However, as between the two approaches—the one being formal through interstate compacts and the other being informal—the better choice would seem to be the interstate compact, whenever feasible, because of its binding nature. The use of interstate compacts to govern regional issues is particularly compelling when the issues are large, complicated, and require continuing administration. For example, the Kansas and Missouri Metropolitan Culture District Compact is but one of several models for using interstate compacts to serve multistate metropolitan areas.[867] That compact provides not only for the creation of a commission to manage a multistate cultural district, but also enables voters within the district to impose a sales tax for purposes of funding district activities.[868] Consequently, while current interstate compacts in metropolitan areas are issue specific, they nevertheless offer metropolitan areas an opportunity to start thinking beyond political boundaries and acting in a way consistent with reality. Additionally, as many metropolitan areas grow across state lines, the need for regional governance and models to achieve regional governance will likely increase. Today, many people identify with regions—not necessarily states—reflecting a growing reality that regional concerns must be addressed by re-

---

866. Bartsch v. Wash. Metro. Area Transit Comm'n, 344 F.2d 201 (D.C. Cir. 1965).
867. Mo. Rev. Stat. § 70.500 (2004).
868. Kansas and Missouri Metropolitan Culture District Compact, art. IV(b)(1) & (c)(1)-(3) (2000).

gional solutions. Although the use of compacts as tools of regional governance has been quite limited, new economic and regional challenges may compel a need to examine truly interstate regional governing on a broader scale. Whether the future holds a different paradigm in which compacts are broadly written to establish regional governments remains an open question. Such a shift in the use of compacts away from governing regional issues toward governing regions would likely prove difficult in the foreseeable future given the deep cultural and political affiliation Americans generally have to the concept of statehood (though not necessarily identification with a particular state) and a purely federal system of government. Several interstate compacts illustrate both the success and failure in the use of such instruments in managing small and large regional matters.

9.5.2   New York–New Jersey Port Authority Compact[869]

The Port Authority of New York and New Jersey (Port Authority) is a self-sustaining bi-state public entity established in 1921 by an interstate compact between the states of New York and New Jersey. Originally called the Port of New York Authority, the name was changed to The Port Authority of New York and New Jersey in 1972, to identify more accurately its status as a bi-state agency. The Port Authority was established as the first of its kind in the western hemisphere and the first interstate agency created by compact. It was originally modeled after the Port of London Authority, then the only public authority in the world. The Port Authority has its roots in 1917 when the governors of New York and New Jersey appointed a commission to study the problem of coordinating port and harbor development in an attempt to resolve disputes between the states concerning such matters as boundaries, marine police jurisdiction, and freight rates. The commission eventually recommended the establishment of a single authority to manage the bi-state interests in the region's port resources. A compact was signed that defined a single Port District and provided for its administration by a Port Authority whose purpose was to coordinate terminal, transportation, and other facilities of commerce.

The principal purpose of the Port Authority is to administer transportation and port activities in the New York–New Jersey Port District, a 1,500-square-mile area defined as a circle with a 25-mile radius centered on the Statue of Liberty. The Port Authority consists of 12 commissioners, six appointed by the governor of each state, subject to confirmation by the senate

---

869. *See generally* Port Authority of New York–New Jersey, *at* http://www.panynj.gov.

of the respective states. Since the commissioners constitute agents of the state, their instructions take the form of legislative mandates. The board of commissioners appoints an executive director to carry out the agency's policies and manage its day-to-day operations. In addition to its domestic responsibilities, the Port Authority also engages in international business activities to develop business for the Port Authority and the New York/New Jersey region. A network of international offices and agents market the agency's maritime, aviation, and world trade businesses overseas. Thus, in addition to managing transportation hubs and port facilities, the Port Authority engages in independent business development seeking to expand not only use of facilities but overall economic development in the New York metropolitan area.

The work of the commissioners, in addition to administration, includes development, construction, operation, and protection of the Port District. The authority finances its activities from income, such as tolls and charges, and by selling revenue bonds in the public market.[870] Since its creation in 1921, the Port Authority has grown to regulate most of the region's transportation systems, including its airports, bridges, and tunnels. Today, the Port Authority manages the Holland Tunnel, the George Washington Bridge, the Lincoln Tunnel, the Port Authority Bus Terminal in New York City, marine terminals in Newark and Elizabeth, and the Port Authority Trans-Hudson Railroad, known as PATH. The Port Authority also manages the New York City airports and Newark International Airport, and built the World Trade Center complex.

Although the Port Authority does run a good portion of the transportation structures, some bridges, tunnels, and other transportation facilities are operated independently of the Port Authority, including the Staten Island Ferry, operated by the New York City Department of Transportation; bridges, tunnels, buses, subways, and commuter rail, operated by the New York Metropolitan Transportation Authority; and buses, commuter rail, and light rail, run by New Jersey Transit. The Port Authority is a financially self-supporting public agency and relies almost entirely on revenues generated by facility users, tolls, fees, and rents. The Port Authority also operates its own police department, which is responsible for providing safety and deterring criminal activity at Port Authority-owned and -operated facilities.

Perhaps most interesting is the evolution of the Port Authority from managing port facilities to managing transportation systems and engaging in

---

870. The self-financing ability of the Port Authority was one factor in the U.S. Supreme Court determining that the Authority did not enjoy Eleventh Amendment immunity. *See* Hess v. Port Auth. Trans.-Hudson Corp., 513 U.S. 30 (1994).

promoting regional economic development. No other compact-created agency
has the scope of responsibilities. The Port Authority is the nation's largest
compact-created agency in terms of span of authority, number of employees,
and annual expenditures.

9.5.3   Bi-State Metropolitan Development District Compact
(Missouri and Illinois)

Created in 1949, the Bi-State Metropolitan Development District compact is an agreement between Missouri and Illinois to promote interstate cooperation in the future planning and development of the St. Louis metropolitan
area, including areas that lie in Illinois. The compact creates the Bi-State
Metropolitan Development District covering the city of St. Louis, three Missouri counties, and three Illinois counties that are considered to fall within
the St. Louis metropolitan area.[871] Additionally, the compact creates the Bi-
State Development Agency and vests it with the power to (1) construct, maintain, own, and operate bridges, tunnels, airports, and terminal facilities, and
to establish policies for sewerage and drainage facilities, and (2) make plans
for submission to the communities involved for the coordination of streets,
highways, parkways, parking areas, terminals, water supply, and sewerage
and waste disposal works, recreational and conservation facilities, and land
use patterns and other matters in which joint coordination of actions will
generally be beneficial.[872]

The Bi-State Development Agency (BSDA), which has changed its name
to "Metro," is primarily involved in the development, construction, and management of transportation systems. Its motto is "Regional Economic Development through Excellence in Transportation."[873] The agency entered the
transportation business in 1963 with the purchase of some 15 privately held
transportation companies and consolidation of those businesses into the "Metro"
transportation system. Today the agency oversees the area's mass transit systems along with the St. Louis Downtown Airport facility. It has also been
instrumental in promoting and constructing a 34-mile, bi-state light rail system in addition to maintaining a bus fleet of some 480 vehicles along 84
routes. Finally, the agency owns and operates the Gateway Arch Transportation System, a ticketing and reservation center, and Gateway Arch Riverboats.

---

871. Bi-State Metropolitan Development District Compact, art. II (1959).

872. *Id.* at art. III(1) & (2).

873. *See* Metro Mission Statement, *available at* http://www.metrostlouis.org/
     InsideMetro/history.asp.

The Bi-State Metropolitan Development District Compact provides that entry into force is accomplished not through legislative adoption but through a process of legislative delegation. The agreement specifically provides that within 60 days of legislative action, the governors of the states "shall appoint three commissioners" to enter into the compact on behalf of the member states.[874] Any two commissioners along with the state attorney general can execute the agreement on behalf of the member states. Thus, the Bi-State Metropolitan Development District Compact, although enacted by the respective state legislatures, only became effective through administrative action.

Like other regional compacts, the Bi-State Metropolitan Development District Compact is overseen by a commission, also known as the "Bi-State Development Agency of the Missouri-Illinois Metropolitan District." The commission is a corporate and political body of the member states. The commission is comprised of 10 members, five of whom are voting residents of Missouri and five of whom are voting residents of Illinois. All commissioners must reside in the district covered by the compact. Like many other multistate commissions, the flat structure of the BSDA and even state representation, creates tension because board members generally represent first the interests of their home state and second the interests of the region. Daily affairs of the BSDA are managed by an executive director. The BSDA is divided into four equal divisions: Operations, Administration and Finance, Engineering and Facilities Management, and Business Development. However, the BSDA lacks a strict traditional chain of command; there are instead different divisions with equal footing, with the ten commissioners, appointed largely on a political basis, at the top. The BSDA is generally considered a distributive policy agency; that is, it uses funds received from a variety of sources to provide the necessary public services of transit and project planning.

The compact empowers the BSDA to:

> [M]ake suitable rules and regulations not inconsistent with the constitution or laws of the United States or of either state, or of any political subdivision thereof, and subject to the exercise of the power of Congress, for the improvement of the District, which when concurred in or authorized by the legislatures of both states, shall be binding and effective upon all persons and corporations affected thereby.[875]

Both Missouri and Illinois are required to enforce any such rules by providing "penalties for violations of any order, rule or regulation of the Bi-

---

874. Bi-State Metropolitan Development District Compact, art. II (1959).
875. *Id.* at art. V.

state Agency, and for the manner of enforcing same."[876] The compact does not, however, establish any procedure for promulgating rules, a flaw similar to that of many other compacts historically.

By comparison to other multistate development commissions such as the Washington Metropolitan Area Transit Authority, the power of the BSDA is quite modest. Although the BSDA has the potential to have sweeping powers, it has lacked the political and regional support needed to propose and implement more aggressive development plans. Moreover, the BSDA does not have taxation powers, which means that the BSDA generally lacks robust self-financing capability and is subject to funds appropriated from transportation sales taxes in the City of St. Louis and St. Louis County. The BSDA also receives limited, though declining, federal funds and some revenue from user fees. The state of Missouri has limited the activities of the BSDA by refusing to commit to a long-term state funding strategy and the St. Louis city and county governments have held funds from the BSDA to ensure that local interests are given paramount consideration. Consequently, absent sufficient political, regional, and financial support, the BSDA cannot do everything that it theoretically has the power to do under its enabling compact.

An additional problem for the BSDA is that the power it possesses is dependent on political support divided between two states and many municipal, county, and parochial interests. As a result, the BSDA is not always able to build needed public support or obtain policy direction from key public officials. Operation of the regional transit system is now the focus of BSDA operations. As a result, the name "Bi-State Development Agency" has little meaning outside the realm of public transportation, and the agency does not advance broad development plans for the entire metropolitan region as was intended. Though arguably structured to be a powerful interstate development commission, on par with the Port Authority of New York–New Jersey or the Washington Metropolitan Area Transit Authority, local and state political interests and a poor independent funding base have limited its effectiveness and relegated the commission to the limited task of developing and running a mass transit system.

Finally, like many compact-created interstate commissions, the BSDA exists in somewhat of a legal limbo, being at once a creation of multilateral state action and a body politic of Missouri and Illinois. As such, the BSDA is subject to the laws of both states as to its operations in those states.[877] Perhaps

876. *Id.*
877. Alhough the BSDA is the creation of a congressionally approved compact, that does not necessarily mean that it is also subject to federal law governing administrative agencies.

because the BSDA is headquartered in St. Louis, the law of Missouri tends to have more controlling interest and the state of Missouri appears to take a greater interest in the operations of the BSDA. The BSDA is considered a Missouri state governmental body for purposes of Missouri's Sunshine Law.[878]

9.5.4   Washington Metropolitan Area Transportation Compacts

The Washington, D.C. metropolitan area's transportation needs are governed by interstate compacts that attempt to coordinate transit needs across the region.[879] A discussion of the breadth and complexity of the transporta-

---

878. 2004 S.B. 1020 (2004).
879. As discussed further, it is important to note that the Washington Area Transportation Compacts can be a source of some confusion, given the manner in which they were constructed. Although the Metropolitan Washington Airports Authority is clearly a separate agreement, there remains some difference of opinion on whether the surface transportation needs of the area are served by one or two compacts. From a purely technical point of view, it can be argued that a single compact of multiple titles manages surface transportation needs: the Washington Metropolitan Area Transit Regulation Compact of 1960 creating the Washington Metropolitan Area Transit Commission (WMATC), which was amended in 1966 by adding Title III, creating the Washington Metropolitan Area Transit Authority (WMATA). However, from a practical perspective, it can also be argued that the area is served by the Washington Metropolitan Area Transit Regulation Compact and the Washington Metropolitan Area Transit Authority Compact. It is not entirely clear why the creation of WMATA was by amendment to the Washington Metropolitan Area Transit Regulation Compact and not by a separate compact. WMATA's creation may have been conceived at the same time as WMATC's creation and, thus, as part of the same plan. Perhaps it seemed to the framers of the agreement that pushing an amendment to an existing compact through three state legislatures and Congress would be easier than getting agreement on an entirely separate compact.
   In any event, there is only the one compact, but it has become accepted to refer to Title III of the Compact as the "WMATA Compact." The Maryland Code references the "Text of Washington Metropolitan Area Transit Authority Compact." MD. CODE ANN. TRANSP. § 10-204 (2004). The District of Columbia Code uses essentially the same title. *See* D.C. CODE §§ 9-1107.01 & 9-1107.08 (2004). *But see* D.C. CODE § 9-1107.06 (2004) ("The Congress hereby consents to, and adopts and enacts for the District of Columbia, amendments to Articles I and XVI of Title III of the Washington Metropolitan Area Transit Regulation Compact as set out in § 9-1107.01[.]"). For purposes of

tion compacts and the authority of the agencies created by these compacts could produce a small book on compact law. Yet, no discussion on interstate compacts would be complete without, at the very least, a high-level discussion of these agreements regarding their creation and how they continue to serve the transportation needs of the Washington, D.C. region. While the Bi-state Development Compact between Missouri and Illinois may serve as an example of the weaknesses of the compact instrument and the fact that all compact-created agencies lie to some extent at the mercy of state and local politics, the Washington, D.C. metropolitan transportation compacts serve as example, of the success of such instruments. Perhaps with the exception of the New York–New Jersey Port Authority Compact and the Tahoe Regional Planning Compact (if only for its regulatory breadth), few agreements have reached the scale and provided services to such a broad regional area as the Washington, D.C. transportation compacts.[880]

Depending on one's viewpoint, two or three transportation compacts are currently in effect: (1) the Washington Metropolitan Area Transportation Compact;[881] (2) the Washington Metropolitan Area Transit Authority (WMATA) amendment;[882] and (3) the Metropolitan Washington Airports Authority agreement.[883] Each of these agreements creates an independent authority to oversee an assigned aspect of the region's transportation systems. In the case of the Washington Metropolitan Area Transit Commission (WMATC), it is the regulation of interstate private passenger carriers, such as taxis and tour bus companies. In the case of the WMATA, it is the design, construction, management, and operation of public mass transit systems, including bus and rapid rail transportation systems.[884] And in the case of the Metropolitan Washington

---

this discussion, however, the authors will refer singularly to the Washington Metropolitan Area Transit Regulation Compact, recognizing that Titles I and II govern the WMATC and Title III refers to the WMATA, two distinct and independent bodies with differing missions.

880. For example, the Washington Metropolitan Area Transit Authority is arguably the second largest compact entity in the nation, surpassed only by the New York–New Jersey Port Authority in terms of budget, personnel, and citizens directly served by the agency. *See* WMATA Facts, *available at* http://wmata.com/about/metrofacts.pdf.

881. Washington Metropolitan Area Transit Regulation Compact, tit. I (1960).

882. *Id.* at tit. III.

883. 49 U.S.C. § 49106 (2004).

884. It is important to note that although the WMATA has regulatory authority, its primary mission is to operation the "Metro." Its regulatory authority is narrowly circumscribed to this purpose and covers such matters as advertising, design and construction, and use of facilities and services.

Airports Authority, it is the management and operation of public airports in the region, primarily Reagan National Airport and Dulles International Airport.[885] Congressional consent was required for each of these agreements.[886]

In response to growing urbanization and resulting transportation problems after World War II, Congress appropriated funds in 1955 and 1956 to study transit problems in the Washington, D.C. metropolitan area, which included the District of Columbia, northern Virginia and areas of Maryland adjacent to the District. As a result of the study, Congress passed the National Capital Transportation Act of 1960 authorizing the District of Columbia to negotiate an interstate mass transit compact with Virginia and Maryland.[887] A major purpose of the compact was to alleviate growing traffic congestion caused by growth in the metropolitan area and the steady rise of private automobiles as the major means of transportation in the area.[888] Out of this process grew an interstate compact that has formed the backbone of surface transportation and economic development in the Washington metropolitan area.

The history of the Washington area transportation compacts provides insight into the evolution of the region's transportation needs and the government's response to managing those needs. The first agreement, the Washington Metropolitan Area Transit Regulation Compact, consists of Titles I and II and created the Washington Metropolitan Area Transit District (Metropolitan District) and the WMATC.[889] An amendment in 1962 clarified the commission's jurisdiction and added the Washington-Dulles International Air-

---

885. Like the WMATA, the MWAA has a regulatory function designed to assist in managing the covered airports. Regulations issued by the MWAA cover such areas as regulatory and personal conduct on airport property.

886. *See, e.g.,* D.C. CODE § 9-1107.01 (2004) (Congress consents to amendments to the Washington Metropolitan Area Transit Regulation Compact by adding Title III and creating the Washington Metropolitan Area Transit Authority); D.C. CODE § 9-1002(a) (2004) (Congress authorizes the transfer of operating responsibility to properly constituted independent airport authority created by Virginia and the District of Columbia).

887. National Capital Transportation Act of 1960, tit. III, § 301, 40 U.S.C. § 671 (repealed).

888. Alexandria, Barcroft & Washington Transit Co. v. Wash. Metro. Area Transit Comm'n, 323 F.2d 777 (4th Cir. 1963).

889. Pub. L. No. 86-794, § 1, 74 Stat. 1031 (1960). The Washington Metropolitan Area Transit Regulation Compact has been amended several times. *See* Pub. L. No. 87-767, 76 Stat. 73 (1962), *amended by* Pub. L. No. 89-774, 80 Stat. 1324 (1966), *amended by* Pub. L. No. 94-306, 90 Stat. 672 (1976), *amended by* Pub. L. No. 100-285, 102 Stat. 82 (1988), *amended by* Pub. L. No. 101-505,

port to the definition of the Metropolitan District.[890] The commission was originally charged with regulating private commercial transportation companies in the Metropolitan District by exercising "jurisdiction coextensive with the Metropolitan District for the regulation and improvement of transit and the alleviation of traffic congestion within the Metropolitan District on a coordinated basis, without regard to political boundaries[.]"[891]

The initial purpose of the WMATC was to license and regulate four private mass transit companies (the largest and best known being D.C. Transit) on a regional basis and to aid in highway planning and traffic management. The regulation of private transportation companies was accomplished through a process by which the WMATC would issue "certificates of public convenience and necessity" as a precursor to private entry into the transportation market. However, although the initial and primary purpose of the WMATC was to regulate privately held mass transit companies, the authority of the WMATC actually extended to other private sector carriers including tour bus companies, charter operators, and interstate taxi services. The WMATC is created and authorized by Title I and Title II of the Washington Metropolitan Area Transit Regulation Compact.

Titles I and II were amended in their entirety in 1990[892] for the purpose of "lowering barriers to market entry . . . while maintaining a regional approach to transportation and keeping those controls necessary for the security of the public."[893] This was accomplished by eliminating the need for a showing of public convenience and necessity and replacing this approach with a

---

104 Stat. 1300 (1990), *amended by* Pub. L. No. 104-322, 110 Stat. 3884 (1996), *amended by* Pub. L. No. 105-151, 111 Stat. 2686 (1997).

890. Pub. L. No. 87-767, 76 Stat. 764 (1962).

891. Washington Metropolitan Area Transit Regulation Compact, tit. I, art. II, 74 Stat. 1032 (1960). It should be noted that, among the three agencies, only the Washington Metropolitan Area Transit Commission can be described as a classic regulatory body. The Washington Metropolitan Area Transit Authority and the Metropolitan Washington Airports Authority are more aptly described as administrative or operational agencies with some regulatory authority. They are not, however, purely regulatory bodies.

892. Pub. L. No. 101-505, § 1, 104 Stat. 1300 (1990).

893. Old Town Trolley Tours v. Wash. Metro. Area Transit Comm'n, 129 F.3d 201, 203 (D.C. Cir. 1997) (citing *Granting the Consent of Congress to Amendments to the Washington Metropolitan Area Transit Regulation Compact: Hearing on H.J. Res. 520 Before the Subcomm. on Admin. Law and Governmental Relations of the House Comm. on the Judiciary,* 101st Cong. 35 (1990) (statement of Carlton R. Sickles, Chairman, WMATRC Review Committee)).

requirement that a carrier obtain a "certificate of authority."[894] To qualify for a certificate of authority the WMATC must find that the applicant is fit, willing, and able to provide transportation services in compliance with the regulations of the commission and that the proposed entry into the market is consistent with the public interest. The WMATC has some discretion in granting certificates of authority, and a decision to issue such a certificate will not be disturbed absent a clear error of judgment.[895]

The second agreement came in 1966 with the amendment of the Washington Metropolitan Area Transit Regulation Compact and the addition of Title III to the agreement.[896] This amendment, known as the Washington Metropolitan Area Transit Authority Compact, created the WMATA, and established a "transit zone" encompassing all of the District of Columbia, and parts of northern Virginia and Maryland.[897] The "transit zone" created by the 1966 agreement is independent of the "transit district" originally created by the 1960 compact. The purpose of the Washington Metropolitan Area Transit Authority Compact is "to create a regional instrumentality, as a common agency of each signatory party" to fulfill three objects: (1) to plan, develop, finance, and operate improved transit facilities; (2) to coordinate the operations of public and private transit facilities into a unified regional transit system; and (3) to serve such other regional purposes as the signatories deem appropriate.[898]

The WMATA was the successor organization to the National Capital Transportation Agency (NCTA) created in 1960 to develop a rapid rail system.[899] Where the WMATC was charged with regulating private commercial mass transit carriers, the WMATA was charged with designing, building, and overseeing a public mass transportation system. It is impor-

---

The amendment also eliminated the Commission's highway planning and traffic management functions.

894. Washington Metropolitan Area Transit Regulation Compact, tit. II, art. XI, § 7, 104 Stat. 1306 (1990).

895. Old Town Trolley Tours v. Wash. Metro. Area Transit Comm'n, 129 F.3d 201, 206 (D.C. Cir. 1997).

896. *See* Pub. L. No. 89-774, 80 Stat. 1324 (1966).

897. *See* Democratic Cent. Comm. v. Wash. Metro. Area Transit Comm'n, 84 F.3d 451 (D.C. Cir. 1996).

898. Pub. L. No. 89-774, 80 Stat. 1324 (1966).

899. Washington Metropolitan Area Transit Authority, Metrorail Specification Collection Papers Finding Aid, *available at* http://www.gwu.edu/gelman/spec/collections/manuscript/metrorail.html#bio.

tant to understand that although the WMATC and the WMATA are arguably creations of a single compact, they create two separate and distinct interstate bodies, each having different authority over different aspects of the Washington, D.C. metropolitan area transportation system. Although the WMATA was originally forbidden to operate a bus system, it was given the power in 1972 to acquire, through negotiation or condemnation, four private bus companies.[900] The WMATA now operates some 900 rails cars over 106 miles of track and a bus fleet of almost 1,500 vehicles.[901] Most people today recognize the WMATA not by its legal designation but by its popular name, "Metro." The WMATA has evolved into the second largest compact-created administrative agency in the nation, with an annual budget now exceeding $1.29 billion and employing more than 10,000 people.[902] Some 336 million passengers travel on the Metro annually.[903]

With the acquisition of private carriers by WMATA in 1973, the mission of WMATC changed. The focus of the WMATC became exclusively regulating private transportation providers within its district, while the WMATA became the prime provider of public mass transit systems in the metropolitan area. Today the WMATC is focused on regulating non–mass transit providers such as tour bus operators, airport shuttle services, charter bus owners, individual ticketed sightseers, and limousines.[904] The WMATC also regulates taxicab operators by setting interstate rates and insurance requirements. The WMATC has no regulatory authority over the WMATA or its operations.[905] Fares, regulations, and practices of transportation companies and interstate taxicabs in the Washington Metropolitan Area Transit District are generally set by the commission. Anyone interested in providing private for-hire transportation in the district must obtain from the commission a certificate of authority. Applicants must provide the WMATC with proof of insurance, the

900. National Capital Area Transit Act of 1972, Pub. L. No. 92-517, 86 Stat. 999 (1972).
901. *See* Washington Metropolitan Area Transit Authority, WMATA Facts, *available at* http://wmata.com/about/metrofacts.pdf.
902. *See* Washington Metropolitan Area Transit Authority, Approve Fiscal 2005 Annual Budget, *available at* http://wmata.com/about/board_gm/FY2005_Budget_Book.pdf.
903. Washington Metropolitan Area Transit Authority, WMATA Facts, *available at* http://wmata.com/about/metrofacts.pdf.
904. For rules and regulations issued by the WMATC, *see* Washington Metropolitan Area Transit Commission, Rules of Practice and Procedures and Regulations (1991), *available at* http://www.wmatc.gov/.

proposed rate schedule, a list of vehicles, and proof of safety inspections. No applicant is permitted to operate within the transit district before obtaining a certificate of authority. The commission takes legal action against any party operating without a certificate.

The final transportation agreement concerns the operation of Washington-Dulles International Airport and Washington National (later changed to Ronald Reagan Washington National) Airport. These were the only two air carrier airports operated exclusively by the federal government under the auspices of the Federal Aviation Administration. In 1984 The U.S. Secretary of Transportation appointed an advisory commission to develop a proposal for transferring the airports to a state, local, or interstate public entity. The District of Columbia and the Commonwealth of Virginia responded to the advisory commission's recommendation by enacting the District of Columbia Regional Airports Authority Act of 1985 and Chapter 598 of the 1985 Virginia Acts of Assembly, which together created the Metropolitan Washington Airports Authority (MWAA). Congress approved the compact and transfer pursuant to the Metropolitan Washington Airports Act of 1986.[906] On June 7, 1987, Dulles International Airport and Reagan National Airport were leased to the MWAA for 50 years.[907] In 2003, the term of the lease was extended to 2067, and it was further amended to grant the federal government a reversionary interest in all real property acquired by the MWAA after

---

905. Washington Metropolitan Area Transit Regulation Compact, tit. III, art. XIII, § 60 (1966).

906. Metropolitan Washington Airports Act of 1986, Pub. L. No. 99-55, 100 Stat. 1783-373, Pub. L. No. 99-591, 100 Stat. 3341-376 (1986). Uniquely, the act conditioned transferring control of the airports upon the appointment of a nine-member congressional advisory board with authority to veto development plans, a requirement that was subsequently held unconstitutional under the separation of powers doctrine. Metro. Wash. Airports Auth. v. Citizens for the Abatement of Aircraft Noise, 501 U.S. 252 (1991) (Congress imposed its will on the MWAA by creation of a board consisting of nine members of Congress and allowed that board to arguably exercise executive power in violation of separation of powers.). Congress also provided that the Baltimore-Washington International Airport could be transferred to the MWAA subject to terms and conditions agreed to by the Airports Authority, the Secretary, the Commonwealth of Virginia, the District of Columbia, and the state of Maryland. *See* Pub. L. 99-591, § 6003, 100 Stat. 3341-376 (Oct. 30, 1986). No such transfer has occurred.

907. 49 U.S.C. § 49104 (2004).

the start of the lease.[908]

The MWAA is responsible for operating, maintaining, developing, promoting, and protecting the two airports.[909] The MWAA may issue bonds,[910] acquire property by eminent domain,[911] and adopt regulations with the full force and effect of law that preempts inconsistent local legislation.[912] The MWAA may also establish, operate, and maintain a foreign trade zone, and otherwise expedite and encourage foreign commerce, a unique feature of its compact.[913] The organization consists of more than 1,000 employees in a structure that includes central administration, airports management, and operations and police and fire departments.

The WMATC, WMATA, and MWAA share several similar characteristics and offer important insights into the use of interstate compacts to address the region's broad transportation needs. First, each is managed by an interstate body having representatives from the jurisdictions that are parties to the compact. The WMATC is overseen by a commission consisting of three members, one named by the governor of Maryland from the Maryland Public Service Commission, one named by the governor of Virginia from the Virginia State Corporation Commission, and one chosen by the mayor of the District of Columbia from the District Public Service Commission.[914] Each member's term coincides with the term of office in the agency from which the member is selected. Commission expenses are allocated annually in proportion to the population of each signatory in the Metropolitan District. The WMATA is managed by a board of directors consisting of representatives from each signatory. The WMATA board consists of two levels of directors: (1) six principal directors, consisting of two representatives from each member jurisdiction, and (2) six alternate directors, likewise consisting of two representatives from each member jurisdiction. Each director serves a term

---

908. 49 U.S.C. § 49104(d) (2004) specifically gives the Secretary of Transportation and the MWAA authority to renegotiate the terms and conditions of the lease at any time.

909. Va. Code Ann. § 5.1-156 (2004).

910. Va. Code Ann. § 5.1-161 (2004).

911. Va. Code Ann. § 5.1-160 (2004).

912. Va. Code Ann. § 5.1-157 (2004).

913. D.C. Code § 9-908 (2004).

914. Washington Metropolitan Area Transit Regulation Compact, tit. I, art. III, § 1(a) (1986).

coincident with his or her term on the body by which they were appointed.[915] The MWAA is governed by a 13-member board, with five members appointed by the governor of Virginia, three by the mayor of the District of Columbia, two by the governor of Maryland, and three by the President of the United States, even though neither Maryland nor the United States are members of the compact.[916]

Second, each compact-created body is a "public body corporate and politic," having the powers and jurisdiction conferred upon it by the member states and the District of Columbia, including the authority to promulgate rules. The MWAA, for example, is empowered to adopt rules and regulations that have the force and effect of law governing the use, maintenance, and operation of its facilities and the conduct of persons and organizations using its facilities.[917] Violations of such regulations are a Class 1 misdemeanor (unless the MWAA sets a lower penalty), are prosecuted by the Commonwealth's attorney, and tried in the Virginia courts of the jurisdiction in which the offense took place.[918] The MWAA has promulgated an extensive system of regulations covering employment practices and collective bargaining procedures, aircraft operations, traffic rules, and motor vehicle control in restricted areas, permits at Reagan National, demonstrations and other First Amendment activities, commercial activity, and security.[919]

The fact that each agency is allowed to promulgate rules under a compact that received congressional consent does not mean they are per se subject to federal rulemaking requirements or federal administrative procedures. While interpreting compacts may present federal questions, it does not follow that management authorities constitute federal agencies governed by the Admin-

---

915. *Id.* at tit. III, art. III, § 5(a) (1966).

916. *See* D.C. CODE ANN. § 9-904(a) (2004).

917. D.C. CODE ANN. § 9-906(a) (2004).

918. *See* Loudoun County v. Murphy, 24 Va. Cir. 337 (Va. Cir. Ct. 1991) (where defendant was ticketed for a state vehicular offense at an airport, the fact that the United States owned the airport did not preclude state officials from prosecuting defendant because the state had concurrent jurisdiction over the airport).

919. *See generally* Metropolitan Washington Airports Authority Regulations (2001), *available at* http://www.metwashairports.com/authority/publications/PDFregs.pdf. *See also* Virginia v. Achu, 54 Va. Cir. 109 (Va. Cir. Ct. 2000) (MWAA was a properly constituted compact agency, and its regulations regarding the unlawful solicitation of passengers were constitutional and enforceable).

istrative Procedure Act.[920] The procedures governing the regulatory process
and judicial review of that process are defined by the terms and conditions of
the compact, not by federal administrative or regulatory law.[921] However,
where the compacts creating an authority are silent on the appropriate
rulemaking standard, the courts have generally applied the "arbitrary and
capricious" standard of review.[922] In regard to bidding procedures, for example, a disappointed bidder bears the burden of establishing that a decision
by a government agency either had no rational basis or involved a clear and
prejudicial violation of applicable statutes or regulations. Thus, a bidder is
required to demonstrate prejudice attributable to either (1) the procurement
procedure's violation of applicable statutes or regulations, or (2) an arbitrary
or irrational decision of the procurement official on matters primarily committed to his discretion.[923]

Third, two of the Washington transportation compacts allow for the creation of limited, multijurisdictional police forces. The MWAA may establish
a regular police force and confer the powers to be exercised with respect to
offenses occurring on its facilities or within 300 yards of such facilities,
subject to its employees meeting the minimal requirements of Virginia's Department of Criminal Justice Services.[924] Similarly, the WMATA is authorized to establish and maintain a multistate police force charged with enforcing
the laws, ordinances, and regulations of the member states and their political
subdivisions in the transit zone, and the rules and regulations of the WMATA.[925]
The Metro Transit Police have concurrent jurisdiction with the law enforcement agencies of the signatories wherever a transit facility is located or where

---

920. *See, e.g.,* Old Town Trolley Tours v. Wash. Metro. Area Transit Comm'n, 129 F.3d 201, 204 (D.C. Cir. 1997).
921. *Id.* at 204.
922. *Id.*
923. Washington-Dulles Transp., Ltd. v. Metro. Wash. Airports Auth., 87 Fed. Appx. 843 (4th Cir. 2004), *cert. denied,* 125 S. Ct. 50 (Oct. 4, 2004).
924. D.C. Code Ann. § 9-907 (a) (2004). *See* Sanders v. Virginia, 1994 Va. App. LEXIS 505 (Va. Ct. App. 1994) (1987 Va. Acts 665, § 7(B) limits MWAA police power to offenses occurring on the Authority facilities or within 300 yards of the facilities; conviction for driving under the influence of alcohol must be dismissed where commonwealth failed to establish that arrest oc-curred within jurisdiction of police.).
925. Washington Metropolitan Area Transit Regulation Compact, tit. III, art. XVI, § 76 (1966).

the WMATA operates a transit service.[926] On-duty Metro Transit Police officers are authorized to make arrests outside of transit facilities but within the transit zone when immediate action is necessary to protect the health, safety, welfare, or property of an individual from actual or threatened harm or from an unlawful act.[927] In the case of MWAA, Virginia state police and local law enforcement agencies have concurrent jurisdiction with the MWAA police on MWAA property.[928] Like other police officers in Virginia, the MWAA police may pursue someone fleeing arrest in the MWAA's jurisdiction and arrest the offender elsewhere in the state.[929] Under both the MWAA and the WMATA compacts, persons arrested by the police are subject to the jurisdiction of the court in the locality where the apprehension occurred.[930] The WMATA police force is the only tri-jurisdictional police agency in the nation.

Financing compact-created interstate agencies has always proven a difficult challenge, generally the result of the lack of independent taxing power or the very nature of public transit systems that require subsidies to meet both operations needs and expansion. Each of the authorities in the Washington region has its own funding approach. Thus, while the WMATC, the WMATA, and the MWAA share similar characteristics in structure and powers, their financing differs. The WMATC is generally financed through a cost allocation procedure in the agreement that calls upon the signatories to cover the costs of the commission's operations. By contrast, the MWAA is largely self-funded relying on its authority to issue debt for major improvements and charge fees for services, chiefly landing fees and concession sales, for operations. Capital

---

926. *See* Saidi v. Wash. Metro. Area Transit Auth., 928 F. Supp. 21 (D. D.C. 1996) (transit police have the same powers, including the powers of arrest and limitations, as the D.C. Metropolitan Police). *But see* United States v. Foster, 566 F. Supp. 1403 (D. D.C. 1983) (Investigative detention of defendant by uniformed, armed Metro transit police officer who accused defendant of driving without a permit, and retained defendant's license and registration pending arrival of D.C. police officers, was patently beyond officer's statutory authority where there was no indication that defendant was involved in criminal activity on or near any subway stations or bus stops; officer's conduct violated defendant's Fourth Amendment rights, and defendant's abandonment of the shotgun which resulted from that conduct was tainted with illegality.).

927. Washington Metropolitan Area Transit Regulation Compact, tit. III, art. XVI, § 76 (1960).

928. *See* VA. CODE ANN. § 5.1-158 (2004).

929. VA. CODE ANN. § 5.1-158 and § 19.2-77 (2004).

930. *Id. See also* VA. CODE ANN. § 5.1-158(B) (2004).

developments are financed though the sale of bonds issued by the MWAA and
to a lesser extent by Federal and State Airport Improvement Program funds,
and Passenger Facility Charges.[931] No general taxpayer fund underwrites the
operations of capital improvement projects of the MWAA. Funding the WMATA
is much more complicated. The WMATA relies upon a combination of fare
box revenue, debt issuance, fees, federal funding, contributions from the signatories (based on the number of riders from each jurisdiction) and the federal
government, and temporary borrowing.[932] The rail operating subsidy allocates
the costs of the WMATA through a formula that takes into account population
density, average weekly ridership by jurisdiction of residence, and the number
of rail stations by jurisdiction.[933] The WMATA budget consists of two portions:
operations and capital improvements.

There are other significant differences between the agencies. In general,
the WMATC is a small and purely regulatory agency whose authority is limited to a very specific purpose—regulating the fares of private transportation
providers in the Washington, D.C. metropolitan area. The MWAA and the
WMATA have significantly broader responsibilities embracing not only "regu-
lation" but equally importantly operational management and development.
As a result, the compact creating the MWAA and the amendments to the
Washington Metropolitan Area Transit Regulation Compact that created the
WMATA reflect the distinction between the purely regulatory nature of the
WMATC and the broader responsibilities of the MWAA and the WMATA.
The scope of their power and the reach of their authority are far more exten-
sive than traditional notions of "regulatory" agencies.

The Washington metropolitan transportation compacts offer important insights into the interaction between compacts, the breadth and limits of the
compact-created regulatory process, and the authority of compact-created entities. These agreements and the accompanying case law reinforce a most critical
principle of compact law: the authority enjoyed by a compact-created agency is
defined by the explicit terms of the agreement.[934] Thus, for example, by the

---

931. Metropolitan Washington Airports Authority, History and Facts, *available
at* http://www.metwashairports.com.

932. *See generally* Washington Metropolitan Area Transit Regulation Compact,
tit. III, arts. VII, VIII & IX. (1960).

933. *See* WMATA Subsidy Allocation Methodology, *available at* http://
wmata.com/about/metro_matters/subsidy_allocation.pdf.

934. *See, e.g.,* Keenan v. Housing Comm'n, 643 F. Supp. 324 (D. D.C. 1986) (Section 80 of the Washington Metropolitan Area Transit Authority (WMATA)
Compact states explicitly that WMATA shall not be liable for any torts occur-

terms of the Washington Metropolitan Area Transit Regulation Compact, the WMATA is excluded from the regulatory authority of the WMATC notwithstanding the overlapping geographic jurisdiction of the two authorities.[935] Likewise, the District of Columbia's taxi commission's licensing power over limousine franchises, vehicles, and operators was not expressly or impliedly preempted by either the Washington Metropolitan Area Transit Regulation Compact or the WMATC's regulations.[936] Although each of the authorities possesses rulemaking power within the realm of its assigned responsibilities, that power is not unlimited. The WMATC, for example, cannot regulate transit providers operating in the nation's Mall because, when Congress established the commission, it did not intend to create dual regulatory jurisdiction by divesting the Secretary of the Interior of long-standing exclusive charge and control over the Mall.[937] By contrast, the MWAA may promulgate rules that "have the force and effect of law," in effect a code of ordinances that is punishable under Virginia law as a misdemeanor.

Though successful, the use of interstate compacts to manage the transportation needs of the Washington, D.C. metropolitan area has not been without controversy. These compacts have produced significant litigation concerning the status of compact-created commissions and the regulatory authority of their agencies. Provisions in these compacts have been used to define employment practices,[938] establish regulatory powers not otherwise

---

ring in the performance of a governmental function.); Teart v. Wash. Metro. Area Transit Auth., 686 F. Supp. 12 (D. D.C. 1988).

935. Washington Metropolitan Area Transit Regulation Compact, tit. I, art. XI(3)(c) (1960). *See also* D.C. CODE ANN. § 9-1103.01 (2004).

936. Boston Coach-Wash. Corp. v. Dist. of Columbia Taxicab Comm'n, 930 F. Supp. 649 (D. D.C. 1996).

937. Universal Interpretive Shuttle Corp. v. Wash. Metro. Area Transit Comm'n, 393 U.S. 186 (1968) (Secretary of Interior has exclusive authority over National Mall, and WMATC cannot impose its own regulatory scheme on the same matter.).

938. *See, e.g.,* Washington Metropolitan Area Transit Regulation Compact, tit. III, art. XIV (1966). *See also* Metro. Wash. Airports Auth. Prof'l Firefighters Local 3217 v. Metro. Wash. Airports Auth., 159 F.3d 630, 633 (D.C. Cir. 1998) (federal court lacked jurisdiction over employment matters because in creating the MWAA, Congress expressly transferred management and operations of the airports—including employment—from federal government to the Authority); Metro. Wash. Airports Auth. Prof'l Firefighters Ass'n Local 3217 v. United States, 959 F.2d 297 (D.C. Cir. 1992) (federal employees transferred to MWAA have no greater rights than previously enjoyed); McKenna v. Wash.

enjoyed by the signatories,[939] determine the geographical boundaries of the authority,[940] define jurisdiction,[941] and create political entities that exist outside traditional notions of state and federal oversight.[942] The compacts have presented fundamental questions of the liability compact-created agencies face and the immunity they enjoy.[943] Jurisdictional controversies continue to

---

Metro. Area Transit Auth., 670 F. Supp. 7 (D. D.C. 1986), *aff'd*, 829 F.2d 186 (D.C. Cir. 1987) (WMATA not liable in damages for the work-related death of employees under the Federal Employers' Liability Act (FELA) where language of D.C. Code Ann. § 9-1107.01 clearly provided an exclusive remedy for the work-related death of an employee under signatory law and expressly precluded coverage for the same injury under any other federal statute); Office & Prof'l Employees Int'l Union, Local 2 v. Housing Comm'n, 569 F. Supp. 797 (D. D.C. 1983) (court lacked jurisdiction to hear dispute between labor union and the WMATA where claims were not first raised before arbitration board under § 66 (c) of the compact).

939. *See, e.g.*, One Parcel of Land v. Wash. Metro. Area Transit Auth., 706 F.2d 1312 (4th Cir. 1983) (Under the compact, proceedings instituted by WMATA to condemn property are controlled by federal law, not state law; WMATA has authority to exercise "quick-take" condemnation notwithstanding provision in Maryland's constitution barring such action.).

940. *See, e.g.*, Washington Metropolitan Area Transit Regulation Compact, tit. III, art. XVI, § 83 (1966) (when advised that geographical areas embraced by compact have enlarged, board of WMATA shall enlarge the transit zone also).

941. *See, e.g.*, Metropolitan Washington Airports Authority Compact (1986) (courts of Virginia have original jurisdiction over all actions brought by or against MWAA); Washington Metropolitan Area Transit Regulation Compact, tit. III, art. XVI, § 81 (1966) (federal district courts have concurrent jurisdiction with courts of Maryland, Virginia, and District of Columbia over all actions brought by or against the WMATA). *See also* Qasim v. Housing Comm'n, 455 A.2d 904 (D.C. 1983) (Section 81 of the WMATA Compact eliminated the $10,000 jurisdictional threshold for actions involving WMATA.).

942. *See, e.g.*, D.C. CODE ANN. § 9-1006(b) (2004) (Airports Authority shall be independent of Virginia and its local governments, the District of Columbia, and the federal government). *But see* Colbert v. United States, 601 A.2d 603 (D.C. 1992) (Agencies created by compacts approved by Congress are not necessarily federal agencies and can be agencies of each of the signatory parties; thus, the WMATA is a District of Columbia agency for the purposes of the bribery statute.).

943. See Chapter 7 for a general discussion of Eleventh Amendment immunity for compact-created agencies. As to liability and immunity considerations for

exist concerning the extent to which state law applies to these agencies.[944] Some have even contended that the current compact agencies are not meeting all of the region's transportation needs and that a new approach is needed to manage the long-range transportation requirements of the area.[945] Although the Washington region might be better served by a single transportation authority exercising the powers of the current three regional authorities, the existing structure has clearly served the region well and provides a model for other forms of compact-created regional governance.

WMATA, *see, e.g.,* Abdulwali v. Wash. Metro. Area Transit Auth., 315 F.3d 302 (D.C. Cir. 2003) (compact did not prescribe design specifications for metro cars; agency made discretionary choices when it established plans, specifications, or schedules regarding the metro system that fell within the scope of a discretionary function, and thus sovereign immunity barred plaintiff's claims); Beebe v. Wash. Metro. Area Transit Auth., 129 F.3d 1283 (D.C. Cir. 1997) (WMATA immune from tort claims where all the challenged actions involved a large measure of discretion by those appointed to oversee reorganization of a department within the transit authority); Diven v. Amalgamated Transit Union Int'l & Local 689, 38 F.3d 598 (D.C. Cir. 1994) (WMATA is a political subdivision of the party states; presence of District of Columbia does not alter the nature of WMATA as a political subdivision, and thus WMATA did not constitute an employer, nor did its employees belong to a labor organization within meaning of federal Labor Management Reporting and Disclosure Act). *But see* E. 56th St. Corp. v. Mobil Oil Corp., 906 F. Supp. 669 (D. D.C. 1995) (WMATA not immune from claims arising out of the maintenance of property, since such activity was proprietary, not governmental); Wash. Metro. Area Transit Auth. v. O'Neill, 633 A.2d 834 (D.C. 1993) (sovereign immunity did not bar suit by bus passenger to recover for injuries incurred in beating by other passengers where suit was premised on the negligence of the driver in carrying out express safety directives).

944. *See, e.g.,* Letter from Marie J.K. Everett, Executive Director, Virginia Freedom of Information Advisory Council, to Mike Stollenwerk (Jan. 6, 2004) (pursuant to the terms of the compact, the MWAA is subject to Virginia law, including Virginia's Freedom of Information Act, notwithstanding its status as an independent political entity). *But see* Lucero-Nelson v. Wash. Metro. Area Transit Auth., 1 F. Supp. 2d 1 (D. D.C. 1998) (WMATA is not subject to District of Columbia Human Rights Act, since the Authority is an interstate compact agency and an instrumentality of three separate jurisdictions).

945. *See generally* Metropolitan Washington Regional Transportation Act, H.R. 2882, 108th Cong. (2003).

9.6   TAX COMPACTS GENERALLY

This section discusses the Multistate Tax Compact.

9.6.1   Multistate Tax Compact

The Multistate Tax Compact was drafted in 1966 and became effective, according to its own terms, on August 4, 1967, after seven states had adopted it. Congressional consent has been sought, but never obtained.[946] The compact was formed in the aftermath of the Supreme Court's 1959 decision in *Northwestern States Portland Cement Co. v. Minnesota* allowing for state taxation of interstate commerce and entities.[947] The Supreme Court held that states could tax interstate commerce and its proceeds, if the entity subject to the tax had some "nexus" to the taxing jurisdiction, and the tax was "fairly apportioned."[948] The purpose of the compact is, therefore, to: (1) facilitate proper determination of state and local tax liability of multistate taxpayers, including the equitable apportionment of tax bases and settlement of apportionment disputes; (2) promote uniformity or compatibility in significant components of tax systems; (3) facilitate taxpayer convenience and compliance in the filing of tax returns and in other phases of tax administration; and (4) avoid duplicative taxation.[949] The existence of the Multistate Tax Compact and participation in that compact does not, however, relieve states of the obligation to ensure that their tax systems are fair. The Supreme Court has pointed out numerous times that in structuring internal taxation schemes, "states have large leeway in making classifications and drawing lines which in their judgment produce reasonable systems of taxation."[950]

The compact is overseen by the Multistate Tax Commission, which is composed of the tax administrators from all the member states.[951] The commission is charged with studying state and local tax systems, developing and

---

946. See S. 3892, 89th Cong. (1966); S. 883, 90th Cong. (1967); S. 1551, 90th Cong. (1967); H.R. 9476, 90th Cong. (1967); H.R. 13682, 90th Cong. (1967); S. 1198, 91st Cong. (1969); H.R. 6246, 91st Cong. (1969); H.R. 9873, 91st Cong. (1969); S. 1883, 92d Cong. (1971); H.R. 6160, 92d Cong. (1971); S. 3333, 92d Cong. (1972); S. 2092, 93d Cong. (1973).
947. Northwestern States Portland Cement Co. v. Minnesota, 358 U.S. 450 (1959).
948. See Michael S. Greve, *Compact, Cartels and Congressional Consent,* 68 Mo. L. Rev. 285 (2003).
949. See generally Multistate Tax Compact, art. I (1967).
950. Lehnhausen v. Lake Shore Auto Parts Co., 410 U.S. 356, 359 (1973).
951. Multistate Tax Compact, art. VI, § 1(a) (1967).

recommending proposals for an increase in uniformity and compatibility of state and local tax laws in order to encourage simplicity and improvement in state and local tax law and administration, publishing information that may assist states in implementing the compact and taxpayers in complying with the tax laws, and to do all things necessary and incidental to the administration of its functions pursuant to the compact.[952] The commission is financed through an allocation and apportionment process, with one-tenth of the costs apportioned in equal shares to the members and the remainder of the costs determined "in proportion to the amount of revenue collected by each party State and its subdivisions from income taxes, capital stock taxes, gross receipts taxes, sales and use taxes."[953]

In addition to its powers to study and recommend changes to tax laws, under limited circumstances the commission is also empowered to adopt uniform regulations and forms. Article VIII of the compact provides:

> Whenever any two or more party States or subdivisions of party States have uniform or similar provisions of law relating to an income tax, capital stock tax, gross receipts tax, or sales or use tax, the Commission may adopt uniform regulations for any phase of the administration of such law, including assertion of jurisdiction to tax or prescribing uniform tax forms.[954]

However, the regulations are advisory only, and each member state has the power to reject, disregard, amend, or modify any rules or regulations promulgated by the commission.[955] Therefore, the regulations promulgated by the commission have no force in any member state until adopted by that state in accordance with its own law. One additional power of the commission is to conduct audits of state accounts when so directed by state statute.[956]

---

952. *Id.* at art. VI, § 3 (a)-(d).
953. *Id.* at art. VI, § 4(b). *See, e.g.,* IDAHO CODE § 63-3706 (2003) ("Unless the legislature determines otherwise prior to adjournment, the amounts which the state tax commission has certified as complying with section 4 (b) of article VI are hereby continually appropriated from the multistate tax compact account to the multistate tax commission.").
954. Multistate Tax Compact, art. VII, § 1 (1967).
955. *See generally id.* at art. VII, § 3. *See also* May Dep't Stores Co. v. Indiana Dep't of State Revenue, 749 N.E.2d 651, 656 n.7 (Ind. Tax Ct. 2001).
956. *See generally* Multistate Tax Compact, art. VIII (1967). *See, e.g.,* ARK. CODE ANN. § 26-5-107 (2003) ("The provisions of Article VIII of the Multistate Tax Compact, § 26-5-101, pertaining to interstate audits, shall not be applicable

In conducting its audits, the commission is empowered to compel testimony and to apply to any court having power to issue a compulsory process for orders in aid of its powers and responsibilities.[957]

From a taxpayer's perspective, the most important article of the compact may be Article IV, which addresses apportionment of taxes between member states and provides arguably complicated formulas for arriving at the appropriate tax apportionment for a wide variety of business and nonbusiness income.[958] As previously noted, one of the major purposes of the compact is the apportionment of taxes between two or more member states or their political subdivisions. Article IV provides, in part: "Any taxpayer having income from business activity which is taxable both within and without this State, other than activity as a financial organization or public utility or the rendering of purely personal services by an individual, shall allocate and apportion his net income as provided in this Article."[959] Article IV then provides that a taxpayer is taxable in another state if: (1) the taxpayer is subject to a net income tax, a franchise tax measured by net income, a franchise tax for the privilege of doing business, or a corporate stock tax; or (2) a member state has jurisdiction to subject the taxpayer to a net income tax "regardless of whether, in fact, the State does or does not do so."[960] To the extent that they constitute nonbusiness income, the article provides for allocation of rents and royalties from real or tangible personal property, capital gains, interest, dividends, or patent or copyright royalties.[961] All business income is apportioned to a member state by "multiplying the income by a fraction the numerator of which is

---

to this state unless the Director of the Department of Finance and Administration shall, with the approval of the Governor, determine that compliance with the interstate audits procedures would be in the better interest of this state and shall notify the commission of this fact in writing."); MINN. STAT. § 290.174 (2004) ("Article VIII of the Multistate Tax Compact relating to interstate audits shall be in force in and with respect to the state of Minnesota.").

957. Multistate Tax Compact, art. VIII, §§ 3 & 4 (1967).

958. Article IV is based on the Uniform Division of Income for Tax Purposes Act (UDITPA). The UDITPA is a tax allocation system approved in 1957 by the National Conference of Commissioners on Uniform State Laws and by the American Bar Association. The UDITPA has been adopted as Article IV of the Multistate Tax Compact. *See* U.S. Steel Corp. v. Multistate Tax Comm'n, 434 U.S. 452, 457-58 n.6 (1978). *See also* Asarco, Inc. v. Idaho State Tax Comm'n, 458 U.S. 307, 310 n.3 (1982).

959. Multistate Tax Compact, art. IV, § 2 (1967).

960. *Id.* at art. IV, § 3.

the property factor plus the payroll factor plus the sales factor and the denominator of which is three."[962]

The Multistate Tax Compact has been the source of important litigation in both the area of general compact law and the area of state taxation.[963] Much of the litigation has been in the arena of apportionment and allocation of state taxes and has centered on the issue of unifying income—that is, treating as the income of a single corporation the income of wholly owned subsidiaries.[964] It is important to recognize that under the compact, allocation and apportionment are distinct concepts. Income is allocated when it is attributable to the particular state or states that are considered to be the source of the income. Income is apportioned when it is divided among the states in which the taxpayer derives apportionable income.[965] Courts have generally found that out-of-state income is subject to apportionment under the compact if it constituted part of a taxpayer's unitary business, or if it was short-term and the income was used to fund the unitary business.[966] Thus, insurance proceeds received by a taxpayer for flood damage to its Virginia manufacturing facility could be apportioned and taxed as business income by the District of Columbia because the property had integral function in the taxpayer's unitary business.[967] Likewise, when a taxpayer and its subsidiary operated similar businesses and the taxpayer had provided the subsidiary with its capital and its directors and officers, the unity of ownership, operation, and use needed for a unitary business was present.[968] Income from disposition of property that was an integral part of a pipeline's regular business operations was properly classified and apportioned as business income.[969] Generally, in determin-

---

961. *Id.* at art. IV, §§ 5-8.

962. *Id.* at art. IV, § 9.

963. *See, e.g.,* Associated Indus. v. Lohman, 511 U.S. 641 (1994); Dep't of Revenue v. ACF Indus., 506 U.S. 811 (1992); Allied-Signal, Inc. v. Director, Div. of Taxation, 504 U.S. 768 (1992); Bacchus Imports v. Dias, 468 U.S. 263 (1984).

964. *See, e.g.,* Asarco, Inc. v. Idaho State Tax Comm'n, 458 U.S. 307 (1982); F. W. Woolworth Co. v. Taxation & Revenue Dep't, 458 U.S. 354 (1982).

965. *Cf.,* Roger Dean Enters., Inc. v. Dep't of Revenue, 387 So. 2d 358 (Fla. 1980). *See also* May Dep't Stores Co. v. Indiana Dep't of State Revenue, 749 N.E.2d 651 (Ind. Tax Ct. 2001).

966. *See, e.g.,* Dep't of Revenue v. OSG Bulk Ships, 961 P.2d 399 (Alaska 1998).

967. Dist. of Columbia v. Pierce Assocs., Inc., 462 A.2d 1129 (D.C. 1983).

968. Albertson's, Inc. v. Dep't of Revenue, 683 P.2d 846 (Idaho 1984).

969. Texaco-Cities Serv. Pipeline Co. v. McGaw, 695 N.E.2d 481 (Ill. 1998). *See also* Citizens Utils. Co. v. Dep't of Revenue, 488 N.E.2d 984 (Ill. 1986)

ing apportionment, the three-part test provided in the compact is applied.[970] For purposes of apportioning income for the payment of state business taxes, the calculation of the tax must take into account the value of the business income of a multistate company that can fairly be attributed to its activity in the state.[971]

Other aspects of the Multistate Tax Compact have also given rise to litigation. Prime among the contentious issues has been the audit provision of the compact, leading one company to attempt to avoid the production of documents by unsuccessfully arguing that a change of the commission's by-laws rendered both the commission and the compact invalid.[972] In general, courts confronted with efforts by the commission to gain access to documents for purposes of audit have supported the commission's efforts.[973] What income is subject to taxation given the interaction between individual state tax laws and the compact has also been contentious. For example, a one-time liquidation of assets has been held not to have occurred within the regular course of business and, therefore, under the Multistate Tax Compact, the business was not liable for taxes on its capital gains from the liquidation.[974] However, a corporation's capital gains from sale of assets of another company that occurred in other regions of the country was subject to state income taxation under the Multistate Tax Compact because the sale of assets occurred in the regular course of business.[975] Similarly, where a multistate financing business borrowed money through its California headquarters for use by Arizona customers, that business must use the apportionment method to compute

---

(public utility, though not involved in transportation, was a unitary business subject to formula apportionment of income); Caterpillar Tractor Co. v. Lenckos, 417 N.E.2d 1343 (Ill. 1981) (unitary method of apportionment applicable to corporation and subsidiaries' determination of taxable state income).

970. Suburban Newspapers v. Director of Revenue, 975 S.W.2d 107 (Mo. 1998).

971. Dow Chem. Co. v. Director of Revenue, 834 S.W.2d 742 (Mo. 1992).

972. Multistate Tax Comm'n v. Int'l Harvester Co., 639 F.2d 493 (9th Cir. 1981); *cf.,* Dorgan v. Int'l Harvester Co., 585 F.2d 1380 (8th Cir. 1978).

973. *See, e.g.,* Franchise Tax Board v. Firestone Tire & Rubber Co., 139 Cal. App. 3d 843 (Cal. Ct. App. 1983) (taxpayer required by injunction not to interfere with audit of tax returns and to allow auditors to photocopy documents because injunction was merely prohibitive and not overly broad in its terms).

974. *Ex parte* Uniroyal Tire Co., 779 So. 2d 227 (Ala. 2001).

975. Atlantic Richfield Co. v. State, 601 P.2d 628 (Colo. 1979).

the amount of total income subject to Arizona tax.[976] Interest earned by a corporate taxpayer from loans to related corporations, which in turn provided services to the taxpayer, was business income and, for taxation purposes, subject to apportionment among the states in which the taxpayer did business.[977] Point-of-sale and point-of-distribution issues can also complicate the determination of apportioning taxes on multistate activity.[978]

Perhaps the Multistate Tax Compact is most famous for its contribution to the law of interstate compacts. In the celebrated case of *U.S. Steel Corp. v. Multistate Tax Commission,* the U.S. Supreme Court was given the opportunity to address the status and enforceability of the agreement in the absence of congressional consent.[979] In that case, taxpayers threatened with audits by the commission filed a suit challenging the compact, arguing that the agreement was unconstitutional because it was never approved by Congress, unreasonably burdened interstate commerce, and violated the Fourth and Fourteenth Amendments through its audit provisions. The Supreme Court once again affirmed that the Compact Clause applied only to those agreements directed to the formation of any combination tending to the increase of political power in the states in a way that would encroach on federal supremacy. The Court found that the compact was not such an agreement because it granted the states no powers that they did not already possess, was entirely voluntary to the states, and did not burden interstate commerce. The Court also held that the taxpayers had failed to allege facts that established a

---

976. Walter E. Heller Western, Inc. v. Ariz. Dep't of Revenue, 775 P.2d 1113 (Ariz. 1989).

977. Qualls v. Montgomery Ward & Co., 585 S.W.2d 18 (Ark. 1979). *But see* Pledger v. Illinois Tool Works, Inc., 812 S.W.2d 101 (Ark. 1991) (foreign corporation's capital gains income from the sale of its stock interest in the relevant corporations was "nonbusiness income," and accordingly not taxable by the state). *See also In re* Kroger Co., 12 P.3d 889 (Kan. 2000) (interest paid on money borrowed by corporation to defend against a hostile takeover was a non-business expense and not deductible because it was not an expense in the regular course of business).

978. *See, e.g.,* Olympia Brewing Co. v. Comm'r of Revenue, 326 N.W.2d 642 (Minn. 1982) (merchandise pickup at a taxpayer's brewery in Minnesota by out-of-state distributors in their own trucks for transportation and resale outside Minnesota did not constitute a sale within the state for income tax apportionment).

979. U.S. Steel Corp. v. Multistate Tax Comm'n, 434 U.S. 452 (1978).

violation of the Fourth or Fourteenth Amendments. Other courts have found likewise.[980]

9.7   EDUCATION COMPACTS GENERALLY

This section discusses the Midwestern Regional Higher Education Compact.

9.7.1   Midwestern Regional Higher Education Compact

The Midwestern Higher Education Commission (MHEC) is one of four compact-created education entities in the nation devoted to improving higher education in its assigned region. Other compact-created entities of similar purpose include the New England Board of Higher Education (NEBHE), the Southern Regional Education Board (SREB), and the Western Interstate Commission for Higher Education (WICHE). The SREB was established in 1948 as the first interstate compact for education. The NEBHE and the WICHE were established in the 1950s, and the MHEC was established in 1991.

Each member state appoints five commissioners to the MHEC's governing body—the governor or the governor's designee, a member of each chamber of the state legislature, and two at-large members, one of whom must come from post-secondary education. The commission meets twice each year to establish goals and priorities, review programs, and approve the operating budget. The work of the commission is financed largely through member-state obligations and foundation grants. A small, full-time staff headquartered in Minneapolis administers the MHEC's daily operation and programming activities.

Established in 1991 as an interstate compact agency, the Midwestern Higher Education Compact (MHEC)—also known as the Midwestern Higher Education Commission—is charged with promoting interstate cooperation and resource-sharing in higher education through three core functions: cost savings programs, reduced tuition, and policy research. As of 2003, the member states of the MHEC are Illinois, Indiana, Kansas, Michigan, Minnesota, Missouri, Nebraska, North Dakota, Ohio, and Wisconsin. The overarching purpose of the MHEC is to provide expanded higher educational opportunities and services in the midwestern region, with the aim of furthering regional access to and choice of higher education for the citizens residing in the member states. Since 1994, the Midwest Student Exchange Program (MSEP) has

---

980. *See, e.g.,* State Dep't of Revenue v. MGH Mgmt., 627 So. 2d 408 (Ala. Civ. App. 1993).

served as the area's largest multistate tuition reciprocity program, with over 130 campuses participating. Public institutions enrolling students under the MSEP agree to charge no more than 150 percent of the in-state resident tuition rate, while private institutions offer a 10 percent reduction on their tuition rates.

In order for a college or university to participate in MSEP, the state higher education office must endorse the program by signing the participation agreement and appointing a representative to the MSEP Council. This agreement allows any institution in that state to voluntarily join MSEP. Institutions participating in MSEP have the ability to tailor the program to their individual campus needs. For example, an institution may select only those degree programs it wishes to increase enrollment in and limit the programs that are already popular among students. The admission requirements are set by each campus along with the available programs of study. When the MSEP began in 1994, only 366 students were participating across the Midwest. As of the 2002-2003 school year, over 2,600 students were enrolled as MSEP students. Since 1994, 14,716 students and families have saved $43 million in tuition, an annual per-student average of $2,900. According to a survey of MSEP students completed in 2000, the vast majority of students used MSEP as a factor in making their college decisions. In addition, the admissions counselors at the MSEP institutions are the best sources of information about the MSEP and the reduced-tuition benefits that it offers. More and more campuses are using the MSEP to attract out-of-state students by offering them an affordable solution.

The compact follows six major goals in carrying out its mission. Those goals are to enhance productivity through reductions in administrative costs; to encourage student access, completion and affordability; to facilitate public policy analysis and information exchange; to facilitate regional academic cooperation and services; to promote quality educational programs; and to encourage innovation in the delivery of educational services. All initiatives supported by the compact are overseen by appointed volunteer committees of practicing professionals from colleges, universities, state agencies located in member states, and some of the MHEC's commissioners. The committee members are identified through peer nominations and selected for their expertise in specific program areas.

APPENDIX:
INDEX OF INTERSTATE
ADMINISTRATIVE COMPACTS

The following is an index of interstate regulatory compacts, by title, in effect as of July 1, 2005. The index does not contain information on all interstate compacts, such as border compacts. Compacts adopted by one state but which did not appear adopted by any other state are likewise not included as those compacts are technically not "active" agreements as compacts are generally understood. Uniform laws, while adopted in substantially the same form by states, do not bear the contractual hallmarks generally associated with compacts and are, therefore, not referenced.

Every effort has been made to provide the user the most up-to-date list, member states, relevant statutory references, and, where applicable, the administrative agency responsible for overseeing the compact. As statutory schemes employed by the states can change and state codes contain references to agreements that, while "on the books," are nevertheless inactive of dormant, the reader is encouraged to verify the information associated with a particular compact to ensure its accuracy information.

- **Alabama-Coosa-Tallapoosa River Basin Compact:** Apportions the surface waters of the Alabama-Coosa-Tallapoosa river basin to include the Alabama River, the Coosa River, the Tallapoosa River, all their associated tributaries as well as the Cahaba River. Creates the ACT Basin Commission manage compact affairs.

  Member States & Enabling Statutes:

  Alabama: ALA. CODE § 33-18-1 (2004)
  Georgia: GA. CODE ANN. § 12-10-110 (2004)
  United States: Pub. L. No. 105-105; 111 Stat. 2233 (1997)

  Administrative Agency:

  ACT Basin Commission
  Suite 451
  7 Martin Luther King Junior Drive
  Atlanta, GA 30334-9004

- **Animas-La Plata Project Compact:** Apportions the surface waters of the Animas and La Plata River system.

  Member States & Enabling Statutes:

Colorado:	COLO. REV. STAT. § 37-64-101 (2004)
New Mexico:	N.M. STAT. ANN. § 72-25-1 (2004)

- **Apalachicola-Chattahoochee-Flint River Basin Compact:** Apportions the surface waters of the Apalachicola-Chattahoochee-Flint River Basin and creates regulatory commission to manage compact affairs.

  Member States & Enabling Statutes:

Alabama:	ALA. CODE § 33-19-1 (2004)
Florida:	FLA. STAT. ANN. § 373.71 (2004)
Georgia:	GA. CODE ANN. § 12-10-100 (2004)
United States:	Pub. L. No. 105-104, 111 Stat. 2219 (1997)

  Administrative Agency:

  ACF Basin Commission
  Suite 451
  7 Martin Luther King Junior Drive
  Atlanta, GA 30334-9004

- **Appalachian States Low-Level Radioactive Waste Compact:** Compact established the Appalachian States Low-Level Radioactive Waste Commission to assure interstate cooperation for the proper disposal of low-level radioactive wastes. The commission identifies a host state (based on the volume and curie content of radioactive waste generated) to receive and dispose of radioactive waste from party states. Costs and benefits are distributed equitably among party states.

  Member States & Enabling Statutes:

Dist. of Columbia:	DEL. CODE ANN. tit. 7, § 8001, et seq. (2004)
Maryland:	MD. CODE ANN. ENVIR. § 7-301, et seq. (2004)
Pennsylvania:	35 PA. CONS. STAT. § 7125.1, et seq. (2004)
West Virginia:	W. VA. CODE § 29-1H-1 (2004)
United States:	Pub. L. No 100-319, 102 Stat. 471 (1988)

  Administrative Agency:

  Appalachian States Low-Level Radioactive Waste Commission
  P.O. Box 8469
  Harrisburg, PA 17105
  (717) 787-2163

- **Arkansas-Mississippi Great River Bridge Construction Compact:** Compact is to promote the construction of a highway bridge or a combined highway-railroad bridge connecting the states of Mississippi and Arkansas at or near Rosedale, Mississippi, and McGehee and Dumas, Arkansas, and to establish a joint interstate authority to assist in those efforts.

  Member States & Enabling Statutes:

Arkansas:	ARK. CODE ANN. § 29-89-301 (2004)
Mississippi:	MISS. CODE ANN. § 62-25-121, et se*q*. (2004)
United States:	Pub. L. No. 99-560, 100 Stat. 3146 (1986)

- **Arkansas River Basin Compact (of 1970):** Compact provides for an equitable apportionment of the waters of the Arkansas River between Arkansas and Oklahoma, promotes the orderly development thereof, creates an agency to administer water apportionment, encourages maintenance of an active pollution abatement program to seek reduction of both natural and man-made pollution in the basin, and facilitates the cooperation of the water administration agencies in Arkansas and Oklahoma to provide total development and management of the water resources in the basin.

  Member States & Enabling Statutes:

Arkansas:	ARK. CODE. ANN. § 15-23-401 (2004)
Oklahoma:	OKLA. STAT. tit. 82, § 1421 (2004)
United States:	Pub. L. No. 93-152, 87 Stat. 569 (1973)

  Administrative Agency:

  Arkansas-Oklahoma, Arkansas River Compact Commission
  10701 Hunters Point Road
  Fort Smith, AR, 72903
  (501) 452-2497

- **Arkansas River Compact of 1949:** Compact apportions the waters of the Arkansas River and establishes an administrative board to supervise apportionment.

  Member States & Enabling Statutes:

Colorado:	COLO. REV. STAT. § 37-69-101, et seq. (2004)
Kansas:	KAN. STAT. ANN. § 82a-520 (2004)
United States:	Pub. L. No. 81-82, 63 Stat. 145 (1949)

Administrative Agency:

Colorado Water Conservation Board
1313 Sherman St., Room 818
Denver, CO 80203:
(303) 8663581

- **Arkansas River Compact of 1955 (Arkansas River Basin Compact, Kansas-Oklahoma):** Compact apportions the waters of the Arkansas River Basin and establishes a commission to administer the agreement and encourage pollution abatement programs.

Member States & Enabling Statutes:

Kansas:	KAN. STAT. ANN. § 82a-528 (2004)
Oklahoma:	OKLA. STAT. tit. 82, § 1401 (2004)
United States:	Pub. L. No. 84-340, 69 Stat. 631 (1955)

Administrative Agency:

Kansas-Oklahoma Arkansas River Commission
11800 S. Midwest Blvd.
Guthrie, OK 73044-8205
(404) 282-3011

- **Atlantic States Marine Fisheries Compact:** The compact promotes better utilization of fisheries (marine, shell, and anadromous) along the Atlantic seaboard by developing programs for the promotion and protection of fisheries and by preventing physical waste of fisheries from any cause. The compact does not limit the production of fish or fish products for the purpose of establishing or fixing the price or creating and perpetuating monopoly.

Member States & Enabling Statutes:

Connecticut:	CONN. GEN. STAT. § 26-295 (2004)
Delaware:	DEL. CODE ANN. tit 7, § 1501 (2004)
Florida:	FLA. STAT. ANN. § 370.19 (2004)
Georgia	GA. CODE ANN. § 27-4-210, et seq. (2004)
Maine:	ME. REV. STAT. ANN. tit. 12, § 4601, et seq. (2003)
Maryland:	MD. CODE ANN. NAT. RES. § 4-301, et seq. (2004)
New Hampshire:	N.H. REV. STAT. ANN. § 213:1, et seq. (2004)
New York:	N.Y. ENVTL. CONSERV. LAW § 13-0371 (2004)
North Carolina:	N.C. GEN. STAT. § 113-251, et seq. (2004)

Pennsylvania:	30 PA. CONS. STAT. § 7101, et seq. (2004)
Rhode Island:	R.I. GEN. LAWS § 20-8-1, et seq. (2004)
South Carolina:	S.C. CODE ANN. § 50-5-2700 (2003)
Virginia:	VA. CODE ANN. § 28.2-1000 (2004)
United States:	Pub. L. No. 77-539, 56 Stat. 267 (1942)

Administrative Agency:

Atlantic States Marine Fisheries Commission (ASMFC)
1444 Eye Street, NW, 6th Floor
Washington, DC 20005
(202) 289-6400

Web Site:

www.asmfc.org

- **Bay State-Ocean State Compact (Compact with Rhode Island Relating to Bay Systems):** Compact establishes a commission to study, develop and make recommendations about the environmental and economic aspects of Narragansett Bay and Mount Hope Bay; provide a clearing house of information on matters relating to the problems of the bays systems; and facilitate the improvement of state and local systems.

Member States & Enabling Statutes:

| Massachusetts: | MASS. ANN. LAWS (SPEC. L.) ch. 137, § 1 (2004) |
| Rhode Island: | R.I. GEN. LAWS § 42-111-1 (2004) |

- **Big Blue River Compact of Kansas-Nebraska:** Compact establishes a commission to promote equitable apportion of water in the Big Blue River basin and to encourage water pollution abatement programs in the member states.

Member States & Enabling Statutes:

Kansas:	KAN. STAT. ANN. § 82a-529 (2004)
Nebraska:	NEB. REV. STAT. (Appendix) § A1-115 (2004)
United States:	Pub. L. No. 92-308, 86 Stat. 193 (1972)

Administrative Agency:

Kansas-Nebraska Big Blue River Commission
P.O. Box 94676
301 Centennial Mall S.
Lincoln, NE 68509
(402) 471-2363

- **Bear River Compact:** The purpose of the compact is regulate the distribution and use of the waters of the Bear River; to provide for efficient use of water for multiple purposes; to permit additional development of the water resources of the Bear River; and to provide an equitable apportionment of the waters of the Bear River among the compacting states.

  Member States & Enabling Statutes:

Idaho:	IDAHO CODE § 42-3402 (2004)
Utah:	UTAH CODE ANN. § 73-16-1, et seq. (2004)
Wyoming:	WYO. STAT. ANN. § 41-12-101 (2004)
United States:	Pub. L. No 85-348, 72 Stat. 38 (1958)

  Administrative Agency:

  Bear River Commission
  106 W. 500 S., Suite 101
  Bountiful, UT 84010-6232
  (801) 292-4633

- **Belle Fourche River Compact:** The purpose of the compact is to provide for the efficient use of the waters of the Belle Fourche river basin for multiple purposes; to provide for an equitable division of waters; and to promote joint action by the states and the United States in the efficient use of water and the control of floods.

  Member States & Enabling Statutes:

South Dakota:	S.D. CODIFIED LAWS § 46A-17-1 (2004)
Wyoming:	WYO. STAT. ANN. § 41-12-201, et seq. (2004)
United States:	Pub. L. No. 78-236, 58 Stat. 94 (1944)

- **(Illinois and Missouri) Bi-State Development Agency Compact:** Creates the Bi-State Development Agency to promote development in the St. Louis metropolitan area, to build and maintain transportation infrastructure and systems, and to assist local communities in planning transportation, water, and sewage systems.

  Member States & Enabling Statutes:

Illinois:	45 ILL. COMP. STAT. 100/1, et seq. (2004)
Missouri:	MO. REV. STAT. § 70.370 (2004)
United States:	Pub. L. No 81-743, 64 Stat. 568 (1950); amended, Pub. L. No. 86-303, 73 Stat. 582 (1959)

Administrative Agency:

Bi-State Development Agency (Metro)
707 North First Street
St. Louis, MO 63102
(314)982-1406
(618) 271-7879

Web Site:

http://www.metrostlouis.org/

- **Boating Offense Compact:** Provides concurrent jurisdiction for Oregon and Washington courts and law enforcement over offenses committed in waters forming a common boundary between the two states.

Member States & Enabling Statutes:

Oregon:	OR. REV. STAT. § 830.080 (2004)
Washington:	WASH. REV. CODE § 88.01.010 (2004)
United States:	Pub. L. No. 73-293, 48 Stat. 909 (1934) (codified at 4 U.S.C. § 112(A) (2004))

- **Breaks Interstate Park Compact:** Compact establishes a commission to administer and operate one of two interstate parks in the nation. The Breaks Interstate Park encompasses land along the Kentucky and Virginia border.

Member States & Enabling Statutes:

Kentucky:	KY. REV. STAT. ANN. §§ 148.022, 148.220, et seq. (2004)
Virginia*	
United States:	Pub. L. No. 83-543, 68 Stat. 571 (1954); amended Pub. L. No. 88-602, 78 Stat. 957 (1964)

---

* Although considered a member of the compact, statutory verification of membership could not be found in the state code. State code does authorize use of state funds to support the Breaks Interstate Park. *See* VA. CODE ANN. § 15.2-6011 (2004).

Administrative Agency:

Breaks Interstate Park Commission
P.O. Box 100
Breaks, VA 24607
(800) 865-4413

Web Site:

www.breakspark.com

- **Bus Taxation Proration and Reciprocity Agreement:** Compact creates a system by which bus fleet owners operating in two or more states may prorate their registration fees on the basis of miles operated within a member state to total fleet miles in all states. Specific consent of Congress is required for participation by new members.

Member States & Enabling Statutes:

Connecticut:	Conn. Gen. Stat. § 14-365, et seq. (2004)
Maine:	Me. Rev. Stat. Ann. tit. 36, § 1492, et seq. (2004)
New Hampshire:	N.H. Rev. Stat. Ann. § 261:49, et seq. (2004)
Ohio:	Ohio Rev. Code §§4503.80, 4503.81 (2004)
Rhode Island:	R.I. Gen. Laws § 31-6.1-1, et seq. (2004)
United States:	Pub. L. No. 8911, 79 Stat. 58 (1965) (District of Columbia, New Hampshire, New York, and Pennsylvania); Pub. L. No. 89312, 79 Stat.1157 (1965) (Connecticut, Rhode Island, and Vermont); Pub. L. No. 89-727, 80 Stat. 1156 (1966) (Massachusetts); Pub. L. No. 90-200, 81 Stat. 583 (1967) (Ohio).

- **California-Nevada Water Compact:** California and Nevada to negotiate and enter into a compact with respect to the distribution and use of the waters of the Truckee, Carson, and Walker Rivers.

Member States & Enabling Statutes:

California:	Cal Water Code § 5976 (2004)
Nevada:	Nev. Rev. Stat. § 538.600 (2004)
United States:	Pub. L. No. 84-353, 69 Stat. 675 (1955)

- **California-Nevada Compact for Jurisdiction on Interstate Waters:** Provides concurrent jurisdiction to arrest, prosecute, and try offenders with regard to acts committed on Lake Tahoe or Topaz Lake, on either side of the boundary line between California and Nevada.

  Member States & Enabling Statutes:

California:	CAL. PENAL CODE §§ 853.3, 853.4 (2004)
Nevada:	NEV. REV. STAT. § 171.076, et seq. (2004)
United States:	Pub. L. No. 73-293, 48 Stat. 909 (1934) (codified at 4 U.S.C. § 112(A) (2004))

- **Canadian River Compact:** Compact creates a commission to allocate and apportion waters of the Canadian River.

  Member States & Enabling Statutes:

New Mexico:	N.M. STAT. ANN. § 72-15-2, et seq. (2004)
Oklahoma:	OKLA. STAT. tit. 82 § 526.1 (2004)
Texas:	TEX. WATER CODE ANN. § 43.001, et seq. (2004)
United States:	Pub. L. No. 82-345, 66 Stat. 74 (1952)

  Administrative Agency:

  Canadian River Commission
  P.O. Box 25102
  Santa Fe NM 87504
  (505) 827-6339

- **Central Interstate Low-Level Radioactive Waste Compact:** Compact creates regime for the disposal of low-level radioactive waste and establishes a commission to manage compact affairs.

  Member States & Enabling Statutes:

Arkansas:	ARK. CODE ANN. § 8-8-201, et seq. (2004)
Kansas:	KAN. STAT. ANN. § 65-34a01, et seq. (2004)
Louisiana:	LA. REV. STAT. ANN. § 30:2131, et seq. (2004)
Nebraska:	NEB. REV. STAT. § 71-3521 (2004)*
Oklahoma:	OKLA. STAT. tit. 27A § 2-8-101, et seq. (2004)
United States:	Pub. L. No 99-240, 99 Stat. 1842 (1986)

---

* Nebraska withdrew per NEB. REV. STAT. § 71-3522 (2004).

Administrative Agency:

Central Interstate Low-Level Radioactive Waste Compact
Commission
1033 O St., Suite 530
Lincoln, NE 68508
(402) 476-8247

Web Site:

www.cillrwcc.org

- **Central Midwest Low-Level Radioactive Waste Compact:** Compact creates regime for disposal of low-level radioactive waste and creates a commission to administer compact affairs.

Member States & Enabling Statutes:

Illinois:	45 ILL. COMP. STAT. 140/0.01 et seq.;
	420 ILL. COMP. STAT. 20/1, et seq. (2004)
Kentucky:	KY. REV. STAT. ANN. §§ 211.859, 211.861,
	et seq. (2004)
United States:	Pub. L. No 99-240, 99 Stat. 1842 (1986)

Administrative Agency:

Central Midwest Compact Commission
1035 Outer Park Drive
Springfield, IL 62704
(217) 785-9982

Web Site:

www.state.il.us/idns/html/CMCC/cmcc.asp

- **Chesapeake Bay Commission:** Compact creates the Chesapeake Bay Commission, which advises member state legislatures on matters regarding the restoration and management of Chesapeake Bay. The commission is also a signatory to the Chesapeake Bay Agreement that includes Virginia, Maryland, Pennsylvania, the District of Columbia, and the Environmental Protection Agency. The commission is mandated to move forward initiatives of the multi-jurisdictional Chesapeake Bay Program.

Member States & Enabling Statutes:

Maryland:	MD. CODE ANN. NAT. RES. § 8-301, et seq. (2004)
Pennsylvania:	32 PA. CONS. STAT. § 820.11, et seq. (2004)
Virginia:	VA. CODE ANN. § 30-240, et seq. (2004)

Administrative Agency:

Chesapeake Bay Commission
60 W. St., Suite 200
Annapolis, MD 21401
(410) 2633420

- **Chickasaw Trail Economic Development Compact:** Compact creates authority to promote development of undeveloped rural area in Mississippi and Tennessee.

Member States & Enabling Statutes:

Mississippi:	MISS. CODE ANN., § 57-36-1 (2002)*
Tennessee:	TENN. CODE. ANN. § 13-2-301, et seq. (2004)
United States:	Pub. L. No. 105-145; 111 Stat. 2669 (1997)

Administrative Agency:

Chickasaw Trail Economic Development Authority

- **Colorado River Compact:** Compact apportions the waters of the Colorado river basin, which is administered by an interstate commission.

Member States & Enabling Statutes:

Arizona:	ARIZ. REV. STAT. § 45-1311 (2004)
California:	CAL UNCOD. INIT MEASURES & STATS § 1929-1 (2004)
Colorado:	COLO. REV. STAT. § 37-61-101, et seq. (2004)
Nevada:	NEV. REV. STAT. §§ 538.010, 538.041-538.251 (2004)
New Mexico:	N.M. STAT. ANN. § 72-15-5, et seq. (2004)
Utah:	UTAH CODE ANN. § 73-12a-1, et seq. (2004)
Wyoming:	WYO. STAT. ANN. §§ 41-12-301, 41-12-302 (2004)
United States:	Pub. L. No. 67-56; 42 Stat. 171 (1921)

---

*   Mississippi withdrew per 2003 Miss. Laws ch. 310, §§ 1-3, effective June 30, 2003.

Administrative Agency:

Colorado River Commission
c/o Colorado River Commission of Nevada
555 E Washington Ave, Suite 3100
Las Vegas, NV 89101
(702) 486-2670

Web Site:

www.state.nv.us/colorado_river/

- **Colorado River Crime Enforcement Compact:** Provides concurrent jurisdiction for Arizona and California courts and law enforcement officers of counties bordering the Colorado River over criminal offenses committed on the Colorado River.

Member States & Enabling Statutes

Arizona:	ARIZ. REV. STAT. § 37-620.11 (2004)
California:	CAL. PENAL CODE §§ 853.1, 853.2 (2004)
Nevada:	NEV. REV. STAT. § 171.079 (2004)
United States:	Pub. L. No. 73-293, 48 Stat. 909 (1934) (codified at 4 U.S.C. § 112(A) (2004))

- **Columbia River Compact:** Compact provides for regulation and protection of fish in waters of the Columbia River.

Member States & Enabling Statutes

Oregon:	OR. REV. STAT. §§ 507.010, 507.040 (2004)
Washington:	WASH. REV. CODE § 77.75 (2004)
United States:	Pub. L. No. 65-123, 40 Stat. 515 (1918)

- **Columbia River Gorge Compact:** Compact establishes a regional regulatory agency to govern the planning and development of the areas designated by the Columbia River Gorge National Scenic Area Act. The compact commission possesses broad land-use powers that include the authority to disapprove county land-use ordinances that are inconsistent with the area's management plan and enacting ordinances setting standards for using nonfederal land within the scenic area.

Member States & Enabling Statutes:

Oregon:	OR. REV. STAT. § 196.150, et seq. (2004)
Washington:	WASH. REV. CODE § 43.97.015 (2004)
United States:	Pub. L. No. 99-663, 100 Stat. 4274 (1986)

Administrative Agency:

Columbia River Gorge Commission
P.O. Box 730
288 E. Jewett Blvd.
White SMass. Ann. Lawson, WA 98672
(509) 493-3323

Web Site:

www.gorgecommission.org

- **Connecticut-New York Railroad Passenger Transportation Compact:** Compact provides for preservation and improvement of interstate rail passenger service between New York City and points in Connecticut.

Member States & Enabling Statutes:

Connecticut: CONN. GEN. STAT. § 16-343 (2004)
New York: NY UNCONSOL. LAWS, ch 110-B, § 1 (2004).*
United States: Pub. L. No 91-159, 83 Stat. 441 (1969)

- **Connecticut River Atlantic Salmon Compact:** Compact promotes the restoration of anadromous Atlantic salmon in the Connecticut River basin through the development of joint interstate programs for stocking, protection, management, research, and regulation.

Member States & Enabling Statutes:

Connecticut: CONN. GEN. STAT. § 26-302 (2004)
Massachusetts: MASS. ANN. LAWS (SPEC. L) ch. 133, § 1
                     (2004)
Vermont: VT. STAT. ANN. tit. 10 § 4651, et seq. (2004)
United States: Pub. L. No. 98-138, 97 Stat. 866 (1983)

Administrative Agency:

Connecticut River Atlantic SMass. Ann. Lawson Commission
103 East Plumtree Road
Sunderland, MA 01375
(413) 548-9138

Web Site:

www.fws.gov/r5crc/who/concrasc.html

---

*   This compact is referred to as the Passenger Services of New York, New Haven and Hartford Railroad Compact.

- **Connecticut River Valley Flood Control Compact:** Compact creates a commission to provide for financial reimbursement for economic losses to political subdivisions in which flood control reservoirs are located.

  Member States & Enabling Statutes:

Connecticut:	CONN. GEN. STAT. §§ 25-99, et seq. (2004)
New Hampshire:	N.H. REV. STAT. ANN. 484:1, et seq. (2004)
Vermont:	VT. STAT. ANN. tit. 10 §§ 1151 – 1160, 1171 – 1178, 1191 – 1196 (2004)
United States:	Pub. L. No. 83-52, 67 Stat. 45 (1953)

  Administrative Agency:

  Connecticut River Valley Flood Control Commission
  Box 511
  Greenfield, MA 01302
  (413) 665-9761

- **Colorado-New Mexico Costilla Creek Compact:** Compact apportions waters of Costilla Creek and creates an administrative agency to manage compact affairs.

  Member States & Enabling Statutes:

Colorado:	COLO. REV. STAT. §§ 37-68-101, 37-68-102 (2004)
New Mexico:	N.M. STAT. ANN. § 72-15-10, et seq. (2004)
United States:	Pub. L. No. 79-408, 60 Stat. 246 (1946); amended 88 Pub. L. No. 198, 77 Stat. 350 (1963)

  Administrative Agency:

  Costilla Creek Compact Commission
  1313 Sherman St., Room 818
  Denver, CO 80203
  (303) 866-3581

  Web Site:

  www.water.state.co.us

- **Cumbres and Toltec Scenic Railroad Compact:** Compact enables member states to acquire and jointly operate scenic railroad as part of the Denver and Rio Grande Railroad.

  Member States & Enabling Statutes:

Colorado:	Colo. Rev. Stat. §§ 24-60-1701, 24-60-1901 (2004)
New Mexico:	N.M. Stat. Ann. § 16-5-1, et seq. (2004)
United States:	Pub. L. No. 93-467, 88 Stat. 1421 (1974)

  Administrative Agency:

  Cumbres and Toltec Scenic Railroad Commission
  P.O. Box 561
  Antonito, CO 81120
  (719) 376-5488

- **Delaware River and Bay Authority Compact:** Establishes an authority to provide for orderly development of transportation, terminal, and other commercial facilities on the Delaware River and Bay.

  Member States & Enabling Statutes:

Delaware:	Del. Code Ann. tit. 17, § 1701, et seq. (2004)
New Jersey:	N.J. Stat. Ann. § 32:11E-1, et seq. (2004)
United States:	Pub. L. No. 87678, 76 Stat. 560 (1962)

  Administrative Agency:

  Delaware River and Bay Authority
  P.O. Box 71
  New Castle, DE 19720-0071
  Tel: (302) 571-6300

  Web Site:

  www.drba.net

- **Delaware River Basin Compact:** Compact establishes a commission to manage regional multipurpose water resources.

  Member States & Enabling Statutes:

Delaware:	Del. Code Ann. tit. 7, §§ 6501, 6511 (2004)
New Jersey:	N.J. Stat. Ann. § 32:11D-1, et seq. (2004)
New York:	N.Y. Envtl Conserv. Law § 21-0701, et seq. (2004)

Pennsylvania: 32 PA. CONS. STAT. § 815.101, et seq. (2004)

United States: Pub. L. No. 87-328, 75 Stat. 688 (1961)

Administrative Agency:

Delaware River Basin Commission
25 State Police Drive
P.O. Box 7360
West Trenton, NJ 08628
(609) 883-9500

Web Site:

www.state.nj.us/drbc:

- **Delaware River Joint Toll Bridge Compact:** Compact creates a commission to acquire, construct, and administer bridges across the Delaware River between New Jersey and Pennsylvania.

Member States & Enabling Statutes:

New Jersey: N.J. STAT. ANN. § 32:8-1, et seq. (2004)

Pennsylvania: 36 PA. CONS. STAT. § 3401, et seq. (2004)

United States: Pub. L. No. 74-411, 49 Stat. 1051 (1935)

Interstate Agency:

Delaware River Joint Toll Bridge Commission
Administration Building
110 Wood St.
Morrisville, PA 19067
(215) 295-5061

Web Site:

www.drjtbc.com

- **Delaware River Port Authority Compact** Compact creates a commission to construct bridges, develop port facilities, enhance economic development, promote commerce, develop and maintain a rapid transit system, and unify the ports of Philadelphia and Camden through the establishment of a subsidiary corporation.

Member States & Enabling Statutes:

New Jersey: N.J. STAT. ANN. § 32:3-1, et seq. (2004)

Pennsylvania: 36 PA. CONS. STAT. § 3503 (2004)

United States: Pub. L. No. 72-76, 47 Stat. 308 (1932)

Administrative Agency:

Delaware River Port Authority
One Port Center
2 Riverside Drive
P.O. Box 1949
Camden, NJ 08101
(856) 968-2001

Web Site:

www.drpa.org

- **Delaware Valley Urban Area Compact:** Compact establishes a commission to plan development in the Philadelphia-Camden-Trenton metropolitan region.

Member States & Enabling Statutes:

New Jersey:	N.J. Stat. Ann. § 32:27-1, et seq. (2004)
Pennsylvania:	73 Pa. Cons. Stat. § 701 (2004)
United States:	Pub. L. No. 83-560, 75 Stat. 170 (codified at 23 U.S.C. § 134(d)(1) (2005))

Administrative Agency:

Delaware Valley Regional Planning Commission
The Bourse Building, 8th Floor
111 S. Independence Mall,
E. Philadelphia, PA 19106
(215) 592-1800

Web Site:

www.dvrpc.org

- **Delmarva Advisory Council Agreement:** Compact creates a council to advise public and private organizations regarding development and other issues on the Delmarva Peninsula.

Member States & Enabling Statutes:

Delaware:	Del. Code Ann. tit. 29 § 11101, et seq. (2004)
Maryland:	Md. Ann. Code art. 32B, § 1-101, et seq. (2003)
Virginia:	Va. Code Ann. § 2.2-5800, et seq. (2004)

Administrative Agency:

Delmarva Advisory Council
P.O. Box 4277
Salisbury, MD 21802-4277
(410) 742-9271

- **Driver License Agreement:** This agreement is intended to replace both the Drivers License Compact and the Nonresident Violators Compact. The agreement is only beginning to make the rounds in state legislatures, which may account for why so few states have joined. Several state legislatures have delegated authority to enter drivers license agreements to executive departments without further legislature action, which presumably would allow states to join this agreement through executive department action. *See* ARK. CODE ANN. § 27-16-809 (2004); FLA. STAT. ANN. § 322.02 (2004). New York allows its commission to enter a drivers license agreement with any province of Canada. *See* N.Y. VEH & TRAF. LAW § 516-a (2004).

Member States & Enabling Statutes:

Connecticut: CONN. GEN. STAT. § 14-111i, et seq. (2003)

Administrative Agency:

American Association of Motor Vehicle Administrators
(AAMVA)
4200 Wilson Blvd., Suite 1100
Arlington, VA 22203-1800
(703) 522-4200

Web Site:

www.aamva.org

- **Drivers' License Compact:** Compact provides for member states to exchange information on citations against nonresident drivers who violate traffic laws and regulations.

Member States & Enabling Statutes:

Alabama: ALA. CODE §§ 32-6-30 to 32-6-36 (2004)
Alaska: ALASKA STAT.§§ 28.37.010 to 28.37.190 (2004)
Arizona: ARIZ. REV. STAT. § 28-1851, et seq. (2004)
Arkansas: ARK. CODE ANN. §§ 27-17-101 to 27-17-106 (2004)

California: CAL.VEH.CODE § 15000, et seq. (2004)
Colorado: COLO. REV. STAT. § 24-60-1101, et seq. (2004)
Delaware: DEL. CODE ANN. tit. 21, §§ 8101, 8111, et seq. (2004)
Florida: FLA. STAT. ANN. § 322.43, et seq. (2004)
Hawaii: HAW. REV. STAT. §§ 286C-1, 286C-2 (2004)
Idaho: IDAHO CODE §§ 49-2001 to 49-2003 (2004)
Illinois: 625 ILL. COMP. STAT. 5/6-700, et seq. (2004)
Indiana: IND. CODE § 9-28-1-1, et seq. (2004)
Iowa: IOWA CODE §§ 321C.1, 321C.2 (2004)
Kansas: KAN. STAT. ANN. § 8-1212, et seq. (2004)
Louisiana: LA. REV. STAT. ANN. 32:1420, et seq. (2004)
Maryland: MD. CODE ANN. TRANSP. § 16-701, et seq. (2004)
Massachusetts: MASS. ANN. LAWS ch. 90, § 30B (2004)
Minnesota: MINN. STAT. ANN. § 171.50, et seq. (2004)
Mississippi: MISS. CODE ANN. § 63-1-101, et seq. (2004)
Missouri: MO. REV. STAT. §§ 302.600, 302.605 (2004)
Montana: MONT. CODE ANN. § 61-5-401, et seq. (2004)
Nebraska: NEB. REV. STAT. (Appendix) § A1-112 (2004)
New Hampshire: N.H. REV. STAT. ANN. § 263:77, et seq. (2004)
New Jersey: N.J. STAT. ANN. § 39:5D-1, et seq. (2004)
New Mexico: N.M. STAT. ANN. § 66-5-49, et seq. (2004)
New York: N.Y. VEH. & TRAF. LAW § 516 (2004) North
Carolina: N.C. GEN. STAT. § 20-4.21, et seq. (2004)
Ohio: OHIO REV. CODE § 4507.60, et seq. (2004)
Oklahoma: OKLA. STAT. tit. 47 § 781, et seq. (2004)
Oregon: OR. REV. STAT. §§ 802.540, 802.550 (2004)
Pennsylvania: 75 PA. CONS. STAT. § 1581, et seq. (2004)
South Carolina: S.C. CODE ANN., § 56-1-610, et seq. (2004)
South Dakota: S.D. CODIFIED LAWS § 32-12-56.1 (2004)
Tennessee: TENN. CODE ANN. § 55-50-702 (2004)
Texas: TEX. TRANSP. CODE ANN. § 523.001, et seq. (2004)
Utah: UTAH CODE ANN. § 53-3-601, et seq. (2004)
Vermont: VT. STAT. ANN. tit. 23 § 3901, et seq. (2004)
Virginia: VA. CODE ANN. § 46.2-483, et seq. (2004)
Washington: WASH. REV. CODE 46.21.010, et seq. (2004)

West Virginia: W. VA. CODE, §§ 17B-1A-1, 17B-1A-2 (2004)

Wyoming: WYO. STAT. ANN. §§ 31-7-140, 31-7-201, 31-7-202 (2004)

Dist. of Columbia: D.C. CODE ANN. §§ 50-1001, 50-1002 (2004)

United States: Pub. L. No. 85-684, 72 Stat. 635 (1958)

Administrative Agency:

Driver License Compact Commission
American Association of Motor Vehicle Administrators
(AAMVA)
4200 Wilson Blvd., Suite 1100
Arlington, VA 22203-1800
(703) 522-4200

Web Site:

www.aamva.org

- **Emergency Management Assistance Compact**: Compact provides mutual assistance between the states in managing any emergency or disaster that is declared by the governor of the affected state or states, whether arising from natural disaster, technological hazard, man-made disaster, civil emergency aspects of resources shortages, community disorders, insurgency, or enemy attack. Compact provides mutual cooperation in emergency-related exercises, testing, or other training activities.

Member States & Enabling Statutes:

Alabama: ALA. CODE § 31-9-40 (2004)
Alaska: ALASKA STAT. § 26.23.135 (2004)
Arizona: ARIZ. REV. STAT. § 26-402 (2004)
Arkansas: ARK. CODE ANN. §§ 12-49-401, 12-49-402 (2004)
Colorado: COLO. REV. STAT. § 24-60-2901, et seq. (2004)
Connecticut: CONN. GEN. STAT. § 28-23a, et seq. (2004)
Delaware: DEL. CODE ANN. tit. 20, § 3401, et seq. (2004)
Florida: FLA. STAT. ANN. § 252.921, et seq. (2004)
Georgia: GA. CODE ANN. §§ 38-3-80, 38-3-81 (2004)
Idaho: IDAHO CODE § 46-1018A (2004)
Illinois: 45 ILL. COMP. STAT. 151/1 (2004)
Indiana: IND. CODE § 10-4-2.5 (2004)

Iowa:	Iowa Code § 29C.1, et seq. (2004)
Kansas:	Kan. Stat. Ann. § 48-9a01 (2004)
Kentucky:	Ky. Rev. Stat. Ann. § 39A.950 (2004)
Louisiana:	La. Rev. Stat. Ann. § 29:751 (2004)
Maine:	Me. Rev. Stat. Ann. tit. 37-B § 921 (2004)
Maryland:	Md. Code Ann. art. 41, §§ 19-101, 19-102 (2004)
Massachusetts:	Mass. Ann. Laws (Spec. L.) ch. S141, § 1 (2004)
Michigan:	Mich. Comp. Laws § 3.991, et seq. (2004)
Minnesota:	Minn. Stat. Ann. 192.89 (2004)
Mississippi:	Miss. Code Ann. § 45-18-1, et seq. (2004)
Missouri:	Mo. Rev. Stat. § 44.415 (2004)
Montana:	Mont. Code Ann. § 10-3-1001 (2004)
Nebraska:	Neb. Rev. Stat. (Appendix) § A1-114 (2004)
Nevada*:	Nev. Rev. Stat. § 415.010 (2004)
New Hampshire:	N.H. Rev. Stat. Ann. § 108.1 (2004)
New Jersey:	N.J. Stat. Ann. § 38A:20-4 (2004)
New Mexico:	N.M. Stat. Ann. §§ 11-15-1, 11-115-2 (2004)
New York:	N.Y. Exec. Law § 29-g (2004)
North Carolina:	N.C. Gen. Stat. § 166A-40, et seq. (2004)
North Dakota:	N.D. Cent. Code, § 37-17.1-14.5 (2003)
Ohio:	Ohio Rev. Code § 5502.40 (2004)
Oklahoma:	Okla. Stat. tit. 63 § 684.1, et seq. (2004)
Oregon:	Or. Rev. Stat. § 401.045 (2004)
Pennsylvania:	35 Pa. Cons. Stat. § 7601, et seq. (2004)
Rhode Island:	R.I. Gen. Laws § 30-15.9-1 (2004)
South Carolina:	S.C. Code Ann. § 25-9-410 (2004)
South Dakota:	S.D. Codified Laws § 33-15-48 (2004)
Tennessee:	Tenn. Code Ann. § 58-2-403 (2004)
Texas:	Tex. Health & Safety Code § 778.001 (2004)
Utah:	Utah Code Ann. §§ 53-2-201, 53-2-202 (2004)
Vermont:	Vt. Stat. Ann. tit. 20, § 101, et seq. (2004)
Virginia:	Va. Code Ann. § 44-146.28:1 (2004)

---

*   Although Nevada does not appear to have adopted verbatim this particular compact, it is listed by the National Emergency Management Association as a member of the agreement. The cite given above for Nevada is reference to the Interstate Civil Defense and Disaster Compact, which some may consider as authorization for this particular compact.

Washington: WASH. REV. CODE § 38.10.010 (2004)
West Virginia: W. VA. CODE § 15-5-22 (2004)
Wisconsin: WIS. STAT. § 166.30 (2004)
Dist. of Columbia: D.C. CODE ANN. §§ 7-2331, 7-2332 (2004)
United States: Pub. L. No. 104-321, 110 Stat. 3877 (1996)

Administrative Agency:

National Emergency Management Association
c/o Council of State Governments
P.O. Box 11910
Lexington, KY 40578
(859) 244-8000

Web Site:

www.nemaweb.org

- **Great Lakes (Basin) Compact:** Compact creates a commission to advise and make recommendations to the member states on water resources matters affecting the Great Lakes, including comprehensive water use, economic development, and maintenance of environmental quality.

Member States & Enabling Statutes:

Illinois: 45 ILL. COMP. STAT. 145/0.01, et seq. (2004)
Indiana: IND. CODE § 14-25-13-1, et seq. (2004)
Michigan: MICH. COMP. LAWS § 324.32201, et seq. (2004)
Minnesota: MINN. STAT. ANN. § 1.21, et seq. (2004)
New York: N.Y. ENVTL. CONSERV. LAW § 21-0901, et seq. (2004)
Ohio: OHIO REV. CODE § 6161.01, et seq. (2004)
Pennsylvania: 32 PA. CONS. STAT. § 817.1, et seq. (2004)
Wisconsin: WIS. STAT. § 14.78 (2004)
United States: Pub. L. No. 90-419, 82 Stat. 414 (1968)

Administrative Agency:

Great Lakes Commission
400 4th St.
Ann Arbor, MI 48103-4816
(734) 665-9135

Web Site:

www.glc.org

- **Great Lakes Forest Fire Compact:** Though formally listed as a compact, the GLFFC appears to be more a formal association of state and provincial administrative agencies than a formal interstate compact adopted pursuant to legislative act.

Member States & Enabling Statutes:

Michigan:	Michigan Dept. of Natural Resources Forest Management
Minnesota:	Minnesota Dept. of Natural Resources
Wisconsin:	Wisconsin Dept. of Natural Resources
Manitoba:	Manitoba Conservation Operations Fire Program
Ontario:	Ontario Ministry of Natural Resources, Aviation & Forest: Fire Management
United States:	Pub. L. No. 81-129; 63 Stat. 271 (1949), amended Pub. L. No. 82-340; 66 Stat. 71 (1952)

Administrative Agency:

Compact Board (also referred to as the Executive Committee)

Web Site:

www.glffc.com

- **Gulf States Marine Fisheries Compact:** Compact promotes better utilization of fisheries, marine, shell, and anadromous, along the seaboard of the Gulf of Mexico. The agreement authorizes the development of a joint program for the promotion and protection of such fisheries and the prevention of the physical waste of the fisheries.

Member States & Enabling Statutes:

Alabama:	ALA. CODE 1975 § 9-12-180, et seq. (2004)
Florida:	FLA. STAT. ANN. § 370.20 (2004)
Louisiana:	LA. REV. STAT. ANN. § 56:71, et seq. (2004)
Mississippi:	MISS. CODE ANN. § 49-15-101, et seq. (2004)
Texas:	TEX. PARKS & WILD. CODE ANN. § 91.001, et seq. (2004)
United States:	Pub. L. No. 81-66, 63 Stat. 70 (1949)

Administrative Agency:

Gulf States Marine Fisheries Commission
P.O. Box 726
Ocean Springs, MS 39566-0726
(228) 875-5912

Web Site:

www.gsmfc.org

- **Historic Chattahoochee Compact:** Compact establishes a commission to promote tourism and historic preservation in the Chattahoochee Valley. The geographic area of the compact includes 18 Alabama and Georgia counties along the Chattahoochee River.

Member States & Enabling Statutes:

Alabama:	ALA. CODE § 41-9-311 (2004)
Georgia:	GA. CODE ANN. §§ 12-10-80, 12-10-81 (2004)
United States:	Pub. L. No. 95-462, 92 Stat. 1271 (1978)

Administrative Agency:

Historic Chattahoochee Commission
P.O. Box 33
Eufaula, AL 36072-0033
(334) 687-8440

Web Site:

www.hcc-al-ga.org

- **Interpleader Compact:** Compact enables courts to acquire personal jurisdiction over adverse claimants to property located anywhere within the member states. The compact brings all claims together in a single action.

Member States & Enabling Statutes:

Maine	14 ME. REV. STAT. ANN. tit. 14, §§ 6351, et seq.; 6401, et seq. (2004)
New Hampshire:	N.H. REV. STAT. ANN. § 5-A:1, et seq. (2004)
New Jersey:	N.J. STAT. ANN. § 2A:41A-1, et seq. (2004)
New York:	N.Y.C.P.L.R. § 1006 (2004)
Pennsylvania:	42 PA. CONS. STAT. § 7521, et seq. (2004)

- **Interstate Agreement (Compact) on Qualification of Educational Personnel:** Agreement facilitates movement of teachers and other professional educational personnel among member states and establishes procedures for the employment without reference to their state of origin.

Member States & Enabling Statutes:

Alabama:	ALA. CODE § 16-23A-1, et seq. (2004)
Alaska:	ALASKA STAT. § 14.20.620, et seq. (2004)
California:	CAL.EDUC.CODE § 12500, et seq. (2004)
Connecticut:	CONN. GEN. STAT. § 10-146c, et seq. (2004)
Delaware:	DEL. CODE ANN. tit. 14, § 8211, et seq. (2004)
Florida:	FLA. STAT. ANN. § 1012.99, et seq. (2004)
Hawaii:	HAW. REV. STAT. § 315-1, et seq. (2004)
Idaho:	IDAHO CODE § 33-4104, et seq. (2004)
Indiana:	IND. CODE §§ 20-1-17-1, 20-1-17-2 (2004)
Iowa:	IOWA CODE § 272A.1, et seq. (2004)
Kansas:	KAN. STAT. ANN. 72-60a01, et seq. (2004)
Kentucky:	KY. REV. STAT. ANN. §§ 161.124, 161.126 (2004)
Maine:	ME. REV. STAT. ANN. tit. 20A § 13901, et seq. (2004)
Maryland:	MD. CODE ANN. EDUC. § 6-601, et seq. (2004)
Massachusetts:	MASS. ANN. LAWS, (SPEC. L.) ch. 105 § 1, et seq. (2004)
Michigan:	MICH. COMP. LAWS § 388.1371, et seq. (2004)
Minnesota:	MINN. STAT. ANN. § 122A.90, et seq. (2004)
Montana:	MONT. CODE ANN. § 20-4-121, et seq. (2004)
Nebraska:	NEB. REV. STAT. § 79-893, et seq. (2004)
New Hampshire:	N.H. REV. STAT. ANN. § 200-E:1, et seq. (2004)
New Jersey:	N.J. STAT. ANN. § 18A:26-11, et seq. (2004)
New York:	N.Y. EDUC. LAW § 3030 (2004)
North Carolina:	N.C. GEN. STAT. § 15C-349, et seq. (2004)
Ohio:	OHIO REV. CODE § 3319.42, et seq. (2004)
Oklahoma:	OKLA. STAT. tit. 70 § 508.1, et seq. (2004)
Pennsylvania:	24 PA. CONS. STAT.§ 2401.1, et seq. (2004)
Rhode Island:	R.I. GEN. LAWS §16-11-5 (2004)
South Carolina:	S.C. CODE ANN. § 59-27-10, et seq. (2004)
South Dakota:	S.D. CODIFIED LAWS § 13-42-18, et seq. (2004)

Utah: UTAH CODE ANN. § 53A-6-201, et seq. (2004)
Vermont: VT. STAT. ANN. tit. 16 § 2041, et seq. (2004)
Virginia: VA. CODE ANN. § 22.1-316, et seq. (2004)
Washington: WASH. REV. CODE § 28A.690.010, et seq.
                 (2004)
West Virginia: W. VA. CODE, §§ 18-10E-1, 18-10E-2 (2004)
Wisconsin: WIS. STAT. § 115.46 (2004)
Dist. of Columbia: D.C. CODE ANN. § 38-2101, et seq. (2004)

- **Interstate Compact for Adult Offender Supervision:** Compact creates an interstate commission to promulgate rules governing the interstate movement of adult offenders (probationers and parolees) subject to community-based supervision programs and to administer the provisions of the compact.

Member States & Enabling Statutes:

Alabama: ALA. CODE § 15-22-1-1 (2004)
Alaska: ALASKA STAT. §33-36-3 (2004)
Arizona: ARIZ. REV. STAT. § 31-467 (2004)
Arkansas: ARK. CODE ANN. § 12-15-101 (2004)
California: CAL. PENAL CODE § 11180 (2004)
Colorado: COLO. REV. STAT. §§ 24-60-2802 (2004)
Conneticut: CONN. GEN. STAT. § 54-133 (2004)
Delaware: DEL. CODE ANN. tit. 11, §§ 4358 & 4359
               (2004)
Florida: FLA. STAT. ANN. 949-07 (2004)
Georgia: GA. CODE ANN. § 42-9-81 (2004)
Hawaii: HAW. REV. STAT. § 353B-1 (2004)
Idaho: IDAHO CODE § 20-301 (2004)
Illinois: 45 ILL. COMP. STAT. 170 (2004)
Indiana: IND. CODE 11-13-4.5 (2004)
Iowa: IOWA CODE § 907B-2 (2004)
Kansas: KAN. STAT. ANN.§ 22-4110 (2004)
Kentucky: KY. REV. STAT. ANN. § 439-561 (2004)
Louisiana: LA. REV. STAT. ANN. § 15-574-31 (2004)
Maine: ME. REV. STAT. ANN. tit. 34-A, § 9871, et
               seq. (2004)
Maryland: MD CODE ANN. CORRECT. SERV. § 6-201, et
               seq. (2004)
Massachusetts: MASS. ANN. LAWS, ch 127 §§ 151A-151L
               (2005), as amended by 2005 Mass. H.B. 4192
               (2005)

Michigan:	MICH CONS. LAWS. § 3-1012 (2004)
Minnesota:	MINN. STAT. ANN. § 243.1605 (2004)
Mississippi:	MISS. CODE ANN. § 47-7-81 (2004)
Missouri:	MO. REV. STAT. § 589.500 (2004)
Montana:	MONT. CODE ANN. § 46-23-1115 (2004)
Nebraska:	NEB. REV. STAT. § 29-2254 (2004)
Nevada:	NEV. REV. STAT. § 213-215 (2004)
New Hampshire:	N.H. REV. STAT. ANN. § 651-A:29 (2004)
New Jersey:	N.J. STAT. ANN. § 2A:168-26 (2004)
New Mexico:	N.M. STAT. ANN. § 31-5-20 (2004)
New York:	N.Y. EXEC. LAW § 259-mm (2004)
North Carolina:	N.C. GEN. STAT. § 148-4B (2004)
North Dakota:	N.D. CENT. CODE § 12-65-01 (2004)
Ohio:	OHIO REV. CODE §5149-21 (2004)
Oklahoma:	OKLA. STAT. tit. 22 § 1091, et seq. (2004)
Oregon:	OR. REV. STAT. §144-600 (2004)
Pennsylvania:	61 PA. CONS. STAT. § 324.1 (2004)
Rhode Island:	R.I. GEN. LAWS § 13-9.1-1 (2004)
South Carolina:	S.C. CODE ANN. § 24-21-1100 (2003)
South Dakota:	S.D. CODIFIED LAWS § 24-24-16A (2004)
Tennessee:	TENN. CODE ANN. § 40-28-41 (2004)
Texas:	TEXAS GOV'T CODE ANN. § 510.00, et seq. (2004)
Utah:	UTAH CODE ANN. § 77-28C-103 (2004)
Vermont:	VT. STAT. ANN. tit. 22 § 1351 (2004)
Virginia:	VA. CODE ANN. §§ 53.1-172 & 53.1-174 (2004)
Washington:	WASH. REV. CODE § 9-94A-745 (2004)
West Virginia:	W. VA. CODE § 28-7-1, et seq. (2004)
Wisconsin:	WIS. STAT. § 304-16 (2004)
Wyoming:	WYO. STAT. ANN. § 7-13-423 (2004):
Dist. of Columbia:	D.C. CODE § 24-133 (2004)
United States:	Pub. L. No. 73-293, 48 Stat. 909 (1934) (codified at 4 U.S.C. § 112(A) (2004))

Administrative Agency:

Interstate Commission for Adult Offender Supervision
PO Box 11910
Lexington KY 40578-1910
(859) 244-8227

Web Site:

http://www.interstatecompact.org.

- **Interstate Compact for Education:** Compact creates an interstate commission to serve as a clearinghouse on educational matters and provide a forum for the developing educational policy.

Member States & Enabling Statutes:

Alabama:	ALA. CODE § 16-44-1, et seq. (2004)
Alaska:	ALASKA STAT. § 14.44.050, et seq. (2004)
Arizona:	ARIZ. REV. STAT. § 15-1901 (2004)
Arkansas:	ARK. CODE ANN. § 6-4-201, et seq. (2004)
California:	CAL. EDUC. CODE § 12510, et seq. (2004)
Colorado:	COLO. REV. STAT. § 24-60-1201, et seq. (2004)
Connecticut:	CONN. GEN. STAT. § 10-374, et seq. (2004)
Delaware:	DEL. CODE ANN. tit. 14, § 8201 (2004)
Florida:	FLA. STAT. ANN. § 1000.34, et seq. (2004)
Georgia:	GA. CODE ANN. § 20-6-20, et seq. (2004)
Hawaii:	HAW. REV. STAT. § 311-1, et seq. (2004)
Idaho:	IDAHO CODE § 33-4101, et seq. (2004)
Illinois:	45 ILL. COMP. STAT. 90/0.01, et seq. (2004)
Indiana:	IND. CODE § 20-11-1-1 (2004)
Iowa:	IOWA CODE § 272B.1, et seq. (2004)
Kansas:	KAN. STAT. ANN. § 72-6011, et seq. (2004).
Kentucky:	KY. REV. STAT. ANN. §§ 156.710, 156.715, 156.720 (2004)
Louisiana:	LA. REV. STAT. ANN. § 17:1911, et seq. (2004)
Maine:	ME. REV. STAT. ANN. tit. 20-A § 601, et seq. (2004)
Maryland:	MD. CODE ANN. EDUC. § 25-101, et seq. (2004)
Massachusetts:	MASS. ANN. LAWS (SPEC. L.) ch. 99, § 1, et seq. (2004)
Michigan:	MICH. COMP. LAWS § 388.1301, et seq. (2004)

Minnesota:	MINN. STAT. ANN. §§ 127A.80, 127A.81, et seq. (2004)
Mississippi:	MISS. CODE ANN. § 37-135-11, et seq. (2004)
Missouri:	MO. REV. STAT. § 173.300, et seq. (2004)
Montana:	MONT. CODE ANN. § 20-2-501 (2004)
Nebraska:	NEB. REV. STAT. § 79-1501, et seq. (2004)
Nevada:	Nev. Rev. Stat. § 399.015 (2004)
New Hampshire:	N.H. REV. STAT. ANN. § 200-G:1, et seq. (2004)
New Jersey:	N.J. STAT. ANN. § 18A:75-1, et seq. (2004)
New Mexico:	N.M. STAT. ANN. § 11-8-1, et seq. (2004)
New York:	N.Y. EDUC. LAW § 107 (2004)
North Carolina:	N.C. GEN. STAT. § 115C-104 (2004)
North Dakota:	N.D. CENT. CODE §§ 15.1-04-01, 15.1-04-02 (20040
Ohio:	OHIO REV. CODE § 3301.48, 3301.49 (2004)
Oklahoma:	OKLA. STAT. tit. 70 § 506.1, et seq. (2004)
Pennsylvania:	24 PA. CONS. STAT.§ 5401, et seq. (2004)
Rhode Island:	R.I. GEN. LAWS §16-47-1 (2004)
South Carolina:	S.C. CODE ANN. § 59-11-10, et seq. (2004)
Tennessee:	TENN. CODE ANN. §§ 49-12-201, 49-12-203 (2004)
Texas:	TEX. EDUC. CODE ANN. § 161.01, et seq. (2004)
Utah:	UTAH CODE ANN. § 53A-27-101, et seq. (2004)
Vermont:	VT. STAT. ANN. tit. 16 § 1501, et seq. (2004)
Virginia:	VA. CODE ANN. § 22.1-336, et seq. (2004)
West Virginia:	W. VA. CODE § 18-10D-1, et seq. (2004)
Wisconsin:	WIS. STAT. §§ 39.75, 39.76 (2004)
Wyoming:	WYO. STAT. ANN. § 21-16-301 (2004)
Dist. of Columbia:	D.C. CODE ANN. § 38-3001, et seq. (2004)

Administrative Agency:

Education Commission of the States
700 Broadway
Suite 1200
Denver, CO 80203-3460
(303) 299-3600

Web Site:

www.ecs.org

- **Interstate Compact for Adoption and Medical Assistance:** Compact is intended to strengthen protections for children with special needs on whose behalf adoption assistance is to be paid. Compact applies when such children are present in or located to states other than the one committed to provide adoption assistance. Compact provides substantive assurances and operating procedures to promote the delivery of medical and other services to children through programs of adoption assistance under the laws of the member states.

  Member States & Enabling Statutes:

Arkansas:	ARK. CODE ANN. § 9-29-301 (2004)
Colorado:	COLO. REV. STAT. § 24-60-2401, et seq. (2004)
Connecticut:	CONN. GEN. STAT. § 17a-116d (2004)
Delaware:	DEL. CODE ANN. tit. 31 § 5401, et seq. (2004)
Florida:	FLA. STAT. ANN. §§ 409.406, 409.407 (2004)
Hawaii:	HAW. REV. STAT. § 350C-1, et seq. (2004)
Idaho:	IDAHO CODE § 39-7501, et seq. (2004)
Iowa:	IOWA CODE § 600.23 (2004)
Kansas:	KAN. STAT. ANN. § 38-335, et seq. (2004).
Maryland:	MD. CODE ANN. FAM. LAW § 5-4A-01 (2004)
Massachusetts:	MASS. ANN. LAWS ch. 18B, § 22 (2004)
Michigan:	MICH. COMP. LAWS §§ 400.115r, 400.115s (2004)
Minnesota:	MINN. STAT. ANN. § 259.71 (2004)
Nebraska:	NEB. REV. STAT. § 43-147, et seq. (2004)
Nevada:	NEV. REV. STAT. 127.400, et seq. (2004)
New Mexico:	N.M. STAT. ANN. § 40-7B-1, et seq. (2004)
North Carolina:	N.C. GEN. STAT. § 7B-3800, et seq. (2004)
Oklahoma:	OKLA. STAT. tit. 10 § 7510-3.1, et seq. (2004)
Rhode Island:	R.I. GEN. LAWS, § 15-7.1-1, et seq. (2004)
South Carolina:	S.C. CODE ANN., § 20-7-2610, et seq. (2004)
Tennessee:	TENN. CODE ANN. § 36-1-201, et seq. (2004)
Texas:	TEX. FAM. CODE ANN. § 162.201, et seq. (2004)
Wisconsin:	WIS. STAT. § 48.9985 (2004)
United States:	Pub. L. No. 96-272 Title I, § 101(4)(B), 94 Stat. 512 (1980) (codified at 42 U.S.C. 673a (2004)).

Administrative Agency:

Association of Administrators of the Interstate Compact on
Adoption & Medical Assistance
c/o American Public Health Services Association
810 First Street, N.E.
Suite 500
Washington, DC 20002
(202) 682-0100

Web Site:

http://aaicama.aphsa.org/

- **Interstate Adoption Assistance Compact:** Compact authorizes state departments of social services to enter into interstate agreements with agencies of other states for the protection of children on behalf of whom adoption assistance is being provided by the departments and provides procedures for interstate children's adoption assistance payments, including medical payments.

Member States & Enabling Statutes:

Alabama:	ALA. CODE §§ 26-10B-1, et seq. (2004)
Delaware:	DEL. CODE ANN. tit. 31, § 5401, et seq. (2004)
Indiana:	IND. CODE § 31-19-29-1, et seq. (2004)
Mississippi:	MISS. CODE ANN. § 93-17-101, et seq. (2004)
Maine:	ME. REV. STAT. ANN. tit. 22 § 4171, et seq. (2004)
Missouri:	MO. REV. STAT. §§ 453.500, 453.503 (2004)
Montana:	MONT. CODE ANN. § 42-10-125 (2004)
West Virginia:	W. VA. CODE, § 49-2C-1, et seq. (2004)

- **Interstate Agreement on Detainers**: Promotes the expeditious and orderly disposition of charges pending against a person detained in one state who is subject to pending charges in another state. The agreement resolves the proper status of any detainers based on untried indictments, information, and complaints, and gives detained persons certain rights. The federal government is a full participant.

Member States & Enabling Statutes:

Alabama:	ALA. CODE § 15-9-81 (2004)
Alaska:	ALASKA STAT. § 33.35.010, et seq. (2004)
Arizona:	ARIZ. REV. STAT. §§ 31-481, 31-482 (2004)
Arkansas:	ARK. CODE ANN. § 16-95-101, et seq. (2004)

California:	CAL. PENAL CODE § 1389, et seq. (2004)
Colorado:	COLO. REV. STAT. § 24-60-501, et seq. (2004)
Connecticut:	CONN. GEN. STAT. § 54-186, et seq. (2004)
Delaware:	DEL. CODE ANN. tit. 11 §§ 2540, et seq. (2004)
Florida:	FLA. STAT. ANN. § 941.45, et seq. (2004)
Georgia:	GA. CODE ANN. § 42-6-20, et seq. (2004)
Hawaii:	HAW. REV. STAT. § 834-1, et seq. (2004)
Idaho:	IDAHO CODE § 19-5001, et seq. (2004)
Illinois:	730 ILL. COMP. STAT. 5/3-8-9 (2004)
Iowa:	IOWA CODE § 821.1, et seq. (2004)
Kansas:	KAN. STAT. ANN. § 22-4401 (2004)
Kentucky:	KY. REV. STAT. ANN. § 440.450, et seq. (2004)
Maine:	ME. REV. STAT. ANN. tit. 34-A § 9601, et seq. (2004)
Maryland:	MD. ANN. CODE art. 27, § 616A, et seq. (2004)
Massachusetts:	MASS. ANN. LAWS, ch. 276, § 11, et seq. (2004)
Michigan:	MICH. COMP. LAWS § 780.601, et seq. (2004)
Minnesota:	MINN. STAT. ANN. § 629.294 (2004)
Missouri:	MO. REV. STAT. § 217.490 (2004)
Montana:	MONT. CODE ANN. § 46-31-101, et seq. (2004)
Nebraska:	NEB. REV. STAT. § 29-759, et seq. (2004)
Nevada:	NEV. REV. STAT. § 178.620 (2004)
New Hampshire:	N.H. REV. STAT. ANN. § 606-A:1, et seq. (2004)
New Jersey:	N.J. STAT. ANN. § 2A:159A-1, et seq. (2004)
New Mexico:	N.M. STAT. ANN. § 31-5-12, et seq. (2004)
New York:	N.Y. CRIM. PROC. LAW § 580.20 (2004)
North Carolina:	N.C. GEN. STAT. § 15A-761, et seq. (2004)
North Dakota:	N.D. CENT. CODE § 29-34-01, et seq. (2004)
Ohio:	OHIO REV. CODE § 2963.30, et seq. (2004)
Oklahoma:	OKLA. STAT. tit. 22 § 1345, et seq. (2004)
Oregon:	OR. REV. STAT. § 135.775, et seq. (2004)
Pennsylvania:	42 PA. CONS. STAT. § 9101, et seq. (2004)
Rhode Island:	R.I. GEN. LAWS, § 13-13-1, et seq. (2004)
South Carolina:	S.C. CODE ANN. § 17-11-10, et seq. (2004)
South Dakota:	S.D. CODIFIED LAWS § 23-24A-1, et seq. (2004)

Tennessee: TENN. CODE ANN. § 40-31-101, et seq. (2004)
Texas: TEX. CRIM. PROC. CODE § 51.14 (2004)
Utah: UTAH CODE ANN. § 77-29-5, et seq. (2004)
Vermont: VT. STAT. ANN. tit. 28 § 1501, et seq. (2004)
Virginia: VA. CODE ANN. § 53.1-210, et seq. (2004)
Washington: WASH. REV. CODE § 9.100.010 (2004)
West Virginia: W. VA. CODE § 62-14-1, et seq. (2004)
Wisconsin: WIS. STAT. § 976.05 (2004)
Wyoming: WYO. STAT. ANN. § 7-15-101, et seq. (2004)
Dist. of Columbia: D.C. CODE ANN. § 24-801, et seq. (2004)
United States: Pub. L. No.91-538, 84 Stat. 1397 (1970),
                        amended by Pub. L. No. 100-690, 102 Stat.
                        4181 (1988), 18 U.S.C. Appx. (2004)

- **Interstate Compact For Mutual Military Aid In An Emergency:**
  Provides for mutual military aid and assistance of the member states
  or the United States in the event of an emergency, allows for hot
  pursuit of insurrectionists, saboteurs, enemies, or enemy forces by the
  military forces of member states, and defines the rights, privileges,
  and immunities of the members of state military forces participating
  in compact activities.

Member States & Enabling Statutes:

Connecticut: CONN. GEN. STAT. § 27-38 (2004)
Massachuesetts   MASS. ANN. LAWS (SPEC. L.) ch. S91 (2004)
New Jersey: N.J. STAT. ANN. § 38A:20-2 (2004)
New York: N.Y. MIL. LAW Appx. § 7 (2004)
Pennsylvania: 51 PA. CONS. STAT. § 4501 (2004)

- **Interstate Compact to Conserve Oil and Gas:** Compact creates a
  commission whose purpose is to conserve oil and gas. The compact
  is unique in that renewal of congressional consent is required.

Member States & Enabling Statutes:

Alabama*
Alaska: ALASKA STAT.§ 46.04.100 (2004)
Arizona: ARIZ. REV. STAT. § 27-601, et seq. (2004)
Arkansas: ARK. CODE ANN. § 15-72-901, et seq. (2004)
California: CAL. PUB. RES. CODE § 3275, et seq. (2004)

---

*   Listed as a full member of the compact by the Interstate Oil and Gas Compact
Commission, however statutory citation could not be found in state code.

Colorado:	Colo. Rev. Stat. § 34-60-123 (2004)
Florida:	Fla. Stat. Ann. § 377.01, et seq. (2004)
Illinois:	45 Ill. Comp. Stat. 55/0.01, et seq. (2004)
Indiana:	Ind. Code § 14-38-3-1 (2004)
Kansas:	Kan. Stat. Ann. § 55-801, et seq. (2004)
Kentucky*	
Louisiana*	
Maryland:	Md. Code Ann. Envir § 14-401, et seq. (2004)
Michigan:	Mich. Comp. Laws § 324.62101, et seq. (2004)
Mississippi:	Miss. Code Ann., § 53-1-101 (2004)
Montana:	Mont. Code Ann. § 82-11-301, et seq. (2004)
Nebraska:	Neb. Rev. Stat. (Appendix) § A1-123
Nevada:	Nev. Rev. Stat. 522.160, et seq. (2004)
New Mexico*	
New York:	N.Y. Envtl. Conserv. Law § 23-2101 (2004)
North Dakota*	
Ohio*	
Oklahoma:	Okla. Stat. tit. 52 § 201, et seq. (2004)
Pennsylvania:	58 Pa. Cons. Stat. § 191, et seq. (2004)
South Dakota:	S.D. Codified Laws § 45-10-1, et seq. (2004)
Texas:	Tex. Nat. Res. Code Ann. § 90.001, et seq. (2004)
Utah:	Utah Code Ann. § 40-7-1, et seq. (2004)
Virginia:	Va. Code Ann. §§ 45.1-381, 45.1-382 (2004)
West Virginia*	
Wyoming:	Wyo. Stat. Ann. § 30-5-201, et seq. (2004)
United States:	76 Pub. Res. 31, 53 Stat. 1071 (1939); renewed Pub. L. No. 86-143, 73 Stat. 290 (1959); renewed Pub. L. No. 88-115, 77 Stat. 145 (1963); renewed, Pub. L. No. 90-185, 81 Stat. 560 (1967)

Associate States:
Georgia
Idaho

---

*   Listed as a full member of the compact by the Interstate Oil and Gas Compact Commission, however statutory citation could not be found in state code.

Missouri
North Carolina
Oregon
South Carolina
Washington.

Administrative Agency:

Interstate Oil and Gas Compact Commission
P.O. Box 53127
Oklahoma City, OK 73152-3127
(405) 525-3556

Web Site:

iogcc.state.ok.us

* **Interstate Compact on Industrialized/Modular Buildings:** Establishes a commission to develop and promulgate uniform rules and regulations governing the design and construction of industrialized/ modular buildings. The compact does not reference congressional consent, but Article I (2)(b) implies that the compact was developed to "provide assurances to the U.S. Congress that would preclude the need for a voluntary, pre-emptive federal regulatory system for modular housing, as outlined in Section 572 of the Housing and Community Development Act of 1987." *NOTE:* Kentucky maintains a reciprocal agreement with the Industrialized Buildings Commission to accept units bearing the commission label. Wisconsin maintains a reciprocal agreement with Minnesota to accept industrialized buildings assembled in Minnesota and bearing the commission label.

Member States & Enabling Statutes:

Minnesota:	MINN. STAT. ANN. § 16B.75 (2004)
New Jersey:	N.J. STAT. ANN. § 32:33-1, et seq. (2004)
Rhode Island:	R.I. GEN. LAWS § 23-27.4-1 (2004)

Administrative Agency:

Industrialized Buildings Commission:
505 Huntmar Park Drive, Suite 210
Herndon, VA 20170
(703) 481-2022

Web Site:

www.interstateibc.org

- **Interstate Compact on Juveniles (ICJ):** Establishes procedures for out-of-state supervision of juveniles and provides procedures for their return. Compact eligibility is nationwide in scope. In addition to the basic compact, a substantial number of jurisdictions have also enacted optional supplemental amendments dealing with runaways, rendition, and out-of-state confinement. *NOTE:* The current ICJ has undergone significant changes and a new version of the compact is currently making the rounds in state legislatures. Among the significant changes is the creation of an interstate commission with broad rulemaking and enforcement powers. Until the new version of the ICJ is approved by at least 35 states, the current version remains in effect.

Member States & Enabling Statutes:

Alabama:	ALA. CODE § 44-2-1, et seq. (2004)
Alaska:	ALASKA STAT. § 47.15.010, et seq. (2004)
Arizona:	ARIZ. REV. STAT. § 8-361, et seq. (2004)
Arkansas:	ARK. CODE ANN. § 9-29-101, et seq. (2004)
California:	CAL. WELF. & INST. CODE § 1300, et seq. (2004)
Colorado:	COLO. REV. STAT. § 24-60-701, et seq. (2004)
Connecticut:	CONN. GEN. STAT. § 46b-151a-q (2004)
Delaware:	DEL. CODE ANN. tit. 31, § 5201, et seq. (2004)
Florida:	FLA. STAT. ANN. § 985.501, et seq. (2004)
Georgia:	GA. CODE ANN. § 39-3-1, et seq. (2004)
Hawaii:	HAW. REV. STAT. § 582-1, et seq. (2004)
Idaho:	IDAHO CODE § 16-1901, et seq. (2004)
Illinois:	45 ILL. COMP. STAT. 10/0.1, et seq. (2004)
Indiana:	IND. CODE § 31-37-23-2 (2004)
Iowa:	IOWA CODE § 232.171 (2004)
Kansas:	KAN. STAT. ANN. § 38-1002, et seq. (2004)
Kentucky:	KY. REV. STAT. ANN. § 615.010 (2004)
Louisiana:	LA. REV. STAT. ANN. § 1623, et seq. (2004)
Maine:	ME. REV. STAT. ANN. tit. 34-A § 9001, et seq. (2004)
Maryland:	MD. ANN. CODE, art. 83C, § 3-101, et seq. (2004)
Massachusetts:	MASS. ANN. LAWS (SPEC. L.) ch. 97, § 1, et seq. (2004)
Michigan:	MICH. COMP. LAWS § 3.701, et seq. (2004)
Minnesota:	MINN. STAT. ANN. § 260.51, et seq. (2004)

Mississippi:	MISS. CODE ANN., § 43-25-1, et seq. (2004)
Missouri:	MO. REV. STAT. § 210.570, et seq. (2004)
Montana:	MONT. CODE ANN. § 41-6-101, et seq. (2004)
Nebraska:	NEB. REV. STAT. § 43-1001, et seq. (004)
Nevada:	NEV. REV. STAT. § 214.010, et seq. (2004)
New Hampshire:	N.H. REV. STAT. ANN. § 169-A:1, et seq. (2004)
New Jersey:	N.J. STAT. ANN. § 9:23-1, et seq. (2004)
New Mexico:	N.M. STAT. ANN. § 32A-10-1, et seq. (2004)
New York:	N.Y. UNCONSOL. LAW § 1801, et seq. (2004)
North Carolina:	N.C. GEN. STAT. § 7B-2800, et seq. (2004)
North Dakota:	N.D. CENT. CODE § 27-22-01, et seq. (2004)
Ohio:	OHIO REV. CODE § 2151.56, et seq. (2004)
Oklahoma:	OKLA. STAT. tit. 10. § 531, et seq. (2004)
Oregon:	OR. REV. STAT. § 417.030, et seq. (2004)
Pennsylvania:	62 PA. CONS. STAT.§ 731, et seq. (2004)
Rhode Island:	R.I. GEN. LAWS § 14-6-1, et seq. (2004)
South Carolina:	S.C. CODE ANN., § 20-7-1980, et seq. (2004)
South Dakota:	S.D. CODIFIED LAWS § 26-12-1, et seq. (2004)
Tennessee:	TENN. CODE ANN. § 37-4-101, et seq. (2004)
Texas:	TEX. FAMILY CODE ANN. § 60.001, et seq. (2004)
Utah:	UTAH CODE ANN. § 55-12-1, et seq. (2004)
Vermont:	VT. STAT. ANN. tit. 33 § 551, et seq. (2004)
Virginia:	VA. CODE ANN, § 16.1-323, et seq (2004)
Washington:	WASH. REV. CODE § 13.24.010, et seq. (2004)
West Virginia:	W. VA. CODE, § 49-8-1, et seq. (2004)
Wisconsin:	WIS. STAT. § 938.991, et seq. (2004)
Wyoming:	WYO. STAT. ANN. § 14-6-101 (2004)
Dist. of Columbia:	D.C. CODE ANN. § 24-1101, et seq. (2004)
United States:	Pub. L. No. 73-293, 48 Stat. 909 (1934), 4 U.S.C. § 112(A) (2004)[1]

---

1. The Association of Juvenile Compact Administrators has opined that congressional consent is not necessary to this compact under the doctrine of Virginia v. Tennessee, 148 U.S. 503 (1893). *See* Association of Juvenile Compact Administrators, Manual § 4 (2004), *at* http://ajca.us/manual/section4/general%20legal%20questions.htm#congcons.

- **Interstate Compact on Licensure of Participants in Live Racing with Pari-Mutuel Wagering:** Compact establishes uniform requirements among the member states for the licensing of participants in live racing with pari-mutuel wagering and ensures that participants licensed under the compact meet certain minimum standards. Compact also facilitates growth of pari-mutuel racing member states and nationwide by simplifying the process for licensing participants.

  Member States & Enabling Statutes:

California:	CAL. BUS. & PROF. CODE §§ 19527, 19528 (2004)
Delaware:	DEL. CODE ANN. tit. 3, § 10200, et seq. (2004)
Florida:	FLA. STAT. ANN. § 550.901, et seq. (2004)
Kentucky:	KY. REV. STAT. ANN. 230.3751 (2004)
Louisiana:	LA. REV. STAT. ANN. § 4: 275, et seq. (2004)
Nebraska:	NEB. REV. STAT. § 2-1247 (2004)
New York:	N.Y. RAC. PARI-MUT. WAG. & BREED LAW § 1101, et seq. (2004)
Washington:	WASH. REV. CODE § 67.17.005, et seq. (2004)
West Virginia:	W. VA. CODE § 19-24-21, et seq. (2004)

- **Interstate Compact on Mentally Disordered Offenders**: Compact authorizes interstate agreements to provide services, care, and treatment to mentally disordered offenders. Agreement also authorizes research and training of personnel on a joint cooperative basis.

  Member States & Enabling Statutes:

Delaware:	DEL. CODE ANN. tit. 16, § 5201, et seq. (2004)
Illinois:	45 ILL. COMP. STAT. 45/0.01, et seq. (2004)
Maine:	15 ME. REV. STAT. ANN. § 2301, et seq. (2004)
Missouri:	MO. REV. STAT. § 630.850, et seq. (2004)
New Hampshire:	N.H. REV. STAT. ANN. §§ 126-C:1, et seq. (2004)
New Mexico:	N.M. STAT. ANN. §§ 31-5-10, 31-5-11 (2004)
North Dakota:	N.D. CENT. CODE §§ 25-14-01, 25-14-02 (2004)
West Virginia:	W. VA. CODE, §§ 27-15-1, et seq. (2004)

- **Interstate Pest Control Compact:** Compact establishes a governing board to provide and administer an insurance fund to which member states apply for financial support to promote pest control or underwrite eradication activities as needed to protect agricultural and forest products.

Member States & Enabling Statutes:

Arizona*
Arkansas*
California: CAL. FOOD & AGRIC. CODE § 8801, et seq. (2004)
Colorado: COLO. REV. STAT. § 35-4-113 (2004)
Delaware: DEL. CODE ANN. tit. 3, §§ 9001, 9022, et seq. (2004)
Georgia: GA. CODE ANN. § 2-7-130, et seq. (2004)
Florida*
Illinois: 45 ILL. COMP. STAT. 5/0.01, et seq. (2004)
Kansas: KAN. STAT. ANN. § 2-2114 (2004) (Repealed but abides by the Compact)
Maine: ME. REV. STAT. ANN. tit. 21 § 8501, et seq. (2004)
Maryland: MD. CODE ANN. AGRIC. § 5-701, et seq. (2004)
Michigan: MICH. COMP. LAWS § 286.501, et seq. (2004)
Minnesota: MINN. STAT. ANN. § 18.62, et seq. (2004)
New Hampshire: N.H. REV. STAT. ANN. § 430:21, et seq. (2004)
New Jersey: N.J. STAT. ANN. § 32:30-1, et seq. (2004)
New Mexico: N.M. STAT. ANN. § 76-6-10, et seq. (2004)
New York: N.Y. AGRIC. & MKTS. LAW § 149 (2004)
North Carolina: N.C. GEN. STAT. § 106-65.55, et seq. (2004)
North Dakota: N.D. CENT. CODE § 4-32-01, et seq. (2004)
Ohio: OHIO REV. CODE § 921.60, et seq. (2004)
Oklahoma*
Oregon: OR. REV. STAT. § 570.650 (2004)
Pennsylvania: 3 PA. CONS. STAT.§ 214-41, et seq. (2004)
Rhode Island*
South Carolina: S.C. CODE ANN., § 46-11-10, et seq. (2004)

---

* Listed as a member in 2004 by the Interstate Pest Control Compact Governing Board. There appears no statutory adoption of the compact in these listed states.

Tennessee:	TENN. CODE ANN. § 43-6-301, et seq. (2004)
Texas*	
Utah:	UTAH CODE ANN. § 4-36-1, et seq. (2004)
Vermont**	
Virginia:	VA. CODE ANN. § 33.1-188.1, et seq. (2004)
Washington:	WASH. REV. CODE § 17.34.010, et seq. (2004)
West Virginia:	W. VA. CODE, §§ 19-12B-1, et seq. (2004)
Wisconsin:	WIS. STAT. §§ 93.07 (2004); 1965 Wis. Laws c. 583, §§ 1 to 7, 9
Wyoming*	

Administrative Agency:

Interstate Pest Control Compact
61 Britton Road
Stockton, NJ 08559
(908) 788-8707

Web Site:

http://www.pestcompact.org/

- **Interstate Compact on the Placement of Children (ICPC):** Compact permits the interstate placement of children subject to adoption or who are under the jurisdiction of a state court or child placement agency. Member states agree to provide certain safeguards and services as though a child was located in a single state. The compact requires notice and proof of the suitability of a placement; allocates specific legal and administrative responsibilities between the sending and receiving state; provides for enforcement of rights; and authorizes actions in member states to improve operations and services. All U.S. jurisdictions and Canadian provinces are eligible. Consent of Congress is not required until a Canadian province seeks to join. *NOTE:* The ICPC is currently undergoing substantial revision.

Member States & Enabling Statutes:

Alabama:	ALA. CODE § 44-2-20, et seq. (2004)
Alaska:	ALASKA STAT. § 47.70.010, et seq. (2004)
Arizona:	ARIZ. REV. STAT. § 8-548, et seq. (2004)
Arkansas:	ARK. CODE ANN. § 9-29-201, et seq. (2004)

---

* Listed as a member in 2004 by the Interstate Pest Control Compact Governing Board. There appears no statutory adoption of the compact in these listed states.
** Appears to have repealed the compact.

California:	CAL. FAM. CODE § 7900, et seq. (2004)
Colorado:	COLO. REV. STAT. § 24-60-1801, et seq. (2004)
Connecticut:	CONN. GEN. STAT. § 17a-175, et seq. (2004)
Delaware:	DEL. CODE ANN. tit. 31, § 381, et seq. (2004)
Florida:	FLA. STAT. ANN. § 409.401, et seq. (2004)
Georgia:	GA. CODE ANN. § 39-4-1, et seq. (2004)
Hawaii:	HAW. REV. STAT. § 350E-1, et seq. (2004)
Idaho:	IDAHO CODE § 16-2101, et seq. (2004)
Illinois:	ILL. COMP. STAT. 15/0.01, et seq. (2004)
Indiana:	IND. CODE § 12-17-8-1, et seq. (2004)
Iowa:	IOWA CODE§ 232.158, et seq. (2004)
Kansas:	KAN. STAT. ANN. § 38-1201, et seq. (2004)
Kentucky:	KY. REV. STAT. ANN. § 615.030, et seq. (2004)
Louisiana*:	LA. REV. STAT. ANN. § 46:1700 (2004).
Maine:	ME. REV. STAT. ANN. tit. 22 § 4191, et seq. (2004).
Maryland:	MD. CODE ANN. FAM. LAW § 5-601, et seq. (2004)
Massachusetts:	MASS. ANN. LAWS (SPEC. L.) ch. 95, § 1, et seq. (2004)
Michigan:	MICH. COMP. LAWS § 3.711, et seq. (2004)
Minnesota:	MINN. STAT. ANN. § 260.851, et seq. (2004)
Mississippi:	MISS. CODE ANN. § 43-18-1, et seq. (2004)
Missouri:	MO. REV. STAT. § 210.620, et seq. (2004)
Montana:	MONT. CODE ANN. § 41-4-101, et seq. (2004)
Nebraska:	NEB. REV. STAT. § 43-1101, et seq. (2004)
Nevada:	NEV. REV. STAT. § 127.320, et seq. (2004).
New Hampshire:	N.H. REV. STAT. ANN. § 170-A:1, et seq. (2004)
New Jersey:	N.J. STAT. ANN. § 9:23-5, et seq. (2004)
New Mexico:	N.M. STAT. ANN. § 32A-11-1, et seq. (2004)
New York:	N.Y. SOC. SERV. LAW § 374-A (2004)
North Dakota:	N.D. CENT. CODE § 14-13-01, et seq. (2004)
Ohio:	OHIO REV. CODE § 5103.20, et seq. (2004)
Oklahoma:	OKLA. STAT. tit. 10 § 571, et seq. (2004)
Oregon:	OR. REV. STAT. § 417.200, et seq. (2004)

---

* Appears to have been repealed. *See* 1991 La. Acts 1991, No. 235, § 17, effective Jan. 1, 1992.

Pennsylvania:	62 Pa. Cons. Stat.§ 761, et seq. (2004)
Rhode Island:	R.I. Gen. Laws § 40-15-1, et seq. (2004)
South Carolina:	S.C. Code Ann., § 20-7-1980, et seq. (2004)
South Dakota:	S.D. Codified Laws § 26-13-1, et seq. (2004)
Tennessee:	Tenn. Code Ann. § 37-4-201, et seq. (2004)
Texas:	Tex. Family Code Ann. § 162.102 (2004)
Utah:	Utah Code Ann. § 62A-4a-701, et seq. (2004)
Vermont:	Vt. Stat. Ann. tit. § 5901, et seq. (2004)
Virginia:	Va. Code Ann. § 63.1-219, et seq. (2004)
Washington:	Wash. Rev. Code § 26.34.010, et seq. (2004)
West Virginia:	W. Va. Code, § 49-2A-1, et seq. (2004)
Wisconsin:	Wis. Stat. § 48.988 (2004)
Wyoming:	Wyo. Stat. Ann. § 14-5-101, et seq. (2004)
Dist. of Columbia:	D.C. Code Ann. § 4-1421, et seq. (2004)

Administrative Agency:

Assoc. of Administrators on the Interstate Compact on the
Placement of Children
c/o American Public Health Services Association
810 First Street, N.E.
Suite 500
Washington, DC 20002
(202) 682-0100

Web Site:

http://icpc.aphsa.org/

- **Interstate Corrections Compact:** Enables state officials to enter into contracts and agreements for cooperative care, treatment, and rehabilitation of offenders sentenced to or confined in prisons and other correctional institutions.

Member States & Enabling Statutes:

Alabama:	Ala. Code § 14-13-1, et seq. (2004)
Alaska:	Alaska Stat.§ 33.36.010, et seq. (2004)
Arizona:	Ariz. Rev. Stat. § 31-491, et seq. (2004)
Arkansas:	Ark. Code Ann. § 12-49-101, et seq. (2004)
California:	Cal. Pen. Code § 11189, et seq. (2004)
Colorado:	Colo. Rev. Stat. § 24-60-1601, et seq. (2004)

Connecticut:	CONN. GEN. STAT. § 18-105 (2004)
Delaware:	DEL. CODE ANN. tit. 11, § 6570, et seq. (2004)
Florida:	FLA. STAT. ANN. § 941.55, et seq. (2004)
Georgia:	GA. CODE ANN. § 42-11-1, et seq. (2004)
Idaho:	IDAHO CODE § 20-701, et seq. (2004)
Illinois:	730 ILL. COMP. STAT. 5/3-4-4 (2004)
Indiana:	IND. CODE § 11-8-4-1, et seq. (2004)
Iowa:	IOWA CODE § 913.1, et seq. (2004)
Kansas:	KAN. STAT. ANN. § 76-3001, et seq. (2004)
Kentucky:	KY. REV. STAT. ANN. § 196.610, et seq. (2004)
Maine:	ME. REV. STAT. ANN. tit. 34-A, § 9401, et seq. (2004)
Maryland:	MD. ANN. CODE art. 41, § 4-1201, et seq. (2004)
Michigan:	MICH. COMP. LAWS § 3.981, et seq. (2004)
Minnesota:	MINN. STAT. ANN. § 241.28, et seq. (2004)
Missouri:	MO. REV. STAT. § 217.535 (2004)
Montana:	MONT. CODE ANN. § 46-19-401, et seq. (2004)
Nebraska:	NEB. REV. STAT. § 29-3401 (2004)
Nevada:	NEV. REV. STAT. § 215A.010 (2004)
New Jersey:	N.J. STAT. ANN. § 30:7C-1, et seq.; 2A:67-6 (2004)
New Mexico:	N.M. STAT. ANN. § 31-5-17, et seq. (2004)
New York:	N.Y. CORRECT. LAW § 100, et seq. (2004)
North Carolina:	N.C. GEN. STAT. § 148-119, et seq. (2004)
Ohio:	OHIO REV. CODE § 5120.50 (2004)
Oklahoma:	OKLA. STAT. tit. 57 §§ 601, 602 (2004)
Oregon:	OR. REV. STAT. § 421.245, et seq. (2004)
Pennsylvania:	61 PA. CONS. STAT.§ 1062, et seq. (2004)
South Carolina:	S.C. CODE ANN. § 24-11-10, et seq. (2004)
Tennessee:	TENN. CODE ANN. § 41-23-101, et seq. (2004)
Texas:	TEXAS CRIM. PROC. CODE ANN. § 42.19 (2004)
Utah:	UTAH CODE ANN. § 77-28a-1, et seq. (2004)
Vermont:	VT. STAT. ANN. tit. 28 § 1601, et seq. (2004)
Virginia:	VA. CODE ANN. § 53.1-216, et seq. (2004)
Washington:	WASH. REV. CODE § 72.74.010, et seq. (2004)
Wisconsin:	WIS. STAT. § 302.25, et seq. (2004)
Dist. of Columbia:	D.C. CODE ANN. §§ 24-1001, 24-1002 (2004)
United States:	Pub. L. No. 73-293, 48 Stat. 909 (1934), 4 U.S.C. § 112(A) (2004)

- **Interstate Compact on Agricultural Grain Marketing**: Compact establishes a commission to promote exporting American produced grain. Membership is limited to any U.S. state in which agricultural grains are produced for national and international markets. The status of the compact is unclear as the commission appears inactive.

  Member States & Enabling Statutes:

Colorado:	COLO. REV. STAT. § 24-60-2001, et seq. (2004)
Kansas:	KAN. STAT. ANN. § 2-3101 (2004)

- **Interstate Compact on Mental Health:** Compact enables member states to provide care and treatment of mentally retarded persons regardless of residence requirements and authorizes supplementary agreements for joint or cooperative use of mental health resources.

  Member States & Enabling Statutes:

Alabama:	ALA. CODE 1975 § 22-55-1, et seq. (2004)
Alaska:	ALASKA STAT.§ 47.30.880 (2004)
Arkansas:	ARK. CODE ANN. § 20-50-101, et seq. (2004)
Colorado:	COLO. REV. STAT. § 24-60-1001, et seq. (2004)
Connecticut:	CONN. GEN. STAT. § 17a-615, et seq. (2004)
Delaware:	DEL. CODE ANN. tit. 16, § 6101, et seq. (2004)
Florida:	FLA. STAT. ANN. § 394.479, et seq. (2004)
Georgia:	GA. CODE ANN. § 37-10-1, et seq. (2004)
Hawaii:	HAW. REV. STAT. § 335-1, et seq. (2004)
Idaho:	IDAHO CODE § 66-1201, et seq. (2004)
Illinois:	45 ILL. COMP. STAT. 40/0.01, et seq. (2004)
Indiana:	IND. CODE § 12-28-2-1, et seq. (2004)
Iowa:	IOWA CODE § 221.1, et seq. (2004)
Kansas:	KAN. STAT. ANN. § 65-3101, et seq. (2004)
Kentucky:	KY. REV. STAT. ANN. § 210.520, et seq. (2004)
Louisiana:	LA. REV. STAT. ANN. § 28:721 et seq.
Maine:	ME. REV. STAT. ANN. tit. 34-B § 9001, et seq. (2004)
Maryland:	MD. CODE ANN. HEALTH-GEN. § 11-101, et seq. (2004)
Massachusetts:	MASS. ANN. LAWS (SPEC. L.) ch. 107, § 1, et seq. (2004)
Michigan:	MICH. COMP. LAWS § 330.1920, et seq. (2004)

Minnesota:	MINN. STAT. ANN. § 245.51, et seq. (2004)
Missouri:	MO. REV. STAT. § 630.810, et seq. (2004)
Montana:	MONT. CODE ANN. § 53-22-101, et seq. (2004)
Nebraska:	NEB. REV. STAT. § 83-801, et seq. (2004)
New Hampshire:	N.H. REV. STAT. ANN. § 135-A:1, et seq. (2004)
New Jersey:	N.J. STAT. ANN. § 30:7B-1, et seq. (2004)
New Mexico:	N.M. STAT. ANN. § 11-7-1, et seq. (2004)
New York:	N.Y. MENTAL HYG. LAW § 67.07 (2004)
North Carolina:	N.C. GEN. STAT. § 122C-361, et seq. (2004)
North Dakota:	N.D. CENT. CODE § 25-11-01, et seq. (2004)
Ohio:	OHIO REV. CODE § 5119.50, et seq. (2004)
Oklahoma:	OKLA. STAT. tit. 43A § 6-201, et seq. (2004)
Oregon:	OR. REV. STAT. § 428.310, et seq. (2004)
Pennsylvania:	62 PA. CONS. STAT. § 1121, et seq. (2004)
Rhode Island:	R.I. GEN. LAWS § 40.1-9-1, et seq. (2004)
South Carolina:	S.C. CODE ANN. § 44-25-10, et seq. (2004)
South Dakota:	S.D. CODIFIED LAWS § 27A-6-1, et seq. (2004)
Tennessee:	TENN. CODE ANN. § 33-9-201, et seq. (2004)
Texas:	TEX. HEALTH & SAFETY CODE ANN. § 612.001, et seq. (2004)
Utah:	UTAH CODE ANN. § 62A-15-801 (2004)
Vermont:	VT. STAT. ANN. Tit. 18 § 9001, et seq. (2004)
Washington:	WASH. REV. CODE § 72.27.010, et seq. (2004)
West Virginia:	W. VA. CODE § 27-14-1, et seq. (2004)
Wisconsin:	WIS. STAT. § 51.75, et seq. (2004)
Wyoming:	WYO. STAT. ANN. § 25-10-301, et seq. (2004)
Dist. of Columbia:	D.C. CODE ANN. § 7-1101, et seq. (2004)
United States:	Pub. L. No. 92-280, 86 Stat. 126 (1972)

- **Interstate Earthquake Emergency Compact:** Compact provides mutual aid among member states in meeting emergencies or disasters caused by earthquakes or other seismic disturbance.

Member States & Enabling Statutes:

Indiana:	IND. CODE § 10-4-3-1 (2004)
Mississippi:	MISS. CODE ANN. § 27-107-301 (2004)
Missouri:	MO. REV. STAT. § 256.155 (2004)
Tennessee:	TENN. CODE ANN. § 58-2-701 (2004)

- **Interstate Forest Fire Suppression Compact:** Compact allows member state to use inmate forest fire-fighting units from the other state when necessary to help fight forest fires.

  Member States & Enabling Statutes:

Idaho:	IDAHO CODE § 38-1601 (2004)
Oregon:	OR. REV. STAT. § 421.296 (2004)
Washington:	WASH. REV. CODE §§ 72.64.150, 72.64.160 (2004)

- **(Interstate) Furlough Compact:** Compact allows states to release incarcerated persons to (a) visit a critically ill relative; (b) attend a funeral of a relative; (c) obtain medical services of both a physiological and psychiatric nature; (d) contact prospective employers; (e) secure a suitable residence for use upon discharge or upon parole; (f) for any other reason that, in the opinion of the appropriate official of the sending state, is consistent with the rehabilitation of the inmate. This compact may be affected by the Interstate Compact for Adult Offender Supervision

  Member States & Enabling Statutes:

Tennessee*:	TENN. CODE ANN. § 41-23-202 (2004)
Utah:	UTAH CODE ANN. § 77-34-1, et seq. (2004)

- **Interstate High Speed Intercity Rail Passenger Compact/Interstate High Speed Rail Compact:** Compact intended to enable Illinois, Indiana, Kentucky, New York, Michigan, Missouri, Ohio, Pennsylvania, and West Virginia to conduct feasibility studies to establish high-speed rail passenger service between the major cities in each state. The compact is referred to as the Interstate High Speed Rail Compact, Midwest High Speed Rail Compact and High Speed Rail Compact.

  Member States & Enabling Statutes:

Illinois:	45 ILL. COMP. STAT. 70/0.01, et seq. (2004)
Indiana:	IND. CODE §§ 8-3-19-1, 8-3-19-2 (2004)
Michigan:	MICH. COMP. LAWS § 462.71 (2004)
Missouri:	MO. REV. STAT. § 680.200 (2004)
New York:	N.Y. TRANSP. LAW § 19 (2004)
Ohio:	OHIO REV. CODE § 4981.35 (2004)

---

*   Although substantially similar, Tennessee's version is more restrictive.

Pennsylvania: 55 PA. CONS. STAT. § 671 (2004)
United States: Pub. L. No. 98-358; 98 Stat. 399 (1984)

Administrative Agency:

High Speed Rail Compact
c/o Missouri Dept. of Transportation
P.O. Box 270
Jefferson City, MO 65102
(573) 751-7476:

- **Interstate Insurance Receivership Compact:** Compact establishes a commission to promote more uniform and coordinated approaches for managing the affairs of insolvent insurance companies, particularly multistate insurance companies.

Member States & Enabling Statutes:

California: CAL. INS. CODE, prec § 1120 (2005)
Illinois: 45 ILL. COMP. STAT. 160/1 (2004)
Michigan: MICH. COMP. LAWS § 550.11, et seq. (2004)
Nebraska: NEB. REV. STAT. § 44-6501 (2004)
Wisconsin: WIS. STAT. § 601.59 (2005)

- **Interstate Insurance Product Regulation Compact:** Creates the Interstate Insurance Product Regulation Commission to (1) develop uniform standards for certain insurance products covered under the compact, (2) give appropriate regulatory approval to those product filings and advertisements satisfying the applicable uniform standard, (3) establish a central clearinghouse to receive and provide prompt review of insurance products covered under the compact and, in certain cases, advertisements, submitted by insurers authorized to do business in one or more member states, and (4) give appropriate regulatory approval to those product filings and advertisements satisfying the applicable uniform standard. The compact becomes effective upon adoption by the 35th state.

Member States & Enabling Statutes:

Colorado: COLO. REV. STAT. § 24-60-3001 (2004)
Hawaii: HAW. REV. STAT. § 431:30-101 et seq., (2004)
Idaho: IDAHO CODE § 41-5702 (2005)
Iowa: IOWA CODE § 505A.1 (2005)
Indiana: IND. CODE § 27-8-31 (2005)
Kansas: Senate Bill 268

Maryland:	MD. CODE ANN. INS. § 29-101 (2005)
Maine:	ME. REV. STAT. ANN. tit. 24-A § 2471 (2005)
Nebraska:	LB 119
New Hampshire:	N.H. REV. STAT. ANN. § 408-C:1, et seq. (2005)
Rhode Island:	R.I. GEN. LAWS § 27-2.5-2 (2005)
Texas:	House Bill 2613, Effective Sept. 1, 2005
Utah:	UTAH CODE ANN. § 31A-39-101 (2005)
Vermont:	House Bill 0352
Virginia:	VA. CODE ANN. § 38.2-6200 (2004)
Washington:	Effective July 24, 2005
West Virginia:	W.VA. CODE § 38-47-1, et seq. (2004)

Administrative Agency:

National Association of Insurance Commissioners
2301 McGee Street
Suite 800
Kansas City, MO 64108-2662
Phone: (816)842-3600

Web Site:

http://www.naic.org/compact/index.htm

- **Interstate Library Compact:** Compact allows state, local, and private libraries to enter into agreements for services and use facilities, including the creation of joint library districts.

Member States & Enabling Statutes:

Alabama:	ALA. CODE § 41-8-21 (2004)
Arkansas:	ARK. CODE ANN. § 13-2-601, et seq. (2004)
Colorado:	COLO. REV. STAT. § 24-60-1501, et seq. (2004)
Connecticut:	CONN. GEN. STAT. § 11-38, et seq. (2004)
Florida:	FLA. STAT. ANN. § 257.28, et seq. (2004)
Georgia:	GA. CODE ANN. § 20-5-60, et seq. (2004)
Idaho:	IDAHO CODE § 33-2505, et seq. (2004)
Illinois:	45 ILL. COMP. STAT. 25/0.01 (2004)
Indiana:	IND. CODE § 20-14-11-1, et seq. (2004)
Iowa:	IOWA CODE § 256.70, et seq. (2004)
Kansas:	KAN. STAT. ANN. § 12-2901, et seq. (2004)
Kentucky:	KY. REV. STAT. ANN. § 171.221 (2004)
Louisiana:	LA. REV. STAT. ANN. § 25:631, et seq. (2004)

Maine:	ME. REV. STAT. ANN. tit. 27 § 141, et seq. (2004)
Maryland:	MD. CODE ANN. EDUC. § 25-301, et seq. (2004)
Massachusetts:	MASS. ANN. LAWS (SPEC. L.) ch. 103, § 1, et seq. (2004)
Minnesota:	MINN. STAT. ANN. § 134.21, et seq. (2004)
Mississippi:	MISS. CODE ANN. § 39-3-201, et seq. (2004)
Montana:	MONT. CODE ANN. §§ 22-1-601, 22-1-602 (2004)
New Hampshire:	N.H. REV. STAT. ANN. § 201-B:1, et seq. (2004)
New Mexico:	N.M. STAT. ANN. § 18-2-19, et seq. (2004)
New York:	N.Y. EDUC. LAW § 293, et seq. (2004)
North Carolina:	N.C. GEN. STAT. § 125-12, et seq. (2004)
North Dakota:	N.D. CENT. CODE § 54-24.1-01, et seq. (2004)
Ohio:	OHIO REV. CODE § 3375.83, et seq. (2004)
Oregon:	OR. REV. STAT. § 357.330, et seq. (2004)
Rhode Island:	R.I. GEN. LAWS, § 29-5-1, et seq. (2004)
South Dakota:	S.D. CODIFIED LAWS § 14-7-12, et seq. (2004)
Tennessee:	TENN. CODE ANN. § 10-6-101, et seq. (2004)
Vermont:	VT. STAT. ANN. tit. 22 § 21, et seq. (2004)
Virginia:	VA. CODE ANN. § 42.1-75 (2004)
Washington:	WASH. REV. CODE § 27.18.010 (2004)
West Virginia:	W. VA. CODE, § 10-1A-1, et seq.
Wyoming:	WYO. STAT. ANN. § 9-2-1026.8, et seq. (2004) (may be dormant)

- **Interstate Mining Compact**: Compact established a commission in 1970 to promote conservation practices, adopt standards for restoration of mined land, and develop mineral and other natural resources. Compact allows for both full membership and associate membership.

Member States & Enabling Statutes:

Illinois:	45 ILL. COMP. STAT. 50/1, et seq. (2004)
Indiana:	IND. CODE § 14-35-4-1, et seq. (2004)
Kentucky:	KY. REV. STAT. ANN. § 350.300, et seq. (2004)
Louisiana:	LA. REV. STAT. ANN. § 30:951, et seq. (2004)
Maryland:	MD. CODE ANN. ENVIR. §§ 15-901, 15-902 (2004)

Missouri:	Mo. Rev. Stat. § 444.400, et seq. (2004)
North Carolina:	N.C. Gen. Stat. §§ 74-37, 74-38 (2004)
Ohio:	Ohio Rev. Code § 1514.30, et seq. (2004)
Oklahoma:	Okla. Stat. tit. 45 § 851, et seq. (2004)
Pennsylvania:	52 Pa. Cons. Stat. § 3251, et seq. (2004)
South Carolina:	S.C. Code Ann. § 48-21-10, et seq. (2004)
Tennessee:	Tenn. Code Ann. § 59-10-101, et seq. (2004)
Texas:	Tex. Nat. Res. Code Ann. § 132.001, et seq. (2004)
Virginia:	Va. Code Ann. § 45.1-271 (2004)
West Virginia:	W. Va. Code, § 22C-10-1, et seq. (2004)
Wyoming:	Wyo. Stat. Ann. § 30-4-101 (2004)

Associate Members:
New Mexico
New York
North Dakota

Administrative Agency:

Interstate Mining Compact Commission
445-A Carlisle Dr.
Herndon, VA 20170-4819
(703) 709-8654

Web Site:

www.imcc.isa.us

- **Interstate Mutual Aid Compact:** Compact provides voluntary assistance between member states in responding to disasters or imminent disasters that supercede the resources of a local or state government. Assistance may include rescue, fire, police, medical, communication, and transportation services and facilities.

Member States & Enabling Statutes:

Idaho:	Idaho Code § 46-1018 (2004)
Montana:	Mont. Code Ann. § 10-3-207 (2004)

- **Interstate Preparedness and Civil Defense (and Disaster Compact):** Compact provides mutual aid among the states in meeting any emergency or disaster whether from human actions or natural cause. Compact allows prompt utilization of the resources of the respective states, including such resources as may be available from the United States government or any other source. This compact may interact with the Emergency Management Assistance Compact.

Member States & Enabling Statutes:

Alabama:	ALA. CODE § 31-9-7 (2004)
Alaska:	ALASKA STAT. § 26.23.120, et seq. (2004)
Arkansas:	ARK. CODE ANN. § 12-76-101, et seq. (2004)
California:	CAL. GOV'T CODE § 177, et seq. (2004)
Delaware:	DEL. CODE ANN. tit. 20, §§ 3301, 3302 (2004)
Georgia:	GA. CODE ANN. § 38-3-70, et seq. (2004)
Indiana:	IND. CODE § 10-4-2-1, et seq. (2004)
Kansas:	KAN. STAT. ANN. § 48-3201, et seq. (2004)
Louisiana:	LA. REV. STAT. ANN. § 29:733 (2004)
Maine:	ME. REV. STAT. ANN. tit. 37-B § 901, et seq. (2004)
Maryland:	MD. ANN. CODE, art. 41, § 17-101, et seq. (2004)
Michigan:	MICH. COMP. LAWS § 30.261 (2004)
Nebraska:	NEB. REV. STAT. (Appendix) § A1-109 (2004)
Nevada:	NEV. REV. STAT. § 415.010 (2004)
New Jersey:	N.J. STAT. ANN. § 38A:20-3 (2004)
Pennsylvania:	35 PA. CONS. STAT. § 7111 (2004)
Rhode Island:	R.I. GEN. LAWS § 30-15-14 (2004)
South Carolina:	S.C. CODE ANN. § 25-9-10, et seq. (2004)
Tennessee:	TENN. CODE ANN. § 58-2-401, et seq. (2004)
Utah:	UTAH CODE ANN. § 39-5-1, et seq. (2004)
Vermont:	VT. STAT. ANN. tit. 20 § 81, et seq. (2004)
Virginia:	VA. CODE ANN. § 44-146.17(5) (2004)
Dist. of Columbia:	D.C. CODE ANN. § 9-11-7.01, et seq. (2004)

- **Interstate Rail Passenger Network Compact:** Compacts allows for joint study to create an interstate rail passenger network to connect major cities in the member states.

  Member States & Enabling Statutes:

Georgia:	GA. CODE ANN. § 32-11-1, et seq. (2004)
Illinois:	45 Ill. Comp. Stat. 77/1, et seq. (2004)
Indiana:	IND. CODE § 8-3-21-1, et seq. (2004)
Tennessee:	TENN. CODE ANN. § 4-42-101, et seq. (2004)
United States:	Pub. L. No. 102-452; 106 Stat. 2255 (1992)

- **Interstate (Solid) Waste Compact:** Compact allows municipalities in New Hampshire and Vermont to enter into agreements to build and maintain solid waste disposal and resource recovery facilities.

  Member States & Enabling Statutes:

New Hampshire:	N.H. REV. STAT. ANN. § 53D:1 (2004)
Vermont:	VT. STAT. ANN. tit. 10 § 1222, et seq. (2004)

- **Interstate Wildlife Violator Compact:** Compact allows member states to develop reciprocal programs to issue and enforce wildlife citations. Agreements provide that states may recognize and suspend wildlife license privileges of someone who has violated the wildlife laws in another member state. Compact is managed by a board of administrators.

  Member States & Enabling Statutes:

Arizona:	ARIZ. REV. STAT. § 17-501, et seq. (2004)
Colorado:	COLO. REV. STAT. § 24-60-2601, et seq. (2004)
Idaho:	IDAHO CODE § 36-2301, et seq. (2004)
Indiana:	IND. CODE § 13-22-41-1 (2004)
Iowa:	IOWA CODE § 456A.24 (2004)
Georgia:	GA. CODE ANN. § 27-2-40, et seq. (2004)
Maryland:	MD. CODE ANN. NAT. RES. § 10-1201, et seq. (2004)
Montana:	MONT. CODE ANN. § 87-1-801, et seq. (2004)
Nevada:	NEV. REV. STAT. §§ 506.010, 506.020 (2004)
New Mexico:	N.M. STAT. ANN. § 11-16-1, et seq. (2004)
North Dakota:	N.D. CENT. CODE § 20.1-16 (2004)
Oregon:	OR. REV. STAT. § 469.750 (2004)

Utah: UTAH CODE ANN. § 23-25-1, et seq. (2004)
Washington: WASH. REV. CODE § 77.75.070, et seq. (2004)
West Virginia: W. VA. CODE, § 20-2C-1, et seq. (2004)
Wyoming: WYO. STAT. ANN. § 23-6-301, et seq. (2004)

- **Jennings Randolph Lake Project Compact:** Compact provides for joint management, planning, operation, and maintenance of the Jennings Randolph Lake Project. Compact establishes concurrent jurisdiction between member states for enforcing civil and criminal laws of the states regarding natural resources, boating, and other regulations over the land and waters of the project.

Member States & Enabling Statutes:

West Virginia: W. VA. CODE §§ 29-1J-1, 29-1J-2 (2004)
Maryland: MD. CODE ANN. NAT. RES. § 8-4A-01 (2004)
United States: Pub. L. No. 104-176; 110 Stat. 1557 (1996)

- **Kansas City Area Transportation (District & Authority) Compact:** Compact creates a metropolitan area transport district to construct, operate, and administer transit systems in the Kansas City area.

Member States & Enabling Statutes:

Kansas: KAN. STAT. ANN. § 12-2524, et seq. (2004)
Missouri: MO. REV. STAT. § 238.010, et seq. (2004)
United States: Pub. L. No. 89599; 80 Stat. 826 (1966);
                amended Pub. L. No.90395; 82 Stat. 338
                (1968)

Administrative Agency:

Kansas City Area Transportation Authority
1200 E. 18th Street
Kansas City, MO 64108
(816) 346-0200

Web Site:

www.kcata.org/

- **Kansas and Missouri Metropolitan Culture District Compact:**
Compact establishes a special district and commission to promote
and coordinate the arts and cultural activities (including sports) in
Johnson County, Kansas, and Jackson County, Missouri.

  Member States & Enabling Statutes:

Kansas:	KAN. STAT. ANN. § 12-2536 (2004)
Missouri:	REV. STAT. MO. § 70.500 (2004)
United States:	Pub. L. No. 103-390; 108 Stat. 4085 (1994); amended Pub. L. No. 106-287; 114 Stat. 909 (2000)

  Administrative Agency:

  Kansas-Missouri Metropolitan Culture District
  600 Broadway, Suite 300
  Kansas City, MO 64105
  (816) 474-4240

- **Klamath River Compact:** Compact creates a commission to promote development, conservation. and control of the resources of the
Klamath River.

  Member States & Enabling Statutes:

California:	CAL. WATER CODE § 5900, et seq. (2004)
Oregon:	OR. REV. STAT. § 542.610, et seq. (2004)
United States:	Pub. L. No. 84-316; 69 Stat. 613 (1955); Pub. L. No. 85-222; 71 Stat. 497 (1957)

  Administrative Agency:

  Klamath River Compact Commission
  280 Main St.
  Klamath Falls, OR 97601
  (541) 882-4436

- **La Plata River Compact:** Compact creates a joint commission to
apportion the waters of the La Plata River between Colorado and
New Mexico.

  Member States & Enabling Statutes:

Colorado:	COLO. REV. STAT. § 37-63-101, et seq. (2004)
New Mexico:	N.M. STAT. ANN. § 72-15-16, et seq. (2004)
United States:	Pub. L. No. 68-346; 43 Stat. 796 (1925)

Administrative Agency:

La Plata River Compact Commission
1313 Sherman St., Room 818
Denver, CO 80203
(303) 866-3581

Web Site:

www.water.state.co.us

- **Maine-New Hampshire School District Compact:** Compact authorizes interstate school districts between Maine and New Hampshire, and allows consolidation of elementary and secondary schools.

Member States & Enabling Statutes:

| Maine: | ME. REV. STAT. ANN. tit. 20-A § 3601, et seq. (2004) |
| New Hampshire: | N.H. REV. STAT. ANN. § 200-F:1 (2004) |

- **Merrimack River Flood Control Compact:** Establishes a commission to manage flood control in the Merrimack River Basin.

Member States & Enabling Statutes:

Massachuetts:	MASS. ANN. LAWS (SPEC. L.) ch. S123 (2004)
New Hampshire:	N.H. REV. STAT. ANN. § 484:7, et seq. (2004)
United States:	Pub. L. No. 85-23; 71 Stat. 18 (1957)

- **Metropolitan Washington Airports Authority:** Compact creates the Metropolitan Washington Airports Authority and charges that authority with administering airports in the Washington, D.C., metropolitan area. The authority currently operates Reagan National Airport and Dulles International Airport under lease from the federal government. Maryland is able to join and upon doing so Baltimore-Washington International Airport could be transferred to the authority.

Member States & Enabling Statutes:

Dist. of Columbia:	D.C. CODE § 9-901, et seq. (2004)
Virginia:	VA. CODE ANN. § 5.1-152, et seq. (2004)
United States:	49 U.S.C. § 49101, et seq. (2004)

Administrative Agency:

Metropolitan Washington Airports Authority
1 Aviation Circle
Washington, DC 20001
(703) 417-8600

Web Site:

http://www.metwashairports.com/

- **Middle Atlantic (Interstate) Forest Fire Protection Compact:** Compact provides mutual assistance in forest fire protection in the middle-Atlantic area and states adjoining that area.

Member States & Enabling Statutes:

Delaware:	DEL. CODE ANN. tit. 3, § 9101, et seq. (2004)
Maryland:	MD. CODE ANN. NAT. RES. § 5-801 (2004)
New Jersey:	N.J. STAT. ANN. § 32:24-1, et seq. (2004)
Ohio:	OHIO REV. CODE § 1503.41 (2004)
Pennsylvania:	32 PA. CONS. STAT.§ 422, et seq. (2004)
Virginia:	VA. CODE ANN. § 10.1-1150 (2004)
West Virginia:	W. VA. CODE § 20-3-25, et seq. (2004)
United States:	Pub. L. No. 84-790; 70 Stat. 636 (1956); Pub. L. No. 100-609; 102 Stat. 3175 (1988)

- **Midwest Interstate Low-Level Radioactive Waste Compact:** Compact creates regime for managing disposal of low-level radioactive waste and establishes a commission to manage compact affairs.

Member States & Enabling Statutes:

Indiana:	IND. CODE § 13-29-1-1, et seq. (2004)
Iowa:	IOWA CODE § 457B.1 (2004)
Michigan:	MICH. COMP. LAWS §§ 3.751, 3.722 (2004)
Minnesota:	MINN. STAT. ANN. § 116C.831, et seq. (2004)
Missouri:	MO. REV. STAT. § 260.700 (2004)
Ohio:	OHIO REV. CODE § 3747.01, et seq. (2004)
Wisconsin:	WIS. STAT. § 14.81 (2004)
United States:	Pub. L. No. 99-240, 99 Stat. 1859 (1986)

Administrative Agency:

Midwest Interstate Low-Level Radioactive Waste Compact
Commission
P.O. Box 2659
Madison, WI 53701-2659
(608) 267-4793

Web Site:

www.midwestcompact.org

- **Midwest Interstate Passenger Rail Compact:** Compact promotes development and implementation of improvements to intercity passenger rail service in the Midwest.

Member States & Enabling Statutes:

Indiana:	IND. CODE § 8-3-22 (2004)
Minnesota:	MINN. STAT. ANN. § 218.75 (2004)
Nebraska:	NEB. REV. STAT. § 74-1601 (2004)
North Dakota:	N.D. CENT. CODE § 8-11-01 (2004)
Ohio:	OHIO REV. CODE § 4982.36, et seq. (2004)

Interstate Agency:

Midwest Interstate Passenger Rail Compact Commission

- **Midwestern (Regional) Higher Education Compact:** Established in 1991 as an interstate compact agency, the Midwestern Higher Education Commission (MHEC) is charged with promoting interstate cooperation and resource sharing in higher education.

Member States & Enabling Statutes:

Illinois:	45 ILL. COMP. STAT. 155/0.01, et seq. (2004)
Indiana:	IDAHO CODE § 20-12-73-1, et seq. (2004)
Kansas:	KAN. STAT. ANN. § 72-60b01, et seq. (2004)
Michigan:	MICH. COMP. LAWS §§ 390.1531, 390.1532 (2004)
Minnesota:	MINN. STAT. ANN. § 135A.20, et seq. (2004)
Missouri:	MO. REV. STAT. § 173.700, et seq. (2004)
Nebraska:	NEB. REV. STAT. § 85-1301, et seq. (2004)
North Dakota:	N.D. CENT. CODE §§ 15-10.2-01, 15-10.2-02 (2004)
Ohio:	OHIO REV. CODE §§ 3333.40, 3333.41 (2004)
Wisconsin:	WIS. STAT. § 39.80 (2004)

Administrative Agency:

Midwestern Higher Education Commission
1300 South 2nd St., Suite 130
Minneapolis, MN55454-1079
(612) 626-8288

Web Site:

www.mhec.org

- **Mississippi-Louisiana-Alabama-Georgia Rapid Rail Transit Compact:** Also known as the Southern Rapid Rail Transit Compact, agreement creates a study of the feasibility of rapid rail transit service within the states of Mississippi, Louisiana, Alabama, and Georgia and to establish a joint interstate commission to assist in this effort.

Member States & Enabling Statutes:

Alabama:	ALA. CODE § 37-11-1 (2004)
Georgia*:	GA. CODE ANN. § 46-9-300 (2004)
Louisiana:	LA. REV. STAT. ANN. §§ 48:1671, 48:1672 (2004)
Mississippi:	MISS. CODE ANN. § 57-45-1 (2004)

Administrative Agency:

Southern Rapid Rail Transit Commission
c/o New Orleans Regional Planning Commission
1340 Poydras Street, Suite 2100
New Orleans, LA 70112
(504) 568-6633

- **Missouri River Barge Traffic Compact:** Compact provides for planning for the efficient use of the Missouri River to increase barge traffic on that segment that flows between and within the compact states; to take steps to develop the Missouri River to handle more traffic; to encourage the use of barges for transporting goods; to insure that an increase in barge traffic does not impose unacceptable damage on the river in all its various uses, including agriculture, wildlife management, and recreational opportunities; to consider the diversion of water as it affects navigation; and to promote joint action between the compact parties to accomplish these purposes.

---

*   Georgia apparently adopted a version of the compact, but is not a member of the compact.

Member States & Enabling Statutes:

Iowa: IOWA CODE § 307C.1, et seq. (2004)

Nebraska: NEB. REV. STAT. APP. §§ A1-118, A1-121 (2004)

Missouri: MO. REV. STAT. § 237.400 (2004)

- **Missouri River Toll Bridge Compact:** Authorizes acceptance for and on behalf of the states of Kansas and Missouri of title to a toll bridge spanning the Missouri River.

Member States & Enabling Statutes:

Kansas: KAN. STAT. ANN. § 68-1601, et seq. (2004)

Missouri: MO. REV. STAT. § 234.190 (2004)

United States: 73 Pub. Res. 8; 48 Stat. 105 (1933)

- **Multistate Highway Transportation Agreement:** Compact encourages uniformity in allowable vehicle size and loads.

Member States & Enabling Statutes:

Arizona: ARIZ. REV. STAT. § 28-1821, et seq. (2004)

Colorado: COLO. REV. STAT. §§ 24-60-2501, 24-60-2502 (2004)

Idaho: IDAHO CODE § 49-1901, et seq. (2004)

Montana: MONT. CODE ANN. § 61-10-1101 (2004)

Nevada: NEV. REV. STAT. §§ 481A.010, 481A.020 (2004)

New Mexico: N.M. STAT. ANN. §11-14-1, et seq. (2004)

Oregon: OR. REV. STAT. § 802.560 (2004)

Utah: UTAH CODE ANN. §§ 41-23-1, 41-23-2 (2004)

Washington: WASH. REV. CODE §§ 47.74.010, 47.74.020 (2004)

Wyoming: WYO. STAT. ANN. §§ 31-18-901, 31-18-903 (2004)

- **Multistate Lottery Agreement:** Agreement enables states to enter agreements for the operation and promotion of multiple jurisdictional lotteries. NOTE: It is questionable whether this agreement constitutes a true compact in as much as the agreement merely authorizes state lottery commission to enter subsequent agreements and does not appear to possess any binding force.

Member States & Enabling Statutes:

Florida: FLA. STAT. ANN. § 24.105 (2004)
Indiana: IND. CODE § 4-30-3-18 (2004)
Kansas: KAN. STAT. ANN. § 74-8731 (2004)

- **Multistate Tax Compact:** Created in 1967, the compact establishes a commission to (1) facilitate proper determination of state and local tax liability of multistate taxpayers, (2) promote uniformity and compatibility in significant components of tax systems, (3) facilitate taxpayer convenience and compliance, (4) seeks to avoid duplicate taxation, (5) conduct audits of major corporations on behalf of group of states, and (6) participate in litigation to require tax-payers to submit to audits. All states and other U.S. jurisdictions are eligible to participate.

Member States & Enabling Statutes:

Alabama:	ALA. CODE § 40-27-1, et seq. (2004)
Alaska:	ALASKA STAT. § 43.19.010, et seq. (2004)
Arkansas:	ARK. CODE ANN. § 26-5-101, et seq. (2004)
California:	CAL. REV. & TAX. CODE § 38001, et seq. (2004)
Colorado:	COLO. REV. STAT. § 24-60-1301, et seq. (2004)
Hawaii:	HAW. REV. STAT. § 255-1, et seq. (2004)
Idaho:	IDAHO CODE § 63-3701, et seq. (2004)
Kansas:	KAN. STAT. ANN. § 79-4301, et seq. (2004)
Maine:	ME. REV. STAT. ANN. tit. 36 § 7107, et seq. (2004)
Michigan:	MICH. COMP. LAWS § 205.581, et seq. (2004)
Minnesota:	MINN. STAT. ANN. § 290.171, et seq. (2004)
Missouri:	MO. REV. STAT. § 32.200, et seq. (2004)
Montana:	MONT. CODE ANN. § 15-1-601 (2004)
New Mexico:	N.M. STAT. ANN. § 7-5-1, et seq. (2004)
North Dakota:	N.D. CENT. CODE § 57-59-01, et seq. (2004)
Oregon:	OR. REV. STAT. § 305.655, et seq. (2004)
South Dakota:	S.D. CODIFIED LAWS §10-54-1, et seq. (2004)
Texas:	TEX. TAX CODE ANN. § 141.001, et seq. (2004)
Utah:	UTAH CODE ANN. § 59-1-801, et seq. (2004)
Washington:	WASH. REV. CODE § 82.56.010 (2004)
Dist. of Columbia:	D.C. CODE ANN. § 47-441, et seq. (2004)

Administrative Agency:

Multistate Tax Commission
444 N. Capitol St., NW
Suite 425
Washington, DC 20001
(202) 624-8699

Web Site:

http://www.mtc.gov

• **National Crime Prevention and Privacy Compact:** Authorizes and requires participating state criminal history repositories and the Federal Bureau of Investigation to make all unsealed criminal history records available in response to authorized noncriminal justice information requests. Such requests include employment background checks for those seeking to work with children or the elderly.

Member States & Enabling Statutes:

Alaska:	ALASKA STAT. § 12.64.010 (2004)
Arizona:	ARIZ. REV. STAT. § 41-1750.01 (2004)
Arkansas:	ARK. CODE ANN. § 12-12-1010 (2004)
Colorado:	COLO. REV. STAT. §§ 24-60-2701, 24-60-2702 (2004)
Connecticut:	CONN. GEN. STAT. § 29-164f, et seq. (2004)
Florida:	FLA. STAT. ANN. § 943.0543 (2004)
Georgia:	GA. CODE ANN. § 35-3-39.1 (2004)
Iowa:	IOWA CODE § 692B.1, et seq. (2003)
Kansas:	KAN. STAT. ANN. § 22-5001 (2004)
Maine:	ME. REV. STAT. ANN. tit. 25 §1701, et seq. (2004)
Michigan:	MICH. COMP. LAWS § 28.244 (2004)
Minnesota:	MINN. STAT. ANN. § 299C.57, et seq. (2004)
Missouri:	MO. REV. STAT. § 43.542 (2004)
Montana:	MONT. CODE ANN. § 44-5-601 (2004)
Nevada:	NEV. REV. STAT. 179A.800 (2004)
New Hampshire:	N.H. REV. STAT. ANN. 106-B:14 (2004)
New Jersey:	N.J. STAT. ANN. § 53:1-32 (2004)
North Carolina:	N.C. GEN. STAT. § 114-19.50 (2004)
Ohio:	OHIO REV. CODE § 109.57, et seq. (2004)
Oklahoma:	OKLA. STAT. tit. 74 § 150.9b (2004)
South Carolina:	S.C. CODE ANN. § 23-3-1010 (2003)

Tennessee: TENN. CODE ANN. § 38-14-101 (2004)
United States: Pub. L. No. 105-251; 112 Stat. 1870 (1998)
                  (codified at 42 U.S.C. § 14616 (2004)).

Administrative Agency

National Crime Prevention and Privacy Compact Council
FBI/CJIS Division
1000 Custer Hollow Road
Module C3
Clarksburg, WV 26306
(304) 625-2803

Web Site:

http://www.fbi.gov/hq/cjisd/cc.htm

- **National Guard Mutual Assistance Compact:** Compact provides for mutual aid in using the National Guard for emergencies, flexibility in deployment of forces, and protection of personnel when serving in other states on emergency duty. This compact may have been superseded by the Emergency Management Assistance Compact.

Member States & Enabling Statutes:

Alaska: ALASKA STAT. § 26.25.010, et seq. (2004)
Florida: FLA. STAT. ANN. § 250.540, et seq. (2004)
Kansas: KAN. STAT. ANN. § 48-1701 (2004)
North Carolina: N.C. GEN. STAT. § 127A-175, et seq. (2004)
South Dakota: S.D. CODIFIED LAWS § 33-9-12, et seq. (2004)
Virginia: VA. CODE ANN. § 44-54.1, et seq. (2004)

- **National Guard Mutual Assistance Counter-Drug Activities Compact:** Compact provides mutual assistance and support among the party states in the utilization of the National Guard in drug interdiction, counter-drug, and demand-reduction activities.

Member States & Enabling Statutes:

Alabama: ALA. CODE § 31-11-1, et seq. (2004)
Florida: FLA. STAT. ANN. 250.533, et seq. (2004)
Louisiana: LA. REV. STAT. ANN. §§ 29:741, 29:742
                  (2004)
Minnesota: MINN. STAT. § 192.88 (2004)
Mississippi: MISS. CODE § 33-7-501, et seq. (2004)

North Dakota:	N.D. CENT. CODE §§ 37-17.2-01, 37-17.2-02 (2004)
South Carolina:	S.C. CODE ANN. § 1-3-490 (2004)
South Dakota:	S.D. CODIFIED LAWS § 33-9-15 (2004)
Virginia:	VA. CODE ANN. § 44-75.1:1 (2004)
Washington:	WASH. REV. CODE § 38.08.500 (2004)
Wyoming:	WYO. STAT. ANN. § 19-9-211 (2004)

- **New England Radiological Health Protection:** Compact mandates that each member state develop an intrastate radiation-incident plan that is compatible with the interstate radiation-incident plan formulated pursuant to this compact. Whenever the compact administrator of a member state requests assistance, compact requires that the requested state render all possible aid to the requesting state, which is consonant with the maintenance of protection of its own people.

Member States & Enabling Statutes:

Conneticut:	CONN. GEN. STAT. § 22a-159 (2003)
Maine:	ME. REV. STAT. ANN. tit. 22 § 751, et seq. (2004)
Massachuetts:	MASS. ANN. LAWS, (SPEC. L.) ch. S109, § 1 (2004)
New Hampshire:	N.H. REV. STAT. ANN. § 125-B:1 (2004)
Rhode Island:	R.I. GEN. LAWS § 23-12.5-1 (2004)
Vermont:	VT. STAT. ANN. tit. 18 § 1601 (2004)

- **New England Higher Education Compact:** Compact establishes a board to foster development and joint use of higher education resources in New England.

Member States & Enabling Statutes:

Connecticut:	CONN. GEN. STAT. § 10a-61 (2004)
Maine:	ME. REV. STAT. ANN. tit. 20-A § 11001, et seq. (2004)
Massachusetts:	MASS. ANN. LAWS (SPEC. L.) ch. 101, § 1, et seq. (2004)
New Hampshire:	N.H. REV. STAT. ANN. § 200-A:1, et seq. (2004)
Rhode Island:	R.I. GEN. LAWS § 16-41-1, et seq. (2004)
Vermont:	VT. STAT. ANN. tit. 16 § 2691, et seq. (2004)
United States:	Pub. L. No. 83-719; 68 Stat. 982 (1954)

Administrative Agency:

New England Board of Higher Education
45 Temple Place
Boston, MA 02111
(617) 357-9620

Web Site:

www.nebhe.org/

- **New England Corrections Compact:** Compact encourages cooperation in the confinement, treatment, and rehabilitation of offenders and authorizes joint use of facilities and other resources.

Member States & Enabling Statutes:

Connecticut:	CONN. GEN. STAT. § 18-102, et seq. (2004)
Maine:	ME. REV. STAT. ANN. tit. 34-A § 9201, et seq. (2004)
Massachusetts:	MASS. ANN. LAWS, (SPEC. L.) ch. 113, §1 et seq. (2004)
New Hampshire:	N.H. REV. STAT. ANN. § 622-A:1, et seq. (2004)
Rhode Island:	R.I. GEN. LAWS § 13-11-1, et seq. (2004)
Vermont:	VT. STAT. ANN. tit. 28 § 1401, et seq. (2004)
United States:	Pub. L. No. 73-293; 48 Stat. 909 (1934) (codified at 4 U.S.C. § 112(A) (2004))

- **New England Interstate Water Pollution Control Compact:** Compact establishes a commission to oversee water pollution control in member states as pertains to the waters within the geographic area covered by the agreement. Commission is charged with water quality planning and standards development to improve groundwater, and engaging in public education of environmental issues:

Member States & Enabling Statutes:

Connecticut:	CONN. GEN. STAT. § 22a-308, et seq. (2004)
Maine:	ME. REV. STAT. ANN. tit. 38 § 491, et seq., 531, et seq. (2004)
New Hampshire:	N.H. REV. STAT. ANN. § 484:17, et seq. (2004)
Massachusetts:	MASS. ANN. LAWS (SPEC. L.) ch. 119, § 1, et seq. (2004)
New York:	N.Y. ENVTL. CONSERV. LAW § 21-0101, et seq. (2004)

Rhode Island: R.I. GEN. LAWS § 46-16-1, et seq. (2004)

Vermont: VT. STAT. ANN. tit. 10 § 1331, et seq. (2004)

United States: Pub. L. No. 80292; 61 Stat. 682 (1947)

Administrative Agency:

New England Interstate Water Pollution Control Commission
Boott Mills South
100 Foot of John Street
Lowell, MA 01852
(978) 323-7929

Web Site:

www.neiwpcc.org

- **New England Police Compact:** Compact establishes procedures for receiving mutual aid from member states in the area of prison control, riots, and general law enforcement.

Member States & Enabling Statutes:

Connecticut: CONN. GEN. STAT. § 29-162, et seq. (2004)

Maine: ME. REV. STAT. ANN. tit. 25 § 1665, et seq. (2004)

Massachusetts: MASS. ANN. LAWS (SPEC. L.) ch. 111, §1, et seq. (2004)

New Hampshire: N.H. REV. STAT. ANN. § 106-D:1, et seq. (2004)

Rhode Island: R.I. GEN. LAWS § 42-37-1, et seq. (2004)

Vermont: VT. STAT. ANN. tit. 20 § 1951, et seq. (2004)

United States: Pub. L. No. 73-293; 48 Stat. 909 (1934) (codified at 4 U.S.C. § 112(A) (2004))

- **New England Truck Permit Agreement for Oversize, Non-Divisible, Interstate Loads** Authorizes executive department officials to enter into regional agreements to make uniform, among member jurisdictions, the administration of overdimensional and overweight permits for nondivisible loads on vehicles in interstate operation; and enable participating jurisdictions to act cooperatively in issuing overdimensional and overweight permits and collecting the appropriate fees.

Member States & Enabling Statutes:

Maine: ME. REV. STAT. ANN. tit. 29-A § 2384 (2004)
Massachusetts: MASS. ANN. LAWS (SPEC. L.) ch. S135, § 2
                  (2004)
New Hampshire: N.H. REV. STAT. ANN. § 266:24-b (2004)

• **New Hampshire-Vermont Interstate Public Water Supply Compact:** Compact allows joint public water supply facilities.

Member States & Enabling Statutes:

New Hampshire: N.H. REV. STAT. ANN. § 485-D (2004)
Vermont: VT. STAT. ANN. tit. 10 § 1231, et seq. (2004)
United States: Pub. L. No. 104-126; 110 Stat. 884 (1996)

• **New Hampshire-Vermont Interstate School Compact**: Establishes board to increase educational opportunities for students.

Member States & Enabling Statutes:

New Hampshire: N.H. REV. STAT. ANN. § 200-B:1 (2004)
Vermont: VT. STAT. ANN. tit. 16 § 771, et seq. (2004)
United States: Pub. L. No. 91-21; 83 Stat. 14 (1969),
                  amended Pub. L. No. 107-352; 116 Stat.
                  2981 (2002)

• **New Hampshire-Vermont Interstate School Compact (Dresden or Hanover-Norwich School District):** Compact establishes an interstate school district.

Member States & Enabling Statutes:

New Hampshire: N.H. REV. STAT. ANN. § 200-B:1, et seq.
                  (2004)
Vermont: VT. STAT. ANN. tit. 16 § 771 (2004)
United States: Pub. L. No. 88-177; 77 Stat. 332 (1963)

• **New Hampshire-Vermont Interstate Sewage and Waste Disposal Facilities Compact:** Compact allows local governments and sewage districts in member states to develop programs, cooperate, and maintain joint facilities for the abatement and disposal of sewage and other waste products.

Member States & Enabling Statutes:

New Hampshire: N.H. Rev. Stat. Ann. § 149-J:1, et seq.
 (2004)
Vermont: Vt. Stat. Ann. tit. 10 § 1201, et seq. (2004)
United States: Pub. L. No. 94-403; 90 Stat. 1221 (1976)

- **New Hampshire-Vermont Compact (on Solid Waste Disposal):**
  Allows cooperative agreements for the construction and management of facilities concerning solid waste disposal.

Member States & Enabling Statutes:

New Hampshire: N.H. Rev. Stat. Ann. § 53-D:1 (2004)
Vermont: Vt. Stat. Ann. tit. 10 § 1222, et seq. (2004)
United States: Pub. L. No. 97-278, 96 Stat. 1207 (1982)

- **New Jersey-Pennsylvania Turnpike Bridge Compact:** Provides
  for construction of a bridge across the Delaware River.

Member States & Enabling Statutes:

New Jersey: N.J. Stat. Ann. § 32:11AA-1, et seq. (2004)
Pennsylvania: 36 Pa. Cons. Stat. § 3511, et seq. (2004)
United States: Pub. L. No. 82-216; 65 Stat. 650 (1951)

Administrative Agency:

Pennsylvania Turnpike Commission
P.O. Box 67676
Harrisburg, PA 17106-7676
(717) 939-9551

Web Site:

http://www.paturnpike.com/

- **Nonresident Violator Compact:** Compact ensures that nonresident
  motorists who violate minor traffic laws in a member state will be
  provided the same treatment accorded resident motorists.

Member States & Enabling Statutes:

Arizona: Ariz. Rev. Stat. § 28-1871, et seq. (2004)
Arkansas: Ark. Code Ann. § 27-54-101 (2004)
Colorado: Colo. Rev. Stat. § 24-60-2101, et seq. (2004)
Florida: Fla. Stat. Ann. § 322.50 (2004)
Hawaii: Haw. Rev. Stat. § 291A-1 (2004)
Idaho: Idaho Code § 49-2501 (2004)

Illinois:	625 ILL. COMP. STAT. 5/6-800, et seq. (2004)
Iowa:	IOWA CODE § 321.513 (2004)
Kansas:	KAN. STAT. ANN. § 8-1219, et seq. (2004)
Kentucky:	KY. REV. STAT. ANN. § 186.860 (2004)
Louisiana:	LA. REV. STAT. ANN. § 32:1441, et seq. (2004)
Maine:	ME. REV. STAT. ANN. tit. 29-A § 2460(3) (2004)
Maryland:	MD. CODE ANN. TRANSP. § 12-401, et seq. (2004)
Mississippi:	MISS. CODE ANN. § 63-10-1, et seq. (2004)
Missouri:	MO. REV. STAT. § 544.046 (2004)
Nebraska:	NEB. REV. STAT. (Appendix) § A1-119 (2004)
New Jersey:	N.J. STAT. ANN. § 39:5F-1, et seq. (2004)
New Mexico:	N.M. STAT. ANN. § 66-8-137.1, et seq. (2004)
New York:	N.Y. VEH. & TRAF. LAW, § 517 (2004)
Ohio:	OHIO REV. CODE § 4511.95, et seq. (2004)
Oklahoma:	OKLA. STAT. tit. 47 §§ 789, 790 (2004)
Texas:	TEX. TRANSP. CODE ANN. § 703.001, et seq. (2004)
Utah:	UTAH CODE ANN. § 53-3-701, et seq. (2004)
Vermont:	VT. STAT. ANN. tit. 23 § 3552, et seq. (2004)
Virginia:	VA. CODE ANN. § 46.2-944, et seq. (2004)
Washington:	WASH. REV. CODE § 46.23.010, et seq. (2004)
West Virginia:	W. VA. CODE §17B-1C-1 (2004)
United States:	Pub. L. No. 73-293; 48 Stat. 909 (1934) (codified at 4 U.S.C. § 112(A) (2004)

Administrative Agency:

Nonresident Violator Compact Board of Administrators
American Association of Motor Vehicle Administrators
(AAMVA)
4301 Wilson Blvd., Suite 400
Arlington, VA 22203
(703) 522-4200

Web Site:

www.aamva.org

- **Northeast Interstate Low-Level Radioactive Waste Management Compact:** Also referred to as the "Atlantic Compact," the compact creates a regime for the disposal of low-level radioactive waste and establishes a commission to manage compact affairs.

  Member States & Enabling Statutes:

Connecticut:	CONN. GEN. STAT. § 22a-161 (2004)
New Jersey:	N.J. STAT. ANN. § 32:31-1, et seq. (2004)
South Carolina:	S.C. CODE ANN. § 48-46-10, et seq. (2004)
United States:	Pub. L. No. 99-240; 99 Stat. 1859 (1986)

  Administrative Agency:

  Atlantic Compact Commission
  1201 Main Street, Suite 600
  Columbia, SC 29201
  (803) 737-1928

  Web Site:

  www.atlanticcompact.org/

- **Northeast Conservation Law Enforcement Compact:** Provides for cooperation and assistance in detecting and apprehending persons engaged in illegal fisheries and wildlife and environmental activities. Allows for mutual aid and assistance, and provides for the powers, duties, rights, privileges and immunities of conservation law enforcement personnel when rendering such aid.

  Member States & Enabling Statutes:

Connecticut:	CONN. GEN. STAT. § 26-26a (2004)
New Hampshire:	N.H. REV. STAT. ANN. § 215-B:1 (2003)

- **Northeastern Water and Related Land Resources Compact:** Compact provides, in the northeastern region, for improved facilities and procedures for the coordination of the policies, programs, and private persons or entities, in the field of water and related land resources. Enables states to study, investigate, and plan the development, use and conservation of water and related land resources; to provide means by which conflicts may be resolved; and to provide procedures for coordination of the interests of all public and private agencies, persons, and entities in the field of water and related land resources; and to provide an organization for cooperation in such coordination on both the federal and state levels of government.

Member States & Enabling Statutes:

Connecticut: Conn. Gen. Stat. § 25-120 (2001)
Massachusetts: Mass. Ann. Laws ch. S121, § 1 (2003)
New Hampshire: N.H. Rev. Stat. Ann. § 484:13, et seq. (2004)
Rhode Island: R.I. Gen. Laws § 46-17-2 (2004)

• **Northeastern (Interstate) Forest Fire Protection Compact:** Compact establishes a commission to promote effective prevention and control of forest fires in the New England states, New York, and adjoining Canadian provinces.

Member States & Enabling Statutes:

Connecticut: Conn. Gen. Stat. § 23-53, et seq. (2004)
Maine*
Massachusetts*
New Hampshire: N.H. Rev. Stat. Ann. § 227-L:26, et seq.
                 (2004)
New York: N.Y. Envtl. Conserv. Law § 9-1123 (2004)
Rhode Island: R.I. Gen. Laws § 2-13-1, et seq. (2004)
New Brunswick*
Nova Scotia*
Quebec*
Vermont: Vt. Stat. Ann. tit. 10 § 2461, et seq. (2004)
United States: Pub. L. No. 81-129; 63 Stat. 271 (1949);
                 granting consent to Canadian participation,
                 Pub. L. No. 82-340; 66 Stat. 71 (1952)

Administrative Agency:

Northeastern Forest Fire Protection Commission
P.O. Box 6192
China Village, Maine 04926-6192
(207) 968-3782

Web Site:

www.nffpc.com

---

*   Listed as a member of the compact by the Northeastern Forest Fire Protection Commission but statutory authorization cannot be located.

- **Northwest Wildland Fire Protection Agreement:** Compact is intended to promote effective prevention, presuppression, and control of forest fires in the Northwest wildland region of the United States and adjacent areas of Canada (by the members) by providing mutual aid in prevention, presuppression, and control of wildland.

   Member States & Enabling Statutes:*

Oregon:	OR. REV. STAT. § 477.200 (2004)
United States:	105 Pub. L. No. 377; 112 Stat. 3391 (1998)

- **Northwest Compact on Low-Level Radioactive Waste Management:** Compact establishes a regime for the disposal of low-level radioactive waste and creates a commission to manage compact affairs.

   Member States & Enabling Statutes:

Alaska:	ALASKA STAT. § 46.45.010, et seq. (2004)
Hawaii:	HAW. REV. STAT. § 339K-1, et seq. (2004)
Idaho:	IDAHO CODE § 39-3025, et seq. (2004)
Montana:	MONT. CODE ANN. §§ 50-79-501, 50-79-502 (2004)
Oregon:	OR. REV. STAT. § 469.930 (2004)
Utah:	UTAH CODE ANN. § 19-3-201, et seq. (2004)
Washington:	WASH. REV. CODE § 43.145.010, et seq. (2004)
Wyoming:	WYO. STAT. ANN. § 9-6-206, et seq. (2004)
United States:	Pub. L. No. 99-240; 99 Stat. 1859 (1986)

   Administrative Agency:

   Northwest Interstate Low-Level Radioactive Waste Compact
   Committee
   P.O. 47600
   Olympia, WA 98504
   (360) 407-7107

---

*   Other states and Canadian provinces participate through Cooperative Fire Protection Agreements (*see, e.g.,* agreement between U.S. Forest Service and California, *available at* http://www.fs.fed.us/r5/fire/cooperators/4-party_agrmt_fina_02.pdf#search=' northwest%20fire%20protection%20agreement) although statutory reference to this specific compact could not be located.

- **Nurse Licensure Compact:** Compact establishes reciprocal licensing between the member states for practical/vocational nurses.

  Member States & Enabling Statutes:

Arizona:	ARIZ. REV. STAT. §§ 32-1668, 32-1669 (2004)
Arkansas:	ARK. CODE ANN. § 17-87-601, et seq. (2004)
Iowa:	IOWA CODE § 152E. (2004)
Maryland:	MD. CODE ANN. HEALTH GEN. § 8-301 (2004)
Mississippi:	MISS. CODE ANN. § 73-15-22, et seq. (2004)
Nebraska:	NEB. REV. STAT. § 71-1795 (2004)
New Jersey:	N.J. STAT. ANN. § 45:11A-1 (2004)
North Carolina:	N.C. GEN. STAT. § 90-171.80, et seq. (2004)
South Dakota:	S.D. CODIFIED LAWS § 36-9-92 (2004)
Texas:	TEX. OCC. CODE § 304.001, (2004)
Utah:	UTAH CODE ANN. § 58-31C-102 (2004)

- **Ohio River Valley Water Sanitation Compact:** Establishes the Ohio River Valley Water Sanitation Commission to improve water quality in the Ohio River Basin so that the river and its tributaries can be used for drinking water, industrial supplies, and recreational purposes.

  Member States & Enabling Statutes:

Illinois:	45 ILL. COMP. STAT. 60/0.01 (2004)
Indiana:	IND. CODE § 13-29-2-1, et seq. (2004)
Kentucky:	KY. REV. STAT. § 224.18-760 (2004)
New York:	N.Y. ENVTL. CONSERV. § 21-0301(2004)
Ohio:	OHIO REV. CODE § 6113.01 (2004)
Pennsylvania:	32 PA. CONS. STAT. § 816.1 (2004)
Virginia:	VA. CODE. ANN. § 62.1-70 (2004)
West Virginia:	W. VA. CODE § 22C-12-1 (2004)
United States:	Pub. L. No. 76739; 54 Stat. 752 (1940)

  Administrative Agency:

  Ohio River Valley Water Sanitation Commission (ORSANCO)
  5735 Kellogg Avenue
  Cincinnati OH 45228
  (513) 231-7719

  Web Site:

  http://www.orsanco.org/default.asp

- **Pacific Marine Fisheries Compact:** Compact establishes the Pacific Marine Fisheries Commission to promote conservation, development and management of Pacific coast fisheries through research, monitoring, and utilization.

  Member States & Enabling Statutes:

Alaska:	ALASKA STAT. § 16.45.010, et seq. (2004)
California:	CAL. FISH & GAME CODE § 14000, et seq. (2004)
Idaho:	IDAHO CODE § 36-2001, et seq. (2004)
Oregon:	OR. REV. STAT. §§ 507.040, 507.050 (2004)
Washington:	WASH. REV. CODE §§ 77.75.030, 77.75.040 (2004)
United States:	Pub. L. No. 80-232; 61 Stat. 419 (1947)

  Administrative Agency:

  Pacific States Marine Fisheries Commission
  45 S.E. 82nd Drive, Suite 100
  Gladstone, OR 97027-2522
  (503) 650-5400

  Web Site:

  www.psmfc.org

- **Pacific States Agreement on Radioactive Materials Transportation:** Compact creates the Pacific States Radioactive Materials Transportation Committee to develop model regulatory standards for member states governing routing and inspecting shipments of radioactive material.

  Member States & Enabling Statutes:

Idaho:	IDAHO CODE § 39-3029 (2004)
Washington:	WASH. REV. CODE § 43.146.010 (2004)
Wyoming	WY. STAT. ANN. § 37-24-101 (2004)

- **Palisades Interstate Park Compact:** Compact establishes a commission to administer parks in New Jersey and New York.

  Member States & Enabling Statutes:

New Jersey:	N.J. STAT. ANN. § 32:17-1, et seq. (2004)
New York:	N.Y. PARKS, REC. & HIST. PRESERV. LAW § 9.01 (2004)
United States:	Pub. Res. 75-65; 50 Stat. 719 (1937)

Administrative Agency:

Palisades Interstate Park Commission
Administration Building
Bear Mountain, NY 10911-0427
(845) 7862701

Web Site:

www.pipc.org

- **Pecos River Compact:** Compact creates a commission to apportion waters of the Pecos River and administer provisions of the compact.

Member States & Enabling Statutes:

New Mexico:	N.M. Stat. Ann. § 72-15-19, et seq. (2004)
Texas:	Tex. Water Code Ann. § 42.001, et seq. (2004)
United States:	Pub. L. No. 81-91; 63 Stat. 159 (1949)

Administrative Agency:

Pecos River Commission
P.O. Box 340
Monahans, TX 79756
(915) 943-5171

- **(Port Authority of) New York-New Jersey Port Authority Compact:** Compact establishes a port district in the New York City-New Jersey metropolitan area and a joint authority to provide and manage transportation, terminal, and other facilities of commerce and trade. Formerly known as the Port of New York Authority.

Member States & Enabling Statutes:

New Jersey:	N.J. Stat. Ann. § 32:1-1, et seq.; 32:2-1, et seq. (2004)
New York:	N.Y. Unconsol. Law § 6401, et seq. (2004)
United States:	Pub. Res. 67-17; 42 Stat. 174 (1921); revised, Pub. L. No. 96-163; 93 Stat. 1242 (1979)

Administrative Agency:

Port Authority of New York and New Jersey
225 Park Avenue South, 18th Floor
New York, NY 10003
Tel: (212) 4357000

Web Site:

www.panynj.gov

- **Portsmouth-Kittery Bridge Compact (Maine-New Hampshire Interstate Bridge Authority):** Compact establishes an authority to build an interstate bridge. In 1985 Congress passed Pub. L. No. 99-190 to enable the Authority to transfer ownership of the approach roadways to the bridge and the overpasses to Maine and New Hampshire. Ownership of bordering real estate located in New Hampshire was also transferred to New Hampshire. The roadways became public highways, and (by administrative action) are in the Federal Aid system, thus qualifying for matching funds for capital improvement projects. The bridge itself is retained by the Bridge Authority, and also qualifies for Federal Aid in the form of matching funds. An amendment to the Compact (Article IV) transfers authority employees to the Maine Department of Transportation and New Hampshire Department of Public Works and Highways.

Member States & Enabling Statutes:

Maine*
New Hampshire: N.H. REV. STAT. ANN. § 234:43, et seq. (2004)
United States: Pub. L. No. 99-190; 50 Stat. 535 (1937)

Administrative Agency:

MaineNew Hampshire Interstate Bridge Authority
P.O. Box 483
One Hazen Drive
Concord, NH 03302
(603) 271-3667

---

*   Maine appears to be a member of the compact by its membership on and participation in the Maine-New Hampshire Interstate Bridge Authority. However, no statutory authority could be located affirmatively establishing that Maine has legislatively adopted the compact.

- **Potomac Highlands Airport Authority:** Compact creates the Potomac Highlands Authority to enable local governments in Maryland and West Virginia to coordinate air transportation facilities and services on a regional basis.

Member States & Enabling Statutes:

Maryland: MD. CODE ANN. TRANSP. § 10-101, et seq. (2004)

West Virginia*
United States: Pub. L. No. 105-348; 112 Stat. 3212 (1998)

Administrative Agency:

Potomac Highlands Airport Authority
Cumberland Regional Airport
Route 1, Box 99
Wiley Ford, WV 26767
(304) 738-0002

Web Site:

www.cumberlandairport.com

- **Potomac River Bridges Towing Compact**: Authorizes law enforcement officers from the District of Columbia, Maryland, and Virginia to direct traffic, move disabled vehicles and conduct related traffic matters on any part of the Potomac River bridges. The District of Columbia and Virginia are reported to be parties to this compact or agreement.

Member States & Enabling Statues:

Dist. of Columbia: D.C. CODE § 9-1117.01 (2004),
Maryland: MD. CODE ANN. TRANSP. § 25-301 (2004)

- **Potomac River Compact of 1958:** Compact creates the Potomac River Fisheries Commission to conserve and improve fishing in the tidewater portion of the Potomac River.

Member States & Enabling Statutes:

Maryland: MD. CODE ANN. NAT. RES. § 4-306, et seq. (2004)

---

    *   West Virginia appears to participate in the compact through an intergovernmental agreement.

Virginia: VA. CODE ANN. § 28.2-1001, et seq. (2004)
United States: Pub. L. No. 87-783; 76 Stat. 797 (1962)

Administrative Agency:

Potomac River Fisheries Commission
P.O. Box 9
222 Taylor St.
Colonial Beach, VA 22443-0009
(804) 224-7148

• **Potomac Valley Compact (Potomac River Basin Compact)**: Compact establishes an interstate commission to preserve water quality and to conserve water and related land resources of the Potomac River Basin. The commission is a nonregulatory body that uses watershed-based approaches to promote water quality management.

Member States & Enabling Statutes:

Maryland: MD. CODE ANN. NAT. RES. § 5-301, et seq.
                       (2004)
Pennsylvania: 32 PA. CONS. STAT. § 741, et seq. (2004)
West Virginia: W. VA. CODE § 22C-11-1 (2004)
Dist. of Columbia: D.C. CODE ANN. §§ 8-1601, 8-1602 (2004)
United States: Pub. Res. 76-93, 54 Stat. 748 (1940); Pub.
                       L. No. 91-407, 84 Stat. 856 (1970)
                       (approving amendments)

Administrative Agency:

Interstate Commission on the Potomac River Basin
Suite 300
6110 Executive Blvd.
Rockville, MD 20852-3903
(301) 984-1908

Web Site:

www.potomacriver.org

• **Pymatuning Lake Compact**: Compact establishes a recreation district, provides for water conservation, and establishes concurrent Ohio and Pennsylvania jurisdiction over Pymatuning Lake.

Member States & Enabling Statute:

Ohio: OHIO REV. CODE §§ 1541.31, 1541.32 (2004)
Pennsylvania: 71 PA. CONS. STAT. § 1840, et seq. (2004)
United States: Pub. L. No. 75-398, 50 Stat. 865 (1937)

- **Red River Compact:** Compact creates interstate commission to apportion waters of the Red River and its tributaries.

Member States & Enabling Statutes:

Arkansas: ARK. CODE ANN. § 15-23-501, et seq. (2004)
Louisiana: LA. REV. STAT. ANN. § 38.20 (2204)
Oklahoma: OKLA. STAT. tit. 82 §§ 1431, 1432 (2004)
Texas: TEX. WATER CODE ANN. § 46.001, et seq.
                         (2004)
United States: Pub. L. No. 84-346, 69 Stat. 654 (1955);
                         Pub. L. No. 96564, 94 Stat. 3305 (1980)

Administrative Agency:

Red River Compact Commission
Arkansas Soil and Water Commission
101 E. Capitol, Suite 350
Little Rock, AR 72201
(501) 682-1611

- **Republican River Compact:** Compact creates a commission to oversee equitable apportionment of the Republican River. Provisions of the compact are administered by existing agencies of signatory states.

Member States & Enabling Statutes:

Colorado: COLO. REV. STAT. §§ 37-67-101, 37-67-102
                         (2004)
Kansas: KAN. STAT. ANN. § 82a-518 (2004)
Nebraska: NEB. REV. STAT. (Appendix) § A1-106 (2004)
United States: Pub. L. No. 78-60, 57 Stat. 86 (1943)

- **Rio Grande Compact:** Compact creates an interstate commission to administer the compact and apportion the waters of the Rio Grande River between member states.

Member States & Enabling Statutes:

Colorado:	COLO. REV. STAT. §§ 37-66-101, 37-66-102 (2004)
New Mexico:	N.M. STAT. ANN. § 72-15-23, et seq. (2004)
Texas:	TEX. WATER CODE ANN. § 41.001, et seq. (2004)
United States:	Pub. L. No. 76-96, 53 Stat. 785 (1939)

Administrative Agency:

Rio Grande River Compact Commission
1313 Sherman St. Room 818
Denver, CO 80203
(303) 866-3581

Web Site:

www.water.state.co.us

- **Rocky Mountain Low-Level Radioactive Waste Compact**: Compact is to develop a regional management system for low-level waste (LLW) generated in the six states eligible for membership: Arizona, Colorado, Nevada, New Mexico, Utah, and Wyoming. Under the compact, any party state generating at least 20 percent of the region's waste becomes responsible for hosting a regional LLW management facility. However, the compact prescribes no system that the host state must follow to develop a facility, but rather calls on the state to fulfill its responsibility through reliance on its own laws and regulations

Member States & Enabling Statutes:

Colorado:	COLO. REV. STAT. § 24-60-2201, et seq. (2004)
Nevada:	NEV. REV. STAT. §§ 459.007, 459.008 (2004)
New Mexico:	N.M. STAT. ANN. § 11-9A-1, et seq. (2004)
Wyoming:	WY. STAT. ANN. § 9-6-201 (2004)
United States:	Pub. L. No. 99-240, 99 Stat. 1859 (1986)

Administrative Agency:

Rocky Mountain Low-Level Radioactive Waste Compact Board
1675 Broadway, Suite 1400
Denver, CO 80202
(303) 825-1912

- **Sabine River Compact:** Compact creates an interstate commission to apportion the waters of the Sabine River and to plan, develop, and conserve water resources in the river basin.

Member State & Enabling Statutes:

Louisiana:	LA. REV. STAT. ANN. § 38:2329 (2004)
Texas:	TEX. WATER CODE ANN. § 44.001, et seq. (2004)
United States:	Pub. L. No. 83-578, 68 Stat. 690 (1954); as amended Pub. L. No. 95-71, 91 Stat. 281 (1977)

Administrative Agency:

Sabine River Compact Administration
15091 Texas Highway
Many, LA 71449-9730
(318) 256-4112

- **Snake River Compact:** Compact apportions the waters of the Snake River and directs that the compact be administered through the official in each state.

Member States & Enabling Statutes:

Idaho:	IDAHO CODE § 42-3401, et seq. (2004)
Wyoming:	WYO. STAT. ANN. §§ 41-12-501, 41-12-502 (2004)
United States:	Pub. L. No. 81-464, 64 Stat. 29 (1950)

- **South Central (Interstate) Forest Fire Protection Compact:** Compact provides mutual aid in forest fire protection and control among states in the south central area and with states that are parties to other regional forest fire prevention compacts.

Member States & Enabling Statutes:

Arkansas:	ARK. CODE ANN. § 15-33-101, et seq. (2004)
Kentucky:	KY. REV. STAT. § 149.320 (2004)
Louisiana:	LA. REV. STAT. ANN. § 3:4296 (2004)
Mississippi:	MISS. CODE ANN. § 49-19-141, et seq. (2004)
North Carolina:	N.C. GEN. STAT. § 113-60.13 (2004)*

---

*   Ratifies specific articles that provide for cooperation with mutual aid agreements and other compacts such as the Middle Atlantic Fire Protection Compact.

Oklahoma:	OKLA. STAT. tit. 2 § 1301-215, et seq. (2004)
Texas:	TEX. EDUCATION CODE ANN. § 88.112, et seq. (2004)
United States:	Pub. L. No. 83-642; 68 Stat. 783 (1954)

Administrative Agency:

South Central States Forest Fire Protection
Compact Commission

• **South Platte River Compact:** Compact creates a commission to apportion the waters of the South Platte River between member states.

Member States & Enabling Statutes:

Colorado:	COLO. REV. STAT. § 37-65-101 (2004)
Nebraska:	NEB. REV. STAT. (Appendix) § A1-105 (2004)
United States:	Pub. L. No. 69-37, 44 Stat. 195 (1926)

Administrative Agency:

South Platte River Compact Commission
1313 Sherman St. Room 818
Denver, CO 80203
(303) 8663581

• **Southeast Interstate Low-Level Radioactive Waste Compact:** Compact establishes a commission to manage the disposal of low-level radioactive waste.

Member States & Enabling Statutes:

Alabama:	ALA. CODE § 22-32-1, et seq. (2004)
Florida:	FLA. STAT. ANN. § 404.30 (2004)
Georgia:	GA. CODE ANN. § 12-8-120, et seq. (2004)
Mississippi:	MISS. CODE ANN. § 57-47-1, et seq. (2004)
North Carolina*:	N.C. GEN. STAT. § 104F-1, et seq. (2004)
Tennessee:	TENN. CODE ANN. § 68-202-701, et seq. (2004)
Virginia:	VA. CODE ANN. § 10.1-1500, et seq. (2004)
United States:	Pub.L. 99-240, 99 Stat. 1859 (1986)

---

*   North Carolina repealed this compact by Session Laws 1999-357.

Administrative Agency:

Southeast Compact Commission
21 Glenwood Ave., Suite 207
Raleigh, NC 27603
(919) 821-0500

Web Site:

www.secompact.org

• **Southeastern (Interstate) Forest Fire Protection Compact:** Compact provides mutual aid in forest fire prevention and control among states in the southeastern area and with party states that are members other regional forest fire prevention compacts.

Member States & Enabling Statutes:

Alabama:	ALA. CODE §§ 9-13-200, 9-13-201 (2004)
Florida:	FLA. STAT. ANN. § 590.31, et seq. (2004)
Georgia:	GA. CODE ANN. § 12-10-60, et seq. (2004)
Kentucky:	KY. REV. STAT. ANN. § 149.310, et seq. (2004)
Mississippi:	MISS. CODE ANN. § 49-19-171, et seq. (2004)
North Carolina:	N.C. GEN. STAT. § 113-60.11, et seq. (2004)
South Carolina:	S.C. CODE ANN., § 48-37-10, et seq. (2004)
Tennessee:	TENN. CODE ANN. § 11-4-501, et seq. (2004)
Virginia:	VA. CODE ANN. § 10.1-1149 (2004)
West Virginia:	W. VA. CODE, § 20-3-20, et seq. (2004)
United States:	Pub. L. No. 83-536; 68 Stat. 563 (1954)

Interstate Agency:

Southeastern States Forest Fire Compact Commission
c/o Southern Area Coordination Center
1954 Airport Road, Suite 105
Chamblee, GA 30341
(770) 456-2464

Web Site:

www.southernregion.fs.fed.us/sacc/

• **Southern Dairy Compact:** Compact promotes a variety of regional dairy issues.

Member States & Enabling Statutes:

Alabama:	ALA. CODE, §§ 2-13A-1, 2-13A-2 (2004)
Arkansas:	ARK. CODE ANN. § 2-33-401 (2004)
Georgia:	GA. CODE ANN. § 2-20-1, et seq. (2004)
Kansas:	KAN. STAT. ANN. § 74-577 (2004)
Kentucky	KY. REV. STAT. ANN. § 260.670, et seq. (2004)
Louisiana:	LA. REV. STAT. ANN. § 3:4021, et seq. (2004)
Mississippi:	MISS. CODE ANN. § 69-36-1 (2004)
Missouri:	MO. REV. STAT. § 262.700 (2004)
North Carolina:	N.C. GEN. STAT. §§ 106-810, 106-811 (2004)
Oklahoma:	OKLA. STAT. tit. 2 § 7-10 (2004)
South Carolina:	S.C. CODE ANN., § 46-50-10, et seq. (2004)
Tennessee:	TENN. CODE ANN. § 43-35-101-110 (2004)
Virginia:	VA. CODE ANN. § 3.1-461.4, et seq. (2004)
West Virginia:	W. VA. CODE, § 19-11C-1, et seq. (2004)

- **Southern Growth Policies Board Agreement:** Establishes a board charged with promoting economic development. The compact permits gubernatorial ratification pending legislative action.

Member States & Enabling Statutes:

Alabama:	ALA. CODE § 41-18-1, et seq. (2004)
Arkansas:	ARK. CODE ANN. § 15-2-101 (2004)
Georgia:	GA. CODE ANN. § 12-10-20, et seq. (2004)
Kentucky:	KY. REV. STAT. § 147.580 (2004)
Louisiana:	LA. REV. STAT. ANN. § 49:61 (2004)
Mississippi:	MISS. CODE ANN. § 57-33-1, et seq. (2004)
Missouri*	
North Carolina:	N.C. GEN. STAT. § 143-490, et seq. (2004)
Oklahoma:	OKLA. STAT. ANN. tit. 74, §§ 3501, 3502 (2004)
South Carolina:	S.C. CODE ANN. § 13-13-10 (2004)
Tennessee:	TENN. CODE ANN. § 13-2-101, et seq. (2004)
Virginia:	VA. CODE ANN. § 2.1-339.1, et seq. (2004)
West Virginia*	

---

*   Missouri and West Virginia are listed as member of the compact by the Southern Growth Policies Board. However, there appears no statutory verification of their membership.

Administrative Agency:

Southern Growth Policies Board
630 Davis Drive, Suite 100
Durham, NC 27713
(919) 9415145

Web Site:

www.southern.org

- **Southern Regional Education Compact:** Created in 1948, the compact establishes a board to promote interstate educational opportunities in the southern region. The board is charged with improving education from kindergarten through higher education. The compact represents the first regional education compact.

Member States & Enabling Statutes:

Alabama:	Ala. Code § 16-5-11, et seq. (2004)
Arkansas:	Ark. Code Ann. § 6-4-101, (2004)
Delaware:	Del. Code Ann. 14 § 3495 (2004)
Florida:	Fla. Stat. Ann. § 1000.32, et seq. (2004)
Georgia:	Ga. Code Ann. § 20-6-1 (2004)
Kentucky:	Ky. Rev. Stat. §§ 164.530, 164.540 (2004)
Louisiana:	La. Rev. Stat. Ann. § 17:1901, et seq. (2004)
Maryland:	Md. Code Ann. Educ. § 25-201, et seq. (2004)
Mississippi:	Miss. Code § 37-135-1, et seq. (2004)
Missouri*:	Mo. Rev. Stat. § 173.715 (2004)
North Carolina**	
Oklahoma:	Okla. St. Ann. tit. 10 §§ 2127, 2128 (2004)
South Carolina**	
Tennessee:	Tenn. Code Ann. § 49-12-101 (2004)
Texas:	Tex. Educ. Code Ann. § 160.01, et seq. (2004)
Virginia:	Va. Code Ann. § 22.1-358 (2004)
West Virginia:	W. Va. Code § 18-10C-1, et seq. (2004)

* Missouri is not listed by SREB as a member of the compact, although it has statutorily adopted the agreement.

** Both North Carolina and South Carolina are listed as members by the SREB. Various statutes in both states make reference to cooperating with the SREB on a variety of matters. However, there is no statutory reference actually adopting the compact.

Administrative Agency:

Southern Regional Education Board
592 Tenth Street, NW
Atlanta, GA 30318-5790
(404) 875 9211

Web Site:

www.sreb.org

- **Southern States Interstate (Energy) (Nuclear) Compact:** Compact creates an interstate commission to provide for regional cooperation in the proper utilization of energy and environmental resources in the southern states.

Member States & Enabling Statutes:

Alabama:	ALA. CODE § 9-18A-1, et seq. (2004)
Arkansas:	ARK. CODE ANN. § 15-10-401, et seq. (2004)
Florida:	FLA. STAT. ANN. § 377.71, et seq. (2004)
Georgia:	GA. CODE ANN. § 12-10-1, et seq. (2004)
Kentucky:	KY. REV. STAT. ANN. § 152.200, et seq. (2004)
Louisiana:	LA. REV. STAT. ANN. § 51:1001, et seq. (2004)
Maryland:	MD. ANN. CODE, art. 41, § 16-101, et seq. (2004)
Mississippi:	MISS. CODE ANN, § 57-25-1 (2004)
Missouri:	MO. REV. STAT. § 18.060, et seq. (2004)
North Carolina:	N.C. GEN. STAT. § 104D-1, et seq. (2004)
Oklahoma:	OKLA. STAT. tit. 74 § 1051, et seq. (2004)
South Carolina:	S.C. CODE ANN. § 13-7-410, et seq. (2004)
Tennessee:	TENN. CODE ANN. § 68-202-601, et seq. (2004)
Texas:	TEX. GOVERNMENT CODE ANN. § 761.001, et seq. (2004)
Virginia:	VA. CODE ANN. § 2.1-336, et seq. (2004)
West Virginia:	W. VA. CODE, § 29-1E-1, et seq. (2004)
United States:	Pub. L. No. 87-563, 76 Stat. 249 (1962)

Administrative Agency:

Southern States Energy Board
6325 Amherst Court
Norcross, GA 30092
(770) 242-7712

Web Site:

www.sseb.org

- **Southwestern Low-Level Radioactive Waste Disposal Compact**: Compact creates the Southwestern Low-Level Radioactive Waste Commission. California, as host state, is required to develop a regional disposal facility. The commission's key duties include controlling the importation and exportation of low-level waste into and out of the region. As a separate legal entity, it can make recommendations and comments appropriate to its charge under law to do whatever is reasonably necessary to ensure that low-level waste is safely disposed of and managed within the region.

Member States & Enabling Statutes:

Arizona: ARIZ. REV. STAT. § 30-721, et seq. (2004)
California: CAL. HEALTH & SAFETY CODE § 115250, et seq. (2004)
North Dakota: N.D. CENT. CODE § 23-20.5-01, et seq. (2004)
South Dakota: S.D. CODIFIED LAWS § 34-21B-3, et seq. (2004)
United States: Pub. L. No. 100-712, 102 Stat. 4773 (1988) (codified at 42 U.S.C.A. § 2021d (2004))

Administrative Agency:

Southwestern Low-Level Radioactive Waste Commission
P.O. Box 277727
Sacramento CA 95827-7727
(916) 448-2390

Web Site:

http://www.swllrwcc.org/

- **Susquehanna River Basin Compact:** Compact creates a federal-interstate commission to provide comprehensive planning, development, and management of water and related resources of the Susquehanna River Basin. The federal government is a full member of this com-pact.

  Member States & Enabling Statutes:

Maryland:	MD. CODE ANN. ENVIR. § 5-301 (2004)
New York:	N.Y. ENVTL. CONSERV. LAW § 21-1301, et seq. (2004)
Pennsylvania:	32 PA. CONS. STAT.§ 820.1, et seq. (2004)
United States:	Pub. L. No. 91575, 84 Stat. 1509 (1970)

  Administrative Agency:

  Susquehanna River Basin Commission
  1721 N. Front St.
  Harrisburg, PA 17102:
  (717) 2380423

  Web Site:

  www.srbc.net

- **Tahoe Regional Planning Compact:** Creates the Tahoe Regional Planning Agency to oversee and manage development in the Lake Tahoe Basin through enforcement of a code of ordinances and environmental quality standards, also referred to as environmental thresholds.

  Member States & Enabling Statutes:

California:	CAL. GOV'T CODE §§ 66800-66801 (2004)
Nevada:	NEV. REV. STAT. § 277.190, et s*eq.* (2004)
United States:	Pub. L. No. 91-148, 83 Stat. 360 (1969); Pub. L. No. 96-551, 94 Stat. 3233 (1980)

  Administrative Agency:

  Tahoe Regional Planning Agency
  PO Box 5310
  128 Market Street
  Stateline, NV 89449
  (775) 588-4547

  Web Site:

  http://www.trpa.org/

- **Taxation of Motor Fuels Consumed by Interstate Buses:** Compact seeks to avoid multiple taxation of motor fuels used by interstate buses, to assure each member state its share of motor fuel taxes, and to facilitate effective tax administration.

  Member States & Enabling Statutes:

Maine:	ME. REV. STAT. ANN. tit. 36 § 3091, et seq. (2004)
Massachusetts:	MASS. ANN. LAWS (SPEC. L.) ch, 129, § 1, et seq. (2004)
United States:	Pub. L. No. 89 11, 79 Stat. 58 (1965)

- **Tennessee River Basin Water Pollution Control Compact:** Compact seeks to establish a cooperative mechanism between the states in the Tennessee River basin for the management and control of water pollution.

  Member States & Enabling Statutes:

Kentucky:	KY. REV. STAT. ANN. § 224.18-780 (2004)
Mississippi:	MISS. CODE ANN. § 49-17-71 (2004)
United States:	Pub. L. No. 85-734, 72 Stat. 823 (1958)

- **Tennessee-Tombigbee Waterway Development Compact:** Establishes an authority to foster and develop navigable waterways connecting the Tennessee and Tombigbee Rivers.

  Member States & Enabling Statutes:

Alabama:	ALA. CODE § 33-8-1, et seq. (2004)
Kentucky:	KY. REV. STAT. ANN. § 182.300 (2004)
Mississippi:	MISS. CODE ANN. § 51-27-1, et seq. (2004)
Tennessee:	TENN. CODE ANN. § 69-9-101, et seq. (2004)
United States:	Pub. L. No. 85-653, 72 Stat. 609 (1958)

  Interstate Agency:

  Tennessee-Tombigbee Waterway Development Authority
  P.O. Drawer 671
  Columbus, MS 39703
  (662) 328-3286

  Web Site:

  www.tenntom.org

- **Texas Low-Level Radioactive Waste Disposal Compact**: Compact provides that Texas will act as the host state for certain radioactive waste disposal. Under the agreement, Maine and Vermont would ship their low-level waste to Texas in exchange for payments.

  Member States & Enabling Statutes:

Maine:	ME. REV. STAT. ANN. tit. 22, § 679-A, et seq. (2004)
Texas:	TEX. HEALTH & SAFETY CODE § 403.001, et seq. (2004)
Vermont:	VT. STAT. ANN. tit. 10 § 7060, et seq. (2004)
United States:	Pub. L. No. 105-236, 112 Stat. 1542 (1998)

  Administrative Agency:

  Texas Low-Level Radioactive Waste Disposal Authority
  7701 N. Lamar Blvd., Suite 300
  Austin, TX 78752
  (512) 451-5292

  Web Site:

  http://link.tsl.state.tx.us/tx/TLLRWDA/homepage.htm

- **Tri-State Lotto Compact:** Compact implements the Tri-State Lotto for the purpose of raising additional revenue for each of the party states. Fifty percent of the gross sales from each state are aggregated in a common prize pool and operating costs will be charged proportionally to the sales made by each of the party states. The remaining revenues generated within each state will remain in that particular state. The compact creates a commission to administer the lottery and compact provisions.

  Member States & Enabling Statutes:

Delaware:	DEL. CODE ANN. tit. 29 § 4830, et seq. (2004)
Maine:	ME. REV. STAT. ANN. tit. 8, § 401, et seq. (2004)
New Hampshire:	N.H. REV. STAT. ANN. § 287-F:1, et seq. (2004)
Vermont:	VT. STAT. ANN. tit. 31, § 671, et seq. (2004)

- **Tri-State Sanitation Compact:** Compact creates an interstate sanitation district and establishes a commission to promote water pollution abatement and control within the tidal and coastal waters in the adjacent portions of Connecticut, New Jersey, and New York.

  Member States & Enabling Statutes:

Connecticut:	CONN. GEN. STAT. § 22a-294 (2004)
New Jersey:	N.J. STAT. ANN. § 32:22B-1, et seq. (2004)
New York:	N.Y. ENVTL. CONSERV. LAW § 21-0501, et seq. (2004)
United States:	Pub. Res. 74-62, 49 Stat. 932 (1935)

  Administrative Agency:

  Interstate Environmental Commission
  311 West 43rd Street, Suite 201
  New York, NY 10036
  (212) 582-0380

  Web Site:

  www.iec-nynjct.org/staff.htm

- **Upper Colorado River Basin Compact:** Compact creates an interstate commission to administer apportionment of the waters of the Upper Colorado river basin system and to promote agricultural and industrial development.

  Member States & Enabling Statutes:

Arizona:	ARIZ. REV. STAT. § 45-1321 (2004)
Colorado:	COLO. REV. STAT. § 37-62-101, et seq. (2004)
New Mexico:	N.M. STAT. ANN. § 72-15-26, et seq. (2004)
Utah:	UTAH CODE ANN. § 73-13-9, et seq. (2004)
Wyoming:	WYO. STAT. ANN. §§ 41-12-401, 41-12-402 (2004)
United States:	Pub. L. No. 81-37, 63 Stat. 31 (1949)

  Administrative Agency:

  Upper Colorado River Commission
  355 S.400 E.
  Salt Lake City, UT 84111
  (801) 531-1150

- **Upper Niobrara River Compact**: Compact apportions the waters of the Upper Niobrara iver basin and the groundwaters in Nebraska and Wyoming.

  Member States & Enabling Statutes:

Nebraska:	NEB. REV. STAT. (Appendix) §A1-112 (2004)
Wyoming:	WYO. STAT. ANN. §§41-12-701, 41-12-702 (2004)
United States:	Pub. L. No. 91-52, 83 Stat. 86 (1969)

  Administrative Agency:

  Upper Niobrara River Commission
  Nebraska Dept. of Natural Resources
  P.O. Box 94676
  301 Centennial Mall S.
  Lincoln, NE 68509
  (402) 471-2363

- **Vehicle Equipment Safety Compact:** Compact expedites the development and adoption of uniform standards for improving automotive safety equipment.

  Member States & Enabling Statutes:

Arizona:	ARIZ. REV. STAT. § 28-1801, et seq. (2004)
Arkansas:	ARK. CODE ANN. § 27-33-101, et seq. (2004)
Colorado:	COLO. REV. STAT. § 24-60-901, et seq. (2004)
Hawaii:	HAW. REV. STAT. §§ 286A-1, 286A-2 (2004)
Indiana:	IND. CODE § 9-28-6-1, et seq. (2004)
Iowa:	IOWA CODE §§ 321D.1, 321D.2 (2004)
Massachusetts:	MASS. ANN. LAWS (SPEC. L.) ch. 127, § 1, et seq. (2004)
Missouri:	MO. REV. STAT. § 307.250, et seq. (2004)
Montana:	MONT. CODE ANN. § 61-2-201, et seq. (2004)
New Jersey:	N.J. STAT. ANN. § 32:26-1, et seq. (2004)
New York:	N.Y. CONSOLID. LAWS, VEH. & TRAF. § 384 (2004)
North Carolina:	N.C. GEN. STAT. § 20-183.13, et seq. (2004)
Rhode Island:	R.I. GEN. LAWS § 31-23.1-1, et seq. (2004)
Utah:	UTAH CODE ANN. § 41-15-1, et seq. (2004)
Vermont:	VT. STAT. ANN. Tit. 23 § 1801, et seq. (2004)
Washington:	WASH. REV. CODE § 46.38.010, et seq. (2004)
United States:	Pub. L. No. 85-684, 72 Stat. 635 (1958)

- **Washington Metropolitan Area Transit Authority Compact:** Compact creates an interstate authority to plan, develop, operate, construct, acquire, and improve mass transit facilities in the Washington metropolitan area.[2]

Member States & Enabling Statutes:

Maryland:	MD. CODE ANN. TRANSP. § 10-204 (2004)
Virginia:	VA. CODE ANN. §§ 56-529, 56-530 (2004)
Dist. of Columbia:	D.C. CODE ANN. §§ 9-1107.01 to 9-1107.12 (2004)
United States:	Pub. L. No. 86-794, 74 Stat. 1031 (1960); Pub. L. No. 87-767, 76 Stat. 764 (1962); Pub. L. No. 89-774, 80 Stat. 1324 (1966); Pub. L. No. 92-349, 86 Stat. 464 (1972)

Administrative Agency:

Washington Metropolitan Area Transit Authority
600 Fifth Street, NW
Washington, DC 20001
(202) 962-1234

Web Site:

www.wmata.com

- **Washington Metropolitan Area Transit Regulation Compact:** Compact creates an interstate commission to regulate passenger transportation by any privately owned carriers between any points in the District of Columbia and adjacent portions of Maryland and Virginia. Transportation exclusively occurring with Virginia is exempted from regulation under the compact.[3]

---

2.   For ease of use, this index refers to the Washington Metropolitan Area Transit Authority (WMATA) Compact as an agreement separate and apart from the Washington Metropolitan Area Transit Regulation Compact. However, technically the creation of WMATA was accomplished by an amendment that added Title III to the Washington Metropolitan Area Transit Regulation Compact. Consequently, legally there is a single transit agreement for the Washington metropolitan area comprised of Titles I, II, and III. Titles I & II refer to the Washington Metropolitan Area Transit Commission, which is charged with regulating private transportation rates. Title III refers to the Washington Metropolitan Area Transit Authority, which is charged with developing, constructing, and operating a public mass transit system. As a result, some will refer to the Washington Metropolitan Area Transit Authority Compact while others may refer to Title III of the Washington Metropolitan Area Transit Regulation Compact. Technically either reference would be accurate.

3.   For a clarifying statement, *see supra* note 2.

Member States & Enabling Statutes:

Maryland: MD. CODE ANN. TRANSP. § 10-201, et seq.
                   (2004)
Virginia: VA. CODE ANN, §§ 56-529, 56-530 (2004)
Dist. of Columbia: D.C. CODE ANN. § 9-1103.01,
                   et seq. (2004)
United States: Pub. L. No. 87-767, 76 Stat. 764 (1962);
                   Pub. L. No. 89-774, 80 Stat. 1324 (1966);
                   Pub. L. No. 94-306, 90 Stat. 672 (1976);
                   amended by Pub. L. No. 100-285, 102 Stat.
                   82 (1988); amended by Pub. L. No. 101-
                   505, 104 Stat. 1300 (1990); amended by Pub.
                   L. No. 104-322, 110 Stat. 3884 (1996);
                   amended by Pub. L. No. 105-151, 111 Stat.
                   2686 (1997)

Administrative Agency:

Washington Metropolitan Area Transit Commission
1828 I Street NW, Suite 703
Washington, DC 20036-5104
(202) 331-1671

- **Waterfront Commission Compact:** Compact establishes a bistate commission to eliminate criminal and corrupt practices in the handling of waterfront cargo and seeks to stabilize and regulate employment of waterfront labor.

Member States & Enabling Statutes:

New Jersey: N.J. STAT. ANN. § 32:23-1, et seq. (2004)
New York: N.Y. UNCONSOL. LAWS §§ 9801-9873 (2004)
United States: Pub. L. No. 83-252, 67 Stat. 541 (1953)

Administrative Agency:

The Waterfront Commission of New York Harbor
39 Broadway, 4th Fl.,
New York, NY 10006
(212) 742-9280

Web Site:

www.state.nj.us/wcnynj

- **Western (Interstate) Corrections Compact:** Compact enables joint use of corrections facilities in the West.

Member States & Enabling Statutes:

Alaska:	Alaska Stat.§ 33.36.060, et seq. (2004)
Arizona:	Ariz. Rev. Stat. § 31-471, et seq. (2004)
California:	Cal. Penal Code § 11190, et seq. (2004)
Colorado:	Colo. Rev. Stat. § 24-60-801, et seq. (2004)
Hawaii:	Haw. Rev. Stat. § 355-1, et seq. (2004)
Montana:	Mont. Code Ann. § 46-19-301, et seq. (2004)
New Mexico:	N.M. Stat. Ann. § 31-5-4, et seq. (2004)
Oregon:	Or. Rev. Stat. § 421.282, et seq. (2004)
Utah:	Utah Code Ann. § 77-28-1, et seq. (2004)
Washington:	Wash. Rev. Code § 72.70.010, et seq. (2004)
Wyoming:	Wyo. Stat. Ann. § 7-3-401, et seq. (2004)
United States:	Pub. L. No. 73-293; 48 Stat. 909 (1934); 4 U.S.C. § 112(A) (2004)

- **Western Interstate Nuclear Energy Compact:** Compact establishes a board to assist member states in dealing with nuclear energy issues. The Western Interstate Energy Board assists in development of regulation of all energy fields.

Member States & Enabling Statutes:

Alaska:	Alaska Stat. § 41.98.110 (2004)
Arizona:	Ariz. Rev. Stat. § 30-701, et seq. (2004)
California:	Cal. Gov. Code § 67400, et seq. (2004)
Colorado:	Colo. Rev. Stat. § 24-60-1401, et seq. (2004)
Idaho:	Idaho Code § 39-3020, et seq. (2004)
Montana:	Mont. Code Ann. § 90-5-201, et seq. (2004)
Nevada:	Nev. Rev. Stat. § 459.001, et seq. (2004)
New Mexico:	N.M. Stat. Ann. § 11-9-1, et seq. (2004)
Utah:	Utah Code Ann. § 63-41-1, et seq. (2004)
Washington:	Wash. Rev. Code § 43.21F.400, et seq. (2004)
Wyoming:	Wy. Stat. Ann. § 9-6-101, et seq. (2004)

NOTE: The Western Interstate Energy Board lists Oregon as a full member although that state does not appear to have adopted the compact. The Canadian provinces of Alberta, British Columbia, and Saskatchewan are identified as associate members. Nebraska is also listed as an associate member of the board.

Administrative Agency:

Western Interstate Energy Board
1515 Cleveland Place, Suite 200
Denver, CO 80202
(303) 573-8910

Web Site:

www.westgov.org/wieb

- **Western Regional (Higher) Education Compact:** Created in 1953, the compact creates an interstate regional commission to assist Western states increase educational opportunities, improve colleges, and univer-sities, and expand the supply of specialized persons.

Member States & Enabling Statutes:

Alaska:	ALASKA STAT. § 14.44.010, et seq. (2004)
Arizona:	ARIZ. REV. STAT. § 15-1741, et seq. (2004)
California:	CAL. EDUC. CODE § 99000, et seq. (2004)
Colorado:	COLO. REV. STAT. § 24-60-601 (2004)
Hawaii:	HAW. REV. STAT. §§ 310-1, et seq. (2004)
Idaho:	IDAHO CODE § 33-3601, et seq. (2004)
Montana:	MONT. CODE ANN. § 20-25-801, et seq. (2004)
Nevada:	NEV. REV. STAT. § 397.010, et seq. (2004)
North Dakota:	N.D. CENT. CODE §§15-10.2-01, 15-10.2-02 (2004)
New Mexico:	N.M. STAT. ANN. § 11-10-1, et seq. (2004)
Oregon:	OR. REV. STAT. § 351.770, et seq. (2004)
Utah:	UTAH CODE ANN. § 53B-4-101, et seq. (2004)
Washington:	WASH. REV. CODE § 28B.70.010, et seq. (2004)
Wyoming:	WYO. STAT. ANN. § 21-16-201 (2004)
United States:	Pub. L. No. 83-226, 67 Stat. 490 (1953)

Administrative Agency:

Western Interstate Commission for Higher Education
P.O. Box 9752
Boulder, CO 80301-9752
(303) 541-0200

Web Site:

http://www.wiche.edu

- **Wheeling Creek Watershed Protection and Flood Prevention District Compact:** Compact creates an interstate commission to administer programs of flood control and preservation of natural resources and recreational facilities in the Wheeling Creek watershed.

  Member States & Enabling Statutes:

Pennsylvania:	32 PA. CONS. STAT.§ 819.1, et seq. (2004)
West Virginia:	W. VA. CODE, § 29-1F-1, et seq. (2004)
United States:	Pub. L. No. 90-181, 81 Stat. 553 (1967)

- **Woodrow Wilson Bridge and Tunnel Compact:** Compact creates the National Capital Region Woodrow Wilson Bridge and Tunnel Authority, charged with alleviating traffic problems related to the inadequacy of the Woodrow Wilson Memorial Bridge.

  Member States & Enabling Statutes:

Maryland:	MD. CODE ANN. TRANSP. § 10-301, et seq. (2004)
Virginia:	VA. CODE ANN. § 33.1-320.2 (2004)
Dist. of Columbia:	D.C. CODE ANN. § 9-1115.01, et seq. (2004)

  Administrative Agency:

  Woodrow Wilson Bridge and Tunnel Authority
  1800 Duke Street, Suite 200
  Alexandria, VA 22314
  (703) 519-9802

- **Yellowstone River Compact**: Establishes the Yellowstone River Compact Commission to apportion the waters of the Yellowstone River among Montana, North Dakota, and Wyoming.

  Member States & Enabling Statutes:

Montana:	MONT. CODE ANN. § 85-20-101 (2004)
North Dakota:	N.D. CENT. CODE § 61-23-01 (2004)
Wyoming:	WYO. STAT. ANN. § 41-12-601 (2004)
United States:	Pub. L. No. 78-257, 58 Stat. 117 (1944); Pub. L. No. 82-231, 65 Stat. 663 (1951)

INDEX